# *Power Transformers and Special Transformers*

***A Book for every Electrical Engineer and Student***



***Coverage :***

- *Principles, Terms and Definitions*
- *Specifications and Ratings, Type Tests*
- *Construction of Tanks, Windings, Bushings, Core etc.*
- *Materials and Production Sequence*
- *Insulation Coordination and Surge Arresters*
- *Magnetic Circuit, Core, Noise*
- *Neutral Grounding Practice and Third Harmonic Paths*
- *Tap Changers and Voltage Control*
- *Insulation Systems, Transient Stresses*
- *Troubles, Abnormal Conditions*
- *Protection and Fitments*
- *Partial Discharge and Measurement*
- *Testing*
- *Installation, Drying Out and Commissioning*
- *Operation and IEC Loading Guide*
- *Maintenance*
- *CTs, VTs, CVT, CCVT*
- *Furnace Transformers, Welding Transfomers*
- *Autotransformers, Phase Regulating Transformers*
- *Distribution Transformers*
- *Large Transformers, Small Transformers*
- *Shunt Reactors and Series Reactors*

**By the Same Author :**

- *Switchgear, Protection and Power Systems*
- *Testing Commissioning, Operation and Maintenance of Electrical Equipments*
- *EHV-AC and HVDC Transmission Engineering and Practice*
- *Electrical Substation Practice (EHV-AC, HVDC and $SF_6$-GIS)*
- *Energy Technology*
- *Electrical Safety, Fire Safety Engineering and Management*
- *Industrial Safety, Health and Environment Management System*
- *Utilization, Generation and Conservation of Electrical Energy*

# *Power Transformers and Special Transformers*

**Sunil S. Rao**

*M.E., M.I.E.*

*Revised by*

**Ashok Kumar**

*B.Tech., M.Tech. (IIT, Delhi)*

*Edited by*

**Vineet Kumar**

**KHANNA PUBLISHERS**

Operational Office

4575/15, Onkar House, Ground Floor,

Darya Ganj, New Delhi 110 002

*Phones* : 011-23243042, 011-23243043 & Mob. 9811541460

*E-mail :* contactus@khannapublishers.in

*Published by :*

Romesh Chander Khanna & Vineet Khanna
*for* **KHANNA PUBLISHERS**
2-B, Nath Market, Nai Sarak
Delhi- 110 006 (India)

**Website : www.khannapublishers.in**



*Hologram & Description*

To all readers of our books, from yourself if being defrauded by pirates to prevent, please make sure that there is an Hologram on the cover of our books with the below specifications. If you find any book without Hologram and Description, please mail us at **contactus@khannapublishers.in**

Thanking you

**ISBN No. 978-81-7409-291-5**

***First Edition : 1997***
***Fourth Edition : 2011***
***First Reprint : 2016***

***Price :* ₹ 349.00**

# Preface

Since the publication of the first edition in 1985, many advances have occured in Transformers Technology. EHV-AC and UHV-AC transmission systems have been introduced. Installed capacities have increased. Interconnections have been added. The demands made by power systems on Power Transformers, Shunt Reactors, Special Transformers etc. have diversified. Power Transformer, Shunt Reactor and Special Transformer Technologies have kept pace with these pressing demands.

The annual growth rate of distribution transformer and power transformer industry is more than 18 per cent. The total installed capacity of power transformers in India is likely to cross, 15,00,000 MVA by the year 2015 AD.

A very wide range of power transformers from a few kVA to several hundred MVA and from LV to UHV are being produced, installed, operated and maintained. There is an urgent need for Human Resources Development to keep pace with the growing demands of manufacturers, erectors and users. This book will serve as a ready reference book to Transformer Engineers, Power Engineers, Polytechnics and Engineering Colleges. The book will also be a useful course material for refreshers courses and workshops for Power Engineers Organized by various Human Resources Development Organizations.

Salient features of this book include neat sketches, reference tables, graphs, terms and definitions, specification, theory and practical aspects. This edition covers all most all practical aspects of applications, selection, manufacturing, testing, installation, commissioning, operation and maintenance of power transformers and special transformers, in a single volume.

Care has been taken to cover advanced topics, recent developments with essential fundamentals and theoretical inputs.

In this revised edition, several new topics have been added and each of the chapter has been fully revised. Importance has also been given to layouts of substations and generating stations, associated electrical equipment, protective relaying, stresses on transformers, etc.

Related power system aspects such as Tap-changers and Voltage Control, Neutral connections, Tertiary and Third Harmonics, Insulation co-ordination, Insulation levels, Surge arrester protect on etc. have by fully covered.

The book will be of interest to almost every power engineer and student.

The encouragement given by the faculty members of Engineering Staff College, VJTI, Bombay; TTTI, Bhopal ; College of Engineering, Pune ; etc. and various Transformer Manufacturers and users is gratefully acknowledged.

Finally, I thank my Wife and my Mother for the affectionate encouragement and patience showered on me during last three years.

**— Author**

# Contents

**15. Partial Discharges and their Location** 

## 16. Polarity, Three-phase Connections 299-309



## 17. Parallel Operations of Transformers 310—316



## 18. Tap-Changer and Voltage Control 317—327



## 19. Loading of Power Transformers 328—340

**32. Distribution Transformers 606—614**



**33. Current Transformer (CTs) 615—630**

# 1

# General Background and Recent Advances

## 1.1. INTRODUCTION

Three phase A.C. system at 50 Hz (60 Hz in USA) is used for generation, transmission, distribution and utilisation of electrical power. Power transformers are necessary between consecutive voltage levels for raising or lowering A.C. voltage at the same frequency. As the transformation of voltages is carried out successively in generating stations, sub-stations, distribution systems and near load points, the total cumulative installed MVA capacity of the power transformer is 8 to 10 times the cumulative installed MVA capacity of generators. Therefore, transformers are very important apparatus in the electrical network. There is hardly any electrical installation where we don't use a power transformer. Transformer is a well known electrical equipment which deserves attention. It is a costly and important equipment. Transformers can give reliable service for than twenty years or so. Transformer is the most important link for transmission and distribution of Electrical Energy.

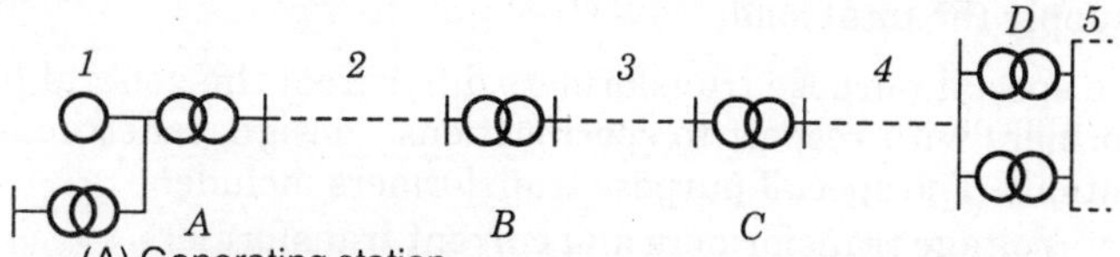


(A) Generating station.
— Generator transformer
— Unit-Auxiliary transformer
(B) Transmission substation
(C, D) Distribution substations
1. Generator voltage level: 11 kV to 28 kV
2. Transmission voltage levels: 220 kV, 400 kV, 765 kV
3. Sub-transmission voltage levels: 66 kV, 132 kV
4. Distribution voltage levels: 400 V, 1.1 kV, 33 kV, 6.6 kV, 11 kV, 33 kV

Fig. 1.1. Power transformers in the Network and Voltage Levels.

The transformers are designed and built in several sizes from a few kVA to several hundred MVA, from low voltage to extra-high voltages (EHV) and ultra high voltages (UHV) and also for convertors in High Voltage Direct Current Transmission (HVDC) Systems.

The KVA ratings of power transformers cover a wide range between say, 5 kVA to 650 MVA. Very large transformers (250 MVA to

650 MVA) are installed generating stations. Very small transformers (a few VA) are used in low voltage systems. The choice for kVA rating of transformers in a particular installations depends upon the kVA load.

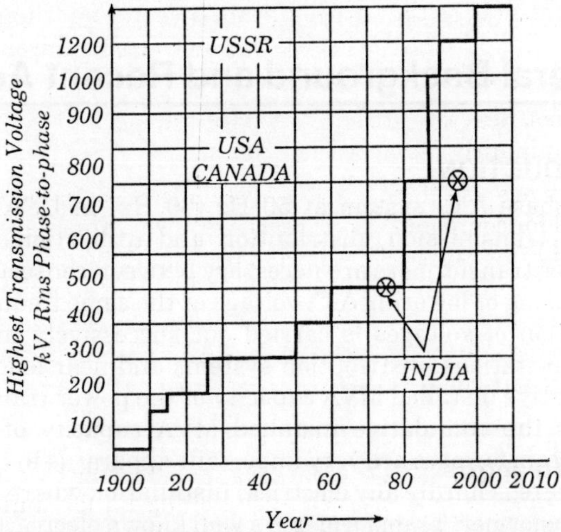


Fig. 1.2. Highest AC voltages in Power Systems over the years. Transformers have been developed to meet the requirements of highest system voltages.

Required number of identical transformers are connected in parallel to supply the total load.

The special purpose transformers differ from the general purpose transformers with respect to specifications, design, construction and applications. The special purpose transformers include:

- Voltage transformers and current transformers
- Furnace transformers
- Regulating transformers
- Convertor transformers
- Rectifier transformers
- Mining transformers
- Phase shifting transformers
- Phase changing transformers (*e.g.*, 3 ph to 1 ph )
- Traction transformers
- High frequency transformers
- Welding transformers
- High voltage testing transformers
- Short-circuit testing transformers, etc.

Large convertor-transformers are installed in conversion sub-stations of HVDC transmission links.

Dry type transformers are used for auxiliaries in generating stations, industrial applications etc. Dry type transformers are available up to 5 MVA capacity either as cast resin or air cooled transformers. These are preferred as they are maintainance free but their cost is more by 40% or so compared to oil cooled transformers of the same capacity. Overloading capacity in also less.

**Reactors.** Reactors are equipment of transformer family. A reactor has a predominantly inductive coil.

Reactors are use in the power system (network) for fault current limiting and for compensation of reactive power. There are two types of reactors (1) Series reactors, connected in series for current limiting and (2) Shunt reactors, connected in shunt, for compensation of reactive power. Oil-insulated Reactors are similar to transformers in external appearance and have some design features similar to those of power transformers. Air-core dry type reactor looks like a large coil.

Reactors are necessary in following applications:

**Series Reactors** are necessary for limiting short-circuit currents, for limiting in rush currents while switching-in, for limiting current surges with fluctuating loads. for smoothing the current waveform, for giving stored energy for satisfactory operation of converters, neutral grounding reactors, etc.

**Shunt Reactors** are necessary for shunt harmonic filters, and for providing reactive power compensation for long EHV-AC lines.

## 1.2. DEFINITION OF TRANSFORMER

Transformer is a static electrical equipment which transforms A.C. electrical power from one voltage to another voltage without changing frequency charge by electromagnetic induction.

From this definition, .

- Transformers are static equipment.
- They transform electrical power from one circuit to another circuit at the same frequency by (usually) at different voltage.
- They operate on the principle of electomagnetic induction.
- They generally operate only with alternating current.

## 1.3. PRINCIPLE OF OPERATION

A transformer has two or more separate windings placed on a common magnetic core. It works on induction principle. The primary winding is supplied with alternating current of supply frequency. There by, alternating magnetic flux of the same frequency is produced in the magnetic core. The flux linkage of the secondary winding also changes at the same frequency, resulting in induced e.m.f. of the same frequency in the secondary winding.

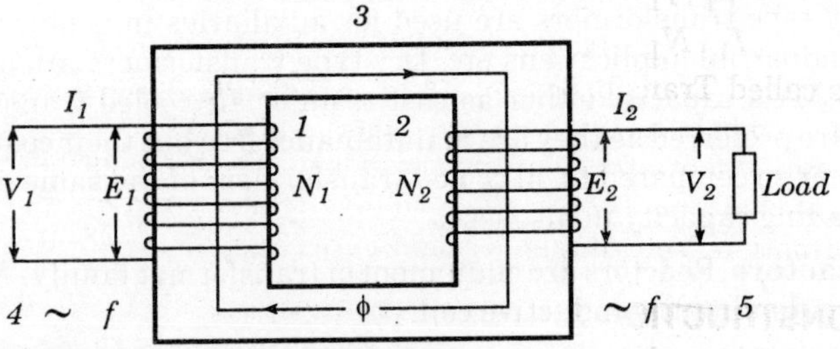


1. Primary winding with $N_1$ turns
2. Secondary winding with $N_2$ turns
3. Core with magnetic flux $\phi$
4. Supply
5. Load.

Fig. 1.3. Principle of a single-phase transformer.

Alternating magnetic flux in the core induces e.m.f. in the secondary windings by electomagnetic induction.

Thus, the transformer works only on alternating current. The above principle is based on the well known Faraday's Law of Electomagnetic induction. "EMF( Electro Motive Force) is induced in a close circuit when the flux linkage with the circuit changes."

In case of transformers, the 'change' in 'flux linkage' occurs due to the continuously varying alternating flux in the core. Hence e.m.f. is induced continuously in the secondary.

The direction of induced e.m.f. in the secondary winding opposes the cause (Lenz's Law) and , therefore, alternates at the same frequency.

If the secondary winding is without electrical load, the transformer is on *no load*. The primary takes only a small current for magnetising the core. If secondary side is loaded with electrical load, the secondary current flows. The flux produced by the secondary winding opposes the flux produced by the primary winding. As a result flux the, e.m.f. induced in the primary winding decreases momentarily. As suppply voltage remains constant, the difference between the supply voltage and the primary induced voltage increases and this difference forces more current from the supply to flow. This increased primary currents compensates for the increased secondary current. The difference between primary flux and secondary flux remains almost constant if leakage etc. are neglected. Hence transformer is also called constant flux device. The primary current increases correspondingly to maintain the same magnetic flux in the core. For a two winding transformers, neglecting magnetization currents

$$V_1/V_2 = N_1/N_2 = k$$
$$I_2/I_1 = N_1/N_2 = k$$

$$V_1 \,.\, I_1 = V_2 \,.\, I_2 = \text{Volt Amperes.}$$
$$I_1 \,.\, N_1 = I_2 \,.\, N_2 = \text{Amperes–Turns}$$

$k$ is called Transformation Ratio. Neglecting no-load current (excitation current), the total ampere-turns of primary winding are equal to the total ampere-turns of the secondary. The transformer does not give higher output. It only gives voltage transformation and current transformation. Volt Amperes remain unchanged.

## 1.4. CONSTRUCTION AND DESCRIPTION

A transformer has the following sub-assemblies and sub-systems:

- Tank
- Core and Magnetic Circuit
- Windings and Insulation system
- Leads and terminal arrangements
- Tap-changer for Voltage-Control
- Bushings, CTs
- Conservator
- Insulating Oil and Oil-preservation means
- Cooling system
- Fitments
- Carriage
- Marshalling kiosk
- Protective system.

A transformer has two or more sets of windings wound on a common magnetic core. The core and the windings are enclosed in a tank filled with dielectric oil or dry gas. The terminals of the winding are connected to the internal end of bushing. The bushing provides the necessary insulating support to the conductor passing through the earthed tank. The bushings are supported on the tank-cover.

A tap-changer may be provided on primary or secondary side but it is generally in HV side. The tap-changer may be mounted on the tank either internally or externally The taps of the winding are connected to the tap changer. Tap changers are either On-load type or off-load type. Tap changing gives change in secondary voltage for given primary voltage. Tap-changing is the basic method for voltage control of AC Networks and HVDC transmission system.

A small transformer is generally naturally cooled as available surface area is adequate to dissipate the losses taking place in a transformer. As capacity of transformer increases the surface area increases in proper time to square of and losses increase in proportion to $k^3$, where $k$ is the ratio of new dimension divided by old dimension. For example, if particular dimension of core for 1 MVA transformer is $X_1$ and the same dimension for 2 MVA transformer in $X_2$, we have

$K = \dfrac{X_2}{X_1}$ and design of 2 MVA will change accordingly. With the increased losses hence, artificial cooling becomes essential for large transformers. The transformer is filled with dielectric oil or dry inert-gas. In case of oil filled transformers a conservator is provided. It is installed at a slightly higher level than that of the tank. During higher loads, the oil in the tank expands and the level of oil in the conservator rises. The air cushion in the conservator permits expansion are contraction of the oil in the tank without contact with moist external air. The air cushion in the conservator is connected to the external atmosphere via a silica-jel breather ensuring dryness of incoming air during the breathing. (Fig. 1.4 items 15)

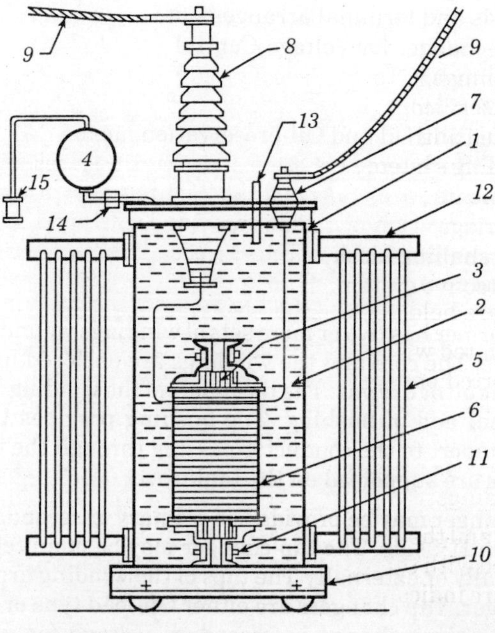


1. Flange for mounting (12).
2. Tank, Tank cover.
3. Core.
4. Conservator.
5. Cooler (Radiator).
6. Windings on 3.
7. LV bushing.
8. HV bushing.
9. Terminals connections.
10. Carriage.
11. Core-bolts.
12. Header.
13. Thermometer.
14. Buchholtz relay.
15. Breather.

Fig. 1.4. Parts of distribution transformer.

Alternatively a rubber bag filled with air is fitted within the conservator. The rubber bag accommodates expansion and contraction of the oil without contact with external atmosphere.

A Buchholtz relay is connected in the pipe between the tank and the conservator. It sounds an alarm when gases are generated in oil due to small discharges or arcing.

A transformer needs adequate cooling to keep the temperature rise of the windings, core and the oil within safe limits. Depending upon the type of the cooling system, the transformer is provided with a radiator and associated cooling system. Large transformers are provided with following types of cooling:

ONAF : Oil Natural Air Forced.

OFAF : Oil Forced Air Forced.

Effective cooling system gives lower temperature rise for same load. With better cooling, the size of transformer can be reduced.

The core is made up of thin laminations (0.33 mm thick ) of special electrical sheet steel. Presently the lowest thickness of commercially available steel is 0.23 mm. The cold rolled grain oriented silicon sheet steel (with 3 % silicon) are used for power transformers. Each lamination is provided with zinc-oxide coating or varnish insulation layer on both the sides. Such a construction of the core ensures low core losses. The core is built-up by placing the laminations in an interleaved fashion. The core is clamped and is provided with rigid insulated bolts. In case of high-power transformers special techniques are used for assembling the laminations of the limbs and core-bolts are avoided. The laminations are held together by fiber glass bands.

The insulated windings are placed on the limbs. The windings are rigidly supported on the core by the insulation system. The design of insulation system is based on the voltage distribution during transient over-voltages and the forces during the short-circuit conditions. There are various types of windings. Choice depends on voltage and current rating of windings.

The tank and the core of the transformer are earthed. A marshalling kiosk provided with the transformer enclosed various instruments such as temperature indicator and controller, relays for tap-changer control, cooler fan control etc. The connections of control and relay instruments in the panel in the control room are through the marshaling kiosk of the transformer.

Three phase transformers are built as single three phase units upto certain maximum MVA rating. Above such a rating a 3 phase transformer bank is formed by connecting three single phase units in required fashion. The choice between one 3-phase unit and 3-single phase depends on transportation limitations. In India, transformers above 300 MVA are generally built in single phase units. In Europe, very large transformers (*e.g.*, 1300 MVA ) have been built as a three phase unit.

The overall dimensions of a transformer are designed by considering permissible transport profile and weight.

## 1.5. Recent Advances

Principles of power transformers were known during 1880's. However the voltage and MVA ratings of power transformers have steadily grown and transformers have been developed too meet several system requirements. There is on going trend to go for higher systems voltage for transmission which increases the voltage rating of transformers. The transformer design, manufacturing and testing techniques have advanced with following objectives:

- High efficiency
- Low material cost, smaller size
- High reliability, long life, low maintenance
- Low noise
- To conform to relevant specifications.

The advances of power transformer technology has been accompanied by the progress in the tap-changers, bushings, surge arresters, protective relays etc. Also computer aided design (CAD) has resulted in optimum and accurate design of transformers as important advances in power transformer technology include:

**1. Improved Magnetic Materials for Core**

- Grain oriented Cold rolled Silicon sheet steel, of 0.3 mm, 0.23 mm, 0.15 mm thickness.
- Laser irradiation for improved grain orientation.
- Lower losses.
- Increased maximum flux density
- Reduced size of core.
- *Amorphous metal cores*—Core loss is 25% of the conventional core loss in a transformer. Core handling is difficult due to brittleness maximum size is 2.5 MVA capacity transformer.

The application of Amorphous metal cores is limited to distribution transformers, specially to smaller rated single-phase units where wound cores are advantageous. Extreme brittleness, mechanical sensitivtiy, cutting and stacking problems are due to the thickness in the range of only 20 to 30 μm and is the necessity of annealing in the magnetic field after fabrication seem to be prohibitive for the application in power transformers. The advantage of low loss values of low flux density is compensated by the higher stacking factor and the low saturation point where losses increase rapidly.

**2. Improved Method of Construction of Core**

- Use of mitred joint between laminations of leg and yoke.
- Elimination of core bolts.
- Use of fibre glass bands impregrated with the thermosetting resins for holdings the laminations in position.

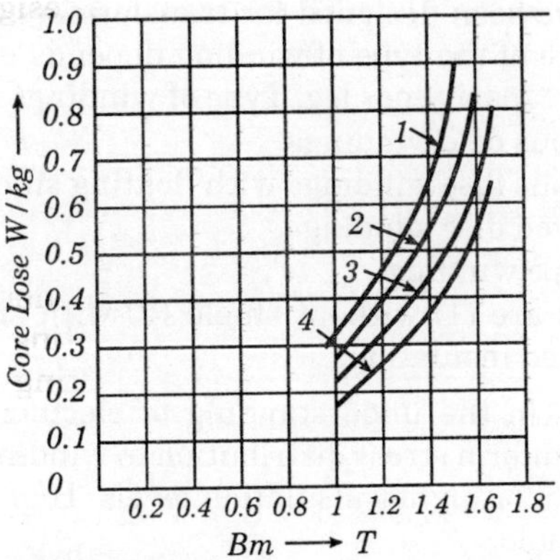


1. 0.3 mm CIRGO (3.25 % Si)
2. 0.25 mm CRGO (3.25% Si)
3. 0.15 mm RGO
4. 0.15. CRGO-Laser Irradiated super oriented.

Fig. 1.5. Improved magnetic material for core laminations.

**3. Improved Conductors and Conductor Insulations.** Multiple wire transposed conductors are now used, thereby the eddy current losses and skin effects are reduced, current distribution is more uniform. The conductors coated with epoxy resins are used. The epoxy resin gets hardened after polymerisation resulting in strong coils.

**4. Reduction in Noise.** Use of superior magnetic sheet steel, improved method of construction of core and tank, appropriate choice of speed of cooling fans for reduced noise of transformers. As the major source of transformer noise is magnetostriction of the core lamination, steel manufacturers startia to develop material with silicon content up to 65%, where magnetostriction disappears. When produced in a conventional manner by rolling Fe-material with more than 4% silicon is extremely brittle. Only a rapid quenching process produce ductile material which can easily be handled by the manufacturer. High temperature annealing is still required to generate a texture which gurantees magnetic properties comparable to those of normal grain oriented sheets of best quality.

**5. Improved Design of Windings and Insulation System.** The distribution of electrical stresses between winding and core, windings, turns of a winding, coil of a winding depends on electomagnetic phenomena. The stresses are severe during lightning impulse waves and switching impules waves. For 400 kV and above voltage levels, switching surges are more severe than lightning surges.

The research carried out on electomagnetic phenomena and winding design have resulted in uniform stress distribution design.

Windings have been designed for transformers of highest voltage ratings. The choice of the type of winding depends upon rated system voltage and MVA capacity per leg. Type of windings include:

- Continuous disc windings.
- Continuous disc windings with floating shield
- Interleaved disc winding
- Layer type winding.

The windings are (1) without shield (2) with shield, (3) uniform insulation or graded insulation.

The advances in the understanding of electomagnetic transient phenomena and uniform stress distribution in windings has resulted in design of windings for higher insulation levels. High speed computers have made it possible.

**6. Fabrication of Tank.** The configurations and design philosophy varies with manufacturers. Advances in design have resulted in reduction in tank size, reduced quantity of oil, reduced manufacturing costs, reduced vibrations.

**7. Improved Conservator Design.** Earlier conservators were with breather fitted in between conservator and external air.

In modern conservators, a rubber bellow (bag) filled with compressed air is held suspended within the conservator. Such a construction gives and effective reliable separation between oil in conservator and the atmospheric air.

**8. Improved Short-Circuit Strength.** Earlier generation of power transformers were weak in short-circuit strengths. The improved design of insulation systems and windings, based on repeated short-circuit performance has resulted in stronger windings and transformers of higher short-circuit strengths.

**9. Improved Efficiency and Improved Methods of Loading.** By improved design of core, windings, and optimisation of design, the transformers of lower losses and higher efficiencies are now available.

The lower losses require higher material cost. Lower losses give higher initial cost and lower operating cost of losses. For proper choice , the methods of capitalisation of losses have been standardised.

Tenders are compared by adding together capital cost of transformer and capitalised cost of losses. This method has resulted in slightly higher size of core and windings and reduced operating losses.

**10. Guide for Loading**. For discontinuous loading, the design of transformer can be optimized by reduced size of core and windings without exceeding temperature limits. IEC Guide 354 for loading of Power Transformers is useful in this regard.

**11.Improved Manufacturing Techniques**. The manufacturing techniques have advanced in several respects including the following:

(*i*) Use of large cropping machines for cropping magnetic core laminations. CNC machines are also frequently used.

Width of strip to be cut 1000 mm length of sheet to be cut: 5000 mm Automatically controlled.

(*ii*) Automatic stacking machines for stacking laminations in the core.

(*iii*) **Presses.** Windings are subjected to vacuum and heating cycles. While they are held under constant axial pressure. High pressure press (up to 800 Ton) is used for holding the windings under axial pressure.

(*iv*) **Vapour Phase Drying.** The assembled core and windings are cleaned and dried by use of vapour phase drying technique. This method gives rapid cleaning and drying with least ageing of dielectric materials of the winding and insulation system.

(*v*) **Improved Manufacture of Tank.** Large tanks are fabricated, welded, short-blasted and painted in modern fabrication shops.

(*vi*) **Improved Testing and Quality Control Techniques.** Quality control techniques are applied during manufacture. Tests are applied on major sub-assemblies and complete transformer. Important advances include:

— Monitoring of hot-spot temperature by measurement of dissolved gases in oil, Infrared thermography to detect hot spots.
— Verification of short-circuit strength.
— Detection of partial discharges.

Partial discharge is defined as a localized electrical discharge in insulating materials, oil. The discharge occurs only partially and does not bridge the conductors completely. Partial discharge test gives location and possible cause and possible defects in the insulation.

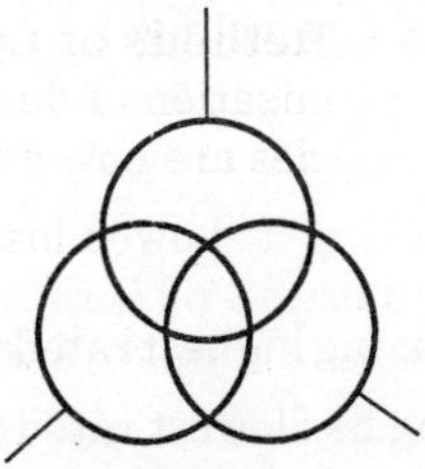

Fig. 1.6. Representation of a 3 winding transformer.

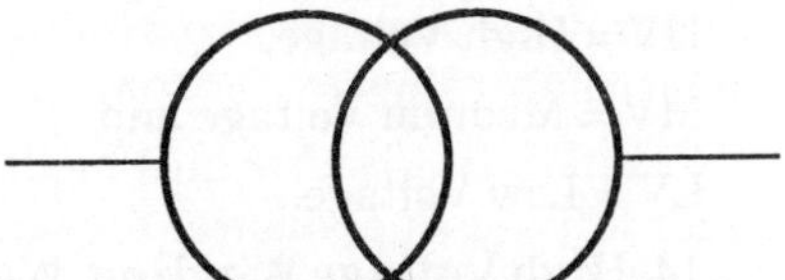

Fig. 1.7. Representation of a 2 winding transformer.

Partial discharge has been introduced as a routine test for transformers and reactors rated 300 kV and above.

## 1.6. TERMS AND DEFINITIONS

1. **Transformer.** A static apparatus which transforms A.C. electrical power from one voltage to another voltage at the same frequency by electomagnetic induction.

2. **Core-type transformer.** A transformer in which the windings surrounded the limbs of the core.

3. **Shell-type transformer.** A transformer in which the core surrounds major portion of the windings.

4. **Auto-transformer.** A transformer in which the primary and the secondary windings have a common portion.

5. **Oil-immersed type transformer.** A transformer which has the core and windings immersed in oil (or synthetic insulating liquid).

6. **Dry type transformer.** The transformer which has no oil or dielectric liquid.

7. **Single-phase transformer.** It has a single phase primary winding and a single phase secondary winding (and may have a single phase third winding).

8. **Three-phase Transformer.** It has a set of three phase primary winding and a three phase secondary winding (and may have a third phase third winding).

9. **Neutral point.** A point common to three phases of a star connected three phase winding. Neutral point is normally at zero potential.

10. **Terminal.** The conducting part to which the line conductor of external system is connected.

11. **Winding.** An assembly of turns of conducting material forming an electrical circuit associated with of the assigned voltage.

12. **Two-winding Transformer.** It has two sets of windings, HV and LV (High voltage, Low voltage).

13. **Three-winding Transformer.** It has three sets of windings, HV, MV, LV (High voltage, Medium voltage, Low voltage).

HV = High Voltage,

MV = Medium Voltage and

LV = Low Voltage.

14. **High Voltage Winding.** Winding having highest rated voltage.

15. **Low Voltage Winding.** The winding has lowest rated voltage.

16. **Intermediate Voltage Winding.** The winding of a multi-winding transformer having rated voltage intermediate between the highest and the lowest rated voltages.

17. **Primary Winding.** The winding to which supply is applied.

18. **Secondary Winding.** The winding to which the load is connected or which delivers output.

19 **Tertiary Winding.** A winding in addition to the primary and the secondary winding which is provided for any of the following purposes:

— To obtain additional voltage
— To stabilize neutral in case of a star/star transformer.
— To reduce third harmonics and control zero sequence impedance.

20. **Auxiliary Winding.** A winding intended only for a small load compared with the rated power of the transformer.

21. **Trappings:**

(*a*) *Principle tapping.* The tapping to which the rated quantities are related.

(*b*) *Tapping Factor Corresponding to given tapping*

Ration $U_d/U_N$ (tapping factor)

or $U_d/U_N \times 100$ (tapping factor as percentage)

Where $U_N$ = Rated voltage of winding

$U_d$ = Voltage which would be developed at no load at terminals of winding, connected on tapping concerned by applying rated voltage to untapped winding.

23. **System Voltages:**

(*a*) *Nominal system voltage.* Nominal value of r.m.s. line to line voltage under normal operating conditions *e.g.,* 220 kV.

(*b*) *Highest system voltage.* Highest r.m.s. line to line voltage permissible to be maintained under normal operating conditions *e.g.,* 245 kV.

24. **Insulation Level.** It is a combination of the rated voltage, power frequency withstand voltage, impulse withstand voltage values which characteristics the insulation of the apparatus. The insulation level refers to that of the respective winding.

'Basic Insulation Level's is a term which includes the following characteristic of a transformer:

— Power frequency voltage withstand level.
— Lightning impulse voltage withstand level.
— Switching impulse voltage withstand level (applicable to transformer windings rated 220 kV and above).

These withstand levels together characteristic the insulation level of a transformer winding.

This is the reference insulation level expressed as an impulse crest (or peak) voltage with a standard wave not longer than a $1.2 \times 50$ microsecond wave. A $1.2 \times 50$ microsecond wave means that the impulse takes 1.2 microsecond to reach the peak and then decays to 50% of the peak in 50 microseconds.

25. **Insulation Coordination.** Insulation coordination is correlation of insulation of equipment and circuit with the characteristic of protective devices such that the insulation is protected from over voltages.

Insulation coordination can be defined as the process of determining the proper insulation levels of various components in a power system as well as their arrangements. It is the selection of an insulation structure that will withstand voltage stresses to which the system, or equipment will subjected to, together with proper surge arrester. The insulation is determined from the known characteristics of voltage surges and the characteristics of surge arresters.

26. **Voltage Regulation of a Transformer** ($\Delta V$). The voltage regulation of a power transformer is the numerical difference between the rated secondary voltage ($V_{2-r}$) and the actual secondary voltage ($V_{2-a}$) cross the secondary terminals for given load and its power factor, with rated voltage applied to the primary winding.

$$\Delta V = (V_{2\,-\,\text{rated}}) - (V_{2\,-\,\text{actual}})$$

Percentage regulation is expressed as a percentage of rated secondary voltage.

$$\text{Thus,} \qquad \%\,\Delta V = \frac{V_{2\,-\,\text{rated}} - V_{2\,-\,\text{actual}}}{V_{2\,-\,\text{rated}}} \times 100$$

27. **Impedance Voltage.** It is also called the short-circuit voltage $V_{sc}$.

It is the voltage required to be applied to drive rated current under short-circuit condition on the other winding. It is a vector sum of Resistance and Reactance voltage drops.

Impedance voltage is determined by conducting sustained short-circuit test.

28. **Losses:**

(*a*) **No Load Losses.** The losses occuring in a transformer when the secondary is not loaded and the primary is supplied with rated voltage at rated frequency. No-load losses are also called Core Losses or Iron Losses and are equal to the sum of hystersis loss and eddy current loss.

(*b*) **Load Losses or Short-Circuit Losses.** These are also called copper losses. The load loss (short-circuit loss) is equal to the active power absorbed by the transformer while carrying rated current in primary and secondary windings under loaded/short circuited condition.

(*c*) **Total Losses.** It is the sum of No-load Loss and Load Loss. It is also the sum of Iron Loss and Copper Loss.

(*d*) Efficiency of the Transformer

$$\% \eta = \frac{\text{Output}}{\text{Input}} \times 100$$

$$= \frac{\text{Output}}{\text{Output + Losses}} \times 100$$

**Note.** Additional definitions have been given in respective chapters.

29. **Rating.** Numerical value assigned to the transformer under specified operating conditions, which denote the capabilities of the transformer and which are proved by tests.

Ratings are in form of Rated Quantities of voltage, current, power etc.

**Ratings include**

| | |
|---|---|
| — Rated Voltage of a Winding | — Rated voltage ratio |
| — Rated power | — Rated current |
| — Rated insulation level | — Rated frequency |
| — Ratings of bushings | — Rating of tap-changer |

30. **Kinds of Tests on a Transformer**

| | |
|---|---|
| — Acceptance Tests | — Type Tests |
| — Routine Tests | — Special Tests |

## 1.7. SUB-STATION EQUIPMENT ASSOCIATED WITH TRANSFORMERS AND PROTECTION OF TRANSFORMERS.

At substation, voltage change takes place and there is assemblage of electrical apparatus. Transformers are necessary in a substation for stepping-up and stepping-down of A.C. voltage. Besides the transformers, the sub-station has several other electrical equipments including bus-bars, circuit-breakers, isolators, surge arresters, CTs, VTs, Shunt-Reactors, Shunt Capacitors etc. A typical layout of a Sub-station circuit is shown in Fig.1.8. The functions of the sub-station apparatus have been mentioned in Table 1.1.

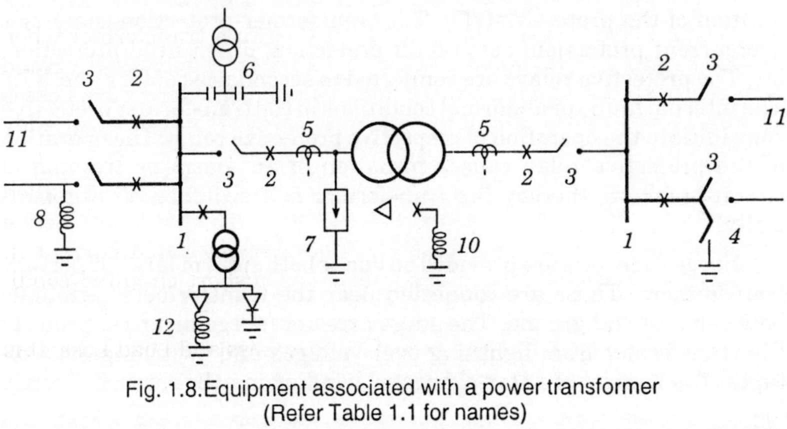


Fig. 1.8. Equipment associated with a power transformer
(Refer Table 1.1 for names)

**Table 1.1. Function of Sub-station Equipment Associated with Power Transformers Ref. Fig. 1.8**

| *Equipment* | *Function* |
|---|---|
| 1. Bus-bars | Incoming and outgoing circuits connected to bus-bars. |
| 2. Circuit-Breakers | Automatic switching on/off during normal or abnormal conditions. |
| 3. Isolators | Disconnection under no-load condition for safety. |
| 4. Earthing Switch | To discharge the voltage on dead lines to earth. |
| 5. Current Transformer | To step-down current for measurement control and protection. |
| 6. Voltage Transformer | To step-down voltage for measurement control and protection. |
| 7. Surge Arrester (Lightning Arrester) | To discharge lightning over-voltages and switching over-voltages to earth. |
| 8. Shunt Reactor | To provide reactive power compensation during low loads. |
| 9. Series Reactors. (Not shown) | To reduce the short-circuit currents or starting currents. |
| 10. Neutral-Grounding Resistor. | To limit the earth fault current. |
| 11. Harmonic Filters | To divert harmonic components to earth and purify the AC waveform. |
| 12. SVC | Static VAr Compensator. Thyristor controlled reactor (TCR) and thyristor controlled capacitor (TCC) for rapid stepless control of reactive power. |

The transformer is covered by a protective zone of transformer-protection. The boundaries of the protective zone are determined by location of the protective CT's. The transformer protection comprises overcurrent protection, earth-fault protection, differential protection, etc. The protective relays are connected to secondaries of CTs and VTs. The internal faults or abnormal conditions in the transformer protective zone initiate the operation of respective protective relay. The operation of the protective relay causes initiation of an alarm or tripping of circuit-breakers, thereby the transformer is a switched off automatically.

Surge Arresters are provided on one or both sides of large important transformers. These are connected near the transformers terminals between line and ground. The surge arrester (surge diverter) protects the transformer from lightning over voltages and switching overvoltages. The neutral of a star-connected winding may be earthed directly (soil earthing) or through a resistance (resistance earthing). The choice of neutral earthing is decided on the basis of system requirements related with the earth fault current, insulation coordination and earth-fault protection.

## 1.8. TRANSFORMERS IN GENERATING STATIONS (Fig.1.9.)

In the *Unit System* adopted universally, each generator is directly connected to the unit step-up transformer (Main Transformer) *without* any circuit-breaker in-between. The connection between the generator terminals and the step-up transformer is usually in the form of *Isolated Phase Busducts.* The generator and its unit step-up transformer form the *unit.* Each unit has its own turbine, control and auxiliaries. The unit auxiliaries are supplied through *unit-auxiliary transformer.*

The MVA rating of the Main Unit Transformers is almost equal to the MVA rating of the generator. The MVA rating of the unit-auxiliary transformer is about 8 per cent of the generator MVA rating in thermal power plants. The Unit-Protection Zone includes the generator protection,auxiliary transformer protection and the main step-up transformer protection. Generator-transformer protection is complex. There are several step-down auxiliary transformers in a power station.

Unit Auxiliaries are supplied via the unit-auxiliary transformer. The station auxiliaries are supplied through another transformer called *Station-Service Transformers.*

While starting the unit, the auxiliaries receive power from the busbars via the station service transformer. Once the unit is started. it feeds its own auxiliaries via the unit auxiliay transformer.

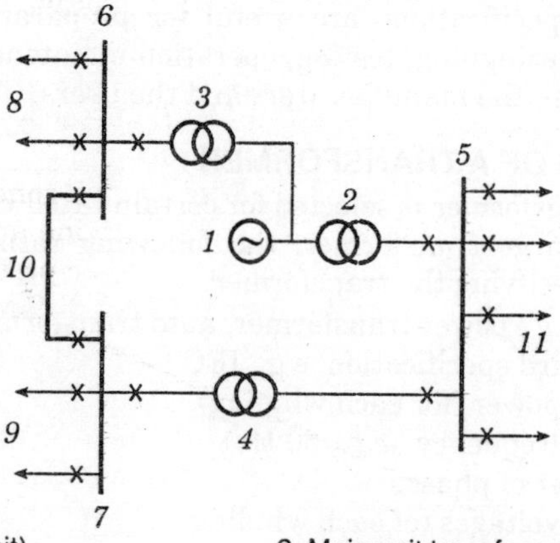


1. Generator (Unit)
2. Main unit transformer
3. Unit -Auxiliary transformer
4. Station service transformer
5. EHV-Bus in Yard
6. Auxiliary-bus (indoor) for the unit
7. Auxiliary bus for the power station
8. Unit auxiliaries
9. Station auxiliaries
10. Bus-coupling
11. EHV-Transmission lines

Fig. 1.9. Power transformers in a Generating Station.

At present the trend is to use generator circuit breaker (GCB) also. This circuit breaker is installed between generator and main tranformer. Use of (GCB) permits crawl of start up power through main transformer unit auxiliary tranformer link. Also main generator tranformer can be isolated completely. Where GCB is not there, it is not possible to isolate completely the main tranformer. In such cases generator keeps on feeding the fault till generator speed reduces to zero. This shortens the life of main transformer.

## 1.9. STANDARD SPECIFICATIONS

IEC and IS standards on power transformers have been published in several parts. They cover several aspects including

— Terms and definitions
— Standard characteristics
— Performance specifications
— Recommended standard ratings
— Test conditions and test methods
— Permissible tolerances
— Service conditions
— Guidelines for selection
— Guidelines for installation and operation
— Guidelines for maintenance etc.

Standards have been published on (1) Transformers (2) Reactors (3) Tap-changers (4) Bushings (5) Fittings (6) Insulation coordination and high voltage testing (7) Short-circuit withstand tests, (8) Transformer oil (9) Various materials, etc.

Standard specifications are useful for preparation of purchase specifications, desingning, testing, operation maintenance etc. Standards are useful to the manufacturers and the users.

## 1.10. RATINGS OF A TRANSFORMER

A small transformer is selected for certain rated voltages and kVA rating. For a large transformer, the following ratings and data is essential for specifying the transformer.

1. Type *e.g* : power transformer, auto transformer
2. Standard specification, e.g., IEC
3. Rated power (for each winding)
4. Rated frequency (*e.g.*, 50 Hz)
5. Number of phases
6. Rated voltages (of each winding)
7. Rated currents (of each winding)
8. Rated insulation levels (of each winding)
9. Connection symbol (*e.g.*, star/delta)
10. Impedance voltage at rated current
11. Type of cooling (*e.g.*, OFAF)

12. Total mass, mass of tank without oil, mass of oil
13. Connection diagram

**Following data is given in certain cases**

14. Temperature class of insulation
15. Insulation levels
16. Temperature rise
17. Transportation mass
18. Untankig mass
19. Insulating liquid if other than mineral oil
20. Details regarding tappings
    — Winding to which tappings are provided
    — Tapping voltage, tapping current, tapping power of each winding
    — Short-circuit impedance on extreme tapping
21. Ability of transformer to operate at voltage exceeding 105% of tapping voltage
22. Other details if any as per specifications.

## 1.11. PURCHASE SPECIFICATIONS

These are prepared by the user for tender enquiry. The essential basic data to be given in the purchase specifications of a power transformer includes the following:

1. Standards *e.g.*, IEC,IS
2. Nominal kVA or MVA rating
3. Rated windig voltages
4. Number of phases
5. Frequency
6. Type of cooling
7. Ambient temperature of cooling medium
8. Phase connections
9. Phase relationship
10. Terminal arrangement
11. Attitude if more than 1000 m
12. Transport limitation, weight and dimensions
13. Impulse levels for lightning surges
14. Impulse levels for switching surges (if applicable)
15. Impedance with acceptable minimum and maximum values for limitation of fault current level and or for voltage regulation.
16. Characteristics of transformers is parallel operation is required.
17. Tapping range: Number of steps, size of step, whether on load or off-load Impedance variation over tapping range.
18. Bushings, clearances, creepage requirements.
19. Performance requirements with load cycle and emergency overloading:

20. Fittings, Paint, Finish
21. Guaranteed maximum losses: The purchaser should advise the manufacturer the basis for minimum first cost, maximum efficiency or capitalisation of losses.
22. Maximum Audible Noise at given distance, dB (A).

The specifications should state clearly the technical and operating conditions. The details on construction should be left to the manufacturer. With competitive market, the manufacturer should bring-out minimum cost design for given specifications without over-designing. Therefore every requirement beyond the standard specifications should be clearly brought out in the purchase specifications.

## 1.12. PROGRESS OF TRANSFORMER TECHNOLOGY

Transformers were invented around 1885 in Europe and USA. As the power demand increased , the size of transformers also increased. 400 kV transformer were manufactured as early as 1950 s. Transformers have played a very significant role in the growth of electrical power system.

— In early years, the core was of ordinary low carbon iron. The core losses were high. Flux densities were low, size of core was large,efficiency was poor (50 to 90 %). Life expectancy was low (5 years).

— Cold-rolled grain oriented silicon steel sheet lamination (CRGO) with oxide coating are used in today's transformers. Manufacturing techniques have advanced. Superior low ageing material is now available. The flux densities of the order of 1.7. Tesla are now possible and with loss of less than 1.1 W/kg (Earlier 1.3 Tesla with loss of 1.9 W/kg).

— Modern transformer cores are built with mitred joints and without any core bolts. The laminations are held together by resin bonded fibre-glass bands.

— Modern transformers are with high efficiency (more than 99%) and with long service life (more than 20 years).

— Better cooling techniques have been developed. This has resulted in compact and efficient coolers and lower hot spot temperatures, longer insulation life.

— Weight/MVA ratios and size of transformers have reduced significantly.

— The oil, insulating materials and design of insulation system have improved.

— Transient phenomena and stresses on insulation system have been understood. This has resulted in successful development of 400 kV, 765 kV, 1000 kV 1200 kV transformers. Transformer have been developed for HVDC transmission systems of rated voltages ± 500 kV, ± 600 kV etc..

— Transformers have been developed to meet all the requirements of transmission distribution and utilization.

## 1.13. TESTING

On a newly designed transformer, comprehensive type tests are carried out in the manufacturers works and testing laboratories to verify the design and transformer capability. Type tests prove the capabilities and guaranteed ratings. The number of tests and nature of tests is as per relevant standard specifications and the agreement between manufacturers and users.

*Routine tests* are carried out on each transformer before despatch from manufacturers works. They are simpler and are conducted to verify that the manufacture and assembly are satisfactory.

*Special Tests* are conducted in testing laboratory or at site to investing at certain phenomena or certain capabilities. They may not be as per particular standard.

*Site Tests* are carried out after completion of installation to confirm that there are no transit damages and installation is satisfactory. Site tests include equipment tests and commissioning tests.

**Quality Checks and Quality Tests.** These are conducted on components, sub-assemblies and complete assembly to confirm that the quality is satisfactory and there are no material/manufacturing defects. Noteworthy quality checks include pressure test, vibration tests, partial discharge tests, tests on oil/gases tests on materials, welding tests, tests on components , etc.

Testing is very important to ensures good health of transformer and trouble free service.

**Table 1.2. Summary of Type Tests and Routine Tests**

| *Routine Tests* | *Type Tests* |
|---|---|
| Ration, Polarity Interphase | Switching impulse |
| Connections winding resistance | Lightning impulse |
| Insulation resistance | Partial discharge |
| Impedance measurement | Temperature rise |
| Load loss | Noise measurement |
| Core loss and magnetising current | RI measurement. |
| Core insulation test | |
| Applied voltage test | |
| Induced overvoltages tests | |

### 1.13.1 Special Tests

—Short circuit withstand
—Radio interference tests
—No load switching tests
—Reliability tests
—Partial discharge tests
—No load switching tests
—Vibration /Earthquake tests
—Environmental tests.

Any other test can be included with the consent of manufacturer and purchaser.

## 1.14. STRESSES ON TRANSFORMER IS SERVICE

A transformer installed in a network is subjected to the following kinds of stresses.

**Dielectric Stresses**

— Continuous service voltage and occasional temporary over-voltage, (power frequency)
— Occasional lightning surges (1.2/50 μ*S* wave).
— Occasional switching surges (250/2500 μ*S* wave).

**Temperature Stresses**

— Due to losses during normal load cycle
— Due to losses during occasional overloads
— Due to high ambient temperature
— Alternate temperature cycles
— Due to harmonics
— During external Short circuits
— Due to failure of cooling system.

**Mechanical Stresses**

— During handling, transportation
— Mechanical vibrations
— During tap-changing on tap-changer parts
— During external short-circuits (on windings, core, insulation system).

**Environmental Stresses**

— Dust, moisture, chemical deposits
— Alternate temperatures
— Extreme temperatures.

The design is based on permissible *stresses* and required factor of safety.

The stresses occurring in service should be limited by effective external means e.g.,

— Reduction in temporary over voltages by dynamic voltage control of network buses.
— Reduction in switching over voltages by use of proper circuit-breakers and associated voltage control techniques.
— Reduction in switching and lightning surges seen by the tranformer by means of surge arresters.

— Reduction in short-circuit levels by appropriate system design.
— Reduction in temperature stresses by appropriate loading and cooling. This requires tripping of fault currents as early as possible.

The external stresses should be controlled by suitable means to get long and trouble free service life. Even a well designed transformer can fail if there are repeated external short circuits or switching surges in the substation; or if it is overloaded continuously without limiting temperature rise.

The transformers are provided with adequate protection systems which include the following:

— Buchholtz relay (Gas operated)
— Over current and earth fault protection
— *Differential protection*—It is provided only for large transformers or where the availability is most important. This is so as the protection cost becomes equal to the transformer cost itself.

Dry type transformers are very much sensitive to temperature. Hence, it must be ensured that the temperature will not rise beyond per- missible limits.

A transformer is also provided with various accessories/fitments to enable measurements, monitoring filling, handling etc. The protective systems and accessories to be provided depends upon the size and importance of the transformer and the cost aspects.

The study and analysis of transformers has been systematized through the years of practical experience, research and development and advancements in the field of transformers. The standards have been evolved and updated regularly.

Under normal operating conditions, the transformer acts as simple voltage-transforming device which is simple to analyse.

During transient conditions and abnormal conditions such as switching-in, switching off, short circuits, over fluxing etc. the phenomenon and independently form the view point of corresponding conditions of operation.

The transformer is an important and vulnerable equipment. It influenes the behaviour of the network during steady state and the transient state. The waveforms of transient over voltages and transient currents depends on the flux density at the instant of occurrences of the system disturbances. The magnitude of the short-circuit current is limited by the impedance of the transformer. The reactances of the transformer is a significant part of the equivalent reactances of the network.

The flow of third harmonic currents is associated with the neutral earthing of the transformers. Thus, there is a close association between the phenomena occuring in the network and the performance of the power transformers. The power transformers should withstand the stresses occuring during the system disturbances. The power transformer should be designed to satisfy the requirements of the power system. The stresses should be limited within guaranteed capabilities by appropriate means.

### 1.14.1 Gas insulated Transformers

$SF_6$ gas is used insulating and cooling medium. First transformer applications were indoor distribution transformers in public buildings because of smaller dimensions, non flammability and non-explosive behaviour. In 1991, The first 300 MVA/275 kV gas insulated transformer was put into service. Further research resulted in 500 kV prototype transformer which passed all tests successfully. The next aim was to realize 500 kV gas insulated transformers of 1000 MVA rating for underground stations. For small rated gas insulated distribution transformers, $SF_6$ is used for both cooling and insulation. Due to the fact that gases have much smaller thermal conductivity and heat capacity, the heat efficient cooling effect of evaporation of liquids is used for gas insulated transformers of large rating.

## 1.15. SUPER CONDUCTING TRANSFORMERS:

Use of super conducting wires can reduce load losses by a large amount. There has always been a strong demand to decrease the amount of load losses that is roughly 3 to 4 times higher than the no load losses. It has been studied to reduce the load losses by operating the transformer at lower temperature. The result of the study was that super conducting transformer exhibits very attractive properties. Only the problem of recovering to super conductivity from normal conductivity after a fault could not be solved conveniently.

The discovery of high temperature conducting (HTSC) of some ceramic alloys and the development of some ceramic alloys and the development of suitable multifilament wires of adequate length received research and studies of large power transformers using super conductive windings at a service temperature of 77°K, the temperature of liquid nitorgen. As this temperature cooling cost reduces considerably.

Recent studies concerning the total cost of large HSTC transformers in comparison with conventional units are promising, provided the progress to develop conductors of lower AC losses and lower cost continues and loss evaluation figures remain at the current level. The inherent fault limiting feature combined with reduced transformer reactance and the over load capacity which is limited only by the cooling capacity permit optimum design and utilisation of the transmission system as a whole.

## 1.16. SCOPE OF THE SUBJECT

The activities related with the power transformers include:

— Finalising the requirements (User)
— Selection and application (User)
— Tender Enquiry, Tender specifications (User)
— Route survey for transportation, handling (manufacturer/transport contractor)
— Installation planning, civil conceptual design (User/Manufacturer)
— Preliminary design and tender submission (Manufacturer)
— Tender negotiations (User/Manufacturer)
— Ordering, pricing, Billing schedule, Despatch schedule (Manufacturer/User)
— Finalising specifications (User)
— Project Planning (User/Project Agency)
— Design
— Ordering materials, components (Manufacturer)
— Final design (Manufacturer)
— Testing (Manufacturer), Acceptance (User)
— Dismantling for transport
— Packing.
— Despatch (Manufacturer), Transport Contractor
— Unloading at site (Transport Contractor)
— Installation (Erection Contractor)
— Testing, Commissioning (Erection contractor)
— Trial operation for a few months
— Acceptance (User), Handling-over
— Operation and maintenance (User).

Transformers are ordered, designed, manufactured, tested, transported, installed, commissioned, operated and maintained. The various activities are inter-related and demand expertise about different aspects of power transformers. The knowledge about the electrical power systems and associated phenomena is useful. These aspects have been presented in this book in later chapters.

# 2

# Construction, Materials and Production Sequence of Distribution Transformers and Large Power Transformers

The essential parts of a *distribution transformer* are core, windings, insulation system, oil, tank, tank cover, bushings, carriage, fitments, radiator, etc. Distribution transformers are made in lot as per standard designs. *Large transformers* have same essential components plus tap-changer, control cabinet, separate cooling system, etc. They are manufactured individually against specific orders.

Correct kind of design, manufacture, test, operation and protection increase the normal life of a transformer.

Essential parts in the construction of a transformer have been described in brief.

The materials used in the construction of power transformers are described in brief.

The details about the construction of core, windings, tank, coolers, tap-changers, bushings etc., have been covered in subsequent chapters.

## 2.1. ESSENTIAL PARTS

Figure 1.4. illustrates the essential parts and subassemblies of a distribution transformer. A large power transformer has additional tap-changer, separate cooling system and modified construction of the core.

The configuration, structural assembly, detailed design philosophy depends upon type and ratings of the transformer and the manufacturers internal standerdization.

The four important applications of power transformers are:

1. In generating stations
2. In transmission substations
3. In distribution substations
4. In consumers premises.

## 2.2. LARGE TRANSFORMERS

The transformers in generating stations and transmission sub-station are characteristised by;

— High MVA rating and kV ratings

— Large size and high transport weight
— With On-load or Off-load Tap-Changers .
— With separately installed coolers and with forced oil and forced air cooling
— Long bushings
— Three of Five limb construction of core. Three limb constructions is no more used on it increases the transformer height.

The configuration and choice of such transformers are decided by permissible transport weight and permissible dimensions and profile.

The dimensions and weight is finalised after the survey of the complete route from the factory to the site including road route, rail route etc., and after getting permission from railways for particular routes. Such large transformers are despatched and transported with the tank (assembled with core, coils, gaskets etc.) filled with dry air or nitrogen. The oil, bushings, tap-changer, accessories are despatched separately. The configuration of core and tank is determined by the conditions of transportation and handling. Choice is made from the following alternatives.

**Table 2.1. Alternatives for Single Phase/Three Phase Units**

| *Alternative* | *Weight and size of Transportable Unit* |
|---|---|
| 1. Single phase two winding | Lowest |
| 2. Single phase three winding | Low |
| 3. Three phase two winding | High |
| 4. Three phase three winding | Highest |

The separately despatchable parts of the large transformer include:
— Tank with core, winding, tank cover, filled with dry air or nitrogen.
— Coolers, cooling system.
— Bushings.
— Tap-changers.
— Accessories.

Large transformers are designed against particular order or repeat order. They are not manufactured in large quantities. Choice of core configuration depends on the transportation limitation.

## 2.3. MEDIUM TRANSFORMERS

The transformers of medium size may be despatched like large power transformers. The design limitations of transportation are generally not applicable. If the road is safe, such transformers are transported by road trailer.

## 2.4. DISTRIBUTION TRANSFORMERS

The kVA and kV ratings are generally standardised by the users on the basis of IS or IEC standards. The variations in applications include:

— Type of mounting: Pole mounted, foundation mounted, mobile.

— Indoor or outdoor.

— Dry or soil filled.

For selection of distribution transformer, the most essential data is kVA rating, kV class of HV winding, kV class of LV winding, Type of connection, *e.g.*, star/delta.

The production of distribution transformers follows standard ratings. Orders are placed in bulk. Production is in large quantities design.

Small and medium transformers are generally despatched with the tank with sufficient oil to cover winding and insulation. Remaining oil is despatched separately in steel drums or by tankers. Alternatively full quantity of oil may be contained in transformer tank under despatch. The following description generally applies to Medium and large transformers.

## 2.5. SINGLE PHASE VERSUS THREE-PHASE UNITS

Transformers are built generally as three phase units except when single three phase units are beyond permissible transportation size/weight. Before 1950, single phase units were more commonly used to form three phase banks. However, this practice is no more followed.

Single phase transformers are used for single phase 25 kV, 50 Hz traction system.

## 2.6. MAIN PARTS OF A TRANSFORMER

The main parts of a transformer are:

1. Tank and tank cover.
2. Core and clamping structure.
3. Primary and secondary windings and clamping arrangements.
4. Insulation of windings.
5. Leads and tappings, support arrangements.
6. Bushings.
7. Tap-changers.
8. Cooling system.
9. Accessories and Fitments.

Table 2.2 gives the brief description.

## 2.7. ACCESSORIES AND FITMENTS

The following accessories and fitments are generally provided.

—Fluid level gauge
—Vacuum gauge
—pressure vacuum switch
—Sudden Pressure Relay
—Pressure Relief valve
—Fluid temperature indicator
—Hot spot temperature indicator
—Gas temperature indicator
—Combustible limit relays etc.
—Conservator
—Breather
—Buchholz relay
—Bushings
—Tap changer
—Marshalling kiosk
—Cooling system
—Neutral grounding arrester
—Truck on rollers etc.
—Surge arrester
—Earthing connection.

The application of these devices depends upon the type of transformer rating and the local needs.

**Table 2.2 Construction Features of Power Transformers**

| *Part* | *Description and Remarks* |
|---|---|
| **1. Core** | **Functions:** |
| | 1. It is a backbone of the transformer from magnetic and mechanical strength aspects. 2. Provides path for magnetic flux. 3. Supports windings. |
| | **Desirable Features.** Low losses, better heat dissipation, low vibrations, low noise, low watts/kg ratio, higher working flux, compact size. |
| | **Important Construction Features.** Material of laminations; specific losses W/kg, permeability, magnetostriction properties. |
| | **Correctness of manufacturing techniques.** for lamination, edge preparation, method of holding jointing, clamping. |
| | **Materials.** Laminated CRGO steel sheets (Cold Rolled Grain oriented silicon sheet steel). Superior properties in direction of rolling, surface treatment: oxide coating or vanish. |
| | **Properties.** Specific core loss W/kg at peak flux density 1.7 T at 50 Hz, Ageing withstand, surface resistance, space factor, waviness, edge camber, burrs, etc., within specified limits. |

*(Contd...)*

| *Part* | *Description and Remarks* |
|---|---|
| | **Configurations.** Shell type preferred in USA, core type preferred in India, Europe, USSR. For single phase units: two leg or three leg or four leg. For three phase unit: three leg or five leg. |
| | **Cooling.** Cooling of core by circulation of oil through ducts and around the core. |
| | **Vibrations.** Due to magnetostriction and loose clamping. Reduced at lower flux densities. |
| **2. Windings and Insulation System** | —Wound concentrically around the core limbs. LV winding placed near the core on the press-board cylinder. |
| | —HV winding away from core. |
| | —Placed on press board cylinders. |
| | —Packings and clamps provided by press boards, laminated resin impregnated wood strips, bars. |
| | —Superior craft paper insulation wrapped over conductors. |
| | —Types include helical, double helical, disc winding, choice depends on voltage and kVA per winding. |
| | —Most sensitive part, subjected to thermal, mechanical and dielectric stresses. |
| **3. Tanks** | —Supports and encloses various parts. |
| | — Should be strong, sturdy free from vibrations. |
| | —Should have good surface finish by shot blasting, painting. |
| | —Should withstand mechanical load during handling, lifting, transport. |
| | —Should withstand vacuum test. |
| | —Should withstand pressure test. |
| | —Boiler plate steel. Fabricated welded construction to obtain box type construction for tank; with Flanges on the top. |
| | —Tank cover supports bushings, tap-changers other fit ments. |
| | —Accessories include: Lifting lugs, pulling eyes, manhole for inspection, valves for filling, draining, earthing terminals, spring loaded pressure relief valve. |
| | —Transformer cover either bolted or welded Gaskets used with bolted construction. |

*(Contd...)*

| Part | Description and Remarks |
|---|---|
| **4.Bushings** | —Oil Impregnated Paper wound condenser bushing (OIP) used for higher voltages. Earlier synthetic resin bonded paper insullated condenser bushings (SRBP) were used. |
| | —Provides insulated supported to conductors connecting the external terminal to the transformer winding. |
| | —Essential parts: Central flange, air-end porcelain enclosure, oil-end porcelain enclosure (optional) central condenser. |
| | —Central copper or Alumuinium tube with surrounding condenser body. |
| | —Oil resistant rubber gaskets. |
| | —Oil filling between condenser and the porcelain. |
| | —Bushing mounted vertically or inclined or tank cover on turrets. |
| | —Essential requirements: Rated voltage rated current, rated insulation level, external creepage, external clearances; flange arrangement, terminal connections oil level indicator, provision of rubber bellows for expansion of oil, turret mounted CTs (optional). |
| **5. Cooling System** | **Small transformers.** Tube welded on the tank. Oil Natural (ON) Oil circulates naturally through tank. |
| | **Medium Transformers.** Radiators fitted on to the tank, oil Natural (ON) oil circulates naturally through tank. |
| | **Large Transformers.** Radiators fitted on to the tank, fans provide forced air on radiator for cooking (ONAF) oil circulates naturally through tank. |
| | **Large High Power Voltage Transformers.** Coolers separately mounted. Oil forced by means of pumps through tank and cooler. Oil flow within tank is directed through windings and cores for effective cooling. Fans provide forced air for cooling to improve heat dissipation. Coolers are mounted on separate foundations. |
| | **Significance.** Transformer size is reduced MVA/kg ratio improved. Loading improved, Hot spot temperature reduced. Transformer life improved. |
| **6.Tap-Changes** | Mounted vertically within the transformer tank. |
| | **Essential components.** Drive housing diverter switch, tap-selector. |
| | **Types.** On load or off-circuit, on-load for daily voltage variation off-circuit for seasonal voltage variation. |

*(Contd...)*

| *Part* | *Description and Remarks* |
|---|---|
| | **Important data for ordering.** Type, phases. step voltage, Number of tap positions, Rated through current in regulating winding, insulation level rated voltages, rated current of connections. |
| | Voltage ratio can be varied in steps either by operators command or by voltage control relay. Each change in step voltage taken approximately 10 seconds. Most complex switching device. Designed for over million operation without need for intermdiate maintenance. |

**Table 2.3. Accessories and Fitments on a Transformer**

| *Item* | *Description* |
|---|---|
| **1. Flow Indicators** | Fitted in oil circulation system. Indiactes flow rate.<br>Used for control purposes in combination with float switches for starting and stopping oil pumps. |
| **2. Pressure Relief Valve** | Fitted on the tank to permit venting out of gasses formed of oil. Protects transformer tank against explosion. Many used for tripping or alarm. |
| **3. Buchholz Relay (Gas Operated Relay)** | Fitted in the pipe between tank and conservator.<br>Gives alarm for incipient faults in the transformer which form gas. Gas pressure operates alarm contacts. Short circuit gives very high pressure and flow of oil through the relay resulting in closing of trip contacts in the relay. Transformer is protected from bursting. Gas sample can be collected and analysed, to obtain indication about type of deterioration of oil/insulation., |
| **4. Sudden Pressure Relay (Rate of rise of pressure relay** | The rate of rise pressure relay responds to sudden rise of pressure due to internal arcing. The relay is fitted on the tank and is actuated by rate of rise in oil pressure. |
| **5. Conservator.** | It is a large cylinder connected by pipe to the transformer. Transformer oil is filled upto certain level in the conservator. Remaining upper portion is filled with air. Conservator oil is in communication with tank-oil. Expansion and contraction of transformer tank oil is accommodated by the air cushion in the conservator. Direct contact with external air is avoided through silica gel breather. Conservators are of two types. |

*(Contd...)*

| *Item* | *Description* |
|---|---|
| | (1) Air cushion connected with external atmosphere through breather. Air which enters conservator is dried by silica gel in the breather.<br>(2) Air cushion contained in rubber bag (bellow) installed within the conservator. Rubber bag is filled with air of positive pressure. Contact with external air is totally avoided. This is used in large transformers. |
| **6. Breather** | Installed in a pipe from conservator. One end connected to air cushion to air cushion in conservator. Other end connected to external air. Air cushion in the upper portion of conservator is in communication with external atmosphere through the breather.<br>Breather is filled with dry silica jel (Pink). When oil in conservator rises, air is let out through breather. When oil is contracted during low loads/low temperature, air is breathed in by the conservator through the breather. Silica jel absorbs the moisture and admits only dry air.<br>Wet Silica jel (Blue) can be dried during periodic maintenance (pink). |
| **7 Oil Temperature thermometer/indicator.** | A thermocouple is placed in the pocket provided with the tank near hot oil. Thermocouple leads are connected to oil temperature indicator placed in marshaling kiosk (control cabinet). |
| **8. Winding Temperature Indicator**<br>**(Hot-spot Indicator) with alarm and tripping contacts** | Winding temperature indicator installed in marshalling kiosk gets input for measurement from<br>(1) Thermocouple placed in the tank near hot oil.<br>(2) CT secondary which measures the current in winding.<br>The indicator is provided with alarm and tripping contacts. Provided with time delays. Typical settings of contacts are:<br>(1) Staring fan : 60°C (2) Alarm 95°C<br>(3) Trip : 120°C. |
| **9. Control Cabinet (Marshaling Kiosk)** | Provided with each large transformer/reactor. Generally placed on the side of the tank fixed on brackets.<br>All instruments for measurements, monitoring and control are placed in the cabinet. |

(*Contd...*)

| *Item* | *Description* |
|---|---|
| | All monitoring, starting, stopping contractors terminal blocks of control wiring etc., are placed in this cabinet.<br><br>All control cables and power cables between transformer, cooler, control room, auxiliary supply switchgear etc., are via control cabinet. Start, stop, switches for fan motors, cooler pump motors etc., are housed in control cabinet. Temperature indicators, temperature controllers etc., are placed in the control cabinet. |
| **10. Trolleys Truck** | Steel carriage with caster wheels placed on rails. Carries transformer weight , Transformer be moved horizontally in manufacturers premises or at site. Without need of road trailer. |
| **11. Surge Arresters (one per phase)** | Separate devices. Installed on separate foundation near the transformer. Single phase units.<br><br>One terminal connected to the lead from transformer terminal. Other terminal connected to earth.<br><br>Lightning surges and switching surges are discharged to earth. Transformer winding and insulation is protected.<br><br>Two types (1) Silicon carbide type gapped surge arrester. It has silicon carbide resistor discs in series with spark gaps. (2) Zinc-oxide surge Arrester (ZnO). This has only ZnO discs. There are no spark gaps. ZnO arresters have Superior V/I characteristics and energy absorption capability. The distance between arrester and transformer should not be more. |

## 2.8. PRODUCTION OF TRANSFORMERS

The production of *Distribution Transformers* is generally a lot production. The kVA and kV ratings are standardized. Several units of certain standard kVA ratings are produced during every month Standaredisation of ratings and lot production aims at low production cost, high rate of production and guaranteed quality.

*Large Transformers* are manufactured against specific orders and to meet customer's specific requirements. The large transformers have to meet several different requirements such as size, weight, capitalization of losses, rated characteristics etc., and standardization of ratings and lot production is not possible. Such transformers are manufactured one or two at a time. Production cycle takes a few months. Type testing is essential to verify the design etc.

### 2.8.1. Production Sequence for Distribution Transformers.

The components/subassemblies are divided into following groups:

— Core — Coils
— Tank — Accessories
— Subassemblies/components like bushings, tap-changers, control cabinets, cooling system etc.

A market survey is conducted to determine the expected demand for basic units and a profitability calculation is carried out to decide which materials and in what quantities should be held in stock. Example of production program for the individual components of distribution transformer of standard kVA ratings is as follows:

— *Magnet cores*: Lots of 10 to 100 units, depending on type.
— *Coils*: Copper for windings and also insulating materials, sufficient for two months.
— *Tanks and accessories*: Corrugated walls, bases, frames and covers in lots of 20 to 100 units, depending on type.
— *Assembly components and subassemblies*: Bushings, tapping switches, seals etc., sufficient for two to three months.

**Coil Shop.** The HV and LV coils are fabricated on special purpose machines either as complete coils or sub-assemblies. All connections and terminals are prepared in advance. The coils are aged and made ready for installation.

**Press Shop and Core Assembly.** The laminations for the limbs and yokes are produced in the press shop, coils of sheet in one operation on special presses are heat-treated in a tunnel oven. They are then transported to the assembly shop. Core assembly is planned such that finished cores are available for a maximum of one week's production.

**Core and Coil Assembly.** The assembly line involves the following operations:

— placing the magnet core on light trolleys
— dismounting the top yoke on a special truck with a U shape channel to accept the upper end yoke plates.
— remove special truck and fit coil
— fit upper yoke
— assemble cover with bushings, switches and other equipment
— fit cover on core and coil assembly
— secure electrical connections.

**Tank Assembly.** The components of the transformer tanks i.e., the walls, bases and frames, are welded together in the tank assembly shop. All tanks of the same type are combined in a weekly production batch. Each tank is leakage tested with transformer oil at about 80°C. In the last stage of production, they pass through the surface treatment bay where they are steam cleaned and degreased. Finally, two coats of paint are applied.

The trolleys are moved on after each operation. Each assembly area has the necessary components and tools within easy reach.

**Drying, Testing, Filling with Oil.** The core and coil assemblies are dried during the night by heating under vacuum. The next day they are checked i.e., the coil pressure is tested, all screwed fixing are tightened and locked. The core and coil assembly is then fitted into the tank and bolted in position. Finally, the tank if filled with dried and degassed oil.

**Final Tests.** The test facility at the end of the assembly line is split into two bays, each of which can accommodated 5 to 8 transformers.

Standard tests are carried out on the transformers in the following sequences:

The resistance and voltage ratio are measured and the polarity checked with a measuring bridge and then the no-load and copper losses, the short-circuit voltage, internal and external voltages are measured. Type tests are also conducted as required.

Test reports are finalised.

**Preparing for despatch.** The final coat of paint is sprayed on after testing. The rating plates are fitted and loose installation material parcelled up and attached to the transformer.

Starting from the point where the laminations are fitted in the upper yoke, five to six working days are taken to produce the tank and about the same time is consumed in making the complete coil. All other parts are drawn from stock. Production of a simple distribution transformer required approximately twelve days.

### 2.8.2. Merits of Standardisation of Distribution Transformers

The standardisation of distribution transformers offers several advantages to the manufacturer and user. These include:

**Product Quality.** Wide-scale use of well-tried components, such as iron frames, coils, main insulation, heat exchangers etc., results in a high-quality end product.

**Flanges and Seals.** Flange dimensions, such as for connecting the oil treatment plant can be standardized. Using clearly defined types of seal simplifies both transformer maintenance and spares storage.

**Transformer Accessories.** Standard equipment which has proved itself in service is used in protection and fault indication,This includes Buchholz relays, oil level indicators, thermometers, thermostats and thermal replicas.

**Transport and Installation Equipment.** By working in close cooperation with transporters, it is possible to steam line the transportation.

Standardized dimensions and location of the lifting lugs and eyes enable the same lifting tackle to be used for a wide range of types. Foundation design and civil work design also gets standardized resulting in fast and correct civil works.

### 2.8.3. Production of Large Transformers

There are so many different versions of large transformers that it is impossible to standardize them according to a fixed code. Although certain users limit themselves to certain standard types which cover their special requirements, these are generally isolated cases.

The designers have to devise a means of producing necessary engineering documentation on an economically acceptable basis. As a result, the transformers are arranged in individual, self-contained groups. The production sequence should be taken into account. The computer is used successfully in processing the orders and producing the necessary engineering documentation. For instance, the necessary workshop data for producing the magnet core, including size, weight, number and shape of the lamination sheets, is printed out from a computer programme.

Large transformers are designed and manufactured against particular order or repeat order. They are not manufactured in a dot.

**Production Sequence.** The production shop comprises separate neighbouring bays for the following; fabrication shop for tanks, press shop for producing laminations of required size, Winding shop for producing coils and windings.

— Insulation shop — Bushing* shop
— Tap-changer* shop — Assembly shop
— Vapour phase drying
— Despatch shop — Final testing
— Core assembly shop for assembly of core
— Core and coil assembly shops

The following sub-assemblies/part are manufactured in different shops:

(1) *Tanks* and tank covers are produced in fabrication shop. Tanks are designed and manufactured to withstand hydrostatic pressure equal to twice the oil head in the tank. Tanks for EHV transformers are designed to withstand full vacuum.

Tanks are manufactured by high grade boiler plate steel. Non-magnetic steels are used wherever there is a problem of stray fluxes. Plates are cut to size bent, prepared, welded. Surface is cleaned. Primer coat is applied. This is followed by two coats of paint.

(2) *Windings* are prepared in winding shop as per specific design. Three types of winding in high power transformer are:

*These may be purchased from different manufacturers.

— Disc winding, Helical winding, Regulating winding.

Individual conductors are insulated with craft paper. Windings are wound on vertical winding machine.

(3) *Press Shop: Preparation of Laminations.* Sheet steel is obtained from steel manufacturers in roll form in suitable widths. The sheets are already treated with surface treatment. The rolls are loaded on automatic cutting machine for getting laminations of required width. The taper is provided by shearing machine. The laminations are cut to required sizes and shapes within close tolerances. Edge camber, waviness, damage to surface insulation by scratches/blisters etc., is not permitted. Lamination are sent to core assembly shop.

(4) *Core assembly shops.* The laminations are placed in required sequence to obtain the three phase cores or single phase cores. This operation is done on core-building platform. Lamination of large cores are held together by insulated bands wound on press-board cylinder by using high density press board spacers.

(5) *Windings.* The winding are prepared on vertical or horizontal winding machine. The number of turns and sequence of turn depends on type of winding and design of winding.

Windings are produced in separate clean area to avoid dust, iron particles etc. Each winding is wound separately on a *winding machine* and then taken to core-and coil assembly shop. Non magnetic steel bands or fiber glass tapes which are wound on tension and applied with thermosetting resin and cured.

(6) *Core and Windings Assembly.* For smaller, cores epoxy cementing technique is used.

Core clamps are provided on top and bottom. Side supports may be provided at each corner. The complete core is taken to core-and-winding assembly shop. The lamination of top-yoke are deassembled. Press board cylinders are placed on the core legs. The insulation strips are placed. The LV winding is placed on the press board cylinder. The press board insulation system is assembled. Interphase insulation cylinder is placed over the LV winding. The HV winding is slided over the interphase insulation cylinder (while still hot) the insulating components are assembled. The entire winding and insulation system is subjected to vertical pressure in large press and is subjected to vacuum and heating cycles for stabilizing and ageing.

During alternate vacuum and heating cycles to core and coil assembly, a constant axial pressure is maintained by means of hydraulic jacks. In early days, clamping plates, springs and clamping structure were used for this operation.

Prior to tanking, the core and coil assembly is subjected to vapour phase drying or hot air drying. In hot air drying, special ovens are used.

Hot dry is circulated through the oven. The moisture is removed from the coils, core and insulation system.

For large transformers, vapour phase drying is used.*

*Tanking.* Tanking of core-and-coil assembly is done immediately after final drying out process. Tanking is done as follows: after taking-out of drying oven, the nut bolts are rechecked for tightness. The complete assembly is blown by dry air to remove dust and iron particles and then vacuumed. Thereafter, the complete assembly is carefully lowered into the tank. Tank cover is fitted. The oil filled as per procedure for the respective voltage class. The oil filling is done with vacuum inside the tank. This eliminates moisture and dust ingress. As the oil is filled under vacuum, the capillaries and voids in the insulation system are filled with oil and air pockets are eliminated.

*Testing.* Complete transformer is taken to the testing bay for conducting (1) agreed type tests (2) Routine test (3) agreed special tests. These tests are conducted in presence of customers representatives in accordance with pre-planned schedule.

*Packing and Despatch.* The complete tank filled with dry nitrogen is transported by special rail-wagon or by road trailer as per preplanned transportation. Bushing are packed as per packing drawing.

Tap-changers are packed as per instructions. The bushings, tap-changers, other components are road transported by trucks upto site. Oil is transported by road in oil drums.

## 2.9.QUALITY PLANS

The complete quality plans are submitted for approval prior to commencement of production.

Quality plans include:

— Quality plans for purchased-items
— Quality plans for raw material and components
— Quality plans for core windings. assembly etc.
— Quality plans for oil
— Quality plans for final drying
— Quality plans for testing.

The quality plans comprise definite instructions for checks, measurements and records during every step in the production sequence from raw materials to finished products. During the production, the checks and measurements are made and recorded. The materials and components which are beyond the specifications in quality/dimensions are rejected. Quality control ensures perfection of raw materials, components subassemblies, final assembly.

*Refer appendix—I.

By strict quality control, the successful type testing and routine testing is ensured.

## 2.10. BUSHINGS

High voltage bushings are generally Oil-impregrated paper type condenser Bushings. Manufacturing sequence includes following major steps;

— Central non-magnetic tube (brass or Alumuinium alloy or Copper) is machined to exact dimensions.
— Oil impregrated Craft paper and tin foil is wound to form the condenser. A resin coating is provided on the condenser.
— Central flange is fitted
— Air end porcelain and oil-end porcelain are fitted.
— Top-hood is assembled over the porcelain.
— Complete bushing is subjected to vacuum drying and is filled with dielectric oil.
— After certain hours of drying, the bushing is sent to testing laboratory.
— After testing, the bushing is sent to transformer assembly shop or it is despatched to site.

## 2.11. TAP-CHANGER

Tap-changer is the most complex and sub-assembly and consists of very accurately dimensioned components of tap-changer assembly. The completed assembly is subjected to rigorous operational tests and routine tests. For testing purpose the tap-changer is mounted on a stand and the motor-drive housing, drive shafts etc., are connected. Mechanical tests are carried out.

The electrical tests are carried out after assembly on a dummy oil filled tank or on actual transformer.

## 2.12. MATERIALS

Materials used in the construction of power transformers are classified as:

— Conducting materials
— Insulating (Dielectric materials)
— Magnetic materials
— Structural (Fabrication) materials
— Sealing materials.

### 2.12.1. Conducting Materials

**Important Properties.** Conductivity/resistivity temperature coefficient of resistivity, working temperature, softening temperature, workability.

**Parts.** Windings, leads, conducting parts in tap changer, bushings, terminals, connections.

**Copper and Alumuinium.** Electrolytic copper is used for conductors in transformer winding, machine windings, busbars, cables.

Alumuinium wound power transformers have been developed but at present only copper is used in transformer windings. When copper becomes scares, alumuinium will replace copper even in transformer winding. Alumuinium alloy is used for the central tube in bushings.

**Properties of Copper.** Properties depend on purity, manufacturing process, heat-treatment etc. Copper is Malleable, ductile, reddish metal, can be cast, forged, rolled, drawn machined.

Specific gravity : 8.9 average

Melting point : 1083°C

Softening temperature : 180°C.

At 180°C it starts oxidizing rapidly in air. It is attacked by Ammonia, Sulphur dioxide. Copper oxide is green and is insulating. Copper is corroded slowly in sea-water. Mechanical working, cold drawing etc., causes hardening of copper.

Anealing causes softening of copper

Before making a joint, the oxide layer on surface should be removed by means of emery-paper. The joint should be made immediately. Anti-oxidising jelley is applied where joints are exposed to air.

Moisture and water should be kept away.

**Table 2.4 Properties of Copper and Alumuinium***

| *Material* | *Specific gravity* | *Conductivity at 20°C % IACE* | *Resistivity at 20°C* | *Temp. Expansion Coeff.per °C* | *Temp. Coefficient of resistance at 20°C* |
|---|---|---|---|---|---|
| **Copper** | | | | | |
| Soft bus rod<br>Soft bus tube<br>Wire bar | 8.89 | 100 | 1.72 | $16.92 \times 10^{-4}$ | 0.00427 |
| Hardbus pipe, round Strong | 8.89 | 9.74 | 1.77 | " | 0.00415 |
| **Aluminium** | | | | | |
| Hard rod | 2.703 | 61.8 | 2.78 | $23 \times 10^{-4}$ | 0.00445 |

*Properties very widely with composition, manufacturing process etc. Refer manufacturer's catalogues and specifications.

**Copper Alloy.** Pure copper is soft and has lesser mechanical properties. Mechanical properties of copper are improved by alloying with elements which are soluble in a solid rotation of copper. These elements include manganese, nickel, zinc, tin. Alumuinium. Alloying with the elements reduces conductivity, and ductility but improves rolling and working properties.

**Brass.** It is binary alloy of copper and zinc. It has low electrical conductivity. It is easily machined and has higher mechanical strength.

### 2.12.2 Dielectic Materials

#### (a) Important Properties

— From : Gas/liquid/solid
— Dielectric strength, kV/cm.
— Permittivity (ε) F/m
— Mechanical properties: Workability, strength etc., depending upon application.
— Temperature properties
— Temperature withstand.
— Moisture absorption
— Uniformity and freedom from voids/gaps.
— Ageing.

#### (b) Application

— For external enclosures: Porcelain/Epoxy resin
— For filling: Dielectric oil or Nitrogen gas
— For winding insulation: Craft paper.
— For insulation system: High density press board
— For cylinders: Press board, glass fiber reinforced synthetic resin cylinders
— For bars, rods: resin bonded laminated wood, resin bonded glass fiber.

#### (c) Significance

— Insulating materials are most vulnerable in the life of a transformer. Principle causes of failures include (1) Moisture (2) Partial discharges (3) Ageing (4) Temperature rise.

**Table 2.5. Dielectric Materials used in Power Transformers and Reactors, CTs,VTS.**

| *Material* | *Application* | *Remarks* |
|---|---|---|
| 1. Porcelain | —Enclosure for CTs VTs. | —Compression strength 6000 kg/cm$^2$ |
| | —Support porcelains for equipment bus bars. | —Tensile strength 4000 kg/cm$^2$ |
| | —Enclosures for Bushing | —High temperature withstand. |

*(Contd...)*

| *Material* | *Application* | *Remarks* |
|---|---|---|
| | —Solid and hollow supports.<br>—Tubes for passage of compressed air, Dielectric oil. | —Suitable for outdoor and indoor applications.<br>—Processed clay by moulding and firing before and after glazing at 1250° to 1400°C. |
| 2. Epoxy Resin | —Support insulators and equipment enclosures in indoor application.<br>—Bonding of core laminations<br>—Insulation for conductors<br>—Insulating covers<br>—Insulating castings<br>—Encapsulated conducting parts such as bus-bars coils, terminals. | —Generally used in solid form obtained by mixing with hardener an curing at appropriate temperature.<br>—Suitable filler used to get strength and economy. |
| 3. Glass Fiber Reinforced Synthetic Resins. | —Insulating components | —High tensile strength high withstand pressure, high dielectric strength |
| 4. Dielectric oil | —As insulation and cooling medium in transformers, CTs, VTs | —Good dielectric strength properties as per IS 335-1993 BS 148, IEC 296 |
| 5. Press Boards | —Solid, soft, Calender pressboards used for cylinders, barriers, spacers, washers, yoke insulation, partitions.<br>—Soft laminated press board used for blocks, supports, cleats, spacers etc.<br>—Precompressed solid press boards for studs, blocks, washers, clamping of winding etc. | IS–1576–1992<br>BS – 5354<br>IEC – 763 |
| 6. Laminated wood. | —Packing between core and winding | Unimpregrated high density laminated wood |

(*Contd...*)

| *Material* | *Application* | *Remarks* |
|---|---|---|
| | —Blocks, wedges for coil supports. | Alternate laminations in perpendicular grain orientation. High strength High dielectric strength |
| 7. Insulating tapes | —For taping on the conductors on turns on winding on loads. | —High dielectric strength |
| | | —Moisture retardon |
| | | —Good ageing properties |
| | | —Compatible with transformer oil |
| | | —High temperature with stand. |
| | —Cotton tape | IS : 1923–2003 |
| | —Class woven tape | IS : 5352–2004 (Part 1 & 2) |
| | —Terylene woven tape | IS : 5351–2006 |
| 8. Insulated copper conductor cables. | 1. Paper insulated rectangular copper conductors for winding | IS : 7404 Part I |
| | 2. Paper covered stranded copper cable. | IS : 8130, 8572–2003–2006 |
| | 3. PVC insulated copper cable single or multicore (Polyvinylechloride) | IS : 1554–1988 |
| | 4. Synthetic resin insulated conductors | |
| 9. Phenolic Laminated Paper base sheet. | —Terminal gear support | IS : 2036–1995 |
| | —Terminal board for core ducts, supports., | |
| 10. Phenolic laminated cotton fabric sheet. | —Terminal boards, | IS: 2036-1995 |
| | —Core ducts | |
| | —Support | |
| | —Cleat | |
| 11. Insulating Papers. | —For winding insulation | Electrical grade insulating craft paper. |

*(Contd...)*

| *Material* | *Application* | *Remarks* |
|---|---|---|
| | —For paper boards | —High dielectric strength<br>—Thermal stability<br>—High temperature withstand.<br>—Moisture retardation<br>—Free from voids, gaps<br>—Good heat dissipation<br>—Chemically compatible with oil<br>—Good mechanical properties. |

### 2.12.3. Insulating Materials Used in Power Transformer

The main properties of insulating materials used in power transformer are the following:

1. High dielectric strength at working temperature.
2. Good thermal conductivity.
3. Long life at working temperatures.
4. Good mechanical properties such as ease for working and application, bending.
5. Resistant to vibrations and abrasion.
6. Compatible with oil and surrounding medium.
7. Non-hygroscopic.
8. Low dielectric loss.
9. Long life, good ageing property.

The various insulating materials used in power transformers are mentioned in Table 2.6.

**Table 2.6. Insulating Components in Power Transformers**

| *Component* | *Function* |
|---|---|
| 1. Press board or synthetic resin bonded paper cylinder (S.R.B.P) | Insulation between Core L.V., winding |
| 2. Press board or synthetic regin bonded paper cylinder (S.R.B.P) | Insulation between L.V. and H.V. winding |
| 3. Synthetic resin bonded paper bars. | For supports, for spacers between core/ L.V. winding H.V. winding. |
| 4. Tape of paper for conductor. | Conductor insulation in oil immersed transformer. |
| 5. Tape of Glass. | Conductor insulation for dry transformer. |

### 2.12.4. Temperature Classification of Insulating Materials

Insulating materials used in power transformers are classified on the basis of maximum permitted temperature. The temperature classification of insulating material is as follows:

Y, A, E, B, F, H, C

**Table 2.7**

| Insulation Class | Y | A | E | B | F | H | C |
|---|---|---|---|---|---|---|---|
| Maximum Temp., °C | 90 | 105 | 120 | 130 | 155 | 180 | 180 |

**Material of Temperature Class**

| *Class* | *Max.Temp.°C* | *Materials* |
|---|---|---|
| Y | 90 | Cotton, Silk, Paper, Wood, Cellulose, Fiber etc., without impregnation or oil immersion. |
| A | 105 | The materials of class Y-impregnated with natural resins, cellulose, esters, insulating oil, etc., also laminated wood, varnished paper, cellulose acetate film, etc. |
| E | 120 | Synthetic resin enamels, cotton and paper laminates with formaldehyde bonding etc. |
| B | 130 | Mica, glass, fiber, asbestos, etc., with suitable bonding substances, built-up mica, glass fiber and asbestos laminates. |
| F | 155 | The materials of class B with more thermally resistant bonding materials. |
| H | 180 | Glass fiber and asbestos materials, and built up mica, with appropriate silicon resins. |
| C | > 180 | Mica, ccramies, glass, quarters and asbestos without binders or with silicon resins of superior thermal stability. |

1. Class A, E, B, C, F and H are all used in dry type transformers. Silicon treated materials are advantageous because of their water repellent property.

2. For oil immersed transformers the coil insulation is generally of class A type, (craft paper, manila paper etc., or paper derivatives such as press boards, craft boards are used). Paper based materials are excellent when dry. But they can readily absorb moisture from oil.

Depending upon requirements of a particular design specified. Number of layer of specially treated tape is applied to the winding conductor.

Parts made from sheet insulation such as phenolic resin bonded paper bars,tubes, cylinders are used to support the winding and to provide insulation barriers.

**3. Insulating Varnish.** Insulating varnish is used for impregnating the transformer winding. The impregnation of transformer windings by insulating varnish increases the mechanical the mechanical strength of the windings insulation and fill up the pores of the paper and reduces the tendency to absorb moisture. Vacuum impregnation is preferable.

**4 Enamel.** Enamel insulation is used for conductors for dry type transformers. Oil resistant, air drying cnamel applied to copper conductors of small size.

**5.Transformer Oil.** The transformer oil (dielectric oil) is used as an insulation and cooling medium power transformers.

### 2.12.5. Dielectic Strength

The property of the insulating material which enable it to withstand high voltage without deterioration or failure is expressed in terms of minimum electric strength/electric stress which will cause break down. It is expressed in terms of breakdown voltage per unit thickness of the dielectric.

$$E_{br} = \frac{V_{br}}{t}$$

where, $E_{br}$ = break-down stress, kV/mm

$V_{br}$ = break-down voltage, kV

$t$ = thickness of the dielectric ,mm

The break-down stress of a dielectric is referred to as the electric strength (or dielectic strength) of the material.

It is one of the main insulation characteristics. The average dielectric strength of the insulating materials used in transformers ranges from 5 to 90 kV/mm at 20°C.

### 2.12.6 Insulation Resistance and Polarisation Index

*Insulation resistance* of an electrical equipment refers to the resistance between conducting part and earth, expressed in megaohms. The insulation resistance can also be measured between two circuits separated by insulation.

Insulation resistance is measured by *Megger*. Megger consists of a built in megaohms meter and a d.c. generator. The generator is driven by hand or by a motor.

One terminal of megger is connected to conducting part, Other terminal is connected to earth frame (or other conducting circuit), the rotor of the generator is driven by hand or by motor.

*The reading $V_{de}/V_{de}$ ready by the megger gives the insulating resistance value in megaohm. The scale of Megger is graduated from zero to infinity in terms of megaohms.*

When DC voltage is applied across the insulation, intial reading of megger gives

$$R_0 = \frac{V_{de}}{I_0}$$

where, $I_0$ = Initial current at t = 0

$R_0$ = Initial insulation resistance

Initial $I_0$ consists of capacitive currents component and leakage current component.

After continuous application of DC voltage for say 60 seconds, the value of megger reading is

$$R_{60} = \frac{V_{de}}{I_{60}}$$

The d.c. current $I_{60}$ has lesser capacitive current component and has mainly leakage current component.

Hence $I_{60} < I_0$ and $R_{60} > R_0$

By continuous application of DC test voltage from megger, the megger reading goes on increasing.

To determine, how dry and clean is the insulation, the insulation is usually measured after 1 minute and 10 minutes. The polarisation index in the ratio of 10 minutes, IR value to 1 minute IR value. This is independent of temperature. PI gives idea about the age of the insulation. PI value have some meaning for large transformers only. For small transformers, PI will always be one as there will be no difference between 1 minute and 10 minutes IR values.

### 2.12.7. Magnetic Materials for Core

**Important Properties**

— Low specific core loss (W/kg) at working flux density.

— Low eddy current loss

— High saturation flux density ($B_m$) e.g., 1.8 T.

— Long life. Good ageing property

— Easy to manufacture.

— Low magnetic striction and noise.

**Parts.** Core consisting of top and bottom horizontal yokes and two or more vertical limbs in the construction of the core.

**Type of Material.** *Cold-rolled grain oriented silicon sheet steels are used for laminations of power transformers.* The commercially available cold-rolled silicon sheet steels have 3% silicon; total loss value 1.7 watts per kg at maximum flux density 1.6 teslas ( = 1.6 Wb/m$^2$) at 50 Hz. The thickness of sheets is 0.33 mm. The cold-rolled grain oriented steel sheets have superior magnetic properties in the direction of rolling. The crystal are aligned in the direction of rolling by cold-rolling and heat treatment process. The magnetic properties of the sheet steels are dependent on the magnetic properties of individual crystals of the material and the direction of orientation of the crystals.

*In non-oriented hot-rolled sheets* (used in early 1930s), the crystals are placed at random so that the magnetic properties of the sheet are independent of the direction of magnetic flux. However. in grain oriented cold rolled sheets, the magnetic properties in the direction of grain orientation (direction of rolling) are superior the properties in other directions.

*The electrical resistivity* of the material increase with the increase in percentage of silicon. However, the saturation flux density reduces with the increase in percentage of silicon. A silicon content upto 3% is used in commercial cold-rolled grain oriented sheets. The diameter if grains is about 3 mm. The sheets are commercially available in various grades. The grade designations and maximum core loss limits are specified by manufacturer.

**Surface Insulation.** Electrical steel lamination is provided with insulation layer on both sides. This insulation prevents eddy currents and reduces eddy current losses. The insulating layer is of oxide coating or varnish or both.

**Table 2.8**

| *Type of material for core lamination* | *Maximum flux density in core $B_m$, Tesla* | | | |
|---|---|---|---|---|
| | 1 | 1.2 | 1.4 | 1.6 |
| | | Core loss W/kg | | |
| 1. 0.33 mm, 3.25% Si commercial CRGO sheet steel. | 1.32 | 0.47 | 0.62 | 0.95 |
| 2. 0.23 mm 3.25% Si commercial CRGO Sheet steel. | 0.27 | 0.4 | 0.55 | 0.85 |
| 3. 0.15 mm 3.25% Si commercial CRGO sheet steel. | 0.23 | 0.35 | 0.47 | 0.75 |
| 4. Laser Irridiated super oriented CRGO | 0.16 | 0.25 | 0.35 | 0.57 |

The core losses increase with working flux density. With superior magnetic the specific core loss W/kg is reduced and higher working flux can be used.

### 2.12.8. Sealing Materials

**Purpose.** Seals (Gaskets) are provided between two mating surfaces to ensure leakage free joint for oil filled, gas filled, dry nitrogen filled equipment. When the two mating surfaces are tightened by means of nutbolts, the seal (gasket) gets squenced to about 20% and provides a leak-free joint . The shapes include:

—Circular cross-section (O-rings)

—Flat gaskets - Special shape.

**Degree of Protection.** The degree of protection against ingress of dust, water etc., are specified by IP code. The control cabinets of transformers, motor-driven housings of tap-changers are assigned with certain degree of protection such as

| *IP* | *Water Ingress* | *Dust Ingress* |
|---|---|---|
| IP 54 | Splash proof | Sealed, dust proof |
| IP 55 | Hose proof | Sealed, dust proof |
| IP 56 | Water tight for decks. | Sealed, dust proof |

The seal design depend upon the degree of protection desired.

**Table 2.9. Materials used for Seals***

| | | |
|---|---|---|
| **Synthetic rubber bonded cork** | —As flat gasket between the transformer tank flange and the tank cover<br>—between turret flange and bushing flange<br>—For inspection covers<br>—For flanges of various fitments. | IS : 4253 |
| **Nitrile rubber Oring or flat gasket** | —Between two flangers to prevent leakage of oil and to give gas-tight joint. | BS : 2751 |

### 2.12.9. Structural Materials

The structural materials are used for tank, tank cover. carriage, clamping plates, lifting hooks, stiffeners etc.

These are classified as:

—Ferrous materials

—Non-ferrous materials.

High carbon cold-rolled steels (IS 513, BS 1449). These are used for making radiator tubes.

---

TITE (Teflon) tape used in threaded joints to give air tight/oil tight threaded joint.

**High tensile strength steel plates (IS 961).** These are used for core-clamp plates, anchoring of core to the bottom tank.

**Nickel Chromium, molybdenum steel.** It is used for roller shaft, lifting pins, eye bolts etc.

**Stainless Steel (Non magnetic) IS : 6911.** Chromium nickel steel alloy. It is used for parts encircling current carrying conductors to prevent eddy current heating. Stainless steel sections are also used for high current and high strength applications.

**Cold Rolled Bright Steel bars, Sections (IS : 7270).** These are used for machined components, threaded components.

# 3

# EMF Equation, Voltage Ratio and kVA Ratings

In this chapter the most important EMF equation has been derived from fundamentals.

The significance of volts per turn and volts per hertz has been elaborated.

The equations for kVA of single phase and three phase transformers have been derived.

The ratings of transformers have been covered in Chapter 4.

## 3.1. NOTATIONS AND UNITS

Subscript 1 for primary.

Subscript 2 for secondary.

$I_1$ = Primary Current, a.c., r.m.s., amps.

$I_2$ = Secondary Current, a.c., r.m.s. amps.

$V_1$ = Applied Primary voltage, volts, r.m.s.

$V_2$ = Voltage at Secondary terminals, volts, r.m.s.

$N_1$ = Primary number of turns

$N_2$ = Secondary number of turns

$\phi_m$ = Main flux in the core, webers, r.m.s.

$\phi_L$ = Leakage flux

$E_1$ = Induced e.m.f. in primary winding

$E_2$ = Induced e.m.f. in secondary winding

$\cos\phi_2$ = Load power factor

$N_1 N_2 = k$ = Turns Ratio, Transformation Ratio

$B$ = Flux density in core, Tesla (wb/m$^2$)

$B_m$ = Peak flux density, Tesla

$S$ = VA load.

## 3.2. TRANSFORMER PRINCIPLE

A transformer is basically a static device, used for stepping up or down alternating voltages.

The principle of a transformer can be explained by means of Faraday's Law of electro-magnetic induction. *Faraday's Law* states that:

"Electromotive force (emf) is induced *in a closed electric circuit whenever there is a change in magnetic flux linkage of that circuit."*

*"The induced emf is proportional to the rate of change of flux linkage."*

The direction of the induced emf is given by *Lenz's law* which states that:

*"The direction of induced emf is such that at every instant, it tries to oppose the cause of induction."*

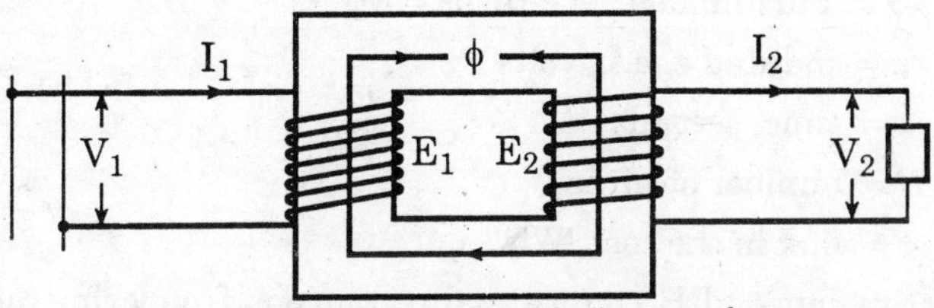


Fig. 3.1. A single phase, two winding transformer.

A transformer has a closed magnetic circuit called the *core.* Two or more windings are placed on the core. One of the winding (called the primary winding) is supplied with alternating voltage of power frequency (50 Hz). The primary winding takes no-load current ($I_0$) from the supply and sets-up alternating magnetic flux of 50 Hz in the core. As the secondary winding is also placed on the same core, the magnetic flux linking with the secondary winding also changes continuously at a rate of 50 Hz. Thereby, e.m.f. is induced in the secondary winding by induction principle. The emf induced in the secondary winding has the same frequency as that of the magnetic flux and primary exciting current.

When the secondary side is connected to a load, the secondary current flows. The primary current increases correspondingly such that the secondary ampere-turns are almost equal to the primary ampere turns, *i.e.*

$$V_2 I_2 \cong V_1 I_1$$

The basic relations between the primary and secondary quantities is given by

$$\frac{V_1}{V_2} = \frac{I_2}{I_1} = k$$

$$V_1 I_1 = V_2 I_2$$

Thus, the transformer transforms electrical power from primary circuit to the secondary circuit at the same frequency, by electro-magnetic induction, with change in voltage and change in current but without change in volt-amperes.

## 3.3 DERIVATION OF EMF EQUATION

From Faraday's Law of electro-magnetic induction, *emf induced in a closed electric circuit is proportional to the time rate of change of flux linkage*. Consider a winding having $N$ number of turns and linking with magnetic flux $\phi$ webers. Then, the flux linkage ($\phi$) is equal to ($N \times \phi$) weber-turns.

$$e = -\frac{d\phi}{dt} \qquad .....(3.1)$$

where $\psi$ = Flux linkage, Wb-turns = $N\phi$

$e$ = induced e.m.f., volts

$t$ = time, seconds

$N$ = number of turns

$\phi$ = flux in the core, Wb.

Negative sign on RHS indicates direction e.m.f. opposing the cause (Lenz's Law).

$$\psi = N\phi$$

$$\frac{d\psi}{dt} = Nd\frac{\phi}{dt} \qquad ....(3.2)$$

These equations are obtained from basic electromagnetic theory. As the flux in the core changes sinusoidally, the equation (3.2) gets modified as follows:

For sinusoidal flux in the core, let

$$\phi = \phi_m \sin \omega t \qquad ....(3.3)$$

where $\phi_m$ = Peak value (Maximum value) of the flux wave $= \sqrt{2}\,\phi_{rms}$

$\omega$ = Radian frequency $= 2\pi f$

Hence, $$e = -N\frac{d\phi}{dt} = -N\frac{d}{dt}(\phi_m \sin \omega t)$$

$$e = -N\phi_m\,\omega \cos \omega t \qquad .....(3.4)$$

**Note.** $e$ is at a phase angle 90° with reference to $\phi$. The peak value of the above sinusoidally varying e is

$$E_m = N\,\phi_m\,(\omega)$$

The rms value is $\frac{E_m}{\sqrt{2}}$

$$E_{rms} = \frac{\omega}{2} N\,\phi_m = \sqrt{2} \times 3.14 f N\,\phi_m$$

For $f = 50\ Hz$, we get

$$E_{rms} = 4.44 f N\,\phi_m \qquad .....(3.5)$$

This is the basic *e.m.f. equation of a transformer* in which $E_{rms} = R.M.S.$ value of Induced e.m.f., volts.

$f =$ frequency of applied voltage, flux in the core and induced e.m.f., in Hz

$N =$ Number of turns in the winding

$\phi_m =$ Peak value of flux in the core, Wb.

Let $A =$ Area of cross-section of core, $m^2$

$B_m =$ Peak flux density in core , Tesla

(1 *Tesla* = $1 Wb/m^2$)

Then, $\phi_m = A \cdot B_m$

Substituting in Eqn. (3.4.),

$$E_{rms} = 4.44\, f N A{\cdot}B_m \qquad ....(3.6)$$

Let $N_1 =$ Number of turns in primary.

$N_2 =$ Number of turns in secondary.

$E_1 =$ RMS value of e.m.f. in primary.

$E_2 =$ RMS value of e.m.f.in secondary.

Then

$$E_1 = 4.44 f N_1 \phi_m \qquad ...(3.7)$$

$$E_2 = 4.44\, f N_2\, \phi_m, f \text{ If there in no leakage} \qquad ...(3.8)$$

$$\frac{E_1}{E_2} = \frac{N_1}{N_2} = k \qquad ...(3.9)$$

where $K =$ Turns Ratio or Ratio of Transformation.

Remember, EMF Equation for a Transformer:

$$\boxed{E = 4.44 f N \phi_m} \qquad ...(3.10)$$

## 3.4. E.M.F. EQUATION OF A TRANSFORMER

The induced e.m.f. (electro-motive force) in each winding of a transformer is given by the e.m.f. equation.

$$E = 4.44\, f \phi_m N \ldots\ldots \text{ volts, } r.m.s. \qquad ...(3.11)$$

where, $E =$ r.m.s. value of induced in a winding of the transformer volts, r.m.s.

$f =$ frequency of applied voltage, $H_z$

$\phi_m =$ Peak (maximum) flux in the core, Wb

$N =$ Number of turns in the winding.

From the basic e.m.f. equation, we get the correlation between the e.m.f. induced in a winding and the number of turns in that winding.

$$\frac{E_1}{E_2} = \frac{4.44 f \phi_m N_1}{4.44 f \phi_m N_2}$$

$$= \frac{N_1}{N_2} = k \qquad ...(3.12)$$

## 3.5. TURNS RATIO, RATIO OF TRANSFORMATION, VOLTAGE RATIO

The e.m.f. induced in a winding is proportional to the number of turns in that winding. The ratio of number of turns in the primary to the number of turns in the secondary winding is called the *turns ratio* or *the ratio of transformation* of the transformer.

Let $$E_1 = 4.44 f \phi_m N_1$$

$$E_2 = 4.44 f \phi_m N_2$$

where subscript 1 is for primary winding and subscript 2 is for the secondary winding. Then,

$$\frac{E_1}{E_2} = \frac{N_1}{N_2} = k \qquad ...(3.13)$$

where $k$ is called the *turns ratio* or *the ratio of transformation. Neglecting* the voltage drops in the internal impedances of the windings, we get

$$\frac{E_1}{E_2} = \frac{V_1}{V_2} = k = \frac{N_1}{N_2} \qquad ...(3.14)$$

$$\left.\begin{aligned} V_2 &= \frac{V_1}{k} \\ V_1 &= k V_2 \\ k &= \frac{N_1}{N_2} \end{aligned}\right\} \qquad ...(3.15)$$

If $k = N_1/N_2$ is more than 1, $V_2 = V_1/k$ is less than $V_1$ and the transformer is called a *step-down transformer*, In case of a step-down transformer, the secondary winding has lesser number of turns than the primary winding turns.

In a 'step-down transformer', $N_2$ is less than $N_1$; and $k = N_1/N_2$ is more than 1.

In a 'step-up transformer', $k$ is less than 1.

Thus by a suitable choice of the turns ratio, the required *Voltage Ratio* can be obtained.

Furthermore, by means of the tap-changing, the turns ratio and the voltage ratio can be changed. Tap-changing of a transformer is an important method of voltage control control in a network. Tap-changing transformers are located in various sub-stations for the purpose of controlling the bus voltages.

## 3.6. VOLT-AMPERES OF PRIMARY AND SECONDARY WINDINGS

Neglecting the no-load current (excitation current), the total ampere-turns of the primary winding is equal to the total ampere-turns of the secondary, as both have a common magnetic core and, therefore, their mmfs are equal. Thus,

$$N_1 I_1 = N_2 I_2 \qquad ...(3.16)$$

(Neglecting no-load current $I_0$ which is only 2 to 3 per cent of rated primary current $I_1$)

Hence, $$\frac{N_1}{N_2} = \frac{I_2}{I_1} = k \qquad ...(3.17)$$

We get $$I_2 = kI_1 \qquad ...(3.18)$$

But, $$K = \frac{N_1}{N_2} = \frac{V_1}{V_2} \qquad ...(3.19)$$

Substituting, $$V_1 I_1 = ( (kV_2) \cdot I_2/k) = V_2 \cdot I_2 \qquad ...(3.20)$$

Thus, neglecting the small no-load current $I_0$, the number of ampere-turns of primary is equal to the number of ampere-turns of secondary. The stepping-up of voltage results in proportionate stepping down of current. Neglecting losses, the volt-ampere input to primary is equal to the volt-ampere output from secondary. The transformer does not step-up or step-down the power. It only transforms a.c. power from one voltage to another voltage and with simultaneous transformation of the current in inverse proportion.

From Eqn. (3.17) and (3.19) we not that

Voltage ratio = 1/ current Ratio

Stepping-up of voltage = Stepping down of current

## 3.7. VOLTS PER TURN, V/N

From the e.m.f. equations, volts per turn:

$$\frac{E_1}{N_1} = 4.44 f \phi_m$$

$$\frac{E_2}{N_2} = 4.44 f \phi_m$$

Hence, $$\frac{E_1}{N_1} = 4.44 f \phi_m$$

$$\frac{E_2}{N_2} = 4.44 f \phi_m$$

For $f = 50$ Hz, Volts per turn $E/N$ is equal to

$$\frac{E}{N} = 4.44 \times 50 \times \phi_m$$

$$= 222\phi_m \quad ...(3.21)$$

$$= 222 \cdot A \cdot B_m \quad ...(3.22)$$

$$\frac{E_1}{N_1} = 222 \cdot A \cdot B_m = \frac{E_2}{N_2} \quad ...(3.23)$$

It is observed that the *volts per turn of primary winding and secondary winding are equal.*

Also, *the increase in volts per turn per turn causes increase in the peak flux density in the core* ($B_m$); *i.e.*, flux density in the core is proportional to volts/turns.

$$V/N \propto B_m \quad ...(3.24)$$

If the applied voltage $V_1$ is increased above highest system voltage or rated primary voltage, the volts per turn, and the flux density. increases. *This may result in saturation of core, over heating of the core, increases leakage flux, increased core-losses and damage to the core-bolt insulation.*

Also, increased applied voltage results in increased voltage stress on transformer winding. Hence, a transformer should not be operated on voltage above the highest system voltage.

**Volts per turn** charts are used for determining the number of turns required for transformer winding of required rated voltage.

## 3.8. VOLTS PER Hz

The standard frequency ($f$) is 50 cycles per second (Hz). The power supply frequency $f$ is maintained within targetted limits of 49 and 51. A transformer is usually designed for frequency variation of ± 3%, *i.e.* for operating frequency range of 48.5 and 51.5.

From the voltage equation,

$$\frac{V}{f} = 4.44N\phi_m \quad ...(3.25)$$

$N$ being constant.

$$V/f \propto \phi_m \propto B_m \quad ...(3.26)$$

Thus, the reduction in frequency $f$ causes the increase in flux density $B_m$ in the core.

The supply frequency is generally held within 49 Hz and 51 Hz. In case of small, isolated power systems the supply frequency may drop below 48 Hz during peak loads resulting in the condition of overfluxing.

In-case of generator transformers, unit-auxiliary transformers, the condition of over-fluxing occurs if excitation is applied to the generators before attaining full synchronous speed or during under-speed operation. Such condition result's in failure of core insulation. Overfluxing protection is provided with generator excitation-system to avoid over-fluxing condition.

## 3.9. VOLT-AMPERE RATING (kVA OR MVA RATING)

Each power transformer is assigned a certain rating of apparent power expressed in terms of kVA or MVA. The power transfer capability of a transformer is expressed in terms of *its apparent power rating* (kVA rating or MVA rating; Notation $S$).

The apparent power $S$ is expressed in terms of kVA or MVA.

### 3.9.1. kVA Rating of a Single Phase Transformer

Assumption: Two winding single phase transformer

$$S = V_{ph} \cdot I_{ph} \times 10^{-3} \text{ kVA} \quad \text{...(3.27)}$$

where, $V_{ph}$ = Rated phase voltage, volts rms, voltage at primary terminals.

$I_{ph}$ = Rated phase current, Amp, rms current through primary terminals.

S = kVA rating.

Equation (3.25) can be applied to the primary winding by using subscript 1,

$$S = S_1 = V_1 I_1 \times 10^{-3} \text{ kVA} \quad \text{...(3.28)}$$

and to secondary winding by using the subscript 2,

$$S = S_2 = V_2 I_2 \times 10^{-3} \text{ kVA} \quad \text{...(3.29)}$$

**Note.** From Eqn. (3.20), we know the volt amperes of primary and secondary are equal. *Hence, for Single Phase Transformers.*

$$S = S_1 = S_2 = V_1 I_1 \times 10^{-3} = V_2 I_2 \times 10^{-3} \quad \text{...(3.30)}$$

where voltage are phase voltage.

From these equations; the currents in respective windings can be calculated for given kVA and $V_1, V_2$ ratings. For single phases transformers,

$$I_1 = (S/V_1)\, 10^{-3}$$

and

$$I_2 = (S/V_2)\, 10^{-3}$$

### 3.9.2. kVA Rating of a 3 Phase Transformer

A three phase two-winding transformer has a three phase primary winding (subscript 1) and a three phase secondary winding (subscript

2). The kVA rating of a three phase three phase transformer is expressed in terms of its rated line voltages,

$$S = \sqrt{3}\, V \times I\, 10^{-3} \text{ kVA} \qquad ...(3.31)$$

where, $S$ = Three phase kVA rating
3 = Factor for 3 phase
V = line-to-line voltage, Volts, rms
I = line current, Amperes, rms.

Applying Eqn. (3.31) to the primary winding,

$$S = S_1 = 3 \cdot V_1 I_1 \cdot 10^{-3} \text{ kVA} \qquad ...(3.32)$$

and to the secondary winding

$$S = S_2 = 3 \cdot V_2 I_2 \cdot 10^{-3} \text{ kVA} \qquad ...(3.33)$$

From these equations, the rated values of currents can be calculated for given values of kVA ratings and rated voltages of windings. Equations apply to *the main tapping of the transformer windings*.

kVA rating of two-winding transformer applies equally to its primary and secondary windings. In case of a three winding transformer, kVA rating of each winding is specified separately.

### 3.9.3. kVA Rating of a Three Winding Transformer

$$S_1 = S_2 + S_3 \qquad ...(3.34)$$

where, $S_1$ = kVA rating of primary winding
$S_2$ = kVA rating of secondary winding
$S_3$ = kVA rating of intermediate winding.

**Example 3.1.** *A single phase transformer has 100 turns on secondary winding. Secondary voltage is 50 V at 50 Hz. The cross-sectional area of core-limb is 1850 mm².*

*Calculate maximum value of flux-density ($B_m$) in the core.*

**Solution.** From equation

$$\phi_m = E_2/4.44 f N_2$$

By substituting given values

$$\phi_m = 50/(4.44 \times 50 \times 100)$$

$$\phi_m = 0.0022.52 \text{ Wb.}$$

$$B_m = \phi_m/\text{area of cross-section}$$

By substituting values

$$= 0.002252/1850 \times 10^{-6} = 1.216 \text{ T.}$$

**Example 3.2.** *A single phase, 50 Hz core type transformer has a voltage ratio of 6000/250 V. Calculate the number of turns in each winding for flux of 0.06 Wb (Crest).*

**Solution.** We know from E.M.F. equation,

$$E_1 = 4.44 f N \phi_m$$

$$E_2 = 4.44 f N \phi_m$$

Therefore
$$\phi_m = \frac{E_2}{4.44 \times f \times N_2}$$

$$N_2 = \frac{E_2}{\phi_m \times 4.44 \times f}$$

$$N_2 = \frac{250}{0.06 \times 222} = 18.76 \text{ turns}$$

Similarly,
$$N_1 = \frac{6000}{0.06 \times 222} = 450.5 \text{ turns.}$$

**Example 3.3.** *A 2 phase; 11 kV/550 V, 50 Hz Delta/star, 300 kVA distribution transformer has core type construction.*

*Gross cross sectional area of core is 400 cm$^2$.*

*Core flux density should be 1.3 tesla maximum.*

*(a) Number of turns of HV winding*
*(b) Number of turns of LV winding*
*(c) Volts/Turn*
*(d) Full load line current of HV side*
*(e) Full load line current of LV side*
*(f) Full load phase current in HV winding*
*(g) Full load phase current in LV winding*
*(h) Power delivered at 0.8 pf lag.*

**Solution.** Calculate voltage ratio per phase.

HV line voltage 11 kV Delta (Mesh)

HV phase voltage 11 kV per phase

LV line voltage 550 V star

LV phase voltage $550/\sqrt{3} = 317.54$V

Cross sectional ares of core 400 cm$^2$ Gross

Net Cross-sectional Area = $0.9 \times 400 = 360$cm$^2$(0.9 factor for core plate insulation, ducting, steps, etc.)

Flux density (Induction) 1.3 tesla, crest $B_m = 1.3$ tesla *i.e.* Wb/m$^2$.

E.M.F. Equation $E = 4.44 f \phi_m N$

Volts/Turn $= \frac{E}{N} = 4.44 f\,\phi_m$

$$\phi_m = B_m A$$

$$V/N = 4.44 \times 50 \times (360 \times 10^{-4} \times 1.3)$$

$$= 10.4 \text{ Volts}$$

Number of turns of secondary winding

$$N_2 = \frac{\text{Volts/Phase}}{\text{Volts/turns}} = \frac{317.54}{10.4} = 30.54 \approx 31 \text{ turns}$$

Volts/Turns would now be

$$\frac{317.54}{31} = 10.243 \text{ Volts/turn}$$

Actual flux density, $B = 1.3 \times \frac{10.243}{10.4} = 1.28$ tesla (crest)

**Primary Turns**

$$N_1 = kN_2 = \frac{11000}{317.54} \times 31 = 1073.88 \approx 1074$$

**Primary phase current**

kVA per phase $= \frac{300}{3} = 100$ kVA

Phase current $= \frac{\text{Phase kVA}}{\text{Phase voltage}} = 100 \times \frac{10^3}{11000} = 9.09$ A

**Secondary phase current**

Secondary phase current

$$= \frac{\text{kVA per phase} \times 10^3}{\text{Secondary V}}$$

$$= 100 \times \frac{10^3}{317.54} = 314.92\text{A}$$

**Primary AT per phase**

$$I_1 N_1 = 9.09 \times 1074 = 9762.52$$

**Secondary AT per phase**

$$I_2 N_2 = 314.92 \times 31 = 9762.52$$

Confirmation : $I_1 N_1 = I_2 N_2$

**Primary line current on full load**

$$\text{KVA} = \sqrt{3}\, V_L\, I_L$$

$$300 \times 10^3 = \sqrt{3} \times 11000 \times I_L$$

$$I_L = \frac{300 \times 10_3}{\sqrt{3} \times 11 \times 10_3} = 15.746$$

For Delta connected primary

$$\frac{I_L}{I_{ph}} = \frac{15.746}{9.09} = 1.73 = \sqrt{3} \text{ (check)}$$

**Secondary line current on full load**

$$KVA = \sqrt{3} V_L I_L$$

$$300 \times 10^3 = \sqrt{3} \times 550 \times I_L$$

$$I_L = \frac{300 \times 10^3}{\sqrt{3} \times 0.55 \times 10^3} = 314.92$$

For star connected secondary

$$I_L = I_{ph} = 314.92 \text{ (check).}$$

**Example 3.4.** *A 3 phase transformer has primary rated voltage (for principle tap) of 240 kV. The maximum flux density for rated voltage is 1.3 T. During no load, bus voltage rose to 250 kV. Calculate maximum flux density. Frequency was constant at 50 Hz.*

**Solution.** $B_m \propto V/N$

$N$ is constant

$$\frac{B_m 1}{B_{m2}} = \frac{V_1}{V_2}$$

Given $V_1 = 240$ kV, $B_{m1} = 1.3$ T

$$V_2 = 250 \text{ kV}$$

$$B_{m2} = B_{m1} \,.\, V_2/V_1$$

$$= 1.3 \times \frac{250}{240}$$

$$= 1.354 \text{ T.}$$

**Example 3.5.** *During starting of a generator unit, full excitation was applied when speed was 50%. For normal 50 Hz frequency rated voltage of primary side of generator transformer is 20 kV and maximum flux density is 1.6 T.*

*Calculate the flux density at the particular situation.*

**Solution.** Full excitation = Full inducded e.m.f.

50% speed = 50% frequency

Magnetic flux density in generator transformer is proportional to $V/f$ ratio, turns being constant

**Case I.** Rated voltage, rated frequency

Let $$B_m = k\frac{V_1}{f}$$

$$1.6 = k\frac{20}{50}$$

$$k = 1.6 \times \frac{50}{20} = 4$$

**Case 2.** Rated Voltage, 50% $f$

$$B_m = k\frac{20}{25} = 4 \times \frac{20}{25} = 8T$$

with such a high flux density, Generator Transformer will fail by overfluxing.

## 3.10. SUMMARY

**1.** EMF Equation of a power transformer is $E = 4.44f\,\phi_m N$. Where $E$=emf induced, rms value, volts; $f$ = frequency Hz ; $\phi_m$ = peak value of flux in the core in Wb; $N$ = Number of turns, in the winding.

**2.** Volts per turn $V/N \propto \phi_m \propto B_m$

**3.** Volts per $Hz$ $V/f \propto \phi_m \propto B_m$

**4.** $$\frac{E_1}{E_2} = \frac{V_1}{V_2} = k = \frac{N_1}{N_2}$$

**5.** $$V_1 I_1 = (kV_2) \cdot (I_2/k) = V_2 \cdot I_2.$$

**6.** Single phase transformer

$$S = S_1 = S_2 = V_1 I_1 \times 10^{-3} \text{ kVA.}$$

$$= V_2 I_2 \times 10^{-3} \text{ kVA.}$$

**7.** Three phase transformer

$$S = \sqrt{3} V \times I \times 10^{-3} kVA$$

$V$ = phase to phase voltage, volts

$I$ = Line current, Amperes

$S$ = 3 phase kVA

$S = S_1 = S_2$ for two Winding Transformers

# 4

# Specifications and Ratings

Manufactures and users follow relevant IEC and IS specifications for finalising the rated characteristics, test requirements, applications of power transformers, bushings, tap-changers, fitments, etc. Specifications and ratings are very important form selection to final use. This chapter covers important ratings and their significance.

## 4.1. STANADARD SPECIFICATIONS

The international standards published by IEC (International Electro-technical Commission) are accepted universally. Indian Bureau of Standards** publishes IS Standards. The Manufacturers and Users in India recognise IS and IEC standard publications.

The Standard Specifications give recommendations, regarding standard definitions, symbol, terminal markings, vector groups ratings, preferred ratings, type tests/ routine test/ special test requirement; test procedures, permissible tolerances, guide for operation and maintenance, information to be supplied with the tender etc.

The *standards* are extremely useful to the manufacturers, users and system designers for selecting designing, testing and other functions. The standards reduce variety and bring uniformity in practices resulting in systematic approach and overall economy. Each manufacturer has his internal standards for drawing practices, materials, and testing procedures etc. The standards are based on the experience of research institutions, working groups of IEC, manufactures and users. The standards are revised regularly on the basis of new experience and technology. It is advisable to refer to the latest standards. The manufacturers offer transformers conforming to *the standards* mentioned by the user in his tender specifications.

The standards for *Power Transformers* are applicable to three phase transformers rated above 5 kVA*. The Special Transformers and transformers below 5 kVA* are covered by separate standards.

A typical standard on power transformer covers the following data:
— Service conditions
— Definitions
— Ratings

---

**Formerly : Indian Standards Insutitution.

* 1 kVA for single phase transformer units.

— Tappings
— Cooling system identification
— Limits of temperature rise
— Ability to withstand short-circuits and corresponding test for shot-circuit withstand capability.
— Information to be given on the Rating Plate and Diagram Plate
— Terminal Markings
— Vector Diagrams, Connection, Method of connections, procedure and interpretation.
— Tolerances
— *Tests*. Acceptance tests, type tests, routine tests, special tests.
— Fitments
— Information for tenders
— Insulation Levels, High voltage testing
— Practice for maintenance.

The standards are published in several parts. They are revised/ammended at times. *The design features are not mentioned in the standards. They are left for the manufacturer and user to decide.*

For large transformers, the specifications and ratings are finalised on the basis of tender specifications, manufacturer's offer and accepted deviations. The quality checks, acceptance tests etc., are performed as per agreement between the manufacturer and user. For special tests such as short-circuit withstand test, environmental, field test etc., testing facilities and testing power should be available.

## 4.2. RATINGS OF POWER TRANSFORMERS

The word Rating denotes the assigned numerical value of capability. The manufacturer *assigns* certain definite ratings to the transformer. These assigned ratings are guaranteed by manufacturer. The assigned ratings are confirmed by conducting the Acceptance Tests and Type Tests to the satisfaction of the user or his consultant. The ratings assigned for a particular transformer conform to the relevant Standard Specifications and the specified service conditions.

The *ratings plate* of a transformer gives the various ratings and data regarding the transformers. Table 4.1 gives an example.

## 4.3. DIAGRAM PLATE (CONNECTION DIAGRAM)

If the vector group does not give the complete information regarding the internal connections, a separate connection diagram is provided in the form of a Diagram Plate. Data includes the vector group, vector diagram, insulation levels, interconnections, markings of tape, neutral, etc.

The details about tapping windings, connections of tap-changer, terminals markings should also be indicated.

**Table 4.1. Rating Plate Data**

| *S.No.* | *Description of Data Required to be given* | *Remarks for example* |
|---|---|---|
| 1. | Kind of Transformer | Power Transformer |
| 2. | Relevant Standard, Year | I.S. 200 |
| 3. | Manufacturer's Name: | |
| 4. | Manufacturer's Serial No.: | 156251 |
| 5. | Year of Manufacture | 2006 |
| 6. | Number of Phases | 3 |
| 7. | Rated Power | 1000 kVA |
| 8. | Rated Frequency: | 50 Hz |
| 9. | Rated Voltages: | HV 33 kV<br>LV 11 kV |
| 10. | Rated currents | HV |
| | | LV |
| 11. | Vector Group Symbol: | |
| 12. | % Impedance Voltage (At Rated Current) | |
| 13. | % Reactance Voltage % : | |
| 14. | Type of Coolling | ONAN |
| 15. | Total Weight | kg |
| | —Mass or Insulating Oil | kg |
| | —Transportation Weight | kg |
| | —Untanking Weight | kg |
| 16. | Insulating liquid (if not oil) type: | |
| 17. | Quantity of oil (Litres): | |
| 18. | Details about Tap-changer | |
| 19. | Rated Insulation Levels: | |
| | —Power-frequency withstand voltage | $kV_{rms}$ |
| | —Lighting impulse withstand voltage | $kV_{peak}$ |
| 20. | Temperature class of insulation (For Dry type transformer) | |
| 21. | Connection Diagram | |
| | Details about Tapping | |
| | —Winding on which tapping provided | |
| | —Table giving tapping, tapping voltage tapping power, of each winding | |

## 4.4. RATED QUANTITIES OF A POWER TRANSFORMER

The significant rated quantities of Power transformer include the following:

- — Rated voltage of each winding i.e., HV/MV/LV winding
- — Rated Voltage Ratios
- — Rated current for each winding
- — Rated apparant power (kVA or MVA) for each winding
- — Rated frequency.

The above mentioned ratings refer to the principal tapping and the values of currents and voltages are generally specified as rms values. The ratings are based on the specified service conditions. The relevant standard specifies the standard tolerances in assigned ratings.

Besides the above mentioned 'rated quantities', the standards also specify other quantities such as Impedance Voltage, No-load current etc., to be assigned by the manufacturer. While studying the particular rated quantity, the significance of the rating and its implications should be studied.

Rated quantities must be confirmed by conducting *type tests*. Type test is performed only on one transformer of particular type, design and rating. Other transformers confirming to the same design are tested only for *routine tests*. Routine test are conducted on every transformer. These tests are conducted to ensure material quality, manufacturing process etc.

### 4.4.1. Rated Voltage of a Winding

It is the voltage assigned (to be applied or developed at no-load) between the line terminals of a winding.

The rated voltage for each winding (HV/MV/LV) should be specified separately.

The rated voltage:

- — It is expressed in rms value in kV.
- — It refers to continuous rating.
- — Capability to withstand power frequency voltage continuously is confirmed by conducting
  1. Power frequency voltage withstand test
  2. Induced voltage test.
- — The value refers to the principal tapping (unless stated otherwise)
- — The transformer should be capable of delivering the rated current at a voltage 5% above the rated voltage.
- — The rated insulation level of the winding corresponds to rated voltage of the winding.
- — The rated apparent power of the winding and the rated current refers to the rated voltage.

— The rated voltage of each winding should be mentioned on the rating plate of the transformer. The rated voltage of each winding should be assigned separately.

— In case of three phase transformer,the rated voltage of winding refer to the no-load voltage between the line terminals of the winding.

— In case of single phase transformer, the rated voltage of winding refers to the voltage between the phase terminals of the winding.

For star connected transformer winding, it is indicated as $V_1/\sqrt{3}$. where $V_L$ is line-to-line voltage.

For example, for a 420 kV, level, rated voltage of a star connected winding would be indicated as $420/\sqrt{3}$ kV.

— In a two or three winding transformer on no load, if rated voltage is applied to one phase, the voltages appearing on terminals of other phases are rated voltage of those phase windings (at no load).

### 4.4.2. Rated Voltage Ratio

It is the ratio of rated voltage of one winding to the rated voltage of another winding.

— It is the voltage ratio at no-load on the principal tapping.

— The actual voltage ratio is confirmed by conducting *Ratio Tests*. This test is conducted during no-load type test and no-load routine test.

— The rated voltage ratio should be mentioned on the rating plate of the transformer.

— The rated voltage is expressed in rms value.

— It refers to continuous voltage rating.

— The value refers to the principal tapping.

— Voltage ratio corresponds to turns ratio between windings.

— The rated insulation level of the winding corresponds to rated voltage of the winding.

— Current ratio is a reciprocal of voltage ratio.

— The rated voltage of each winding should be mentioned on the rating plate of the transformer.

**Note.** The value of voltage at the location of the transformer varies with changes in load and reactive power flow. The permissible value of system highest voltage is specified. The transformer winding is designed for the same. The following terms are important (1) System highest voltage (2) Lowest system voltage.

### 4.4.3. System Highest Voltage for Each Winding

The system highest voltage for each winding should be specified by the manufacturer and should be mentioned on the rating plate of the transformer. The value of system highest voltage is r.m.s value of line to line voltage at the location of the transformer. This occurs at no load.

Many times lightly loaded long transmission line terminating in a transformer can lead to over voltage across the transformer.

**Note.** While specifying the rated voltage of a winding, the system highest voltage also should be specified. The test voltages correspond to the system highest voltages.

The system design should be such that voltage at substation busses does not rise above highest system voltage. Appropriated voltage control actions should be taken to keep busbar voltages within specified limits. Large power transformers are provided with over voltage protection. During no-load, the system voltage tends to rise. Voltage is controlled by means of tap-changers and shunt compensation.

### 4.4.4. Permissible Lowest System Voltage

It is specified in the standards of rated voltage for A.C system.

The rated kVA capacity of the transformer corresponds to rated voltage. The rated current also corresponds to rated voltage. Reduction in supply voltage results in reduction in permissible kVA loading, by keeping rated current unchanged. For three phase transformer.

$$S = \sqrt{3}\, V_L I_L$$

Keeping $I_L$ unchanged, $S$ should be reduced whenever $V_L$ is reduced.

When the bus voltages is lesser than rated voltage, the kVA loading on transformer should also be lesser than rated kVA.

### 4.4.5. Rated Insulation Levels

The rated insulation levels of a transformer denote the combination of voltage values (rated voltage, highest system voltage, switching impulse withstand voltage, lightining impulse withstand voltage and power frequency withstand voltage) which characterize the insulation of *each winding* and associated parts with regard to their ability to withstand the dielectric stresses. Normally Basic Impulse Level (BIL) of a winding is called as insulation level.

The insulation level of each winding should be specified separately as each will face different voltage during service.

The insulation levels of a *transformer* should be specified by the purchaser. The choice of insulation levels for a transformer is governed by the system requirements*.

The insulation level of *a transformer* winding is characterized by the following values:

---

* The insulation levels of the system are influeced by several factors such as type of earthing, exprosure to overvoltage, characteristics of protective devices as surge arresters and protective gaps. Insulation levels are co-ordinatd such that protective level of a surge arrester is lower than the withstand level of the equipment to be protected.

— rated voltage, highest system voltage
— power frequency withstand test voltage,
— impulse withstand test voltage (Refer Table 4.2 for standard Test Values).

**Normal System Voltage.** The rms value of line-to-line voltage for which the system is designated. This voltage is not necessarily the same as the rated voltage of the transformer winding connected to the system at that voltage level. Each transformer winding is assigned with certain rated voltage which corresponds to the rated nominal system voltage and relevant highest system voltage. *The rated voltage of HV winding is regarded as the voltage class of the transformer*. The test voltages for power frequency and impulse voltage withstand tests on each winding correspond to the rated voltage of the winding.

**Table 4.2 Reference Values of Insulation Levels Nominal System Voltage, Highest System Voltage, Power-frequency Test Voltage and Impulse Test Voltage**

| *Nominal system voltage kV rms* | *Highest system voltage kV rms* | *One minute power-frequency test voltage kV, rms* | *Impulse test voltage kV peak* |
|---|---|---|---|
| 3.3 | 3.6 | 16 | 45 |
| 6.6 | 7.2 | 22 | 60 |
| 11 | 12 | 28 | 75 |
| 15 | 17.5 | 38 | 95 |
| 22 | 24 | 50 | 125 |
| 33 | 36 | 70 | 170 |
| 45* | 52 | 95 | 250 |
| 66 | 72.5 | 140 | 325 |
| 90* | 100 | 150 185 | 380 450 |
| 110 | 123 | 115 230 | 450 650 |
| 132 | 145 | 230 275 | 550 650 |
| 150* | 170 | 275 325 | 650 750 |
| 220 | 245 | 395 460 | 900 1050 |
| 275* | 300 | 460 — | 1050 — |
| 350* | 362 | 510 — | 1175 — |
| 400 | 420 | 630 — | 1425 — |

### 4.4.5. Rated Power, kVA or MVA

The power rating of a transformer is given in terms of conventional value of the apparent power (kVA of MVA) assigned to the transformer.

These voltages not preferred in India.

The transformer is designed, manufactured, guaranteed and tested for the assigned rated power. The values of *rated current* of each winding is determined correctly from the assigned value of rated power and rated voltage of that winding. This value is referred for conducting relevant test.

In case of a *two-winding transformer*, each winding (HV and LV) has the same rated power which by definition is equal to the rated power of the transformer. In case of a three-winding transformer (having HV/MV/LV windings) the rated power of each winding should be stated separately. The respective value is used for calculation of the rated current of that winding.

The rated power (kVA or MVA) is used as a basis of design, for guarantees, for tests and for calculation of rated currents, under specific conditions.

— If power varies with cooling conditions, rated power applies to the highest power.

— For a three winding transformer, the rated power of *each* winding should be stated separately.

For designing the *main dimensions*, of a multiwinding transformer, the nominal rated power is given by

$$S = \frac{S_1 + S_2 + S_3 + \ldots}{2} \text{ kVA}$$

where, $S$ = Nominal rated power of a multiwinding transformer *for calculation of main dimensions.* $S_1$, $S_2$, $S_3$ .... are Rated power of winding 1, 2, 3.....

For a two winding transformer

$$S = S_1 = S_2$$

The rated power assigned to a winding should take into account the service conditions and should be related to the product of rated voltage, rated current and appropriate phase factor.

**Phase Factors**

| Number of Phases | 1 | 2 | 3 |
|---|---|---|---|
| Phase Factors | 1 | 2 | $\sqrt{3}$ |

Thus, the rated power of a *single phase* transformer is given by

$$S = V_{ph} \cdot I_{ph}$$

Rated power of a two-phase transformer is given by

$$S = 2V_{ph} \cdot I_{ph}$$

Rated power of a 3 phase Transformer is given by

$$S = \sqrt{3}\, V_L\, I_L$$

The rated power corresponds to continuous duty unless specified otherwise.

The transformer should be designed to deliver the rated current at an applied voltage 5% above and below the rated voltage.

The rated power corresponds to principal tapping. Table 4.3 gives the standard preferred values of Rated Power for 3 phase power transformers and distribution transformers.

**Table 4.3. Standard Preferred Value* of Rated Power of 3 Phase Transformer in kVA**

| | | | | | | | | |
|---|---|---|---|---|---|---|---|---|
| 5 | 6.3 | 8 | 10 | 12.5 | 16 | 20 | 31.5 | 40 |
| 50 | 63 | 10 | 100 | 125 | 160 | 200 | 315 | 400 |
| 500 | 630 | 800 | 1000 | | and likewise | | | |

### 4.4.6. Rated Frequency of a Transformer

It is the frequency at which the transformer is designed to operate. The standard frequency of a commercial power supply is 50 Hz (60 Hz in USA ) with targeted limits 49.5 Hz and 50.1 Hz. The term Hertz is equal to number of cycles per second.

The flux density in the core depends upon applied frequency

$$B_m \propto V/f \text{ for constants voltage}$$

or

$$B_m \propto \frac{1}{f}$$

In generator transformers units auxiliary transformer in power stations, there is a possibility of lower frequency during starting of a generating unit. If full excitation is applied before reaching synchronous speed, high $V/f$ values are obtained. Thereby the core gets saturated and core may fail due to overfluxing.

In Network transformers, such a situation does not arise because frequency does not fall below 48.5 Hz.

During under frequency conditions, load shedding is resorted to maintain frequency above 48.5 Hz.

— Transformer designed for one rated frequency cannot be used for other higher lower frequencies without derating of voltage and power. Rated quantities are with reference to rated frequency.

— The waveform of applied voltage should be nearly sinusoidal (within ± 3% variation). If the applied voltage contains harmonics, the kVA rating should be reduced to take care of additional heating due to harmonic currents.

---

*The rated values may be preferably from this table but not essential Values ar related by factor 1.26.

— No load loss measurement and temperature rise tests are conducted at rated frequency.

### 4.4.7. Rated Current

It is the assigned value of current flowing through the line terminals of the winding at rated frequency.

It is derived from the rated power, rated voltage and appropriate phase factor.

The rated current of each winding should be specified separately. It is mentioned on the rating plate of the transformer.

The assigned current rating is confirmed by conducting temperature rise test (Type Test) and by measurement of load losses (Routine Test). The rated current is for specified reference ambient temperature. For higher ambient temperature, suitable derating factor is used. The rated current of a winding refers to continuous rating unless specified otherwise. For higher operating currents, the permissible duration is recommended by the manufacturer. The design of current carrying conducting parts cooling system and insulation is based on permissible temperature rise of windings and oil.

— For single phase transformers to be used for a three phase bank, the rated current of winding for delta connection is indicated by $I = I_1/I_3$.
  For example, if line current is 1000 A on delta connected side, the rating of winding is indicated as $1000/\sqrt{3}A$.

— If windings are in pairs and are connected externally by links, the rated current refers to the value for the pair, connected together and not for individual path.

## 4.5. OPERATION AT HIGHER THAN RATED VOLTAGE

The transformer should have a design margin to deliver rated current at an applied voltage equal to 105% of rated voltage.

At 105% V, the temperature rise would correspond to 5% over-voltage leading to higher no-load loss. Since no-load losses are a small fraction of load losses, this increase is neglected.

In special applications, such as interconnections, the power may flow in either directions, the transformer should be designed to deliver rated power at continuous voltage upto 110% of rated voltage.

Volts per Herz ratio for design of core is taken as $1.1V_n/f_n$ where $V_n$ = Rated highest voltage and $f_n$ is rated frequency.

## 4.6. RATING PLATE DATA

Each transformer is provided with a Rating Plate. The rating plate should be weather-proof and should be fitted in a suitable visible position. The quantities are etched, engraved or stamped. The rating plate gives the rating and other data.

Typical data to be mentioned on the rating plate is given in Table 4.1.

## 4.7. TOLERANCES

The standard specifications specify the tolerances applied to certain rated quantities and other quantities. The relevant standards should be referred by manufacturer and user. Tolerances are specified because of inherent difference in basic raw materials, variation in manufacturer measurement errors etc. Guaranteed ratings and data is subjected to certain tolerances ( ± variation) refer Table 4.4.

**Table 4.4. Permissible Tolerances for Rated Data**

| *Data* | *Permissible Tolerance* |
|---|---|
| 1. (*a*) Total losses | + 10% of the total losses |
| (*b*) Component losses | + 15% of each component loss. provided that the tolerance for total losses is not exceeded. |
| 2.Voltage ratio at no load on the principal tapping (rated voltage ratio) | The lower of the following values: |
| (*i*) **Note.** Tolerances on other tappings should be the subject of agreement between the manufacturer and the user. | (*a*) ± 0.5% of the declared ratio.<br>(*b*) A percentage of the declared ratio equal to 1/10 of the actual percentage impedance voltage at rated current (see note 2 on page 76). |
| (*ii*)Voltage ratio on other tappings. | ± 1% unless otherwise specified. |
| 3.Impedance voltage at rated current (principal tapping) | |
| (*a*)If the principal tapping corresponds with the mean tapping position or with one of the two middle tapping positions: | |
| (*i*) two winding transformers. | ± 10% of the declared impedance voltage for that tapping. |
| (*ii*) Multi-winding transformers. | ± 10% of the declared impedance voltage for one specified pair of windings.<br>± 15% of the declared impedance voltage for a second specified pair of windings.<br>Tolerance of the agreed and stated for further pairs of windings. |

(*Contd...*)

| *Data* | *Permissible Tolerance* |
|---|---|
| 4. Short circuit impedance for any tapping. | Not less than a indicated above in 3 (*a*). |
| 5. No load current | + 30% of the declared no-load current. |

**Notes to Table 4.4.**

1. The loss tolerances of multi-winding transformers apply to every pair of windings unless the guarantee states that they apply to a given loading condition.

2. Alternative (*b*) does not apply in the case of auto-transformers and booster transformers, where the smallness of the impedance would result in an exceptionally small tolerance.

3. Sound power level has no plus tolerance.

## 4.8. TESTS

The ratings are confirmed by conducting type tests (Table 4.5). Type tests are conducted on completely assembled new transformer to confirm the rated capabilities. The routine tests are conducted on every transformer to confirm quality of components and manufacture.

**Table 4.5. Tests for Confirming Capabilities against Assigned Ratings**

| *Ratings and Data* | *Relevant Type Test** |
|---|---|
| Rated voltage | Power frequency voltage withstand test.<br>—Applied voltage test.<br>—Induced voltage tests. |
| Rated Insulation level | —Lightning impulse test. |
| | —Switching impulse test. |
| Rated kVA | Load test. |
| | Temperature rise test. |
| Rated frequency | —No load test |
| Losses | —No-load test. |
| | —Sustained short-circuit test. |
| Impedance voltage | —Sustained Short-circuit test. |
| Short-circuit withstand | —Sudden short-circuit test. |

Rated Quanitites of Tap-changers and Bushings are covered in subsequent chapters.

*Test produceures covered in a seprate chapter.

# 5

# Phasor Diagrams and Equivalent Circuit Diagrams

## 5.1. INTRODUCTION

In the phasor diagram of a transformer, the sinusoidally varying quantities $\phi$, $E_1$, $I_1$, $V_1$, $E_2$, $I_2$, $V_2$ are represented by respective *phasors* (vectors) having appropriated phase angles with reference to reference vector flux $\phi$.

A phasor diagram is a *conceptual aid* to analyse the performance of a transformer. Phasor diagrams are drawn for *no-load condition, full-load lagging p.f.; leading p.f. loads, short-circuit condition*, etc.

For mathematical calculations of transformer performances, the transformer is represented by *its equivalent circuit diagram*. The equivalent circuit diagram can be drawn *as seen from the primary side*, by *referring* the secondary quantities to the primary side by using appropriate multiplying factors, or alternatively by *referring* the primary quantities to the secondary side, as seen from the secondary by using appropriate multiplying factors.

In balanced 3 phase networks, the single-phase equivalent circuits are drawn to represent the actual three phase circuits. The currents in 3 phases are equal in magnitude and displaced mutually by 120° electrical.

For performance calculations for various load conditions and supply conditions, the transformer is represented by its equivalent circuit. The performance calculations comprise:

— Determination of voltage regulation
— Determination of losses and efficiency
— Calculation of power factors
— Calculation of short-circuit currents etc.

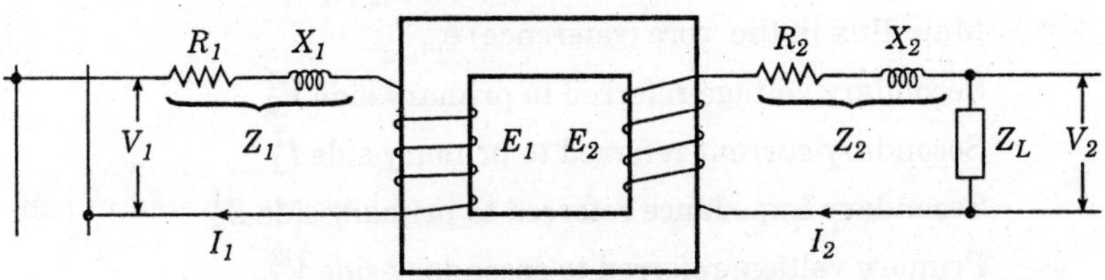


Fig. 5.1. Notations of a single phase transformer.

## 5.2. NOTATIONS

Subscript 1 for primary quantities.
Subscript 2 for secondary quantities.
Primary terminal voltage $V_1$
Primary induced e.m.f. $E_1$
Primary current $I_1$
No-load primary current $I_0$
Magnetising component of $I_0$, $I_m$
Core-loss component of $I_0$, $I$
Primary winding resistance $R_1$
Primary winding leakage reactance $X_1$
Primary winding impedance $Z_1$
Primary impedance voltage drop $I_1Z_1$
Primary reactance voltage drop $I_1R_1$
Primary reactance voltage drop $I_1X_1$
Primary number of turns $N_1$
Primary current p.f. cos $\phi_1$
Secondary terminal voltage $V_2$
Secondary induced e.m.f. $E_2$
Secondary current (load current) $I_2$
Secondary current (load current) p.f. cos$\phi_2$
Secondary resistance $R_2$
Secondary leakage reactance $X_2$
Secondary impedance $Z_2$
Secondary resistance voltage drop $I_2R_2$
Secondary reactance voltage drop $I_2X_2$
Secondary impedance voltage drop $I_2Z_2$
Secondary number of turns $N_2$
Load Impedance on secondary side $Z_L$
Load reactance on secondary side $X_L$
Load resistance on secondary side $R_L$
Secondary load power factor cos$\phi_2$
Turns Ratio (Transformation Ratio) $N_1/N_2 = k$
Main flux in the core (reference) $\phi_m$
Secondary voltage referred to primary side $V_2^1$
Secondary current referred to primary side $I_2^1$
Secondary Impedance referred to primary side $Z_2^1$
Primary voltage referred to secondary side $V_1^2$
**Primary voltage referred to secondary side $I_1^2$**

Primary impedance referred to secondary side $Z_1^2$

Equivalent impedance referred to primary $Z_e^1$

Equivalent impedance referred to secondary $Z_e^2$

## 5.3. PHASOR DIAGRAM FOR NO-LOAD CONDITION

Under *no-load condition* the terminals of secondary winding are not connected to any impedance. The secondary winding does not feed any active or reactive power to any load. The primary winding is supplied with rated voltage at rated frequency.

**Ideal Transformer on No load.** Let us consider an ideal transformer on no-load. The ideal transformer has no resistances, no losses, noleakage reactance and has 100% efficiency.

**Under no-load condition**

$$I_2 = 0 \; ; P_2 = P_1$$

Since $P_L = 0$

$$V_2 = -E_2$$

Since $I_2 Z_2 = 0$

$$V_1 = -E_1$$

Since $I_1 Z_1 = 0$

$$\frac{V_2}{V_1} = \frac{N_2}{N_1} = 1/k$$

$$I_2 = 0$$

Since $\frac{I_1}{I_2} = 1/k$

Hence $I_1 = 0$

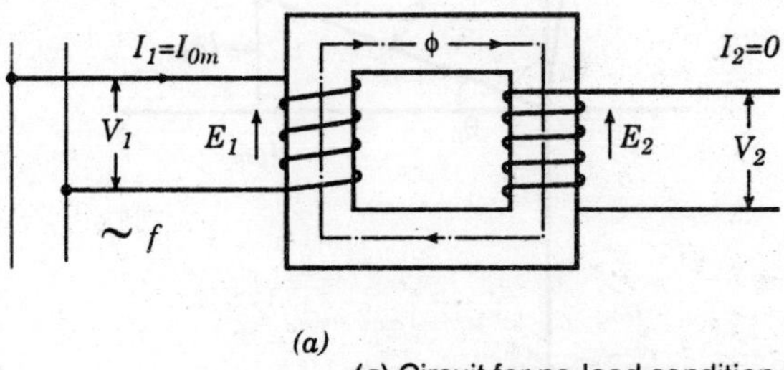


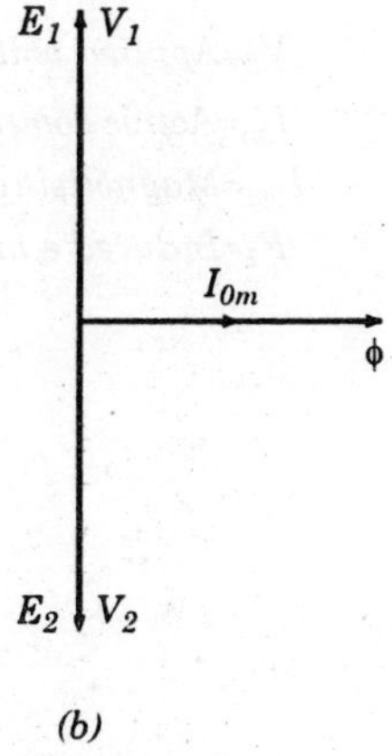


(*a*) Circuit for no-load condition
(*b*) Phasor diagram for no-load condition-ideal transformer
Fig. 5.2.

Hence transformer primary would not take any current from supply and would not set up any magnetic flux in the core.

Hence this situation is impossible. An assumption is made that the primary takes a very small current ($I_{om}$) on load for setting up magnetic flux $\phi_m$ in the core.

Figure. 5.2 (*a*) illustrates the representation of a single phase transformer and Fig. 5.2(*b*) illustrates the phasor diagram, $V_1$ is the applied voltage equal to induced voltage ( $-E_1$). $V_2$ is terminal voltage at secondary equal to ( $-E_2$). The no-load current $I_{om}$ has only magnetising component which sets up magnetic flux $\phi_m$ in the core. Fig. 5.2 (*b*) is for ideal transformer which has no losses.

Hence, $I_0$ does not have any active component. Since there is no load, the vectors $I_2$,$I_1$ are not appearing.

**Real transformer on No-load.** This will have resistance $R_1$, reactances $X_1$, Loss $P_L$, and there will be voltage drops $IZ_1$. The efficiency will be less than 100%. The no-load current will have two components:

(1) $I_{om}$ for setting up flux $\phi$

(2) $I_{or}$ for supplying to the no-load losses.

As a result $I_o$ is not at 90° behind $E_1$, but at an angle less than 90°.

Figure 5.3 illustrates the phasor-diagram (vector diagram) of a non-ideal transformer under no-load condition. The main flux $\phi$(which

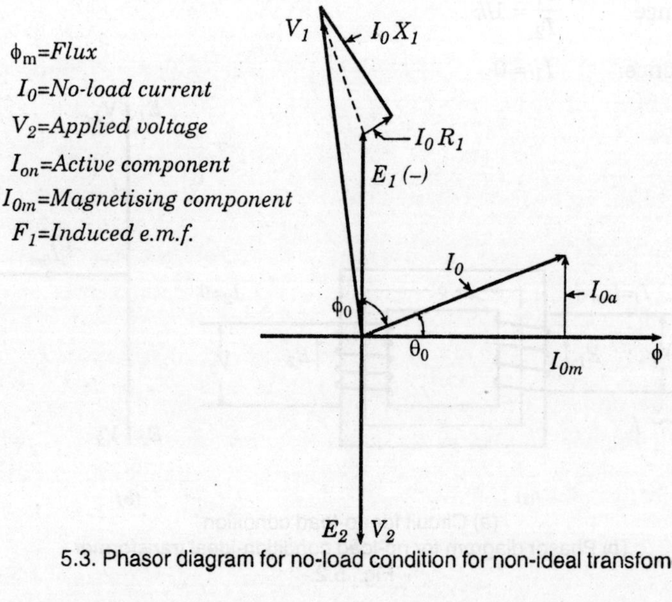


5.3. Phasor diagram for no-load condition for non-ideal transfomer.

is common to the primary winding and the secondary winding) is taken as a reference and is drawn on $X$-axis.

**Primary terminal voltage** $V_1$ differs from *primary induced e.m.f.* $E_1$ by *negligible* voltage drop in the primary winding due to small magnitude of *no-load primary current* $I_0$. Hence, $V_1$ is nearly equal to $E_1$ for no-load condition. $V_1$ and $-E_1$ are 90° ahead of flux $\phi_m$ as explained in Eqn.(5.1) and (5.2).

No-load current $I_0$ is at an angle $\phi_0$ lagging behind vector $V_1$. The power factor of no-load current ($\cos\phi_0$) is about 0.15 lagging because of the high self-inductance of the single winding. No-load current $I_0$ is about 0.05 p.u. of normal rated current.

The voltage equation for no-load condition is given by

$$\bar{V} = -\bar{E} + \bar{I}_0(Z_1) \quad \text{...(5.1)}$$

Since $I_0$ is very small, the voltage drop in primary inductance is usually neglected for no-load condition and the equation is simplified to

$$V_1 = -E_1 \quad \text{...(5.2)}$$

These vectors are drawn 90° ahead of $\phi_m$.

Secondary emf $E_2$ is equal to $E_1/k$. The secondary emf $E_2$ is drawn on the same axis as $E_1$.

The no-load current $I_0$ has an active component $I_0$ which is in-phase with $V_1$ and a magnetizing component $I_{0m}$ in quadrature with $V_1$. The component $I_{0m}$ is in phase with flux $\phi_m$. The vector sum of $I_0$ and $I_{0m}$ gives $I_0$.

As seen from Fig.5.3 primary current $I_0$ has two components.

(i) One in phase with $V_1$. The is known as active component $I_{oa}$ because it supplies the iron-loss plus a small quantity of primary loss

$$I_{0a} = I_0 \; Cos \; \theta_0 \quad \text{...(5.3)}$$

(ii) The other component is in quadrature with $V_1$ and is known as magnetizing component because its function is to produce the alternating flux in the core, It is a reactive or loss-less component

$$I_{0m} = I_0 \sin \theta_0 \quad \text{...(5.4)}$$

$$I_0 = \sqrt{I_{0a}^2 + I_{om}^2} \quad \text{...(5.5)}$$

The no-load primary current $I_0$ is very small as compared to full-load primary current. As $I_0$ is very small, hence no-load primary copper-loss is negligibly small. The no-load primary input power is practically equal to the iron-loss in a transformer.

Hence by conducting no-load test, the core loss (iron loss) of a transformer can be measured.

The no-load current is determined for applied primary voltage and the magnetisation curve of the core. No-load current is usually specified for given rated voltage.

## 5.4. TRANSFORMER ON LOAD

When the secondary terminals are connected to load impedance and the primary terminals are connected to supply terminals, the transformer starts feeding power to the load. Secondary current starts flowing to the load. The transformer is said to be loaded. The work load corresponds to secondary current and kVA supplied by secondary.

Full load condition refers to rated secondary current and rated kVA.

When $I_2$ flows, mmf $N_2 I_2$ is generated. This has component of magnetic flux $\phi_2$ which opposes main flux $\phi$ created by $I_0$.

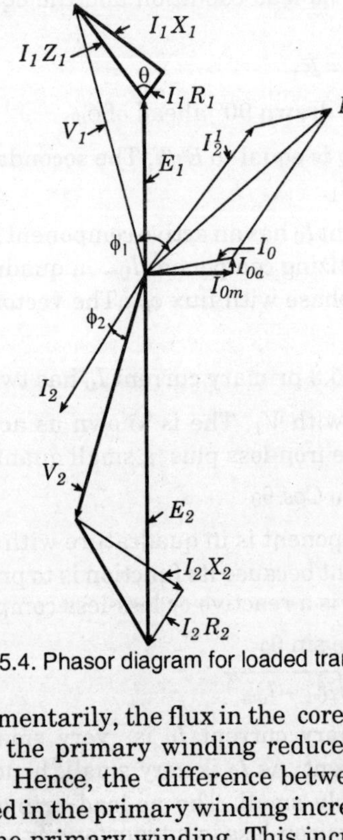


Fig. 5.4. Phasor diagram for loaded transformer.

As a result momentarily, the flux in the core reduces and the value of emf induced in the primary winding reduces. The supply voltage remains constant. Hence, the difference between the supply voltage and the emf induced in the primary winding increases. This forces more current through the primary winding. This increases the flux till the supply voltage minus the drop in primary winding resistance and leakage reactance becomes equal to the voltage generated in primary winding. This way, the core flux tries to remain constant in power transformers.

However the primary supply voltage tries to maintain value of flux $\phi$ to obtain mmf balance $I_1N_1 = I_2N_2$

$$I_1 = I_2\frac{N_2}{N_1}$$

Therefore, increase in $I_2$ is accompanied by increase in $I_1$.

## 5.5. PHASOR DIAGRAM FOR LOADED TRANSFORMER

Figure 5.4. illustrates the phasor diagram of a transformer on load. Main flux in the core $\phi_m$ is drawn along $X$-axis.

$E_2$ lags behind $\phi_m$ by 90°.

— Leakage flux produces leakage reactance which is responsible for voltage regulation.

— Leakage flux causes additional stray losses.

— Leakage flux gives higher impedance and thereby, reduces through short-circuit currents.

— By controlling design parameters, leakage reactance is controlled within required range, a very important consideration for deciding circuit breaker ratings.

The vector-relationship between $E_2$ and $V_2$ is given by the equation:

$$E_2 - I_2 Z_2 = V_2$$

The vector $V_2$ is obtained from the above equation. The vector $I_2Z_2$ is obtained by vector sum $(I_1R_1 + jI_1X_1)$. Current $I_2$ is at a phase angle $\phi_2$ behind vector $V_2$ for lagging power factor loads.

The primary current $I_1$ is the vector sum of no-load current $I_0$ and reflected secondary current $I_2^1 = I_2/k$. Thus, $I_1 = I_0 + I_2^1$. The vector $I_1$ lags behind $V_1$ angle $\phi_1$. The vector relationship between the $V_1$ and $E_1$ is given by the equation,

$$V_1 - I_1 Z_1 = E_1 \quad \text{or} \quad V_1 - E_1 = I_1Z_1$$

or

$$V_1 = E_1 + I_1Z_1 = E_1 + (I_0 + I_2/k)\, Z_1$$

$$I_1Z_1 = I_1R_1 + jI_1X_1$$

The vector $I_1 R_1$ is drawn in phase with $I_1$. The vector $I_1 X_2$ is drawn in quadrature with $I_1$ such that $I_1$ lags behind $I_1 X_1$ by 90°.

## 5.6. CONCEPT OF LEAKAGE MAGNETIC FLUX

Figure 5.5 shown main flux $\phi_m$ and leakage flux $\phi_L$. The magnetic flux which does not link with the two windings and which is not flowing in the core is called leakage flux ($\phi_L$). The leakage flux is minimised by placing the HV winding and LV winding concentrically and as close as possible without much gap. Further, both the winding are placed as close to the core as practically as possible with required insulation present.

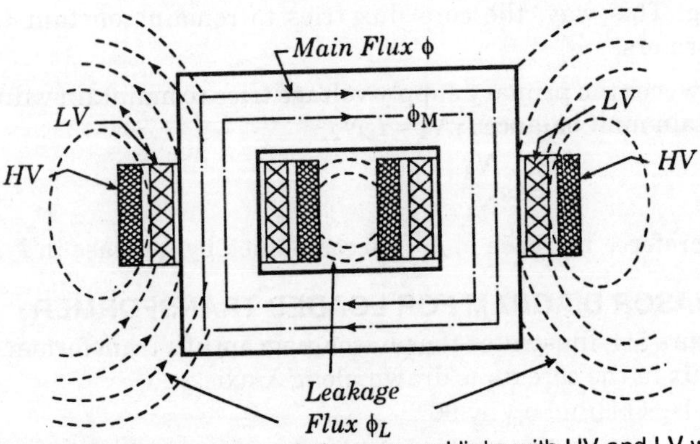


Fig. 5.5. Main flux $\phi_M$ flows through the core and links with HV and LV windings. Leakage flux $\phi_L$ leaks out of the main core and does not link with both the windings.

## 5.7. TRANSFORMER WITH RESISTANCE AND LEAKAGE REACTANCE FOR EACH WINDING

Figure 5.6 shows the circuit diagram. Each winding is shown separately on the core. The constants $R$ and $X$ of each winding are shown separately. The impedance of the primary winding is given by

$$Z_1 = \sqrt{(R_1^2 + X_1^2)}$$

And the secondary impedance is given by

$$Z_2 = \sqrt{(R_2^2 + X_2^2)}$$

$$V_1 = E_1 + I_1 (R_1 + jX_1) = E_1 + I_1 Z_1$$

and $$E_2 = V_2 + I_2 (R_2 + jX_2) = V_2 + I_2 Z_2$$

## 5.8. DEVELOPMENT OF EQUIVALENT CIRCUIT DIAGRAM OF A TRANSFORMER

**The Concept of Equivalent Circuit Diagram.** Electrical network comprises generators, transmission and distribution lines, and connected loads. For calculating voltages, currents, power factors, active and reactive powers at various points in the network, the network components are represented by their *equivalent circuits*.

The equivalent circuit has the resistances and reactances connected in such a way that the calculations give the values of currents voltages, etc., equal to the respective values in the actual network. Some *assumptions* are made to simplify the circuit and the calculations.

Though, the transformer has two or more windings at different voltages, there are definite relationships between $I_1$, $I_2$ and $V_1$, $V_2$.

Therefore, secondary quantities can be referred to primary side by applying appropriate multiplying factors such that the currents and voltages on primary side or secondary side remain unchanged. Such an equivalent diagram is called equivalent diagram as seen from primary or secondary depending upon from which side we are seeing from or vice versa.

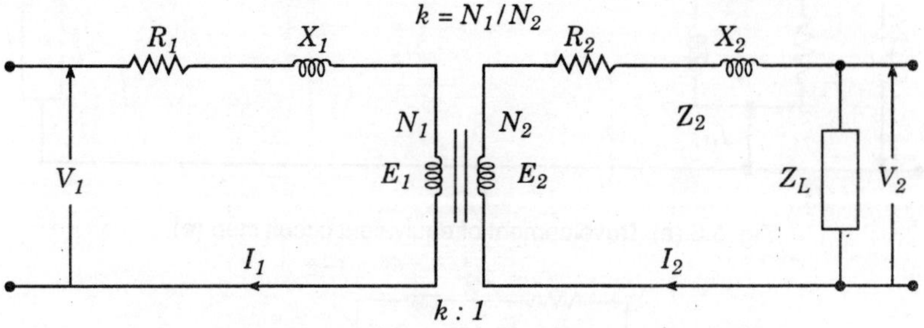


Fig. 5.6 (*a*). Development of equivalent circuit step (a).

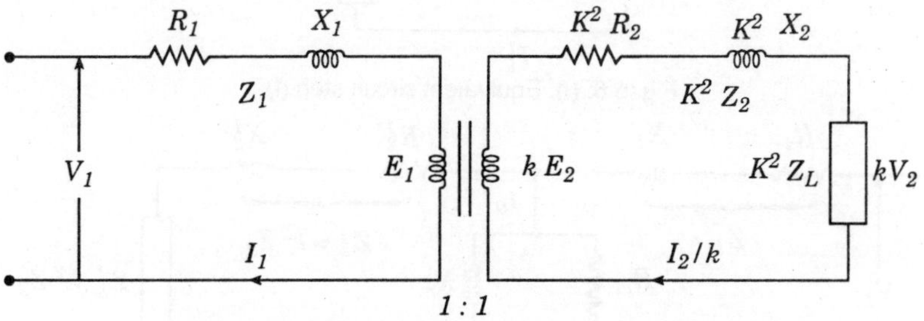


Fig. 5.6(*b*). Development of equivalent circuit step (b).

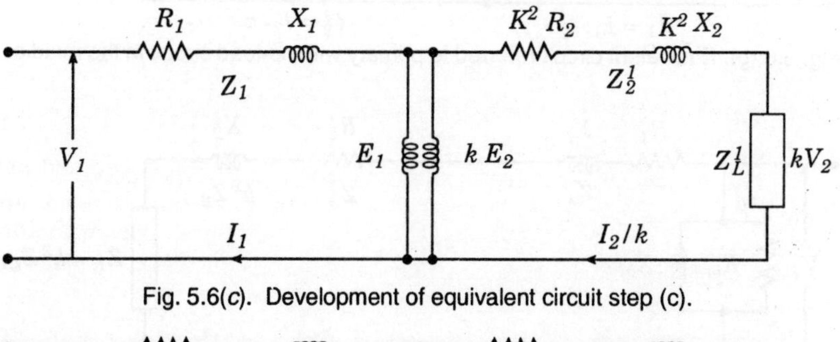


Fig. 5.6(*c*). Development of equivalent circuit step (c).

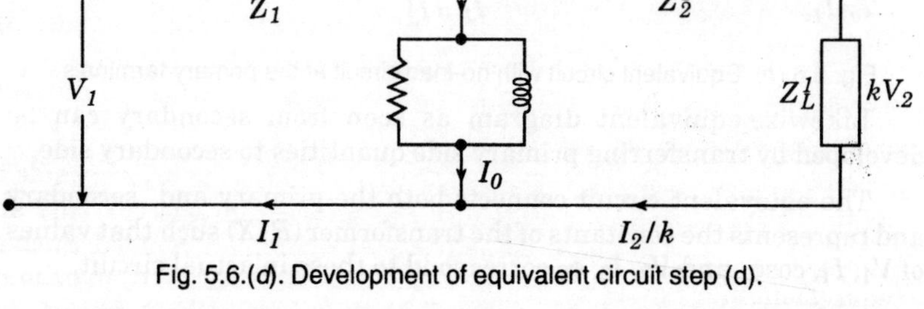


Fig. 5.6.(*d*). Development of equivalent circuit step (d).

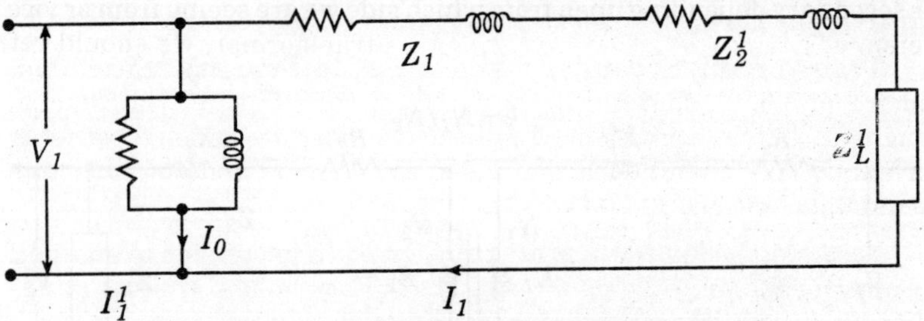


Fig. 5.6.(e). Development of equivalent circuit step (e).

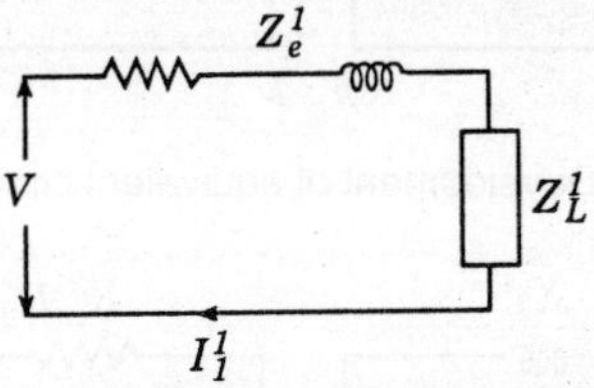


Fig. 5.6. (*f*). Equivalent circuit step (f).

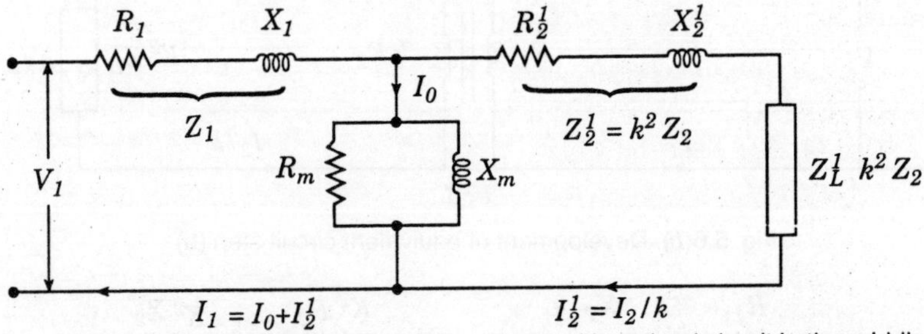


Fig. 5.6.(*g*). Equivalent circuit referred to primary with no-load circuit in the middle.

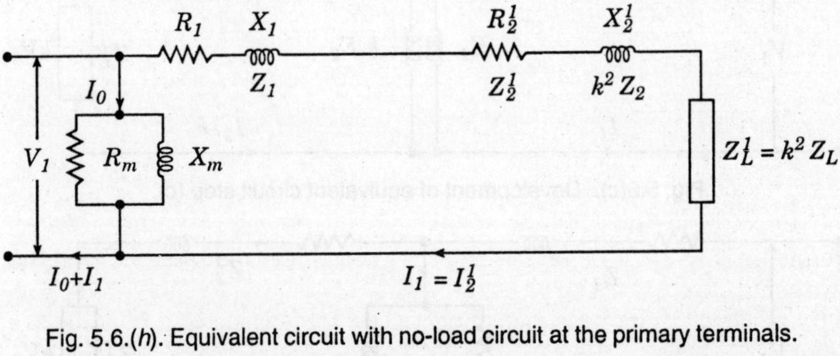


Fig. 5.6.(*h*). Equivalent circuit with no-load circuit at the primary terminals.

Likewise,equivalent diagram as seen from secondary can be developed by transferring primary side quantities to secondary side.

The equivalent circuit connects both the primary and secondary and represents the constants of the transformer ($R, X$) such that values of $V_1$, $I_1$, $\cos\phi_1$ and $V_2$, $I_2$, $\phi_2$ correspond to those in actual circuit.

## Equivalent Circuit-Referred to Primary Side

**Transferring Secondary Quantities to Primary Side.** Consider Fig. 5.6.(*a*), showing two separate circuits linked by a common magnetic core. In equivalent circuit,the two sides are joined together to form only one circuit such that voltages. currents and power factors remain unchanged.

For, this, the impedances are transferred from one side to another, by appropriate multiplying factors. The voltage values are also multiplied by appropriate multiplying factor.

For basic equations, we know

$$K = N_1/N_2$$

$$E_1E_2 = k, \text{ the transformation ratio.}$$

If we multiply $E_2$ by $k$, we get $E_1$. The secondary side can be connected to primary as shown in Fig. 5.6. (b).

In Fig. 5.6. (b) the following multiplying factors are used:

where $$k = N_1/N_2$$

$$V_1/V_2 = I_2/I_1$$

| *Secondary Quantity* | *Quantities and Multiplying factors for referring to the primary side* |
|---|---|
| $V_2$ | $V_2^1 = kV_2$ |
| $E_2$ | $E_2^1 = kE_2$ |
| $I_2$ | $I_2^1 = I_2/k$ |
| $Z_2$ | $Z_2^1 = \dfrac{V_2^1}{I_2^1} = \dfrac{kV_2}{I_2/k} = K^2Z_2$ |

$V_2^1$ is secondary voltage referred to primary

$E_2^1$ is secondary emf referred to primary

$I_2^1$ is secondary current referred to primary

$Z_2^1$ is secondary impedance referred to primary

By multiplying appropriate factors ($k$, $1/k$, $k_2$, $1/k_2$) the primary quantities are made equal to respective secondary quantities. Then the two separate circuits can be joined without changing circuit values. Fig. 5.6. (c). Two circuits can be connected when voltage and current are same.

Consider the secondary circuit in Fig.5.6.

*Emf* = $E_2$, Voltage = $V_1$, Current = $I_2$, Secondary impedance = $Z_2$. Let us *refer* the secondary quantities to primary side by using multiplying factors.

| *Original Secondary Quantities* | *Secondary Quantity referred to primary* |
|---|---|
| $E_2$ | $E_2 k = E_2^1$ |
| $V_2$ | $V_{2k} = V_2^1$ |
| $I_1$ | $I_2/k = I_2^1$ |
| $Z_2 = V_2/I_2$ | $Z_2/k^2 = Z_2^1$ |

But $\quad V_2^1 = V_2 k = V_1$

$$I_2^1 = I_2/k = I_1$$

**Note:** $\quad k = N_1/N_2 = V_1/V_2$

Likewise, Load impedance referred to primary is

$$Z_L^1 = Z_2/k^2$$

Also $\quad X_2^1 = X_2/k^2$

$$R_2^1 = R_2/k^2$$

**Representation of No-load Current** and *No-load losses.* The no-load current $I_0$ and no-load losses $P_0$ are represented by *no-load equivalent* circuit comprising resistance $R_m$ and reactance $X_m$ in parallel and connected across terminals having emf $E_1$. The values of $R_m$ and $X_m$ are calculated from no-load test result as follows:

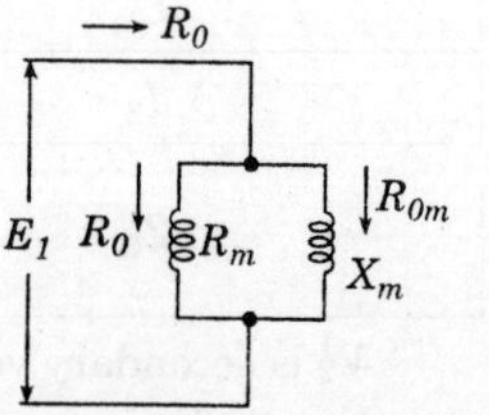


$$R_a = \frac{P_a}{I_{0a}{}^2}$$

$$X_m = E_1/I_{0m}$$

$I_{0a}$ and $I_{0m}$ are components of $I_0$.

**Approximate Equivalent Circuit Referred to the Primary**

The secondary quantities are referred to primary side

Total resistance as seen from primary side:

$$\text{Re}^1 = R_1 + R_2^1 = R_1 + R_2/k_2$$

Total reactance as seen from primary:

$$Xe^1 = X_2 + X_2^1 = X_1 + X_2/k^2$$

Total impedance as seen from primary side

$$Z_e{}^1 = R_1{\cdot}l + jX_1{\cdot}t$$

In approximate equivalent circuit, the no-load equivalent is connected near primary terminals. Fig. 5.6.(*e*).

**Exact Equivalent Circuit Referred to the Primary.**

The no-load circuit is connected in between $Z_1$ and $Z_2^1$ as shown in Fig.5.6. (*g*) and 5.6 (*h*).

**Figure 5.6(*c*) gives the equivalent circuit of a transformer.** As seen from the primary side $V_2^1 =$ Secondary voltage referred to primary side, $\dot{I}_2^1 =$ Secondary current referred to primary side; $Z_2^1 =$ Secondary impedance referred to primary side. $Z_L^1 =$ Load impedance referred to primary side.

The no-load equivalent circuit comparison $R_m$ and $X_m$ is added as shown in Fig. 5.6. (*d*). Fig. 5.6.(*d*) gives the complete equivalent circuit of a transformer as seen from the primary side.

**Equivalent circuit as seen from the load side.** Using same principles, the primary quantities can be transferred to the secondary side to obtain the equivalent circuit as seen from the secondary side. Fig. 5.7.

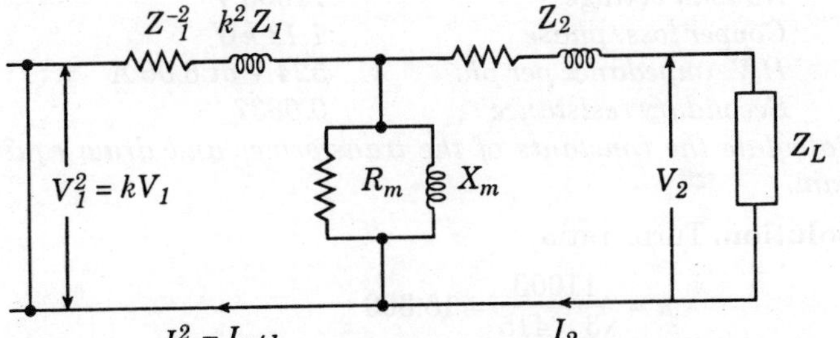


Fig. 5.7. Equivalent circuit referred to the secondary side (load side).

Let $V_1^2 = V_1$ as seen from secondary side

$E_1^2 = E_1$ as seen from secondary side

$I_1^2 = I_1$ as seen from secondary side

$Z_1^2 = Z_1$ as seen from secondary side

$$\frac{V_1}{V_2} = k = \frac{N_1}{N_2} \text{ Transformation Ratio}$$

$$V_1 = kV_2$$

$$\frac{V_1}{k} = V_2$$

Hence by dividing $V_1$ by $k$, we get $V_2$ and both circuits can be connected by using the appropriate multiply factors as follows:

| *Primary quantity* | *Referred to secondary side and multiplying factor* |
|---|---|
| $V_1$ | $V_1^2 = kV_1$ |
| $E_1$ | $E_1^2 = kE_1$ |
| $I_1$ | $I_1^2 = D_1/k$ |
| $Z_1$ | $Z_1^2 = \frac{V_1^2}{I_1^2} = k^2 Z_1$ |
| $R_1$ | $R_1^2 = k^2 R_1$ |
| $X_1$ | $X_1^2 = k^2 X_1$ |

**Example 5.1.** *Equivalent diagram. A 3 phase, 11 kV/0.415 kV, Delta/Star, 50 Hz, 200 kVA distribution transformer is tested with the following results:*

| | |
|---|---|
| *Core loss/phase* | *270 watts* |
| *Resistance of primary* | *16.6 *Ω* |
| *No-load current* | *0.212 A* |
| *No-load voltage* | *11000 V* |
| *Copper loss/phase* | *1.13 kW* |
| *H.V. impedance per ph.* | *524 V at 6.06 A* |
| *Secondary resistance* | *0.0637* |

*Calculate the constants of the transformer and draw equivalent diagram.*

**Solution.** Turns ratio

$$k = \frac{11000}{\sqrt{3} \times 415} = 15.303$$

$$k^2 = 234.189$$

No-load loss $P_0 = 270$ W (measured)

No-load current $I_0 = 0.212$ (measured)

**Components of No-load Current** (calculated)

Active component $I_{oa} = \frac{P_0}{V} = \frac{270}{11000} = 0.0245$ A

Magnetising component

$$I_{om}^2 = I_0^2 - I_{oa}^2 = (0.212)^2 - (0.0245)^2$$

$$I_{om} = 0.21057\text{A}$$

Primary No-load p.f. $= \cos\phi_0 = \frac{0.0245}{0.212} = 0.1155$

$$\phi_0 = 83.3°$$

Primary resistance $R_0 = 16.6$ (measured)

Copper loss/phase $= 1130$ (measured)

HV impedance voltage/phase

(at 6.06 A per phase) = 524 V (measured)

Secondary resistance

$$R_2 = 0.00637$$

Secondary resistance referred to primary

$$R_{21} = R_2k^2 = 0.00637 \times 234.189 = 1.419\ \Omega$$

Equivalent impedance (see from HV side)

$$Z_e^1 = \frac{V_{sc}}{I^1} = \frac{524}{6.06} = 86.468\ \Omega$$

Equivalent reactance

$$X_e^1 = (Z_e^1)^2 - R_t^1)^2$$

Total Equivalent Resistance

$$= R_1 + R_2^1 = 16.6 + 1.419 = 18.019\ \Omega$$

Equivalent Reactance

$$X_e^1 = \sqrt{(Z_e^1)^2 - (R_t^1)^2} = \sqrt{86.468^2 - 18.019^2} = 84.57\ \Omega$$

Assuming $X_1 = X_2 = 42.285\ \Omega$

The constants of the transformer per phase are as follows:

$k = 15.303$ $\quad k^2 = 234.189$

$I_0 = 0.212\text{A}$ ; $\quad I_{oa} = 0.0245$ A , $I_oV = 0.21057$ A

$\phi_0 = 83.3°$

$R_1 = 16.6$ $\quad R_2^1 = 1.419\ \Omega$

$X_1 = 42.285\ \Omega$ $\quad X_2 = 42.285\ \Omega$

The equivalent diagram is drawn as in Fig.5.6 (d). It is a single phase equivalent referred to the HV side.

**Example 5.2. Equivalent Circuit.** *A single phase transformer has a voltage ratio of 240/24 V. The constants are as follows:*

$R_1 = 6.0\Omega/ph$ $\quad X_1 = 20\Omega/ph.$

$R_2 = 0.05\Omega/ph$ $\quad X_2 = 0.18\Omega/ph.$

*The load connected on 24 V side is* $3.9 + j1.9\ \Omega$. *Calculate primary current for following data from no-load test.*

*No load test. Supply voltage 240 V, No-load current taken 0.02 A at 0.3 p.f. lag.*

**Solution.** As we have to calculate primary current of loaded transformer, we should refer the load inpedance and secondary impedance to primary side.

Secondary resistance referred to primary:

$$R_2^1 = k^2 R_2$$

$$k = \frac{240}{24} = 10$$

$$R_2^1 = 0.05\left(\frac{240}{24}\right)^2 = 5\ \Omega$$

$$X_2^1 = 0.18\left(\frac{240}{24}\right)^2 = 18\ \Omega$$

**Load impedance $Z_L$ referred to primary ($Z_2^1$)**

$$Z_L^1 = k^2 Z^2 = \left(\frac{240}{24}\right)^2 Z_2$$

$$= \left(\frac{240}{24}\right)^2 (3.9 + j\,1.9)$$

$$= 433.82\ \angle 25.974°$$

The Equivalent Circuit is drawn referred to primary

$$I_1 = \frac{V_1}{Z_1 + Z_2^1 + Z_L^1}$$

$$= \frac{240}{(6 + 390 + 5) + j(20 + 190 + 18)}$$

$$= \frac{240}{401 + j\,228} = 0.52 - \angle 29.62°\ \text{A}$$

$$= 0.452 - j\,0.257\ \text{A}$$

**No load current $I_0$**

$$I_0 = 0.02\ \angle - \cos^{-1} 0.3$$

$$= 0.02\ \angle\,(-\ 72.5°)$$

$$= 0.02\,(\cos 72.5 - j \sin 72.5)$$

$$= 0.02\,(0.3 - j\,0.95)$$

$$= 0.006 - j\,0.0191\ \text{A.}$$

**Total primary current**

$$\bar{I}_1 = \bar{I}_0 + \bar{I}_1$$

$$= 0.458 - j0.276$$

$$= 0.535\angle - 31.07°$$

$$I_1 = 0.535\ \text{A}\ \angle - 31.07° \qquad \text{...Ans}$$

### Summary

The transformer can be represented by its equivalent circuits

- — referred to the primary, or
- — referred to the secondary.

The interrelationship between primary quantities and secondary quantities is shown by phasor diagrams.

Phasor diagrams are drawn for

- — no-load condition (open circuit)
- — loaded condition
- — short circuit test condition

# 6

# Impedance Voltage and Voltage Regulation

Impedance Voltage of a transformer is defined as the voltage required to circulate full load current in one winding with the other winding(s) short-circuited.

Impedance $Z$ is usually expressed as a percentage or per unit for rated base $V$ for rated current *i.e.* $\% Z = (IZ/V) \times 100$ and p.u. $Z = IZ/V$.

Impedance cause *voltage regulation*. Impedance also limits the short-circuit current. Impedance voltage comprises of IR and $IX_L$ components. The $IX_L$ component predominates. The impedance depends upon the leakage flux, hence on the configuration and relative position of primary and secondary windings.

Higher impedance gives higher losses. higher voltage regulation and lesser short-circuit currents.

The terms and definitions, significance, measurement aad design aspects related with impedance voltage and voltage regulation have been covered in this chapter. The losses and efficiency are covered in the next Chapter.

## 6.1. INTRODUCTION

A transformer has a certain equivalent impedance. The impedance is composed of resistance and reactance. Reactance predominates.

The impedance of a transformer is expressed in terms of *impedance voltage* and is measured by conducting sustained *short circuit test*. As the transformer is loaded, the current causes *voltage drop* in the impedance. Therefore, with rated primary applied voltage, changes in secondary voltage. This change is called Regulation.

Impedance of a transformer influences

— Short-circuit level on secondary side

— Voltage regulation

— Load sharing in parallel operation

— Efficiency

## 6.2.. DEFINITIONS

**1. Impedance voltage at rated current ($V_{sc}$).** It is defined as the voltage required to be applied to the line terminals of a winding to cause rated current flow through these terminals, with the terminals.

of the other winding being short circuited. The value is related to the reference temperature.

**Note.** The impedance voltage is usually expressed as a percentage of the rated voltage of the winding to which the voltage is applied during the short-circuit test. *Impedance voltage* is also called *short-circuit voltage* and is designated by $V_{sc}$.

**2. Resistance Voltage ($V_R$)** is the component of the impedance voltage which is in phase with the current.

**3. Reactance Voltage ($V_L$)** is the component of the impedance voltage which is perpendicular (in quadrature) with the current.

**4. Voltage Drop or Voltage Rise (Voltage Regulation) for a specified load condition.** It is defined as the difference between the *rated voltage of the winding and the voltage at the specified load and power factor, the voltage applied to the other winding being at its rated value.*

It is generally expressed as a percentage of the rated voltage of the former winding.

*Voltage Regulation $\Delta V$ of a transformer* is by definition, the difference between the rated secondary voltage $V_2$-rated and actual secondary voltage $V_2$-actual for given load and at specified power factor of load, the primary voltage $V_1$ being at rated voltage and rated frequency.

Thus, the % Regulation:

$$\%\Delta V = \frac{V_2 \text{ rated} - V_2 \text{ actual}}{V_2 \text{ rated}} \times 100 \qquad \text{....(6.1)}$$

at specified load current and load p.f.

## 6.3. TRANSFORMER IMPEDANCE

The primary winding (1) has its resistance $R_1$ and leakage reactance $X_{L_1}$. The secondary winding (2) has its resistance $R_2$ and leakage reactance $X_{L_2}$.

The secondary impedance is $Z_2 = R_2 + jX_{L_2}$

The primary impedance is $Z_1 = R_1 + jX_{L_1}$

*The secondary impedance can be referred to the primary side by multiplying by factor $K^2$*, where, $K = N_1/N_2$.

Thus $Z_2^1$ = Secondary Impedance referred to the primary side $= K^2 Z_2$

Total transformer impedance seen from primary side would be

$$Z_{1t} = Z_1 + Z_2^1 = Z_1 + k^2 Z_2$$

The total Impedance $Z_1 + Z_{1t}$ is usually expressed in terms of percentage impedance (Refer Sec. 5.8).

Likewise, the secondary resistance $R_2$ and secondary reactance $X_{L2}$ can be referred to primary side as

$$R_2^1 = K^2 R_2$$

$$X_{L_2}^1 = K^2 X_{l2}$$

*Total Resistance seen from the primary side*

$$R_{1t} = R_1 + R_2^1 = R_1 + K^2 R_2$$

*Total Reactance as seen from primary side*

$$X_{1t} = X_1 + X_2^1 = X_1 + K^2 X^2$$

Where $k = N_1/N_2$

*Total Transformer Impedance as seen from primary side is*

$$Z_{1t} = R_1 t + j X_{1t}$$

where $Z_{1t}$ = Equivalent Impedance of the transformer seen from primary side.

*Consider the voltage drops in the resistances and reactances.* Primary current $I_1$ flowing through $Z_{1t}$ produces a voltage drop $I_1 Z_{1t}$. This voltage drop has tow components $I_1 R_{1t}$ which is in phase with $I_1$, and $I_1 X_{1t}$ which is in quadrature with $I_1$.

Let $V_2^1$ = Secondary voltage $V_2$ referred to primary side = $kV_2$

Applying Kirchoff's voltage law to the primary side,

$$V_1 = V_2^1 - I_1 Z_{1t} = 0$$

or

$$V_1 = V_2^1 + I_1 Z_{1t}$$

## 6.4. RELATION BETWEEN THE TRANSFORMER IMPEDANCE, IMPEDANCE VOLTAGE AND SHORT-CIRCUIT CONDITION.

If the secondary winding is short-circuited, Load impedance is zero. A very small per cent of rated voltage is sufficient to circulate rated current in the primary winding. Under such a situation.

— Entire applied voltage is consumed by the *IZ* drop in the transformer.

If transformer has higher impedance, higher applied voltage would be necessary to circulate rated current under short-circuit condition and vice versa.

— If rated voltage had been applied to primary and secondary were shorted, the short-circuit current ($I_{sc}$) would be high. It would be limited only by the Impedance of the transformer as load impedance is zero.

$$I_{sc} = \frac{V}{Z} \quad ...(6.2)$$

where $I_{sc}$ = Short circuit current

$V$ = Applied voltage

$Z$ = Impedance of transformer

$Z_L$ = Load impedance = 0

## 6.5. IMPEDANCE VOLTAGE

When the secondary winding is short-circuited and the primary is supplied with voltage $V_{sc}$ such that rated current flows through the primary terminals, the applied voltage $V_{sc}$ is required to overcome the impedance voltage drop in the transformer, *i.e.*,

$$V_{sc} = I_{sc} Z_{1t}$$

Where $V_{sc}$ = Applied voltage to primary called impedance voltage.

$I_{sc}$ = Rated current through primary terminals, with secondary shorted.

$Z_{1t}$ = Equivalent Impedance of the transformer as seen from the primary.

The voltage $V_{sc}$ is called Impedance Voltage of the transformer for rated current (referred to primary)

— Impedance voltage is determined by conducting short-circuit test.

— Impedance voltage determines the regulation and efficiency of a transformer

— Impedance voltage should be mentioned in the tender as one of the service parameters.

— High Impedance voltage means higher impedance, higher voltage regulation, higher losses, lesser efficiency.

— The Impedance or Impedance voltage of a transformer is generally expressed as a percentage of rated voltage. The percentage impedance is in the range of 4.5% to 15% (Refer Table 4.1)

*Relation between impedance voltage and short-circuit current*

Let $I_1$ = Rated Primary Current

$V_{sc}$ = Impedance Voltage

$Z_{1t}$ = Impedance

by definition $V_{sc} = I_1 Z_{1t}$ ...(6.3)

$I_1$ is constant for given kVA, kV ratings

Hence, $V_{sc} \propto Z_{1t}$

Impedance voltage ∝ Impedance

Let $V_1$ be applied voltage

$$I_{sc} = \frac{V_1}{Z_{1t}} \qquad ...(6.4)$$

where $V_1$ = applied voltage

$I_{sc}$ = Short circuit current for a fault beyond transformer

$Z_{1t}$ = Impedance.

From Eqn. (6.3), $Z_{1t} = \frac{V_{sc}}{I_1}$

where $V_{sc}$ = Impedance voltage and $I_1$ = Rated Current

Substituting the value in Eqn. (6.4)

$$I_{sc} = \frac{V_1}{V_{sc}} I_1 \qquad ...(6.5)$$

*i.e., Short circuit current $I_{sc}$ is inversely proportioned to the impedance voltage $V_{sc}$. Higher the impedance voltage, lesser will be through short-circuit current.*

*Though higher impedance voltage results in higher voltage regulation, higher losses and reduced efficiency, it ensures reduced through short-circuit currents and therefore safety of the transformer form excessive short circuit currents during external faults.*

## 6.6 STANDARD VALUES OF PERCENTAGE IMPEDANCE

The Impedance of a transformer ($Z_{1t}$) is often expressed as a percentage and is called percentage impedance of the transformer. *The percentage impedance is the value of impedance voltage expressed as a percentage of rated voltage*. Thus

% Impedance = % impedance voltage

$$\% \, V_{sc} = I_1 \frac{Z_{1t}}{V_1} \times 100 \qquad ...(6.6)$$

where, I = Rated primary current

$Z_{1t}$ = Impedance seen from primary

$V_1$ = Rated primary voltage.

The reference values of % impedance of transformers has been given in Table 6.1. These are used while designing the transformer.

**Table 6.1. Reference Values of Percentage Impedance (Voltages) for Single Phase Transformers at Normal flux Densities**

| *Rated kVA* | *Rated kV of HV winding* | | | | | | | |
|---|---|---|---|---|---|---|---|---|
| | *3.3* | *6.6* | *11* | *15* | *22* | *33* | *66* | *110* |
| | *Percentage Impedances* | | | | | | | |
| 5 | 4.5 | 4.5 | 4.5 | 5.25 | — | — | — | |
| 10 | 4.5 | 4.5 | 4.5 | 4.75 | 4.75 | 4.75 | — | |
| 50 | 4.5 | 4.5 | 4.5 | 4.5 | 4.5 | 4.5 | | |
| 100 | 4.5 | 4.5 | 4.5 | 4.5 | 4.5 | 4.5 | 5.5 | |
| 500 | 4.75 | 4.75 | 4.75 | 5 | 5 | 5 | 6 | |
| 1000 | — | 5.5 | 5.5 | 6 | 6 | 6 | 6.5 | |
| 2500 | — | — | 6 | 6 | 7 | 7 | 7.5 | |
| 5000 | — | — | 6 | 6.5 | 7 | 3 | 8.5 | |
| 10000 | | | | | 10 | 10 | 10 | |

**Note.** Value of % impedance is higher for higher kVA rating and higher kV rating of *HV* winding. This is related with design of transformer winding and its reactance.

The choice is made on the basis of short-circuit level and over all cost.

**Table 6.2. Reference Values of Percentage Reactance (Voltages) for 3 Phase Transformers at Normal flux Densities**

| *Rate kVA* | *Rated kV of HV winding* | | | | | | | | |
|---|---|---|---|---|---|---|---|---|---|
| | *3.3* | *6.6* | *11* | *15* | *22* | *33* | *66* | *110* | *220* |
| 5 | 4.75 | 4.75 | 4.75 | 5.5 | 5.5 | 6.6 | — | — | |
| 10 | 4.75 | 4.75 | 4.75 | 4.75 | 4.75 | 4.75 | — | — | |
| 50 | 4.5 | 4.5 | 4.5 | 4.5 | 4.5 | 4.5 | — | — | |
| 100 | 4.75 | 4.75 | 4.75 | 5 | 5 | 5.5 | — | — | |
| 500 | 4.75 | 4.75 | 4.75 | 5 | 5 | 5 | 6 | 7 | |
| 1000 | 4.75 | 4.75 | 4.75 | 5 | 5 | 5 | 6 | 7 | |
| 5000 | — | — | 6 | 6.5 | 7 | 7 | 7.5 | 7.5 | |
| 10000 | — | — | — | — | 9 | 9 | 9 | 10 | |
| 20000 | — | — | — | — | 10 | 10 | 10 | 10 | |
| 25000 | — | — | — | — | 10 | 10 | 10 | 10 | |
| 30000 | — | — | — | — | 10 | 10 | 10 | 10 | |

## 6.7. SIGNIFICANT ASPECTS ABOUT TRANSFORMER IMPEDANCE VOLTAGE

The impedance voltage of a transformer is the voltage required to drive rated current in winding with other winding(s) short circuited. Impedance voltage has two components:

— IR drop in the resistance

— IX drop in leakage reactance.

IX drop is required for overcoming induced emf due to leakage reactance. The leakage flux $\phi_L$ is dependent on the winding ampere-turns, length and area of paths of leakage flux. By selecting design parameters of the windings, the transformer can be designed to have required leakage reactance.

The economical design of core and winding gives certain value of leakage reactance called the 'natural value of reactance'. This value can be changed to some limited extent by changing the winding configuration without affecting the cost of transformer.

Interleaving the winding reduces the leakage paths and leakage reactance. High leakage reactance results in higher stray losses due to leakage flux. The leakage reactance is mainly due to the leakage flux and the flux linkage of leakage flux with primary winding and secondary winding. The distribution of leakage flux depends upon the configuration and geometry of the windings and the neighbouring ferrous materials such as tank, structural steel.

In case of transformer with tappings, the impedance is conventionally expressed in terms of rated voltage of concerned tapping.

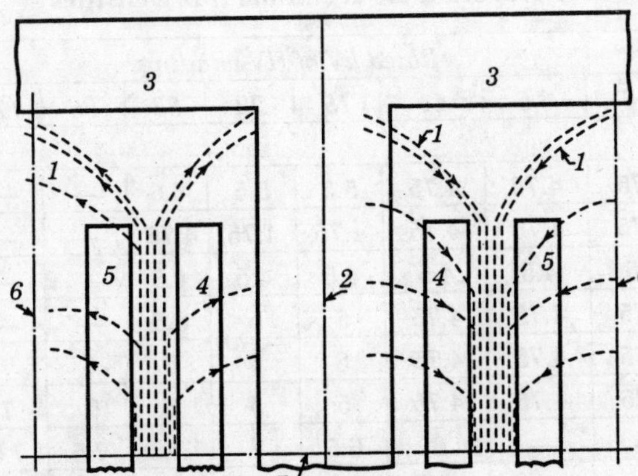


1. Leakage flux 2. Centre line of Limb
3. Yoke. 4. LV winding.
5. HV winding 6. Centre line of window
7. Centre line of core-limbs.

Fig. 6.1. (a) Leakage flux for windings of equal lengths.

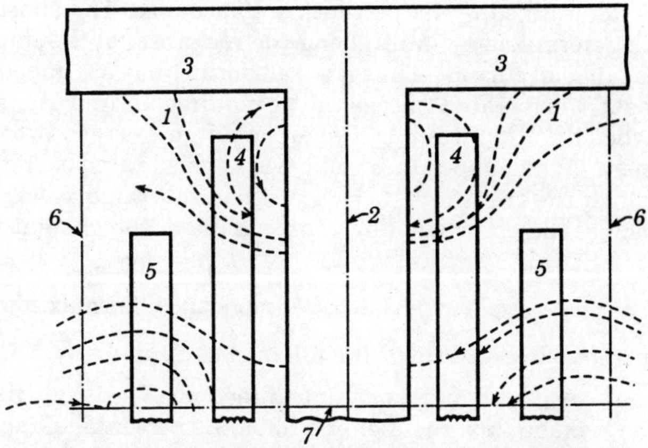


Fig. 6.1. (b) Leakage flux for windings of equal lengths.

What should be the impedance of a transformer? Higher impedance gives lesser short-circuit currents on secondary and safer transformer design. But voltage regulation is poor, losses are more. Hence balance should be reached.

For parallel operation the two or more transformers should have equal per cent impedances.

Figure 6.1. (*a*) shows flux distribution of two concentric windings of equal lengths. The lines of leakage flux flow mostly through the gap between the windings. Figure 6.1(*b*) shows flux distribution of two concentric windings of unequal length.

The path of leakage flux lines are now alterered significantly resulting in increase in flux linkage of leakage flux. Therefore the leakage reactance increases.

## 6.8. PER UNIT IMPEDANCE

Another method of specifying the impedance in terms of p.u. value as

$$\text{p.u.z.} = \frac{IZ}{V} \qquad \text{...(6.7)}$$

where $I$ = Rated current, A

$Z$ = Equivalent impedance.......

$V$ = Voltage of the winding

**Percentage impedance** Impedance basically represents the unavoidable voltage drop in the transformer itself and it is expressed as per cent. The percentage impedance represents the amount of normal rated primary voltage that needs to be applied to the transformer to pass full load current when the secondary winding in short circuited. The maximum short circuit current that can flow through the transformer is determined by its percentage impedance. The short circuit current is determined by multiplying the reciprocal of the impedance times the full load current. Thus if a transformer has 5% impedance, it means that 5% of its rated voltage will be required to circulate the rated current when the other winding in short circuit in case of a two winding transformer. When impedance voltage is applied, rated current circulates through the transformer. Hence, when full rated voltage is applied, keeping the other winding short circuited, the current passing through the transformer will be equal to $\frac{1}{\%\ \text{impedance}} \times$ rated current. For 5% impedance, the maximum short circuit current will be 20 times the full load current.

Percentage impedance is mainly function of leakage flux. The higher the leakage flux, the higher will be the percentage impedance, the higher the percentage impedance, the lower will be short circuit current and it will require small circuit breaker fuse etc. On the other hand, higher percentage impedance will lead to higher voltage drop under normal operating conditions. So we will have to meet these conflicting requirements while selecting percentage impedance of a transformer.

The curve in figure 6.2. give the amount of short circuit current of the secondary terminals v/s percentage impedance of a transformer. In the figure, we can see that the optimum value of % age impedance is at *C*. If we select a lower value than this, the fault current increases drastically and it will make transformer design costly, with expensive protective devices etc., except that will result in lower voltage drop. we can not select to low percentage impedance also as it may not be possible to design the transformer. On the other hand, percentage impedance higher than at point *C* does not decrease fault level considerably and this results in a higher voltage drop under normal operating conditions. So percentage impedance at *C* is optimum. Sometimes, we may have inverse transformer capacity to keep the voltage drop, especially during induction motor starting, within permissible limits.

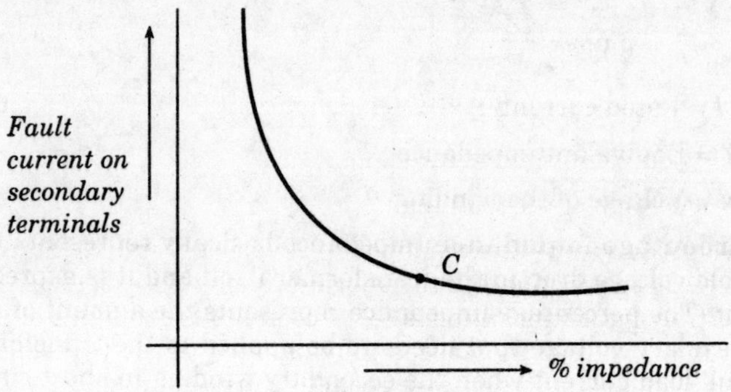


Fig. 6.2

**Example 6.1.** *A 3 phase 6.6 kV/0.433 kV, 1000 kVA distribution transformer is supplied with 6.6 kV and a dead 3 phase short-circuit occurs on the secondary bus bars. The full load impedance voltage of the transformer is 4.75%. Calculate the fault current flowing through primary terminals.*

**Solution.** $I_{sc} = \frac{V_1}{V_{sc}} I_1 \times 100$

$V_1$ = rated voltage or applied voltage

$V_{sc}$ = % impedance voltage

$I_1$ = rated primary current. $= \frac{1000 \times 10^3}{\sqrt{3} \times 6.6 \times 10^3}$

$= \frac{6.6}{4.75} \times 87.477 \times 100 = 12154.69$ Amp.

## 6.9. DETERMINATION OF IMPEDANCE VOLTAGE $V_{sc}$, RESISTANCE VOLTAGE $V_R$ AND REACTANCE VOLTAGE $V_x$

Refer Definitions in Sec 6.2,

Let $V_{sc} = V_R + jV_x$

where, $V_{sc}$ = Impedance voltage

$V_R$ = Resistance Voltage

$V_X$ = Reactance voltage

Since $V_R$ and $V_x$ are quadrature,

$$V_{sc} = \sqrt{V_R^2 + V_x^2} \quad \text{...(6.8)}$$

The impedance voltage $V_{sc}$ is determined by conduction short-circuit test. *It is the voltage required to drive rated short-circuit current.* Hence, the voltmeter reading gives $V_{sc}$ directly. For determining $V_R$ and $V_x$, the $V_R$ is calculated first, as described below and then $V_x$ is calculated from Equation 4.4.

**Determination of Resistance Voltage.** $V_R$ is the resistive component of the impedance voltage $V_{sc}$. The short-circuit losses (copper losses) are equal to $I^2R$ and $V_R$ is equal to $IR$. Hence $V_R$ can be calculated as follows:

Let $V_R$ be expressed as a % of rated voltage $V_1$.

$$\%V_{R_1} = \frac{V_{R_1}}{V_1} \times 100 = \frac{I_1 R_1}{V_1} \times 100$$

Multiplying numerator and denominator by $I_1$

$$\%V_{R_1} = \frac{I_1^2 R_1}{V_1 I} \times 100 = \frac{P_{sc} \cdot 1}{S} \times 100 \quad \text{...(6.9)}$$

where $P_{sc \cdot 1}$ = short circuit loss in primary

$S = VA$ rating

Similarly, $$\%V_{R_2} = \frac{I_2^2 R_2}{V_2 I_2} \times 100 = \frac{P_{sc \cdot 2}}{S} \times 100 \quad ...(6.10)$$

$$\% V_R = \% V_{R_1} + \% V_{R_2}$$

$$= \frac{P_{sc \cdot 1}}{S} \times 100 + \frac{P_{sc \cdot 2}}{S} \times 100$$

$$= \frac{P_{sc \cdot 1} + P_{sc \cdot 2}}{S} \times 100 \quad ...(6.11)$$

$$= \frac{P_{sc}}{S} \times 100 \quad ..(6.12)$$

Hence $$\% V_R = \frac{P_{sc}}{S} \times 100 \quad ...(6.13)$$

where $\%V_R$ = Precentage Resistance Voltage

= Impedance voltage expressed as a percentage of rated voltage

S = Rated VA of transformer

$P_{sc}$ = Short-circuit losses at rated current in watts.

The short-circuit losses (copper losses or load losses) are usually expressed in watts and volt-ampere rating in kVA. Equation 6.12 should be suitably modified.

**Determination of Reactance Voltage $V_\infty$**

$V_{sc}$ is determined directly from the short-circuit test.

$V_R$ is determined from Eqn. (6.13)

$V_X$ is given by the equation:

$$V_{sc}^2 = V_R^2 + V_X^2 \quad ...(6.14)$$

**Example 6.2.** *A 3 phase, 6.6 kV/0.433 kV, 1000 kVA transformer was tested for open circuit (no-load test) and short-circuit test. The following data was obtained.*

***Open circuit test (No-load test):*** *Total power taken 1.77 kW Short-circuit test:*

*(a) Voltage applied to get rated current 4.75% of rated voltage.*

*(b) Power consumed during S.C. test at rated current 11.64 kW.*

*Calculate the following at (A) Full load and (B) at 3/4 load.*

*(1) Percentage impedance voltage, $\%V_{sc}$*

*(2) Percentage resistance voltage, $\%V_R$*

*(3) Percentage reactance voltage. $\%V_X$*

**Solution.** (A) From S.C. test, the % impedance voltage on full load $= 4.75 = \%V_{sc}$.

Full load % resistance voltage

$$= \frac{P_{sc} \times 100}{S} \% V_R$$

$$\% V_R = \frac{11640 \times 100}{1000 \times 1000} = 1.164 \%$$

Full load Reactance Voltage % $V_X$:

$$\% V_x = \sqrt{V_{sc}^2 - V_R^2} = \sqrt{(4.75^2 = 1.164^2)} = 4.6\%$$

Hence, for full load condition

$$\%V_{sc} = 4.75, \%V_R = 1.164, \% V_x = 4.6$$

(B) **Now, for 3/4 load,**

$\%V_R$ for 3/4 load = 3/4 × 1.164 = 0.873%

$\% V_x$ for 3/4 load = 3/4 × 4.6 = 3.45%

## 6.10. VOLTAGE REGULATION Δ V UNDER SPECIFIED LOAD CONDITION

One of the basic objectives of a power supply company is to supply the electric power to the consumers at specified voltage, within targeted limits of the voltage. *During every day and seasons of the year, the load varies. With the variation of load, the busbar voltages tend to vary.* The bus voltages are held within permissible limits by means of tap-changing transformers and also by providing compensation of reactive power. *Regulation of a transformer is very significant aspect in the voltage control of the sub-station buses.*

*Voltage Regulation of a transformer is defined as the algebraic difference between rated secondary voltage* ($V_2 \cdot r$) *and actual secondary voltage* ($V_2 \cdot a$) *for given secondary (load) current* $I_2$ *at given power factor* ($\cos \phi_2$), *with primary applied voltage of rated value and rated frequency. The change in the secondary voltage ΔV is generally expressed as a percentage of rated secondary voltage and is called the percentage regulation of the transformers.*

Writing the definition in the forms of an equation,

% Regulation = %ΔV (at specified-load current and p.f.)

$$= \frac{V_{2\,rated} - V_{2\,actual}}{V_{2\,rated}} \times 100 \qquad ...(6.15)$$

for given $I_2$ and $\cos\phi_2$, with rated $V_1$. The difference $\Delta V$ is an *algebraic* difference. The change in voltage $\Delta V$ occurs basically due to the voltage drop in the impedance of a transformer.

Since $V_{2\text{-}rated} = V_1/k$, where $k$ is the ratio of transformation $= V_1/V_2$, the voltage regulation equation can be also written as

$$\% \, \Delta V = \frac{V_1/k - V_{2\,actual}}{V_1/K} \times 100$$

$$= \frac{V_1 - k\,V_{2\,actual}}{V_1} \times 100$$

**Note: The Regulation is a numerical quantity and not a complex quantity.** It is an algebraic difference between $V_{2-rated}$ and $V_{2-actual}$. This difference is caused by $IZ$ drop in the transformer itself.

## 6.11. FULL LOAD VOLTAGE REGULATION

The voltage regulation is often specified for full load rated current at certain p.f. of secondary current. For such a condition.

With rated $V_1$ applied to primary, ...(6.16)

$$\text{Full Load \% Regulation} = \frac{V_{2-rated} - V_{2-full\ load}}{V_{2-rated}} \times 100$$

But $V_{2-rated} = V_2$ No load

Hence, Full load % regulation is

$$\text{Full Load \% Regulation} = \frac{|V_2\,N_L| - |V_{2-FL}|}{|V_2 - NL|} \times 100$$

for rated $V_1$ and $I_2$ and given$\phi_2$.

## 6.12. IMPEDANCE VOLTAGE IZ

On no-load, the secondary voltage $V_{2-actual}$ is nearly equal to the rated voltage $V_{2-rated}$; neglecting small voltage drop $I_0Z_1$. Transferring the secondary voltage to the primary side.

$$V_2^1 = kV_2 \text{ where } k = N_1/N_2$$

**On full load,** referring quantities to the primary side,

$V_{2-actual}^1 = V_{2-actual}$ referred to primary side

$V_{2-rated}^1 = V_2k = V_{1-rated} - I_1Z_{1t}$

Hence, we get the vector relation,

$V_{2-actual}^1 = V_{1-rated} - I_1\,Z_{1t}$

$V_{2-actual\ refferred\ primary}$

$I_1$ = Full load primary current

$Z_{1t}$ = Impedance of transformer seen from the primary.

Therefore, $V_{1-rated} - V_{2-actual}^1 = I_1\,Z_{1t}$

$I_1 Z_{1t}$ = Impedance voltage of transformer on rated current.

The scalar difference between $V_{1-rated}$ and $V_{2\,-\,actual}^1$ depends on the power factor of load current.

*In practice, it is convenient to express the Regulation of a transformer in terms of Resistance Voltage $V_R$, Reactance Voltage $V_x$ and power factor of secondary current $I_2$,* because these values are obtained form the tests and subsequent calculations as described in a subsequent chapter.

**IEC Definition of Voltage Regulation**

(Voltage Drop or Voltage Rise)

(*Under Specified Load Condition*).

Arithmetic difference between no-load voltage of a winding and the voltage developed at the terminals of the same winding at specified load and power factor, with the voltage applied to one of the other winding(s) being equal to

— Rated value for principle tapping
— Tapping voltage if the transformer is connected to tapping

For principle tapping, the no-load voltage of the winding would be equal to rated value of the transformer winding.

The difference is generally expressed as a percentage of no load voltage of the former winding.

For multi-winding transformer, the voltage drop or voltage rise depends on the load and power factor on the other windings as well.

## 6.14. SIGNIFICANCE OF VOLTAGE REGULATION

— With rated voltage applied to the primary winding, the terminal voltage varies with load current and load power factor.
— This variation is called voltage regulation.
— Voltage regulation occurs mainly due to the voltage drop in the impedance of the transformer, load current and load p.f.
— For lagging p.f. load the secondary voltage is reduced on load current.
— For leading p.f. load, the secondary voltage increases slightly with load current.

## 6.15. PHASOR DIAGRAM AND EQUATION FOR REGULATION

Refer Fig. 6.3. referred to the primary side.

$$I_2^1 = \text{Secondary current referred to primary}$$

$$= I_2/k$$

$$k = \frac{N_1}{N_2}$$

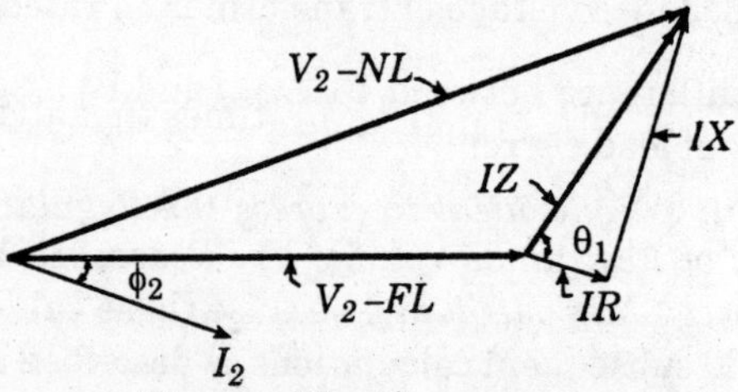


$$\Delta V = \frac{|V_{2\,.\,NL}| - |V_{2\,.\,FL}|}{V_{2\,.\,NL}} \times 100$$

$|V_{2\,.\,NL}| = V_2$ Rated

Fig. 6.3. Vector diagram explaining voltage regulation.

$R_e^1$ = Total equivalent resistance of transformer referred to primary

$X_e^1$ = Total equivalent leakage reactance of transformer referred to primary = $X_1 + X_2{}^1$.

From phasor diagram;

$$\% \text{ Regulation } = \frac{V_{2 \cdot NL} - V_{2 \cdot FL}}{V_{2 \cdot NL}} \times 100$$

$$= \frac{V_{2 \cdot NL} - V_{2 \cdot FL}}{V_{2 \cdot NL}} \times 100$$

From Fig. 6.3, neglecting small vertical component,

$V_{1 \cdot NL} - kV_{2 \cdot FL} = I_1 R_e{}^1 \cos \phi_1 + I_1 X_e{}^1 \sin \phi_1$

$$\Delta V = \frac{|V_2 \cdot NL| - |V_2 \cdot FL|}{V_2 \cdot NL} \times 100$$

$|V_2 \cdot NL| = V_2$ Rated

Hence, % Regulation is given by approximate equation referring to primary as follows:

$$\% \text{ Regulation } = \frac{I_1 R_e^1 \cos \phi_1 + I_1 X_e^1 \sin \phi_1}{V_{1 \cdot NL}} \times 100 \qquad \text{...(6.17)}$$

Alternatively, referring to secondary, approximate regulation

$$\% \text{ Regulation } = \frac{I_2 R_e^2 \cos \phi_2 + I_2 X_e^2 \sin \phi_2}{V_{2 \cdot NL}} \times 100 \qquad \text{...( 6.18)}$$

These are approximate equations neglecting vertical components in Fig. 6.3.

## 6.16. REGULATION IN TERMS OF RESISTANCE VOLTAGE $V_R$ AND REACTANCE VOLTAGE $V_X$.

In practice it is convenient to express % regulation in terms of the following:

$V_R$ = Resitance voltage

$\phi_2$ = Phase angle of $I_2$ with respect to $V_2$.

$V_R$ and $V_X$ are obtained from test results and subsequent calculations.

The equation for full load regulation is as follows:

**Full-load Voltage Regulation**

$$\% \Delta V = (V_R \cos \phi_2 \pm V_x \sin \phi_2) + \frac{(V_x \cos \phi_2 \mp V_R \sin \phi_2)^2}{200} \quad ...(6.19)$$

The *upper sign* is for lagging load p.f.

The *lower sign* for leading load p.f.

where $V_R$ = Per cent resistance voltage on full load

$V_x$ = Per cent reactance voltage on full load

$\phi_2$ = Angle of lag for full load $I_2$.

**Assumption.** % Impedance, $Z_e$ is less than 20%.

**Note.** *For lagging loads* the upper negative sign is taken.

**The Standard Formula for Full Load Percentage Regulation of a Transformer at Full Load and Lagging p.f. cos $\phi_2$.**

$$\% \Delta V = (V_R \cos\phi_2 + V_X \sin\phi_2) + \frac{(V_X \cos \phi_2 - V_R \sin \phi_2)^2}{200} \quad ...(6.20)$$

where, $V_X$ = Percentage Reactance Voltage on Full-load

$V_R$ = Percentage Resistance Voltage on Full-load

$\cos \phi_2$ = Power Factor (lagging) for Full-load

## 6.17. STANDARD EQUATION FOR REGULATION ON PARTIAL LOAD

**For loads other than full loads,** the above *formula gets modified with respect to* $V_R$ and $V_X$ *as follows.*

Let, $\frac{\text{Actual load current}}{\text{Full load current}}$ = Load factor

$V_{RP}$ at partial load $= V_{R\,-\,full\,load}$

$V_{XP}$ at partial load $= V_{x\,-\,full\,load}$.

The voltage regulation at partial load is calculated by substituting $V_{RP}$ and $V_{XP}$ in above equation.

**% $V_p$ at Partial Load:**

$$\%V_P = (V_{RP} \cos \phi_2 + V_{XP} \sin \phi_2) + \frac{(V_{XP} \cos \phi_2 - V_{RP} \sin \phi_2)}{200} \quad ...(6.21)$$

where $V_{RP}$ = % Resistance voltage at partial load

$V_{XP}$ = % Reactance voltage at partial load.

**Note.** 1. Positive ΔV indicates drop in voltage from rated voltage.
2. Negative ΔV indicates rise in voltage above rated.

**Example 6.3. *Voltage regulation*** *A 3 phase, 6.6 kV/0.433 kV, 1000 kVA distribution transformer has at full load, % impedance voltage 4.75%, Copper losses at full load 11.64 kW, Iron losses at no-load 1.77 kW. Calculate % regulation at*

*(a) Full load, unity p.f.* *(b) 3/4th load, p.f. 0.8 lag.*

**Solution.** Refer Ex.6.1.

(*a*) **At full load, unity p.f.**

$$\%V_R = \%\text{resistance voltage}$$

$$= P_{sc} \times \frac{100}{S} = 1.164\%$$

$$\%V_X = \sqrt{V_{sc}^2 - V_R^2}$$

$$= \sqrt{(4.75)^2 - (1.164)^2} = 4.6$$

$$\cos \phi_2 = 1, \phi_2 = 0, \sin \phi_2 = 0$$

For unity p.f. $\Delta\%V = V_R + \frac{VX^2}{200}$

$$= 1.164 + \frac{(4.6)^2}{200} = 1.27\% \quad \textbf{Ans.}$$

**(*b*) At ¾th Full load, 0.8 lag p.f.**

$$\% \Delta V = (V_R \cos \phi_2 + V_X \sin \phi_2) + \frac{(V_X \cos \phi_2 + V_R \sin \phi_2)^2}{200}$$

$$\cos \phi_2 = 0.8, \sin \phi_2 = 0.6$$

$$V_R = \% \text{ resistance voltage at } \frac{3}{4}\text{th load}$$

$$= 0.874\% \quad \text{...sec.Ex.6.1}$$

$$V_X = \% \text{ reactance voltage at } \frac{3}{4}\text{th load}$$

$$= 3.4\% \quad \text{...sec.Ex.6.1}$$

$$\%\Delta V = \% \text{ regulation at } \frac{3}{4}\text{th load p.f. 0.8 lag}$$

$$= (0.874 \times 0.8) - (3.45 \times 0.6)$$

$$+ \frac{[(0.45 \times 0.8) - (0.874 \times 0.6)]^2}{200}$$

$$= 2.8\%. \quad \textbf{Ans.}$$

**Example 6.4.** ***Regulation.*** *Calculate the % regulation of a transformer at p.f. 0.8 lag, Resistance voltage $V_R = 2.4\%$ and Reactance voltage $V_X = 5\%$.*

**Solution.** $\% V = (V_R \cos \phi_2 + V_X \sin \phi_2)$

$$+ \frac{(V_X \sin \phi_2 - V_R \sin \phi_2)^2}{200}$$

$$= 1.92 + 3 + 0.03 = 4.95\%.$$

**Example 6.5** *Calculate percentage regulation of a transformer at p.f. 0.7 lead, $V_R = 4\%$, $V_X = 4.5\%$.*

**Solution.** % resistance voltage = 4%

% resistance voltage = 4.5%

% regulation = % V for leading p.f. is (with change in signs)

$$= (V_R \cos \phi_2 - V_X \sin \phi_2) + \frac{(V_X \cos \phi_2 + V_R \sin \phi_2)^2}{200}$$

$\cos \phi_2 = 0.7$

$\phi_2 = \cos \phi^{-1} 0.7 = 45.57°$

$\sin \phi_2 = 0.71$

$$\% \text{ Regulation } = (4 \times 0.7) - (4.5 \times 0.71) + \frac{(4.5 \times 0.7 - 4 \times 0.71)^2}{200}$$

Second term on R.H.S. in neglected

$$= 2.8 - 3.2 = 0.4\%$$

Negative sign indicates rise in voltage on leading load.

**Example 6.6** *Calculations of performance from no-load test results.*

**Solution.** A no-load test and a short-circuit test was conducted on a 3-Phase, 50 Hz, 300 kVA, 11 kV/0.4 kV, Delta/Star transformer. The result were as follows:

**No-load test:** Applied voltage to LV = 440 V

Current = 21.1 A

Power = 1.30 kW

**Short-Circuit Tests :** Applied Voltage to HV : 630 V

Current15.7 A

Power = 3.6 kW

Winding temperature 75°C.

**Calculate the following:**

(*a*) Total loss at rated load (*b*) Impedance voltage

(*c*) Efficiency at rated load (*d*) p.u. resistance
(*e*) p.u. reactance
(*f*) Regulation on full load, p.f. 0.8 lag.

No-load loss $P_0 = 1.30$ kW

No-load current $I_0 = 21.1$ A..

**Impedance Voltage.** Voltage applied to HV winding to get rated s.c. current was 630 V. Hence impedance voltage 630 V (HV side).

$$\%V_{sc} = \text{Percentage impedance voltage}$$
$$= \frac{630}{11{,}000} \times 100 = 5.7\%$$

Per-unit impedance voltage

$$= \frac{5.7}{100} = 0.057$$

$$\%V_R = \%\text{ resistance voltage}$$
$$= \frac{P_{sc}}{S} \times 100 = \frac{3.08}{300} \times 100 = 1.02\%$$

p.u. resistance voltage

$$= \frac{\%\text{ resistance voltage}}{100} = \frac{1.02}{100} = 0.01 \text{ p.u.}$$

p.u. reactance voltage

$$= \sqrt{V_{sc}^2 - V_R^2}$$
$$= \sqrt{(0.057)^2 - (0.01)^2} = 0.057 \text{ p.u.}$$

[**Ans.** p.u. impedance voltage 0.057
p.u. resistance voltage 0.01]

**Calculations of losses and efficiency**

Iron loss $P_0 = 1.3$

Copper loss $P_c = 3.6$

Total loss $P_t = P_0 + P_c = 4.9$ kW

$$\%\, n = \frac{\text{Output}}{\text{Output + Losses}} \times 100$$
$$= \frac{\text{Input} - \text{Losses}}{\text{Input}} \times 100 = \left(1 - \frac{\text{Losses}}{\text{Input}}\right) \times 100$$
$$= \left[1 - \frac{4.9}{(300 \times 0.8) + 4.9}\right] \times 100 = 97.99\ \%$$ **Ans.**

**Regulation (%V)**

$$\%V = V_R \cos \phi_2 + V_X \sin \phi_2$$
$$= (1.02 \times 0.8) + (5.7 \times 0.6)$$
$$= (0.816 + 3.42) = 4.236\ \%$$ **Ans.**

## 6.18. FACTOR INFLUENCING THE REGULATION OF A TRANSFORMER

The full-load voltage regulation of a transformer depends upon

— Per cent resistance voltage $V_R$

— Per cent resistance voltage $V_X$

Power factor of full load current.

Figure 6.4 illustrates the variation in $V_2$ at full load with changes in load power factor for a typical value of per ent $V_R$ and per cent $V_X \cdot I_2$ and $V_2$ no-load are kept constant

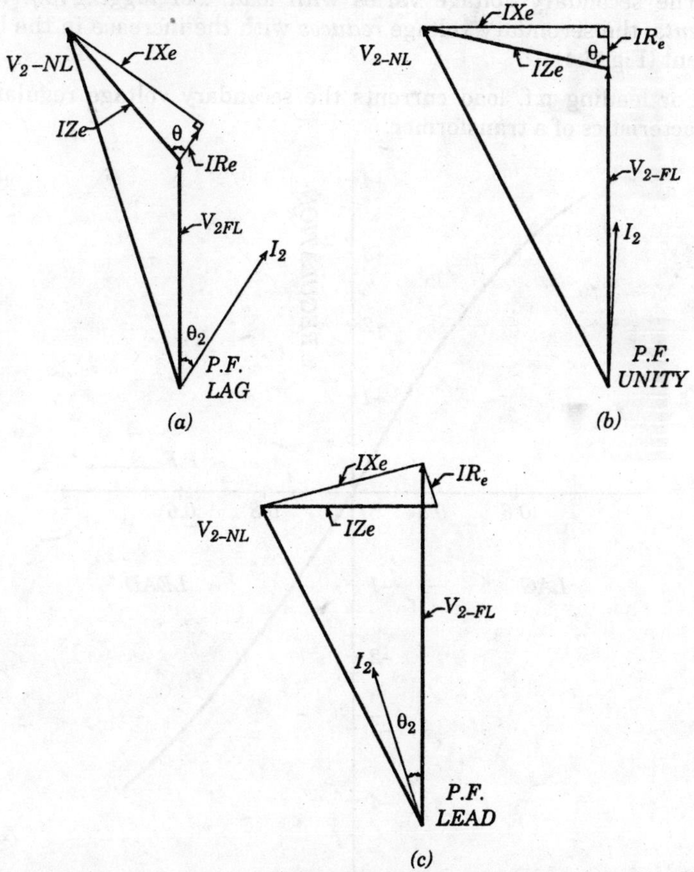


Fig. 6.4a. Effect of load power factor on secondary full load voltage $V_2 - FL$.

The per cent Regulation of a transformer varies with load current. As the per cent resistance voltage and per cent reactance voltage is proportional to load current, regulation is also proportional to the load current.

For leading p.f. loads, the regulation is negative (rise in voltage)

For lagging p.f. loads, the regulation is positive (fall in voltage)

Maximum regulation occurs when load p.f. angle $\phi_2$ is equal to the angle $\theta$ given by $\cos^{-1} X/Z$ of the transformer.

## 6.19. SECONDARY VOLTAGE REGULATION CHARACTERISTICS OF A TRANSFORMER

The output voltage regulation characteristic of a transformer is a curve of secondary voltage *versus* secondary load for given power factor of load; for constant rated primary voltage ($V_1$).

The secondary voltage varies with load. For *lagging p.f. load currents*, the secondary voltage *reduces* with the increase in the load current (Fig. 6.4)

For leading p.f. load currents the secondary voltage regulation characteristics of a transformer.

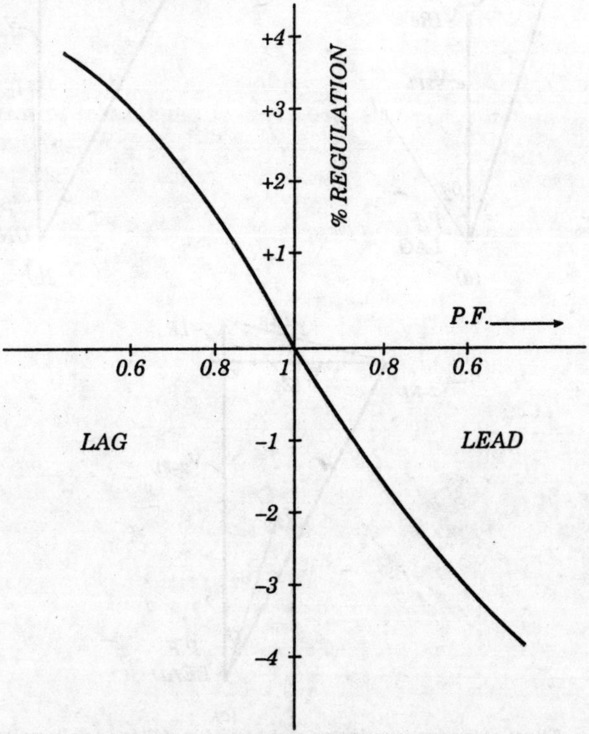


Fig. 6.5. Variation in regulation with changes in load p.f.

## Summary

A transformer has inherent impedance ($Z_e$). The impedance has two components called resistance $R$ and leakage reactance $X$. Leakage reactance predominates.

Leakage reactance is caused by leakage flux which does not flow through the core and does not link with both primary and secondary.

For measurement and calculation purposes the impedance is specified in terms of Impedance voltage. Impedance voltage is further divided into two components.

— Resistance Voltage $V_R$

— Reactance Voltage $V_X$

$$V_Z^2 = V_R^2 + V_x^2$$

**Impedance Voltage** ($V_z$) is determined by conduction short-circuit voltage and is called *short-circuit voltage* ($V_{sc}$)

$$V_Z = V_{sc}$$

**Impedance Voltage** is the value of voltage to be applied to the primary terminals to drive rated current through those terminals with other winding short-circuited. It is expressed as a percentage of rated voltage. Higher impedance voltage signifies higher impedance, lower short-circuit current, higher regulation, lower efficiency. Values of transformer impedance is in the range of 4.5% to 15%. Impedance voltage is stated in the transformer specifications.

**Impedance Voltage** $V_{sc}$ is obtained from short-circuit test. Resistance voltage $\%V_R$ is given by $\%V_R = P_{sc} / s \times 100$. Reactance voltage $\%V_X$ is calculated from the equation

$$V_X^2 = V_{sc}^2 - V_{R_2}$$

**Voltage Regulation** (Voltage Rise/Fall)

When the secondary is loaded, the secondary voltage changes even though primary supply voltage is held constant at rated value.

For Full load Regulation:

$$\% \text{ Regulation} = \frac{V_{2 \cdot NL} - V_{2 \cdot FL}}{V_{2 \cdot NL}} \times 100$$

For Partial Load Regulation

$$\% \text{ Regulation} = \frac{V_{2 \cdot NL} - V_{2 \cdot PL}}{V_{2 \cdot NL}} \times 100$$

$V_{2 \cdot PL}$ = Voltage at Part Load

$V_{2 \cdot NL}$ = Voltage at No-Load

$V_{2 \cdot FL}$ = Voltage at Full load

Voltage regulation depends upon

— Impedance voltage. Higher impedance voltage gives higher voltage regulation.

— Magnitude of load current.

— Power factor of load current. Maximum regulation occurs when load p.f. angle $\theta_2$ angle $\theta$ of $Z_e$ ( Fig. 6.3)

Voltage regulation is specified for principle tapping, rated voltage, rated current.

For other tapping, corresponding tapping voltage is considered.

Transformer impedance limits the through short-circuit current.

Regulation of a transformer is significant for voltage control. Short-circuit current ($I_{sc}$) beyond a transformer is given by

$$I_{sc} = I_1 \frac{V_1}{V_{sc}} \times 100$$

$$= \frac{I_1}{\% \, V_{sc}} \times 100$$

where, $V_{sc}$ = Impedance voltage

$V_1$ = Rated voltage

$I_1$ = Rated current.

# 7

# Core Losses, Copper Losses, Efficiency and All Day Efficiency

The transformer has no moving parts, the losses include:

**Core Loss** resulting from the alternating core magnetization.

**Dielectric Loss** in insulating materials, particularly in the oil and solid insulation of high-voltage units.

$I^2R$ **Loss** in the windings.

**Load (Stray) Loss.** Largely the result of leakage magnetic fields inducing eddy currents in the tank walls and conductor.

The losses are evaluated by conducting no-load test and sustained short-circuit test. No load losses depends on voltage. Load losses increase with the load. Efficiency of transformers is high (95 to 99%).

The fundamentals of losses, loss measurement, efficiency calculation etc., have been covered in this chapter.

## 7.1. INTRODUCTION

During the normal operation of the transformer, the values of currents,voltage, power factors,temperatures, magnetic flux, efficiency, etc., vary with the load. The term 'Performance' is associated with values of these quantities under specified operating conditions. The performance of transformer is usually analysed under following *service conditions*:

— *No-load condition* under which the secondary winding does not feed any load, and the primary winding is supplied at rated voltage of rated frequency.

— *Full-load condition* under which the secondary winding supplies rated active power at rated secondary current at rated voltage.

— *Short-circuit condition* under which one of winding terminals are short-circuited and *reduced voltage* is applied to the other winding such that rated current flows through it . *Short-circuit condition is a test condition.*

The values of constants (parameters) of the transformers are determined by conducting *No-load Test* and sustained *short-circuit Test*. The performance at any load condition can be predicted from the calculations based on these parameters. The transformer can be represented by its *Equivalent Circuit.* The behaviour of the transformer is illustrated by means of the *phasor diagrams* (Vector Diagrams).

Under the normal operating conditions, the load on the transformer (secondary current and its power factor) varies. Therefore, the *voltage regulation losses and efficiency* of the transformer also vary during normal operation with the variation of load.

The *voltage regulation* is significant because the secondary voltage should be maintained within specified limits under every load condition.

The *efficiency* and losses are significant as is desirable to operate the transformer economically at its maximum efficiency and, hence, at lowest operating costs.

The *loading* of the transformer is related with kVA load and power factor of the load. It determies copper losses and efficiency, and the temperature rise of windings and oil. The analysis of the transformer is useful in formulating the guidelines for *economical and safe loading* of the transformers and steps to be taken to maintain the secodary voltage within specified limits.

## 7.2. DEFINITIONS

**1. No-load Current.** The current flowing through a line terminal of a winding when *rated* voltage is applied at *rated* frequency, the other winding ($S$) being left open-circuited (on no-load).

**2. No-load Loss.** The active power (kW) absorbed when rated voltage at rated frequency is applied to the terminals of one winding, with the other windings(s) being open circuited.

**3. Load Loss.** (for two-winding transformer). The active power absorbed by the transformer at rated frequency when rated current is flowing through the line terminal(s) of one of the windings, the terminals of the other winding being short-circuited. (The value is related with the reference temperatures).

**4. Total Losses.** It is the sum of the non-load and load loss.

**Note.** From the above definitions, the Load Loss is the same as short-circuit loss. In practice, the following terms are commonly used.

No-load Loss = Open-circuit Loss
= Core Loss
= Iron Loss.

Load Loss = Short-circuit Loss
= Copper Loss

*No-load Loss is specified at rated voltage. Load Loss is specifeid for rated current.* For voltage/current other than rated values, *appropriate calculations* should be made to arrive at the respective losses.

**5. Stray Losses.** Losses due to leakage (stray) magnetic fields. These include eddy current losses in surrounding metals of tanks, structures, clamps, other metallic parts other than in magnetic and conducting circuits.

**6. Dieletric Loss.** Losses in insulating materials (oil solid insulation) at high AC voltage.

**7.** $\text{Efficiency} = \dfrac{\text{Output}}{\text{Input}} \times 100 = \dfrac{\text{Output}}{\text{Output} + \text{losses}} \times 100$

**8. Losses and no-load current**

**Note.** Unless otherwise specified, the values are related to the principal tapping; consequently, the follwing definitions are related to this tapping.

(a) *No-load loss*. The active power absorbed when rated voltage at rated frequency is applied to the terminals of one of the windings, the other windings (s) being open-circuited.

(b) *No-load current*. The current flowing through a line terminal of a winding when rated voltage is applied at rated frequency, the other windings (s) being open-circuited.

**Notes:** 1. The no-load current of a winiding is often expressed as a percentage of the rated current of the same winding. For multi-winding transformers, this percentage is referred to the winding with the highest winding rated power.

2. For polyphase transformers, the no-load currents through the different line terminals may be unequal. If, in this case, the values of the different no-load currents are not given separately, the no-load current is assumed to be the arithmeic mean value of these currents.

**9. Load loss**

(*a*) *Of two winding transformers.* The active power absorbed at rated frequency when rated current is flowing through the line terminal(s) of one of the windings, the terminals of the other winding short-ciruited. The value is related to the reference temperature shown in Table 7.1.

(*b*) *Of multi-winding transformers, rated to a certain pair of windings*. The active power absorbed at rated frequency when a current flows through the line terminals(s) of one of the windings of the pair, corresponding to the smaller of the rated power values of both windings of that pair, the terminals winding of the same pair being short-circuited and the remaining windings(s) being open-circuited. The various values for the different pairs of windings are related to the reference temperature shown in Table 7.1.

**Total losses.** The sum of no-load loss and load loss.

**Notes : 1.** For multi-winding transformers, the total losses refer to a specified loading combination. **2.** The losses in the auxiliary plants are not included in the total losses; they should be stated separately.

**Table 7.1.Reference Temperatures for Measurement of Losses and Parameters of Transformeres**

| *Temperature class of insulation* * | *Reference temperature* |
|---|---|
| A<br>E<br>B | 75°C * * |
| Other temperature classes of insulation | 115°C |

## 7.3. NO-LOAD PERFORMANCE AND CALCULATIONS

A transformer is on *no-load* or *open-circuit* when a.c. supply is given to its primary winding and the secodary winding is open. Under no-load condition, the primary winding carries no-load current (excitation current), the core carries alternating magnetic flux, emf's are induced in each winding but transformer does not supply any load current from the secondary.

Some of the operating characteristics, constants and operational data of a transformer are obtained from the *no-load test* (also called open-circuit test). No-load test is a *routine test* and is, therefore, conducted on each transformer . *The important characteristics determined from the no-load test include*:

1. No-load Current, $I_0$
2. No-load Loss, $P_0$ (core loss)
3. Turns-ratio (Transformation Ratio), $k$
4. Magnetisation characteristc of the transformer (Applied voltage versus Exciting current).

The relevant standards of a power transformer recommend the test procedures, interpretation and tolerances for the above quantities. The *minimum* values of no-load current and losses are usually *not* specified in the standards, however, they are guaranteed by the manufacturer at the tendering stage. No-load values should be *with in required* values and not too much below or above the required values. *No-load values as per requirements confirms proper design and manufacture of magnetic circuit.* Higher no-load current indicates insufficient magnetic material or defects in the magnetic or electric circuit. Lower no-load current indicates excess magnetic material and higher material cost of the transformer.

*In accordance with IEC Publication 85, Recommendations for the Classification of Materials for the Insulation of Electrical Machinery and Ap paratus in Relation to their Thermal Stability in Service.

**80°C when the oil circultion is forced directed.

**Note:** No load test is conducted at site and performance is comparec with that of factory test.

No load test is conducted on failed transformer to determine whether the magnetic circuit has developed some defects.

**Table 7.2 Classification of Losses**

| *Category* | *Component losses* | *Tests for determination* |
|---|---|---|
| **1. No load Loss** (Iron loss, core loss) | —$I_0^2 R$ due to no load current (usually negligible) | No load test |
| | —Dielectric loss (usually negligible except for EHV, UHV testing transformers | |
| | —Hysteresis loss in core | |
| | —Eddy current loss in core, conductors. | |
| | —Stray losses in tank, clamping plates. | |
| **2. Load Losses** (Call copper loss, Short circuit loss). | —$I^2R$ losses due to load current | Short-circuit test |
| | —$I^2R$ losses due to current which supply the losses | |
| | —Eddy current losses in conductors due to leakage flux | |
| **3. Loss in auxiliaries** | —Cooling fans | Loss measurement |
| | —Cooling pumps | |
| | —Auxiliary heaters | |
| | —Losses in tapchanger operation etc. | |

## 7.4. NO-LOAD CURRENT $I_0$

**The no-load current $I_0$ is of lower magnitude** in comparison with the rated primary current, 2 to 3.5% of rated current in low capacity transformers and 0.5 to 1.5% in high capacity transformers.

If rated voltage $V_1$ is applied to the primary winding while the secodary windings is open-circuited, the transformer is under no-load conditon. The *no-load current* $I_0$ flowing through the windings has a magnetizing component $I_{0m}$ and *an active component* $I_{0a}$. The vector sum fo $I_{0a}$ and $I_{0a}$ is equal to $I_0$. These components are in quadrature with each other.

No-load current = Active Component + Magnetizing Component

$$\bar{I}_0 = \bar{I}_{0a} + \bar{I}_{0m}$$

$$|I_0| = \sqrt{I_{0a}^2 + I_{0m}^2}$$

The reactive component $I_{0m}$ produces main flux $\phi$ in the core and a very weak leakge flux $\phi_{11}$ around primary.

The magnetic flux which leaks out from the core is called the leakage flux. The *magnetizing component* predominates and is about 90% of the total no-load current. Therefore, no-load current is mainly utiltised for settig up magnetic flux in the core is exciting the core. Hence, *no-load current is* also called *exctiting current* or *magntizing current.*

The active component $I_{0a}$ produces $I_0^2R$ losses and voltage drop in resistance. $I_{0a}$ is only about 10% of total $I_0$ the $I_{0a}^2$ $R$ loss is not considered separately and is usually merged with the *core loss*.

## 7.5. NO-LOAD LOSS (CORE LOSS)

Under no-load condition, the secondary winding does not give any kW (real power) output. The total power input to primary (kW) is totally consumed in the transformer itself, hence it is called *No-Load Loss.*

No-load $I_0^2 R$ losses (copper losses) are negligible and are not considered separately.

*No-load losses occur mainly in the form of Hysteresis Loss and Eddy Current Loss in the core. Dielectric losses are usually neglected. No load losses are also called Core Losses or Iron Losses.*

The no load losses result in heating of core. The losses get converted into heat. No-load loss $P_0$ is the sum of hysteresis loss $P_0$ and Eddy Current Loss $P_{0e}$.

No Load Loss = Core Loss

= Hysteresis loss + Eddy current loss

$$P_0 = P_{0n} + P_{0e}$$

Normally the No-load loss is measured together by conducting no-load test.

## 7.6. HYSTERESIS LOSS ($P_{0h}$)

The Hysteresis Loss occurs in the magnetic material of the core due to cyclic magnetization of the core. During every cycle of alternating magnetic flux, certain energy is lost in the magnetic material due to alternate magnetisation in forward and reverse direction. This energy per cycle is proportional to the area of the hysteresis loop (*B-H* curve taken through a cycle of magnetization). The hysteresis loss for a given material is proportional to the frequency and *n*th power of maximum flux density $B_m$, where *n* varies from 1.5 to 2.5.

$$P_{0h} = K_h f B_{\max}{}^n$$

where, $P_{0h}$ = hysteresis loss, watts/kg

$K_h$ = constant of material

$f$ = frequency

$B_m$ = Maximum flux density, tesla

$n$ = Depends on material, is in the range 1.5 to 2.5, say $n = 2$

**Note.** $P_{0h} \propto f \propto P_{oh} \propto B_m^2$.

Higher frequency —Higher core loss.

Higher flux density —Higher core loss.

The flux density $B_m$ in the core is related with volts/turn. Hence higher applied voltage $V_1$ gives higher core loss.

### 7.6.1 MAGNETISATION CHARACTERISTIC AND HYSTERESIS LOOP

The hysteresis loss occurs in the core due to alternating magnetic flux. Refer Fig. 7.1. The excitation current $I_0$ is gradually increased by increasig the applied voltage $V_1$. The magnetic flux density $B$ is plotted against magnetising force $H$. The Magnetization characteristic is obtained.

The cycle of magnetisation is then completed. The magnetisation ($B$) lags behind, the magnetisation force ($H$). This phenomena is called Hysteresis. This occurs due to the time and energy required for the elementary magnetic particles to align themselves in the direction of alternating applied field. The process of taking the magnetic material through each cycle of magnetisation requires certain energy for cycle. This loss is called hystersis loss. Hysteresis loss appears as heat in the core. The hysteresis loss depends on properties of material,volume or weight of the core, frequency, and to the $n$th power of the flux density $B$ in the core, and the wave-shape.

$$P_{0h} = K_h f B_{max}^n$$

The flux density in the core is related with volts/turn and volts/Hz (Refer Sec.)

E.M.F. induced in the winding is given by

$$= 4_{kf} f A B_m N$$

where, $E$ = r.m.s. value of induced voltage in the winding (primary or secondary), volts

$K_f$ form factor of e.m.f. wave 1.1 for sinusoidal wave

1 for flat topped wave.

$A$ = Cross sectional area of core $cm^2$

$f$ = frequency, Hz

$N$ = Number of turns (primary of secondary whichever considered).

If e.m.f. wave is flat topped, factor $K_f$ is reduced. Consequently for the same value of $E$, the flux density $B_m$ increases and hysteresis loss increases in the proportion of $B_n$.

Hysteresis loss is an inherent property of the material of laminations and construction of core. If the material properties deteriorate with time/cyclic temperature stresses, the effect is called *ageing of material*. By ageing of laimintions of core,the hysteresis loss increases substantially resulting in excessive no load currents, no load losses, heating of core and ultimately the failure of core and the transformer winding.

In practice the hysteresis loss and eddy current losses are not separated. They are measured together and are called core loss.

**Table 7.3. Methods to Reduce Hysteresis Loss in Core**

| | |
|---|---|
| Material | —Use of low loss CRGO material for laminations |
| Cross-section of core | —Use adequate cross-section of core |
| Lower flux densities | —Use of lower volts/turn and volts/hertz for design |
| Purity of waveform | —Eliminate harmonics by using filters |
| | —Avoid saturation of core |
| | —Proper path for zero sequence current. |

## 7.7. EDDY CURRENT LOSS $P_{0e}$

The eddy current loss ($P_{0e}$)occurs in the conducting materials in the alternating magnetic field. The currents is induced in the conducting materials (core, tank, shields, conductors) due to alternating magnetic field are called *eddy currents*. They are given by

$$P_{oe} = K_e\, t^2 \cdot B_m^2 \frac{f^2}{\rho}, \text{ W/kg.}$$

where, $K_e$ = constant of material of core

$B_m$ = peak flux density in material of core

$f$ = frequency of flux, Hz

$\rho$ = electrical resistivity of material of core

$t$ = thickness of laminations.

Eddy currents are reduced by

— Using stranded, transposed conductors.

— Using thin laminations for the core. Thickness $t$ is reduced

— Providing insulating layer on each side of a lamination

— Increasing resistivty of the material by alloying with silicon.

— Reducing flux density ($B_m$). Reduction in leakage flux.

Eddy current losses occur in

1. Core laminations
2. Conductors
3. Tank and clamping plates.

The transformer core is made of metal parts and carries alternating magnetic flux. This flux linking with the core produces *eddy currents* in the core which are in a plane perpendicular to the direction of the flux. The *eddy currents* are minmised by using *thinner* sheets of higher, electrical resistivity. *If the core were made solid, eddy currents would be too high, core would heat up.*

In practice, the transformer cores are made-up of thin lamination (0.2 to 0.35 mm thick) of electrical sheet steel having higher electrical resistivity. Each lamination is provided with oxide layers or varnish layer on both the sides. Sharp corners are removed. Proper heat treatment is given for stress-relieving.

*In practice,* hystersis-loss and eddy-current loss are not considered separately and are taken together as No-load Loss or Core loss. The core loss is expressed in Watts per kg for given maximum flux density and conditions of frequency, lamination thickness, etc. Core loss depends upon type of core material and B in the range of a few fractions of watts to several watts per kg.

*No-load loss is only about 0.3 to 0.5% of the rated capacity of the transformer. However, it occurs continuously, therefore, it should be within specified limits.*

*For the given applied voltage, the flux density in the core is constant and the core losses are constant. They dot not vary with the load. Hence they are called fixed losses.* (Copper losses are variable losses).

The core loss is measured by conducting the no-load test.

### 7.7.1. Eddy Current Loss in Conductors

Eddy currents are produced in the conductors of winding and leads due to the flux linkage with them. Due to eddy current loss, the temperature rise of conductor increases. Eddy current loss in a coil are given by the expression.

$$P_{ae} \propto \frac{K_{ec}\, b^4\, n^2\, f^2\, \beta}{\rho^2}$$

where, $P_{oe}$ = Eddy currents loss in a coil

$b$ = Radial dimension of conductor in direction perpendicular to axis

$n$ = Number of conductors in radial direction

$f$ = Frequency

$\beta$ = A factor which takes into account the cross-section of conductor and total cross-sectional area of coil.

$\rho$ = Resistivity of conductor material.

Eddy current loss in conductors is as important portion of no load loss. It is a practice to sub-divide the conductors in to several stands/sub-sections in parallel. The multiple wire transposed conductors are used for windings. The eddy current loss of reduces due to small cross-section of conductors.

Continuously transposed stranded conductor is used for windings.

### 7.7.2. Eddy Current Loss due to Leakage Flux

Leakage fluxes produce eddy current losses in tank wall, core plates, clamps and other metallic parts in the vicinity of winding and core. They are called stray losses.

Table 7.4 gives the summary of means for reducing eddy losses and stray losses.

**Table 7.4. Methods of Reducing Eddy Current Losses and Stray Losses**

| *Part* | *Eddy Loss affected by* | *Means of Reduction in Eddy Loss* |
|---|---|---|
| Lamination in the core | —Thickness | —0.33 mm, 0.25 mm, 0.15 mm |
| | —Resistivity | —Surface insulation |
| | | —Silicon added for higher resistivity |
| Conductors | —Cross-sectional area | —Use of lower flux densities. |
| | | —Sub-divided into several strand/parts insulated from each other |
| | | —Transposed conductors to minimise circulating currents |
| Tank, Clamps and other metallic parts | —Leakage flux | —Reduction in leakage flux |
| | —Permiability of material. | —Non-magnetic material in closed paths surrounding conductor |
| | | —Cut in closed path |
| | | —Addition shields near tank walls. |

### 7.7.3. Means of Reducing Eddy Losses and Stray Losses

These are listed in Table 7.4

Stray losses and eddy losses must be minimised by appropriate design measures. These include:

**(1) Magnetic Circuit:**
- Use of laminations with surface insulation
- Superior silicon iron cold rolled sheet steel, Silicon content increases resistivity but brittleness increases so we have to optimize
- Lamination reduce eddy currents
- Proper mitred joints at corners reduce leakage flux
- Proper assembly of core. Avoid clamping bolts
- Insulation of core bolts
- Use of lower flux densities reduces leakage flux
- Use of non magnetic material for clamping plates

**(2) Conductors,Coils**
- Stranded,Conductors or sub-divided conductors to reduce individual cross sectional area
- Transposed conductors to reduce circulating currents.

**(3) Bushing flanges and closed paths**

To reduce circulating currents
- Use of non-magnetic material in closed path surrounding bushing. Earth metal parts and both ends.
- Use of a slit in the plate supporting the bushing.

**(4) Tank and Clamping parts**
- Reduction in leakage flux by proper design of windings
- Use of shields between tank and the winding to minimise leakage flux entering into tank.

## 7.8. NO-LOAD TEST

The 'No-load current measurement and No-load loss measurement' are included in the Routine Test, Type Test of power transformer. One of the winding is supplied with rated voltage of rated frequency. The other windings are left open circuited. The applied voltage, current taken from supply, power taken from supply are measured under steady condition.

From the no-load test at rated voltage the following data is obtained:
- Total No-load loss : $P_0$
- No-load current : $I_0$
- Magnetising characteristic
- Transformer ratio.

Figure 7.1. shows the circuit diagram for conducting no-load test, on a single phase two winding transformer.

Figure 7.1. shows the phaser diagram for no-load condition.

Let $P_0$ = No load loss at applied rated voltage $V_1$ at rated frequency $f$, watts

$V_1$ = Applied voltage, Volts

$I_0$ = No load current,Amp.

The no-load current $I_0$ is for setting up magnetic flux $\phi$ in the core, to supply for hysteresis loss, eddy current loss and stray losses during no-load.

$I_0$ is divided into two components.

Active Component; $I_{0a}$

It is calculated as follows:

$$I_{0a} = \text{Active Component} = \frac{\text{No–load Loss}}{\text{Applied voltage}} = \frac{P_0}{V_1}$$

**Magnetizing Component : $I_{0m}$**

It is calculated as follows:

$$I_{0m} = \sqrt{I_0^2 - I_{0a}^2}$$

## 7.9. LOAD LOSSES, SHORT-CIRCUIT LOSSES AND COPPER LOSSES

Load losses occur when the transformer is loaded. It means load impedance is connected to the secodary and load current $I_L$ flows through the transformer.

Load = kVA supplied by Transformer

Increase in secondary current and primary current is called increase in load.

**Transformer on Load.** The transformer is considered to be operating under loaded condition when the primary winding is supplied with voltage $V_1$ and the secondary winding supplies active power to the connected load. The primary winding is electromagnetically linked with the secodary winding. The change in the secondary current causes corresponding change in the primary current beause the *magnetomotive force* (m.m.f.) always remains in equilibrium.

As the applied voltage ($V_1$) across the primary winding remains practically constant,the counter e.m.f. ($E_1$) also remains almost unchanged. Therefore, the exciting current ($I_0$) and secodary e.m.f. ($E_2$)

also remain constant.Consequently *for the given applied voltage* ($V_1$) *which does not depend on load, the magnitudes of no-load current* ($I_0$), flux($\phi$) *primary counter e.m.f.* ($E_1$), *secondary induced e.m.f.* ($E_2$) *of a loaded transformer remain at their respective values under no-load condition.*

In other words, when the transformer is loaded,the secondary current $I_2$ flows, producing mmf $I_2N_2$. This is countered by increase in primary mmf $I_1N_1$ such that

$$I_1 N_1 \approx I_2 N_2 \text{ or } I_1 = I_2(N_2/N_1)$$

The mmfs $I_2 N_2$ and $I_1 N_1$ are in opposite direction. The flux in the core $\phi$ remains constant corresponding to the non-load flux. This is true only for power transformers.

The total primary current under loaded condition is the vector sum of the no-load current $I_0$ and the current $I_2$.

where $I_2^1$ is secondary current as seen from the primary side

$$I_1 = \overline{I}_0 + \overline{I}_2 \,(N_1/N_1)$$
$$\overline{I}_1 = \overline{I}_0 + \overline{I}_2$$

*Total Losses* ($P_t$) *uder loaded condition are equal to the sum of no-load losses* ($P_0$) *and load-losses* ($P_L$).

Under load condition, the load losses ($I^2R$ loss, copper loss) in the primary the secodary winding result in heating of the transformer. These losses are *variable losses*, as thery vary with the load

$$P_{total} = P_0 + P_L.$$

### 7.9.1. Components of Load Losses

Load losses are also called copper losses and short-circuit losses because:

— Load losses occur mostly in copper winding in form of $I^2R$ loss
— Load losses are measured by conducting short-circuit test, components of load losses are
— $I^2R$ loss due to no-load current and load current is not taken into account as $I_0^2 R$ is small compared with $I_L^2 R$.
— $I^2R$ losses consumed by current supplying the losses.
— Stray losses, eddy current losses under loaded condition.

### 7.9.2. Load Losses

Load losses increase in the proportion of $I^2R$. As $R$ depends on temperature, the $I^2R$ losses depend on temperature (Ref. Table 7.1.).

By appropriate design of winding, using parallel paths, reducing the length of winding etc. The resistance of winding is minimised, and load losses are minimised.

If crosssection of core is increased,the Core losses are reduced. But length of turns of winding increases. Hence at design stage, the choice is made between core loss and copper loss.

Since copper loss is proportional to square of load current, the transformer with higher copper loss will have limited margin for over-loading.

Transformer with higher copper loss has higher impedance voltage (*IZ*).

A transformer with higher ratio of copper loss to core loss will have higher ratio of material for winding to core

$$\frac{\text{Copper loss}}{\text{No–load loss}} = \frac{\text{Weight of copper}}{\text{Weight of core}}$$

Higher copper loss gives higher hot-spot temperature, higher oil temperature etc.

## 7.10. SHORT-CIRCUIT TEST (STEADY SUSTAINED)

The sustained steady state short circuit test is different from sudden short-circuit withstand test. In steady short circuit test, rms values of steady short-circuit currents are measured. In sudden short-circuit withstand tests, the oscillograms of transient short circuit currents are recorded for a few tens of cycles after application of short-circuit.

Figure 7.1. shows a circuit diagram and Fig. 7.1 gives the phasor diagram for steady short-circuit test condition.

Steady short-circuit test is performed by applying reduced power frequency voltage to one winding with other winding (s) short-circuited. The following data is recorded:

(1) Power consumed by transformer at rated current under short-circuited condition. This gives copper loss or load loss ($P_L$).

(2) Voltage required to drive rated current under short-circuit condition. This gives Impedance voltage (*IZ*).

Let $P_L$ = Power consumed during short-circuit condition at rated current $I_1$.

$V_{sc}$ = Voltage applied to primary (1) get rated current $I_1$.

Equivalent resistance ($R_e^1$) referred from primary side (1) is given by

$$R_e{}^1 = \frac{PL}{I_1{}^2}$$

$$= \frac{\text{Power}}{\text{Square of current}}$$

$$Z_e{}^1 = \frac{V_{sc}}{I_1} = \frac{\text{Voltage}}{\text{Current}}$$

$$X_e^1 = \sqrt{(Z_e{}^1)^2 - (R_e{}^1)^2}$$

From short current test data

$$X_e{}^1 = \sqrt{\left(\frac{V_{sc}}{I_1}\right)^2 - \left(\frac{P_L}{I_1{}^2}\right)^2}$$

## 7.11. EFFICIENCY OF A TRANSFORMER (%η)

The efficiency of a transformer is defined as the ratio of Output to Input (as a percentage) for given load and power factor.

$$\%\ \eta = \frac{\text{Output}}{\text{Input}} \times 100$$

*i.e.,* $$\%\ \eta = P_2/P_1 \times 100 \qquad \text{...(3.4)}$$

where $P_2$ = power output from secondary, kW

$P_1$ = power input to primary, kW.

The efficiency can also be expressed as

$$\%\ \eta = \frac{\text{Output}}{\text{Input}} \times 100$$

$$= \frac{\text{Output}}{\text{Output + Loss}} \times 100$$

*i.e.,* $$\%\ \eta = \frac{P_2}{P_2 + P_L} \times 100$$

$$= \frac{P_2}{P_2 + P_0 + P_{cu}} \times 100$$

where, $P_2$ = Output, kW

$P_0$ = No load loss

$P_{cu}$ = Load loss

$P_1$ = Input, kW

$$\%\ \text{Efficiency} = \left(\frac{\text{Output Watts}}{\text{Output Watts + Losses}}\right) \times 100$$

$$\%\ \text{Efficiency} = \left(\frac{\text{Input Watts} - \text{Losses}}{\text{Input Watts}}\right) \times 100$$

**Calculation of Full Load Efficiency.** From *No-load Test*, no-load loss $P_0$ is measured at no-load, rated voltage and rated frequency.

From *Short-Circuit Test* at rated current (and reduced voltage and rated frequency) full load loss (copper loss) $P_L$ is measured.

**Total loss** $= P_0 + P_L$

Full Load Effieciency $\eta$ %

$$= \frac{P_2}{P_2 + (P_0 + P_L)} \times 100$$

where, $P_2 =$ Power delivered by transformer at full load at given p.f.

When short-circuit test is conducted at a particular load at reduced applied voltage, the short-circuit losses are almost equal to load losses (as iron losses at reduced voltage are negligible).

Hence $P_L = P_{sc}$

where, $P_L =$ Load losses, kW

$P_{sc} =$ Short-circuit losses, kW

Hence $$\eta \% = \frac{P_2}{P_2 + (P_0 + P_{sc})} \times 100$$

$$\eta \% = \frac{P_2}{P_2 + (\text{No–load loss} + \text{Short circuit loss})} \times 100$$

$\eta$ % is calculated for given load ($P_2$) at given power factor of secondary current $\phi_2$.

Transformers have high efficiency in the range of 98 to 99. The efficiency of large transformers is higher. The high efficiency is due to absence of rotating parts and perfection in the design of the magnetic and electrical circuit. Also there is no air gap.

## 7.12. VARIATION EFFICIENCY OF A TRANSFORMER

The load on a transformer varies over a wide range during the day and the seasons of the year. Let the rated real power of the transformer be $P_2$ (kW) at a power factor $\cos \phi_2$. Then, actual real power output at a load factor $\alpha$ is given by

$$P_2 = \alpha S \cos \phi_2$$

where, $\alpha =$ Load factor

$$= \frac{\text{Acutal kVA}}{\text{Rated kVA}} = \frac{S_a}{S}$$

$\cos \phi_2 =$ Power factor

$S =$ Rated kVA

$S_a =$ actual kVA.

The *no-load losses* $P_0$ are proportional to the square of flux density $B$ and, therefore, to emf $E_1$.

Hence $P_0 \propto E_1 \propto V_1$

$P_0$ = Constant for given $V_1$

$\alpha$ = sign of proportionality.

*The load losses $P_L$ are proportional to the square of current, i.e.,*

$$P_L \propto \alpha^2 P_{sc\,.\,rated}$$

where, $P_{sc\,.\,rated}$ = short circuit losses at rated current

$P_L$ = load losses at load factor $\alpha$

Therefore, we get Efficiency

$$\%\,\eta = \left(\frac{P}{P_2 + \text{Losses}}\right) \times 100$$

$P_2$ = Power delivered by secondary

$$= \left(\frac{P_1 - \text{Losses}}{P_1}\right) \times 100$$

$$= \left(1 - \frac{\text{Losses}}{P_1}\right) \times 100$$

$$\%\eta = \left(1 - \frac{P_0 + \alpha^2 P_{sc}}{S \cos \phi_2 + P_0 + \alpha^2 P_{sc}}\right) \times 100$$

This equation gives efficiency in terms of no-load loss, load factor, short-circuit loss, rated kVA, power factor $\cos\phi_2$

$$\%\,\eta = \left(\frac{P_a + \alpha^2 P_{sc}}{S \cos \phi_2 + P_0 + \alpha^2 P_{sc}}\right) \times 100$$

where, $P_0$ = no-load loss

$\alpha$ = load factor = output/rated output

$P_{sc}$ = Rated short-circuit loss

$S$ = kVA rating

It is observed that the efficiency varies with $S \cos \phi_2$.

## 7.13. CONDITONS FOR HIGHEST EFFICIENCY

The condition of maximum efficiency can be determined by considering load factor $\alpha$ as an independent variable and differentiating $\eta$ with respect to $\alpha$. From the Maxima Theorem in differential calculus, we know, maximum where $d\eta/d\alpha$ is zero. Let us derive value of $d\eta/dx$ by differentnaiting.

$$\% \eta = \left(1 - \frac{P_0 + \alpha^2 Psc}{S \cos \phi_2 + P_0 + \alpha^2 Psc}\right) \times 100$$

where, $\eta$ = efficiency of the transformer at load factor $\alpha$ and p.f. $\cos \phi^2$

$\alpha$ = load factor (independent variable)

$P_{sc}$ = Short-circuited loss at full load

S = Rated kVA

$\cos \phi_2$ = Power factor at load

Output = $S \cos \phi_2$

$$\% \eta = \frac{\text{Output}}{\text{Output} + \text{Losses}} \times 100$$

$$= \frac{\alpha S \cos \phi_2}{S \cos \phi_2 + P_0 + \alpha^2 P_{sc}} \times 100$$

For maximum efficiency $d\eta/d\alpha = 0$. Differentiating equating the numerator of right hand side of the equation to zero. Simplifying, we get

$$P_0 S \cos \phi_2 - \alpha^2 P_{sc} S \cos \phi_2 = 0$$

Dividing by $S \cos S_2$

$$P_0 - \alpha^2 P_{sc} = 0$$

$\therefore$ $\boldsymbol{P_0 = \alpha^2 P_{sc}}$ for any value of $\cos \phi_2$

where $\alpha$ = Transformer load factor.

This is the condition for maximum efficiency of a transformer. In other words, for maximum efficiency:

*The maximum efficiency of a transformer occurs at a load factor $\alpha$ at which the iron losses are equal to the copper losses.*

Load factor for maximum efficiency is

$$\alpha = \sqrt{\frac{P_0}{P_{sc}}} = \sqrt{\frac{\text{No-load loss}}{\text{Short-circuit loss}}}$$

$$= \sqrt{\frac{\text{Core loss}}{\text{Copper loss}}}$$

**Core loss = Short-Circuit loss**

**Iron loss = Copper loss.**

### 7.13.1. Significance of the condition of maximum efficiency

The efficiency of a transformer changes with the load (and load factor). The efficiency reaches its maximum value when the copper losses ($\alpha^2 P_{sc}$) become equal to the iron losses ($P_0$). [In other words,

when the short-circuit losses ($\alpha^2 P_{sc}$) become equal to no-load losses $P_0$].
This condition is the guiding factor for

— designing the transformer for maximum efficiency at most average load factor

— for economical loading of transformeres in a sub-station for operation at maximum efficiency.

The average load factor $\alpha$ for a transformer is estimated from the load demand charts/curves. The average estimated value of transformer load factor is taken as a guiding factor for designing the transformer. *The average load factor of a typical power transformer used in distribution systems is about 0.5 and those used in generating stations and major sub-stations is about 0.8.*

For example, Let $\alpha = 0.5$

for maximum efficiency,

$$P_0 = P_{sc} = 0.25 P_{sc}$$

For maximum efficiency, with $\alpha = 0.5$ copper losses should be four times the iron losses,

*i.e.* $P_{sc} = 4\,P_0 \cdots\cdots$

If a transformer is designed for full load copper losses equal to four items iron losses, the efficiency is maximum at load factor 0.5. From the graph of load factor versus % $\eta$, it is observed that after reaching the maximum value, the efficiency curve drops only slightly. Hence even on higher loads, the efficiency would be above 96%.

The efficiency of a transformer reduces rapidly at lower loads than the load for maximum efficiency.

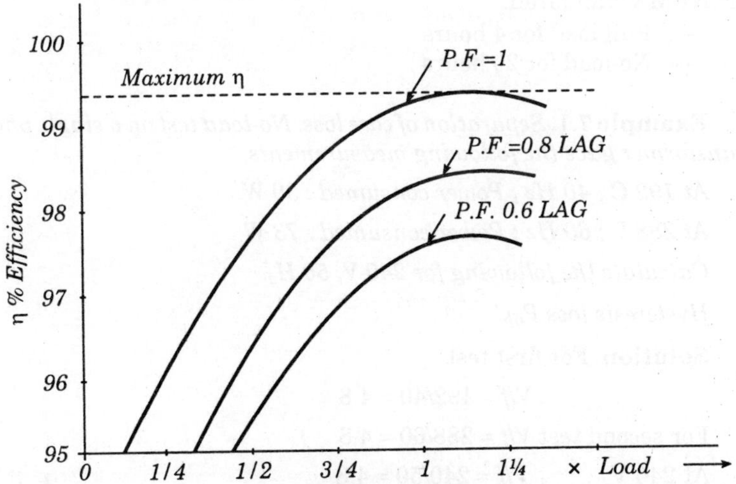


Fig. 7.1. Efficiency of a transformer.
[Maximum efficiency occurs at load for which Copper losses = Iron losses]

*While designing a transformer, the weight of iron and copper are selected such that copper loss is equal to iron loss for average transformer load factor. This ensures high efficiency during the operation.*

**All-day Efficiency of a Transofmer.** The efficiency change with the load. The load changes during a day as per daily load curve. All-day efficiency is an average efficiency of a transformer for a particularly daily load curve of load against hours.

$$\text{All–day Efficiency} = \frac{\text{kWh Output}}{\text{kWh Input}} \times 100$$

for given 24 hours load curve

Let $P_1$ = Output kW for $t_1$ hours = $(V_2 I_2 \cos \phi_2)_1$

$P_2$ = Output kW for $t_2$ hours = $(V_1 I_2 \cos \phi_2)_2$

and likewise for $t_3, t_4$ . . . . etc., hours corresponding to subscripts 1, 2...., etc.

$(I_1^2 R_e)_1$ = Copper loss for condition 1

$(I_1^2 R_2)_2$ = Copper loss for condition 2

and likewise $P_0$ = No-load losses common to condition 1, 2......... etc.

All-day efficiency

$$= \frac{P_1 t_1 + P_2 t_2 ...}{(P_1 t_1 + P_2 t_2 + ...) + [(I_1^2 R_e)_1 t_1 + (I_1^2 R_e)_2 t_2 + ...] + P_a}$$

If daily load curves is not available, follwing load is assumed as per NEMA standarad.

— Full load for 4 hours
— No-load for 20 hours

**Example 7.1.** *Separation of core loss. No-load test on a single phase transformer gave the following measurements:*

*At 192 C ; 40 Hz ; Power consumed : 39 W*

*At 288 V ; 60 Hz ; Power consumed : 73 W*

*Calculate the following for 240 V, 50 $H_z$.*

*Hysteresis loss $P_{oh}$.*

**Solution.** For first test

$$V/f = 192/40 = 4.8$$

For second test $V/f = 288/60 = 4.8$

At 240 V $V/f = 240/50 = 4.8$

Since $V \approx E = 4.44 \, f N \Phi_m$

Then $V/f = K\Phi_m$

where $K$ is a constant.

Since $V/f$ is constant, the flux and flux density are constant.

Hence hysteresis los $P_{oh} \propto f$

or $P_{oh} = af$

Eddy-current loss $P_{oe} \propto f^2$

or $P_{oe} = bf^2$

Total iron loss $= P_{oh} + P_{oe} = af + bf^2$

Therefore $39 = 40a + 1600b$

and $73 = 60a + 3600b$

Thus $a = 0.4916$

and $b = 29/2400 = 12.083 \times 10^{-3}$

At 50 Hz $P_{oh} = 50a = 24.583$ W

and $P_{oe} = 2500b = 30.208$ W

*i.e.* the hysteresis loss is 24.583 W and the eddy-current loss is 30.208 W at 50 Hz.

**Example 7.2.** *Efficiency from No-load and S.C.Tests. A 500 kVA transformer's test result were as follows:*

*No-load test power input = 4.5 kW.*

*Short-circuit test at rated current,power input = 7.8 kW.*

*Calculate the % efficiency at*

*(a) Half rated load, unity p.f.*

*(b) Half roted load, 0.866 p.f. log.*

**Solution.** Short-circuit Loss

$= \text{Copper loss} = I^2R_e$

$\propto (\text{kVA})^2$

Let $\alpha = \text{Load factor}$

$S = \text{kVA full load}$

$\alpha S = \text{Part load kVA}$

$\cos\phi_2 = \text{Load P.F.}$

$P_L = \text{Full load copper loss}$

**(*a*) At half load and unity p.f.**

$\alpha = 0.5$

$\cos\phi = 1$

Copper loss at = 0.5

$$= \alpha^2 \cdot P_L$$

$$= 0.5^2 \times 7.8 = 1.95 \text{ kW}$$

**Total loss at 0.5 load factor**

= Copper loss + Core loss

= 1.95 + 4.5 = 6.45 kW

**Transformer output**

= Load factor × S cos ϕ

= 0.5 × 500 × 1 = 250 kW

% Efficiency at 0.5 load factor and unity p.f.

$$= \frac{\text{Output}}{\text{Output} + \text{Losses}} \times 100$$

$$= \frac{250}{250 + 6.45} \times 100 = 97.5\% \qquad \textbf{Ans.}$$

**(*b*) Half load at 0.866 p.f. lag.** As in (a)

Copper loss at = 0.5 = 1.95 kW

No-load loss = 4.5 kW

Total losses = 6.45 kW

$$\% \text{ Efficiency} = \frac{\text{Output}}{\text{Output} + \text{Losses}} \times 100$$

$$= \frac{S \cos \phi}{S \cos \phi + \text{Losses}} \times 100$$

$$= \frac{(0.5 \times 500 \times 0.866)}{(0.5 \times 500 \times 0.866) + 6.45} \times 100$$

= 97.1% **Ans.**

**Example 7.3. Maximum Efficiency.** *A transformer is rated at 500 kVA.*

*Total no load loss is 4.5 kW*

*Total short circuit loss at rated current is 7.8 kW.*

*Calculate load at which efficiency would be maximum assuming load p.f. is (a) unity (b) 0.7 lag.*

**Solution.** Load factor α is given by

$$\alpha = \frac{\text{Actual kVA load}}{\text{Rated kVA load}}$$

Efficiency is maximum at value of α:

$$\alpha = \sqrt{\frac{\text{Core loss}}{\text{Copper loss}}}$$

$$= \sqrt{\frac{4.5}{7.8}} = \sqrt{0.577} = 0.759$$

Efficiency is maximum at load

$$= \alpha S = 0.759 \times 500 = 379.5 \text{ kVA}$$

**Maximum Efficiency**

(*a*) **At unit p.f.**

$$\% \eta_{max} = \left[\frac{\text{Output}}{\text{Output + Losses}}\right] \times 100$$

For maximum efficiency

Coppr loss = Core loss

Total loss = 2 × Core loss

$$\% \eta_{max} = \left[\frac{379.5 \times 51}{(379.5 \times 1) + (2 \times 4.5)}\right] \times 100$$

$$= \frac{379.5 \times 100}{388.5} = 97.68\%$$

**Example 7.4. Maximum efficiency and all-day efficiency.**

*A 50 kVA, 3.3 kV/250 V, 50 Hz single-phase transformer has a copper loss of 750 W at full-load current. The iron loss at the rated voltage and frequency is 480 W. At what kVA is the efficiency maximum? What is the maximum efficiency if the transformer supplies power to a 0.8 power factor load?*

*The transformer operate at maximum efficiency (supplying a 0.8 power factor loads) for 8 hours of the day and is left on open circuit (no load) thereafter. Determine its all-day efficiency.*

**Solution.** Maximum efficiency occurs at load factor α when

$$P_0 = P_{sc}$$

$$\alpha = \frac{\text{Actual kVA}}{\text{Rated kVA}}$$

**α for maximum**

$$\alpha = \sqrt{\frac{P_0}{P_{sc}}} = \sqrt{\frac{\text{Core loss}}{\text{Copper loss}}}$$

$$= \sqrt{\frac{480}{750}} = 0.8$$

For maximum efficiency

$$S = 0.8 \times 50 = 40 \text{ kVA}$$

**All Day Efficiency.** Let subscript 1,2... be for 8 hours loaded condition and remaining 16 hours of no load period respectively

$$\text{All Day } \% \, \eta = \frac{\text{Total cummulative kwh Output}}{\text{Total cummulative kwh Input}} \times 100$$

(For period of 24 Hours)

**For 8 Hours**

$$\text{Output} = 40 \text{ kVA at } 0.8 \text{ pf}$$

$$\text{kW} = S \cos \phi = 0.8 \times 40$$

$$\text{Energy output} = 40 \times 0.8 \times 8 = 256 \text{ kWh}$$

$$\text{Energy input} = (\text{Output kWh} + \text{Loss kWh})$$

$$= [40 \times 0.8 + 0.48 + 0.48] \times 8$$

$$= 263.7 \text{ kWh}$$

(Since for maximum efficiency copper loss = iron loss = 0.48 kW each).

**For Rest 16 Hours**

$$\text{Output kWh} = 0$$

$$\text{Input kWh} = \text{Iron losses}$$

$$= 0.48 \times 16 = 7.68 \text{ kWh}$$

Thus the total input to the transformer over the whole day

$$= 263.7 + 7.68 = 271.4 \text{ kWh}$$

$$\text{All–day per cent efficiency} = \frac{\text{output kWh}}{\text{input kWh}} \times 100$$

$$= \frac{256}{27.14} \times 100 = 94.32\%$$

**Example 7.5. All-day Efficiency.** *A 10 kVA substation transformer has efficiency of 96% at half-load and unity p.f. The load for a 24 hours maximum period was as follows:*

*Unity p.f. for all loads*

*1/3 × full load = 6 hours*

*2/3 × full load = 5 hours*

*Full load = 5 hours*

*No load = 8 hours*

*Calcualte All-day Efficiecny unity p.f. for all loads.*

**Solution.** Efficiency = [output power/(output power + losses)] × 100 losses. At half-load and unit power factor, output power = 5000 W

Hence  0.96 = 5000/(5000 + losses)

Hence losses at half-load = 208.3 W

Thus iron loss = 104.2 W

and half-load copper loss = 104.2 W

The output in kWh is

$(10/3) \times 6 + (2/3)10 \times 5 + 10 \times 5 = 103.3$ kWh

copper loss on 1/3 full load $= 0.1042 \times (0.333/0.5)^2 = 0.0463$ kW

copper loss on 2/3 full load $= 0.1042 \times (0.667/0.5)^2 = 0.1852$ kW

copper loss on full load $= 0.1042 \times (1/0.5)^2 = 0.4168$ kW

The losses over the day are

iron loss of 0.1042 kW for 24 hours = 2.5 kWh

copper loss of 0.0463 kW for 6 hours = 0.28 kWh

copprer loss of 0.1852 kW for 8 hours = 1.48 kWh

copper loss of 0.4168 kW for 5 hours = 2.08 kWh

Total losses = 6.34 kWh

Total input kWh = 103.3 + 6.34 = 109.6 kWh

Hence All-day per cent efficiency = $(103.3/109.6) \times 100$

= 94.2%

## 7.14. HEATING

All the losses occuring in the core,windings and other parts of a loaded transformer are converted into heat. The heat results in temperature rise of core, windings and oil. The limits of temperature rise for the inividual parts of a transformer are specified in the relevant standards.

Transformer needs cooling to dissipate the heat caused by losses.

The loading of a transformer should be such that the temperature rise is within specified limits and also maximum efficiency is achieved.

**Capitalization of Losses.** When a transformer is proposed for a particular application, the user should specify the requirements based on expected service conditions related with core losses and load losses. The loading guide-lines are covered in a subsequent chapter.

**Core losses** occur continuosly and do not vary with load. By using more magnetic materials of superior properties, the core losses can be reduced. However the cost of core and initial capital cost increases but cost of continuous core losses reduces.

**Load losses.** (Copper losses) vary in proportion of square of current and kVA load. Since the load varies hours to hour and from season to season, the commulative load losses depend upon *load* curve. By increasing the copper in the transformer the intial capital cost increases and cost of cummulative copper losses is reduced.

Increased capital cost of core → Reduced cost of continuous core loss

Increased capital cost of copper → Reduced cost of copper loss copper

With the continuing trend of cost effective designs, transformer design should be improved with the aim towards (1) low capital cost of core and copper (2) low cost of core losses and load losses.

These two demands are opposite. It is possible to sell a cheaper transformer having higher losses or costlier transformer having lower losses.

At tender stage, customers insist on a reduction in losses and compares various tenders by adding together the capital cost of the transformer and capitalized cost of losses. This policy has resulted is slight oversizing of core and windings to reduce the losses during the service.

## Summary

Under no-load condition, the primary winding takes only the *no-load* (excitation) *current* $I_0$ for setting-up flux $\phi$ in the core. No load current $I_0$ is only 2 to 3.5% of rated current. The no-load losses are also called core losses or iron-losses. No load loss is the sum of hysteresis loss and eddy current loss. No load losses are called fixed losses as they do not vary with load. No-load loss is constant for constant supply voltage.

Under loaded condition, the primary current $I_1$increases with the increase in secodary current $I_2$ such that $I_1N_1 = I_1N_2$.

Load losses are equal to copper losses or short-circuit losses. Load losses are variable losses as they vary with load.

*Efficiency of a transformer is maximum at a load factor when copper losses are equal to iron losses.* Transformer is designed for maximum efficiency at average transformer load factor.

The losses get converted into heat. Cooling is provided to dissipate heat.While loadig the transformers, the temperature rises should be within specified limits. The loading should be based on economic loading criterion. Transformer is a highly efficient device (97 to 99.4%).

**No-load Test** is conducted to determine *no-load loss* and *no-load current.* **Short-circuit Test** is conducted to determine *load losses* and *impedance voltage.* From the result of no-load test and short circuit test, the voltage regulation and efficiency of the transformer can be calculated for *any load factor*.

**All-day efficiency** is calculated as a ratio of total kWh output divided kWh input for 24 hours.

**Capitalisation of losses** is used for comparing tenders of the transformers. The trends are towards increased core size and winding size and reduce the losses.

**Loading Guide.** Transformer loading is generally based on permissible temperature rise of windings, oil for given ambient temperature and given load cycle.

# 8

# Magnetic Circuit and Materials for Laminations

The magnetic core is the backbone of a transformer. This chapter covers the various types of cores, the constructional details of 5 limb and 3 limb cores, interleaved mitred joints, etc. The second part of this chapter deals with magnetic materials for laminations. The various properties and characteristics have been described along with reference data.

## 8.1. INTRODUCTION

The core is a backbone of a transformer from electromagetic and mechanical considerations. Magnetic flux passes through the core and links the primary winding with the secondary winding. The energy transfer takes place through the core. The performance of a transformer is analysed in terms of losses, temperature rise, vibrations, audible noise (sound) etc. and depends upon the following.

- — Core material properties such as specific core losses (W/kg).
- — Method of holding the laminations together.
- — Method of jointing (*e.g.,* interleaved mitred joints at corners).
- — Correct method of manufacturing processes to ensure full benefit of properties of superior magnetic materials.
- — Ageing properties.

From mechanical considerations, the important points are:

- — Mechanical stresses during shop handling and transportation to site.
- — Clamping of windings.
- — Stresses during earthquakes.
- — Stresses during short-circuits
- — Vibrations and audible noise.

The thermal considerations include cooling of core laminations, oil-ducts,temperature rise and stresses due to alternate heating and cooling, thermal stability etc.

## 8.2. THE TRANSFORMER CORE

The function of the transformer core is to provide a path of high permeability to the magnetic flux and to support the transformer windings. The transformer core forms a close magnetic circuit. It is made up of thin laminations of special electrical sheet steel. The main magnetic flux passes through the core.

The functions and requirements of the core include:

- — To provide a closed path for magnetic flux linking with primary and secondary windings.
- — Mechanically strong
- — Low core loss
- — Adequate heat dissipation and thermal stability
- — Low magnetizing current
- — Lesser weight and compact size
- — To support the windings
- — To facilitate cooling
- — Low vibrations and low audible noise
- — Minimum loss ratio (W/kg)
- — Good ageing properties (Long life)
- — Easy methods of manufacture
- — Dimensions suitable for transportation.

## 8.3. CORE TYPE AND SHELL TYPE CONSTRUCTIONS

In a core type construction, the limbs are the vertical members of the core. The yokes are the horizontal members of the core, which close the magnetic circuit. The core laminations are thin (0.3 to 0.2 mm) and are provided with insulating coating of varnish or oxide.

There are two types of configurations of the core (1) Core type magnetic circuit and (2) Shell type magnetic circuit.

The choice of the type of construction depending upon the design and manufacturing practices.

The core type magnetic circuit has three or five limbs placed vertically. Two horizontal yokes, one at the top and the other at the bottom, close the magnetic circuit. Most of the power transformers are of core type.

In the core type construction, the windings encircle the core and in the shell type construction, the core encircles the windings. In the shell type construction, the winding is enclosed by the core. The core encircles the winding. The yoke has two branches and the magnetic flux leaving the limb branches off into parts.

In shell type transformers, the cross-section of the limb is twice that of the yoke.

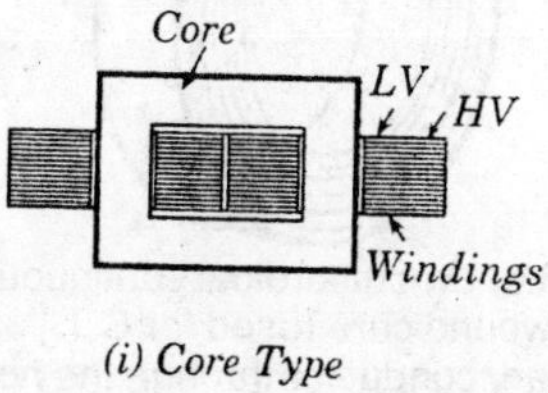


*(i) Core Type*

Fig. 8.1. Core type construction.
(windings encircle the core)

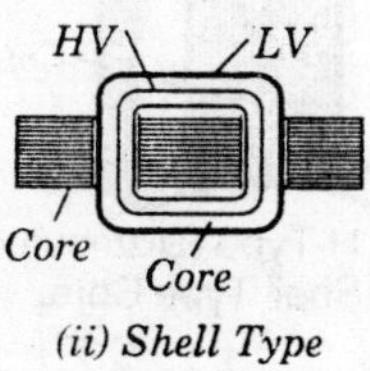


*(ii) Shell Type*

Fig. 8.2. Shell Type construction
(core encircles the winding)

The core type construction is commonly used in India, U.S.S.R. and Europe for small and large transformers. The shell type construction is preferred for small single phase transformers all over the world. However, it is preferred in U.S.A. for large transformers also.

Core type transformers are easy to manufacture. The HV and LV winding-coils are manufactured independently and are then inserted on the limbs. The windings are spiral or helical and are placed concentrically over the limbs.

In shell type construction, the LV and HV windings are flat and Pan-cake type. The core surrounds the windings. Shell type core has minimum cutting of leakage flux.

The manufacturing process of shell type core is slower and costlier than that of a core type. The further description is for core type construction.

## 8.4. CORE OF SINGLE PHASE CORE TYPE TRANSFORMERS. (Refer Fig.8.3 and Fig. 8.4).

Single phase core type transformers are built in following types of cores (i) 2-Limb (ii) 3-Limb.

In 2-Limb construction, windings are placed on both the limbs. In 3-Limb single phase construction, single phase windings are placed on the central limb only.

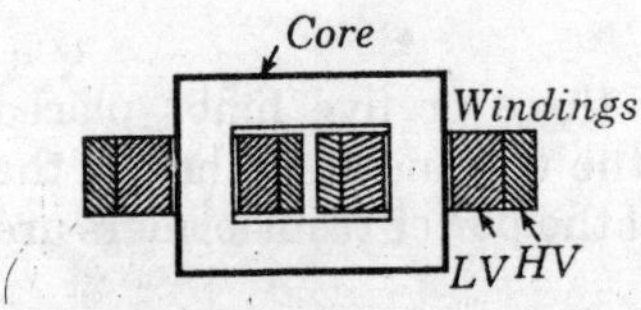


Fig. 8.3.Single Phase Core Type Transformer with 2-Limbs.

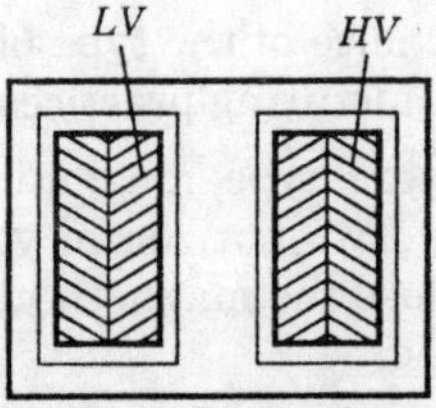


Fig. 8.4. Single Phase Core Type Transformer with 3-Limbs.

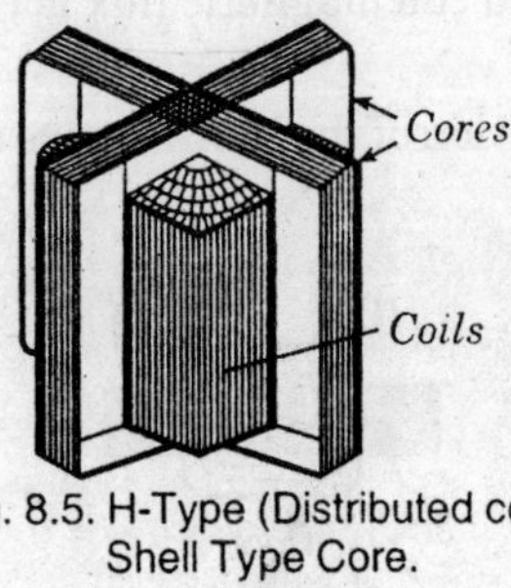


Fig. 8.5. H-Type (Distributed core) Shell Type Core.

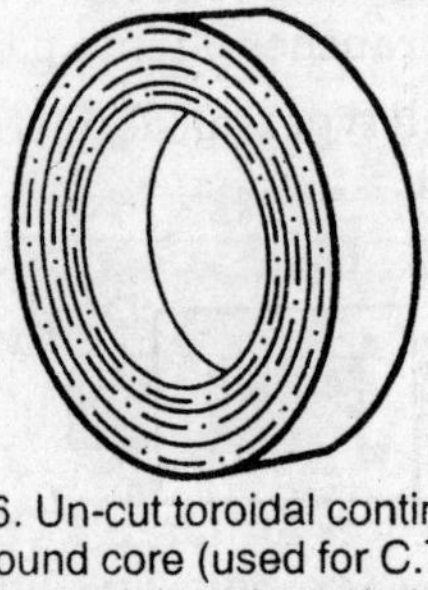

Fig. 8.6. Un-cut toroidal continuously wound core (used for C.T.) Primary conductor through the hole. Secondary wound on core.

## 8.5. HY-TYPE CORE (DISTRIBUTED CORE)

Figure 8.5. illustrates an isometric view of the shell type transformer core having four parallel magnetic circuits. Cores are joined in cruciform (as seen from top). The HV and LV coils are placed on central limb and are surrounded by the four vertical limbs.

## 8.6. TOROIDAL CORES

Figure 8.6. shows a typical toroidal core used for small current transformers having very small VA rating as compared to power transformer. Ref. Chapter 33.

The core is made by continuously wound long thin cold rolled steel strips spirally. The primary winding is a single conductor passing through the central hole. The secondary is wound on the core.

## 8.7. CUT-C OR CUT-TOROIDAL CORES

Such cores are used for small distribution transformers. The core is formed by continuously wound metal tape. The would core is bonded into a solid mass. Then it is cut into two halves. The mating surfaces are specially treated to get accurate butt joint (Fig. 8.7. and 8.8).

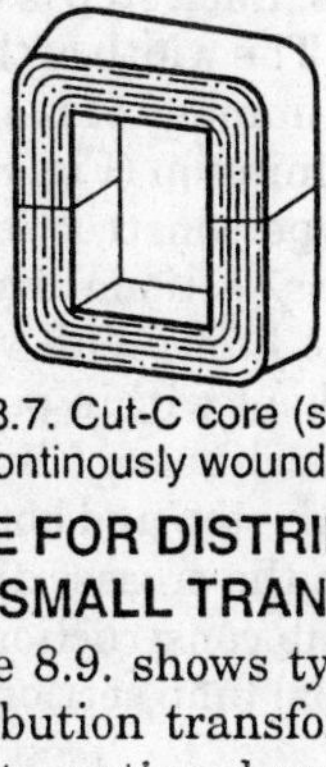

Fig. 8.7. Cut-C core (strip is continously wound).

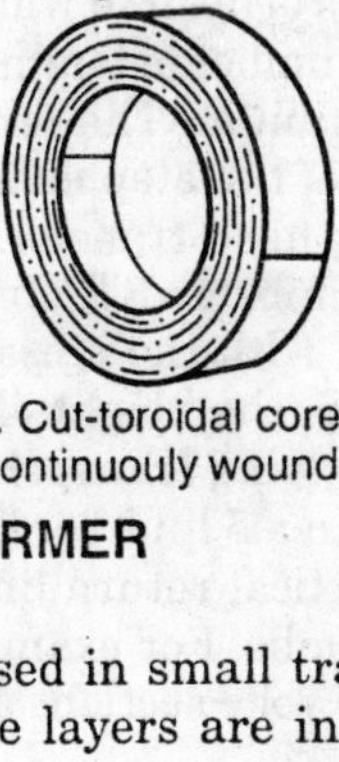

Fig. 8.8. Cut-toroidal core (strip is continuouly wound).

## 8.8. CORE FOR DISTRIBUTION TRANSFORMER AND SMALL TRANSFORMERS

Figure 8.9. shows typical laminations used in small transformer and distribution transformers. The alternate layers are interleaved. Several alternative shapes are possible.

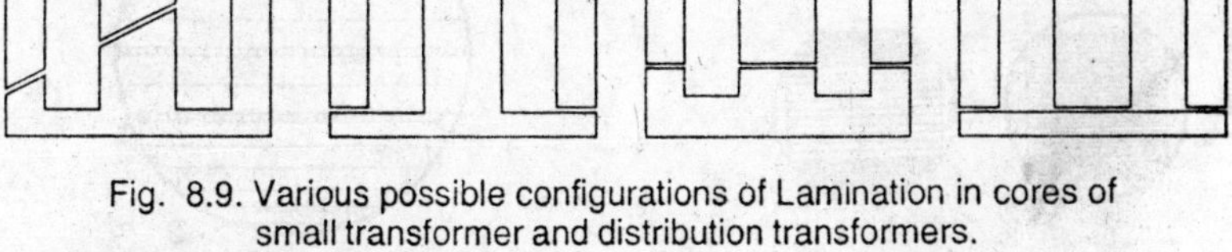

Fig. 8.9. Various possible configurations of Lamination in cores of small transformer and distribution transformers.

## 8.9. 3-LIMB AND 5-LIMB CORE

The cores for large 3 phase transformers are of "Core type", with either three limbs or five limbs depending upon designer's choice based on transportation limitations. Medium transformers are with 3-limb cores (Fig. 8.11) whereas large ones are with 5-limb core (Fig. 8.12.).

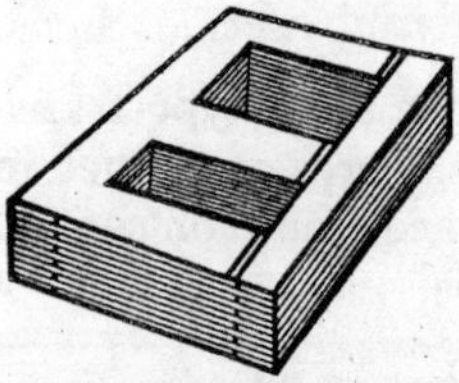

Fig. 8.10. Isometric view.

The cores of single phase transformers are eigther with 2 Limbs or three limbs.

Table 8.1 gives the details.

## 8.10. CONFIGURATION OF CROSS-SECTION OF CORE

The crosssection of the limb and the yoke is built up of a number of steps of achieve ap-

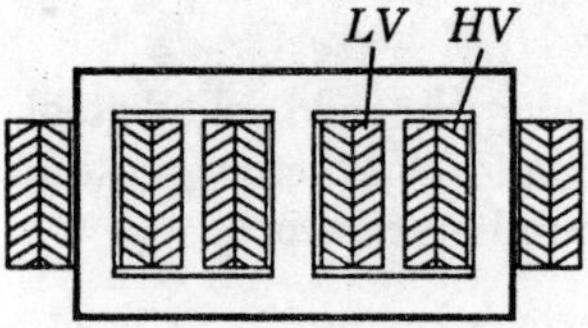


Fig. 8.11. 3-leg core for 3-Phase Core Type Transformer.

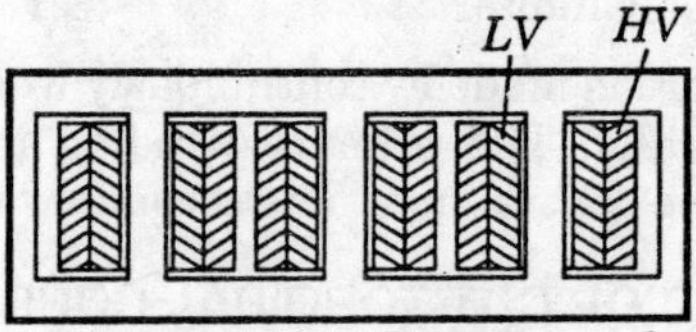


Fig. 8.12. 5-Leg core for 3-Phase Core Type Transformer

proximately a circular shape. The shape is obtained by placing a set of laminations of desired width in respective steps. Each step is composed of certain number of lamination of equal width. The width of the central step is maximum. The central step has larger number of laminations. The width of the step near circumference is minimum (Fig. 8.13). The cores of 3 phase transformers employ core type construction with 3 limbs or 5 limbs. In 3 limb construction, the cross-sectional area of yoke is identical with the cross-sectional area of the limb. With very large transformer, the height of the core should be kept within permissible limits for solving transportation problems. In such cases 5 limb core is preferred. In a 5 limb core, the cross-section of the top and bottom yoke and the vertical return limbs are smaller than the crosssection of the principal limbs. For example, in a typical 5 limb construction, the top and bottom yoke sections are 58% of the principal limb section, and the

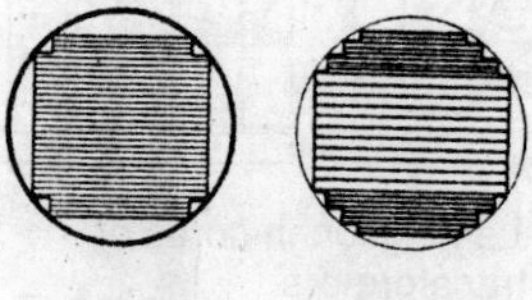

*Two step core section* *Multi step section*

Fig. 8.13. Cross-sections of limbs of core-type transformer.

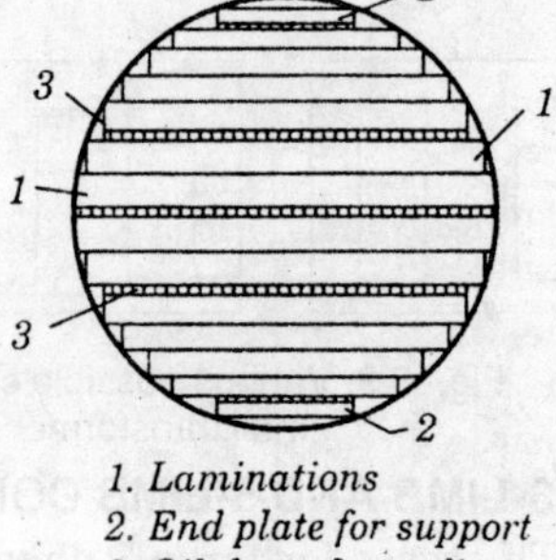


*1. Laminations*
*2. End plate for support*
*3. Oil ducts for cooling*

Fig. 8.14. Details of cross-section

vertical return limb section is 45% of the principal limb section. Such a design gives optimum choice of weight, height and iron losses.

**Table 8.1. Types of Cores in Core-type Construction**

| *Transformer Type* | *Type of Core* | *Description* |
|---|---|---|
| 1.1. Single phase core type transformer | Two-Limb construction | —Core sections of two vertical limbs and two yokes are identical.<br>—Core are bulkier than three core type.<br>—Percentage leakage reactance is higher than three core type.<br>—Primary and secondary windings are split in two parts and placed around two separate limbs. |
| 1.2. Single phase core type transformer | Three Limb construction | —Main central limb has a cross-section twice that of two auxiliary limbs.<br>—Primary and secondary windings placed on central limb.<br>—Top and bottom yokes have equal cross-section as that of auxiliary limbs.<br>—For high capacity single phase transformer, this type of core requires much bigger tank. |
| 2.1. Three phase core type transformer | Three limb construction | —Three vertical limbs of equal crosssection.<br>—Top and bottom yokes of equal cross-section and equal to cross-section of limb.<br>—The phase windings are placed on each Limb.<br>—This type of core is used for medium and small three phase transformers. Such a core cannot be used for very large transformers as the height of tank exceeds the transport limits. |
| 2.2. Three phase core type transformer | Five Limb construction | —Three main limbs are of same cross-section.<br>—Auxiliary limbs have fifty per cent crosssection.<br>—Height of core is reduced compared with three limb construction.<br>—This type of core used for large EHV transformers for limiting height of tank within transport limits. |

## 8.11. CORNER JOINTING OF YOKES WITH LIMB, BUTT JOINT AND MITRED (BEVELLED) JOINTS, INTERLEAVED CONSTRUCTION

While using cold-rolled grain oriented steel laminations, the laminations are placed such that the lines of flux in the core coincide with the grain orientation, *i.e.*, the direction of rolling. At the joint where the direction changes from yoke to limb and *vice-versa*, Inter leaved, Bevelled (Mitred) joints are used. This reduces reluctance of magnetic path, iron losses and the exciting current. The interleaved Mitred joints in each layer reduce the no load losses of transformers by about 12% and exciting currents by about 25%.

Figure 8.15 shows the magnetic flux distribution in a *Butt Joint*. The flux gets distorted at the corner. Leakage flux at corners is more. The grain orientation of CRGO is not utilized in the corner joints.

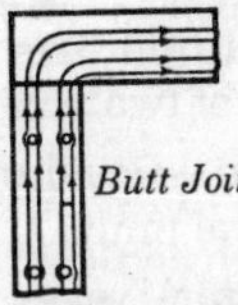


Fig. 8.15. Flux-distribution in Butt-Joint and effect of punched holes.

Fig. 8.16. Flux-distribution in Mitred Joint.

Figure 8.16. shows the flux distribution with *Mitred Joint*. (Bevelled joint). The distortion of flux at joints is minimized. The lines of magnetic flux are along the direction of rolling even at corner joints.

To make the best use of grain oriented silicon steel, it is necessary to make the flux run parallel to the direction of grain-orientation i.e., the direction of rolling. This is achieved by matching the yoke and leg section of identical cross-section and shape having mitred corners and by either eliminating or reducing the number of clamping studs.

Figure 8.17. illustrates the configuration of a 3 phases core type magnetic circuits. The core is built up of thin laminations. The vertical members of the core are called the legs or limbs of the core. The short horizontal parts of the core which do not have windings on them are called the yokes. The windings are placed on the limbs. The yokes complete the magnetic circuit. The core limbs and yokes are built up of separate laminations of electrical sheet steel of 0.33 mm to 0.2 mm thickness. The limbs and the yokes are stacked up to build the complete core. The laminations of the yoke and the limb are interleaved (Ref. Fig. 8.18). In the interleaved construction, a long lamination of the limb is matched with a short lamination of the yoke. In the next layer a short lamination of the limb is matched with the long lamination of the yoke. Thus the core is built up of alternate long and short laminations of the yoke interleaved with alternate short and long laminations of the limb to form interleaved construction. The joint between the lamination of the yoke and the limb is either of Butt type or Bevelled type (Mitred). The interleaved right angle joints between laminations was widely used for laminations made from hot-rolled steels used during 1950s. With hot rolled steel, the direction of flux need not be in the direction of the rolling. Hence the right angle interleaving was used. However with cold rolled grain-oriented silicon steel laminations, the butt joint is not preferred.

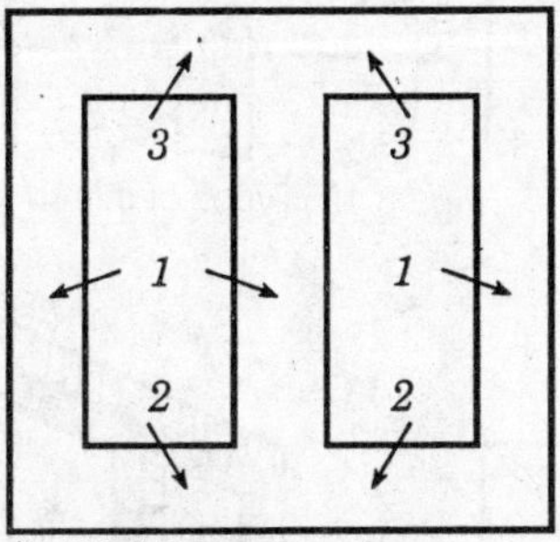


Fig. 8.17. A 3-Leg core for a 3-phase core type transformer
1. Limbs or legs
2. Bottom yoke
3. Top yoke.

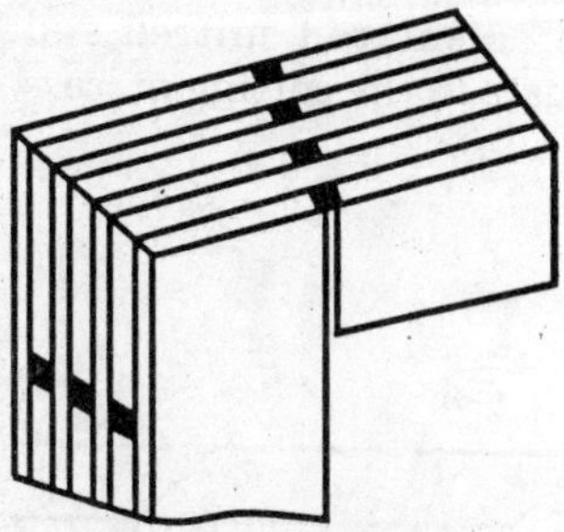

Fig. 8.18. Interleaved butt joint alternate layers are by interleaving short and long lamintions.

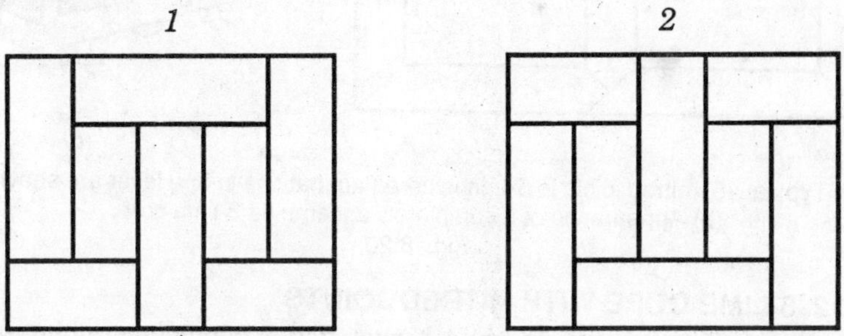


Fig. 8.18. (a) Alternate layers (1 and 2) forming interleaved construction of a 3-Limb core with butt-joint. (The line of joint of two laminations in first layer is covered by flat surface of adjucent laminations).

**Choice of Corner Joint**

| | |
|---|---|
| Butt Interleaved Joint | For hot rolled non-oriented laminations. |
| Bevelled Interleaved Joint | For Cold Rolled Grain-oriented Laminations. |

The advantage of mitred joint and minimum clamping studs is illustrated in Fig. 8.20 (b). Two common forms of mitred joint (bevelled joint) for a 3-phase 3 limb core type construction are shown in Fig. 8.19.

The full lines denote the joint in one layer of the laminations. The dotted lines represent the joint in the next layer. The mitred joints in one layer are displaced from the joint in the next layer to prevent leakage flux. 35° to 55° mitred improves the flow of flux, path round the corner and the 45° displaced mitred reduces the waste in the cutting process.

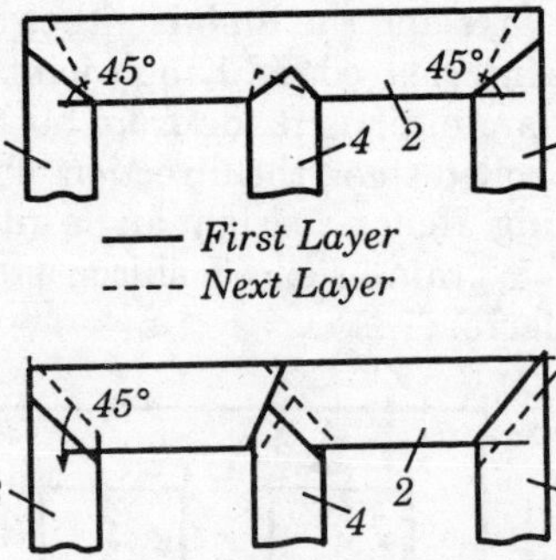


Fig. 8.19. Types of mitred joints

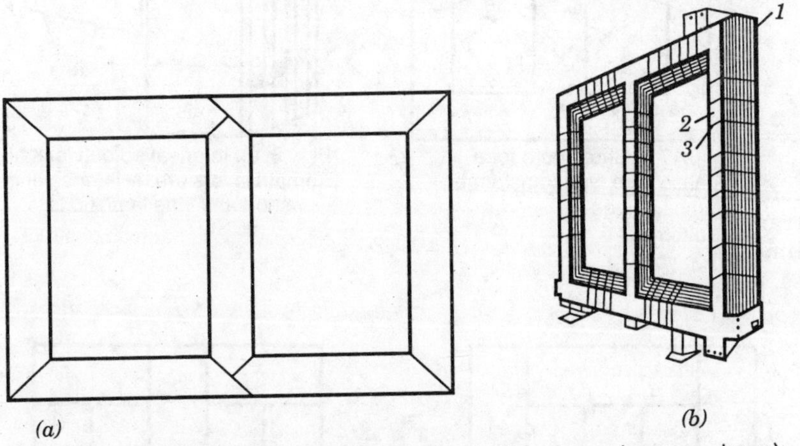


(a) Typical 45° mitred joints in 3-Limbs core (laminations in one layer are shown).
(b) Appearance of a completely assembled 3-limb core.
Fig. 8.20

## 8.12. 3-LIMB CORE WITH MITRED JOINTS

Figure 8.20 (a) shows a typical construction of one layer of laminations with mitred joint for a 3-Limb core. This corresponds approximately to the dark line layer in the lower Fig. 8.19. The next layer would be interleaved as shown by dashed line of lower Fig. 8.19. *All large transformers core are built with interleaved mitred joints without through clamping bolts in the core laminations.*

## 8.13. 5-LIMB CORE

Figure 8.21. shows the configuration of a 5-Limb core. The main limbs (1) carry full flux. The yokes and auxiliary limbs carry lesser flux. Auxiliary limbs and yokes have lesser cross-section than the limbs. Therefore, the height of core and tank is reduced and the length of core is increased. The reduced height is useful in designing the transformer within the given limits dictated by railway tunnels.

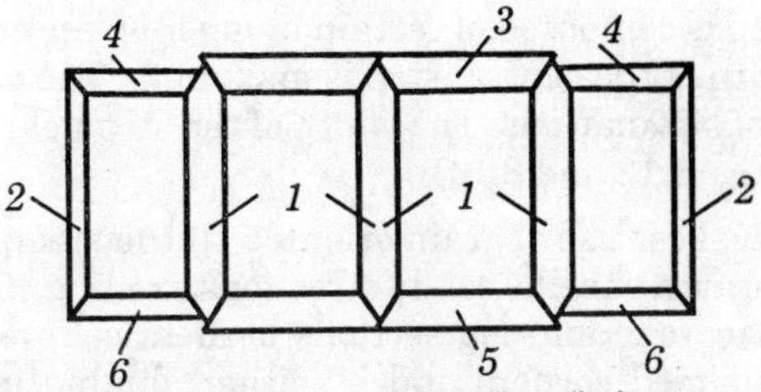


1. Main limbs. 2. Auxiliary limbs.
3. Top main yoke, 4. Auxiliary top yoke.
5. Bottom main yoke. 6. Auxiliary bottom yoke.

Fig. 8.21. Shape of 5-Limb core used for large 3-phase transformers.

Figure 8.22. shows one layer of laminations with 5-Limb core having mitred joints.

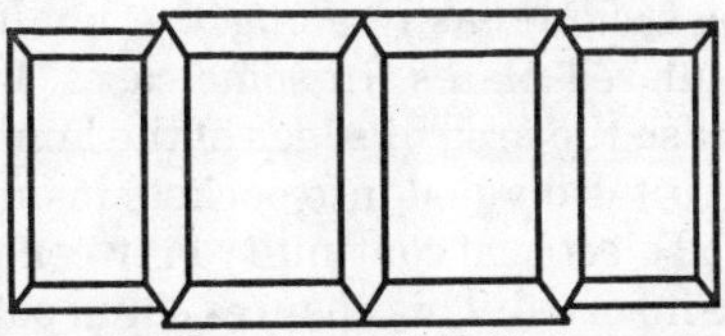

Fig. 8.22. Mitred joints in 5-Limb construction

**Five-Limb Core Transformer Versus Three-Limb Core Transformer.** For large power transformers, five-limb cores are more economical and transportable than the three-limb core transformers of the same rating.

— Height of 5 limb core transformer is lesser than that of a 3 limb core transformer of the same rating and voltage class. This permits profile within railway gauge.
— 5-Limb core is lighter than equivalent 3 limb-core.
— Mean specific core losses (W/kg) of 5-Limb core are higher than those in equivalent three limb core.
— Economic comparison is based on material cost, manufacturing cost and cost of losses.

5-Limb core construction is preferred for transformers rated 100 MVA and above, Comparison of a 5-Limb core and 3-Limb core for a 140 MVA, 320/10.5 kV, 50 Hz. Power transformers shows the following:

| | |
|---|---|
| Weight of core | 60 metric tons for 3-L core<br>57 metric tons for 5-L core |
| Height of transformer | 5-L core is lesser by 1 m |
| Length of transformer | 5-L core longer by 1 m |
| Core losses | Almost same for 5-L and 3-L |
| Leakage flux | Reduced for 5-L core. |

## 8.14. CROSS-SECTION OF A CORE

The cross-section of the limb and the yoke is built up of a number of steps to achieve approximately a circular shape. The shape is obtained by placing a set of laminations of desired width in respective steps. Each step is composed of certain number of laminations of equal width. The width of the central step is maximum. The central step has large number of laminations. The width of the step near circumference is minimum (Fig. 8.13 and 8.14).

To make the best use of grain oriented silicon steel, it is necessary to make the flux run parallel to the direction to rolling. This is achieved by matching the yoke and leg sections of identical cross-section and shape having mitred corners and by either eliminating or reducing number of clamping studs.

The choice of cross-sectional areas of main limbs, auxiliary limbs, top and bottom yokes depends on flux distribution.

Large cores have a relatively small surface/volume ratio, therefore, the cooling surface is increased by providing ducts parallel to laminations in sufficient numbers to obtain desired thermal gradient. Heat flows more easily along the laminations to the edges than between insulated plates. In some cases, transverse ducts are provided to increase the area of edges of the laminations. In such cases the magnetic circuit is divided into pockets insulated from each other and to provide good electrical continuity between the pockets,bridges of tinned copper are inserted. This ensures equal potential on various pockets of the core and effective earthing of the core.

With large core, the uses of ½ width laminations with a central vertical cooling duct enables the core bolts to be inserted through the cooling duct without reduction in effective core oil. The core studs are insulated from the core by tubes of SRBP (Synthetic resin bonded paper) or tubes of apoxy resin bonded fibre glass. The stiffening plates for the core bolts are either of laminated densified wood (Peramalli) or SRBP or non-magnetic material such as stainless steel or aluminium.

## 8.15. METHOD OF CLAMPING THE LIMBS AND MECHANICAL DESIGN

The core has yokes and limbs are formed by thin laminations.

To obtain the required magnetic characteristic and mechanical rigidity, the laminations of the core limbs and yokes are clamped (held rightly), to required tightness.

Two alternatives are available:

1. Clamping without through studs.

2. Clamping with the help of studs. This method was used earlier with hot-rolled laminations. This is not followed any more for large transformers.

### Methods of Clamping the Limbs Without Using Core Studs

The stud-less cores can be clamped by various methods mentioned-below:

1. Stainless steel bands with insulating layers or glass fibre tape are tightened by insulating laminated wood bolts or glass fibre reinforced synthetic resin bolts.

2. Resin impregnated glass fibre bands. The bands are tightened on the core limbs after assembly. The bands are tightened impregnated with resin and baked at high temperature under tension.

3. The core is temporarily taped to keep the lamination in position and then a closely fitting SRBP cylinder is placed on to the limb to insulate the limbs and clamp the lamination.

The boltless arrangement using above techniques can be used for the yoke also. The studs used for clamping should be of non-magnetic material such as stainless steel.

The cores of transformers above 1000 kVA may be clamped without using clamping studs. The vertical limbs are interleaved and mitred with the horizontal yokes. The top and bottom yokes are clamped by steel sections held together by a number of insulated yoke studs. These studs do not pass through the core but are held between the steel sections. The steel sections provide the clamping force to the laminations of yoke. The clamping studs holding the steel sections together are insulated from that steel section and the core. This prevents closed magnetic path and conducting path through these studs. Another modern technique is the use of glass-fibre bands, which are wound over the limbs, tighten, applied with a tension and then heat treated. These glass-fibre bands provide the required insulating clamping to the core limbs.

The steel sections which hold the top yoke which held by vertical and horizontal tie-bolts. These tie-bolts provided rigidity to the magnetic circuit.

**Mechanical Design.** The core and its mechanical parts are designed to withstand stresses arising during normal shop handling, transportation, and earthquake vibrations. The laminations of large cores are held together by fibreglass tapes wound on core cross-sections under tension and then thermally cured to form a homogeneous cylinder. Alternatively, the laminations can be held together by means of insulated non-magnetic steel bands. For smaller cores, epoxy cementing technique is used by some manufactures. The core yokes are pressed together with core clamps to achieve required frictional grip in interleaved joints at the core corners. The windings are placed under pressure by flitchplate tie bolts.

To prevent the movement of the core sheets during the manufacture and transportation, special side supports are placed at each corner. In addition the core is fixed to the tank-bottom and tank-cover of the transformer.

**Clamping by through studs.** The earlier practice was to punch holes through the laminations of the yoke and the limbs and provide insulated clamping studs passing through the cross-section of the limb and the core. Such an arrangement was used *with hot-rolled laminations.* Such a construction caused reduction in the cross-sectional area of the core and also destortion of magnetic field passing through the core stud. The core studs are provided with insulation. Hence, such a method of using through studs passing through the limbs or yokes is nor more preferred now. As per existing practice, the cores made up of cold-rolled grain oriented steel laminations are clamped without making use of through clamping studs. The laminations of limbs and yokes are not be punched with holes. This ensures better utilisation of cold-rolled grain oriented steel material.

The steel sections holding the bottom yoke are supported on horizontal base-frame structure with insulating compounds in between.

## 8.16. MANUFACTURE OF CORE LAMINATIONS

The sheet steel rolls are loaded on the mandrel of the decoiler unit of the cutting machine. The sheet is fed down into the looping pit. It is passed over the main frame. Several annealing and punching tools are mounted on the frame. The other end of the sheet is firmly held by cropping head.

The punching tools and annealing tools are operated hydraulically. The machine gives an output of 10 to 15 components per minute. The laminations are passed through annealing furnaces for stress releaving. The speed of the belt is about 5.5 m/min. The heat treatment is 70 to 80 seconds at temperature in the range of 730° to 840°C. After passing through the furnaces, the laminations are passed through air blast cooling section where the temperature of laminations is reduced from about 500°C to about 50°C.

The laminations are then passed through varnishing machine or oxidising machine. The laminations are fed into the machine through pairs of rollers. The varnish rollers operate in consumption with a pressure roller. The required thickness of varnish coating or oxide coating is applied on each side of the lamination. The laminations coated with the varnish or oxide are passed through backing ovens and then through a cooling chamber. After this, the laminations are stacked and sent to core assembly section.

## 8.17. ANNEALING OF LAMINATIONS OR CORES

Annealing is a type of heat-treatment given for stress releaving in fully processed material or decarborisation and grain growth in semi-processed material. Batch type annealing furnaces are used for small volume of laminations. Continuous annealing furnaces are employed for high volume production.

## 8.18. EARTHING OF CORE

All the internal non-current carrying metallic parts of the transformers require earthing, the only exception are individual limitations and the core bolts. The top yoke clamping plates are bonded to the tank with aluminium strap. The bottom yoke clamped structures are connected with the following:

1. Top yoke clamping structure.
2. Tank base.
3. Top clamped structure and the vertical tie-rod.

A connection is provided between the above bonded parts and the earthing bolt. The earthing bolt should be accessible externally. It is connected to bars and finally the earthing bars are connected to the earthing mat in the sub-station/switch yard/power station.

The magnetic circuit is bonded to the top clamping structure by means of a removable link at one point only. Multiple earth parts are avoided. Multiple earth parts cause difficulties in sensitive earth fault detection during impulse test. Multiple earthing can even initiate partial discharges under normal operating conditions, due to the circulating induced currents.

## 8.19. INSULATION RESISTANCE OF CORE BOLTS

The top and bottom yokes are clamped with the help of insulated clamping studs. These studs are of non-magnetic material and are provided with SRBP tube insulation. The nuts are provided with insulated washers. The core studs and nuts are insulated from the clamping sections and the core limitations. The insulation resistance between the core studs and the core is of the order of 100 Megaohms. The insulation resistance is measured by means of a Megger (D.C megaohms meter). One terminal of the megger is connected to the clamping stud and the other terminal is connected to the core.

The megger is cranked. The pointer of megger indicates the insulation resistance between the core and the clamping studs.

*To eliminate eddy currents in the core, the core clamping plates are insulated and the core-earthing is provided only at one place, e.g., the cover.* In large transformers such connection can be reached from outside to enable easy checking of insulation condition.

The insulation between the core and core clamps is tested at 3.5 kV (DC) for one minute. The measured insulation resistance should exceed 10 Megaohms.

**Finally the insulation resistance is measured on assembled transformer of the core and the core clamps. Initial shop values can be compared with final values after transport and erection. Many times battery operated meggars are also used for IR measurement.**

## 8.20. COOLING

The cooling of the core is achieved by circulation of oil inside and around the core. The quantity and route of inner cooling ducts ensures sufficiently low temperature rise in the -core and windings to ensure long life.

## 8.21. VIBRATIONS AND AUDIBLE NOISE (SOUND)

The audible noise (sound) produced by the core is mainly due to vibrations caused by magnetostriction and defective clamping techniques. The noise level (AN) is determined by maximum flux density ($B_m$), type of material for laminations, dimension of core.

Straight, smooth laminations with low magnetostriction and uniform distribution of surface pressure on the laminations result in reduction of vibrations and audible noise of the core.

Reduced airgaps and prevention of resonance near the multiple of the power frequency (50 Hz) give reduced audible noise. Further details about audible noise reduction have been given in a separate chapter.

## 8.22. QUALITY CONTROL CHECKS

The core steel material is tested against the specifications.

The manufacturing process is such that mechanical stresses and deformation of the core sheets is minimised. Close dimensional tolerances of individual lamination piece is checked. Each lamination piece is laid carefully by skilled workers during stacking of the core. Core assembly takes place in special horizontal cradles. These cradles can be raised/tilted without displacement of laminations.

During entire manufacturing process, the samples are tested for:

— Specific core loss (W/kg) is measured on pieces of different widths during several stages of manufacture.

— Checking of ageing.

— Surface insulation is tested for surface resistivity and thickness.

— Height of burrs resulting from cutting and slitting is checked by optical burr height gauge.

— Each lamination is checked for dimensional accuracy.

The cores are built in core shop under close supervision. The laminations are carefully placed to form the magnetic circuit. Dust, iron particles etc., are removed from surfaces, Defective laminations are rejected.

## PART B

## Fundamental Principles of Magnetic Field and Properties of Magnetic Materials

### 8.23. FERROMAGNETIC MATERIALS

The core is made up of laminations of ferromagnetic materials. Depending upon their magnetic behaviour, materials are classified into diamagnetic, paramagnetic and ferromagnetic materials. *Diamagnetic materials get magnetised in direction opposite to applied magnetic field and have relative permeability less than 1.* Paramagnetic and ferromagnetic materials get magnetised in the direction of applied magnetic field and have relative permeability more than 1. *Ferromagnetic* materials contain iron and are strongly paramagnetic materials. *Their relative permeability is several thousands.* For example, silicon iron with 3.5% silicon has high relative permeability and high electrical resistivity. Ferromagnetic materials exhibit strong magnetic effects. *The permeability of these materials is not a constant, but is a function of applied field (H) and also the previous magnetic history of the material.* In view of the variable nature of the permeability of the ferromagnetic materials, several properties and characteristics should be considered to achieve low core loss, compact size and long life. These properties and characteristics include the following:

- — Permeability
- — B-H curve (Magnetization curve)
- — Hysteresis loop and hysteresis loss
- — Saturation flux density
- — Loss per kg at working flux density (specific core loss)
- — Mechanical properties for manufacture
- — Electrical resistivity and surface resistance.
- — Ageing properties
- — Ease of manufacturing
- — Cost, etc.

A very wide range of magnetic materials have been developed and used for various types of transformers.

All cores of power transformers are manufactured from *Cold Rolled Grain Oriented Electrical Sheet Steels, (CRGO).* There are two varieties of CRGO electrical steels (1) Normal, (2) Super. The choice is dictated by the permissible limits of audible noise level (AN) and evaluation of losses.

Several electrical, mechanical and magnetic properties are specified for electrical sheet steels. The most important include:

- — Specific core losses (W/kg) at 50 Hz, 1.6 Tesla or 1.7 Testa (Bm).
- — Ageing withstand test
- — Surface resistance

— Space factor
— Waviness
— Edge camber
— Height of burs after cutting.

## 8.24. RELATIVE PERMEABILITY ($\mu_r$)

While dealing with magnetic materials, it is often convenient to specify the relative permeability. The relative permeability of a magnetic material denoted by the symbol $\mu_r$ and is defined as

$$\mu_r = \mu/\mu_0$$

where, $\mu_r$ = Relative permeability (Dimensionless)

$\mu$ = Permeability (Henry/meter)

$\mu_0$ = Permeability of vacuum ($4\pi \times 10.7$ Henry/metre.)

The relative permeability is a dimensionless ratio. By definition, the relative permeability of vacuum or free space is one. The relative permeability of vacuum or free space is one. The relative permeability of ferromagnetic materials is very high (Table 8.3).

Higher permeability is a desirable properties for the laminations of the core.

**Table 8.3. Relative Permeability**

| *Materials* | *Relative Permeability* |
|---|---|
| Vacuum | 1 |
| Air | 0.999 |
| Copper | 0.999 |
| Aluminium | 1.0002 |
| Nickel | 600 |
| Cobalt | 250 |
| Mild Steel (0.2°C) | 2000 |
| Iron 0.2 impurity | 2000 |
| Silicon Iron* (4 Si) | 7000 |
| Permalloy (78 Ni) | 100000 |
| Supermalloy (5 Mo 75 Ni) | 1000000 |

## 8.25. MAGNETISATION CURVE

The permeability $\mu$ of a magnetic material is given by the ratio.

$$\mu = \frac{B}{H} \text{ henry/m}$$

$$\mu = \mu_0 \mu_r$$

* Used in power Transformer with Si upto 3%.

where, $B$ = Magnitude of flux density (webers/metre$^2$)

$H$ = Magnitude of field $H$ (amp/metre) also called magnetising force.

$\mu_0$ = Permeability of vacuum ($4\pi \times 10^{-7}$ henrys/metre)

$\mu_r$ = Relative permeability substance (Dimensionless).

The permeability $\mu$ of a ferromagnetic material is not a constant, but depends upon the magnetising force $H$ and the history of magnetisation of the material. It is a ratio of $B/H$ on the $B/H$ curve at a given point. The $B/H$ curve is plotted with flux density $B$ on ordinate ($Y$-axis) and applied field $H$ on abscissa ($X$-axis). The line or the curve showing $B$ has a function of $H$ is called the magnetisation curve of the material. It is to be noted $\mu$ is not the slope of the curve but is given by the ratio $B/H$. A typical magnetisation curves for a ferromagnetic material is shown Fig. 8.24. In this case, the specimen was initially unmagnetised. As $H$ increases from zero to maximum value, $B$ also increases. The permeability at any point with the magnetisation curve is given by :

$$\mu = \frac{B}{H} \text{ (Dimensionless)}$$

$B$ = Ordinate of the point (webers/metre)$^2$

$H$ = Abscissa of the point (amp/metre)

It is observed that initially $\mu$ goes on increasing and after reaching peak value, the $\mu$ starts reducing. Initial magnetisation curve where $\mu$ goes on increasing is the region of easy magnetisation. The flat region corresponds to low relative permeability and hard magnetisation. The curve of $\mu$ is shown in Fig. 8.23.

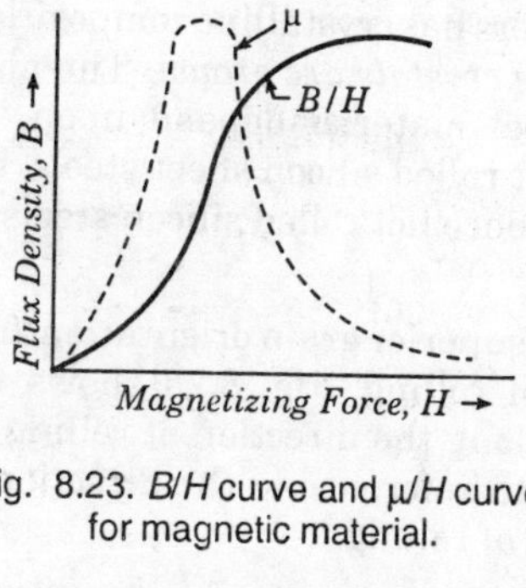


Fig. 8.23. $B/H$ curve and $\mu/H$ curve for magnetic material.

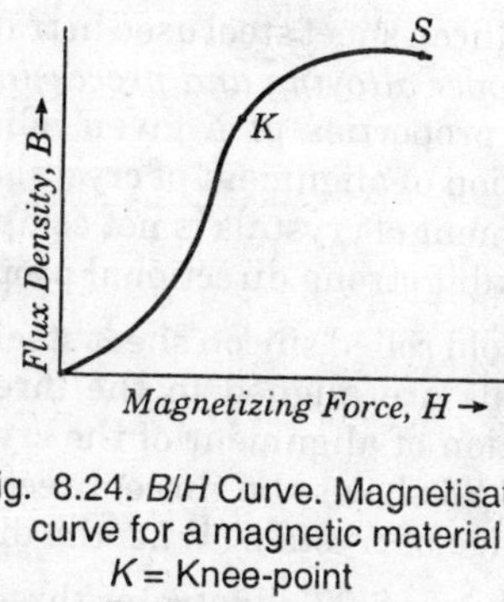


Fig. 8.24. $B/H$ Curve. Magnetisation curve for a magnetic material
$K$ = Knee-point
$S$ = Saturation point.

## 8.26. THEORY OF MAGNETISATION

The magnetic material comprises an aggregate of small crystals scattered at random. Each crystal has a magnetic property along its certain axis.

Because the crystals are scattered at random, on magnetic property is obtained externally. However, when the magnetic field is applied some of the crystals get aligned in the direction of applied field and the material gets magnetised in the direction of the alignment. With the increase in $H$, the alignment increases and $B$ increases. When all the crystals get aligned, the material gets saturated and no further increase in $B$ is possible. After reducing $H$, the $B/H$ curve follows a different path. Value of $B$ remains higher due to previous history of alignment of crystals. This phenomena is called *Hysteresis*.

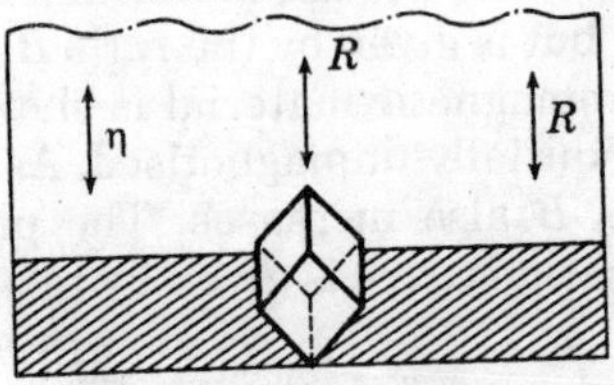


*R=Direction of cold rolling.*

Fig. 8.25. Alignment of crystals in a cold rolled silicon steel sheet

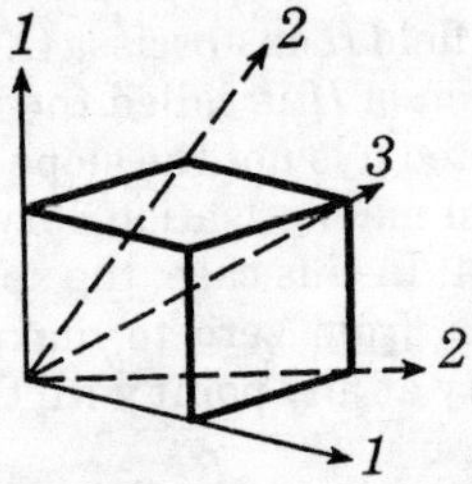


1. Along edge of crystal; direction of rolling R.
2. Across adjacent corners of a crystal.
3. Across opposite corners of a crystal.

Fig. 8.26. Three directions with reference to the direction of the rolling.

## 8.27. HOT ROLLED AND COLD ROLLED ELECTRICAL SHEET STEELS

Silicon sheet steel used in transformers has crystalline composition. *By proper alloying and processing, large crystals are grown.* The magnetic properties of a given silicon steel material depend upon the direction of alignment of crystals. In hot rolled silicon sheet steels, the alignment of crystals is not complete. Hence hot rolled silicon steels do not exibit strong directional properties.

Cold rolled silicon sheet steels have superior grain orientation. The crystals are aligned in the direction of rolling. Fig. 8.25 shows the direction of alignment of the crystals along the direction of rolling '*R*' Fig. 8.26 shows the three directions with reference to the direction of the edge of crystals (1) *i.e.* the direction of rolling.

Figure 8.27. illustrates three magnetisation curves for commercial Cold Rolled Grain Oriented (CRGO) silicon sheet steel. Curve 1 corresponds to the magnetic field in the direction of rolling (Parallel to edges or crystals as shown in Fig. 8.25. by arrow *R*).

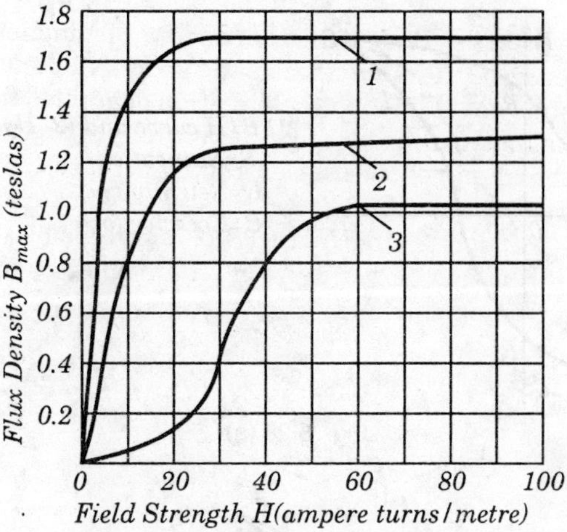


1. Along direction of rolling.
2. Perpendicular to direction of rolling.
3. Along opposite edges of crystals.

Fig. 8.27. Magnetisation curves for a typical commerical Cold Rolled Grain Oriented silicon sheet steel alon three directions shown in Fig. 8.26.

## 8.28. SUPER ORIENTED ELECTRICAL STEELS

Super Oriented electrical sheet steel has an extremely high degree of grain orientation of cubical crystals aligned in the direction of rolling. The average deviation from the direction of rolling is only 3° (against 7% for normal oriented steels). Super grain orientation is achieved by laser irradiation. Super orientared sheet steels are used when the permissible noise levels and permissible losses are of lower limit.

## 8.29. CORE LOSSES

About 80 per cent of no-load losses (core losses) are due to properties of material. Remaining 20% core losses are due to design and manufacturing process. By using 45° mitred joint, interleaved construction, proper clamping etc. the influence of change in direction of flux from/at yoke-to-limb joints is minimised.

## 8.30. HYSTERESIS LOOP (Fig. 8.28.)

If the applied field to a specimen is increased upto the saturation and then decreased. The flux density $B$ also decreases, but not as rapidly as it increased during intial magnetisation. The phenomenon which causes $B$ to lag behind $H$, so that the magnetisation curve for increasing $H$ is not the same as that for decreasing $H$, is called hysteresis. The closed loop traced out by the magnetisation curve by increasing and reversing $H$ cycle is called the Hysteresis Loop. The value of flux density $B$ at zero $H$ is called residual flux density. The residual flux density ($R$) on a saturation loop is called retentivity. The value of $H$ at zero $B$ is called the corrective force ($C$). The coercive force for a saturation loop

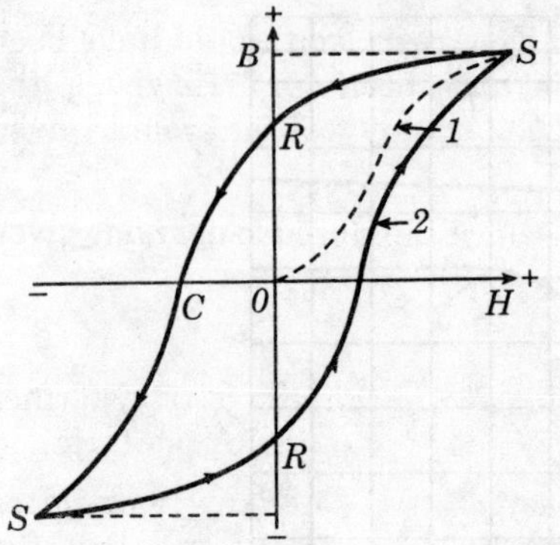


Fig. 8.28 (a)

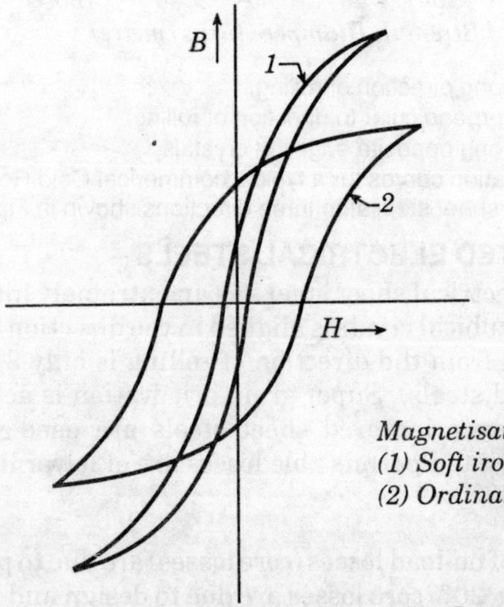


Fig. 8.28. (b) Magnetising Curves

is called coercivity. Thus retentivity of a substance is maximum value which the residual flux density attains ($R$). The coercivity of a substance is the maximum value of coercive force for the substance.

The Hysteresis Loop of a substance gives an information about its magnetic properties. The hysteresis loop of the soft magnetic material and a hard magnetic is useful for comparison. The area of the hysteresis loop of a soft magnetic material is less and such a material requires less energy, per cycle of magnetisation. Such material is preferred for transformer core.

## 8.31. ENERGY LOSS BY HYSTERESIS

While stressing the crystal in the specimen during alternate magnetisation, energy is spent within the material and appears as heat. If there were no hysteresis, the area of hysteresis loop would have been zero and energy lost for cycle would have been zero. However, the hysteresis loop has certain area and the energy lost for cycle is given by the area of hysteresis loop.

It is equal to the line integral of $H$ along the closed loop and is given by:

$W_h \propto \phi H \cdot dB$ . . . . . . per cycle, watts.

The hysteresis loss occurs continuously in the core of transformer because the core is subjected to alternating magnetic flux of 50 Hz.

**Steinmetz's Law of Hysteresis Loss.** This law correlates hysteresis loss ($P_h$) with flux density ($B$). According to this law, the hysteresis loss is proportional to the following:

— Frequency $f$.
— Hysteresis constant of material $h$.
— Volume of the material $v$, $m^3$.
— $B^x$ where $B$ = maximum flux density Wb/m$^2$ (Tesla) and $x$ = Steinmetz's index ranges from 1.6 to 4.

Thus, we get $W_h = h \cdot v \cdot f \cdot B^x \cdot 10^{-7}$.

## 8.32. EDDY CURRENT LOSS

When alternating magnetic flux flows through the iron core, small e.m.f. is induced in the magnetic material itself due to the changes its own flux linkage. The e.m.f. induced causes circulating currents in the metal. Such currents are called Eddy currents. Eddy currents flowing through the metal cause $I^2R$ loss in metal which appear as heat. Such losses are called Eddy currents Losses. To minimized Eddy Current Losses, the following methods are used:

— Laminated Core
— Insulation of lamination
— Use of material of high electrical resistivity.

The Eddy Current Loss $Pe$ is given by the formula

$$Pe = kt^2 B^2 f^2 v \text{ watts/kg}$$

$t$ = thickness of lamination

$B$ = Peak flux density Wb/m$^2$

$f$ = frequency, Hz

$v$ = Volume

$k$ = Eddy loss constant is

$K = \frac{1}{\rho}$ *i.e.*, $k$ is inversely proportional to the resistivity of magnetic material $\rho$.

If core is not laminated, Eddy currents would have been high and core would have got heated, leakage flux would be very high.

By using thin laminations for the core, thickness($t$) is reduced, Thereby, the eddy current losses in the core are reduced.

By using superior grain oriented material having higher electrical resistivity, eddy loss constant $k$, is reduced and flux density $B$ can be increased. Thereby core weight and size is reduced for same KVA rating.

## 8.33. HOT-ROLLED AND COLD ROLLED MAGNETIC MATERIAL USED FOR TRANSFORMER CORES

The materials used for core-laminations of transformers and reactor are of the category soft alloys. These are;

— Low carbon steels
— Silicon steels
— Nickel iron (permalloy)
— Carbon-Nickel iron (perminvar)
— Cobalt iron etc.

A number of variations have been developed in each categories, each alloying agent and manufacturing process has a distinct effect on particular characteristics. Each manufacturer gives a distinct trade name called the 'Grade'. The choice for a particular application is made by evaluating alternatives technically and economically.

In early years of transformer manufacture (1890–1930), ordinary low carbon steels were used. The ageing properties were poor. The losses were higher. The weight of cores was higher.

During the period 1930–1960, hot rolled silicon sheet steel (on grain oriented) was used. This is even used today where cost of CRGO sheets cannot be accepted.

*During 1970's Cold-Rolled Grain Oriented Silicon steels having superior magnetic properties in the direction of rolling have been used. Silicon alloy up to 3% is used.*

Cold-rolled grain oriented silicon sheet steels are used for laminations of power transformers. The commercially available cold-rolled silicon sheet steels have 3% silicon, total loss value 1.7 watts per kg at maximum flux density 1.6 teslas ( = 1.6 Wb/m$^2$ at 50Hz). The thickness of sheets is 0.33 mm to 0.25 mm. The cold-rolled grain oriented steel sheets have superior magnetic properties in the direction of rolling. The crystals are aligned in the direction or rolling by cold-rolling and heat treatment process. The magnetic properties of the sheet steels are dependent on the magnetic properties of individual crystals of the material and the direction of orientation of the crystals.

The properties of CRGO silicon steels are improved by composition, manufacturing process, heat treatment, laser irradiation etc.

Figure 8.29 shows the characteristics resistivity versus silicon content. Higher silicon content increases the resistivity and reduces eddy current losses. But silicon content above 3.5% makes the material brittle. *Silicon content of 3 to 3.25 % is used in commercial grades of CRGO steels.*

Figure 8.30. shows curves of saturation flux densities of commercial CRGO sheet steels. Fig.8.31. shows the specific loss (W/kg) for various values of maximum flux densities (Bm) for (1) 50 Hz flux and (2) 60 Hz flux. Fig. 8.32 shows the specific core loss for various grades CRGO silicon steels. Curve 4 for laser Irradiated 0.15 mm., thick CRGO silicon sheet material has superior magnetic properties and lowest core loss per kg. Maximum flux densities ($B_m$) of 1.6 tesla to 1.7 tesla are used for core design of modern CRGO steels. Superior CRGO steel gives less weight, lower losses and longer life.

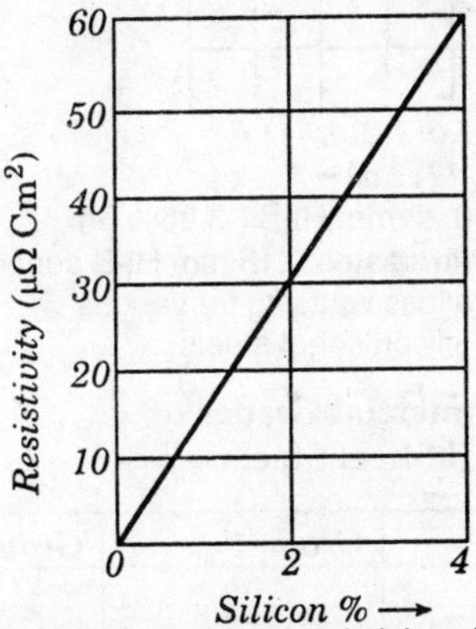


Fig. 8.29. Increase in resistivity with increase in silicon percentage.

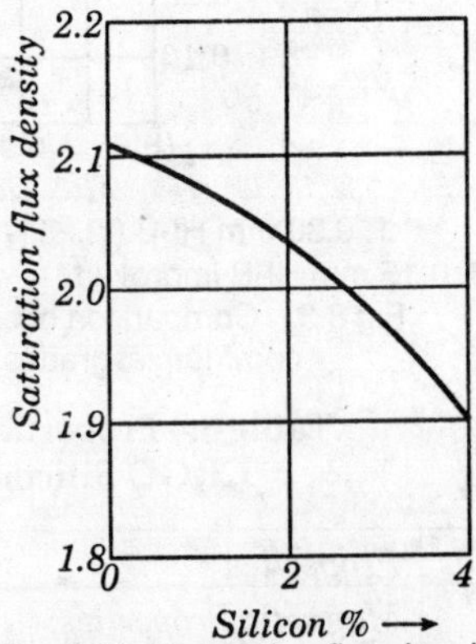


Fig. 8.30. Saturation flux density reduces with increased silicon content.

**Note.** 1.6. Tesla is design reference for $B_{max}$. By superior material, specific core loss can be reduced from 0.9 W/kg to 0.5 W/kg.

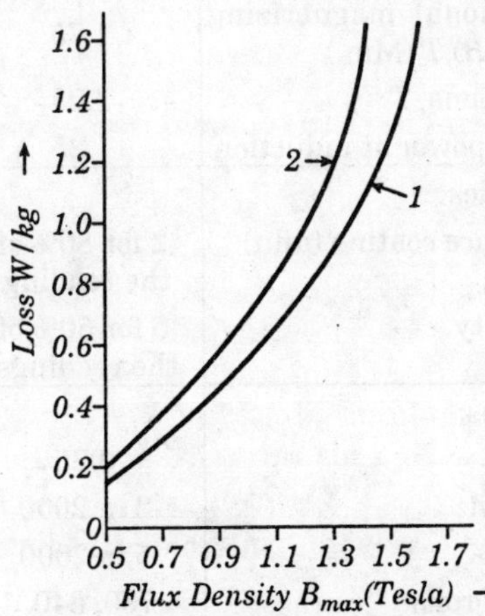


Fig. 8.31. Increase in specific core loss with the increase in Bm.

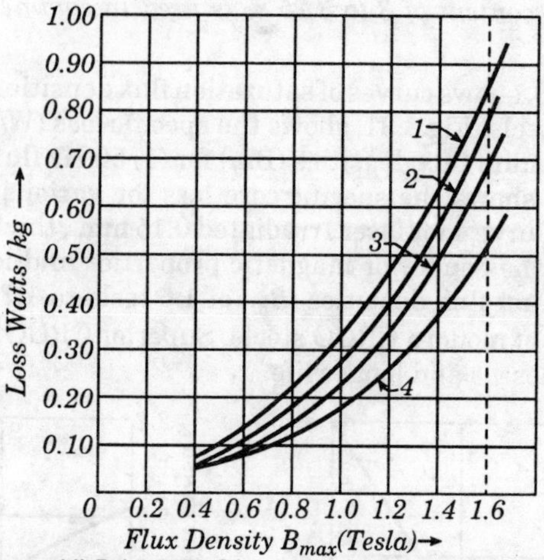


1. 0.30 mm HI-B ( 3.25% Si) 2. 0.23 mm HI-B ( 3.25% Si)
3. 0.15 mm HI-B improved 4. Laser-irradiated 0.15 mm HI-B super.

Fig 8.32. Comparison of specific core loss watts/kg for various commercial grades of CRGO silicon sheet steels.

**Table 8.4 Properties of Commercial Grades of CRGO Silicon Electrical Sheet Steels**

| *S.No.* | *Properties* | *Grade 1* | *Grade 2* |
|---|---|---|---|
| 1. | *Magnetic Properties:* | | |
| 1.1 | Specific core loss at 1.7 tesla W/kg | 1.40 | 1.17 |
| 1.2 | Ageing test (Increase in core-loss after ageing at 150°C for 14 days) % (max.) | 3 | 3 |
| 1.3 | Magnetic inductional magnetizing force of 800 A/m (*B*) *T* (Min.) | 1.75 | 1.85 |
| 1.4 | Saturation inductions, *T* | 2.03 | 2.03 |
| 1.5 | Specific apparent power at induction | 1.25 | 1.0 |
| 2. | Electrical Properties: | | |
| 2.1 | Resistance of surface coating (min) | 2 for 80% of the reading | |
| 2.2 | Electrical resistivity | 5 for 50% of the readings | |
| 3. | Physical Properties: | | |
| 3.1 | Thickness (mm) | 0.25 | 0.33 |
| 3.2 | Edge chamber, mm | 2 in 2000 | 0.05 |
| 3.3 | Edge burr, mm | 5 in 2000 | |
| 3.4 | Standard widths of rolls | 760, 840, 915, 1000 | Same as Grade I |

## 8.34. RELUCTANCE AND PERMEANCE OF MAGNETIC CIRCUIT

Kirchhoff's law of Electric circuit states that the total voltage is equal to total voltage drop in the circuit, *i.e.,*

$$V_t = IR_t \text{ volts}$$

where,
$V_t$ = Total voltage
$I$ = Current, amperes
$R_t$ = Total resistance

Now, consider the law of Magnetic circuit. We have reluctance corresponding to resistance and flux corresponding to current.

**Table 8.5**

| *Electrical Circuit* | *Magnetic Circuit* |
|---|---|
| Current I | Flux I |
| E.M.F.(voltage)$V$ | M.M.F.$F$ |
| Resistance $R$ | Reluctance $R$ |

**Table 8.6**

| *Reluctance* | $R$ | *1/henry* |
|---|---|---|
| M.M.F. | F | Amp. turns |
| Flux | $\phi$ | Webers |

In Magnetic Circuit, the reluctance $R_t$ is given by the equation

$$R_t = \frac{F_t}{\phi_m}$$

where, $R_t$ = Total reluctance of magnetic circuit 1/henry.
$F_t$ = Total M.M.F. weber turns
$\phi_m$ = Flux through magnetic circuit webres

Since

M.M.F. = NI, we get

$$R_t = F_t/\phi_m = NI/\phi_m$$

where, NI = M.M.F. in ampere turns, the above equation concerns the total magnetic circuit.

**Reluctance of a magnetic core path.** Reluctance of a Magnetic path having uniform cross-section $A$, length $L$ and permeability $\mu$ is given by

$$R_t = \frac{L}{\mu A} \text{ 1/henry}$$

**Example 8.1.** *Find the reluctance between the ends of a rectangular iron bar having length L = 10 cm., cross sectional* area = 3 × 5 *cm.*

*Uniform B in the cross-section. Relative permeability.......is 500.*

**Solution.** The reluctance of the block between the two faces having cross sectional area $A$ and length $L$ between the faces is equal to $L$ is given by

$$R_t = \frac{L}{\mu A} = \frac{0.1}{5000 \times 4\pi \times 10^{-7} \times 15 \times 10^{-4}}$$

$$= 1.06 \times 10^5 .....1/\text{henry}.$$

## 8.35. RULES OF MAGNETIC CIRCUIT

1. Reluctances in series get added *i.e.*,

$$R_t = R_1 + R_2$$

2. Reluctance is in parallel are given by

$$\frac{1}{R_t} = \frac{1}{R_1} + \frac{1}{R_2}$$

Permeances is reciprocal of reluctance *i.e.*,

$$P = \frac{1}{R}; P = \text{permeance unit henry}$$

Permeance is in parallel get added *i.e.*,

$$P_t = P_1 + P_2$$

### Summary

The transformer core is either of shell type or core type. Core type is preferred in India, Europe, USSR for distribution transformers and power transformers. 3 Phase core type transformers are built in 3-*L* or 5-*L* construction. Laminations of CRGO electrical sheet steel with 3% silicon are used in thickness of 0.25 or 0.33 mm. Mitred, interleaved joints are preferred. Core should have low loss, low noise, long life and higher saturation flux density.

# 9

# Transformer Tanks and Cooling Systems

The function of a Transformer Tank is to provide a protective cover to the core, windings and other internal parts including transformer oil. The transformer tank also provides external surface for dissipating heat. The tank provides a rigid support to the fitments and accessories.

The cooling system removes the heat and maintains the temperature rise within specified limits. The limits of permissible temperature are specified in accordance with the 'temperature classification of insulating materials'. The maximum temperature of the winding, insulation and the oil depends upon the loading, cooling and ambient temperature. The oil provides a medium for insulation and heat dissipation. The heat from core and windings is dissipated by means of the circulating oil. Several types of cooling systems have been developed. Medium units are oil natural, forced air or oil natural, air natural. Large units are generally oil forced, directed flow type.

The tank and cooling system contribute to the heat dissipation. The design features of the tank and cooling system should be such that the oil circulates without leakage and without contamination by external moist air. Conservator and breather or conservator with air cell and breather are installed to permit expansion of oil and to conserve the properties of the oil. Dry type transformers without oil are used for medium size transformers of medium voltages.

### Part A — Tanks

## 9.1. TYPES OF TANKS AND METHODS OF COOLING

The following three aspects are interrelated:

— Design of tank, tank cover, and sealing system.

— Flow of cooling and insulating medium viz oil and cooling system.

— Conservator, breather and oil preservation.

The types of tanks and cooling systems include;

1. Plain sheet steel tanks without external cooling tubes.
2. Tank with external cooling tubes.
3. Tank with detatchable radiators.
4. Tank and separately installed forced oil type cooler.
5. Tank with externally installed forced oil and forced water type cooler and separate heat exchanger.
6. Dry type transformer tank.

## 9.2. FUNCTIONAL REQUIREMENTS OF THE TANK ASSEMBLY

— To provide enclosure to the winding, oil and other internal parts.
— To provide rigid and mechanically strong unit to withstand mechanical stresses occuring during handling, transportation and internal short-circuits.
— Minimum vibration and audible noise.
— To support various fitments, tank cover, bushings, tapchanger etc.
— To provide sealed construction.
— To provide surface for heat dissipation.
— Should be dimensioned within the tunnel profile specified by railway authority.
— Should be transportable economically by suitable railway wagon/road trailer.
— Should be rust free and should have specified paint of long life.
— Should have minimum eddy currents. Should have minimum external magnetic field.

## 9.3. PLAIN SHEET STEEL TANK

Such tanks are made of thin sheet steel of about 3 mm thickness. Cooling tubes are not provided. The tank's surface is plain. Such tanks are used for small transformers upto 50 kVA rating for low voltages. Upto this output, there is no need of providing additional cooling. The surface of the tank itself is adequate.

In a rectangular box type tanks, the four sides of the tank are made from a single sheet folded and welded at a single vertical welded joint. Electrical welding is preferred. Similar but thicker material is used for base sheet. The vertical sheet is welded to the base sheet. A flange is welded to the vertical sheet on the top. This flange is provided with drilled holes of suitable size at regular intervals. The top sheet also has matching holes. A flat gasket of neoprene bonded cork is placed between the flange and the top sheet. The gasket provides sealing. The gasket is squeezed between the top sheet and the flange. Bushings are provided at a suitable location.

**Heat transfer.** In small oil filled plain sheet tanks, the oil circulates within the tank by natural convection from the windings to the surface of the tank. Heat is radiated to external atmosphere from the tank surface. With increase in the load, the oil expands within the tank and during no load the oil contracts. The temperature of the tank varies from bottom to top. If windings are located near the bottom, entire tank will be hotter and there will be better heat transfer.

Heat transfer from a plain sheet tank is proportional to the square of surface area of tank and weight of material is proportional to cube of dimensions. Hence, for larger kVA transformer material used for core and tank will increase at a higher rate than the corresponding increase in surface area. Therefore, plain sheet tanks can be used only for small transformers.

For increasing the heat dissipation, plain sheet tanks are made taller than those with cooling tubes.

## 9.4. PLAIN TANKS MODIFIED WITH FIN AND PLATES (Fig. 9.1)

The surface area of plain sheet tanks can be increased by adding fins or plates for higher heat dissipation. The fins or plates are welded to the sheet/plate surface of the tank.

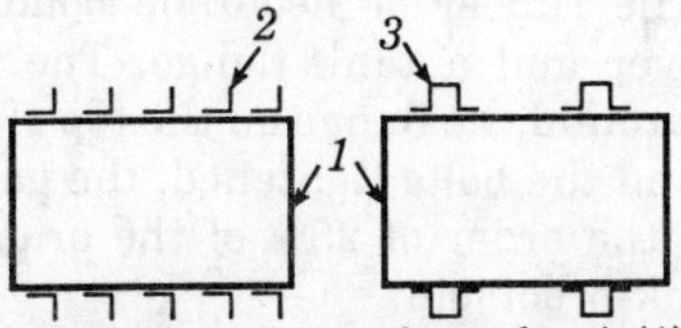


Fig. 9.1. Increase in cooling surface of tank (1) by means of angle-fins (2) or box-type fins (3) (Top-view).

Hollow radiating fins or tubes may be welded to the tank on sides or on top and bottom surfaces.

## 9.5. BOILER PLATE TANK WITH EXTERNAL COOLING TUBES

This type of tank construction is used for self-cooled distribution transformers of all sizes above 50 kVA. External cooling tubes are welded to the tank walls to obtain additional cooling surface and circulation of oil. High quality boiler plate steel (5 to 10 mm) thick, is cut, prepared and welded to get rigid construction. Stiffeners are welded to the sides at an interval of above 1 mm to prevent bulging. The tank should be proof-tested for pressure test and vacuum test. The tubes are arranged at a spacing of about 8 cms centre to centre and the rows are placed at a distance of 10 cms vertical . The bottom plate of the tank is thicker than the side wall plates (8 to 12 mm). The tank is cover formed from boiler plate steel of 3 to 6 mm thickness.

The cooling tubes on the tank sides may be arranged in one, two or three rows depending upon the transformer rating. Tubes of circular cross-section were used earlier. However, tubes with elliptical shape give higher cooling effect and can be placed closer to another and more number of tubes can be accommodated. Hence elliptical tubes are preferred. Elliptical tube fabrications somewhat more complicated.

The transformer tanks are tested for leakage by filling them with oil and keeping them under pressure of 0.5 kg/cm$^2$or above, for several hours. During this test all the joints may be applied with a solution sprinkled with light blue chalk powder which turns dark in presence of oil indicating location of minute leaks.

Four lifting lugs are provided at the four corners of the transformer tank. These are welded to the tank plates.

The stiffeners of large transformer tanks are usually of box type design. The optimum dimension of stiffeners (braces) and the distance between them is determined experimentally so that tank resonance is eliminated. The interior sides of the tank corners are welded to get added strength and to prevent leakage paths.

All external joints such as lifting lugs, flanges, indicator windows etc., are welded properly to prevent ingress of moisture and to prevent leakage of oil. The tank covers are bolted on to the flange on the tank. Flat gaskets of nitrile rubber or neoprene bonded cork are placed between the top cover and a tank flange. The gaskets (seals) are confined in grooves around the flange on the top of the tank. When the top cover is bolted and the bolts tightened, the gasket gets squeezed. The squeezing is of the order of 25% of the original thickness. The squeezing gives a leak-proof joint.

All the other joints such as openings for oil entry, oil drainage, auxiliary fitments etc., have flanges which are provided with proper gaskets. None of the joint should leak.

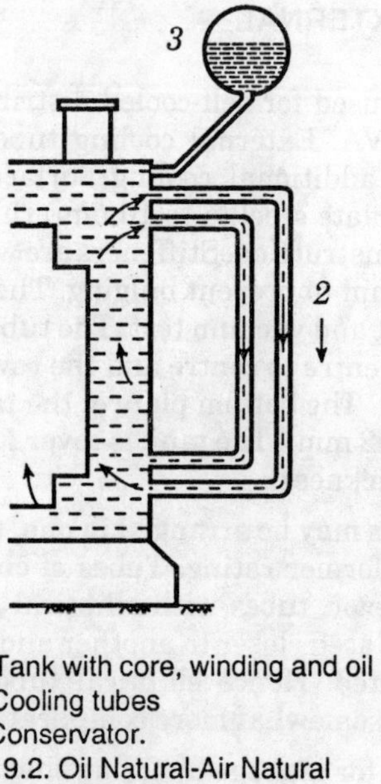


1. Tank with core, winding and oil
2. Cooling tubes
3. Conservator.

Fig. 9.2. Oil Natural-Air Natural (ONAN). Tank with external cooling tubes.

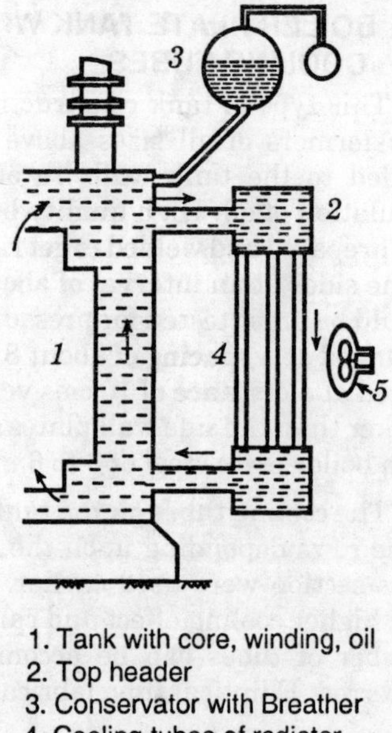


1. Tank with core, winding, oil
2. Top header
3. Conservator with Breather
4. Cooling tubes of radiator
5. Fan for forced air
6. Valves (Not shown) optional.

Fig. 9.3. Oil Natural-Air Forced (ONAF). Tank with detachable radiator.

**Heat Transfer.** The oil circulates through the tubes, the tubes provide additional cooling surface. The tubes are welded near the top and bottom of the tank and the oil circulates by natural convection.

## 9.6. TANK WITH DETACHABLE RADIATORS

For transformers rated 5000 kVA and above, it is not possible to accommodate sufficient number of cooling tubes on the tank sides unless the tank dimension and oil quantity is increased uneconomically. Instead of providing cooling tubes on the tank itself, separate detachable radiators are mounted. The radiator consists of several elliptical tubes or finned tubes or tubes formed by pressed steel plates. These tubes are welded into top header and bottom header. The complete radiator is bolted to the tank wall with one inlet an one outlet valves in between. In case of large transformers, the radiators are packed and despatched separately for assembly on the transformer tank at site. Thus, the tank can be filled with oil or nitrogen and despatched. By adopting detachable radiator, the shipping dimensions can be reduced. Single tubular radiator is sufficient for transformer of 650 to 4000 kVA. In such radiators, the tubes are arranged on only one side of the headers and the flanges are connected on the opposite side of the tubes.

While in operation, hot oil rises to the top of the transformer tank by natural thermal head and enters took of header. The large cooling surface of the radiators cause cooling of oil. Since there is a difference in density between hot and cold oil, the cooled oil descends down the radiator tubes, give away heat to the tubes walls. The heat is transferred into ambient air. Fresh hot oil from the tank enters the top radiator header and moves downwards. Thus, the radiators provided natural path for circulation of oil for cooling.

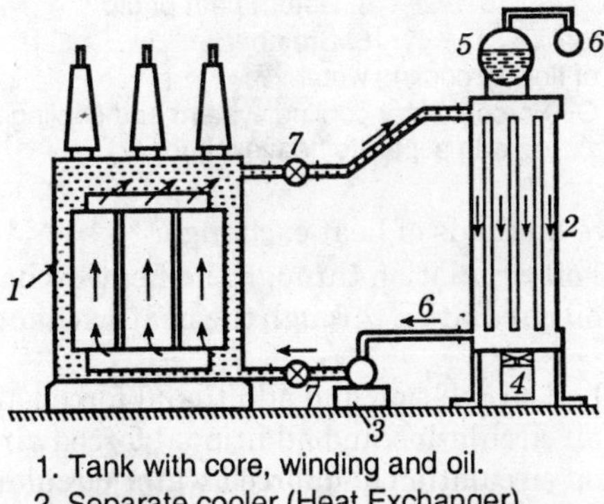


1. Tank with core, winding and oil.
2. Separate cooler (Heat Exchanger).
3. Oil-pump
4. Forced air
5. Radiator
6. Cooled oil
7. Valves for detatching the cooler without leakage of oil from 1.

Fig. 9.4. Oil Forced Air-Forced (OFAF) and tank with separate cooler

## 9.7. TANKS WITH SEPARATE COOLERS (HEAT EXCHANGERS)

(Figure 9.4. and 9.5). In case of high capacity transformers, where the surface of the radiator with natural oil circulation is not adequate to dissipate enough heat, forced air cooling is adopted. Fans are mounted to provide air blast to each radiator. The fans are mounted on a separate bracket.

The cooler (heat exchanger) consists of (1) Cooler element housing and (2) Fan. The cooler elements are either tubes or oil ducts formed by zig-zag sheet metal sections welded together in pairs.

The oil is circulated through the cooler-element by means of an oil-pump. A fan mounted suitably opposite the cooler-element housing provides an air-blast over the cooler element surface. The oil is pumped continuously through the cooler elements. The heat is dissipated by forced air projected on the cooler-elements.

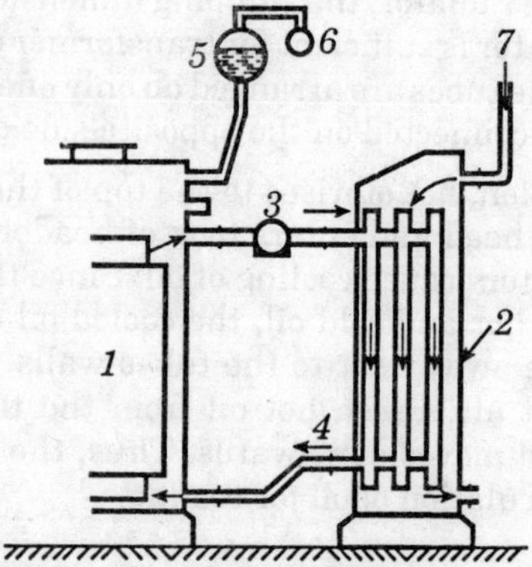


1. Transformer tank. 2. Cooler for (Forced oil-forced water).
3. Oil-pump 4. Return path of oil.
5. conservator. 6. Breather.
7. Direction of flow of cooling water.

Fig. 9.5. Oil-Forced water cooling system and cooling system with separate heat exchanger.

There are five methods of heat exchanger

1. Natural oil circulation through the heat-exchanger.
2. Forced oil circulation through the heat-exchanger, without air blast.
3. Natural oil circulation and additional forced air.
4. Forced oil circulation and additional forced air.
5. Forced oil circulation and forced water circulation.

The natural oil circulation in enough for no-load operations. The coolant oil pumps are started at certain load. The air-blast fans are started at yet a higher load.

The control of cooler pumps and fans is arranged such that the starting of pumps corresponds to the load-on the transformer.

## 9.8. MATERIALS AND MANUFACTURING TECHNIQUES

The tanks are fabricated of high grade boiler plate steel. Special measures are taken to combat the effects of stray flux resulting both from high current carrying conductors and from leakage flux with non-magnetic steel applied where necessary.

Welding is carried out in accordance with strict standards, with double weld is provided where oil lightness in required. All oil tight welds are tested to ensure that no oil leakage will occur. Double threaded studs are provided for the mounting of accessories.

## 9.9. SURFACE TREATMENT AND PAINTING

The tanks are shot-blasted from inside and outside to prepare a good, clean surface. The rough beads on welded joints are chipped off and ground. The tank and the joints are thoroughly cleaned with blast off compressed air. A red oxide premier coat (of zinc oxide, zinc chromite and iron oxide pigments with synthetic alkyd-resin base) is applied to the surface. After drying, paint of grey colour or that required by the customer is given.

Low gloss finish is a better appearance than the high gloss finish. The defects in surface are not clearly visible with low glass paint.

All surfaces are thoroughly cleaned and treated to remove all rust and the scales prior to painting. A primer coat with two-layer paint on epoxy base is then applied. Over this primer a finishing coat with two-layer paint on epoxy-urethane base is applied to a total thickness of not less than 80 microns. The paint is applied in continuous coats without visible running drops, blisters, pinholes or any other defects, to achieve a smooth, uniform surface.

After applying, each paint-coat is cured in an oven at 125°C. The air in the oven is circulated and filtered to ensure that no particles will contaminate the wet paint.

Before applying the next paint-coat, the parts are cooled off to room-temperature. The thickness of the coatings is individually tested and kept within close tolerances.

In addition to external painting, all transformers are painted internally with white epoxy based two layer paint. Besides constituting protection against corrosion, this ensures that no metal particles can loosen from the surfaces and also makes it easier to keep the details clean during the following assembly operations.

**Extra painting.** If the environmental conditions with respect to humidity, salt etc., are severe, it is advisible to apply two coats of both primer and finishing paint to the tank and thus achieve a total thickness of minimum 140 microns.

## 9.10. STANDARD FEATURES AND ACCESSORIES WITH THE TANK

Transformer tanks are provided with welded or bolted covers. High quality nitrile rubber gaskets, inserted in grooves, are used for bolted covers. Alternatively for smaller units a synthetic rubber impregnated cork gasket can be used. A flat base, or a base plate reinforced with a channel construction designed for skidding, is available. Wheels can also be provided.

The following accessories are included as standard features with the tank.

— Lifting lugs and pulling eyes
— Manholes for inspection and assembly
— Valves for oil treatment and draining
— Earthing terminals
— Spring loaded pressure relief device with alarm contacts (optional)

## 9.11. ASSEMBLY OF COMPONENTS

The tank and the various other components are brought in the assembly shop. The core and coil assembly is dried out in a separate chambers by vapour drying process or other suitable process. The dried core and coil assembly is lowered into the tank. The tank cover is placed properly with the gasket in its place. The nuts and bolts between the flange of the tank and the top plate are tightened by torque spanners to the required tightness. The assembly is evacuated to remove dust and moisture. The tank is filled with oil of required purity and dielectric strength. The other fitments such as bushings, cooler, voltages etc., are fitted and the transformer sent to the test bed.

## 9.12. INSTALLATION OF COOLERS

The coolers for large transformers incorporate the following:

— Pipe for flow of oil
— Valves in oil-flow circuit
— Motor-pumps, for oil circulation
— Radiators
— Cooling fans and motors
— Supply circuit for fan-motors.

A wall is provided between neighbouring transformers.

## 9.13. ARRANGEMENT OF TERMINAL BUSHING AND OTHER FITTINGS

The fitments and provisions on the top cover include the following:

— HV Terminal Bushings

— LV Terminal Bushings
— Neutral Bushings
— Lifting eye-bolts for top plate
— Flange for connecting the tank with the conservator
— Flange for mounting the tap changed head
— Pocket for thermometer, etc.

## 9.14. FITMENTS WITH THE TRANSFORMER TANK

The various components fitted to the transformer tank include the following:

1. Oil Conservator
2. Breather
3. Oil Sampler
4. Buchholz Relay
5. Pressure Relief Relay
6. Oil Indicator
7. Oil Temperature Indicator
8. Winding Temperature Indicator
9. HV Bushings, LV Bushings and MV Bushings, Neutral Bushings.
10. Oil Filling System
11. Tap Changer
12. Cooling System
13. Lightening Arrestor
14. Neutral Grounding Arrestor
15. Truck on Rollers
16. Marshalling Kiosk etc.

**Part B—Cooling Systems**

## 9.15. METHODS OF COOLING

The losses in a transformer are of the order of 1% of its full load kW rating. These losses get converted into heat. Thereby the temperature of core, windings, oil and tank rises. The heat is dissipated from the transformer tank and the cooler into the atmosphere. The cooling of transformer helps in maintaining the temperature rise in various parts within permissible limits. In case of transformers, there are no rotating parts and the heat transfer takes place by circulation of oil. When thermal convection is not sufficient, forced circulation is adopted.

Small transformers have adequate cooling surface to radiate all the heat caused by the losses. The surface area is increased by means of cooling tubes and radiators.

As the size and rating of the transformer increase, the losses increase at a faster rate than the tank surface. Thus the tank surface area becomes inadequate and tubes/radiators become necessary. For yet higher ratings, the size of the tank and cooler by natural convection of oil becomes uneconomical and forced oil cooling becomes necessary. The oil is circulated through the transformer tanks by means of oil pumps. Within the tanks, the oil is directed to flow through the space between coils of the windings. Such a design is known as directed oil flow type. In directed oil flow, heat transfer is more effective than in plain self cooled transformers.

Several different combination of natural,forced, air, oil, cooling are applied to transformer. The choice depends on rating, size and local conditions.

## 9.16. DESIGNATIONS AND NOMENCLATURE

The type of cooling is identified by the standard designation, A.N., A.F., O.N., A.N., O.N.A.F., O.F.A.N., O.N.W.F., O.F.W.F, and combinations thereof several cooling methods are possible for transformers. The symbols used are:

(a) *Medium*
- Air—A
- Gas—G
- Synthetic oil—L
- Mineral oil—O
- Solid insulation S
- Water—W

(b) *Circulation*
- Natural—N
- Forced—F

**Table 9.1. Types of Cooling of Power Tr insformers**

| *Symbol* | *Title* | *Description* |
|---|---|---|
| O.N.A.N. | Oil Natural Air Natural | This is widely used for transformer upto 30 MVA. Transformer are fitted with penal type radiators for Oil Natural circulation. |
| O.N.A.F. | Oil Natural Air Force | This is widely used for transformers between 30 MVA and 60 MVA the panel type radiators are provided with cooling fans. Fans are switched on during heavy loads only. |
| O.F.A.F. | Oil Forced Air Forced | This method is used for transformers above 60 MVA. The oil is circulated through coolers. The coolers have cooling fans to exchange heat from oil to air. |
| O.F.W.F. | Oil Forced Water Forced | The heat is exchanged from oil to cooling water. Both oil and cooling water are circulated through heat exchanger. Oil is kept at slightly more pressure than water to avoid the chances of water ingressing into oil. |
| A.N. | Air Natural | The ambient air is used for cooling. This method is useful for oil less transformers (dry type) upto 5 MVA. |

**Methods of Cooling:**

1. *Air cooling for dry type transformer:*
1.1 A.N. — Air Natural
1.2 A.F. — Air Forced
2. *Cooling for oil immersed transformers:*
2.1 O.N.A.N. — Oil Natural Air Natural
2.2 O.N.A.F. — Oil Natural Air Forced
2.3 O.F.A.N. — Oil Forced Air Natural
2.4 O.F.A.F. — Oil Forced Air Forced
3. *Oil Immersed Water Cooling:*
3.1 O.N.W.F. — Oil Natural Water Forced
3.2 O.F.W.F. — Oil Forced Water Force

Details are given in the table 9.1.

## 9.17. AIR NATURAL COOLING

This is applicable to dry type transformers only. The ambient air is used. The surface of the tank provides the heat transfer from the transformer to the ambient air. Plain sheet steel tanks can transfer about 12 $W/m^2$ per °C temperature rise. Small transformers below 25 kVA can be readily cooled by air natural cooling. However, air natural cooling is also used for large dry type transformers.

The cooling takes place by convection currents of air within the transformer tank and by radiation from the tank's surface to the ambient air. Convection of air currents is suitable only in case of small machines.

## 9.18. AIR FORCED COOLING

This is also used for dry type transformers. The air is forced on to the tanks surface to increase the rate of heat dissipation. The fans are switched on when the temperature of winding increases above permissible limits.

## 9.19. OIL NATURAL AIR NATURAL (Figure 9.2)

This is the most widely used method of cooling for oil filled transformers upto about 30 MVA. In Oil Natural cooling, the oil in the tank gets heated due to the heat generated in the core and the windings. The hot oil flows upwards and the cold oil comes downwards according to the principle of convection. The oil flows within the transformer tank by natural convection of oil, hence, the cooling method is known as oil natural cooling. The heat is transferred from the core and the windings to the surrounding oil. The oil transfers the heat to the tank's surface. The tank transfers the heat to the air.

Plain tanks are used for transformers rated upto about 50 kVA. Above this rating, the cooling area is increased by providing cooling tubes. However, for transformers above 5 MVA, the losses are of the order of 50 kW and oil natural cooling is not adequate and forced cooling becomes essential.

## 9.20. OIL NATURAL AIR FORCED COOLING (Fig. 9.3)

In this method, air fans are mounted near the transformer and the forced air is directed on to the cooling tubes to increase the rate of cooling. The fans are provided with automatic starting. When the temperature of oil windings increases above specified limits, the thermostats switch on cooling fans. This happens during heavy loads/higher ambient temperatures.

In high capacity transformers, where the surface of the radiators with natural circulation of oil cannot dissipate enough heat, forced air cooling is used. Two fans are used to force air blast on each radiator. Forced air cooling increases the heat dissipation rate (refer table). The cooling system in which the oil circulates by natural thermal heat and the blast of the air is directed towards radiator is called (O.N.A.F.) oil natural air forced cooling.

Table 9.2. Heat Dissipation Rates

| *Oil natural cooling* | *Oil natural air forced* | *Oil forced air forced* |
|---|---|---|
| 450 W/m$^2$ | 750 W/m$^2$ | 1000 W/m$^2$ |

## 9.21. OIL FORCED AIR FORCED COOLING (Fig.9.6.)

Transformers above 60 MVA employ a combination forced oil and forced air cooling. Oil natural and the forced oil cooling is not adequate to remove the heat caused by the losses which is approximately equal to 1% of the transformer rating (6 kW). In case of forced oil, forced air cooling system, a separate cooler is mounted away from the transformer tank. The cooler is connected with the transformer tank with two pipes, one at the top and the other at the bottom. The oil is circulated by pump from the top of the transformer tank to the cooler. The cold oil from the cooler is returned to the transformer tank by the bottom pipe. The cooler (or radiator) is equipped with fans which give an air blast on the cooling tubes.

## 9.22. OIL FORCED WATER FORCED COOLING (Fig. 9.5)

Such cooling system needs a heat exchanger in which the heat of transformer oil is given to cooling water. The cooling water is taken away and cooled in separate coolers. The oil is forced through the tubes of heat exchanger. The oil from transformer tank is taken out from top pipe and forced into the heat exchanger. Oil from the heat exchanger is sent back to the transformer tank through the bottom pipe.

In the heat exchanger, the oil is cooled by the water which is forced through the cooling pipes of the exchanger. *The hot oil enters the header of the heat exchanger at the bottom* and leading it at top, while the cooling

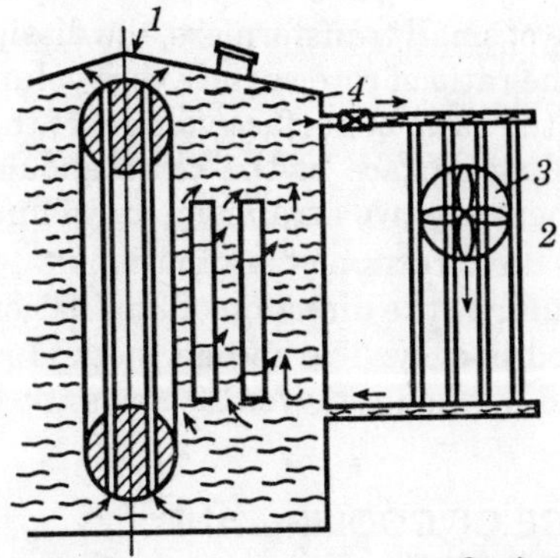


1. Tank 2. Cooler
3. Fan 4. Oil-pump

Fig. 9.6. Oil Forced Air Forced (OFAF)
(Oil Directed Flow through core ducts and winding ducts.)

water flows through the pipes in the opposite direction, *i.e.*, from the top of the heat exchanger downwards.

With detachable radiators or separate coolers, flange connections are provided between the transformer tanks and the pipes. Valves are provided in the top and bottom pipes. The valves enable dismantling of radiators, without draining the transformer tank. Furthermore the transformer can be dispatched, filled with oil and the radiator and cooling system can be assembled at site.

## 9.23. CHOICE OF TYPE OF COOLING FOR LARGE TRANSFORMERS

The choice depends upon power rating, local ambient temperature, installation conditions, method of operation etc.

Natural cooling is most economical and reliance for small and medium transformers upto about 15 MVA. Forced cooling increases the initial cost and maintenance cost.

Depending upon cost of civil works, area transportation,weight etc., artificial cooling becomes economical for transformers above 10 MVA. Between 10 and 100 MVA, forced ventilation or radiators becomes economical. Air blast coolers are preferred above 100 MVA.

Cooling by forced water is preferred only in certain condition of high ambient, steel work, underground substations etc.

## 9.24. HEAT TRANSFER

Heat transfer is a complex phenomena as it involves several variables. The heat is dissipated by conduction, convection and radiation.

Cool oil is passed through passages in the windings and conducts away the heat. The flow of oil is directed through passages in the winding by means of arrangement of baffles and cylinder as illustrated in the figure. In case of small transformers, the dissipation of heat from the core is easy as the ratio of core surface/core volume is large. In case of very large cores, the ratio of surface/volume of the core is relatively small. So that, cooling surface of the cores should be increased by additional ducts. There are two arrangements of ducting:

1. Parallel to the direction of laminations.
2. Perpendicular to the direction of laminations.

The first method is easy. The second method requires punching. However, the second method removes 20 times the heat than the first method.

## 9.25. SIGNIFICANCE OF COOLING AND TEMPERATURE RISE

The permissible load for a given transformer is determined by the limits of temperature rise for oil, windings and other parts. The copper losses are proportional to the square of current. The copper losses causes heating of windings. The heat causes temperature rise of the oil. The insulating materials used in transformers have limits of temperature rise. The loading of the transformer should be such that these limits of temperature rise are not crossed. If temperature rise is more than the permissible limits, the life of insulation is drastically reduced. The temperature rise depends upon loading. The actual temperature is given by the ambient temperature plus the temperature rise. Since the maximum temperature for various insulating materials is specified, the limit of temperature rise (therefore the loading) will depend upon the ambient temperature. The insulating materials used in transformer are classified on the basis of maximum permissible temperature. The temperature classification of insulating materials is as given below:

$Y — A — E — B — F — H — C$

Table 9.3.

| *Insulation Class* | *Y* | *A* | *E* | *B* | *F* | *H* | *C* |
|---|---|---|---|---|---|---|---|
| *Maximum permissible temperature* °C | 90 | 105 | 120 | 130 | 155 | 180 | 180 above |

A transformer is provided with oil temperature indicator and winding temperature indicator. The permissible oil temperature is 65°C and hot spot temperature is 80°C at rated load. By providing better cooling, with the given limits of temperature rise, the load on the transformer can be increased. In other words, the transformer can be up-rated. Alternatively in the same rating, the requirements of active material in a transformer are reduced with better cooling.

Figure 9.7 shows temperature curve for a oil natural and air natural cooled transformer. Fig. 9.8 illustrates a typical temperature diagram for a OFAF transformer.

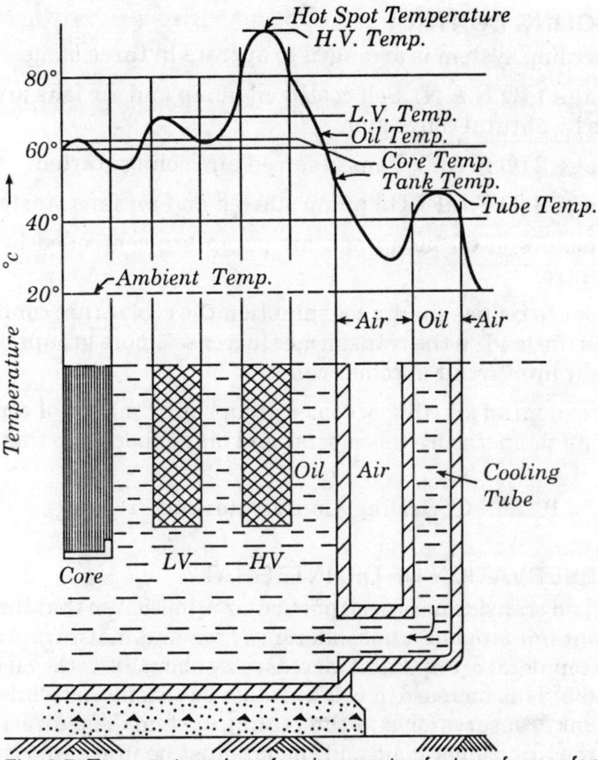


Fig. 9.7. Temperature rise of various parts of a transformer for Oil Natural, Air-Natural (ONAN) Cooling

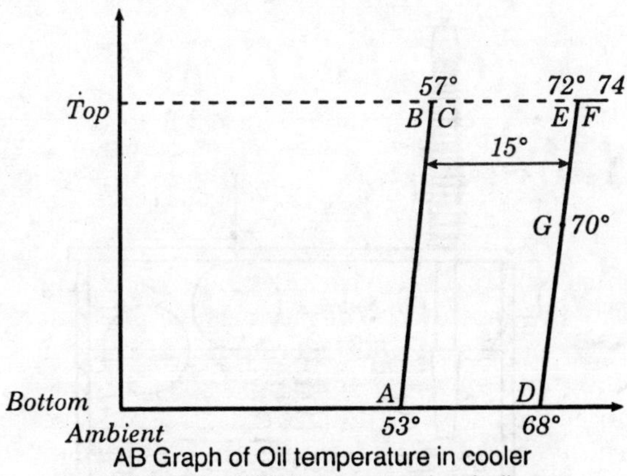


AB Graph of Oil temperature in cooler

AC Graph of Oil temperature in winding

DE Graph of copper temperature in windings

F Hot-spot temperature in winding copper

G Average temperature rise of copper in winding.

Fig. 9.8 Temperture Diagram for OFAF

## 9.26. COOLING CONTROL

The cooling system is arranged to operate in three stages.

1. **Stage 1** (O.N.A.N). Self cooled oil pump and air fans are off. Oil circulates by natural convection.

2. **Stage 2** (O.N.A.F). Fans of forced air cooling started.

3. **Stage 3** (O.F.A.F). Oil pump started and air fans started.

The motors of oil pump and air pump are controlled by cooling system control.

In order to reduce energy consumption,the coolers are connected in groups. As the load on the transformer increases,more groups of coolers are brought into circuit automatically.

The sequential starting of cooler groups is by means of contacts in the winding temperature thermostat and oil temperature thermostat.

### PART– C : Sealing, Conservator and Breathers

## 9.27. PRESERVATION OF OIL INTEGRATY

Oil filled transformers need particular attention so that the oil does not get contaminated by atmospheric oxygen and moisture. However, when the temperature of the oil increases by about 80°C the oil expands by about 6%. This increase in volume must be considered while designing the tank, conservator and the cooling system, The direct contact between the atmospheric air and the oil must be prevented by proper sealing of the tank and use of modern conservator with air bag.

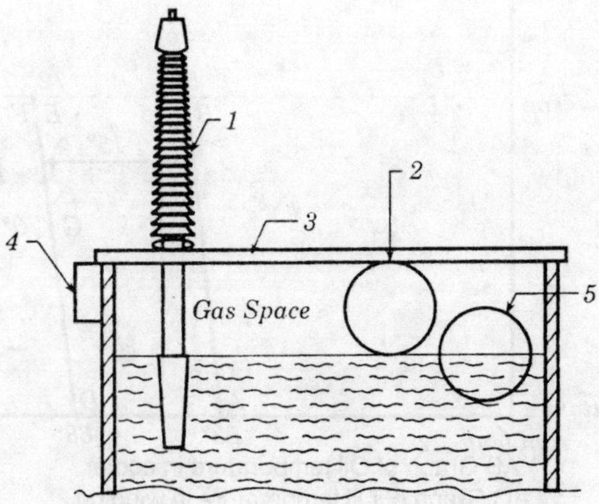


1. Bushing, 2. Gas=pressure gauge 3. Tank cover
4. Pressure-vacuum bleeder 5. Oil-level gauge
Fig. 9.9 Sealed tank filled with dry nitrogen in vacant space.

## 9.28. SEALED TANK

Some small transformers are sealed. Practically all the distribution transformers and some power transformers upto 50 MVA are with sealed tanks. Above 50 MVA, this method is not used and oil is allowed to expand into the conservator.

Figure 9.9. shows sealed tank construction. The space between the oil level and the tank cover is filled with dry nitrogen.

The automatic nitrogen system is shown in Fig. 9.10.

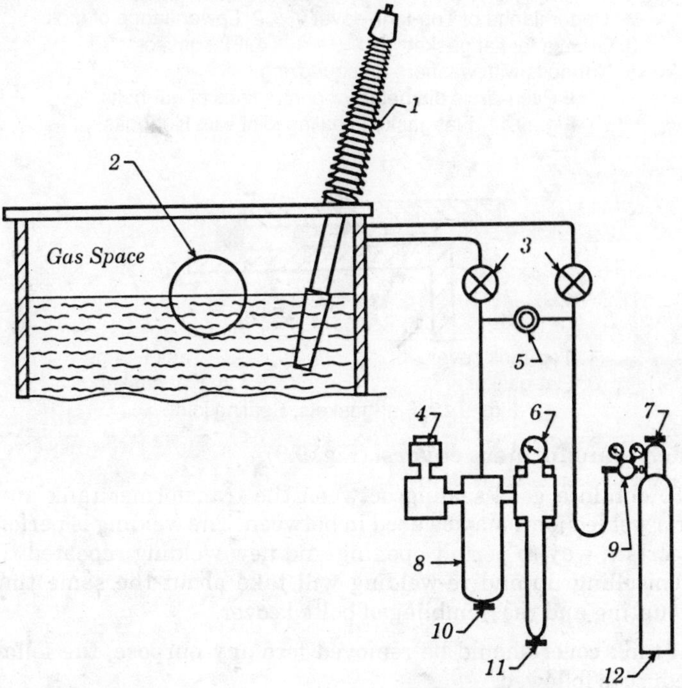


1. Bushing
2. Oil-level gauge
3. Shut-off valves
4. Low-pressure alarm
5. By-pass valve
6. Pressure gauge
7. High pressure control valve
8. Nitrogen receiver (sump)
9. Prressure regulator
10. Exhaust valve
11. Relief valve
12. Gas-cylinder

Fig. 9.10. Nirtrogen filling system.

## 9.29. METHOD OF FIXING THE TANK COVER WITH THE TANK. (Figure 9.11 and 9.12)

The sealing should be leakfree. In order to ensure good sealing, the flange of the tank cover in fixed on the fixed on the flange of the tank with a gasket in between. The gaskets is squeezed to about 20%. This ensures leak free joint.

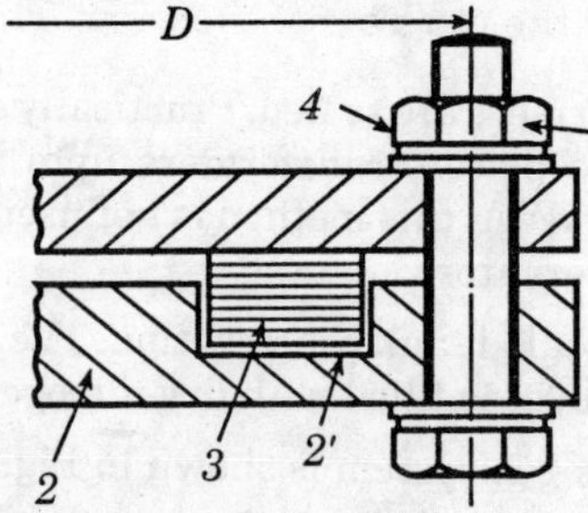


1. Upper flange of Top-tank cover 2. Lower flange of tank
3. Groove for flat gasket 4. Flat gasket
5. Nut-bolts with washers for squeezing

D = Pitch-circle diameter for centre lines of nut-bolts.

Fig. 9.11. Flat-gasket, sealing joint with Nut-bolts

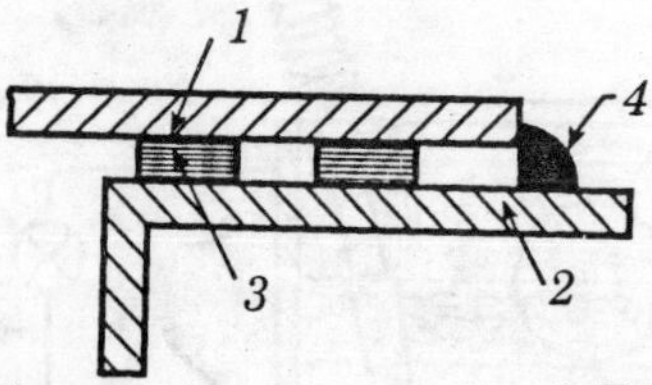


1. Top-tank cover 2. Tank Flange
3. Flat-gasket 4. Flat gasket

Fig. 9.12. Flat-gaskets, Sealing joint.

**Welded transformers covers.** (Fig. 9.9)

To obtain a good sealing between the transformer tank and the cover a welded joint may be used in between. The welding is performed in a certain way to permit opening and new welding repeated times. The chiselling up and re-welding will take about the same time as dismounting and reassembling of bolted cover.

If tank cover should be removed fore any purpose, the following procedure is followed:

When opening the cover the welding joint are to be removed by a suitable emery wheel, the cover should be clamped to the frame by means of G-clamps to prevent iron chips from penetrating the tank. Any parts of the weld which may possibly remain on the tank flange should be removed by a chisel to enable a good result of the re-welding. When fitting the cover again, nitrite-rubber bonded cork gaskets, $25 \times 5$ is fitted on the tank flange (see figure).

The gasket is kept in the correct position with glue based on neoprene-rubber base. The cover should be clamped to the tank flange by means of G-clamps evenly distributed along the flange with about 600 mm spacing. Tank welding is carried out over about 100 mm spacing. An extra G-clamp is used during the tank welding and is moved along the flange during the progress of the work. The continuous weld is then applied. Finally the weld should be cleaned and painted.

When welding, a fire-extinguishing equipment should be available, and the work supervised by fire protection personnel.

### Material for Gaskets

For sealing the joints between the transformer tank flange and the tank cover flange, other flanges fitted on the tank cover and fitments etc., seals (Gaskets) are used. Following materials are used.

— Nitril rubber bonded cork
— Nitril rubber
— PTFE Washers and tapes etc.

### Gaskets for Porcelain Bushing (Fig. 9.13)

The bushing porcelain (1) is cemented with its (3) is porous and does not give leak-free joint. O-ring (6) is squeezed between the ground surface of porcelain and the surface of the groove. The squeezing of

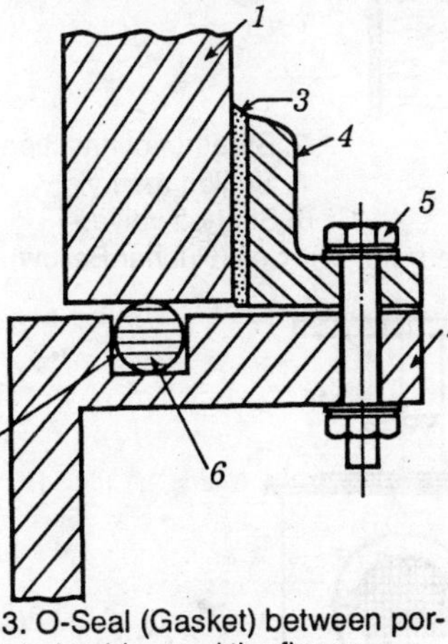


1. Porcelain
2. Flange of Turret
2'. Groove in the flange
3. Cement
4. Flange of porcelain
5. Nut-bolts for squeezing the O-ring

Fig. 9.13. O-Seal (Gasket) between porcelain-bushing and the flange.

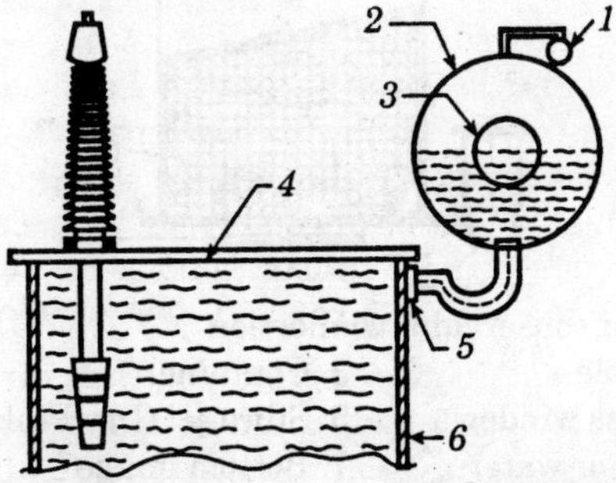


1. Breather 2. Conservator
3. Oil-level gauge 4. Tank-cover
5. Shut-off valve 6. Tank.

Fig. 9.14. Schematic diagram of conservator system.

O-ring by about 20% is obtained by tightning the nut-bolts to exact pressure by using torque spanners.

## 9.30. CONSERVATOR (Figure 9.14 and 9.15)

During the alternate load cycles, the oil of transformers expands and contracts. The conservator is connected to transformer tank by means of a pipe. The conservator volume is used for expansion of oil during higher loads.

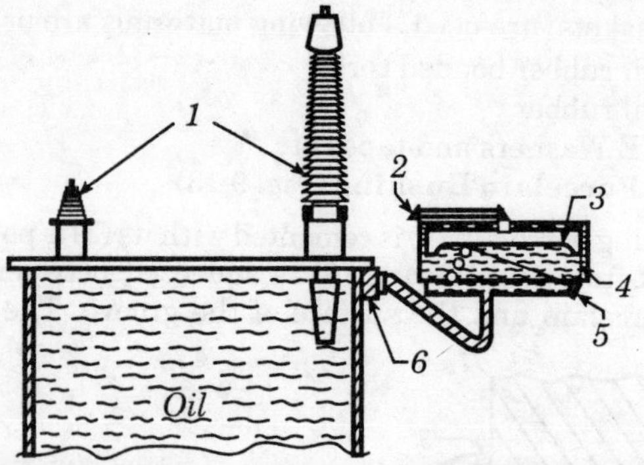


1. Bushings 2. Breather connection
3. Air-Cell (Rubber bellow.) 4. Sealed reservior
5. Oil-level gauge 6. Shut-off valve.

Fig. 9.15. Conservator system with Air-Cell (Rubber Bellow)

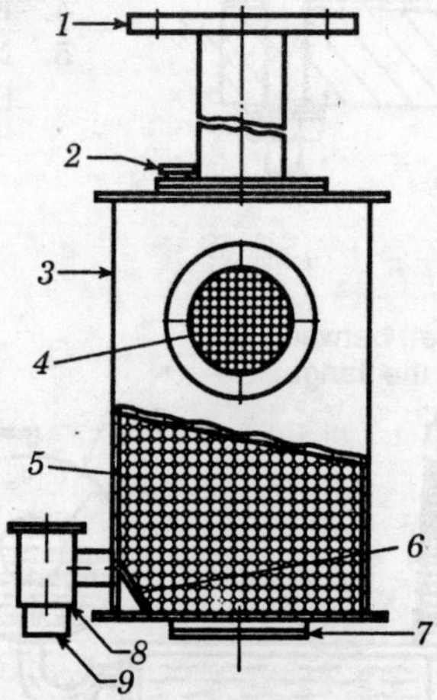


1. Flange for conservator connection
2. Filling-hole 3. Container
4. View-glass window 5. Silica-jel (Dry:Pink; Wet:Blue)
6. Strainer for water 7. Bottom flange
8. Fresh air inlet 9. Oil-seal.

Fig. 9.16. Silica-jel Breather.

The communication of air between the top of the conservator and outside air is through the breather. Breather lets-out expanded air and test-in dry air.

## 9.31. SILICA-JEL BREATHER

(Fig. 9.16)

**Breather.** The breather is filled with silica jel. The silica jel absorbs moisture. The breather is fitted between the air space of conservator and the outside vent. The breathing of transformers during load cycles takes place through the breather. When the load increases, the oil expands and the air from conservator is expelled.

During reduced load, the oil level in the conservator falls down and the atmospheric air is breathed in. This incoming air is taken through the silica-jel breather or activated alumina breather. The silica jel or activated alumina absorb moisture.

Dry silica jel is of pale pink colour.

It turns blue as it absorbs moisture. The wet silica jel can be regenerated by drying.

## 9.32. CONSERVATOR WITH RUBBER AIR-CELL (BELLOW)

Referring Fig 9.15. A rubber Bellow (Air-cell) is attached within the conservator on upper half. It is filled with air at positive pressure by means of a value on upper side of the conservator.

When the load on the transformer increases, losses increase and the oil temperature increases. The oil expands.

The oil in the tank is in communication with the lower part of the conservator. The changes in the level of oil are accommodated by the Rubber. Air-Bellow (Air cell) in the upper half of the conservator. The air in the bellow is dried by the silica-jel in the breather.

# 10

# Audible Noise and Noise Reduction

Transformer noise is due to magnetostriction in core-laminations, air-cooling fans, oil-pumps and vibrations in the tank. For large EHV Transformers, special care is taken in design, manufacture and installation to limit Audible Noise (AN) below specified level. Obviously these activities result in increase in the material cost, manufacturing cost and installation cost of large transformers.

## 10.1. INTRODUCTION

Audible noise (sound) has received attention during recent past due to environmental concern. Large power transformers produce audible noise due to the following:

— Magnetostriction of laminations and vibrations of core.
— Vibrations of tank
— Cooling fans
— Oil-pumps, etc.

The specifications of large transformers include the maximum audible sound level *e.g.*, 65 dB (A) with test performed as per IEC 551.

The Audible Noise is minimised by giving attention to the design features, manufacturing and installation. Audible Noise tests are conducted in the factory and at site to verify that sound levels are within guaranteed values.

## 10.2. NATURE OF SOUND

Sound or Audible Noise is generated by mechanical vibrations in the material, parts; air, oil etc. The sound waves travel through air, oil, solid bodies from the source to the human ears. Above about 53 dB(A), the sound becomes objectionable.

The sound level at listing location reduces as the distance between the source and the listener increases.

Sound is of subjective nature. The response of human ears to sound varies with the frequency.

The response of sound-level meter is calibrated in terms of deci Bel and is denoted by dB(A).

The response of human ear can be different than that of the sound-level meter.

Standard *A* curve of sound level meter corresponds to the response of human ears. Hence audible noise of electrical equipment is measured in dB(A), the *A* corresponds to the measurements by *A* curve meter. Background sound is important. During day time, background noise is higher. Hence the objection to transformer noise is lesser.

## 10.3. CAUSES AND METHODS OF REDUCTION OF TRANSFORMER NOISE

These include the following:

— Magnetostriction
— Vibrations of tank and other members
— Air fans
— Oil pumps
— Corona of busbars/connectors.

**1. Magnetostriction.** The length of laminations increase in the direction of magnetisation and the width reduces accordingly. During AC excitation, the magnetostriction follows 50 Hz wave and the core laminations vibrate at various harmonic frequencies. The frequency of vibrations is higher if some predominate harmonics are present in the magnetic flux. The magnetostriction at 100 Hz is predominate for 50 Hz excitation.

Noise due to magnetostriction is called 'Hum'. It cannot be eliminated totally. But it can be reduced by the following means.

— Use of superior CRGO laminations. Material of laminations should have lesser magnetostriction.
— Better quality of laminations. Waviness, uneven thickness etc. causes more vibrations.
— Better clamping technique for the core.

The laminations should not become losses even after repeated through short-circuits.

— Reduced peak flux density ($B_m$)in the core by using higher cross-section of limbs and yoke (*e.g.,* 1.5 *T* instead of 1.6.*T*).
— Improved technique of core mounting such that core vibrations are not passed on to the tank.

**2. Cooling Fans.** In AF cooling, fans are installed opposite radiator tubes. The sound produced by fans is proportional to the square of the speed of the fan. *A few low speed fans of lower speed produce lesser sound than more number of smaller fans at higher speeds.*

**3. Tank Vibrations.** Leakage flux passing through tank walls produce vibrations-some vibrations are passed on to the tank by the core. Reduced flux density in core, additional stiffners on tank wall at strategic locations are helpful in minimising tank vibrations and associated sound.

**4. Coolant Pumps.** In OF cooling oil pumps used for circulation of oil cause audible sound. Proper foundation and anti-vibration pads help in reducing the noise made by the oil-pumps.

## 10.4. METHODS FOR NOISE REDUCTION

The design and manufacturing methods have been described in Sec. 10.2. The following methods are used in installation;

1. Install the transformer away from office rooms, control rooms, roads, residential and commercial areas.
2. Sound-Absorbing panels fixed on radiators.
3. Sound absorbing wall on two sides.
4. Sound absorbing wall on three or four sides.
5. Sound absorbing enclosure for the complete transformer and cooling system.

**Table 10.1 Summary of Transformer Sound Reduction**

| *Cause* | *Effect* | *Remedial Measures* |
|---|---|---|
| 1. Magneto-striction in core laminations. | Core laminations vibrate at various frequencies giving hum. | —Superior CRGO sheets<br>—Quality of laminations<br>—Lower flux densities<br>—Better clamping. |
| 2. Air fans | Cooling air produces vibrations. | —Reduced speed<br>—Lesser number of low speed, high diameter fans.<br>—Improved mounting<br>—Use of silencers. |
| 3. Oil pumps | Pump-motor vibrations | —Improved alignment<br>—Proper mounting<br>—Better lubrication. |
| 4. Tank vibrations | Vibration of vertical walls. | —Use of stiffners<br>—Reduction of stray flux. |
| 5. Installation | | —Foundation of correct level reduces vibrations in tank. Use stims if necessary.<br>—Proper fastners on foundation bolts.<br>—Use of sound absorbing panel on radiators, coolers.<br>—Sound absorbing wall opposite cooler. (This is required for preventing spread of fire also.<br>—Complete enclosure of transformer tank and cooler by sound-absorbing fire retardant enclosure. |

## 10.5. SOUND OF SHUNT REACTORS AND SERIES REACTORS

Oil Immersed Reactors have much higher sound level due to higher stray fluxes. Details are covered in Chapter 31.

## 10.6. TRANSFORMER SOUND MEASUREMENT

These are carried out as per recommendations of IEC 551 or other relevant standard. A standard calibrated sound-level meter with '*A*' curve is used. The transformer is excited to rated voltage on no-load.

Readings of Audible Noises are taken at specified distance and locations around the tan (*e.g.*, 1 metre from tank in three or four directions, 2 m, 3 m, etc.). Readings are taken at each location.

1. With AF cooling in action.
2. With AF cooling switched off.
3. With AFOF cooling in action.

### Summary

Transformer sound needs consideration at material, design, manufacturing, installation stages. The sound levels are measured at site:

(1) without cooling system energization.
(2) with cooling system energized.

The sound levels dB (A) should be below guaranteed limits.

# 11

# Types of Windings for Distribution Transformers and Large Transformers

The configurations of various types of windings used in distribution transforms and large power transformers have been illustrated in this chapter. Continuous or crossover type winding is with circular conductors are used in smaller transformers.

## 11.1. INTRODUCTION

In core type transformers, concentric, cylindrical windings are placed over each limb. A winding has several turns. The turns can be wound in different forms such as in horizontal disc form or vertical spiral or helical form. The type of a winding is identified in accordance with the method of winding the turns in the coil and placement and connections of consecutive coils. The choice of winding type generally depends upon kV rating and kVA per leg.

## 11.2 FUNCTIONAL REQUIREMENTS AND THEIR SIGNIFICANCE

Windings and associated insulation system should satisfy several diverse requirements such as:

— Ampere-turns and ampere-turn balance.
— Turns ratio.
— Tappings.
— Reactance values, leakage flux.
— Eddy current losses and copper losses.
— Power frequency voltage withstand level.
— Lighting impulse voltage withstand level. Full wave, stopped wave.
— Switching impulse voltage withstand level.
— Temperature size of hot-spot.
— Average temperature rise during loads and overloads by effective cooling.
— Mechanical strength to withstand repeated short-circuit currents, etc.
— Dimensions, size and overall weight within required limits.

Windings and insulation system are sensitive to various hostile stresses such as temperature stresses, electro-mechanical dynamic stresses, dielectric stresses, environmental stresses. During the service, the stresses should be within specified limits and the transformer should withstand them without failure.

## 11.3. TERMS AND DEFINITIONS

**1. HV Winding.** High voltage winding refers to the winding of higher voltage class.

**2. LV Winding.** Low voltage winding refers to the winding of lower voltage class.

**3. MV Winding.** Medium voltage winding refers to intermediate voltage class between HV and LV.

**4. Two winding transformer.** The transformer whose cores carry two independent winding, *i.e.*, HV and LV.

**5. Three winding transformer.** Refers to a transformer whose core carries three independent windings, *i.e.*, HV, LV and MV.

**6. Single phase transformers.** has single phase windings.

**7. 3-phase transformer** has a core having 3-phase magnetic field.

**8. Insulation level** of an apparatus is defined as the combination of voltage values both power frequency and impluse which characterize the insulation of that apparatus with regard to its capability of withstanding dielectric stresses.

**9. Cylindrical winding.** A winding which is of cylindrical shape having its axis in line with the axis of the limb of the core. The coils are held rigidly by press-board sections.

**10. Concentric winding.** A winding having its axis in line with the axis of the core limb. Concentric winding may be of any type such as disc type, spiral type, helical type etc.

*Cylindrical winding is also a concentric winding.* The core type transformer has two or more cylindrical, concentric windings on each limb.

**11. Stranded conductor.** A conductor having several parallel paths formed by sub-conductors (strands). All are bunched together to form one conductor. This is done to reduce the effect of eddy currents.

**12. Turn.** A single loop of a insulated conductor insulated from other turns.

**13. Coil.** It has several turns coil may be either spiral type of disc-type or any other type.

**14. Winding.** It has several coils in series.

**15. Layer.** Generally refers to continuous turns in one cylindrical surface. Alternatively layer may refer to a horizontal layer.

**16. Insulation system.** Assembly of insulating items which supports the windings and leads etc.

**17. Shield.** A metallic sheet or ring having a smooth surface and connected to certain conducting point so as to improve electrical field distribution and reduce the electric stress. The shielding is by capacitive protective rings and by electrostatic shields.

**18. Transposed conductor.** A conductor having several parallel sub-conductors in its cross-section. The position of the sub-conductors is changed with respect to one another along the length. (Continuously)

**19. Transposed winding.** A winding formed by two or more parallel conductors. The relative position of conductor 1, 2, 3, 4....etc., is changed (transposed) along the length of the windings to say 1, 3, 2, 4, then 1, 4, 2, 3 etc.

**20. Pancake winding.** A typical winding used in shell type transformers having consecutive turns in horizontal plane, the side edge of one turn touches those of adjacent turns

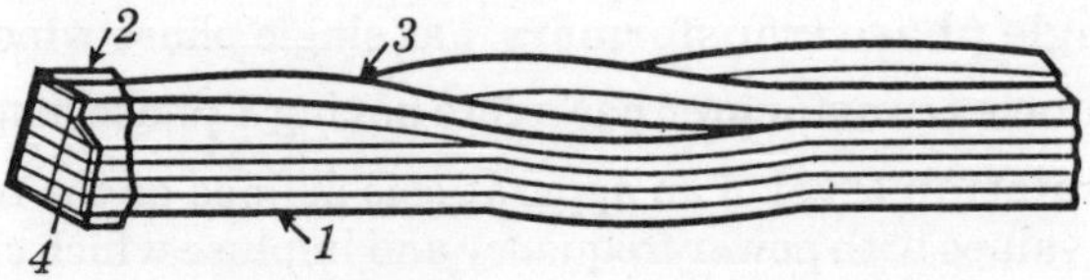


1. Sub-conductor
2. Overall insulation on the transposed conductor
3. Transposition (change in relative position)
4. Insulation over sub-coductor.

Fig. 11.1 Continuously transposed conductor.

## 11.4. CONTINUOUSLY TRANSPOSED STRANDED CONDUCTORS

**A conductor** may be a single conductor or a stranded/transposed conductor. Stranded, continuously transposed conductor (Fig.11.1) is preferred for large cross-sections of a conductor. Stranding reduces eddy current losses and gives flexibility. Transposition results in reduced skin effect, reduced eddy current losses and reduced leakage flux and reduced reactance.

The Disc winding and Helical winding used in large transformers is generally made of continuously transposed, stranded conductors.

For lower currents, lesser cross-section is sufficient and **single conductors** without stranding are preferred. The cross-section of single conductors is either circular or rectangular. Fabricating rectangular conductors is a bit difficult.

## 11.5. TURN, COIL, WINDING

A turn is a single circular loop of an insulated conductor. **A coil** has one or more turns. A **winding** has several continuously wound coils or series-connected coils. The winding may have parallel paths formed by the central entrance divided into two halves or parallel conductors wound together.

The turns may be wound to form the coils in a horizontal plane **(Disc winding, Pan-cake winding).**

The turns may be continuously wound in a concentric cylindrical form **(Spiral winding).** The adjacent edges touch each other.

The turns may be wound helically in a cylindrical concentric shape such that consecutive turn has certain gap filled with oil. **(Helical winding).**

The turns of a circular winding coil may be in the form of thread wound on a bobbin (continuous cylindrical winding with circular conductors). Such coils may be connected in series to form a winding **(cross-over winding).**

The turns may be wound in cylindrical layers (layer winding).

Thus the types of windings are identified according to the configuration of the turns, coils in the three-dimensional space.

A **pane-cake** winding is used only for shell type core (used in USA).

**Cylindrical, concentric windings are used for core-type transformer for LV and HV.** The axis of such a winding coincides with the axis of the vertical limb (leg) of the core, hence the name **concentric**. Windings form a cylindrical sub-assembly with a central hollow portion.

## 11.6. TYPES OF WINDINGS AND CHOICE

The choice of a type of winding depends on

— kVA per leg — kV rating

— Current (kVA/kV) — Number of turns/dimensions.

To obtain required mechanical strength, insulation strength, cooling, etc., for a particular transformer, certain type of winding is preferred for LV and certain type for HV.

Generally LV is placed near the core and HV near tank. This facilitates insulating design.

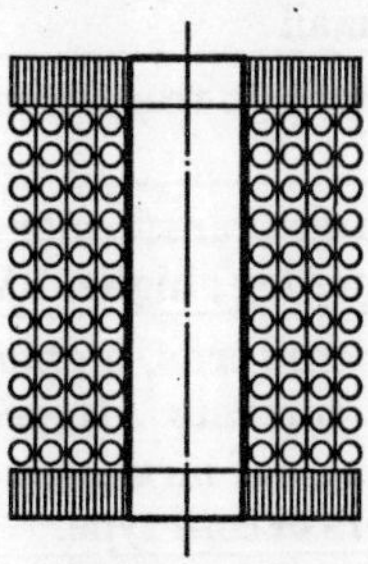

Fig. 11.2.(a) Continuous cylindrical winding with circular conductors (Bobbin type)

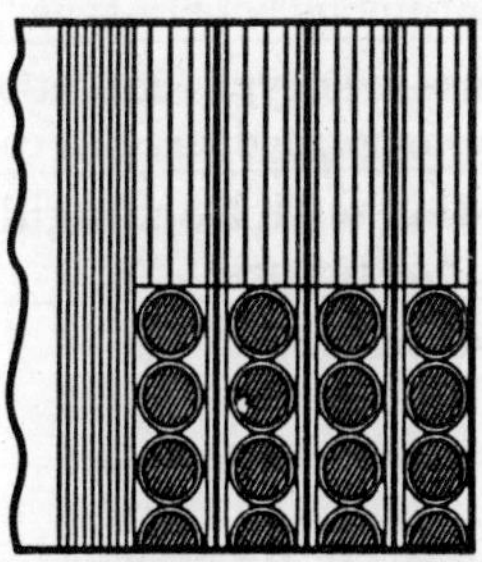

Fig. 11.2.(b) Details of insulation in Bobbin type winding.

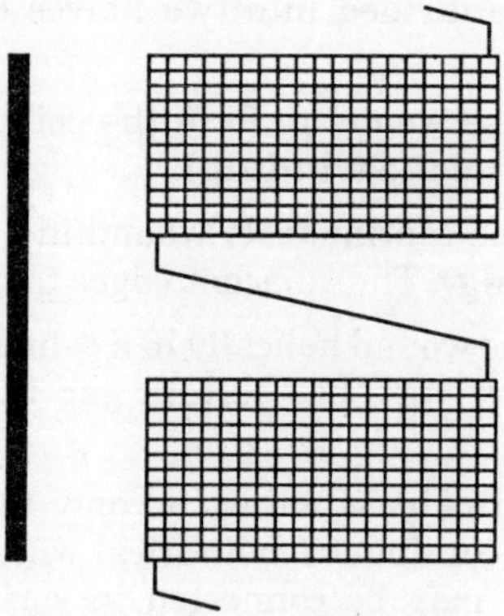

Fig. 11.3. Cross over winding.

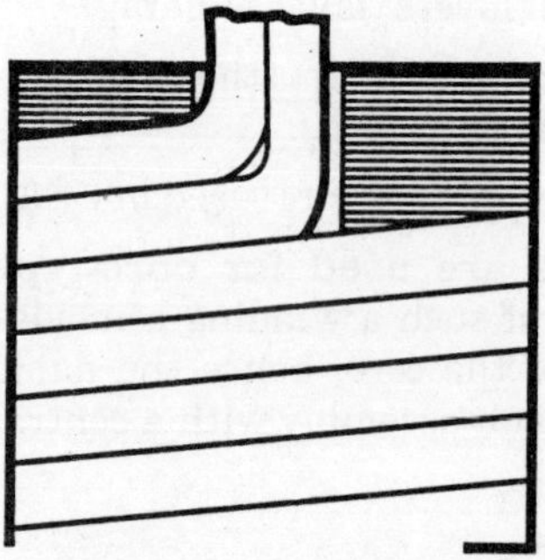

Fig. 11.4. Cylindrical, concentric spiral winding with double conductor spiral. (Used for higher current ratings)

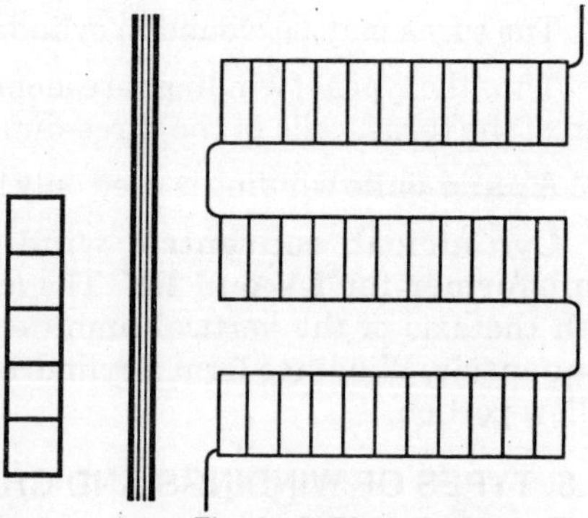

Fig. 11.5. Disc winding.

**Table 11.1 Classification of Windings**

| *Type* | *Remarks* |
|---|---|
| **1. Windings with circular conductors** | |
| 1.1. Continuous bobbin-type | For small |
| 1.2. Cross-over type connections between coils formed circular conductors. | Distribution transformers up to 33 kV |
| **2. Winding with Rectangular Insulated Conductors** | For large transformer of higher kVA per leg ; higher kV |
| 2.1. Disc winding | For more turns, higher voltage, lower currents. Hence for HV windings of large power transformers of core type. |
| *Type* | *Remarks* |

*(Contd...)*

| | |
|---|---|
| 2.2. Helical winding | For lesser turns, lower voltage, higher currents. Hence for LV winding of large transformers of core-type. |
| 2.3. Pan-cake type | For shell type transformers. |

**Table 11.2 Preferred Type of Winding Type**

| *Type of transformer* | *Type of winding* |
|---|---|
| 1. Small transformers | Bobbin type, cylindrical continuous winding with circular conductor. |
| 2. Distribution transformer | —Bobbin type cylindrical winding with circular winding either.<br>1. Continuous type, or<br>2. Cross-over type |
| 3. Medium transformers | 1. Continuous cylindrical winding with rectangular conductors.<br>2. Continuous cylindrical winding with circular conductors<br>3. Above windings with cross-over connections. |
| 4. Large Power Transformers of core type construction | 4. Continuous spiral type winding with rectangular, insulated conductor cylindrical, concentric winding with rectangular, insulated conductors. |
| 4.1. Disc winding | For large number of turns, low current. Hence for LV winding. |
| 4.2. Spiral winding | Only for small kVA/leg. Hence not preferred for larger transformers. |
| 4.3. Helical winding | For lesser number of turns, higher short-circuit strength, higher normal currents. |
| 4.4. Layer winding in multiple layers. | For higher voltages and higher short-circuit strength. |

## 11.7. CYLINDRICAL WINDINGS WITH CIRCULAR CONDUCTORS

Figures 11.2 and 11.5 show a continuous bobbin type windings. The winding is wound on rigid central insulating cylinder. The winding has several cylindrical layers. Flexible insulation of craft paper may be provided in between the layers.

Vertical oil-ducts may be provided between the insulating cylinder and inner cylindrical layer and between intermediate layers (Fig. 11.5. C).

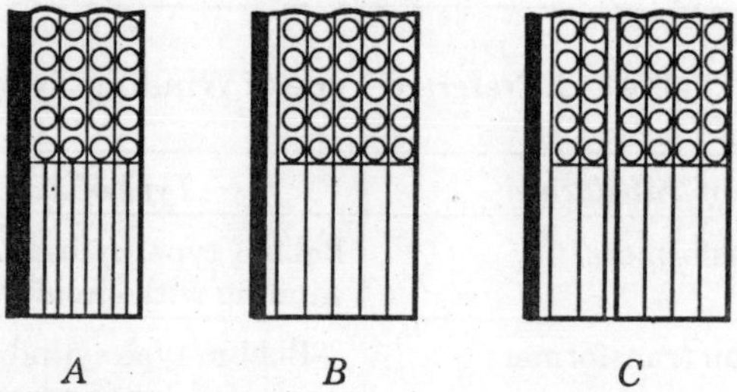


A. Without oil-ducts.

B. With one oil-duct between support insulating cylinder and the winding.

C. With oil-ducts at the beginning and after second layer.

Fig. 11.5 Cylindrical winding with circular conductors (half-cross-section).

For voltages above 33 kV, *electrostatic shield* may be provided below the inner layer (Fig. 11.6).

The shield is of cylindrical metal (brass) sheet (approx. 2 mm thick) and its end is connected to the winding end. Thereby the voltage stress distribution over the inner layers is reduced and becomes more uniform. *Tappings* may also be provided as shown in Fig. 11.6.

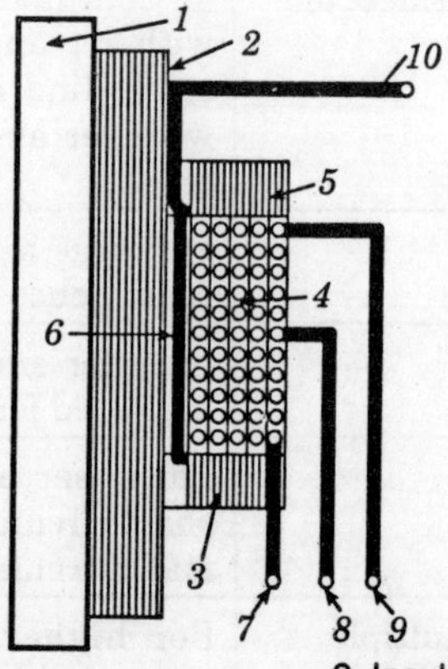


1. Core. 2. Insulating cylinder.
3. Insulating collar. 4. Winding
5. Insulating collar. 6. Voltage grading shield.
7, 8, 9. Tapping leads 10. Shield-terminal.

Fig. 11.6 Shielding and tappings for a bobbin type winding with circular conductors.

**Application.** Cylindrical winding with circular conductors is used for small, distribution transformers for HV windings rated 6.6 kV, 11 kV, 15 kV, 33 kV and with ratings 200 to 300 kVA/leg.

Current density of 3 A/mm$^2$ and cross-sectional area of 13.2 mm$^2$ gives permissible current rating of approx. 40 A for this type of winding with one conductor and 80 A for winding with two conductors wound in parallel.

## 11.8. CROSS-OVER TYPE WINDING WITH CIRCULAR CONDUCTORS

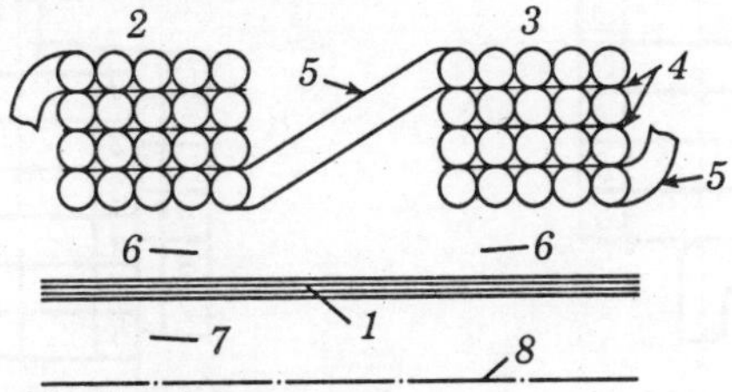


1. Cylindrical insulator support.
2, 3. Coils with circular conductors.
4. Flexible insulation. 5. Cross-over connection.
6. Oil duct. 7. Core.
8. Cente line of core.

Fig. 11.7. Cylindrical winding with circular-conductors and cross-over connections cross-over winding.

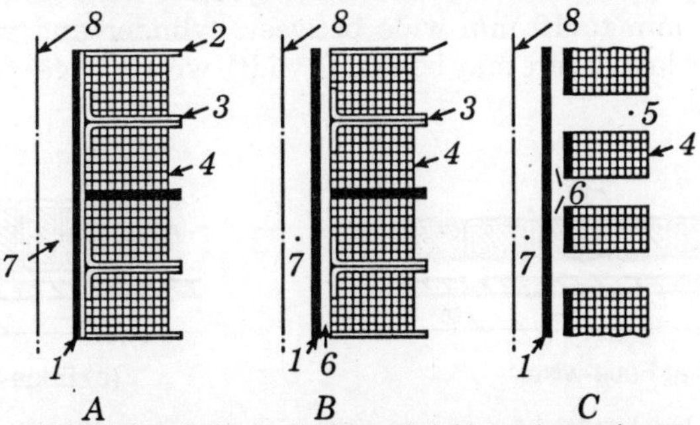


(A) With insulating cylinder and right-angle washers.
(B) With vertical oil duct between cylinder and coils.
(C) With vertical and radial ducts.

1. Insulating cylinder 2. Horizontal insulating washer.
3. L-Shapped insulating washer. 4. Winding.
5, 6. 0.1 duct 7. Core with centre line 8.

Fig. 11.8 Cross-over coils with alternative insulation systems.

Figure 11.7. shows a cross-over connection. Figure 11.8 *A*, *B*, *C* illustrate the insulation systems. Cross-over winding has higher mechanical strength and lower impulse withstand strength. It has the same application range as that of bobbin type continuous cylindrical winding with circular conductors but is preferred for higher short-circuit levels and lower impulse levels.

### 11.8.1. Cylindrical Continuous Spiral Winding with Rectangular Conductors

**Single Layer Type.** Figure 11.9 (a) and Fig.11.9.(b) show the cross-section of a spiral windings with rectangular cross-section.

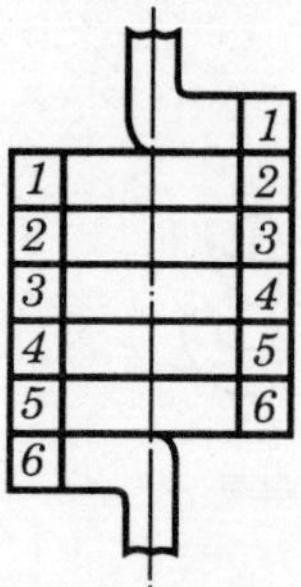


Fig. 11.9. (a) Spiral winding-single layer concentric, cylindrical.

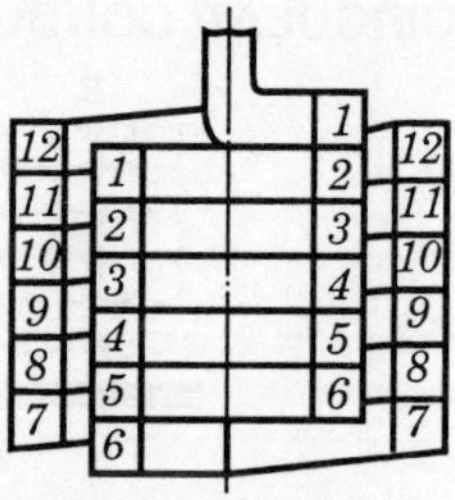


Fig. 11.9. (b) Sprial winding double layer.

[In spiral winding, the sides of insulated conductor touch the adjacent conductor side].

The coil sides touch each other without a gap. The winding is continuously wound over an insulating cylinder with suitable vertical oil ducts 4 mm to 10 mm wide between cylinder and winding and between two layers core may be wound width wise or edge wise as shown in Fig.11.10.

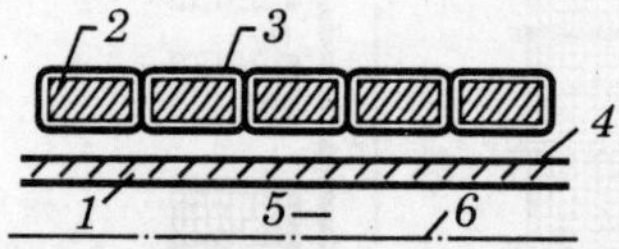


(a) Flat Face-wise

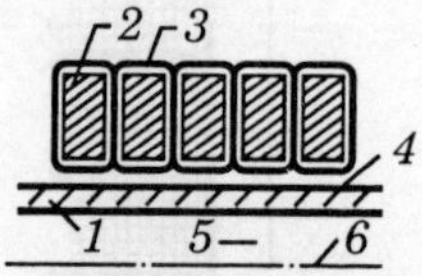


(b) Edge-wise

1. Insulator barrier-press board.
2. Conductor-continuously transposed multi-subconductor with insulation.
3. Conductor insulation.
4. Oil duct.
5. Core limb of core type transformer.
6. Centre line of core limb.

Fig. 11.10. Cylindrical, concentric,spiral winding with rectangular conductors.

**Note.** In spiral winding, the adjucent conductors touch each other without a gap. In Helical winding a gap equal to conductor width is provided between consecutive turns.

**Width OF Oil Ducts in Cylindrical Spiral Winding.**

| | |
|---|---|
| Vertical Ducts between windings | 4 mm to 10 mm. |
| Vertical ducts between winding and insulating cylinder | 4 mm to 8 mm. |
| Vertical duct between winding and core | 4 mm to 10 mm. |
| Horizontal radial ducts | 5 mm to 7mm. |

**Applications.** Cylindrical continuous spiral winding is used mainly for LV windings of distribution transformers for voltages upto 6.6 kV and upto 200 to 250 kVA per leg. (3 phase rating 600 to 750 kVA). It is most common for low voltages upto 1000 V. As the number of turns is less, this type of winding is used only for LV winding of distribution transformer, crosssections of conductors are between 5 m $m^2$ and 200 $mm^2$ with current density of 3 A/$mm^2$, current ratings range is 10 to 600 A.

As there are no intermediate supports, the turns rest against each other. The cooling is not substantial and the mechanical strength is low. Hence such winding is not used for large transformers.

**Multi-Conductor Spiral Winding.** Figure 11.4. shows the concept. Two (or more) conductors are wound simultaneously to form parallel spirals. The two spiral windings are connected in parallel. Cross-section per conductor is reduced resulting in reduced eddy current losses.

## 11.9. CYLINDRICAL HELICAL WINDING

Such a winding is cylindrical, concentric and is wound continuously in the form of a helex. (or a screw-line) as shown in Fig. 11.11.

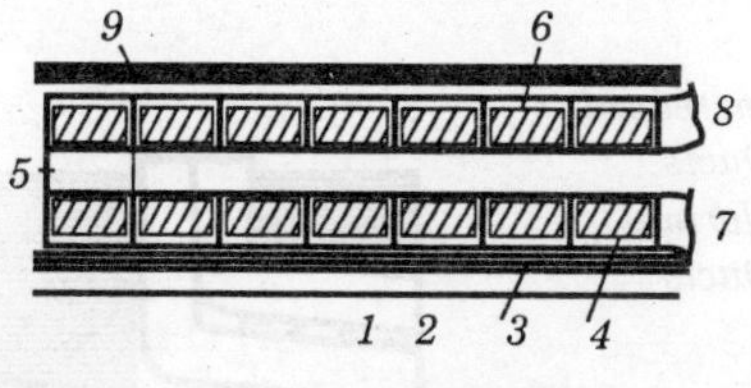


1. Core-limb
2. Centre line of limb.
3. Insulating cylinder.
4. First layer of LVW.
5. Oil duct between 3 and 5.
6. Second layer of LVW
7,8. Start and finish.
9. Barrier between LVW and HVW.
10. HV winding not shown.

Fig. 11.11. Ore side of Cylindrical, Concetric, Double Layer Spiral Winding.

Adjucent conductors are spaced apart by ($\Delta l$) equal to one conductor width ($W$). The space between adjacent conductors is filled with oil.

Winding is made of cable or of predisposed stranded continuously transposed conductor shown in Fig. 11.1.

Helical winding may be with single conductor (Fig. 11.12) or two conductors in parallel (Fig. 11.13) In double conductor helix, two conductors are wound simultaneously in helical form. They are connected in parallel.

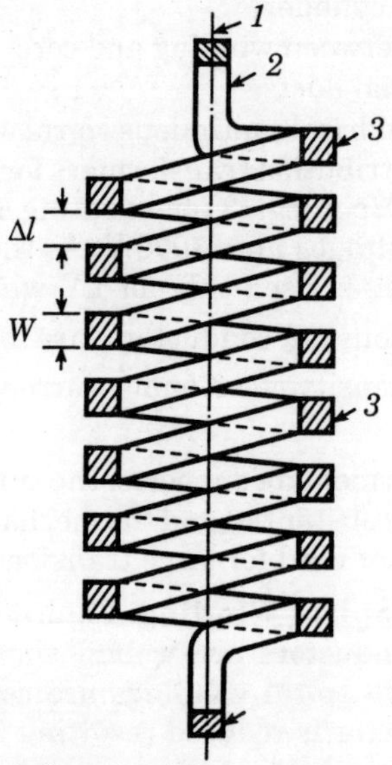


(In helix winding $\Delta L = W$)

1. Axis of the winding. 2. Start.
3. Insulating conductor. 4. End of winding.

Fig. 11.12. Helix winding single helix with a single conductor.

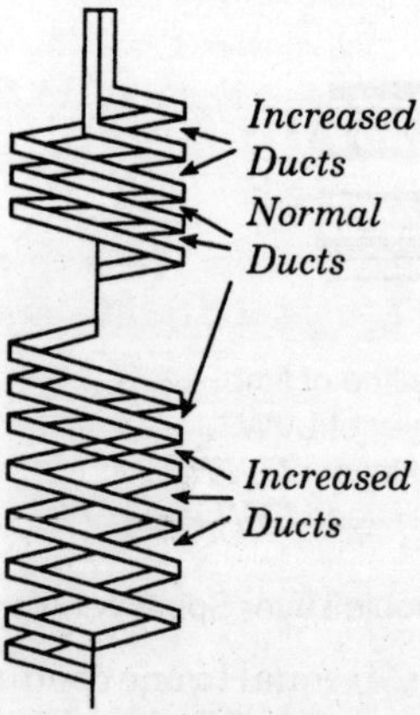


Fig. 11.13 (a) Double conductor Helix-Windings. It has two parallel conductors wound simultaneously in helical form.

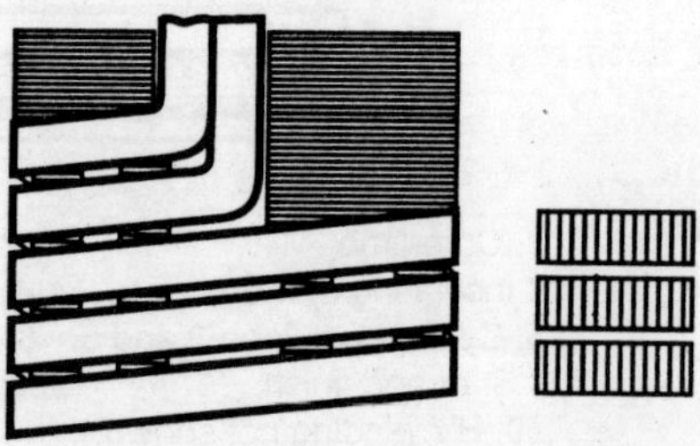

Fig. 11.14. Double conductor Disc Helix Winding. Two conductors are wound helical as shown in Fig. 11.12 (A). However, each horizontal plane has a disc-coil formed by one conductor with seven turns in the disc.

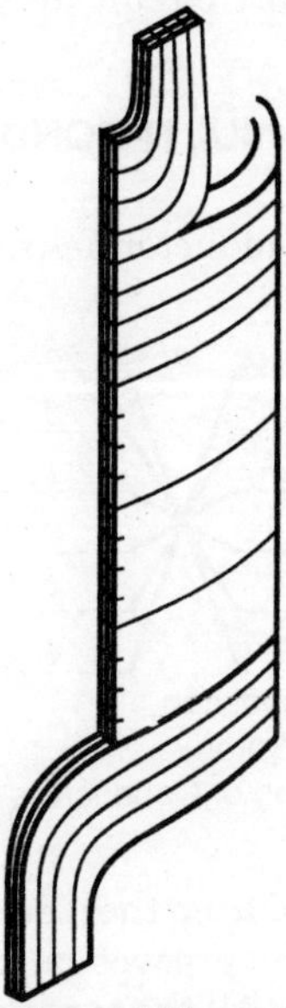

Fig. 11.14. (*a*) Regulating winding : Multi-conductor helical or spiral winding.

## Application

*Helical winding* has less number of turns and each turn is supported on press-board support. Hence the winding is suitable for low number of turns (LV) and higher currents and short-circuit forces, (more kVA/leg). It is seldom used for lesser than 2000 kVA/leg.

Helical winding is used for LT winding of large power transformers. Typical application range is kV 6 to 220 kV, kVA per leg 2000 to 3000. For very large short-circuit strength requirements, long helical cools are not preferred semi-helical windings may be used.

With parallel conductor helical winding, the eddy currents are reduced. Paralled conductor heleix winding is used for larger current ratings.

| **Helical Winding → Low Voltage Winding Less Turns High kVA per leg** |
|---|

## 11.10. REGULATING WINDING-HELICAL WINDING WITH SEVERAL CONDUCTORS WOUND TOGETHER

Whereas the main windings are either of Disc Type or Helical type, the regulating windings can be helical windings in which the winding bunch consists of several conductors. These conductors are then connected in series loops. Connections to tap changer contacts are made between consecutive loops. In any tap changer position, the ampere-turn distribution will be uniform along the limb and the mechanical stresses in the event of a short circuit ar minimised. Figgure 11.14. shows the configuration.

## 11.11. TRANSPOSITION IN MULTI-CONDUCTOR HELIX WINDING

The conductors in multi-conductor helix winding are transposed as shown in Fig. 11.15.

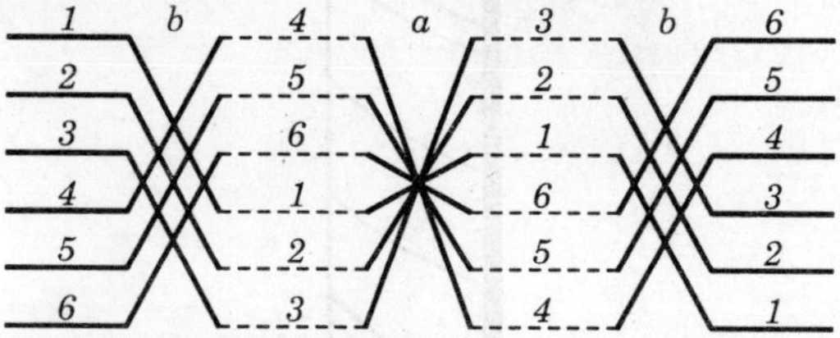


(a) Standard transpositon
(b) Partial Transpositon

Fig. 11.15. Transposition of Conductors in Helical Winding.

## 11.12. DISC WINDING

The name has been derived from the disc coil which is like a musical disc, and the turns are like the grooves on the disc. The disc coil has conductors wound in disc form. All the conductors in one disc coil are in one horizontal plane and follow a continuous circular path of increasing diameter (Fig. 11.16). A disc coil has several turns in a horizontal plane. Number of turns can be a complete integer (4, 6, 8) or a fraction (4.5, 6.5. etc.) several disc coils can be in series to form in a cylindrical concentric winding and in electrical series circuit is without soldered joints.

Each disc coil is supported on press-board sections as shown in Fig. 11.18. The coil has several turns in a horizontal plane. Therefore a large

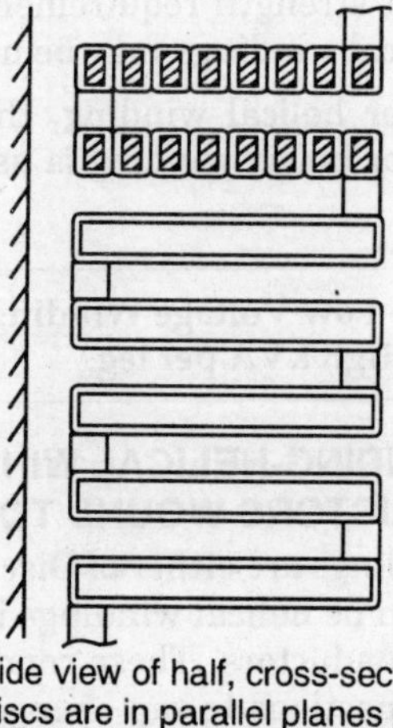

Fig. 11.16. Dic winding. (Side view of half, cross-section) It has several horizontal disc-coil. Consecutive discs are in parallel planes perpendicular to the axis of the coil anld axis of the limb. The consecutive disc coils are continuous connected electrically to form a complete cylindrical : concentric winiding.

number of conductors can be provided per winding. Therefore winding can be used for HV applications.

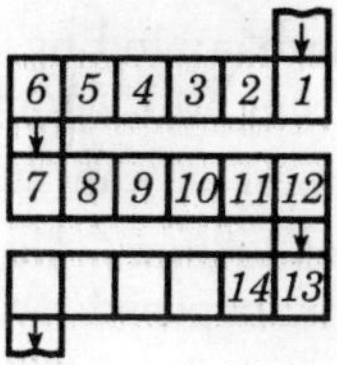


1, 2.......5, 6 : Turns of first disc coil
7, 8,.....11, 12 Turns of second disc coil
13, 14........... Turns of third disc coil

(The conductors are wound continously without any soldering joint in between).

Fig. 11.17. Continuous disc winding

As the coils are of large diameter with flat configuration, short-circuit forces between adjacent coils is large. Hence the winding is comparatively weak.

A series of disc-coils are arranged in parallelly spaced concentric formation to obtain a cylindrical concentric winding (Fig.11.18). Disc winding may be formed by (*A*) parallel discs in pair (Fig. 11.20-*A*). Two disc windings thus formed are connected in parallel. The complete windings are continuous from one end to the other. Alternatively, the winding is in two parallel halves as shown in Fig. 11.20-*B* and 11.19.

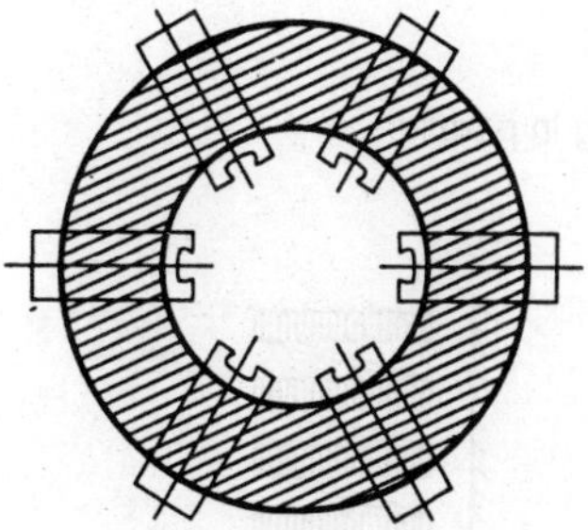

Fig. 11.18. Support for Disc-coil (as seen from Top). Each disc coil is firmly supported on press board brackets.

Fig 11.19. Disc winding with central entrance. Half the disc winding is on upper side and another half on lower side. The disc coils are in horizontal plane. Each disc coil has six turns as seen above. Total cylindrical concentric winding has 14 disc coils as seen above.

The starting is in the middle of the length and at the finishing at two ends which may be connected together to form two parallel halves.

**Application.** Continuous disc winding is used for a very wide range form 3.3 kV to 400 kV and from 50 kVA/leg to several ten thousands kVA/leg, with the cross-section of conductors between 4 m m$^2$ and 50 mm$^2$ and current density of 3 A/mm$^2$. Current range of 12 A to 600A is common. For 600 A rating transposed/stranded conductor with 4 sub conductors may be used.

## 11.13. MULTI-CONDUCTOR DISC WINDING TRANSPOSITION OF CONDUCTORS

Instead of using one conductor to form the disc coil, two to four parallel insulator conductors are wound together to form the disc coil. This ensures reduced eddy current losses *as the cross-section per conductor is reduced.*

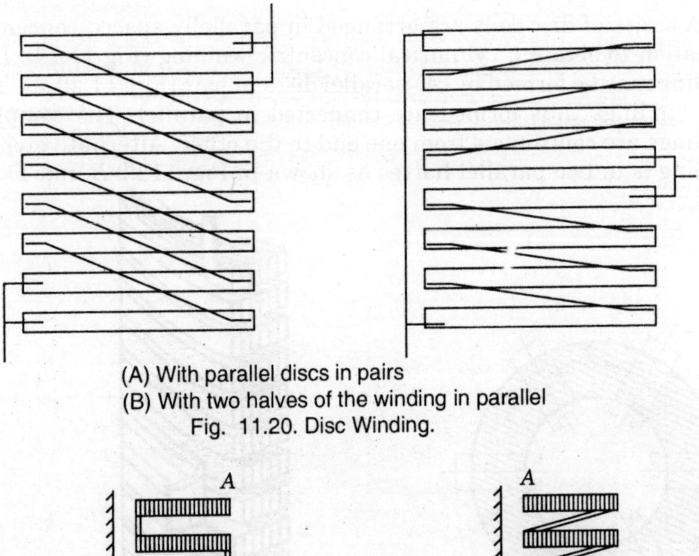

(A) With parallel discs in pairs
(B) With two halves of the winding in parallel
Fig. 11.20. Disc Winding.

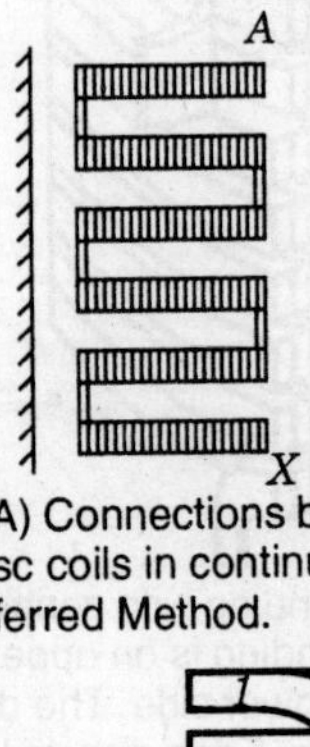


Fig. 11.21. (A) Connections between consecutive disc coils in continuous disc winding. Preferred Method.

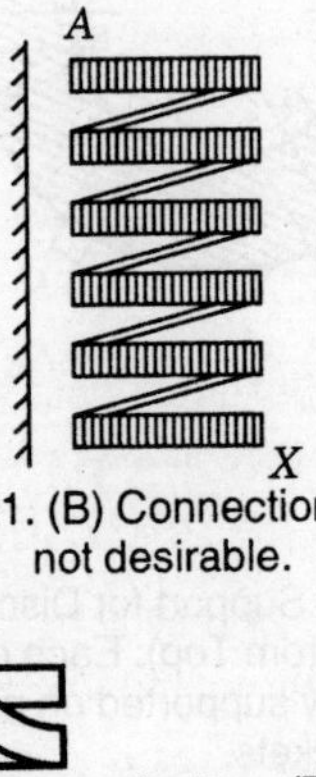


Fig. 11.21. (B) Connection method not desirable.

Fig. 11.22. Typical transposition between four sub conductors. (The relative positions of sub conductors 1, 2, 3, 4 are changed (transposed).

The sequence of the parallel conductor is changed (transposed) while shifting from one disc-coil to the next disc-coil.

A coil turn can have of one or more parallel conductor, its number does not usually exceed four, *as otherwise forming the winding becomes difficult.* The winding is wound on a paper pressboard cylinder and separated from if by pressboard vertical strips. Pressboard spacers are fixed on the strips and form the radial oil ducts between the coils. Figure 11.21. shows a typical configuration.

## 11.14. CHOICE OF WINDING-TYPE

The choice depends on kV rating and kVA per leg. Following choice has emerged from the experience and design requirements.

**For Distribution Transformers (Core Type)**

— Continuous bobbin type, circular conductors
— Cross-over coil connection, circular conductors
— Continuous spiral with rectangular conductors
— Disc winding.

**Table 11.1. Preferred Types of Winding for Distribution Transformer and Large Transformers**

| *No.* | *Name of the winding* | *Voltage in kV* | *Current in a turn in Amps.* | *kVA per leg* | *Cross section-al area of a turn sq.mm.* | *Num-ber of conduc-tors in parallel* |
|---|---|---|---|---|---|---|
| **1.** | For **Distribution Transformers** | | | | | |
| 1.1. | Cylindrical,of circular conduc-tors | Upto 33 | Upto 100 | Upto 200–300 | Upto 30 | 1 to 2 |
| 1.2. | Cross-over type with circular conductors | Upto 33 | Upto 50 | Upto 300 | Upto 15 | 1 |
| **2.** | For Large Power Transformers | | | | | |
| 2.1. | Cylindrical of rectangular con-ductors | Upto 66 often upto 1 kV | 10–600 | Upto 200–250 | 5–200 | 1 to 4 |
| 2.2. | Continuous disc type | 3.3–220 | 10 and above | From 60 to tens of thous-ands | From 4 to 200 and above | 1 to 4 some-times more |
| 2.3. | Helical type in-cluding double-helical | Upto 12 some-times upto 33 | From 300 and above | From 50 to some tens of thous-ands. | 75 to 100 and above | 4 to 16 some-times still more |

**For Large Transformers (Core Type)**

— Disc winding for HT winding
— Helical winding for LT winding
— Modified Helical winding for regulating winding.

## 11.15. MULTI-LAYER WINDING OF SPIRAL OR HELIX TYPE

In spiral or helix type layer winding, each layer has a cylindrical winding in concentric axial form. In multi-layer winding, called popularly as *Layer Winding* three or four concentric layers are placed concentrically as shown in Fig. 11.22. The conseutive layer windings are connected in series to get a complete cylindrical concentric winding.

Multi-layer winding can be used for very high voltages due to its inherent better distributed capacitance. The voltage stress distribution can be further improved by providing cylindrical concentric electro-

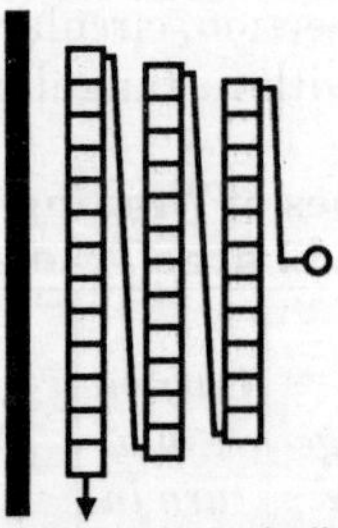

Fig. 11.22. Multi-layer cylindrical spiral winding. (Three to five concentric cylindrical layers are connected in series. Shields are provided as described in chapter 12).

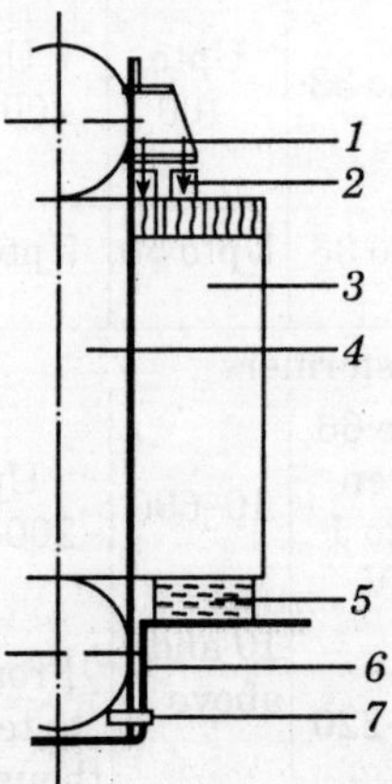


1. Tie-rod
2. Clamping jack
3. Cylindrical winding.
4. Core.
5. Bottom support.
6. Tank with reduced width at bottom
7. Locking pin.

Fig. 11.23. Clamping of cylindrical concentric winding

static screens near core end or outer-end or both-ends. (Refer Chapter 12).

## 11.16. SUPPORTS FOR THE WINDINGS

The winding should be firmly supported by means of clamping jacks and tie rods. Figure 11.23 illustrates a typical arrangement of axial support. Radial support is provided by vertical insulating cylinders and horizontal insulating ribs wedged on the vertical cylinder.

### Summary

The windings for core type transformers are concentric, cylindrical windings of following types:

1. Cross-over type or continuous bobbin type winding with circular cross-section of conductors (only for distribution transformers and small transformers).

2. Spiral type with rectangular crosssection for lower currents, higher voltage, for more number of turns and less kVA/leg.

3. Continuous spiral type with single layer or double layer for higher current and higher short-circuit strength.

4. Helical for higher current, higher short-circuit strength, lesser voltage, lesser number of turns.

Choice depends on kVA/leg, voltage of winding, short-circuit level, etc. Insulation system has been covered in the next chapter.

# 12

# Insulation System, Bushings Shielded Windings and Transient Voltage Distribution

The windings have associated insulation system. The insulation system is exposed to hostile thermal, electro-mechanical, environmental and dielectric stresses simultaneously. It is the weakest part of the transformer. The details have been illustrated in this chapter.

## 12.1. INTRODUCTION

The primary and secondary windings have different potential with respect to the earthed tank and the earthed core. Insulation is necessary between the following:

— HV and LV winding.
— HV winding and earth.
— LV winding and earth.
— Between the turns of the same winding.
— Other conducting parts at different potential with respect to each other and with respect to the tank and core.

The transformer windings are subjected to power frequency voltage stress during normal working condition. The windings are subjected to temporary power-frequency over-voltages during load throw-off. The windings are subjected to transient over voltages due to lightning surges and switching surges. The transformer windings and insulation is subjected to dielectric test to verify the ability to withstand the over-voltages. The various insulation characteristics of a winding are defined by the term *insulation level* of the winding. The insulation level of a winding is co-ordinated with the protective characteristic of surge arresters and the insulation levels of the other sub-station equipments.

For normal power frequency voltage, the voltage distribution along the length of a winding is almost uniform. Hence all the coils are almost equally stressed. During the impluse, surge voltage, the voltage distribution is non-uniform. Initially the stresses on end-turns are higher than the middle turns. However after a few microseconds the oscillations are set-up in the winding due to the inductance, capacitance combinations. *Due to these oscillations, the middle turns are severely stressed.* For obtaining uniform stress distribution under impulse voltage condition, *the windings are provided with suitable electro-static shields.*

## 12.2. MAJOR INSULATION AND MINOR INSULATION OF WINDINGS

**Major Insulation** refers to the insulation between:

1. LV winding and core
2. LV winding and HV winding
3. Winding and yoke
4. The coils
5. The adjucent limbs.

Voltage stress across major insulation is higher than that across minor insulation.

**Minor Insulation** refers to the insulation between:

1. Individual turns of the winding
2. Consecutive layers of the winding.

Voltage stress across *Major Insulation* is generally in cylindrical form. The cylinders are formed by several layer of specially selected pressboards or synthetic resin bonded paper. The cylinders are mechanically strong, dense and have excellent insulating properties.

The end-insulation is usually formed by several press-board washers, spacing blocks or built-up cylindrical blocks.

The dimensions of cylinders are selected to match with the diameters of core limb/yoke and the winding. Space blocks placed over the cylinders give desired oil-ducts between the cylinder and core, cylinder and winding etc.

*Minor Insulation* between consecutive turns, between consecutive layers and consecutive coils of the same winding is of varnished cloth, craft paper or pressboards.

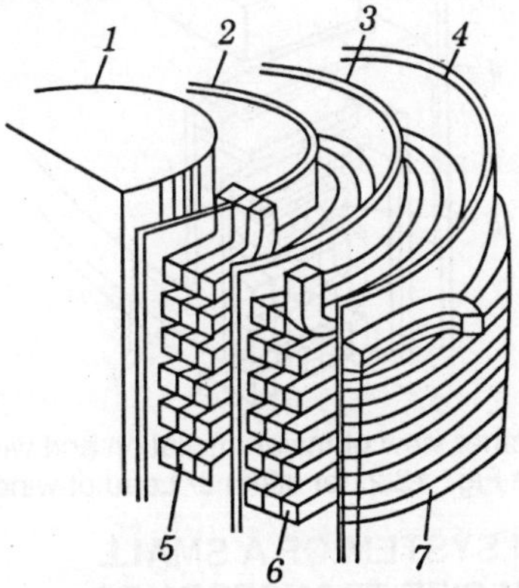


1. Core
2. Insulating cylinder between the core and LV winding (5)
3. Insulating cylinder between the LV winding (5) and HV winding (6)
4. Insulating cylinder between HV winding (6) and regualting winding (7)
5. LV winding
6. HV winding
7. Regulating winding

Fig. 12.1 Major insulation of cylindrical shape.

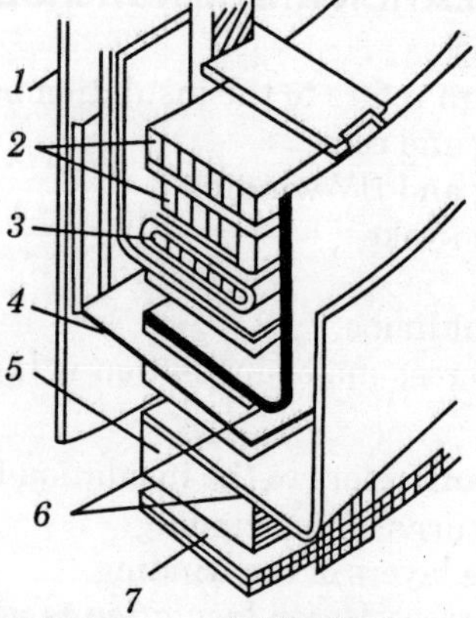


1. Vertical press board
2. Winding
3. Shield
4. Press board L shape sheet
5. Insulating block
6. L shaped insulatling sheets
7. Flat insulating sheet

Fig. 12.2. Major insulation between a winding and Core, Yoke, Another winding.

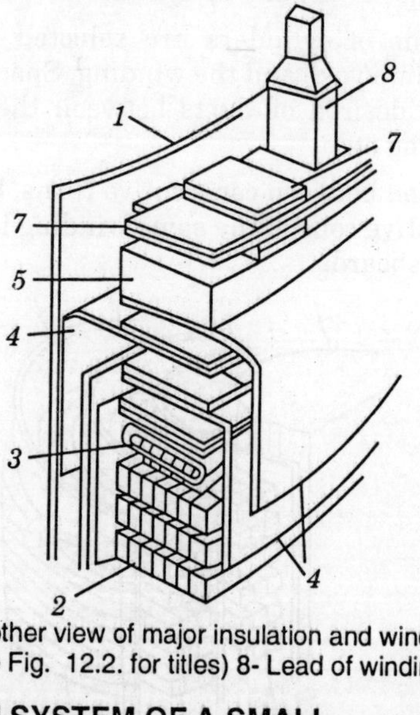


Fig. 12.3. Another view of major insulation and winding support (See Fig. 12.2. for titles) 8- Lead of winding.

## 12.3. INSULATION SYSTEM OF A SMALL AND MEDIUM SIZE TRANSFORMER

Referring Fig.12.4. The LV winding is insulated from the core by a cylinder of press-board or synthetic resin bonded paper (SRBP), with axial bars of press-board or similar material arrange symmetrically around the cylinder to form cooling ducts between the cylinder and the

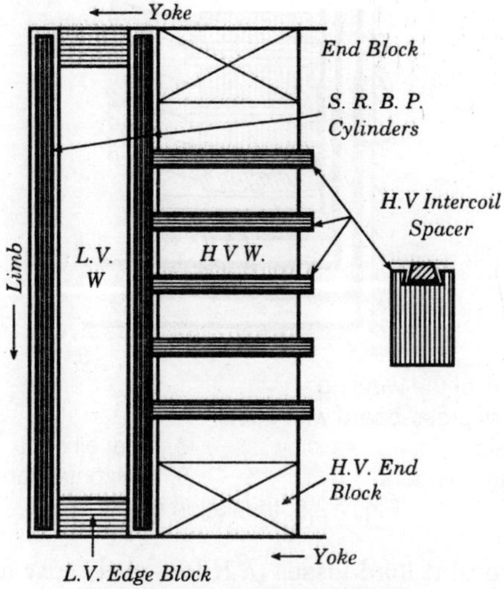


L.V.W.= Low voltage winding.
H.V.W.= High voltage winding.

Fig. 12.4. Insulation system of a small and medium size distribution transformers.

inner surface of LV winding. Another cylinder is placed between the LV and HV to provide major insulation. With disc windings or disc-helix, coils for HV winding, the inter coil spacer has a wedge shaped joint with the cylinder. Similar spacers are placed between consecutive turns of helical winding. Insulation to earthed core at the ends of the windings is in the form of blocks keyed to the axial bar in line with the spacers to form a clamping system. Figure 12.2 gives the details.

When operating voltages are higher (132 kV and above), thicker major insulations is required between windings. Fig.20.1. shows the details.

Paper is used exclusively for interturn (minor) insulation of HV windings.

## 12.4. INSULATION DESIGN OBJECTIVES

The design objectives are:

1. To provide adequate insulation strength to the winding and the insulation system for withstanding.

- Power frequency test voltage (applied or induced tests) to prove the insulation between windings and insulation to earth.
- Induced voltage test to withstand inter-turn, inter-cost, phase to phases stresses.
- Lightning impulse voltage tests (full wave and dropped wave)
- Switching impulse voltage tests (if applicable)
- Environmental tests

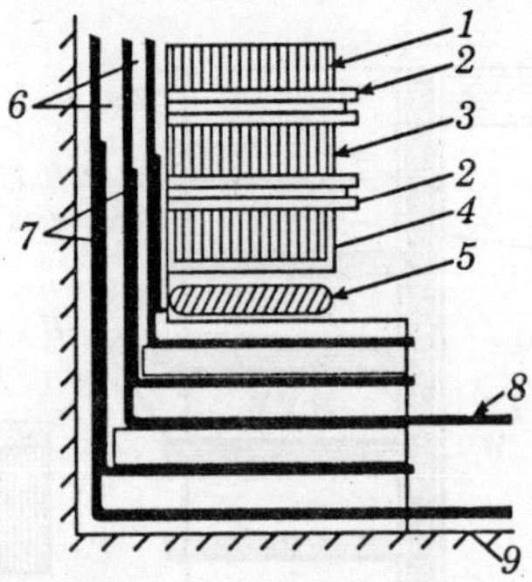


1, 3, 4. Coils of the winding.
2. Horizontal press-board with ducts
5. End shield
6. Axial oil duct
7. Insulating cylinders
8. Horizontal flanged collar.

Fig. 12.5. Insulation details.

2. To ensure that load losses ($I^2R$ loss and stray losses) are within guaranteed limts.

3. To provide sufficient mechanical strength to withstand axial and radial stresses occurring during repeated short-circuits.

4. To obtain required percentage impedance

5. To ensure adequate cooling and flow of coolant through the winding-ducts so as to limit temperatures of oil and winding within guarateed limits.

## 12.5. FULLY INSULATED WINDING

All the points of the winding have equal insulation strength with respect to earth and can withstand separate source voltage test specified of for line terminals. All delta windings and star windings with insulated neutral are provided with full insulation.

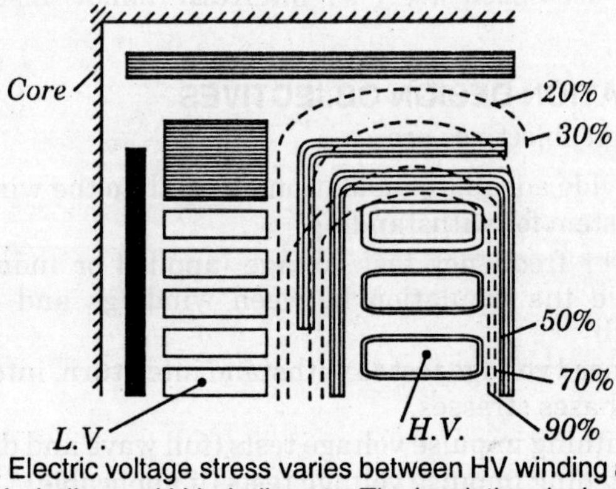


Fig. 12.6. Electric voltage stress varies between HV winding and core, HV winding and LV winding etc. The insulation design is optimised with the help of electric field plots.

1. Vertical rectangular press board strip
2. Horizontal spacer
3. Insulating cylinder
4. Coil

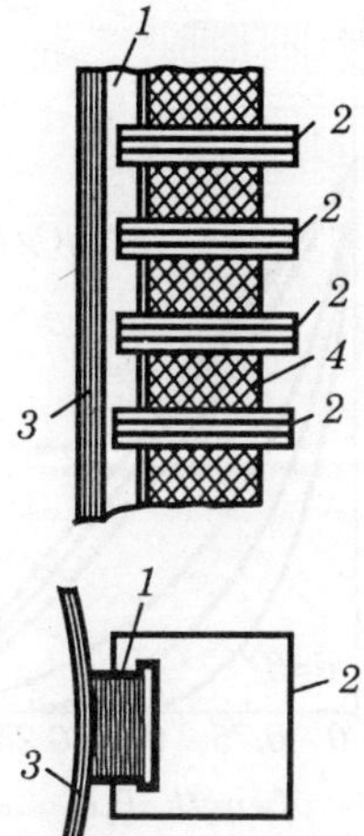

Fig. 12.7. Insulation for a typical helicial·winding.

## 12.6. GRADED INSULATION

Insulation to earth is more for line terminal and is less for neutral terminal. Such winding withstands separate source test corresponding to the neutral terminal insulation level only.

Graded insulation may be provided for star winding with effectively earthed neutral.

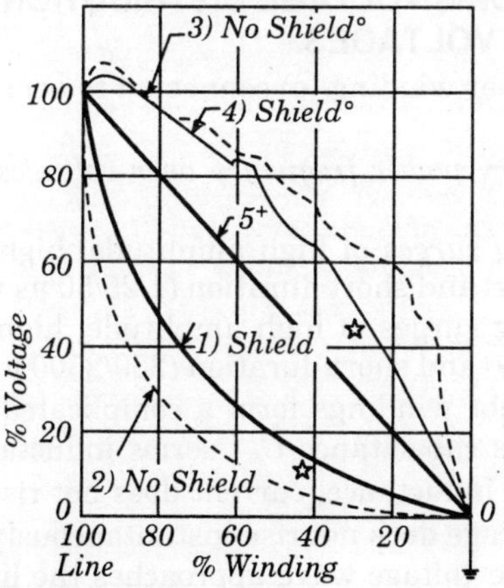


* Initial distribution 1 and 2

** Distribution during severe oscillations after a few microseconds.

*** Ideal distribution.

Fig. 12.8. Distribution of Impulse voltage in a 132 kV star connected winding.

The required insulation level of line terminal is normally designated as Basic Installation Level (BIL). The details are covered in the topic insulation coordination.

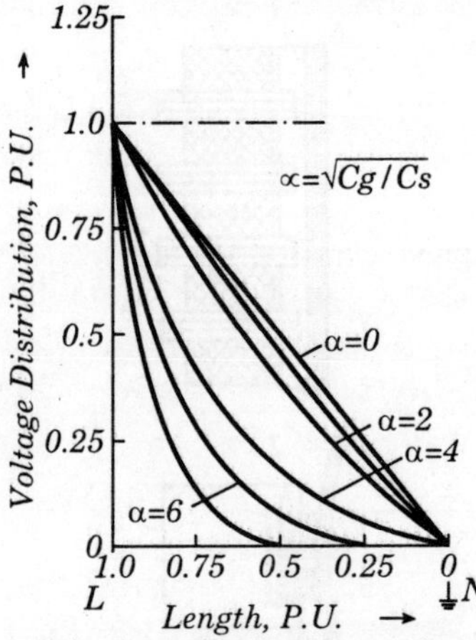


Fig. 12.9. Initial voltage distribution or voltage along the winding for earthed neutral.

Full, uniform insulation should be provided for

1. All delta connected windings.
2. Star connected windings without neutral earth.

Graded Insulation is applied to star connected winding with neutral earth provided earthing condition permits graded insulation.

## 12.7. NON-UNIFORM VOLTAGE DISTRIBUTION OF SURGE VOLTAGES

The transformer winding (s) connected to over head line side are subjected to:

— *Temporary power frequency over voltages* lasting for a few seconds.

— *Lightning surges* of high amplitude, high rate of rise (high frequency) and short duration (1.25/50 μs wave).

— Switching surges of high amplitude, high rate of rise (high frequency) and short duration (250/2500 μs wave).

The transformer windings form a complicated network of series resistance $r$, series capacitance $C_s$ , series inductance $L_s$ and shunt capacitance $C_g$. In inductance, current does not rise instantaneously. In capacitance voltage does not rise instantaneously. Therefore as the steep-fronted surge voltage wave approaches the line terminal of the transformer winding, the voltage distribution along the winding is:

— Non-uniform along the length of the winding (Fig. 12.10, curve 1).

— Changes with time within a few micro-seconds due to oscillations.(Fig.12.11).

For power frequency voltage, the voltage distribution is substantially uniform as shown by (Fig. 12.11. curve 3). This is because, power frequency voltage wave-form has relatively low $dv/dt$ and sufficient time is available for charging $C_g$ and $C_s$.

For steep fronted impulse waves, time available for charging $C_g$ and $C_s$ is short. $dv/dt$ is high and the initial voltage distribution is non-uniform (Fig. 12.10, curve 1).

The end-turns of the winding are subjected to maximum stress during the initial time. The oscillations are set-up within the windings by the way of exchange of energy between capacitance ( $\frac{1}{2} CV^2$) and inductance ($\frac{1}{2} i^2L$). These oscillations result in changing the voltage distribution continuously in time and along the winding.

The oscillations occuring during the later duration of impulse wave result in time-changing oscillatory voltage transient which produces different and higher stresses in the middle portion of the winding. The oscillation-voltage occurring during the later time-portion of the wave may stress the middle part of winding to a much higher voltage than the initial stress on the end-turns. Therefore the non-uniform voltage distribution produces higher stresses on:

1. End-turns during initial time-portion.
2. Middle-turns during later oscillatory time portion.

Such non-uniform voltage distribution calls for sufficient insulation withstand for

1. End-turns.
2. Between turns.
3. Between coils.
4. Major insulation between phases.
5. Major insulation between phases and core.

The objective of designers is to achieve uniform ideal voltage distribution (Fig. 12.8, curve 5). However, without shielding, the voltage distribution is as per curve 2 initially and to curve 3 during oscillations.

By using shields in the windings, the initial voltage distributions is improved to curve 1 and distribution during oscillations is improved to curve 4.

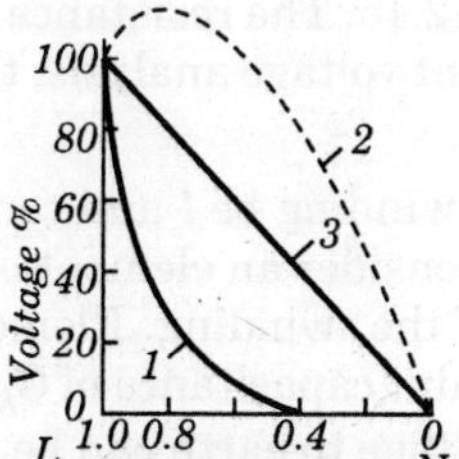


1. Initial.
2. Envelope of maximum voltage at various points.
3. Final steady state

Fig. 12.10. Distribution of voltage changing with time.

Figure 12.10. gives the three curves for voltage distribution along the length of the winding. It is observed that during impulse voltage, the stress distribution exceeds the final voltage distribution and some parts of windings are stressed severely.

Figure 12.11. gives variation of voltage distribution at different instants of time $t = 0$ to $t = 50$ μs, along the length of the winding. Initial voltage distribution (curve 1) gives very high stress on line-end turns and least stress on neutral-end turns. However after a few microseconds (curve 6 – 40μs) the middle portion of winding (60%) is subjected to highest stress.

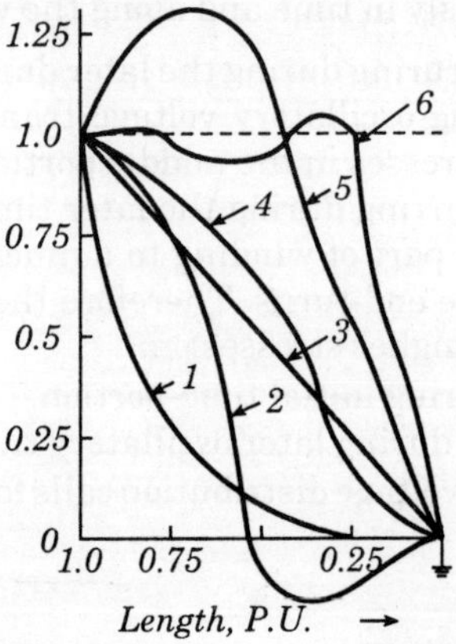


(1) $t = 0$ (2) $t = 10$ μs
(3) Steady state (4) $T = 20$ μs
(5) $t = 30$ μs (6) $st = 40$ μs.

Fig. 12.11. Voltage distribution after at different time instants, along the length of the winding with earthed neutral.

## 12.8. ANALYSIS OF TRANSIENT VOLTAGE DISTRIBUTION

Two conductors separated by a dielectric medium have certain capacitance. The transformer winding has distributed series capacitance $C_s$ between turns, coils etc. and distributed shunt capacitance $C_g$ between the winding and earthed core. A model of the winding is shown in Fig. 12.15. The resistance is neglected. Neglecting inductance for the transient voltage analysis, the model is simplified to Fig.12.16.

Let the length of the winding be $l$ and consider a surge voltage $V$ approach from line end. Consider an element of length $dx$ at a distance $x$ from the neutral end of the winding. Element $dx$ consists of series capacitance $C_s l/dx$ and shunt capacitance of $C_g ldx$. Then the charge on the element $dx$ and its voltage to earth can be written as:

$$\frac{\partial q}{\partial x} = \frac{C_g \cdot dx}{l} \cdot \frac{\partial v}{dt} \qquad ...(12.1)$$

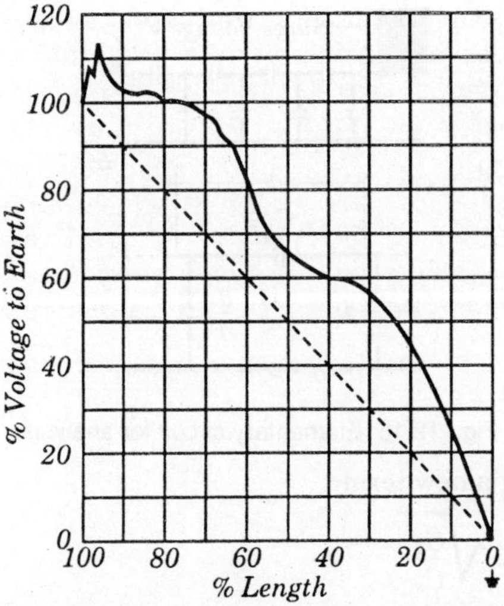


Fig. 12.12. An example of a maximum voltage envelope for winding with neutral earthed (during the entire duration of oscillations due to the surge voltage).

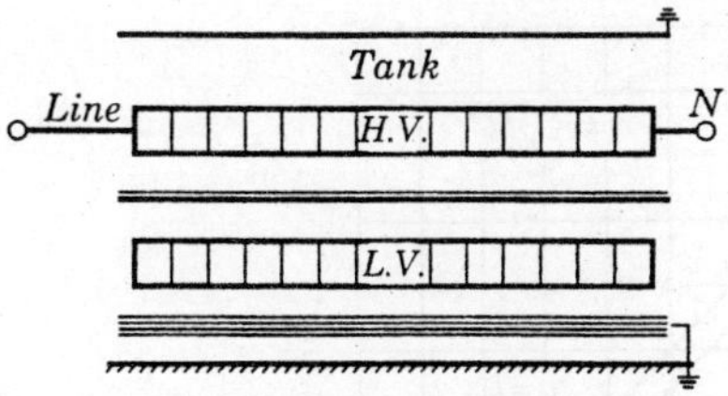


Fig. 12.13. Configuration of winding and insulation to earth.

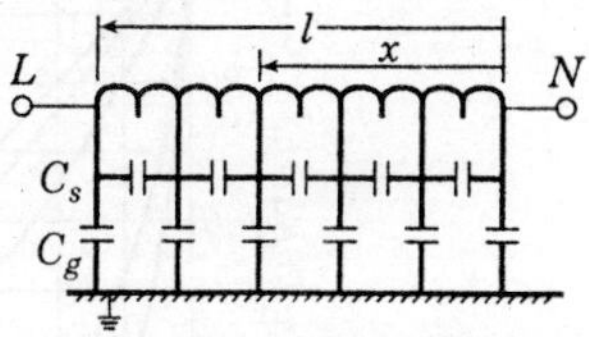


Fig. 12.14. Simplified model of the winding for derivation of voltage distribution.

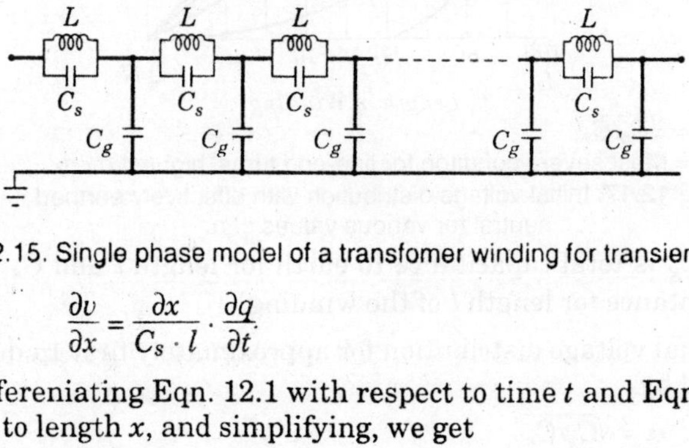


Fig. 12.15. Single phase model of a transfomer winding for transient analysis.

$$\frac{\partial v}{\partial x} = \frac{\partial x}{C_s \cdot l} \cdot \frac{\partial q}{\partial t} \qquad \text{...(12.2)}$$

Differeniating Eqn. 12.1 with respect to time $t$ and Eqn. 12.2 with respect to length $x$, and simplifying, we get

$$\frac{\partial^2 v}{\partial x^2} = \frac{1}{l^2} \frac{C_g}{C_s} \cdot \frac{\partial^2 v}{\partial t^2} \qquad \text{...(12.3)}$$

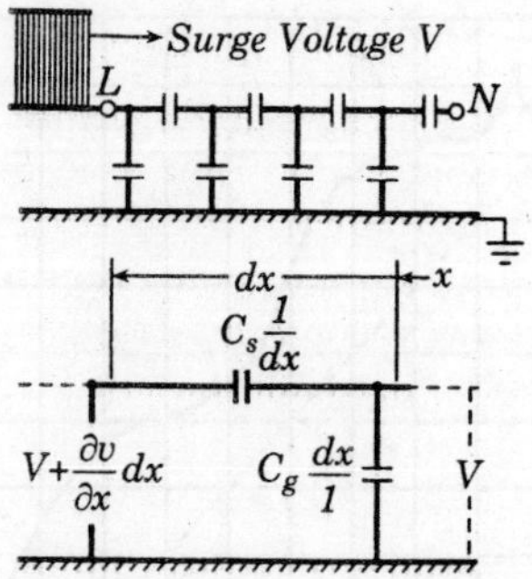


Fig. 12.16. Elementary circuit for analysis.

Substituting a new term

$$\alpha = \sqrt{\frac{C_g}{C_s}} \quad ...(12.4)$$

$$\frac{\partial^2 v}{\partial x^2} = \frac{\alpha^2}{l^2}\frac{\partial^2 v}{\partial t^2} \quad ...(12.5)$$

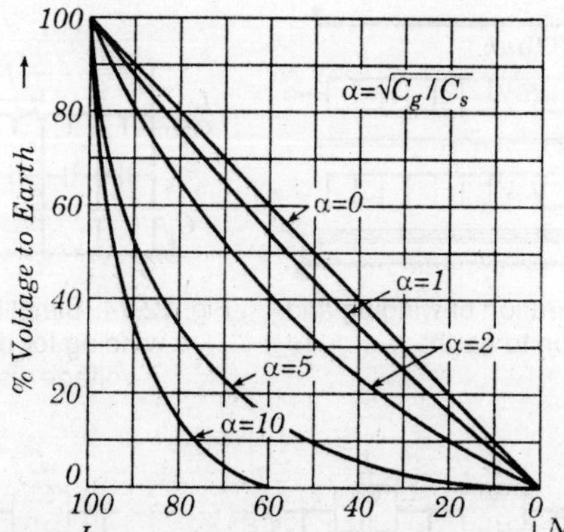


$\alpha = \sqrt{C_g/C_s}$

$x$ = Most severe conditon for line-end turns, highest $dv/dx$.

Fig. 12.17. Initial voltage distribution with effectively earthed neutral for various values of α.

Hence $C_g$ is total capacitance to earth for length $l$ and $C_s$ is total series capacitance for length $l$ of the winding.

The initial voltage distribution for approximately first 1μ duration is influenced by

$$\alpha = \sqrt{C_g/C_s}$$

Fig. 12.17. shows the effect of α *on the intial voltage distribution in the winding with earthed neutral and Fig. 12.18. shows the voltage distribution with isolated neutral.* It is observed that higher is the value of α, higher is the non-uniformity and therefore higher intial voltage stress on the end-turns. Maximum initial voltage stress on end turns in α times that of uniform voltage stress. In practice, with disc type HV winding and spiral type LV winding, the value of α is in the range of five to thirty. In worst case of α = 30, end turns will be stressed 30 times the normal uniform stress during initial 1μs duration of impulse voltage.

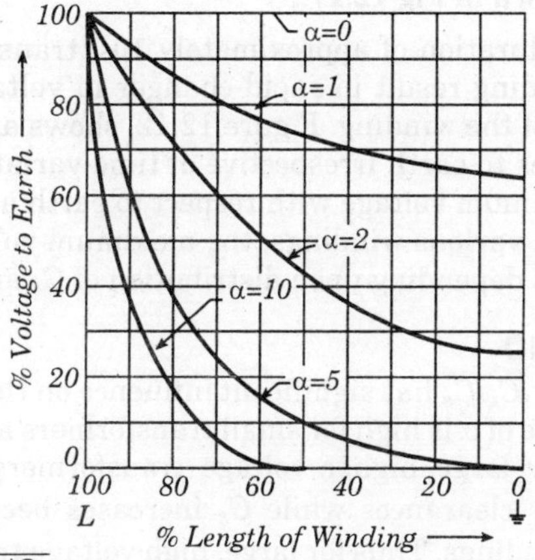


$\alpha = \sqrt{C_g/C_s}$

x = Most severe conditon for line-end turns, maximum *dv*/*dx*.

Fig. 12.18. Initial distribution of voltage with isolated neutral for various values of α.

After about 1.2 μs, the oscillations are set-in and very great variation in the voltage distribution occurs along the length of the winding and with time.

Solution of Eqn. 12.3. gives the voltage $v$ in the form

$$v = A \exp.\left[\alpha\left(\frac{x}{l}\right)\right] + B \exp\left[-\alpha\left(\frac{x}{l}\right)\right] \quad ...(12.6)$$

If the neutral end is earthed

$$v = 0 \text{ at } x = 0$$

and $A = -B$

At line end $x = l$ and $v = V_0$, we get

$$v = V_0 \frac{\sin h\ \alpha(x/l)}{\sin h\ \alpha} \quad ...(12.7)$$

where, $V_0$ = applied surge voltage at $t = 0$

$v$ = voltage at $x$ from neutral end for initial period (1μs)

$l$ = length of winding

$\alpha = \sqrt{C_g/C_s}$

$x$ = distance from neutral, earthed

$l$ = total length of winding

Similarly, if neutral is isolated, we get

$$v = V_0 \frac{\cos h\ \alpha\ x/l}{\cos h\ \alpha} \qquad ...(12.8)$$

A family of curves of voltage distribution are obtained for various values of α as shown in Fig 12.17.

After initial duration of approximately 1μs, transient, oscillation set up in the winding result in rapid changer in voltage in time and along the length of the winding. Figure 12.12. shows an envelop of the maximum voltages to earth irrespective of time variation. It gives an indication of maximum voltage with respect to earth at various points of the winding. In various windings, the maximum voltage may occur at different points depending upon distribution of $C_s$ and $C_g$.

## 12.9. THE α RATIO

The ratio $\alpha = \sqrt{C_g/C_s}$ has significant influence on the initial voltage distribution. Value of α is high for small transformers and low for large transformers. For large higher voltage transformers, $C_g$ decreases because of higher clearances while $C_s$ increases because of greater radial depth of windings. Thus for large, high voltage transformers α is lower and initial voltage distribution is more closer to the uniform distribution line.

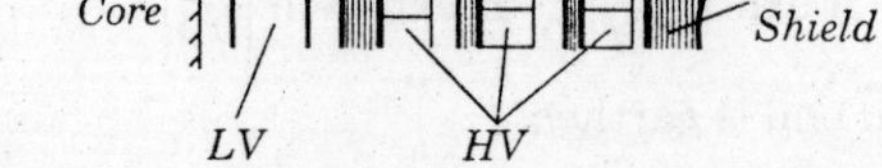


Fig. 12.19. Insulation details with voltage grading shield.

## 12.10. ELECTROSTATIC SHIELDS

To reduce initial stress concentration at end turns, disc-coil winding is provided with stress-rings which act as radial shields. They do not improve the axial stress distribution significantly.

Axial stress distribution is improved by additional rib-shields connected to the line-end turns.

In designing high voltage windings, the distribution of voltage stress is made as uniform as possibly by adopting several means.

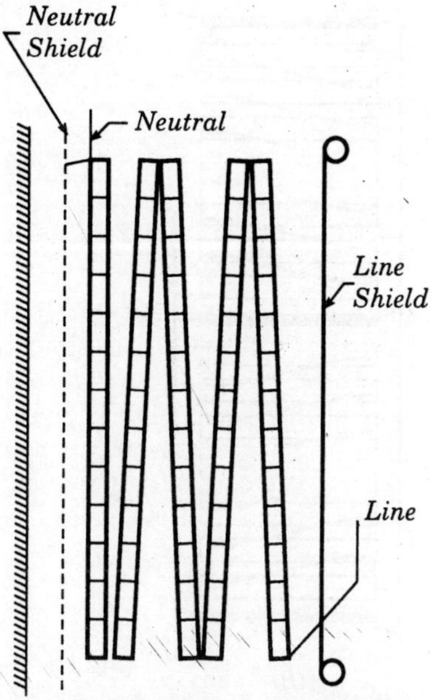


Fig. 12.20. Multi-layer shielded winding.

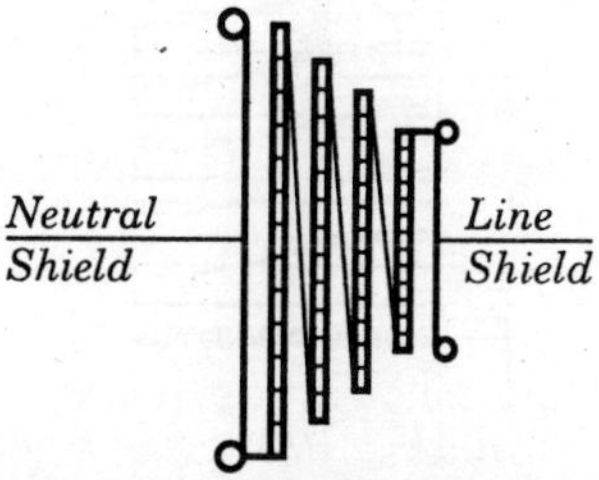


Fig. 12.21. Connection of neutral shield and line shield for a multi-layer winding.

The aim is to reduce the α factor by increasing $C_s$ and reducing $C_g$.

The shunt capacitance $C_g$ depends upon surrounding core, tank and adjucent winding.

The series capacitance $C_s$ depends on inter-turn gaps and inter-coil gaps of the windings.

For higher voltage windings, the reduction in α is more important.

*Compared with the disc winding, the multi-layer winding has higher series capacitance, hence superior initial voltage distribution. The choice between disc winding and layer winding depends on required impulse withstand level.*

## 12.11. DISC-WINDING WITH FLOATING POTENTIAL SHIELD-TURNS

The voltage distribution in disc windings can be improved by floating potential shield-turns as shown in Fig. 12.23. These *non current carrying turns* are connected together and form a floating shield. The voltage between the shield turn and adjucent turns is higher than turn-to-turn voltage. Therefore, the capacitance between the floating shield turns and adjucent shield turns absorbs a high portion of transient voltage.

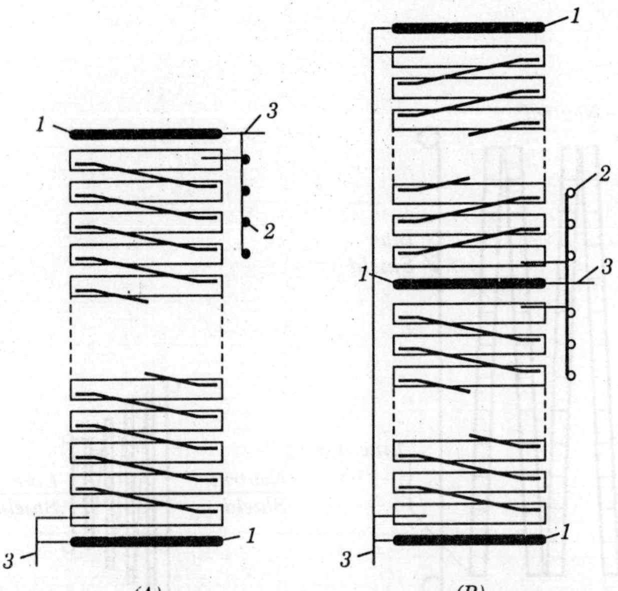


(A) *Entrance from two ends.*

(B) *Entrance from one end and the middle.*

*1. Stress distribution ring* *2. Rib shield* *3. Line lead.*

Fig. 12.22. Disc windings with stress distribution rings and rib shields.

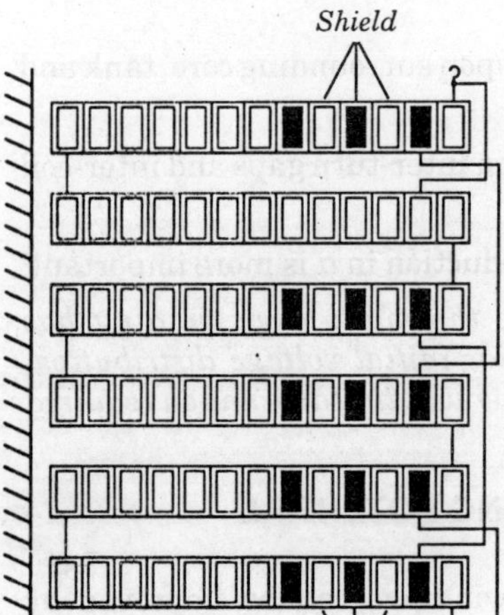


Fig. 12.23. Disc winding with shielding turns.

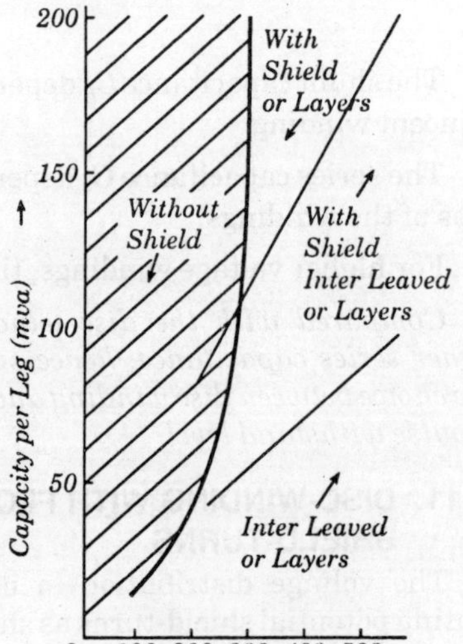


Fig. 12.24. Choice of winding for large transformer depends on kV and MVA per leg-(limb).

Another arrangement is of interleaved disc winding. Additional capacitance is obtained by interleaving the turns of one coil with the turns of the next disc coil as shown in Fig. 12.25.

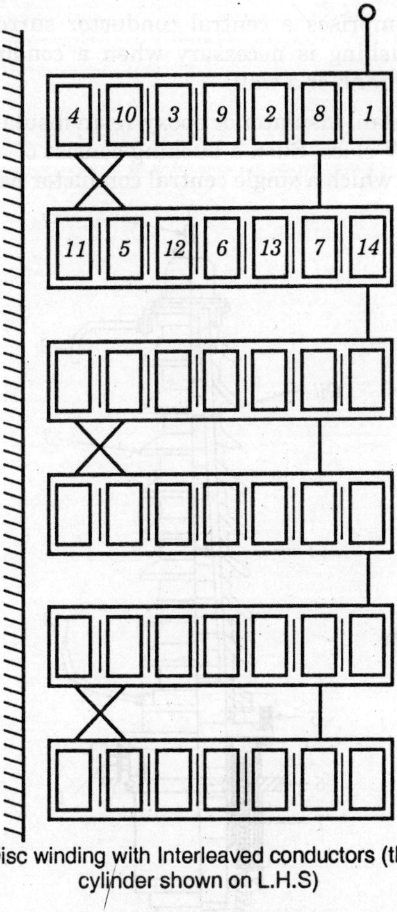


Fig. 12.25 Disc winding with Interleaved conductors (the insulating cylinder shown on L.H.S)

For higher voltages, layer type windings are preferred. (Fig. 12.20). In such a winding the adjucent turns are arranged axially and the winding has certain number of concentric layers separated by paper-oil insualtion with layer winding the shunt capacitance is decreased.

For yet higher voltages the shunt capacitance $C_g$ is reduced by electrostatic shields arranged in concentric layers and connected to

1. Line end
2. Neutral end
3. Both line end and neutral end.

Such winding is preferred for high voltage windings of auto-transformers interconnecting two high voltage systems (*e.g.*, 765 kV/400 kV).

## 12.12. BUSHINGS

Bushings comprises a central conductor surrounded by graded insualtion. A bushing is necessary when a conductor is taken out through metallic tank or a wall.

Simple porcelain insulator or epoxy-resin insulator bushing can be used upto 1.1. kV class. Such a bushing consist of a single insulating support through which a single central conductor passes.

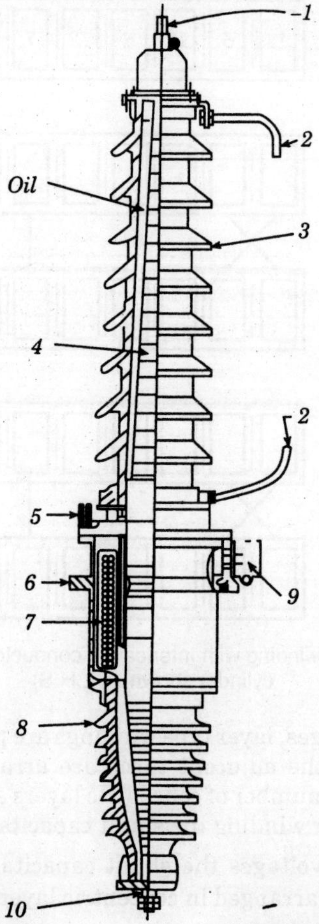


1. Air-end terminal.
2. Arcing horn (optional).
3. Air-end porcelain.
4. Condenser core.
5. Voltage tap-plug.
6. Flange for support.
7. CT.
8. Oil-end porcelain (optional).
9. Terminal box for CT secondaries.
10. Oil-end terminal.

Fig. 12.26. Cross-section of a condenser bushing.

Oil filled bushing is used of 33 kV applications. For making the bushing compact, synthetic resin bonded condenser bushings (S.R.B.P. condenser bushing) is used for 33 kV and 66 kV applications. For 132 kV and above oil impregnated paper condenser bushing is used. (O.I.P. condenser bushings).

The condenser bushing consists of a central conductor surrounded by alternate layers of insulating paper and tin foil. The capacitor formed by alternate layers of tin foil and paper insualtion result in uniform

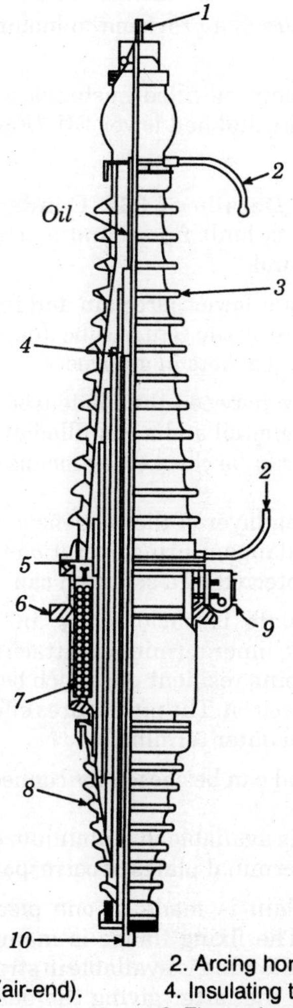


1. Air-end terminal.
2. Arcing horns.
3. Porcelain housing (air-end).
4. Insulating tubes with spacers.
5. Voltage-tap plug.
6. Flange for mounting the bushing.
7. CT.
8. Oil-end porcelain.
9. Terminal box for CT secondaries.
10. Oil-end terminal through the central con ducting tube.

Fig. 12.27. Oil-filled bushing without condenser.

electric stress distribution between conductor surface and the earthed flange.

The bushing core is coated with suitable resin. The assembly is enclosed in hollow porcelain and is provided with support flange and top hood. The porcelain is filled with dielectric oil.

One end of the bushing goes into transformer tank. The other end is in the outside air.

In some cases there is a provision to mount currents transformer on the bushing.

In early years, plain oil-filled bushings without condenser were built. These were bulky and had lower BIL (Fig. 12.27).

**Constructional Details of OIP Condenser Bushing.** Figure (12.26). The bushing is built up around a centre tube on which the condenser body is wound.

The upper porcelain,lower porcelain and fastening flange are held between the end plates by the centre tube and sealing is accomplished by oil-resistant rubber gaskets in grooves.

The annular space between the condenser body and the porcelain is filled with transformer oil and a gas-filled expansion space is left at the top. The oil level can be checked by means of a dip-stick in the oil filling hole.

The outer conducting layer of the condenser body is connected to an insulated test on the flange. During operation the test tap is automatically earthed and protected by a screw on cap'.

The lower end-plate is enclosed by an epoxy resin insulated aluminium shield. The inner terminal is attached to the centre tube by means of a through-going resilient pin which becomes locked when the outer terminal is screwed on. The pin ensures effective electrical contact between the inner and outer terminals.

The inner terminal can be chosen for connection to leads either by brazing or crimping.

The outer terminal is available in aluminium or copper alloy and can be supplemented by terminal plates of corresponding material.

The upper porcelain is made in one piece of the high quality electrical porcelain. The fixing flange is manufactured of corrosion-resistant aluminium alloy and is available in straight or, for some types, also inclined designs, the latter giving the bushing an inclination of 15°.

The flange as well as the other metal parts on the exterior side of the bushing are protected by painting with two-component primer and a grey-blue finishing of paint.

The bushings are delivered oil-filled and ready for use. They can be stored in any position in warm dry storage.

If the bushing is mounted with an inclination of more than 45° from the vertical, special measures may have to be taken to ensure sufficient filling of oil in the bushing.

High voltage bushings are subjected to the following *type tests*:

— Measurement *of d.c. resistance* between terminals of conductor
— *Temperature rise test* (with one end placed in hot-oil corresponding to the transformers oil temperature).
— *Short-circuit test for* one second. A current of the order of 25 times normal rated current is passed through the conductor for one second. The test is followed by dielectric test.
— *Dielectric test.* These include the one minute power frequency voltage withstand test (dry); One minute power frequency voltage withstand test (wet); for outdoor bushings only, Switching impluse voltage withstand test; Lightning impulse voltage withstand test.
— *Partial Discharge Test.*

The *routine tests* on the bushing include:

— Measurement of *Insulation Resistance*
— Measurement of *resistance*
— Power frequency voltage withstand test for one minute.

After installing the bushing on the transformer, the tests are conducted on the complete transformer.

**Technical Particulars of Bushings**

— Rated voltage
— Impulse withstand test level
— Rated current
— Rated short-circuit current and duration.
— Oil-impregnated condenser body of high-voltage insulation paper
— Great adaptability—available with or without space for current transformers, with straight or, for some types, also inclined flanges, alternative connection details, normal or anti fog porcelain in brown or light grey colour.
— Free from partial discharges in the insualtion.
— Thermal stability—withstands system voltage to earth for unlimited time.
— Equipped with test tap for tan δ measurement and measurement of partial discharges in the transformer.
— Maintenance free and non-susceptible to aging.
— Hermetically sealed with own oil system.

— The technical data fulfil the requirements for insulation according to the following standards:
IEC, IS, ANSI, BS, DIN.

### Summary

The insulation system comprises:

— Vertical cylinders of press-board
— Horizontal press-boards, wedges
— Conductor insulation
— Interturn insulation
— Inter layer insualtion
— Insulating supports, packings
— Insulation over leads
— Oil
— Bushings, etc.

Insulation is the weakest part and needs very careful design and processing. Grading rings are used for reducing stress on end turns.

Transient behaviour in response to lightning surges consists of variation of stress along the winding with time.

# 13

# Transformer Oil

Transformer oil provides insulation and cooling. The standard specifications, typical impurities and important tests have been described in this chapter. Maintenance has been covered in a subsequent chapter.

Transformer oil plays a very important role in oil cooled transformers as the oil affects transformer life and service ability. Transformer oil should thoroughly be checked before it is filled in the transformer. While in service, transformer oil deteriorates in the course of time due to unavoidable thermal and electric stresses and chemical contamination the oil undergoes. Hence, regular monitoring of oil becomes essential. Dissolved gas analysis and from analysis of the oil samples give information about healthyness of the transformer. From this, incipient faults, deterioration of insulation etc., can be determined before occurrence of any major failure, thereby saving costly transformers.

## 13.1. TYPES OF TRANSFORMER INSULATING MEDIA

The tank is filled with one of the following:

1. Dielectric-oil (Transformer-oil). Most preferred filling medium.

2. **Askarel**. Now banned due to harmful effects of decomposition products.

3. Dry-air or Nitrogen for dry transformers.

4. $SF_6$ Gas, Developed but not commercially successful.

5. Solid for dry transformers in conjunction with dry air.

Most common medium for large transformers is transformer oil. For 'dry' type transformers, solid insulation and dry air or dry nitrogen filling is used.

## 13.2. SPECIFICATIONS OF TRANSFORMER OILS

Following specifications are applicable.

— IEC 296

— IS 335-1983 (3rd Revision)

— BS 148—1972.

The summary of specifications is given in Table 13.1.

**Table 13.1. Specifications of Transformer Oil (IS 335:1983)**

| *Sr.No.* | *Characteristics* | *Unit* | *Requirement* |
|---|---|---|---|
| 1. | Appearance | | The oil shall be clear, transparent and free from suspended matter or sediments. |
| 2. | Density at 29.5 °C | gm/cc | 0.89 |
| 3. | Kinematic Viscosity at 27 °C (Max.) | Cst | 27 |
| 4. | Interfacial tension at 27 °C (Min.) | N/m | 0.04 |
| 5. | Flash Point (Min.) | °C | 140 |
| 6. | Pour Point (Max.) | °C | – 6 |
| 7. | Neutralisation value (Total acidity) (Max.) | mg/KOH/g | 0.03 |
| 8. | Corrosive sulphur: | | Non-corrosive |
| 9. | Electric strength (breakdown voltage) (Min.) | | |
| (*a*) | New untreated oil. | kV (rms) | 30 (If the above value is not obtained the oil shall be filtered in laboratory). |
| (*b*) | After filtration | kV (rms) | 60 |
| 10. | Dielectric dissipation factor (tan δ) at 90°C (Max.) | | 0.002 |
| 11. | Water content (Max.) | ppm | 50 |
| 12. | Specific resistance (Min.) at 90°C<br>at 27°C | ohm-cm<br>ohm-cm | $35 \times 10^{12}$<br>$1500 \times 10^{12}$ |
| 13. | Oxidation stability | | |
| (*a*) | Neutralisation value (Max.) | mg/KOH/g | 0.4 |
| (*b*) | Total sludge after oxidation (Max.) | mg/KOH/g | 0.10% |
| 14. | Ageing characteristics after accelerated ageing (open beaker method with copper catalyst). | | |
| (*a*) | Resistivity (Min.) at<br>at 90°C<br>at 27°C | ohm-cm<br>ohm-cm | $0.2 \times 10^{12}$<br>$2.5 \times 10^{12}$ |

(*Contd...*)

| Sr.No. | Characteristics | Unit | Requirement |
|---|---|---|---|
| (b) | Tan δ at 90°C (Max.) | | 0.2 |
| (c) | Total acidity (Max.) | mg/KOH/g | 0.05 |
| (d) | Sludge content by weight (Max.) | | 0.05% |
| 15. | Presence of oxidation | | Oil shall not contain inhibitor oxidation inhibitor |

## 13.3. SIGNIFICANCE OF IMPORTANT CHARACTERISTICS

Oil serves as a dielectric medium and cooling medium. Hence its dielectric properties and cooling properties are important. The service-reliability of an oil-immersed transformer depends, therefore, to a great extent on the quality of the oil. Properties of special improtance, when determining the oil quality,are:

**1. Freedom from Dust Particles, Moisture and Impurities.** The fresh dielectric oil has pale clear yellow colour. A dark colour or cloudy appearance indicate deterioration. Impurities have a bad effect on the properties of the oil.

The dielectric oil should never contain suspended particles, water soluble acids and bases, active sulphur or colloidal carbon.

These impurities accelerate deterioration of the insulating properties of the dielectric oil resulting in internal flashovers.

The dust particles, carbon particles and sludge in the oil which as in suspended form in the oil gathers along the conductor and insulator surfaces in presence of electric field. Thereby, a thin conducting layer is formed gradually along the surface of internal insulation during service. The flashover can occur along the surface of the insulation or tank due to tracking. Dust and other particles are removed by means of filters in the oil filtering unit.

Presence of water in oil is highly undesirable as it adversely affect the dielectric properties of oil. It also affects the paper insulation in a transformer. As paper is highly hygroscopic in nature, it absobs the moisture from oil which affects its insulation properties as well as reduces its life.

Moisture in oil lowers the dielectric strength, thereby causing, internal flashover. Moisture is introduced in the transformer through defective seals. Sometimes, oil filled in the transformer may itself have higher moisture content.

2. The viscosity, which is the main factor for determining the cooling properties of the oil. Other factors affecting the cooling properties are practically the same for all qualities of transformer oil.

Viscosity indicates fluidity. Oil with low viscosity has more fluidity and give better cooling. At lower ambient temperatures, the viscosity sharply rises and the speed of oil circulation reduces. Hence viscosity should be measured at various temperatures.

Specifications recommend maximum limit of viscosity at given temperature (Ref. Table 13.12).

3. The *flash point*, which is the temperature at which combustible gases are emitted by the oil in such a concentration that they may be ignited.

Higher flash point (145°C) is preferred. Flash point indicates tendency to evaporate. For flash point lower than 135°C, the oil tends to evaporate rapidly at full load thereby the viscosity rises and total volume of oil reduces.

Specifications recommend minimum flash point (Table 13.14).

4. The *lowest flow-temperature*, which is the temperature at which the oil begins to change to such a viscous consistence that the cooling of the transformer is jeopardized.

This property is applicable to transformers installed in colder countries or at very high attitudes.

**Pour Point.** The temperature at which oil will just start flowing under prescribed conditions is called *Pour Point*. (Table 13.15). If oil temperature falls below its pour point, it will stop flowing and cooling will be affected.

5. The *breakdown voltage* (*Electric strength*), which is the voltage required to obtain a flashover in the oil between two electrodes of specified shape, and at a certain distance from each other. The breakdown voltage is an indicator of the purity from moisture conducting particles, organic acids and other electrolytes.

BDV is the single most important and popular test to gauge oil condition at site. Its lower value indicates presence of solid impurities and moisture in oil.

6. The *moisture content* is also an important factor, which to a great extent affects the insulating properties of the oil. However, the moisture can relatively easily be removed before filling the transformer. Oil is protected against absorption of moisture and oxidation by (1) Filtering (2) Preventing contact with atmospheric oxygen and moisture by conservators with rubber bellows.

7. The *resistance against ageing*, which is the ability of the oil to maintain its properties for a long time as an insulating and cooling medium. Because of the ageing, which is mainly and oxidation process, the oil darkness, becomes acid and forms finally insoluble sludge. The oil will thus gradually be damaged and cannot be used for its purpose any more.

*The oxidation process is depending on the oxygen feed, and the speed of the reaction increases rapidly with rising temperature.* By providing oil conservators, protection by inert gas or closed oil system, the life of the transformer can be considerably increased.

**8. Oxidation Inhibitor.** The oil within the charged transformer is continuously subjected to electrical and thermal stresses, presence of oxygen and heat with copper of the windings acting as catalyst, causes oil to slowly oxidise. The resistance of oil to this oxidation is called oxidation stability of oil. The degree of oxidation is measured by measuring sludge content and total acidity of the oxidized oil. Transformer oil should give good stability against oxidation. In order to improve the oil further and increase its life, an *oxidation inhibitor* is added. The name of an inhibitor is *disobutyl paracresol*, or in abbreviation DBPC. The inhibitor breaks the chain reaction, leading to formation of sludge and acid. DBPC is electrically neutral and has no harmful effect on the solid insulation. Furthermore, it is insoluble in water and cannot, therefore, be washed out from the oil. The inhibitor DBPC, which has been widely used in the oil industry, and is produced by European as well as American manufacturers, is thus easily obtainable in the market.

Transformer oil, inhibited with DBPC, can without disadvantages be mixed with uninhibited transformer oils. However, the ageing properties of the mixture are generally not as good as for the inhibited oil.

**9. Stability of Oil.** The oils manufactured in India are generally Paraffin Base Oils. The oils produced in USA and Eurpoe are generally Napthenic Base Oils. *The properties of transformer oils with paraffin base deteriorate at a slightly faster rate* acting as catalyst,causes oil to to slowly oxidise. The resistance of oil to this oxidation is called oxidation stability of oil. The degree of oxidation is measured by measuring sludge content and total acidity of the oxidized oil.

**10. S K Value.** It is percentage rise in concentrated sulphuric acid volume what mixed with equal volume of oil. It gives an understanding of degree of refinement of oil. A lesser value is considered to be better value.

## 13.4. COMMERCIAL OIL AND TREATMENT OF OIL

Supplies of transformer oils give test certificates for the oil complying with IS 335 or IEC 296. After treatment of the oil the dielectric strength higher than 60 kV is reached in Europe/USA and higher than 45 to 50 kV in India.

**Treatment Specified in IEC Publication 296**

Heating of the oil to 90°C, filtration under vacuum (<20 Torr) through a filter with pore diameter 3–20 μm.

Examples on transformer oils complying with the demands according to IEC Publication 296 and the demands of ASEA:

| | |
|---|---|
| *Inhibited oils*: | Esso Univolt N 61<br>Shell Diala DX<br>BP Energol-JSH-V<br>Nynas TRO 10 X<br>Mobilect 44 |
| *Uninhibited oils* : | Esso Univolt 60<br>Univolt 62<br>Shell Diala D<br>Gulf Transcrest H |

## 13.5. DIELECTRIC PROPERTIES OF TRANSFORMER OIL

**1. Electric Strength (Breakdown Voltage).** Electric strength test provides the indication regarding the purity of the oil/contamination etc. Electric strength is the basic parameter for the insulation system design of the transformers. The electric strength reduces due to contaminants like moisture, dust, carbon particles, sludge, sediments etc. Electric strength is measured.

(*i*) Before acceptance of oil

(*ii*) Before filling in the tank in works, for testing the transformer.

(*iii*) During installation

(*iv*) During treatment prior to commissioning

(*v*) During periodic maintenance.

**Testing of Oil-for Dielectric Strength**

A sample of insulating oil is taken from the bottom of the tank. Dark and brown, clouds indicate deterioration. Oil in good condition has pale yellowish uniform colour. It is tested by means of portable oil testing set which consists of a auto transformer, voltmeter, tripping device etc. The voltage can be gradually increased. Oil in good condition should withstand 45 kV r.m.s. for one minute in a standard oil testing cup with 4 mm gap between electrodes. A gap of 2.5 mm should have break-down value above 45 kV.

The test cell has standard dimension as per relevant standard.

**2. Resistivity (Specific Resistance).** This is another important property of transformer oil. Resistivity is expressed in Ω-cm. It is equivalent to the resistance between opposite faces of a centimeter cube of the oil. Insulation resistance of winding of a transformer is influenced by the resistivity of oil. A low value of resistivity indicates the presence of moisture and conductive contaminants and need for filteration. The resistivity is measured in standard test cell. For d.c. resistivity measurement, the current flowing between the electrodes is measured when a specified voltage, normally 500 V, is applied to the cell. The current is noted after the direct voltage has been applied for one minute, and again after reverse polarity has been applied for one minute, with the electrodes short circuited for five minutes, between the two measurements. Average resistivity values are calculated from the readings taken after application of direct and reverse polarity.

For measurement, an instrument capable of detecting $10^{-11}$ amperes is required. A standard test cell is described in the following paragraph:

The electrodes of copper, brass, bronze or stainless steel, are either spherical and of 12.5 to 13 mm. diameter. The surface is smooth and clean.

The electrodes are mounted on a horizontal axis with a test spacing of 2.5 mm. Test cells, due of glass or transparent plastic-material, with effective volumes of 300 ml to 500 ml, preferably fitted with suitable lids.

The oil is subjected to a steadily increasing alternating voltage until breakdown occurs.

The first application of the voltage is made as quickly as possible after the cell has been filled, provided that there are no longer any air bubbles in the oil, and within 10 minutes after filling. After each breakdown, the oil is gently stirred between electrodes with a clean, dry, glass rod, care being taken to avoid as for as possible the production of air bubbles. For the five remaining tests, the voltage is reapplied one minute after the disappearance of any air bubbles that may have been formed. If observation of the disappearance of air bubbles is not possible, it is necessary to wait five minutes before a new breakdown test is commenced. It is generally recognized that the precision of the electric strength is not high, and it is not surprising that, in a test so susceptible to the presence of minute traces of impurities may not be distributed uniformly over the bulk of the oil, or even the oil sample itself. Accordingly, care is essential in sampling, to avoid the introduction of contaminants not previously present in the oil.

## 13.6. IR TEMPERATURE RELATION

It has always been the question from our customers as to how the IR value can be converted at different temperatures. We have drawn a curve (Fig.13.1) for guidance of the operating staff on the basis of our experience. So that they can judge the IR Value at any temperature. This curve cannot be taken for absolute value but will serve as a good guide for conversions of IR values at different temperatures. A simple example is given as to how to calculate the value at different temperature.

Suppose IR value of 70°C is 300 M ohms and we want to convert at 40°C, the curve will give you a factor K for difference in temperature *i.e.*, (70°C – 40°C) = 30°C.

K for 30°C temperature difference = 4.2

So the value at = 40°C = 4.2 × 300 = 1260 M · Ohms

Value thus converted fairly tally with the actual

Value when cooling the transformer. The factors are tabulated as below:

| Difference in temp. | 10°C | 20°C | 30°C | 40°C | 50°C |
|---|---|---|---|---|---|
| Factor K | 1.65 | 2.6 | 4.2 | 6.6 | 10.5 |

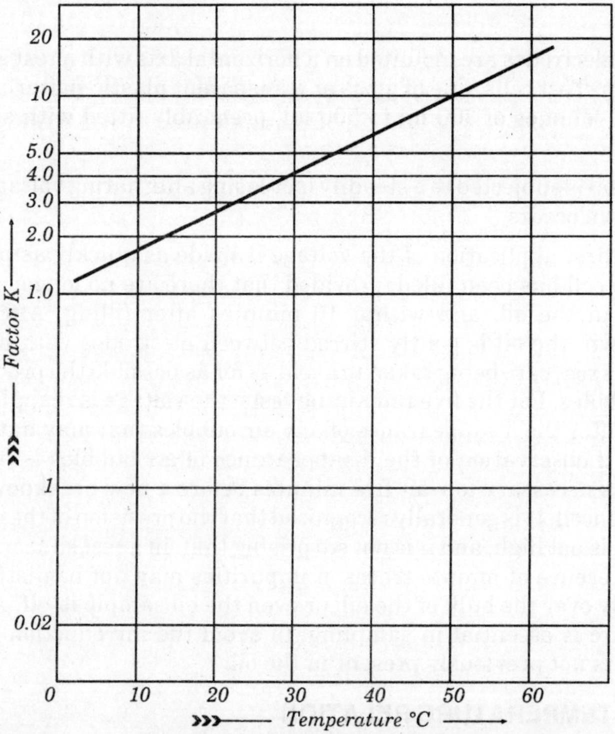


Fig. 13.1 I.R. Temperature Curve

## 13.7 LOSS ANGLE OF DIELECTRIC AND DIELECTRIC DISSIPATION FACTOR

Loss angle is an important property of dielectric oil. In ideal dielectric material, the phase angle between voltage and current is 90°. However, due to impurities, certain leakage current flows through the dielectric and the actual phase angle is slightly less than 90° by angle δ° called loss angle. As angle δ is very low, tan δ should also be low. tan δ gives an indication of the leakage currents through the oil and dielectric loss. For good oil, tan δ should be as less as possible.

The sine of loss angle δ is called Dielectrc Dissipation Factor (DDF). DDF is numerically equal to sine of the loss angle (approximately equal to tangent of loss angle for dielectrics) and is a good tool to indicate the quality of an insulation. A high value of DDF is an indication of the presence of contaminants such as moisture,, metal-oxides, resins,varnishes, dust, carbon particles, etc.

For measurement of the loss tangent, an alternating current (40 Hz to 62 Hz) bridge (Schering Bridge) is used, which should be capable of measuring loss tangent down to $1 \times 10^{-4}$ for normal applications, but preferably down to $1 \times 10^{-5}$ with a resolution of $1 \times 10^{-5}$ in a capacitance of 100 pF. The voltage applied during the measurement must be sinusoidal. Measurement is made at a stress of 0.5 to 10 kV/mm at 90°C, and is started when the inner eletrode attains a temperature within plus or minus 0.5°C of the desired test temperature.

**Tan δ Test on Complete Transformer.** Before commissioning a transformer, the following tests are repeated:

— Dielectric strength of oil
— Tan δ test on transformer
— Other commissioning checks
— Insulation resistance measurement

Tan δ test is conducted as follows. The terminals are disconnected. Test voltage of suitable value (*e.g.*, 30 kV) is applied between terminals connected together and earthed tank. The tan δ is measured by the bridge. The record of tan δ is useful for annual maintenance verification for comparison.

## 13.8. DISSOLVED GAS ANALYSIS

It is very powerful technique to find out incipient faults in a transformer. Certain gases are released by decomposition of oil and/or paper insulation where transformer undergoes abnormal thermal and/or electrical streses. The composition and quantity of the gases generated depends on type and severity of the fault. Regular monitoring of these dissolved gases reveals useful information about healthiness of a transformer and prior information can be had by observing the trend of a various gas contents.

The periodic analysis of the dissolved gases provides an easy method of assessing the transformer behaviour. It can show the presence of a latent defect, which if found early enough can avoid the possibility of serious damage.

The ultimate failure of a transformer involves breakdown of some part of the electrical system, windings, leads, tap changers or bushings. Any such breakdown in almost always preceded by partial discharges.

The analysis of gas collected in the relay chamber indicates the type of incipient fault. The presence of ; (*a*) $C_2H_2$ and $H_2$ shows arcing in oil between constructional parts; (*b*) $C_2H_2$, $CH_4$ and $H_2$ shows arcing with some deterioration of plastic insulation, e.g., fault in tap changer ; (*c*) $CH_4$, $C_2H_4$ and $H_2$ indicate hot spots in core joints; (*d*) $C_2H_4$, $C_3H_6$ and $H_2$ also indicate hot spots in core joints, (*e*) $C_2H_4$, $C_3H_6$, $H_2$ and $CO_2$ shows a hot spot in the winding.

# 14

# Testing of Transformers

Tests are conducted for verifying the capabilities of a transformer to withstand

— Thermal stresses
— Dielectric stresses
— Short-circuit electro-dynamic stresses
— Environmental stresses, etc.

The tests are conducted as per standard specifications and also as per agreement between the manufacturer and the user.

The various checks and tests enable the purchaser to ensure the correct functioning of the transformer and compliance with the guarantees in accordance with the technical specifications.

The various tests are reviewed in this chapter with respect to the following categories:

— Characteristics check (Polarity, connections, Ratios, Losses)
— Dielectric tests (Power frequency and Impulse)
— Operational Tests (Temperature rise, Audible, Noise, Sudden Short-circuits, etc.).

## 14.1. INTRODUCTION

The standards divide the tests into three categories.

Routine tests. These are carried out on every transformer without exception, and include:

1. Measurement of winding resistance.

2. Verification of the polarity of the windings, the connections between windings and terminals and the transformation ratio.

3. Measurement of load losses and the impedance voltages.

4. Measurement of no-load losses and no-load current.

5. Electrical tests at power frequency (by induced voltage, or by applied voltage).

6. Test of ability to withstand full-wave impluse transformers of rated voltage ≥ 220 kV.

7. Check on the level of partial discharges during overvoltages (transformers of rated voltage ≥ 220 kV).

8. Test on ability to withstand switching impulse (transformers of rated voltage ≥ 220 kV).

**Type test,** intended in principle to prove a new design or a series of transformers, include:

9. Test of ability to withstand full-wave impulse (transformers of rated voltage < 220 kV).

10. Test for switching impulse withstand. (≥ 220 kV).

11. Temperature rise test.

**Special tests** correspond to particular service conditions or investigations.

12. Measurement of zero phase-sequence impedance.

13. Measurement of noise.

14. Check on the level of radio interference voltage.

15. Test on the ability to withstand chopped impulse wave.

16. Tests of ability to withstand sudden short circuit.

During earlier years the distinction between type tests, routine tests and special tests was well defined. Gradually, this distinction is getting reduced. Today the standards give general recommendations. The test schedule is drawn by mutual agreement between the manufacturer and the client with relevant standards for guidance.

**Table 14.1 Example of a Test Certificate**

| | |
|---|---|
| *Client:* | *Certificate No* : |
| | Date of test : |
| Client's Order No.: 89 /T&D / 1056 | *Internal Order No* : 901286 |
| | Specification |
| | Rating : Continuous Type : Indoor |

| | | | |
|---|---|---|---|
| Rated kVA 500 | 3-phase 50 Hz | | |
| Winding | | HV | LV |
| Rated line voltage | | 6430 | 400 |
| Rated line current | | 448 | 723 |
| Connection | | Delta | Star |
| IS | Phasor group Dy 11 reference | | |

Connections Diagram No. Outline drawing No.: DIS 6320

Tapping on h.v. wdg. for full capacity, controlled by off-circuit switch.

Cooling ONAN Oil quantity 800 litres

No-load voltage ratio 6756-6596-6435-6274-6112/400

**Test Witnessed by:**

Transformer serial No. 54119 C *(Contd...)*

| | | |
|---|---|---|
| Winding referred to, at 75°C | | 6430/400 |
| No-load loss at normal voltage ratio | watts | 996 |
| Load loss to rated current | watts | 7140 |
| Impedance voltage at rated Current | % | 4.49 |
| No-load average line current at normal voltage ratio | % | 0.75 |
| Average resistance per phase ohms | HV | 1.605 |
| | LV | 0.00204 |
| Excitation current with ref. to l.v. winding | A phase | — |
| | B phase | — |
| | C phase | — |
| Percentage efficiency at unity Power factor | 100% rated current | 98.42 |
| | 75% " " | 98.68 |
| | 50% " " | 98.90 |
| | 25% " " | 98.88 |
| Percentage efficiency at 0.8 lagging power factor | 100% rated current | 98.02 |
| | 75% " " | 98.36 |
| | 50% " " | 98.64 |
| | 25% " " | 98.56 |
| Percentage regulation at full load | 1.0 unity p.f. | 1.53 |
| | 0.8 lagging p.f. | 3.71 |
| Temperature rise, from type test | °C by the thermometer in oil | 45 |
| | by resistance HV Winding | 54 |
| | LV Winding | 58 |
| Insulation resistance, megohms to other windings, core, frame and earth at 23°C (2500 volts d.c.) | HV winding | 2500 |
| | LV winding | 2500 |
| Separate-source voltage withstand test from indiacated winding to other windings, core frame and earth for 60 s at 23 °C | HV Winding | 22kV |
| | LV Winding | 25 kV |
| Induced overvoltage withstand test at 100 Hz for 60 s at 23°C. | | 100% |

*Testing Engineer* *Design Engineer*

Singnature Signature

Date

## 14.2. CATEGORIES OF TESTS

The tests are identified into following categories:

—Type tests. —*Routine tests.*

—*Special test* —*Commissioning test.*

*Type tests* are performed on the first transformers of one type and are intended to check the design characteristics. Type test usually related to the first unit manufactured by a firm to a given specification. It is presumed that every such transformer would also comply with the type test, since its design is identical.

*Routine tests* are tests are made on every transformer before despatch,to ensure that it is in accordance with the specification. These are basically conducted to take care of variation in raw material quality, manufacturing tolerances etc.

*Special tests* are conducted in the presence of the purchaser or his representatives as specified in the tenders.

*Commissioning tests are* conducted at site before commissioning.

The following tests are required as per B.S. 17.1

| *Routine test* | *Types tests* |
|---|---|
| 1. Ratio and polarity | 1. Temperature rise test. |
| 2. Load losses. | 2. Impulse voltage test. |
| 3. Impedance. | 3. Noise level test. |
| 4. Insulation resistance. | *Special tests* |
| 5. Resistance of windings. | |
| 6. No-load losses. | |
| 7. No-load current. | 1. Partial discharge. |
| 8. Voltage tests-on windings. | 2. Radio interference. |
| (*a*) Separate source. | 3. Vibration test. |
| (*b*) induced overvoltage. | 4. Short-circuit withstand test. |
| 9. Core insulation voltage test. | 5. Noise level. |
| | 6. Few sequence impedance test. |

## 14.3. WINDING DC RESISTANCE MEASUREMENT

Measurements of winding DC resistance can be made with a Wheatstone or a Kelvin Bridge. Volt-ampere method can also be used for medium resistance values. A heavy current of 100 amps. DC and sensitive meters would give accurate results. Test may be made when the transformer is cold or hot. Winding and oil temperatures should be recorded when the measurements are made.

Winding resistances are measured for each winding in order to verify the continuity of windings, their correct connections and to create a basis for loss and temperature determination.

Resistance is determined by DC measurement, either using a voltmeter/ammeter method or a resistance bridge method (Wheat-stone or Kelvin bridge, as applicable).

An important parameter for resistance measurement is the winding temperature. Therefore, it is a prerequisite for good measurement that the winding temperature is stable and known.

An important error source during the resistance measurements is the induced voltage due to the large inductance of the transformer windings. This induced voltage may be created by the switching transient or by an unstable power source. The settling time of the switching transient may be several minutes. Precautions to minimise this error could be pre-saturation of the core and an accurately controlled constant-current source.

If a heat run is made, the resistance measurements are repeated rapidly after the completion of heat run in order to determine the temperature of the windings.

DC Volt-Ampere Method is generally used for winding resistance measurement. This well know, simple and straight-forward method is illustrated in Fig. 14.1. Earlier, when only analogue dial instruments were available, this method was considered to be *inaccurate* because current passing through ammeter is the sum of winding current and voltmeter current. The higher the resistance of the voltmeter, the lower will be the error. In addition, it was very often necessary to include corrections for the power consumption in the measuring instruments themselves.

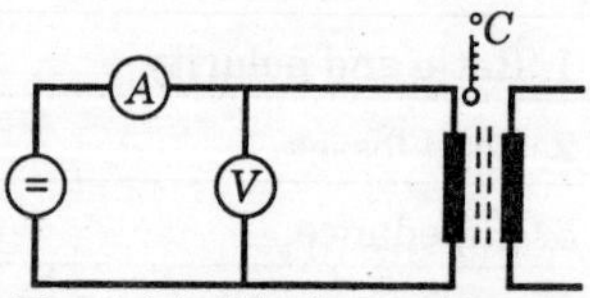

Fig. 14.1. Winding resistnace measurement by volt-amp method.

With modern, *high impedance, digital measuring instruments,* sufficient nominal accuracy is obtained. These instruments also permit automatic data collection, which speeds up the measurements and eliminates operators mistakes in instruments readings.

One advantage of volt-ampere method compared with the bridge method is that no time-consuming balancing of circuits is necessary.

The requirements regarding the stability of the DC source are stringent. Because of the inductive effect of the core, care must be taken to ensure that a steady d.c. value is reached before voltage and current readings are recorded.

**Bridge Method of Resistance Measurement.** In bridge method for measurement of transformer winding resistances, either the

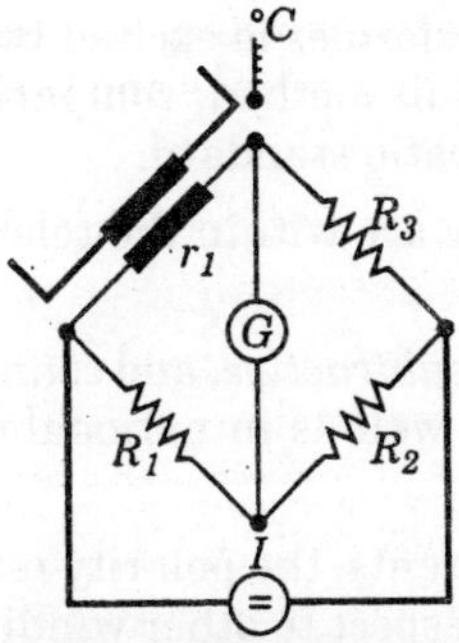


Fig. 14.2. The Wheatstone bridge method, bridge shown, $V_1$ is the transformer winding, $R_1 - R_3$ adjustable standard resistors, G galvanometer for balance indication. The DC source includes devices for setting the current at a suitable value, reversing switch etc.

Wheatstone bridge or the Thomson bridge is used. The choice between them is dependent on the actual resistance value to be measured, and in most cases the Wheatstone bridge circuit illustrated in Fig. 14.2 is preferred.

Bridge measurement of the resistance is based on comparison with standard resistors. The sensitivity and accuracy of the equipment is such that expected relative error is less $10^{-4}$.

Connection to the transformer must be made with both current and potential leads, so that errors caused by contact resistances are excluded.

Before each reading, the bridge must be balanced, which is a manual operation. This delays work, which is of significance when resistances have to be determined in rapid succession after a heat run.

The error in the measurement caused by the inductance of transformer windings must be taken fully into consideration in the bridge measurements. It is not sufficient that the supply current to the bridge is constant. If the resistance of the transformer winding varies with time, as in the case after a heat run, current variations may occur inside the closed bridge even though the total supply current is kept constant.

## 14.4. POLARITY TEST AND RATIO MEASUREMENT TEST

These are no-load, routine tests. These measurements are made to verify the voltage ratio of the windings, their interconnections and their polarity.

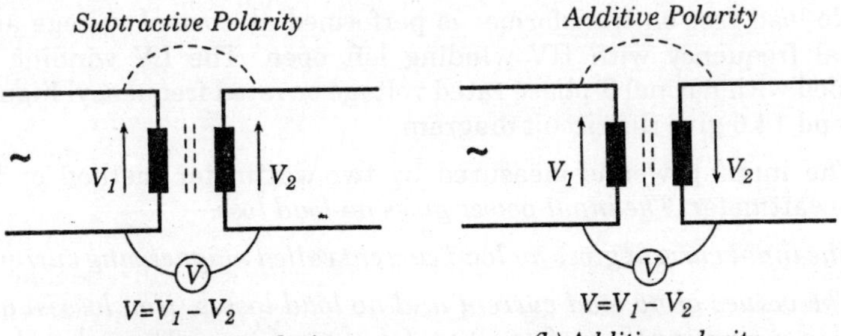


*(a) Subtractive polarity* *(b) Additive polarity*

Fig. 14.3. Explaining polarity of windings.

For purposes of measurement, the transformer is excited by a low voltage (some tens of volts) and, using a null method, comparison is made with an accurate, adjustable voltage ratio standard.

The observed ratios are accepted if they are within the tolerances of the ratings.

Polarity definitions, usually *additive or subtractive*, and connection designations are stated in international as well as in national standards.

Referring Fig. 14.3 with alternating currents, the polarity refers to the direction of voltage at an instant with respect to other windings.

### 14.4.2. RATIO TEST (FIG.14.4)

This test can be carried out using a calibrated voltmeter. But it is preferable to do it by a *special ratio-testing apparatus* called *ratiometer transformer*. This consists of a small portable transformer with a fixed primary, and secondary winding having a large number of taps connected to two selector switches, one coarse and the other fine, so that any voltage desired could be obtained for direct reading (Fig.14.4). The HV side of the transformer under test is connected to a low voltage mains supply say 400 or 220 V and the induced voltage on the secondary winding is compared with the voltage output of the ratiometer, after ensuring that the two voltages are in opposition. Accurate readings are obtained by ammeter connected between the two windings so that the circulating current, due to the difference in potential may be detected.

Ratio test should be conducted on every transformer, as any ratio error detected in the windings may then be readily rectified. The permissible tolerance is ± 0.5 per cent of the declared ratio. This test should be conducted for position of every tap.

## 14.5. NO-LOAD TEST

No-load test is a routine test and should be performed on every transformer manufactured by a manufacturer before dispatch.

No-load test on transformer is performed at normal voltage and normal frequency with HV winding left open. The LV winding is supplied with normal 3-phase rated voltage or rated frequency. Figure 14.5 and 14.6 give the circuit diagram.

The input power is measured by two-wattmeter method or by three-wattmeter. *The input power gives no-load loss.*

*The input current gives no-load current called magnetising current.*

*The values of no load current and no load losses (iron losses) are useful in evaluating the performance of the transformer.* The no load loss is useful in evaluating transformer efficiency.

The defects in magnetic circuit of the transformer cause an increase in the no load-current and losses and hence, reduce the efficiency of the

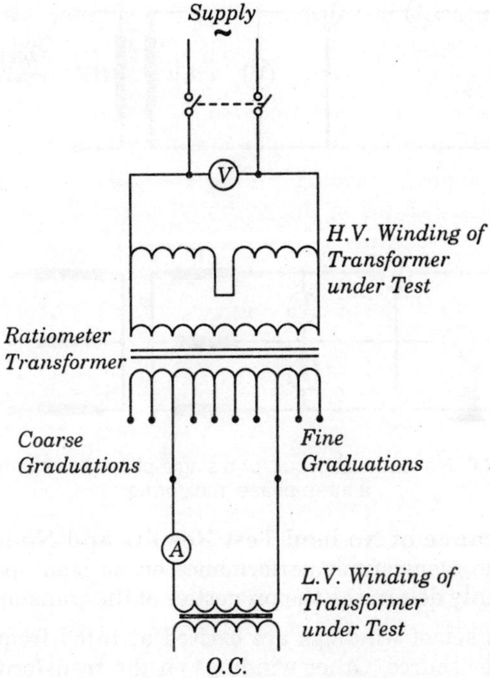


Fig. 14.4 Ratio test on a transformer by using ratiometer transformer.

transformer, and may lead to excessive over heating reducing the life span.

Under no-load condition, the transformer takes no load (magnetising) currents. No-load current is less than 4% of full load current. Hence $I^2R$ losses (copper losses) are negligible under no-load condition. *However, the iron losses (hysterersis losses + eddy current losses) are present during no-load condition.*

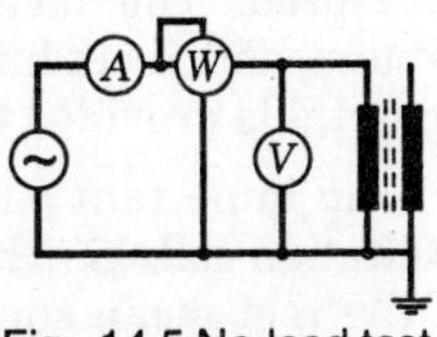

Fig. 14.5 No-load test circuit for a single phase transformer.

To check the transformer for such defects, its no-load (exciting) current and losses are measured and compared with the design data. For this purpose, the no-load loss and exciting-current measurements are carried out. One of the transformer windings (usually the LV) is excited with a 3-phase symmetrical 50 Hz voltage. The voltage is gradually raised from zero to the rated value. The HV winding is left open-circuited. The active power consumed by the transformer is measured by three wattmeter method, line currents are also measured with ammeters. The test is frequently made at a lower, rather than rated, voltage and the test results are corrected to the rated voltage.

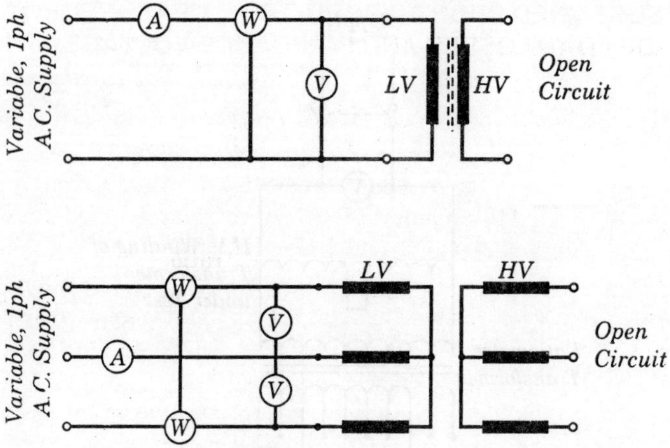


Fig. 14.6. No-load test-circuit for a single-phase transformer and a three-phase transformer.

**Significance of No-load Test Results and No-load Characteristics.** The transformer performance on no load operation is observed to mainly determine the properties of the transformer core.

A chosen set of windings are excited at rated frequency from a suitable power source. Other windings on the transformer are open-ended.

During the test, excitation voltage, current and power are measured. The measurements are made at several voltage levels around and including rated voltage. The performance is considered acceptable provided that currents and losses are within specifications.

An important parameter during this test is the wave shape of the excitation voltage. This may be monitored by simultaneous observation of the root mean square and the average value of the voltage. In the case of noticeable distortion of the voltage wave, correction factors for the power losses may be applied as described in international or national standards.

Deviations from specified performance during the no load test may often have contractual economic consequences. It is therefore important that measuring accuracy be taken under active consideration and monitored.

*No-load tests are conducted after every routine maintenance, after overhaul, after a failure.* Test results of no-load current and no-load losses are compared with the earlier readings of a new transformer. Excessive increase in no-load current/core losses indicate defect in magnetic circuit.

## 14.6. SUSTAINED SHORT CIRCUIT TEST, MEASUREMENT OF LOAD LOSSES AND IMPEDANCE VOLTAGE

*If the secondary winding is short circuited, and rated secondary current is circulated, the power input represents total $I^2R$ losses in primary plus secondary windings and also stray losses.*

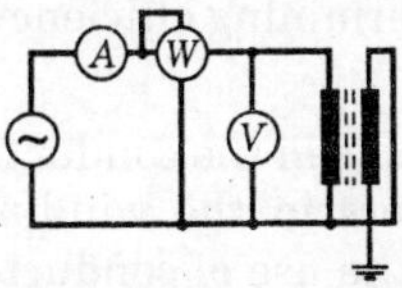


Fig. 14.7 Circuit for measurement of load losses and impedance voltage by sustained snort-circuit test.

Short-circuit test at rated current and frequency gives approximately load loss (also called short-circuit loss).

Short-circuit test also gives information about leakage impedance, load losses, impedance voltage of power transformer.

The short-circuit test, load loss test, impedance voltage measurements are performed during a single test.

In this test the terminals LV side are short-circuited by means of copper jumpers. Three phase symmetrical adjustable low voltage is applied to HV winding. The applied voltage is gradually increased till rated currents are circulated through secondary winding. Note: Supply voltage is only a fraction or rated voltage (5–10%).

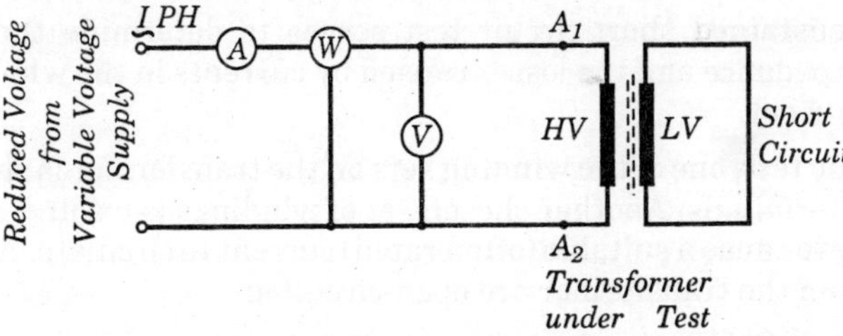


Fig. 14.8. Short-circuit test of one phase transformers.

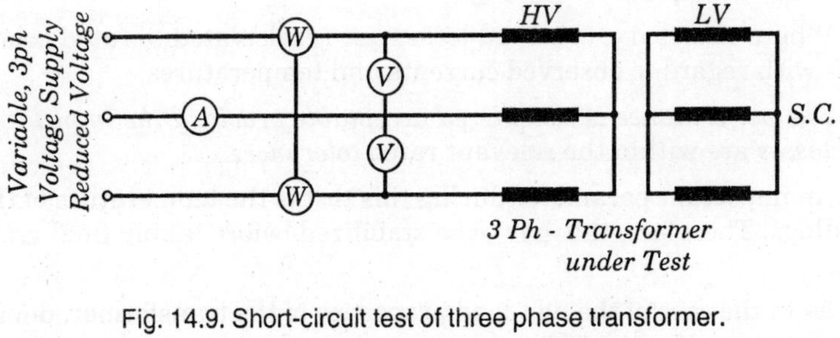


Fig. 14.9. Short-circuit test of three phase transformer.

The measurements of primary voltage, primary current and power input, secondary current are made.

With rated current on secondary side, the input power represents total load loss. This is measured and is adjusted to standard reference temperature (75°C for class *A*, *E*, *B* insulation).

The total loss includes copper loss ($I^2R$), a small core loss (5% of copper loss).

The loss measured in this test is useful in determining efficiency of power transformer.

The short-circuit test reveals the various defects in the conducting circuit *e.g.*, wrong transposition of the conductors in the windings, breaks and fractures in the parallel conductors, the use of conductors of wrong section, bad contacts etc.

*The voltage to be applied to transformer to circulate rated current in the short-circuited secondary is called leakage impedance voltage or impedance voltage or short-circuit voltage of the power transformer.* It is measured by conducting short-circuit test as described above.

The leakage impedance voltage is given by voltage $V_{sc}$ required to circulate rated current at reference temperature. The ratio $V_{sc} / I_{sc}$ gives the leakage impedance $Z_1$ (if the measurements are made on the primary) from which the leakage reactance can be calculated.

The sustained short-circuit test serves to determine the transformer impedance and the losses caused by currents in the windings at *rated frequency*.

For the test, one of the winding sets on the transformer is short-circuited at terminals. Another chosen set of windings is excited at rated frequency to cause a suitable (often rated) current to circulate. All other windings on the transformer are open-circuited.

In the excitation circuit, currents voltages and power are measured.

If the transformer has more than two sets of windings, the test is repeated for all pairs of windings.

Where necessary, observed losses are recalculated to rated conditions with regard to observed currents and temperatures.

*The performance is considered acceptable provided the impedance and losses* are within the relevant rated *tolerances.*

An important parameter during this test is the temperature of the windings. Therefore, this has to be stabilized before taking final readings.

As in the case of the non-load properties of the transformer, deviations from specifications often have *contractual economic consequences.* Low losses, low temperature use indicate higher cost of materials. Therefore the measuring accuracy has to be properly taken into account.

## 14.7. CALCULATION OF EFFICIENCY OF TRANSFORMER FROM THE RESULTS OF NO-LOAD TEST AND SUSTAINED S.C. TEST

The transformers have no moving parts, and have high efficiency. The losses in power transformers include:

1. *Core loss* resulting from the alternating core magnetisation.

2. *Dielectric loss* in insulating materials, particularly in the oil and solid in solid insulation of high voltage units.

3. $I^2R$ *loss* in the windings.

4. *Load (stray) loss*, largely the result of leakage magnetic field including eddy currents in the tank walls and conductors.

The losses can be obtained from open and short-circuit tests, without operating the transformer on load.

$$\% \text{ Efficiency} = \eta\% = \frac{\text{Output}}{\text{Output} + \text{loss}} \times 100 \quad \text{....(14.1)}$$

$$\eta\% = \frac{V_2 I_2 \cos\phi_2 \times 100}{V_2 I_2 \cos\phi_2 + \Sigma \text{ losses}} \quad \text{...(14.2)}$$

$$\eta\% = \frac{V_2 I_2 \cos\phi_2 \times 100}{V_2 I_2 \cos\phi_2 + P_i + K^2 Pc} \quad \text{...(14.3)}$$

where, $\eta\%$ = Percentage efficiency at fractional load $P_L$, where

$K = P_l/P_f, P_L$ = fractional load $P_f$ = full load

$P_c$ = Full load copper loss (from S.C. test).

$P_i$ = No-load loss (from O.C. test).

$V_2$ = Rated secondary voltage.

$I_2$ = Rated secondary current.

$\cos\phi$ = Power factor for calculations of efficiency (given).

**Example.** *Efficiency of a power transformer is to be determined on the basis of test results of O.C. test and S.C. test.*

*Date : Transformer ratings: 11 / 0.44 kV*

*50 Hz, 3-phase, Delta-star, 300 kVA .*

**Results of O.C. Test:**

No-load current 21.1 A, at 440 V,

At L.V. side with loss 1.3 kW.

**Result of S.C. Test:**

Readings from HV side: 630 V; 15.7 A, Loss 3.08 kW at winding temperature 30°C.

Calculate efficiency at full load and p.f. lag.

From O.C. Test (No load test):

No-load loss $P_i = 3.08$ kW

From S.C. Test:

Full load copper loss $P_i = 3.08$ kW

$$\% \text{ Efficiency} = \frac{\text{Output}}{\text{Input}} \times 100 = \frac{\text{Input} - \text{Losses}}{\text{Input}} \times 100$$

Let $P_e =$ Full load copper loss

$P_i =$ No-load loss

$$K = \text{load Factor} = \frac{\text{Acutual load}}{\text{Full load}}$$

$S =$ Rated kVA loading

$\cos \phi =$ Load p.f.

% Efficiency can be expressed as

$$\% \eta = \frac{KS \cos \phi}{KS \cos \phi + P_i + K^2 P_c} = 1 - \frac{P_i + K^2 P_c}{KS \cos 2\phi + P_i - K^2 P_c}$$

In this problem $K = 1$

$$\% \eta = 1 - \frac{1.3 + 3.08}{(300 \times 0.8) + (1.3 + 3.08)} = 1 - \frac{4.38}{240 + 4.38}$$

$$= (1 - 0.01792) \times 100 = 98.2\% \qquad \textbf{Ans.}$$

## 14.8. TEMPERATURE RISE TEST (HEAT RUN)

*Temperature rise test* is one of the type tests conducted on power transformers. This test is also called *heat run test.* This test reproduces conditions of continuous rated load and the temperature rise occurring during the load.

When a transformer is provided with a standard tank, it is not necessary to make a test for temperature rise, as in such cases the tank dissipation constant is known and consequently it is only necessary to measure the transformer losses and to calculate the temperature rise of the oil and the windings on continuous full load. If however, the tank is non-standard, it may be necessary to carry out a temperature rise test on the transformer, and the various methods of conducting this test are as follows:

(*a*) Short-circuit equivalent test.

(*b*) Back to back test.

(*c*) Delta/Delta test.

The general procedure under method (*a*) is as follows: One winding of the transformer is short-circuited and a voltage applied to the other winding of such a value that the power input is equal to the total normal full-load losses of the transformer at the temperature corresponding to continuous full load. The test is carried out two stages.

1. Current adjusted for value of current which will give calculated losses equal to full load losses.

2. Current adjusted to full load rated current.

In the *first stage*, when the normal temperature rise is approached the copper loss should be measured and any necessary current adjustment should then be made in order to current the power input to obtain the true losses under normal full-load conditions, *i.e.*, as regards current and temperature rise are concerned.

*The short-circuit equivalent test should not be adopted when the ratio of copper loss to iron loss is less than two to one; for loss ratios below two, the open-circuit test is preferable.*

The temperature rise test is made to verify the thermal design of the transformer including the capability of its cooling equipment to maintain the temperature of all operating components at specified levels.

The test is made in short circuit operation, like the impedance and load test described in Sec. 14.6. However, during this test all auxiliary heat-transfer equipment such as pumps, heat exchangers fans, etc. must be assembled and be in operation.

The currents circulating in the windings are adjusted to create winding losses equal to the calculated sum of no-load losses and load losses.

Electrical quantities as well as the temperatures at various spots, including temperatures of heat transfer media (oil, air), are measured periodically. Operation is maintained until thermal steady state has been reached or is very close to steady temperature (1°*C* rise in one hour).

*In the second stage*, the currents are slightly reduced to create the actual winding losses, at rated load, and operations is continued for another hour to stabilies these conditions.

*After disconnection, the winding resistance is quickly and repeatedly measured.* The results are then extrapolated backwards in time to the disconnection moment and serve as a base value for determination of the winding temperatures. If there are more than two winding sets on the transformer, the test has to be repeated for the different combinations.

An important parameter during these tests is the temperature of the final cooling medium.

**Duration of temperature-rise tests.** In general,temperature-rise tests last from five to fifteen hours. The duration may be shortened, if necessary, by overloading the transformer at the commencement of the test and then reverting to full-load losses as the final temperature is approached. This method should only be adopted in special cases for if insufficient time is allowed for the windings to attain their correct steady temperature, errors will be introduced. As an alternative it is possible, in the case of separate radiator or coolers, to restrict the normal oil flow and accelerate the temperature rise of the oil in the easy stages of the test.

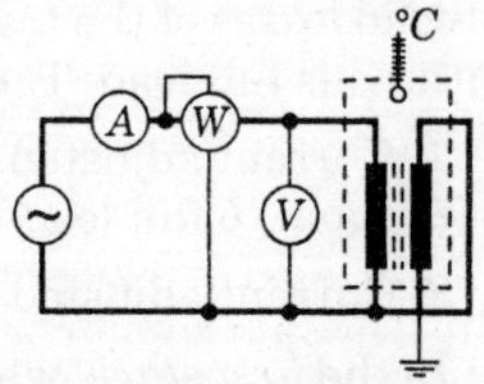


Fig. 14.10. Circuit for a temperature rise test on a single phase transformer.

**Test Measurement.** A temperature rise test takes several hours to perform.

The temperature time constant for large transformers is 3–5 hours.

Electrical quantities and temperatures are measured and recorded at regular time intervals, so that steady state conditions can be recognised. When these have been achieved, the repetition rate of measurements is increased.

During short-circuit operation, core losses are negligibly small During the temperature rise test, this has to be compensated. Therefore, at the beginning, and until temperatures have stabilised; the current is increased above rated current to such an extent that the measured losses are equal to the sum of the measured short-circuit losses and the core losses as measured in a no-load test. This operation

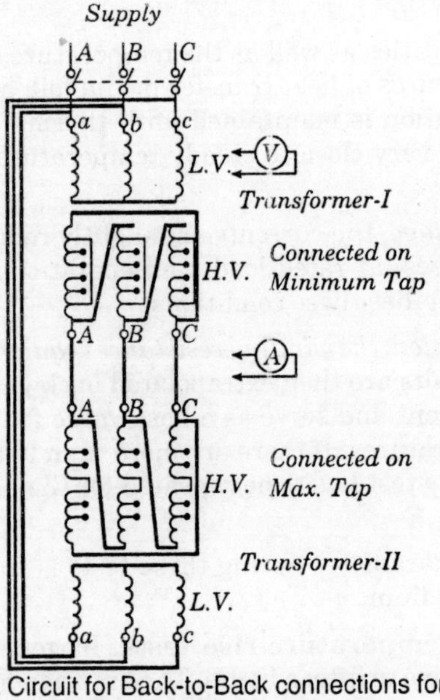


Fig. 14.11. Circuit for Back-to-Back connections for heat-run test on two similar transformers.

with losses created like the calculated total losses serves to establish the correct oil temperatures. This kind of operation is maintained until thermal steady state has been achieved, or according to standardised rules, is in the vicinity.

When steady state and the correct oil temperature have been reached in this manner, the currents are slightly reduced to rated values to create active windings losses and this new state of operation is maintained for another hour to achieve correct temperature of the windings.

After this, the power supply is disconnected and the winding resistances are measured quickly and repeatedly on both the windings simultaneously for a time of at least 10 minutes.

The procedure described above is directly applicable to a transformer, with two sets of windings. For a multi-winding transformer, it may be necessary to employ more than two of the windings to create the total losses by circulating currents. In order to create a suitable current distribution, it may then be necessary to load one of the windings with an impedance. In this manner appropriate oil temperatures may be created. The correct winding temperature rise may thereafter have to be created for one of the windings at a time, operating the other windings below rated current.

### 14.8.1. Back-to-back Test for Temperature Rise

Each transformer of a new design should be subjected to a temperature rise test to ensure that the temperature rise at *rated load* do not exceed the guaranteed values. It is *uneconomic*, to test a large transformer at the manufacturer's works with both full voltage applied and full-load current in the windings, as the total output load is not available on large transformers where the rating of the available test plant is equal to or greater than twice the rating of the transformer under test. Two units are tested simultaneously by connecting in back-to-back as shown in Fig.14.11. If the ratio of both units is identical, no current will identical, no current will flow in the widnings, but if the ratio is changed (by connecting the two units on different tappings), a circulating current would flow through the two transformers. The value of the circulating current is determined by the out-of-balance voltage and the total impedance of the two units in series. The current is predominantly reactive, and the *net power taken from a supply is equal to the total power loss in the two transformers under test*. If tappings are not available, or are unsuitable to circulate rated full-load current, it is a practice to inject the required circulating current through a small booster transformer connected in the leads between the two main transformers.

*The back-to-back connection, or direct loading, method is employed when making temperature rise tests on dry-type transformers, because the heat transformers from the core and windings to the cooling medium (air) are largely independent.* The test conditions therefore represent actual conditions in service when the core is heated by the magnetisation loss and the windings are heated by the load current.

### 14.8.2. Short-Circuit Test for Temperature Rise

In oil filled and oil-cooled transformers, the heat generated in both core and windings is transferred to the oil, and the total heat is dissipated from the oil to the cooling medium. The loss in the core is usually appreciably less than the loss in the windings, it is possible to employ the short-circuit method for temperature rise test. Fig. 14.8. and 14.9 show the circuit diagram.

As the S.C. test is conducted at reduced applied voltage, the core loss is almost negligible. Therefore, the current in the windings is adjusted to a value slightly above the rated value, so that the total loss in the windings is equal to the sum total of the separately measured load losses and core losses. The procedure during a short-circuit temperature rise test is to load the transformer with this increased current till observed oil *temperature rise becomes almost constant*, or is not rising at more than 1°C/hour. This part of the test proves that the cooling system of the transformer is capable to dissipate the total losses under normal full-load conditions and the oil temperature rise is recorded accordingly.

The increased current results in the higher temperature gradient between windings and oil than that is at the rat d value. The thermal time-constant of the windiness is relatively low. *Any change in current is quickly followed by a corresponding change in the temperature gradient between winding and oil.* After reaching final steady temperature, the winding and the oil temperature rise are recorded. Then the current is reduced to the normal rated value and maintained at this level for about 30 minutes. The supply is then switched-off and the d.c. resistance of the windings is measured by taking three temperature measurements in at regular intervals and plotting a graph of temperature versus time, from shut-down and extrapolating back the time of shut-down, the resistance of the windings at the instant of the shut down can be determined. *The winding temperature rise is then calculated by comparing the cold and hot resistances, with an allowance being made for any fall in oil temperature during the last half-hour at rated current.* Details are given in relevant standards such as BS 171.

## 14.9. INSULATION RESISTANCE MEASUREMENTS

The insulation resistance between windings and from each winding to earth is measured by a Megger.

Higher insulation resistances reveals that the transformer has been properly dried out. Insulation Resistance varies widely and inver-

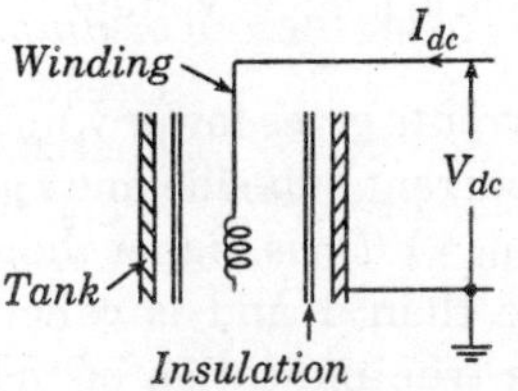


$I_n.R = V_{dc}/I_{dc}$

Fig. 14.12 (a) Concept of Insulation Resistance

sely with temperature, and care is necessary to ensure that the readings are correctly interpreted.

Insulation resistance is normally in Mega-ohms. If insulation is moist or if a track of conducting layer is formed on the surface, IR value would be low. IR measurement gives indication of the health of the insulation.

*Meggers* (mega ohms meters) are available for d.c. voltage of 500, 1000, and 2500 V. In transformer practice, the 500 V Meggers are used for measuring insulation resistance in the oil immersed transformers of up to 60 kVA and in all dry-type transformers of up to 1 kV. The 2500 V meggers are employed for larger transformers operating at voltages of 11,33 110,220 kV and above.

*The insulation resistance of a transformer is measured as follows*:

1. Between the windings collectively (*i.e.* which all the windings being connected together), and the grounded tank (ground).

2. Between each winding, and the tank, the rest of the windings being grounded.

For a *two-winding transformer* the following *three* measurements are to be taken:

— Between LV winding and tank, the HV winding being grounded;

— Between the HV winding and tank, LV winding being grounded;

— Between the LV/HV windings collectively and the tank necessary:

For a *three-winding transformers, five* measurements are necessary:

— Between the HV winding and the tank, the MV and LV windings being grounded;

— Between the MV winding and tank, the HV and LV windings being grounded;

— Between LV winding and tank, the HV and MV windings being grounded;

— Between the HV and MV windings collectively and the tank, the LV winding being grounded;

— Between the HV, MV and LV windings collectively, and the tank grounded.

For testing large transformers, motor-driven meggers are necessary. Following readings are taken

$R_0$ = Initial Reading

$R_{10}$ = Reading after continuous application of megger voltage for 10 minutes.

$R_{10}$ is higher than $R_0$. Initial capacitive currents gives lower value of $R_0 = V/I_0$. After some minutes DC charging current sub-side and $I_{10}$ has only due to leakage currents. Hence final $R_{10} = V/I_{10}$ is higher than intial $R_0 = V/I_0$. The ratio $K = R_{10}/R_0$ is more than 1 and is called *Polarization Index.* Polarisation Index gives a true indication of the dryness of insulation because it does not depend on capacitive currents. PI value also indicates ageing of the insulation. PI value goes down as the insulation ages.

$$K = \frac{R_{10}}{R_0}$$

should be more than 1.3, where

$R_{10}$ = 10th minute Megger reading

$R_0$ = Initial Megger reading.

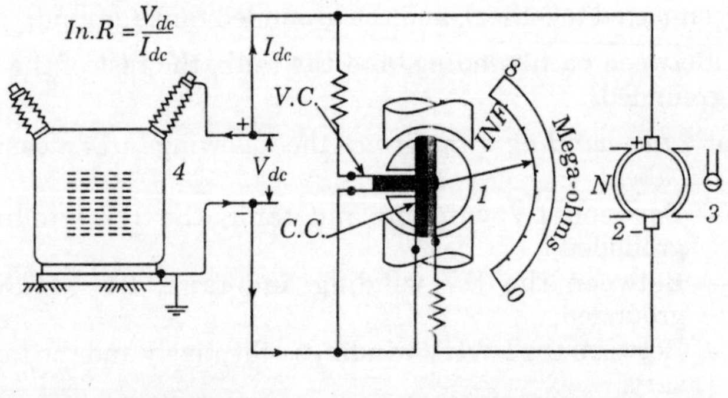


1. Mega-ohm meter 2. DC Generator
3. Drive motor 4. Test-object.
VC = voltage coil, CC = current coil.

Fig. 14.12. Measurement of Insulation Resistance by means of a Megger.

*Insulation resistance measurements and Polarisation Index reveal quality of the transformers insulation and the degree of the dryness. The subsequent high voltage tests can be avoided if insulation resistance is low.*

Measurement of the insulation resistances serves as a reference for repeated measurements after insulation tests and especially at site during the installation and periodic maintenance:

The resistance includes leakage resistance of external parts which may be sensitive to contamination and the internal insulation resistance which may be temperature dependent. Allowance for this must be given when using the results for reference.

The insulation resistance is measured at a direct voltage of 500, or 1000, 2500 V DC (Fig.14.12).

The main feature of this measurement process is the simplicity of the megger. It is therefore very suitable for applications in the site.

Insulation resistance is measured by *Megger*, Megger consists of a built in mega ohm meter and a d.c. generator. The generator is driven by hand or by a motor. Many times, battery operated Meggers are also used.

## 14.10 INSULATION CAPACITANCE AND ITS POWER FACTOR MEASUREMENTS

Measurement of insulation capacitance and its power factor serves as a reference for repeated measurement after the insulation tests and especially on site during installation.

The measurements are made with a capacitance bridge (Schering Bridge) at low voltage. A special capacitance bridge operates at 10 kV and power frequency.

If the measurements are made at power frequency, they are susceptible to interference from the power system. This requires stringent precautions and screening.

In new insulation, this type of measurement would provide indication only in the event of a serious failure.

Insulation Resistance Measurement and capacitance measurement are Special Tests. They are performed before applying the high voltage tests or switching-in the transformer to high voltage bus.

## 14.11. TESTS OF AUXILIARY CONTROL WIRING, AUXILIARIES OPERATION AND TAP-CHANGERS

These tests serve to verify the proper connections, the integrity of the insulation and the power losses of the control and auxiliary system.

For the test, the control system insulation is exposed to a specified test voltage. During the test, ordinary operation of the control system is executed as well as applicable sequence checks. This includes a check of all current transformers for ratio and polarity (often done during the impedance test). It also involves investigation of the performance of thermometers, protective relays, oil and air circulation equipment, etc.

The tap changer is operated over its full range and the performance of its control gear, including voltage measuring equipment if any, is verified.

The losses in auxiliary motors are measured.

The performance is considered acceptable if the insulation withstands the test voltage and the equipment operates properly and the losses are within guaranteed values.

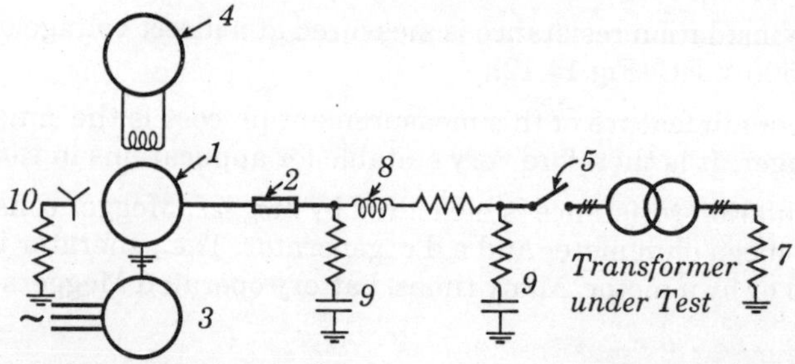


1. Short-circuit current generator.
2. Master circuit-breaker.
3. Drive motor for 1.
4. Impulse exciter for1.
5. Make switch.
6. Transformer under test.
7. Shunt.
8. Series impedance.
9. Shunt impedance.
10. Neutral grounding.

Fig. 14.13. Circuit diagram of a short-circuit test plant.

## 14.12. SHORT-CIRCUIT WITHSTAND TEST*

This is a special test. It is conducted in a short-circuit testing station.

The ability of a transformer to withstand external short-circuits (through short-circuits) is proved by conducting sudden short circuit tests.

A power transformer must be designed and manufactured such that it can withstand the mechanical and thermal stresses caused by external short-circuit currents.

When the short-circuit currents flow through transformer winding, the winding is subjected to radial electromagnetic force. The radial forces produce hoop stress on outer winding and compressive stress on inner winding.

The winding also experiences axial forces tending to the collapse the winding, fracture the end rings, bending of conductor between spacer.

The windings of transformers should be designed such that the windings does not get deformed during permissible short-circuit currents. The winding should withstand repeated short-circuits. The coil should be provided adequate sports and clamps.

The transformer is tested for short-circuit withstand test. Short circuit withstand test is special test on power transformers and is performed as per the agreement between manufacturer and user. In the short-circuit withstand test of a transformers, the secondary is short circuited. Low voltage is applied to transformer primary for specified short duration of the order of 2 seconds.

---

* Short-circuit tests for loss measurement are of steady state. They are different than short-circuit withstand test.

The short circuit withstand tests are performed as follows. HV terminals are connected to supply bus of the test plant. The LV side is short-circuited through measuring shunts.

As per the various standards on the distribution transformers, power transformers and regulating transformers, the transformer should be capable of withstanding mechanical and thermal stresses caused by external short circuit with following conditions:

— the magnitude of r.m.s. value of symmetrical short circuit current in any winding does not exceed *25 times the base current in that windings.*

— the duration of external short-circuit is limited to time period indicated in the table.

**Capabilities of Power Transformers to Carry High Currents for Short Time**

| *R.M.S. value of symmetrical current in a winding (Time rated current)* | *Time period in seconds or minutes* |
|---|---|
| 2 | 30 minutes |
| 3 | 5 minutes |
| 4.75 | 60 seconds |
| 6.7 | 30 seconds |
| 11.3 | 10 seconds |
| 14.4 | 5 seconds |
| 16.6 | 4 seconds |
| 20 | 3 seconds |
| 25 | 2 seconds |

The short-circuit withstand test is conducted in high power short-circuit laboratory. *e.g.,* CPRI's short-circuit. Testing and Development Station (STDS), Bhopal. The test sequence is discussed in advance with the testing authorities. The test shifts are booked will in advance. The transformer for test is taken to the testing laboratory and is installed in the test bay. Figure 14.13 shows a typical test circuit. The parameters of test circuit are arranged to get required S.C. current and peak of first loop. Short-circuit is initiated by closing the make switch 5 and is opened by opening the master breaker 2 and the desired time. The current waveform is automatically recorded on U.V. recorder. After the test, the transformer is subjected to dielectric tests. Tests may be as per standard or as per requirements of customer.

## 14.13. PARTIAL DISCHARGE TEST

Partial discharge testing is a refined, *non-destructive* technique for supervision of the insulation. It permits a more detailed supervision of the insulation without overstressing the insulation or causing breakdown.

The procedure during this test is similar to that described in clause 14.7'2 for in-winding insulation with induced voltage. Additional measuring equipment for observation of high frequency phenomena created by local, non-catastrophic insulation breakdown is necessary. Such equipment is normally connected to capacitive taps on the bushings. This measuring equipment may be wideband (20–600 kHz) or narrowband (9 kHz at 1 MHz).

The measuring technique calls for a special voltage sequence, with the total testing time of the order of 30 minutes.

The insulation is considered to have successfully passed the test if the partial discharge level was below specified values.

The sensitivity of this test method necessitates very high quality in the high voltage test equipment.

(Further details in Chapter 15).

## 14.14. ZERO SEQUENCE IMPEDANCE MEASUREMENTS

Measurement of the Zero sequence impedance test is conducted to verify calculated values.

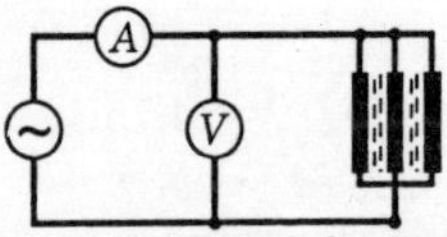


Fig. 14.14. Circuit for zero sequence Impedance test.

For this measurement, all three phases in a *Y*-connected winding are paralleled with the remaining windings on the transformers *open ended*. The *Y*-connected winding is energised by rated frequency and impedance measured by voltmeters and ammeters.

This test is usually performed together with a no-load test.

## 14.15. AUDIBLE SOUND LEVEL MEASUREMENT

This is a special test. The measurement is carried out in accordance with relevant standard with sound level meter having weighted calibration. (Ref. Chapter 10)

This test will verify the audible sound created by the transformer and its auxiliary plants.

As the audible sound from a transformer is essentially created by magnetostrictive effects in the core, the test is executed with the transformer excited in no-load operation.

The test area has to be carefully chosen with respect to other noise sources and with respect to surrounding walls, buildings, etc., that may reflect sound in an unfavourable manner.

Microphones are located around the transformer and the sound is analysed by frequency in accordance with standardised weighing curves. Because of the growing importance of noise as an environmental factor, the sound level measurement for power transformers is increasingly common. The specifications for various sizes of transformers stipulate maximum acceptable sound levels for each size of transformer. The sound level tests are normally carried out at the manufacturer's works. Such tests can only be satisfactorily conducted at times when factory background noise (including that of running test plant) can be kept to a level much below that of the noise of the transformer on test. The transformer on test should be well clear of walls or other large areas which would reflect sound and cause a build-up of noise which would give a false reading.

BS 171: Part 1: 1978 includes the measurement of acoustic sound level as a special test which is carried out according to IEC Publication 551.

## 14.16. COMMISSIONING TESTS

These are performed at site in accordance with an approved Field Quality Plan (FQP). *Commissioning tests differ considerably with the size and importance of the transformer.*

For a *small or medium-sized distribution transformer*, the minimum requirements would be a visual examination for transport damage and an insulation test with a portable instruments. There should be a check of the ratio (by applying a medium voltage to the high-voltage terminals and measuring the induced voltage at the low-voltage terminals), and on the oil level and condition to confirm that ingress of moisture has not occurred. Measurements of ratio and of polarity are essential if a transformer is to be connected in parallel with other transformers.

On large units which are normally dispatched either without oil or only partially filled, checks must be made on the filling procedure and of the condition of the oil prior to filling, in addition to ensuring that the insulation has not become were during transport.

*Auxiliary equipment* such as on-load tap changing gear and any protective relays and current transformers associated with the main transformer must also be checked for correct operation.

A repetition of high-voltage tests carried out at the works is not considered to be necessary. Where the transformer is subjected to retesting on site at high voltage, the test voltage level is normally restricted to 75% of that applied during tests before despatch from works. Further details are given in a separate chapter. Many times, no load current is also measured and compared with factory value.

## 14.17. HIGH VOLTAGE TESTING OF TRANSFORMERS

The windings and insulation system in a transformer are subjected to dielectric stresses of various magnitudes and wave-shapes. The effect of dielectric stress is felt in proportion to (1) Peak-value (crest-value) (2) Rate-of-rise (3) Duration. A power frequency over voltages at 50 Hz has comparatively low magnitude but is of very long duration. *Temporary power-frequency over voltages* occurring occasionally due to line-voltage regulation, sudden load throw-off etc., last for a few seconds. *Lightning impulse voltages* are of high crest value and short duration (a few tens of micro-seconds) Lightning surges are represented by a standard 1.2/50 micro-second wave having specified crest value. *Switching-impulse wave* has longer wave front and longer wave tail. It is represented by a standard 250/2500 μS wave having a specified crest value. The high voltage testing includes:

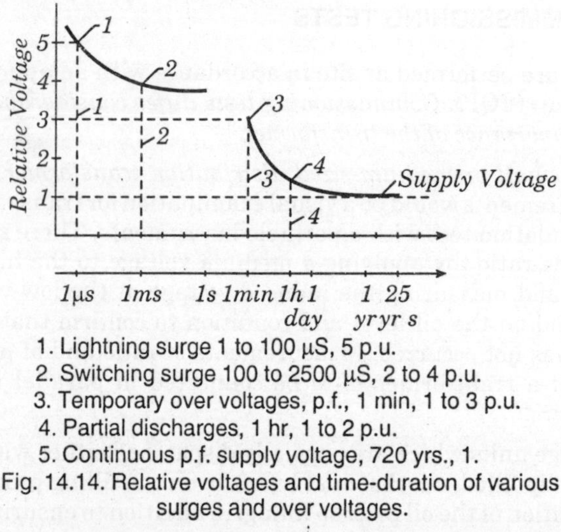


1. Lightning surge 1 to 100 μS, 5 p.u.
2. Switching surge 100 to 2500 μS, 2 to 4 p.u.
3. Temporary over voltages, p.f., 1 min, 1 to 3 p.u.
4. Partial discharges, 1 hr, 1 to 2 p.u.
5. Continuous p.f. supply voltage, 720 yrs., 1.

Fig. 14.14. Relative voltages and time-duration of various surges and over voltages.

— Power-frequency Tests
— Lightning Impulse Tests: Full Wave and Chopped Wave
— Switching Impulse Test.

These are conducted on a transformer to confirm that the windings and insulation system are capable of withstanding the relevant voltage stresses. The word 'Surge' is for network. The word impulse is for test wave. The stresses produced by these four types of voltages on a transformer are different due to the differences in crest value, rate-of-rise, frequency, duration of the waves.

The dielectric-stress distribution in the winding of a transformer is more uniform for power-frequency voltages and is nonuniform for lightning-impulse voltage waves. The end-turn insulation is stressed severely due to the initial voltage stresses during the lightning surges.

After a few micro-seconds, the oscillations are set-up in the winding and the other turns are stressed more resulting a certain curve of maximum voltage stress.

A transformer connected in the system is subjected to high voltage transients due to switching and lightning. The insulation of should not fail due to such voltage surges. The characteristics of the insulation are specified by *standards.* These characteristics should be proved by conducting high voltage tests. According to the standard specifications, certain type tests and certain routine tests should be performed. The standards pertaining to H.V. testing cover the following aspects:

(1) To define the insulation characteristics.
(2) To standardize the insulation levels.
(3) To specify the tests intended to verify insulation level and conditions under which the tests are made.
(4) To specify the markings on the rating plates.

International Electrotechnical Commission (I.E.C.) and standards institutions like Bureau of Indian Standards., B.S.I., specify standards covering the above aspects. The manufacturer normally conducts the type tests and routine tests in accordance with the above standards.

*Type tests* are performed to confirm the design. *Routine tests* are performed on every transformer before its despatch to ascertain manufacturing defects.

High voltage tests are also called Dielectric tests. They are performed to prove the specified insulation level of power transformer, bushing, tap-changer etc.

Following categories of high voltage tests are applicable to high-voltage transformer.

1. **Power-frequency withstand tests**

(a) Applied-voltage tests in which the test voltage is obtained from high voltage testing transformer.

(b) Induced voltage tests in which the voltage is stepped-up in the transformer under tests.

2. **Lightning Impulse Tests.** In which the standard lightning impulse wave 1.2/50 microsecond) is applied to the windings. The full lightning impulse wave is a routine/type test. A chopped lightning impulse test with the wave chopped during the wave front or wave tail is performed as a special test. Such a test simulates the stresses occurring due to sudden chopping of a lightning surge wave by a flash-over on line insulator or an external spark-gap.

The voltage levels, test-levels, test sequence, test procedures etc., are specified in relevant standards on insulation coordination and transformer testing.

Power frequency overvoltages are called *temporary over voltages*. The power frequency phase to ground and/or phase to phase voltage may exceed highest system voltage due to (1) Ferranti-effect (2) Sudden load throw-off (3) Single-phase to ground fault on other phase (4) Fero-resonance etc. Temporary overvoltages are of the order of 1.1 p.u. and may last for a few tens of seconds until the reactive power compensation and tap-changer control acts and brings the voltage back within targetted limits. Temporary over-voltage produces stresses of longer duration. The capability of the winding for such stresses is verified by power frequency withstand tests.

### 14.17.1. Applied Voltage Power-frequency Withstand Test

This is a type test and routine test. Specified test voltage is applied for one minute. There shall not be any flashover or break-down.

The test voltages depend upon the type of transformer (dry or oil immersed) applicable standard and specified insulation level. Typical reference values for power frequency test voltages are as follows:

**Table 14.2. Reference Values of Applied Power Frequency Test Voltage for Oil Immersed Transformers**

| *Normal system voltage* $kV_{rms}$ | *Highest System Voltage* $kV_{rms}$ | *Power frequency test Voltage 1 minute 50 Hz* $kV_{rms}$ | *Insulation* |
|---|---|---|---|
| 3.3 | 3.6 | 16 | |
| 6.6 | 7.2 | 22 | |
| 11 | 12.0 | 28 | |
| 15 | 75.5 | 38 | Uniform |
| 22 | 24 | 50 | |
| 33 | 36 | 70 | |
| 45 | 52 | 95 | |
| 66 | 12.0 | 140 | |
| 90 | 100 | 150 | |
| 110 | 123 | 185 | Graded |
| 132 | 145 | 230 | |
| 150 | 170 | 275 | |
| 220 | 245 | 395 | |
| 275 | 300 | 460 | Graded |
| 350 | 362 | 510 | |
| 400 | 420 | 630 | |

**Table 14.3**
**Power Frequency Voltage Withstand Test and Impulse Voltage Withstand Test For Voltage up to72.2 kV (Reference Values)***

| *Rated Insulation Level* | | *One Minute Power Frequency Withstand Voltage* | |
|---|---|---|---|
| *Rated voltage of circuit-breakers kV (r.m.s.)* | *Standard impulse withstand Voltage positive or negative polarity kV (peak)* | *For type test kV (r.m.s.)* | *V (r.m.s.) test kV (r.m.s.)* |
| 3.6 | 45 | 21 | 16 |
| 7.2 | 60 | 27 | 22 |
| 12 | 75 | 35 | 28 |
| 17.5 | 95 | 45 | 38 |
| 24 | 125 | 55 | 50 |
| 36 | 170 | 75 | 70 |
| 52 | 250 | 105 | 110 |
| 72.5 | 325 | 140 | 140 |

* These value are for familiarity.

For actual practice refer the relevant standards.

**Table 14.4.** (Above 72.5 kV Reference Values)*

| *Rated Insulation Level* | | | *One Minute Power Frequency Voltage withstand* | |
|---|---|---|---|---|
| *Standard Impulse Withstand Voltage* | | | *For Type and Routine Tests* | |
| *Rated voltage kV (r.m.s.)* | *Full insulation kV (r.m.s.)* | *Reduced insulation kV (r.m.s.)* | *Full insulation kV (r.m.s.)* | *Reduced insulation kV (r.m.s.)* |
| 100 | 450 | 380 | 185 | 150 |
| 123 | 450 | 380 | 230 | 185 |
| 145 | 650 | 550 | 275 | 230 |
| 170 | 750 | 650 | 325 | 275 |
| 245 | 1050 | 900 | 460 | 395 |
| | — | 1050 | — | 460 |
| 420 | | 1425 | | 680 |

Applied high-potential test are normally made, sequentially, between each winding, and the core and all other windings connected to earth.

*Figure 14.15* shows the circuit for the high-voltage winding under test and the low-voltage windings and core connected together and to earth.

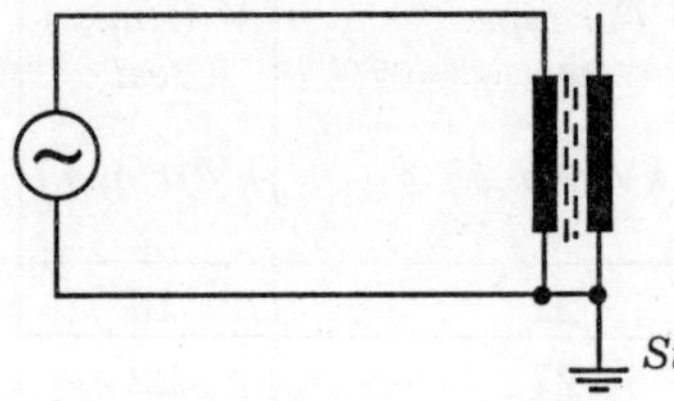

Fig. 14.15. Circuit for applied high voltage test.

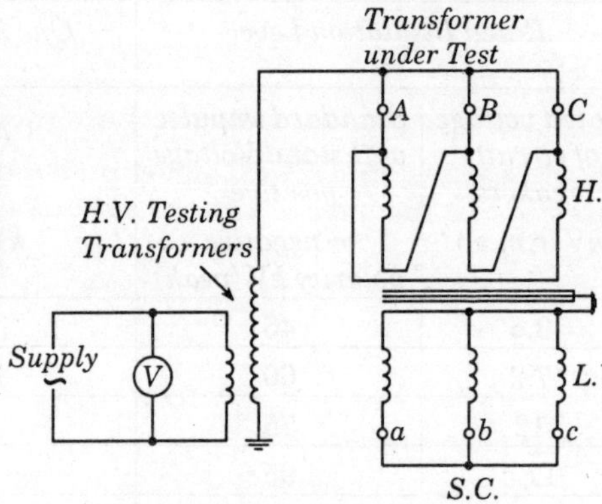


Fig. 14.16. Circuit for applied high voltage tests.

This test will demonstrate the capability of the insulation between windings, and between windings and structural (core) parts, to withstand the stresses from specified, sinusoidal powers frequency test voltages.

For transformers with graded insulation, further testing of the interwinding insulation is made by induced voltage.

The test voltage from a suitable power source is applied on winding sets (structures). on each side of the insulation. The voltage is quickly raised to the specified level and kept there for a certain fixed duration, usually one minute.

This procedure does not excite the transformer core electromagnetically. The voltage is measured as a crest value.

The performance is considered as satisfactory provided there is no noticeable breakdown of the insulation. The test is monitored by measurements of the voltages and currents.

The value of the applied voltage depends on the rated voltage of the winding in question and on whether the major insulation between it and earth is uniform or graded. For a uniformly insulated winding, the applied voltage provides the principal dielectric test of the main insulation. It is usually of the order of $(2V_h + 1)$ kV, where $V_h$ is the 'highest system voltage' for the winding in question. On a 3-phase transformer, an applied voltage test of $2V_h$ raises the line terminals of $3.46 \times$ their normal operating voltage to earth.

For graded insulation windings, the applied test voltage is at a value appropriate to the insulation level at the neutral point and therefore, does not adequately prove the strength of the line-end insulation.

### 14.17.2. Induced High Voltage Tests

In order to demonstrate the capability of the *interturn* and other *in-winding insulation* to withstand stresses from specified test voltages, this test with induced voltage is performed.

For transformer with graded insulation, induced voltage is also used to test the *inter-winding insulation.*

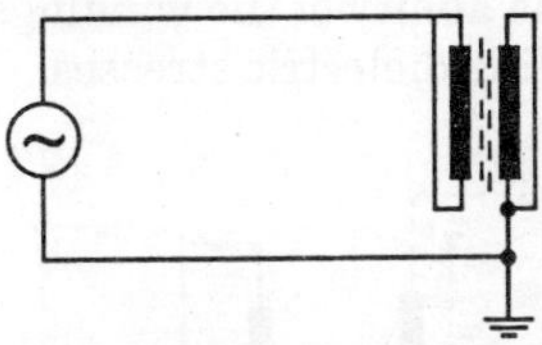

Fig. 14.16. Circuit for induced voltage tests.

The test voltage from a suitable power source is supplied to one of the windings sets so that the core is excited. Consequently, voltages corresponding to the turns ratio are induced in all the windings of the transformer.

The voltage is quickly raised to the specified level and kept there for a predetermined duration.

The test voltage is always much higher than the rated voltage. Therefore, in order to avoid over excitation of the core, a correspondingly higher frequency is needed for the test voltage than the rating of the transformer.

The duration of the test is usually chosen with regard to the frequency of the voltage, so that the specified number of cycles are included.

The test is performed with the transformer connected normally.

If the transformer is equipped with multiphase windings with graded insulation, tests have also to be made in special single-phase connections in order to expose those windings to proper test voltages.

The performance during the test is considered acceptable if there is no noticeable breakdown of the insulation. This is monitored by observation of voltages and currents and of acoustic effects.

In a special test, performance is monitored by observation of partial discharges.

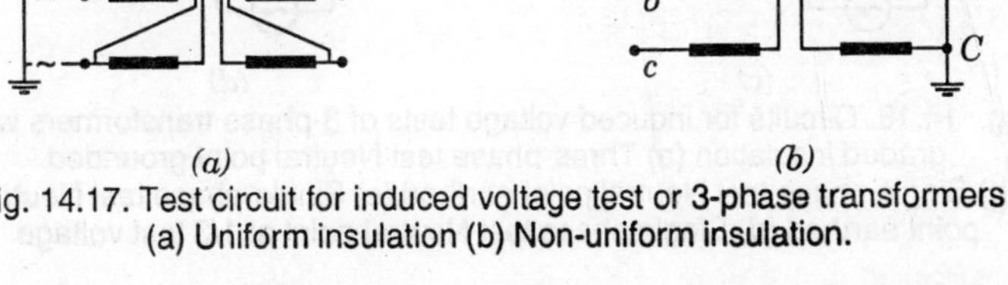


Fig. 14.17. Test circuit for induced voltage test or 3-phase transformers (a) Uniform insulation (b) Non-uniform insulation.

The induced overvoltage test is performed by exciting the transformer on open circuit at a voltage higher than normal for a short period. On transformers, with uniform insulation on which the applied high-potential test provides the principal check on the strength of the major insulation, the objective of the induced test is to prove the strength of the insulation between turns and between other points of the transformer operating at different potentials. The value of test voltage is usually twice rated voltage, and to prevent overexcitation of the core the frequency of supply also should be increased to at least twice normal.

The induced voltage test demonstrates the ability of the windings and insulation system to withstand the following dielectric stresses:

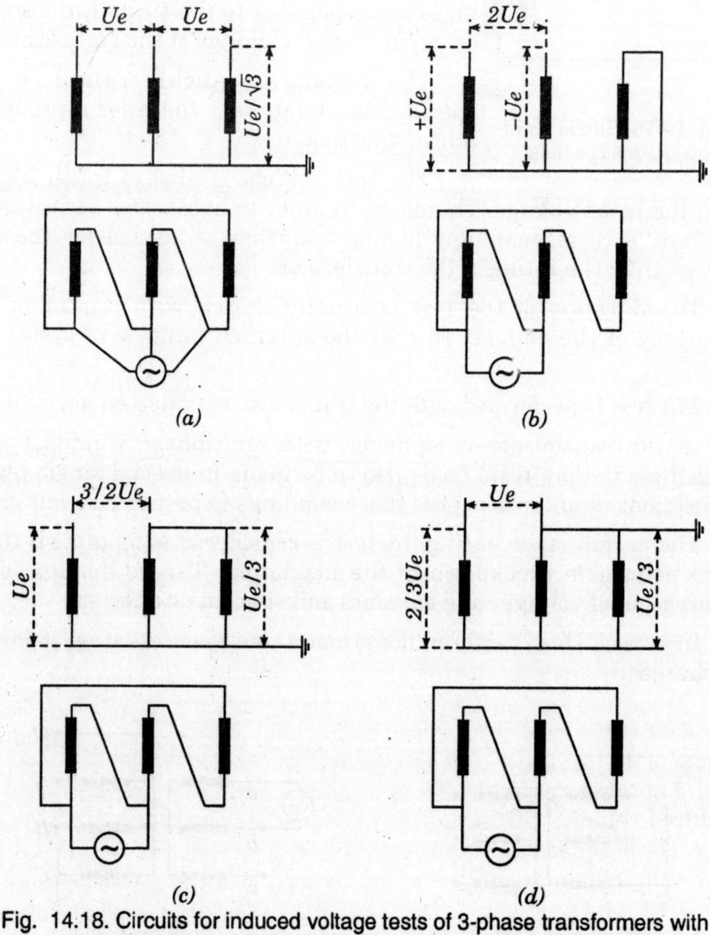


Fig. 14.18. Circuits for induced voltage tests of 3-phase transformers with graded insulation (a) Three-phase test Neutral point grounded (b) Single phase test Neutral point earthed (c) Single-phase test Neutral point earthed (d) Single phase test Neutral point at 1/3 test voltage.

1. In-winding insulation to withstand operational voltage stresses.
2. Inter-winding insulation to withstand operational stresses.
3. Winding-to-earth insulation to withstand operational stresses.

During the dielectric test with induced voltage, the insulation will, for short time, be exposed to dielectric stresses that are a certain multiple of those at rated operational voltage.

During a test with induced voltage, the transformer is excited on one winding (single-phase or three-phase, as applicable) with remaining windings in open circuit. Voltages are then induced in all the windings according to the turns ratio.

The test voltage is always a multiple of the rated voltage and in order not to over-excite the core, the test is always made with increased frequency, normally four to five times the rated frequency.

Energy for the test is created with a rotary converter,operating through a step-up transformer.

There are two main classes of test circuits to consider, those for transformers with uniform insulation and those for transformers with non-uniform insulation.

As an example of a transformer with uniform insulation, consider Fig. 14.17 and 14.18.

One of the windings on the transformers is excited from the test power source and the remaining windings are earthed at one end and left open-circuited. Voltage are induced in the different windings according to their turn ratio.

For a transformer of this kind, with uniform insulation between windings, the inter-winding insulation is tested with applied voltage, a test that is not discussed here.

For a transformer with non-uniformly insulated windings, the test with induced voltage also serves to demonstrate the capability of the inter-winding insulation. This requires a different circuit and a number of possibilities exist. Many of these eases are elaborated in the Standards. Fig. 14.18. gives an example.

This transformer is assumed to have three legs with two windings on each of the legs. The test voltage is supplied between terminals $a$ and $b$. With terminals $B$ and $C$ earthed, the neutral will then be exposed to 1/3 of the induced voltage and the remaining terminal $A$ to the full induced voltage. This test must be repeated for all three phases.

The standard duration of the induced voltage test is 60 seconds for any test frequency up to and including twice the treated frequency. When the test frequency exceeds twice the rated frequency the duration of the test should be equal to

$$60\left(\frac{2 \times \text{rated frequency}}{\text{test frequency}}\right), \text{ seconds}$$

but in no case should the duration of the test be less than 15 seconds. In the case of polyphase transformers, especially three-phase high-voltage units, it is permissible to apply the test voltage to individual phases in succession.

### 14.7.3. Full Lightning Impules Voltage Test

This test serves to verify the capability of the insulation to withstand the stresses from a standardized voltage impulse applied at the winding terminal.

The voltage impulse is created by Impulse Generator, by the discharge of a capacitor bank into a suitable circuit connected to the transformer terminal.

The circuit is adjusted (if necessary, during pre-tests are reduced amplitude) to create standardised impulse shape of specified amplitude. (Typical 1.2 microsecond front time and 50 microseconds to half value).

The shape of the impulse is carefully compared with the shape of the reduced amplitude pre-test. Good similarity in the shapes indicates that the insulation has successfully withstood the test. Additional information regarding the insulation can be obtained by anlaysis of oscillograms of the current in the winding and of other physical phenomena, such as audible noise.

The standardised lightning impulse insulation test is the result of considerable industrial experience and research. It is a good, practical representation of stresses on the insulation, create by atmospheric over-voltages induced in overhead lines due to lightning strokes.

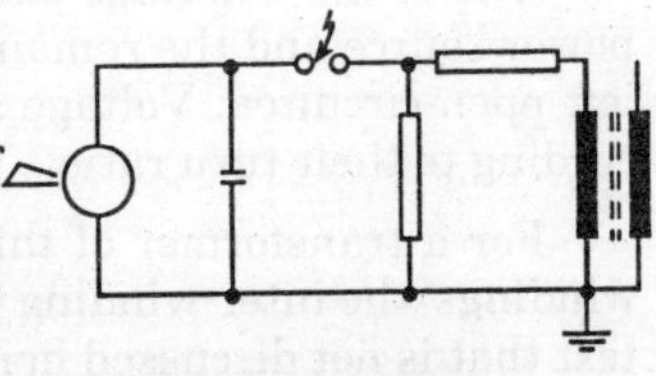

Fig. 14.19. Lightning impulse test.

The full lightning impulse test simulates the stresses occurring when a transformer is subjected to an incoming high-voltage surge due to lightning or other disturbances on the associated transmission line.

The tests are conducted as per recommendations of relevant standards. (Ref. Table 14.3,4).

A typical test sequence for impulse tests is as follows:

(1) One reduced-level full-wave (voltage between 50% and 75% of the full-wave voltage test level).

(2) One full-wave at specified test level.

(3) Two chopped waves with a crest value not less than the specified full-wave test level.

(4) One full-wave at the test level.

During the tests, print-out are obtained for each tests-shot each test result is analysed.

The photo-print of current and voltage wave shapes are carefully compared with each other and with the trial taken during the preliminary reduced voltage shots. Any discrepancy, however slight, in the wave shape of any one of the records compared with the others indicates a change in the conditions either in the test sets or in the transformer under test. Such discrepancies must be investigated and satisfactorily explained. The doubts should be removed. Any failure to do so involves the risk of despatching a transformer with damaged insulation to site and subsequent failure in service.

If any oscillogram differs from the trial oscillogram and doubt persists regarding possible weakness in the winding, three more impulse shots of full 100% wave are recommended by BS 171.

### 14.7.4. Chopped Lightning Impulse Voltage Wave Test

The chopped wave test represents the conditions that arise when an incoming surge is suddenly chopped because of a flashover of an insulator in or near the substation, and it is prudent to ensure that the transformer is capable of safely withstanding events of this nature.

This test is like the previous lightning impulse test with full wave, except that after a pre-determined time, usually on the tail of the impulse, an intentional collapse of the voltage is created in a standardised manner (usually by triggered spark gaps).

When this test is carried out, it is interwoven with the lightning impulse test with full wave so that the latter test can be used for indication that the insulation has successfully withstood the test with the chopped wave as well.

This test with the standardised chopped lightning impulse simulates the action of overvoltage protection in the field, located close to the transformer (for instance, spark gaps or surge arresters).

The main purpose of the chopped wave test as part of the impulse-type test series is to increase the stress in the insulation within and between the coils adjacent to the transformer line terminal.

#### Application of Test Voltage

Tests are conducted separately in the following order:

— HV winding.
— MV winding.
— LV winding.

Test voltage is applied to the each winding and earth. The terminals of winding to be tested are connected together to HV terminal of HV test transformer. All the other winding terminals are con-

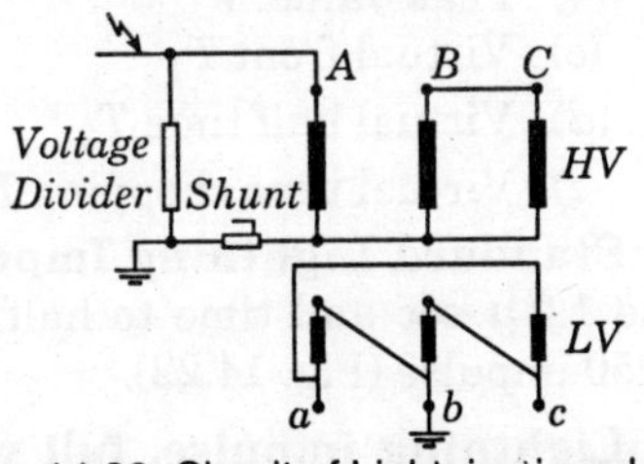

Fig. 14.20. Circuit of Lightning impulse test on HV terminal A.

nected together to earthed tank, and are earthed.

Figure 14.20. shows a circuit connection for lightning impulse test for a 3-limb transformer. Figure 14.26 shows test circuit for switching impulse tests.

### 14.7.5. Standard Impulse Wave Shapes

IEC 60.1. 'High voltage test techniques', gives the following definitions:

All impulse is an intentionally applied a-periodic transient voltage.

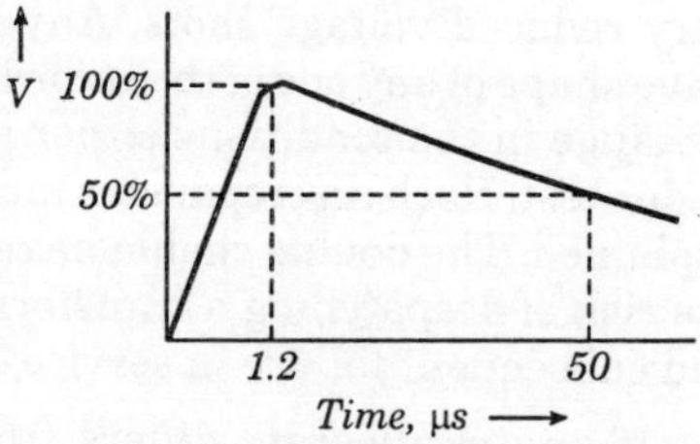


Fig. 14.21. Full Lightning impulse (1.2/50 wave).

The term '*impulse*' is to be distinguished from the term '*surge*' which refers transients occurring in electrical equipment or networks in service."

Following standard impulse wave-shapes are specified:

1. Full lightning impulse.
2. Chopped lightning impulse (*a*) Front chopped (*b*) Test-chopped.
3. Switching Impulse.

**Standard Lightning Impulse Wave Shape**

In an electrical transmission system, lightning surges may occur during natural thunderstorms, either because of direct lightning strokes, or when charges are suddenly released by lightning to ground close by. These surges have a very short rise time (MV/μs) and are of relatively short duration (100μs).

In a laboratory these are represented by *lightning impulse* with a standardised wave shape, the definition of which is given in Fig. 14.21 and Fig. 14.22.

**Impulse Voltage Wave.** An impulse voltage wave is characterized by

(*a*) Polarity, positive or negative
(*b*) Peak value, $V$
(*c*) Virtual front $T_1$
(*d*) Virtual half time $T_2$
(*e*) Virtual time chopping $T_e$.

**Standard Lightning Impulse** is a full impulse having a front time 1.2 μ–sec and time to half value of 50 μ–sec. It is described as 1.2/50 impulse (Fig. 14.22).

**Lightning impulse, full wave test.** According to IEC 60 the lightning impulse test, full wave, should be made with one initial

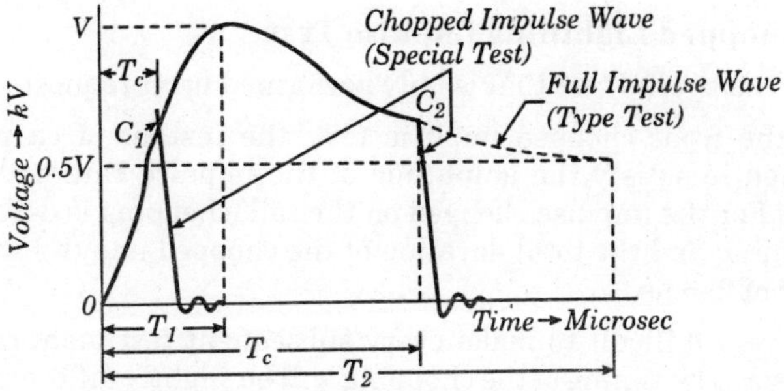


$T_1$ = Wave front : 12 μ sec

$T_e$ = Chopping time : $C_1 < 1.2$ μs, $C_2 > 1.2$ μs. (2 to 6 μs).

$T_2$ = Wave tail: 50 μ sec

Fig. 14.22. Standard impulse voltage wave.

impulse at reduced amplitude followed by three impulses at full level. This test sequence is applied to each terminal of the transformer.

The amplitude of the impulse is related to the insulation level of the system to be connected to the terminals and if the transformer is designed with uniform or non-uniform insulation.

The first impulse with reduced amplitude (normally, 60%) is to check the adjustment of the impulse circuits and to establish a reference for future evaluation of the full amplitude tests. The oscillograms taken both during the reduced amplitude test and during the three full amplitude impulse tests are all carefully compared. If they show the same impulse wave shape in every detail, this is considered an indication that the transformer has passed the tests and that its insulation is in good condition.

If there are any deviations between the oscillograms, this is interpreted as evidence of the presence of irregularities and a thorough investigation is then necessary.

### Chopped Impulse Wave

In a transmission system, a lightning surge may create a flash-over in air on external insulation. Such flashover imply a sudden dramatic voltages breakdown, which propagates through the system and stresses the internal insulation of transformers.

To simulate this in the laboratory, two different chopped impulse tests are used, one when the impulse is chopped already on the rising front at a specified voltage level, and the other when the impulse is chopped on the tail after a specified time.

The total duration of the front chopped impulse is about **1** μs. whereas the impulse chopped on the tail has a duration of **2–6** μs.

### 14.7.6. Chopped Lightning Impulse Test

This is a special test that is only performed upon request.

For the front chopped impulse test, the instant of chopping is determined to satisfy the amplitude of the impulse rather than the duration. For the impulse chopped on the tail, chopping is determined by the timing and the total duration of the chopped impulse will be of the order of 2–6 μs.

It is very difficult to make every subsequent test identical to its predecessor. The timing of the chopping will be slightly different for the different impulses and this makes direct comparison of the oscillograms unsuitable for detection of any defects. The differences between oscillograms may easily be caused by different test conditions.

Considering these difficulties, in analysing test results tests with chopped impulses are always interwoven with tests with full wave lightning impulse in the following manner:

The sequence begins with one reduced amplitude and one full amplitude full wave lightning impulse.

One reduced amplitude chopped impulse.

Two full amplitude chopped impulses.

Finally two full amplitude full wave lightning impulses.

The criterion for successfully passing of this test sequence is the comparison of the oscillograms of the full wave impulse tests at the beginning and the end of the sequence.

### 14.7.7. Switching Impulse Wave

Long duration surges in transmission systems (100 μs and even several ms) usually occur with the operation of circuit breakers and disconnectors. They may be unipolar pulses or they may have oscillatory waves shapes. In order to ascertain the transformer's ability to withstand such long duration stresses, research has been carried out into extremely severe wave shapes that create the highest probability of failure of the insulation. This critical wave shape is dependent on the type of insulating structure. For transformers where the insulation consists of a combination of oil and cellulose, the switching impulse wave shape has been standardised.

Due to the difficulties of generating the switching impulse, the criteria are only minimum values. The virtual front time should exceed 20μs and duration above 90% of crest value should exceed 200 μs. The total duration to first zero passage should be at least 500 μs.

Due to the non-linear magnetic properties of the transformer core, the actual wave shape of the switching impulse may be as illustrated in Fig.3 with a "saturation collapse". This is created when the transformer core is driven into saturation by the switching impulse.

**Standard switching impulse** wave is characterized by prolonged wave-front and wave tail. The typical switching impulse wave has front time of the order of 250 μs and half-time of 2500 μs. The permissible deviation in the crest value is of the order of 4 to 12%. The switching impulse wave has been specified for high voltage transformers rated above 220 kV.

### 14.7.8. Switching Impulse Test

Switching surges occur in electrical networks whenever a circuit-breaker operates. The wave shapes are characterized by longer wave front and longer wave tail. A representative standard wave is called standard switching impulse. It has a wave front of 250 μs and wave tail of 2500 μs. Ref. Fig. 14.24.

This test is similar to the lightning impulse test except that the wave shape has a much longer duration (typical rise time 20 microseconds and total duration exceeding 500 microseconds).

During this test, the voltage is essentially evenly distributed along the winding and also magnetically transferred to the other windings. This may create saturation of the core upon repeated tests and consequently overloading of the surge generator. Therefore polarity reversal may be necessary between consecutive impulses.

Observation of internal audible noise through microphones attached to the tank walls may assist in identification and location of failures.

During a switching impulse test, the voltage distribution in the transformer is not capacitive but inductive, and follows the turns ratio.

In order that the proper switching impulse wave shape should be created, the transformer must be so connected the winding under test presents its open-circuit impedance to the generator. In order to achieve this, the other windings on the transformer should be open-circuited or short-circuited in a suitable way. The circuit must be selected so that induced impulses in the other windings will not overstress the insulation level.

A commonly used connection for a 3-phase transformer is shown in Fig. 14.23.

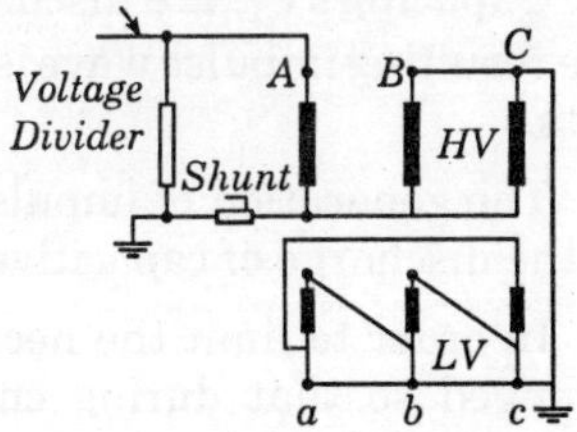

Fig. 14.23. Circuit for switching impulse test on terminal A.

If a winding is short-circuited during the switching impulse test, the magnetic flux is prevented from passing this winding. This can be utilized to reduce phase to phase voltage during the test.

For voltage $U$ on terminal $A$, Terminals $B$ and $C$ will receive voltage $+ U/2$ and thus $1.5\ U$ will appear between $A$ and $B$.

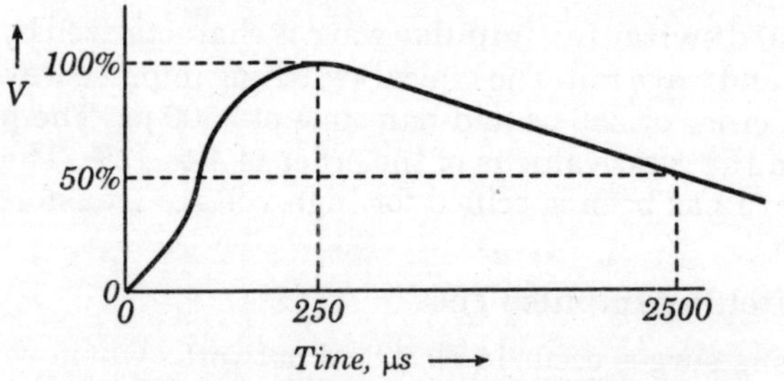


Fig. 14.24. Full switching impulse (250/2500 wave).

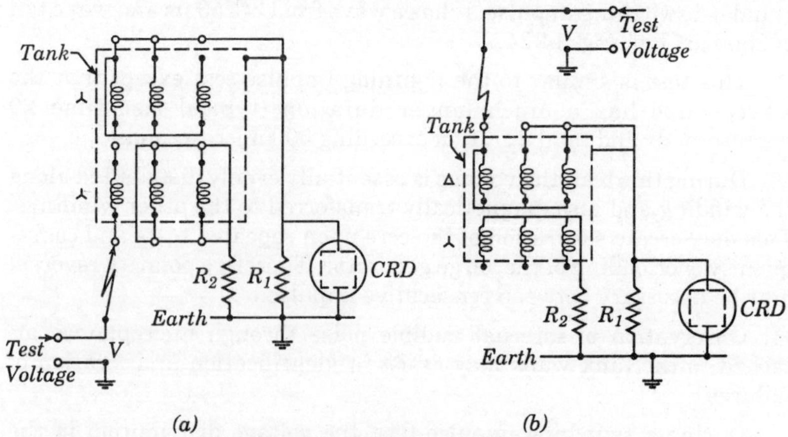


Fig. 14.25. Application of impulse test.

**Test Plant for Impulse Tests.** Impulse tests are conducted in high voltage test laboratory. Figure 14.26. illustrates the test setup.

**Impulse Generator.** Figure 14.27 shows a three stage impulse generator impulse waves of steep wave front and flat wave tail are obtained from the same. This is also called Marx generator.

Capacitors $C_G$ are discharged simultaneously by triggering gap 4. The resulting impulse wave is applied to the transformer winding under tests.

The generation of impulse voltages for insulation testing is based on the discharge of capacitive energy.

In order to limit the necessary charge voltage, the capacitors are arranged so that during charging they are parallel-connected and during discharge they become series-connected.

During charging, the capacitors are all parallel-connected through the resistor $R_P$ and the sphere gaps withstand the voltage. At the moment of "firing" the generator, all stages are series-connected by triggering the sphere gaps. Only the bottom sphere gap need by trig-

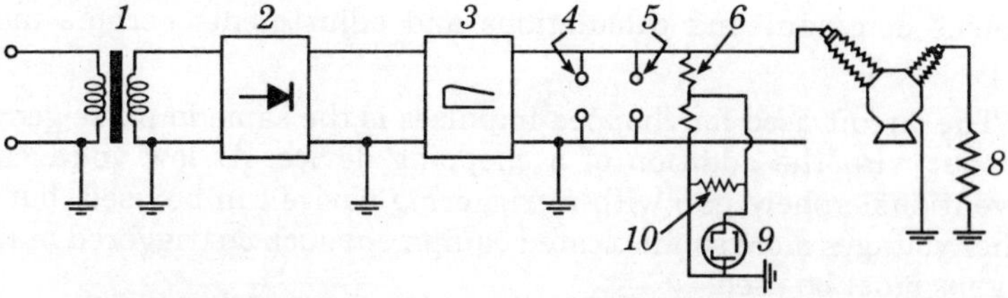


1. AC voltage source.
2. Transformer and rectifier.
3. Impulse generator (Fig. 14.26)
4. Road gap.
5. Sphere gap.
6. Voltage divider.
7. Transformer under test.
8. Low resistance.
9. C.R.O.
10. Low resistance shunt.

Fig. 14.26. Circuit for impulse test.

gered externally. All the other will spark over spontaneously as a consequence of the sudden change in voltage distribution. In order to make this possible, the spacing of the sphere gaps are mechanincally adjusted to match the charge voltage, which is chosen with regard to the test object.

Correct wave shapes are created by proper selection of the parallel and series resistors. Keeping in mind that it is mainly a question of charging and discharging capacitors through the resistors, it will be understood from Fig. 14.27. that the front time is essentially determined by the charging of the test object capacitance $C_1$ through the series resistors $R_s$ whereas the tail of the impulse is essentially determined by the discharge of the impulse generator capacitors $C_G$ through the parallel resistors $R_P$. For approximate calculations the following formula can be used:

$$T_1 = 2.5\, R_S\, C_1$$

$$T_2 = 0.7\, R_P\, C_G$$

where $T_1$ = rise time

$T_2$ = time of half value .

These formulae are applicable to lightning impulse wave shapes only. For switching impulse waves, the impedance of the test object

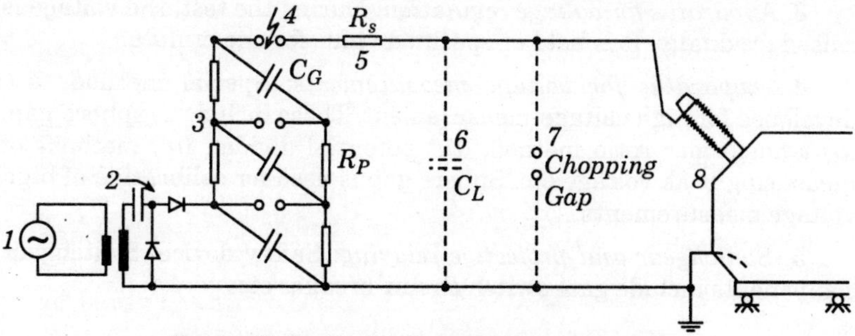


Fig. 14.27. Circuit of a 3-stage impulse generator.

becomes dominant and calculations and adjustments become more complicated.

The circuit used for chopped impulses is the same impulse generator but with the addition of a chopping device. At low voltages a conventional sphere gap with a triggering device can be used, but at higher voltages more sophisticated equipment such as triggered multiple gaps must be used.

### 14.7.9. Test Plant for Applied Power Frequency Test.

Figure 14.28 shows a simplified circuit diagram.

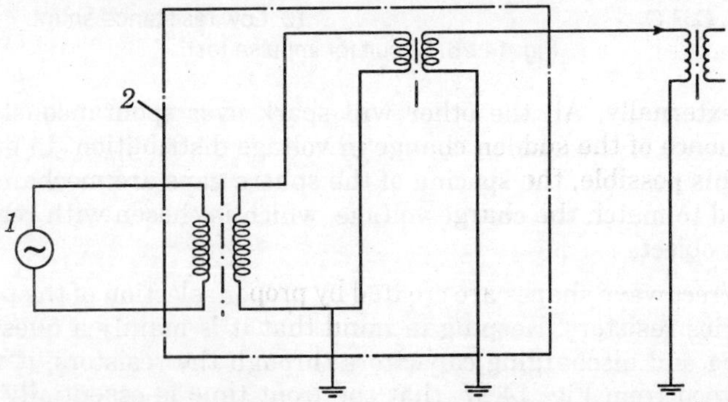


1. Variable voltage p.f. source. 2. High voltage testing transformer.
3. Transformer under test.

Fig. 14.28. Circuit of power-frequency voltage test by applied potential method.

These tests are conducted in high voltage tests laboratory. The equipment for conducting power frequency high voltage tests are the following:

1. *Voltage source*: Single phase generator driven by a.c. motor. The terminal voltage can be varied widely by changing the field current.

2. *High voltage testing transformers*: These are single phase transformer units. For obtaining high voltage the units are connected in cascade.

3. *Apparatus for voltage regulation*: During the test, the voltage is raised gradually. It is held at specified value for one minute.

4. *Apparatus for voltage measurements*: Special methods are developed for high voltage-measurement. These include (*i*) sphere-gap, (*ii*) transformer ratio method, (*iii*) potential divider, (*iv*) methods of measuring peak voltage etc. Sphere gap is used for calibration of high voltage measurements.

5. *Switchgear and protective relaying*: Safety device. Switchgear components include gate switch circuit-breaker etc.

In addition to the equipments (1) to (5) mentioned above, the following equipment is usually provided to conduct D.C. test, high frequency tests and impulse test.

1. Instruments for measurement and record.
2. Devices to obtain high voltage D.C.
3. Devices to obtain high frequency supply.
4. Devices to obtain impulse wave.
5. Equipment for testing dielectric oil, etc.

The test voltage is obtained from a single phase a.c. generator driven by an induction motor. The terminal voltage can be varied widely by changing the field current. The generator voltage is stepped up by high voltage transformer. The test voltage is supplied to the apparatus under test. The sphere gap is connected in parallel with the test specimen. The voltmeter on generator side, *i.e.,* L.T. side can be calibrated by means of sphere-gap. In addition instruments for measurements may be connected on H.T. side by means of potential divider. Resistances are connected in the H.T. side to limit the current after breakdown.

**H.V. Testing Transformer.** Such transformers are single phase units. For obtaining test voltages upto 500 kV, usually a single unit is used. For higher voltage of 1000 kV and upwards two or more transformers are generally used and are connected in *Cascade.* This method is convenient because a single unit for very high voltage is very large and costly. Cascade condition gives flexible test conditions. Cascade connection is illustrated in Fig. 14.28.

**Sphere Gaps.** The break-down voltage between sphere-gaps can be precisely calculated. Sphere gaps are used for calilbration of voltmeters used for high voltage measurement.

Sphere-gaps can be used for (1) D.C. voltage, (2) Power-frequency voltage (3) Impulse voltage.

The procedure consists of establishing a relation between high voltage as measured by the sphere gap and indicating voltmeter,an oscillograph or device connected for voltage measurement. Under standard test conditions, the voltage measured by sphere-gap can be derived from the spacing. It means from the known diameter of spheres, known test conditions and known spacing of gaps the peak value of disruptive discharge voltage can be derived from the standard table. From this value the other measuring insturment can be calibrated.

As per IEC Standard sphere-gaps are of following dimensions.

D – 2 – 5 – 6.25 – 10 – 12.5 – 15 – 25 – 50 – 75 – 100 – 150 – 200 cm (12 standard Diameters).

Standard sphere-gap is a peak voltage measuring device constructed and arranged according to the rules specified by the standards, some of which are given below. Before conducting a test, the standards pertaining to High Voltage Testing Techniques and Sphere Gaps should be thoroughly studied. The sphere gap consists of two metal spheres of equal diameter (*D*) with their shanks, operating gear, insulating support, supporting frames, leads upto the point at which the voltage is to be measured.

One sphere is preferably connected directly to earth and the tank of the transformer under test. If resistance is connected in this, circuit should be of a low value.

The other sphere is connected to high voltage conductor. The lead coming from high voltage transformer or impulse generator.

## Summary

Testing of transformers is a specialised and advance science. Test procedures, test requirements, interpretations etc., have been standardised. As per standards the tests are classified as Type Tests, Routine Tests, Special Tests, Commissioning Tests. However the distiniction is reducing as the tests are generally decided between the manufacturer and the user. Important tests have been listed in Sec. 14.1.

# 15

## Partial Discharges and their Location

The breakdown in a transformer or a reactor is usually preceeded by local discharges at weak points in insulation. Partial discharge (PD) is a localized, low-energy dielectric discharge in insulating material without complete dielectric breakdown. PD occurs in contaminated insulation, defective insulation, in voids, flows etc., at overstressed points due to excessive electric field. PD measurement gives advance warning about possible failure. For high voltage transformers, the measurement of PD is an important non-destructive method of testing which provides valuable information concerning the state of insulation. Partial Discharge Measurement techniques have been developed during 1970's and have now been introduced as *Routine Tests*.

Three types of measuring techniques have been developed.

— Measurement of high frequency (h.f) charge ($\rho C$).

— Measurement of h.f. voltage ($\mu V$ at 1 MHz).

— Ultrasonic measurements.

By locating the partial discharge, the weak points in the insulation are known. Thereby corrective action can be taken in time and the failure of the transformer can be avoided. Locating partial discharges in a transformer or a reactor is an extremely complicated task. Efforts during 1970's and 1980's have resulted in effective methods of locating PD.

Partial discharge monitoring provides a warning to remove the transformer service before catastrophic failure occurs. In fact, PD monitoring is the only mechanism for preventing those failures as PD can deteriorate rapidly to breakdown. It is helpful to monitor it continuously.

### 15.1 DEFINITION AND NATURE OF PD

Partial Discharge is defined as localised, low energy discharge in insulation which does not result in complete flashover or breakdown. Partial discharge is also defined as a partial dielectric rupture in the insulating material without complete flashover or breakdown.

### 15.2 CAUSES OF PARTIAL DISCHARGE

When dielectric stress on the insulating material is gradually increased, the partial discharges begin at weak points such as voids, cavities, gas bubbles, dirty surface, impurities, conducting particles, moisture particles etc. As the stresses increase, the partial discharge of electrical charge occurs over the local defect in small duration of less than 0.1 microsecond. The electric charge jumps/flows through the defect causing a local discharge which generates high frequency signals of several 10 MHz.

Some causes of P.D. in transformers and reactors include.

— Defects in insulating material due to improper processing
— Presence of moisture.
— Surface defects
— Non-uniform voltage stress distribution resulting in high stress pockets.
— Sharp edges on conducting parts or earthed parts.
— Gas bubbles in oil.
— Solid impurities in oil.

Although partial discharges are of low energy and lesser duration, they are the origin of possible runaway effects leading to progressive deterioration of the dielectric properties and subsequent failure of insulating materials.

Low energy partial discharges appearing in gaseous bubbles produce a substantial amount of hydrogen with small quantity of saturated hydrocarbons, methane and ethane in smaller operations. High energy discharges or small arc causes the formation of acetylene. Additionally, ą significant amount of CO and $CO_2$ indicate that cellulose is degrading.

## 15.3 PHYSICS OF PARTIAL DISCHARGE

As mentioned, the partial discharges occur at discontinuities in the insulation, often gaseous voids or other weaknesses.

Fig. 15.1 illustrates a region with a void of this type between two electrodes.

The void $C$ in the insulation is the weak spot. When the local electric field strength in this void exceeds the withstand ability of the gas, a breakdown of this insulation occurs and this void is electrically short-circuited. This creates a relocation of electrical charges in the vicinity of the weak spot, which is accompanied by a current pulse in the whole test circuit.

Fig. 15.2 gives a simplified equivalent electrical circuit for the test object. The three capacitances represent the three regions around the weak spot before the discharge. The voltage across $C_c$ was $U_c$ before the discharge. The voltage across the whole system, $U_i$ which may extend all the way to the external terminals of the transformer, changes by the quantity $\Delta U$, when $U_c$ collapses. The relation between these voltages is:

$$\Delta U = U_c \cdot \frac{C_b}{C_a + C_b} \qquad ...(15.1)$$

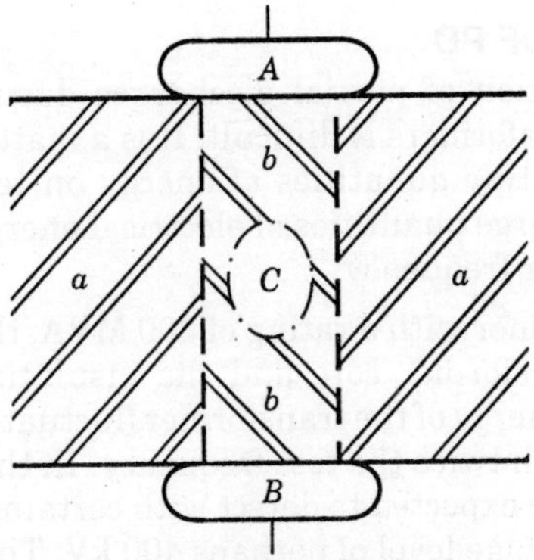


A, B = Electrodes ; C = Cavity;
b = Region of C

Fig. 15.1. Insulation with a cavity

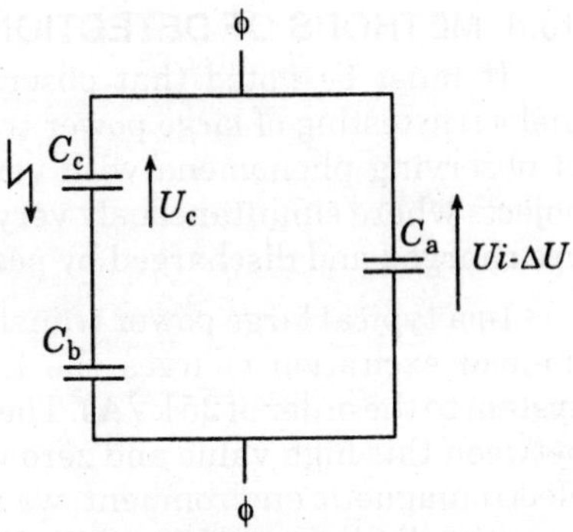


Fig. 15.2. Simplified equivalent electrical circuit of the test object.

where $C_a$ = capacitance shown in Fig. 15.1

$C_b$ = capacitance shown in Fig. 15.1

$U_c$ = voltage across $C_c$ before discharge

$\Delta U$ = the step in voltage $U_i$ across the insulation system

At the terminals of the system (the transformer bushing) an equivalent apparent step in the charge may be defined according to:

$$\Delta Q = U \,.\, (C_a + C_b) = U_c \,.\, C_b \qquad ...(15.2)$$

where $\Delta Q$ = step in charge at the terminals of the system.

During the discharge, electrical energy is converted to other kinds of energy, mostly heat. It can be shown that this energy, with some approximation can be expressed in terms of quantities measurable at the terminals of the system. This is expressed as:

$$W = \frac{Q \,.\, U_i}{2} \qquad ...(15.3)$$

where $W$ = electrical energy converted to other energy (mostly heat) at discharge

A partial discharge phenomenon is matter of less then 1/10 of one microsecond, thus the frequencies that characterise the information propagated from this partial discharge are of the order of several 10 MHz.

The deduction of equation (15.3) is oversimplified with regard to the propagation of the signal from the actual discharge region to the terminals where the observation is being made. This propagation is always subject to attenuation, which will be discussed in the following section.

## 15.4 METHODS OF DETECTION OF PD

It must be noted that observation of partial discharges during dielectric testing of large power transformers is difficult. It is a matter of observing phenomena with very tiny quantities of energy on test objects where simultaneously very large quantities of electrical energy are charged and discharged by power frequency.

In a typical large power transformer with a rating of 300 MVA, the no-load excitation charges the transformer core and the insulation system to the order of 25 kVAs. The energy of the transformer fluctuates between this high value and zero with twice the test frequency. In this electromagnetic environment, we are expected to detect with certainty a partial discharge of 500 pC at a voltage level of perhaps 400 kV. This partial discharge represents an energy of $1.25 \times 10^{-4}$ VAs. This means a ratio between the peak value of the energy in the environment and of the energy in the phenomenon to be observed of $2 \times 10^8$.

However, there is a noticeable difference in frequency range for the two phenomena, the environment fluctuating with twice the test frequency and the discharge with 10 MHz. If we approximate the discharge with a pulse of the duration of 10 ns, the instantaneous power developed in the discharge can be calculated at 12.5 kW and this gives for the measurements a more favourable ratio of 400 between the no-load apparent excitation power of the transformer and the instantaneous discharge power.

Electrical observations of the partial discharges have to be made at the terminals of the test object , *i.e.*, the bushings of the transformer. It has been shown by research measurements that the attenuation of the signals of the partial discharge in the transformer may be appreciable, so that in some cases only 1/10 of the energy reaches the bushing. In order to increase the probability of a successful observation, measurements should, therefore, be made simultaneously on all available bushings on the transformer, including the neutral. One could then expect that for at least one of the bushings more than half the energy would be observed at the bushings.

Upon partial discharge, some of the electrical energy is converted into mechanical energy and radiated as sound. Therefore detection of partial discharges can also be performed by acoustic means using detectors on the outside of the transformer tank.

Following methods have been developed for locating the Partial Discharges.

**1. Electrical Methods:**

**1.1. Narrow-band method** called NEMA method or Radio Interference Method (RIV).

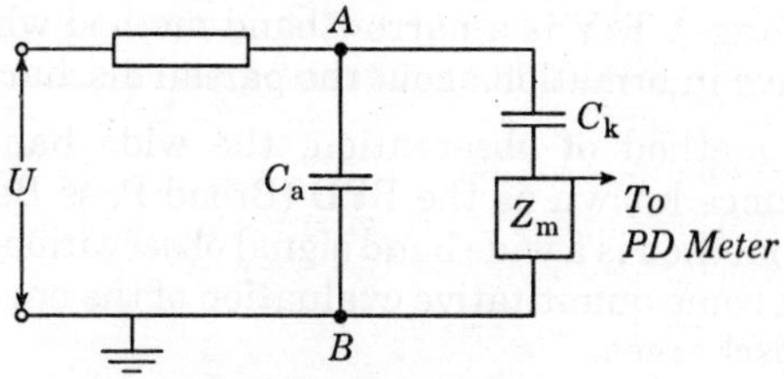


$C_a$ = Capacitance under test.
$C_k$ = Coupling capacitor.
$Z_m$ = Measuring impedance

Fig. 15.3 Basic test circuit for partial discharge test.

**1.2. Wide-band information method.** (BPD-Broad Pass Band) or Pico Coulomb (PC) method.

2. Acoustic Detection Method.
3. Visual Dellection Method.
4. Ultrasonic Method.

**Electrical Methods.** Several methods based on different principles have been developed by various researchers. Fig. 15.3 shows a basic test circuit. Applied AC voltage $U$ is gradually increased when partial discharge occurs in the capacitance under test ($C_a$) the voltage across the terminals $A$, $B$ will be $U - \Delta U$ at $t = 0$. The voltage drop $\Delta U$ is caused by the charge transfer through the *PD*. Hence, the voltage across the coupling capacitor $C_k$ at $t = 0$ would still be $U$ due to the time constant of series impedance $Z_m$ ( called measuring impedance).

The charge will transfer from coupling capacitor $C_k$ to the test capacitor $C_a$ *via* measuring impedance $Z_m$. The charge transfer will be

$$qm = \int_0^\infty i(t)\, dt$$

The apparent charge is given by, $q = qm.\ K$

where $|q|$ is the absolute value apparent charge transferred during the discharge. The factor $K$ is the correction factor for multiplying with the measured charge.

**Measuring Circuit.** For transformers and reactors, the connection of measuring circuit is usually made between the bushing tap (when available) and the tank so that the bushing capacitance acts like coupling $C_k$ to HV terminals. It may be necessary to connect a adjustable impedance across the necessary terminals or a matching reactance network for giving maximum response over the required frequency band.

For detection of partial discharges using electrical means, two methods have developed over the years. The oldest, the narrow band method, originally developed out of concern about interference with radio communications. This method, known as the NEMA or (radio interference voltage). RIV is a narrow band method which gives very little quantitative information about the partial discharge.

The other method of observation, the wide band information method, sometimes known as the BPD (Broad Pass Band) or the pC (pico Coulomb) method is a wide band signal observation method which permits at least some quantitative evaluation of the energies. involved in the partial discharges.

It is quite possible to make observations using both these electrical methods simultaneously and this is normally utilised in transformer test laboratories.

Fig. 15.4 illustrates a set-up for dielectric testing of insulation with observations of partial discharges using different methods.

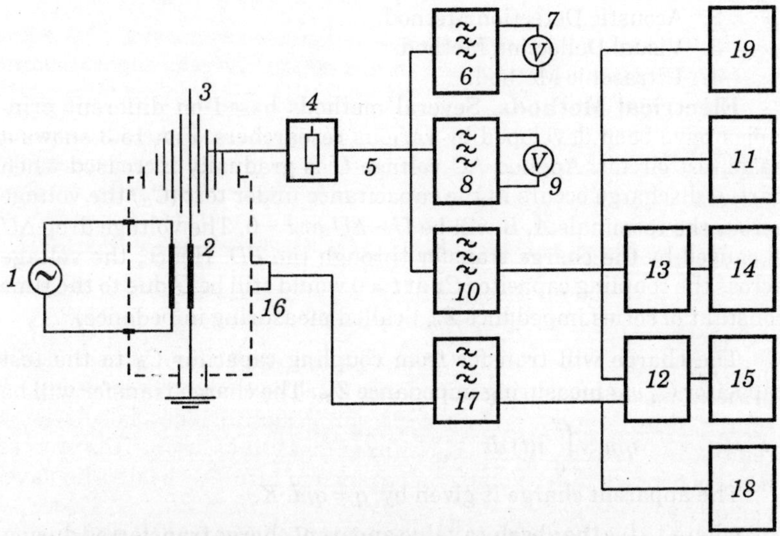


**Note:** 1. Items 16 and 17 repeated up to 10 times.
2. Items 3—6, 8, 10 and 19 repeated for each terminal to be observed.

1. Voltage source AC.
2. Transformer or Reactor under test.
3. Bushing of (2) when a test-tap 3′
4. Terminating impedance
5. Cable
6. Low pass filter.
7. Test voltage-Peak voltage meter
8. Narrow band filter (band width 8 MHz, centre 1 MHz)
9. Indicator for radio-interference voltage
10. Multi-channel filter 20 to 600 kHz.
11. CRO
12. Taper recorder
13. Computer for digital information
14. Display
15. Magnetic oscillogram
16. Microphone
17. Filter (20 to 45 kHz)
18. CRO
19. Peak voltmeter.

Fig. 15.4. Block diagram for electrical method for PD test.

The power source 1 excites test object 2. If partial discharges occur, the electric signals are picked up from the measuring tap on bushing 3 or as acoustic signal with *microphone 16.*

In case of a multi-phase, multiwinding transformer, electrical signal are picked up from several bushings (*10* measuring channels available) and several microphones located around the transformer (10 acoustic channels available).

The electrical signal from the bushing measuring tap is matched to the measuring equipment with its different frequency regions in the terminating impedance 4 located close to the transformer. From this cable 5 runs to the control room and the signal is divided up for various purposes using filters.

In the low pass filter 6, the power frequency component is separated and used for monitoring the applied **test** voltage in the peak voltmeter 7.

In the narrow-band, filter 8 with a centre frequency of 1 MHz and a bandwidth of 9 kHz the radio interference voltage is separated and fed to an indicator 9.

In the wideband, multi-channel filter 10 with a bandwidth extending from 20 to 600 kHz, a signal for indication of apparent discharge at the test object terminals is separated. This information is then propagated for processing in various ways.

In cathode ray oscilloscope 18 and on peak voltmeter 19 the discharges can be visually monitored throughout the tests so that decisions can be taken immediately on the progress of events.

In computer 13 information is digitised, stored and processed. The processing includes separating the discharge signals according to source (transformer bushing) and level. It also includes calculation of relative magnitude, which is later used for fault location. This processing is controlled by a computer program and results are later displayed visually or printed.

In the magnetic tape recorder 12, which is usually kept running continuously during the test, the primary information is stored for later frequency conversion (replay at lower speed) and tracing using a magnetic coil oscillograph for detailed studies of individual pulses.

This magnetic tape recorder is also used for storage and processing of the acoustic signals from the microphones.

This complex measuring system includes components which are unique for each test object, such as the bushings and the transformer windings themselves in the electrical path, and the transformer tank walls in the acoustic path. Therefore, each channel is calibrated before commencement of the test by injection of known signals. Electrical charges and radio frequency voltages are injected in the transformer terminals, one at a time, and the response is each time observed in every channel.

This permits not only calibration of the channel connected directly to the terminal where injection has taken place but also an estimate of attenuation of signals propagated through the windings to the other terminals. This is useful in trouble-shooting.

Acoustic signals are injected in the tank wall beside the microphone, one at a time and the response is monitored.

### 15.4.1 Typical Test Facilities

To provide power for dielectric tests with induced voltage the High voltage test lab, usually has several rotating convertors available, the largest rated at 240 Hz, 4 MVA, three-phase.

Step-up transformers are available for three-phase, 170 kV and 900 kV. The partial discharge measuring equipment according to the principles indicated in Fig. 15.4 includes 10 electrical channels with a measuring range from 10 pC to 100.00 pC as well as ten acoustic channels.

The magnetic tape recorder can handle all the above mentioned 20 channels plus a few more for monitoring operational conditions. Its upper frequency limit is 600 kHz at ½ hour of recorded time.

The on-line digital computer sorts out the pulses according to amplitude and counts them, as well as recording information of operational conditions. This information is processed so that it can displayed and printed in an orderly fashion.

### 15.4.2 Tracing the Location of PD

Partial discharges of excess magnitude have been observed during the test conducted in an attempt to pinpoint the location of the partial discharge. This is necessary to guide the repair team to the proper location, which may otherwise escape visual inspection after untanking. The partial discharge may cover only a small region (a few centimeters) in the vast and complex insulation structure of the large transformer.

The apparent discharge signals observed at the different transformer terminals are compared in magnitude and using the calibration matrix the position is evaluated. However, if the discharge occurs in a geometrically extensive but electrically limited part of the transformer, the result is very to noise.

Analysis of the acoustic signals contributes to the information. The acoustic signals are also severely affected during their propagation in the complex mechanical structure of the transformer. Therefore shape and intensity information is of little value, leaving only the arrival time. In practice, the microphone to which the signal arrives first is assumed to be nearest to the fault and other microphones are thereafter relocated to this neighbourhood and repeated tests made in an attempt to identify a location on the transformer tank, right opposite the fault.

**Acoustic Methods for Detecting PD.** For locating corona type partial discharges in an directionally selective high sensitivity microphones in Audio frequency range are used.

Fig. 15.5 gives block diagram. The acoustic effects from the partial discharges are picked up at the transformer tank using devices usually called microphones but which are more accurately described as acceleration transducers. This acoustic measuring system operates in the ultrasonic frequency range 20 to 45 kHz., where the signal-to noise ratio is favourable.

The acoustic measuring is not so much a performance measuring equipment as a trouble-shooting device for diagnosis purposes once a fault has been identified by electrical measurements.

Basically, the acoustic observations are used for tracing the actual location of the fault. This triangulation is built on measurements of the time differences of the arrival of the signal to the different microphones. However, the power transformer structure is extremely complex and the acoustic signals are severely diverted and distorted during propagation.

### 15.4.3 Test Sequence and Performance Criteria

For transformers of moderate voltage (145 kV) rating, the dielectric test with induced voltage is a short duration test (120 cycles) withstand test. Measurements of partial discharges are not performed for these transformers. The performance limit stipulation is that no breakdown of the insulation such as creates an overcurrent in the test power source is permitted.

For transformers of higher voltage rating or of large power rating (more than 80 MVA), the dielectric test with induced voltage is a long-duration test with observation of partial discharge phenomena. A typical test sequence (IEC recommendations) is 5 minutes at 1.5 times rated voltage, followed by 5 seconds at 1.73 times rated voltage in turn followed by another 30 minutes at 1.5 times rated voltage. After this the test is terminated.

During this test sequence the apparent charge of the partial discharges should always be less than 500 pC. In addition, for all partial discharges, if any, the extinciton voltage should be above the crest value of the maximum operating voltage.

### 15.4.4 Ultrasonic Testing of Partial Discharge Location

The electrical method for locating PD described above is not specific to a particular type of equipment. It can be applied to generators, bushings or transformers. The ultrasonic method is only applicable to insulation impregnated with a dielectric liquid.

When a PD occurs in an impregnated with a dielectric, it generates a pressure wave that travels through the various media. It is a sound wave having certain frequency band.

Using adequately sensitive transducers mounted on the tank, the distance between the source and the transducers can be determined by measuring the time that elapses between the discharge and arrival of the wave at a transducer. A triangulation method is then used to pinpoint the location of the source.

As the discharge duration is very short, the pressure wave emitted will include *high frequency components* well above the audible range. The locating method is therefore referred to as an *ultrasonic method.*

A locating operation includes two main phases:

— signal acquisition.

— analysis of results by determining signal transit times and pinpointing the discharge.

The frequency range is between 20 to 50 kHz. Fig. 15.5 gives a block-diagram for ultrasonic method of locating PD source. After amplifying the sensor signal, its frequencies are shifted to lower range. From this signal which contains interfernce noise such as iron noise, reflections, refractions of ultrasonic waves etc., the original partial discharge signal is filtered out in a storage signal analyser with oscillographic display, employing a band of averaging process. To this end the analyser has to be triggered by part of the partial discharge signal selected by an interval selector.

For checking purposes the electric signal due to the partial discharge, picked up from the bushing capacitance tap or from NEMA circuit is indicated in the noise meter and observed on oscilloscope which

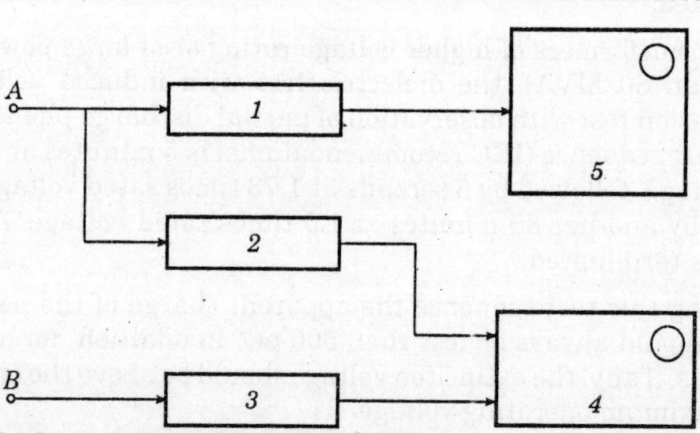


1. Device to measure PD interference signal
2. Amplifier with interval selector
3. Ultrasonic Amplifier with frequency shifter
4. Storage type signal analyser with oscillographic display
5. A To NEMA circuit or to bushing capacitance tap or test object
   B To ultrasonic sensor on the tank wall

Fig. 15.5 Block-diagram for locating the PD source by Ultrasonic.

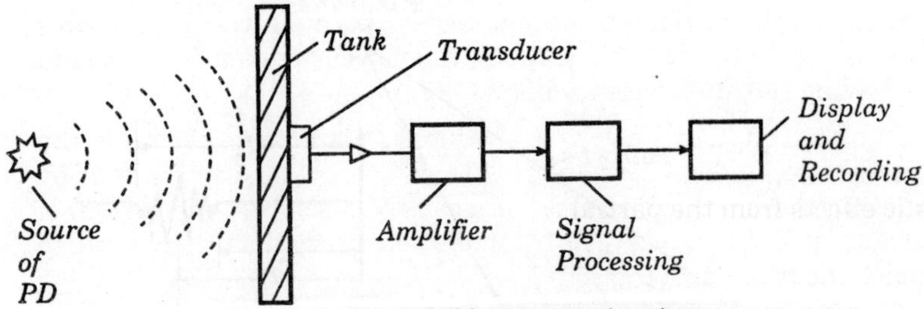


Fig. 15.6 Ultrasonic Measurement system.

is triggered or synchronised by a reduced voltage derived from the test voltage. The extracted ultrasonic signals appear gradually on the screen of the signal analyser.

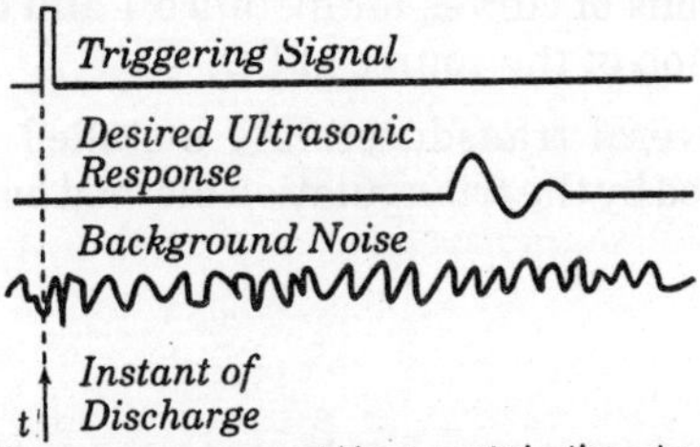


Fig. 15.7 Ultrasonic pressure wave takes certain time to reach the sensor. Waveform of partial discharge differs from background noise waveform.

The front of this wave is delayed relative to start of the recording trace because of the analyser is instantaneously triggered by electrical signal of the partial discharge, whereas the ultrasonic pressure wave takes a certain time to reach the sensor. The time lag corresponds to the distance between the location of the service and the location of sensor. In principle, it is possible to locate the exact location of partial discharge by triangulation from at least three measurements with the sensors at different points. For example, by ultrasonic test, partial discharge from a poor contact at 110 cm was located. In another test a weak insulation at the end of a cable from bushing end was located. Fig. 15.8 shows the concept of triangulation method used for ultrasonic detection of the location of PD source.

Path-1 is direct and gives most intense response by time $t_1$.

Path-2 is shortest and gives fastest test respond in time $t_2$

Time $t_3$ corresponds to the fadeout.

In the first step, the section of the transformer in which PD source is located is determined second step is to place a maximum number of transducers in the postulated area and record the responses and coordinates of the transducers in relation to a reference point. The operator then identifies on the recordings the times that appear to correspond to the direct paths through the oil.

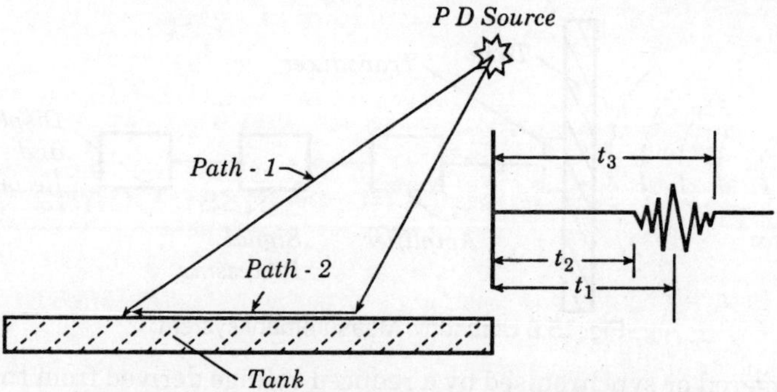


Fig. 15.8. Triangulation method of locating PD source in a transformer or a reactor.

The intersections of curves for distance 1 and distance 2 gives the approximate location of the source of PD.

In practice several transducers are installed and the location of source is determined by the triangulation method by successive elimination.

# 16

# Polarity, Three-phase Connections

Polarity conveys the sense of direction of instantaneous induced e.m.f. with respect to the various other terminals. Polarity is particularly important in parallel operation. Terminal markings have been standardised. The standard notations have been described. Third harmonics phenomena is also described.

## 16.1 POLARITY

The polarity of a winding refers to the direction of induced e.m.f. in the winding at a particular instant. The windings are wound on the same core. At a particular instant of time, the direction induced e.m.f. in a winding can be indicated by an arrow to indicate 'start' and 'finish' with a common reference. It should be clearly understood that though the e.m.f. in individual winding is alternating, at a particular instant of time the direction of e.m.f. is from one-end to the other. The polarity has significance in parallel operation and in three phase connections.

## 16.2 TERMINAL MARKINGS OF A 3-PHASE TRANSFORMER

A 3-phase transformer is either in the form of a 3-phase unit or in the form of a bank of 3 single phase units.

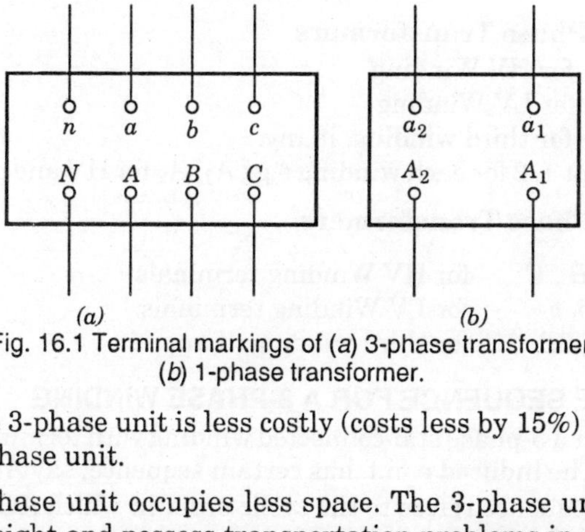


Fig. 16.1 Terminal markings of (*a*) 3-phase transformer (*b*) 1-phase transformer.

A single 3-phase unit is less costly (costs less by 15%) than a bank of 3 single phase unit.

The 3-phase unit occupies less space. The 3-phase unit is larger, has more weight and possess transportation problems in case of large power transformers (300 MVA). Hence where transport limitations do not permit 3-phase unit, 3 single phase units are preferred.

Secondly, a two winding transformer has a 3-phase H.V. winding and 3-phase L.V. winding. These windings are connected either in star or in delta. The choice between star and delta connections requires separate considerations in each case. Star connection is cheaper, since delta connection needs more turns and more insulation. The difference is small, however at voltages below 11kV. With very high voltage, a saving of 10% may be achieved mainly on account of the insulation. An advantage of the star-connected winding with earthed neutral is that the maximum voltage to the core (frame or earth) is limited to 58% of the line voltage, whereas with a delta-connected winding the earthing of one line (due to fault) increases the maximum voltage between windings and core to the full line voltage. Technically the delta connected primary is essential where the LV secondary is a star-connected 4-wire supply to mixed 3-phase and 1-phase loads.

The windings of one 3-phase transformer unit or 3-single phase transformer unit are connected in the similar manner-either in star or delta (Mesh). The primary windings may be star or delta-connected and the secondary windings may be also connected in star or delta. This gives four possible combinations of the transformer windings as follows:

1. Star to star
2. Star to delta
3. Delta to delta
4. Delta to star.

Some of these combinations are approved and are in common use and some have objections and are not used.

Following *terminal markings* are recommended by IEC, BS and IS. Ref. Fig. 16.1.

**Single Phase Transformers**

A for HV Winding
*a* for LV Winding
3*A* for third winding, if any.

Subscript 1, 2 for each winding e.g., $A_1, A_2$ for HV and $a_1$, $a_2$ for LV.

**Three Phase Transformers**

*A, B, C* for HV Winding terminals
*a, b, c* for LV Winding terminals
3*A*, 3*B*, 3*C* for third winding, if any.

## 16.3 PHASE SEQUENCE FOR A 3-PHASE WINDING

Consider a 3-phase star connected winding with terminal markings $A_1$, $B_1$, $C_1$. The induced e.m.f. has certain sequence, say $A_1 \rightarrow B_1 \rightarrow C_1$. The phase sequence refers to the cyclic order in which *AC* wave-forms attain the peak value.

Phase sequence is important for parallel connections and also for direction of rotation of AC motors, for synchronising check etc.

## 16.4 STANDARD VECTOR GROUPS

A 3-phase transformers polarity alone is insufficient to represent the relation between H.V. and L.V. windings. In addition to the terminal markings on H.V. side and L.V. side voltage vector diagrams are required to show the angular displacement between H.V. and L.V. winding.

The angular difference between vectors representing the voltages between H.V. and L.V. terminals having the same marking letters and the corresponding neutral point (real or imaginary expressed with reference to H.V. side is termed as phase displacement of the transformer.

Even under normal condition, the line-to-line voltages on H.V. side are displaced from corresponding voltages on L.V. side. Also line to neutral voltage on H.V. side are displaced from corresponding voltages on L.V side. This displacement depends upon transformer connections (star/delta). IS 2026—1972 gives four vector groups of standard connections. These whole groups are explained below:

Terminal markings on H.V. : *A, B, C*

Terminal markings on L.V. : *a, b, c*

Each windings has two subscripts 1, 2

*e.g.*, $A_1, A_2$ for H.V. winding

$a_1, a_2$ for L.V. winding etc.

Transformers are classified in 4 vector groups 1, 2, 3, 4 depending upon phase displacement as follows:

**Standard Vector Groups**

| *Group* | *Phase displacement* | *Connections* |
|---|---|---|
| 1 | zero | Yy0, Dd0, Dz0 |
| 2 | 180° | Yy6, Dd6, Dz6 |
| 3 | 30° lag | Dy1, Yd1, Yz1 |
| 4 | 30° lead | Dy11, Yd11, Yz11 |

The phase displacement is indicated by the angle in terms of clock face. The H.V. vector being at 12 O'clock (zero) and the corresponding L.V. vector at hour hand number thus,

Phase displacement zero=0

Phase displacement 180° = 6

Phase displacement 30° lag = 1

Phase displacement 30° lead = 11

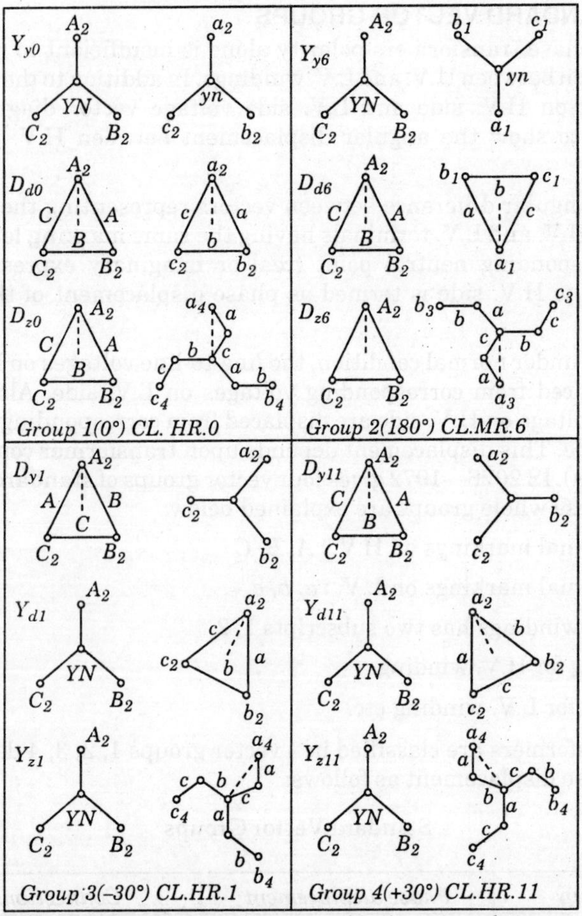


Fig. 16.2 Standard vector groups of 3-phase transformers.

Letter *Y* represents star-connected H.V.

Letter *y* represents star-connected L.V.

Letter *D* represents star-connected H.V.

Letter *d* represents star-connected L.V.

Letter *Z* represents star-connected zig-zag.

Thus the symbol *Yy*0 represents a star/star winding with 0° displacement.

## 16.5 SIGNIFICANCE OF VECTOR GROUPS IN 3-PHASE PARALLEL CONNECTIONS

Vector groups I, II, III, IV are defined as follows:

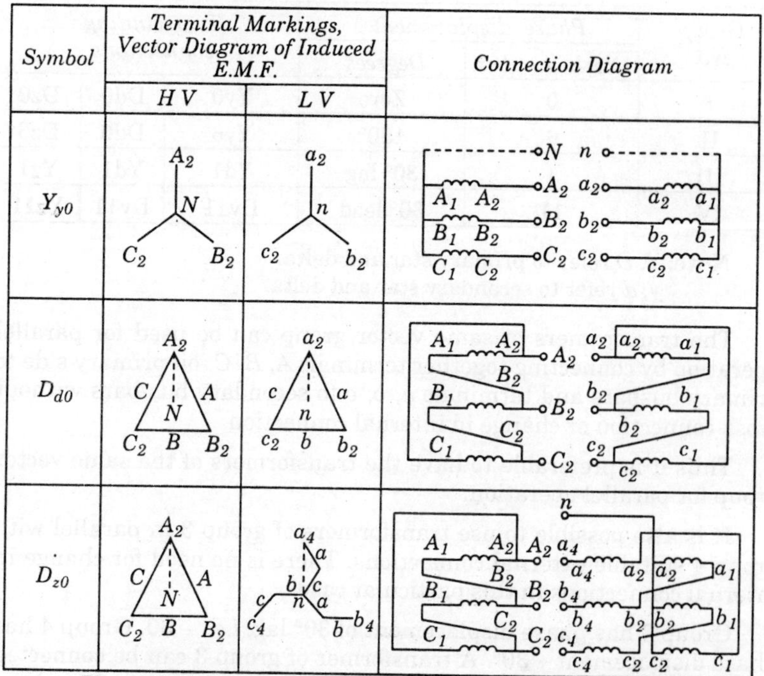


Fig. 16.3 (*a*) Standard vector groups and winding connections.

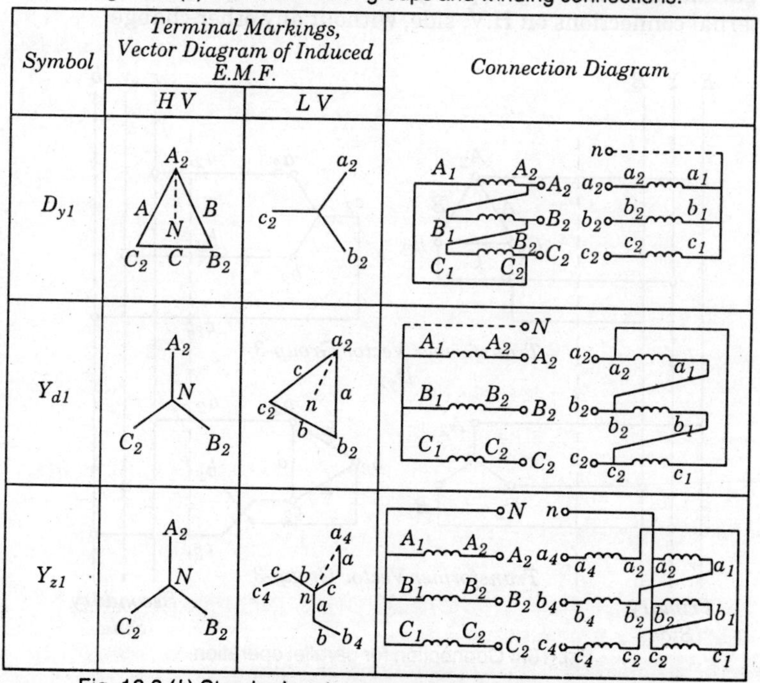


Fig. 16.3 (*b*) Standard vector groups and winding connections.

| Group No. | Phase displacement | | Two winding connections | | |
|---|---|---|---|---|---|
| | Clock number | Degrees | | | |
| I | 0 | Zero | Yy0 | Dd0 | Dz0 |
| II | 6 | 180° | Yy6 | Dd6 | Dz6 |
| III | 1 | 30° lag | Yd1 | Yd1 | Yz1 |
| IV | 11 | 30° lead | Dy11 | Dy11 | Yz11 |

**Note:** *Y*, *D* refer to primary star and delta.
*y*, *d* refer to secondary star and delta.

The transformers of same vector group can be used for parallel operation by connecting together terminals *A, B, C,* on primary side to primary busbars and terminals *a, b, c* to secondary bus-bars without cross-connection or change in internal connection.

Thus it is preferable to have the transformers of the same vector group for parallel operation.

It is also possible to use transformers of group 3 in parallel with group 4 suitable external connections. There is no need for change in internal connections in this particular case.

Group 3 has phase displacement of 30° lag, *i.e.*, – 30. Group 4 has phase displacement + 30°. A transformer of group 3 can be connected in parallel with that of group 4 by cross-connecting any two of the three external connections on H.V. side, without any other change.

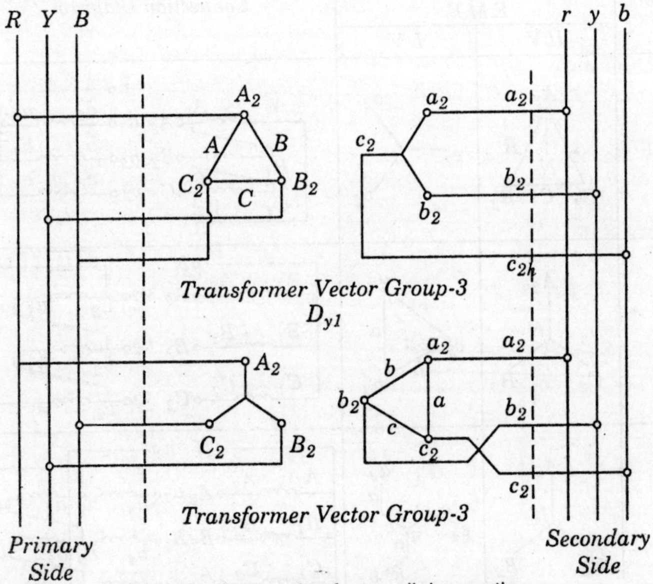


Fig. 16.4 Connection for parallel operation.

Alternatively any two L.V. connections may be cross-connected without other change.

Thus connect $A$, $B$, $C$ of transformer $X$ and transformer $Y$ to bus-bars $R$, $Y$, $B$.

Connect $a,c,b$ of transformer $X$ to bus-bars $r$, $y$, $b$ and $a,b,c$ of transformer $Y$ to bus-bars $r$, $y$, $b$ to adjust the phase displacement difference between group 3 and group 4.

It is possible to use transformers of group 1 in parallel with group 2 by suitable internal connections.

Group 1 has zero displacement group 2 has 180° phase displacement. For parallel operations, one of the internal connections of all the three windings of one of the transformers on one side only (either H.V. or L.V.) is necessary to be changed. Thus bringing same phase shift, *i.e.*, zero degrees or 180° in both transformers.

## 16.6 STAR-DELTA CONNECTION ALTERNATIVES

**1. Star-star 3-phase Transformer Connection.** The star-star connection has advantages and disadvantages. The disadvantages predominate. One of the advantage is that the voltage of each single phase unit connected to form star-star connection is only 57.7 per cent of the line voltage. This tends to make the connection suitable for power transmission, as the individual transformers are wound for a relatively low voltage and nearly double (173%) is obtained on the line.

The star connection also permits the earthing of the natural on either or both primary and secondary windings. If the primary neutral carried back to the generator, unequal loads may be taken off the secondary windings between the secondary neutral and any of the three line loads. The unbalanced current will flow through the neutral back to the alternator. This permits lighting loads to be connected between the neutral and any of the three phase loads.

(The star-star connection is used for connecting together two high voltage transmission systems of unequal voltage). In this case it is necessary that the connection used to be such as not to cause a shift in phase from primary to secondary. Therefore, only two connections are

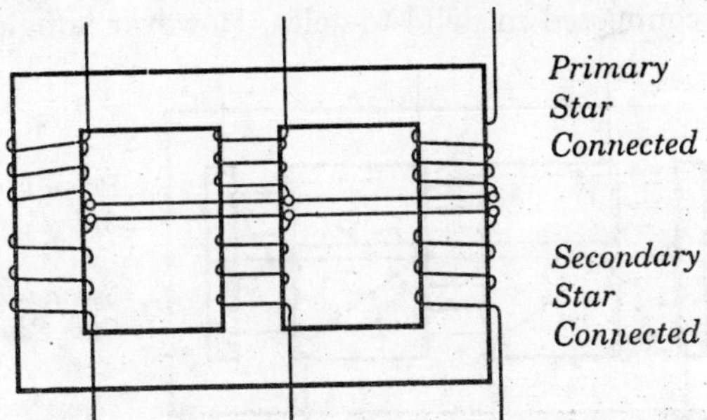


Fig. 16.5. Star-star connection of 3-phase Windings.

applicable, namely, the star-to-star connection and the delta-to-star connection. (For high voltage the star-to-star connection is preferred because the voltage stresses of the windings to ground with the neutral grounded are only 58% of the voltage stress to ground of similar units connected delta-to-delta). When the star-to-star connection is used for this purpose a tertiary winding is provided to supress the third harmonic voltages which would otherwise appear on the system). Tertiary in generally Δ connected.

The tertiary is a third winding and is often used in power transformers to provide station power requirements or for connecting SVS.

In many case, unless a tertiary winding is added to provide a path for third, harmonic currents to flow through, interference with telephone circuits may occur. When using single-phase transformers, this trouble may be avoided by grounding the primary and secondary neutrals.

The disturbances from harmonic voltages and currents constitutes one of the objections to the use of star-star transformer. Another objection in its use is that unbalanced loads cannot be carried on the secondary side unless the primary neutral or fourth wire is provided. Another objection is that it is practically impossible to construct 3-single phase units, or even a three phase-unit, in which the magnetising currents of each of the three-windings are exactly identical. This makes it impossible to have perfectly balanced voltages in each of the three windings of the star-star connection.

**2. 3-Phase delta-star connection.** 3-phase delta-star connection is used for distribution transformer. Star side is used on load side. 3-phase 4 wire supply is available on star side and can be loaded with single phase and 3-phase load. The third harmonic currents flow through delta winding and stable star point is obtained.

**3. 3-Phase star-to-delta connection.** Such connection is used to a great extent for power transmission and distribution. Delta connected side can be loaded with single phase load or 3-phase load.

**4. 3-Phase delta-delta connection.** 3-phase transformer units are rarely connected in delta-to-delta. However, single phase trans-

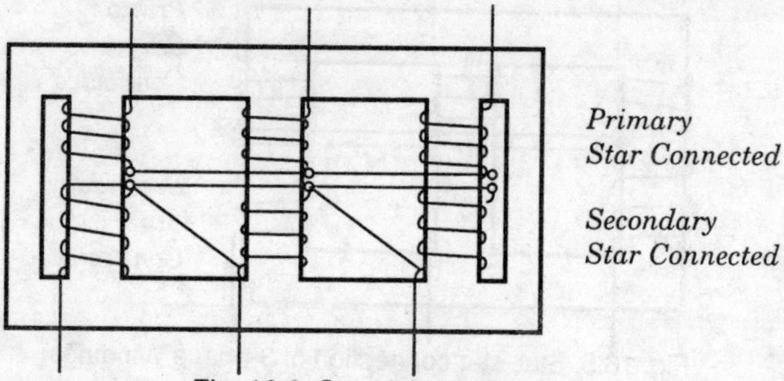


Fig. 16.6. Star-delta connection.

former units are sometimes connected in delta-delta. Delta-delta connection may be used only for low voltage transformers as it requires more turns per phase as full phase-to phase voltage comes across winding. Large load unbalance can be tolerated. Triple harmonic voltages are damped out. Neutral point is not available.

## 16.7 HARMONICS AND TRANSFORMER CONNECTIONS

A sinusoidal waveform of current or voltage consists or only one frequency component called fundamental. Such a sinusoidal waveform does not contain harmonics of other frequencies.

A *non-sinusoidal waveform can be considered to be composed of several sinusoidal waveforms of fundamental frequency and other harmonics frequencies.* According to fourier series a non-sinusoidal periodic function can be expressed in terms of a sum of several sinusoidal periodic functions. Thus a non-sinusoidal waveform can be considered to be made of the following:

— Fundamental component having same frequency as that of original waveform.

— Even harmonics such as 2nd, 4th etc.

— Odd harmonics such as 3rd, 5th, 7th etc.

The frequency of $n$th harmonics is $n$ times fundamental frequency. The r.m.s. value of the $n$th harmonic is $1/n$th of r.m.s value of fundamental.

Harmonics currents cause additional $I^2R$ loss, core loss magnetic interference with protective relays and interference in communication circuits.

Harmonic voltages, cause increased dielectric stress, interference with communication circuits and resonance between inductance of the transformer winding and the capacitance of the transmission line. Therefore, harmonics should be avoided.

**Causes.** Harmonics are caused by the use of high flux densities in the cores of power transformers. If the core is of insufficient cross-section, the core gets saturated. The operating point comes in the non-linear region of $B/H$ curve. Even if primary voltage has sinusoidal waveform, the secondary waveform may be non-sinusoidal because of magnetic core. Hence the basic requirement of the transformer is to provide a sinusoidal secondary voltage wave-form which is achieved by sufficient cross-section of core and operating point in the linear-region of $B/H$ curve.

If cross-section of core is inadequate and core gets saturated the third harmonics are generally present in the secondary wave form.

### Effect of Transformer Connections on Harmonics

**Single phase Transformer.** If core is not saturated, *i.e.*, if operating point of magnetising current is in the linear portion of $B/H$ curve, harmonics are not present. If core saturates, 3rd harmonic e.m.fs. and 3rd harmonic currents are induced on the secondary side.

**(A) Three phase banks of 3 single phase transformers :**

The method of connections decides the harmonics generation.

(*a*) **Delta-delta connection.** Delta connection provides closed path to 3rd harmonics e.m.f. which circulates 3rd harmonic currents in the closed delta, causing 3rd harmonic voltage drop within the closed delta. As a result no 3rd harmonic voltages appear at line terminals. Similar behaviours occur in the delta-delta connection for 5th and 7th harmonics.

(*b*) **Star-delta connection and delta-star connection without neutral wire or neutral grounding.** Triple frequency voltages and currents circulate in closed delta and are absent on line terminal on delta side however the waveform departs from true sinusoidal wave form as 3rd harmonic currents cannot circulate on star side.

(*c*) **Star-star connection without neutral grounding.** There is no path for circulation of 3rd harmonic current, the neutral point oscillates. The line to neutral point voltages of all the 3 phases fluctuates.

(*d*) **Star-star connection with neutral grounding.** The presence of neutral connection provides path for 3rd harmonic compensating currents.

**(B) Three-phase transformer units:**

It is desirable to distinguish between the cases where the phases are magnetically separate and those where they are magnetically (as well as electrically) interlinked. In 3-phase shell type transformer, the magnetic circuits are separated and do not interact and the discussion in (A) for the bank of 1-phase transformers will apply. In the more common 3-phase 3-limb core type unit, however, this in not so, 3rd harmonics fluxes are all upward or all downward at a given instant in the limbs, and their return path must be external (*i.e.*, in the air, oil or the walls of the tank). These paths have a high reluctance and there is a strong tendency to suppress 3rd harmonic, core fluxes. The residuals may cause eddy current loss in the tank, an effect cancelled if a copper band is fitted around the inside perimeter of the tank.

In five-limbed cores the end limbs provide a magnetic path for 3rd harmonic fluxes.

## Summary of 3-phase Connections

| *Connection* | *Salient Aspects* | *Third Harmonics* |
|---|---|---|
| Star/star Yy0 or Yy6 | —Economical for small H.V transformers.<br>—Possibility to provide neutral connection.<br>— No triplen currents flow.<br>— Neutral voltage may oscillate and triplen voltages may be high in shell -type units. | 3rd harmonic currents and voltages circulate in the delta. They are not present in the line. |
| Delta/Delta Dd0 or Dd6 | —Suitable for large H.V. transformers.<br>—Large load unbalance can be tolerated, triplen voltages are damped out.<br>—The absence of a star point may be a disadvantge | 3rd harmonic current circulate in delta winding. |
| Star/Delta Dy or Yd | —Very common for supply networks.<br>—One star point for a neutral to serve mixed 1-ph and 4-ph loads. | |
| | —Delta winding can carry triplen currents and so stabilize the star-point voltage. | |
| Interconnected Star/Star Yzl or Yzll | —Reduces triplen voltages and not sensitive to conditions of unbalnced loading.<br>—Restricted to low-voltage windings. Phase voltages are composed of half-voltages with a 60° displacement, 15% more turns are required.<br>—Sometimes used in rectifier supply. | |

# 17

# Parallel Operation of Transformers

## 17.1 ESSENTIAL REQUIREMENTS FOR PARALLEL OPERATION OF TWO OR MORE TRANSFORMERS

The essential requirements for satisfactory parallel operation of two or more transformers are as follows:

1. The polarity should be the same.
2. The voltage ratios should be same.
3. The percentage impendance should be equal.
4. The phase rotation should be the same.
5. The vector diagrams and the phase displacement should be the same.
6. X/R ratio should be same.

**Voltage Ratio.** If voltage ratios are not identical, for the same primary voltage, the secondary voltages would be different. Thus the different secondary voltages would result in circulating currents within the secondary circuits and heating of transformers even on no load. The kVA ratings will reduce accordingly.

**Percentage Impendance and kVA Ratings.** Two transformers need not be of same kVA capacity for parallel operation but their percentage impedances should be nearly equal. If percentage impedances are equal. the loading of these transformers would not be proportional to their kVA ratings.

If percentage impedances are different the load sharing will not be proportional to kVA ratings.

As percentage impedances of transformers of different kVA ratings cannot be exactly equal, it is preferable to operate transformers of the same kVA rating in parallel.

As a general rule ratio of kVA ratings of transformers operating in parallel should be within 3:1.

**Phase Sequence.** The phase sequence refers to the cyclic order in which the voltage waves of 3-phase reach their peak values *e.g., R, Y, B*.

If any two of the terminals are interchanged, the phase sequence becomes *R, B, Y*. The phase sequence *R, B, Y* is reverse of the phase sequence of *R, Y, B*.

For parallel operation, the phase sequence of terminals to be paralleled should be identical. *e.g. RYB* and *RYB*.

**Polarity.** The polarity of windings to be connected in parallel should be the same. Polarity refers to the instantaneous direction of induced e.m.f. in the winding at a given instant. If the two terminals of parallel transformers connected to the same bus have same polarity, there will not be local circulating currents. If polarities of two terminals are different, there will be heavy local circulating currents losses and heating even on no load.

## 17.2 VECTOR GROUPS OF 3-PHASE TRANSFORMERS AND PARALLEL OPERATION

Vector groups I, II, III, IV are defined as follows:

| *Group No.* | *Phase displacement* | | *Two winding connections* | | |
|---|---|---|---|---|---|
| | *Block numbers* | *Degrees* | | | |
| I | 0 | Zero | Yy0 | Dd0 | Dz0 |
| II | 6 | 180° | Yy6 | Dd6 | Dz6 |
| III | 1 | 30° lag | Dy1 | Dd1 | Dz1 |
| IV | 11 | 30° lead | Dy11 | Dy11 | Yz11 |

**Note:** *Y, D* refer to primary star and delta.
*y, d* refer to secondary star and delta.

The transformers of same vector group can be used for parallel operation by connecting together terminals *A, B, C* on primary side to primary busbars and terminals *a, b, c* to secondary bus-bars without any cross-connection or change in internal connection.

Thus it is preferable to have the transformers of the same vector group for parallel operation.

It is possible to use transformer or group I in parallel with group 2 by suitable changes in internal connections.

It is also possible to use transformers of groups 3 in parallel with group 4 by suitable external connections. There is no need for change in internal connections in this particular case.

Group 3 has phase displacement of 30° lag, *i.e.* – 30°. Group 4 has phase displacement + 30°. A transformer of group 3 can be connected in parallel with that of group 4 by cross-connecting and two of the three external connections on H.V. side, without any other change.

Alternatively any two L.V. connections may be cross-connected without other change.

Thus connect *A, B, C* of transformer *X* and transformer *Y* to bus-bars *R, Y, B*.

Connect *a, c, b* of transformer *X* to bus-bars *r, y, b* and *a, b, c* of transformer *Y* to bus-bars *r, y, b* to adjust the phase displacement difference between group 3 and group 4.

## 17.3 POLARITY CHECK AND VOLTAGE CHECK BEFORE PARALLEL CONNECTIONS

Polarity refers to direction of instantaneous e.m.f. in a winding with reference to the direction of e.m.f.s. in other windings at that instant. (Ref. Sec. 16.1)

The term polarity in parallel operation of transformers refers to a phase relationship between two or more units. It can be applied to indicate the directional relationship of primary and secondary terminal voltages of a single unit. Any two single-phase transformers have the same polarity when their instantaneous terminal voltages are in phase. With this condition a voltmeter connected across similar terminals will indicate zero.

### Single Phase Transformers

*Single phase transformers* are essentially simple to test, as for any given pair of transformers, there are only two possible sets of external connections, one of which must be correct. If two single-phase transformers say, *X* and *Y*, have to be phased in for parallel operation, the first procedure is to connect both primary and secondary terminals of, say, transformer *X*, to their corresponding bus-bars, and then to connect the primary terminals of transformer *Y* to their busbars. If the two transformers have the same polarity, corresponding secondary terminals will be at the same potential, but in order to ascertain if this is so, it is necessary to connect one secondary terminal of transformer *Y* to what is thought to be its corresponding busbar. It is necessary to make the connection from one secondary terminal of transformer *Y*, so that when taking readings there is a return path for the current flowing through the voltmeter. The voltage across disconnected secondary terminal of transformer *Y* and the other busbar is then measured. If zero, the polarity and phase sequence are same and permanent connection can be made. If voltage is double, the polaritites are incorrect and

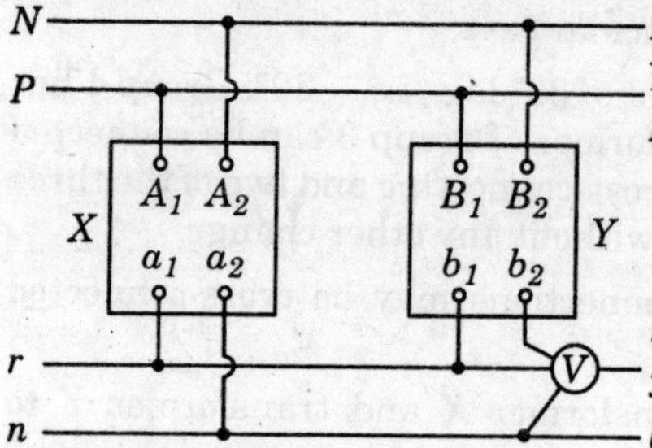


Fig. 17.1. Check on single phase transformer before final connection. (C.B. not shown)

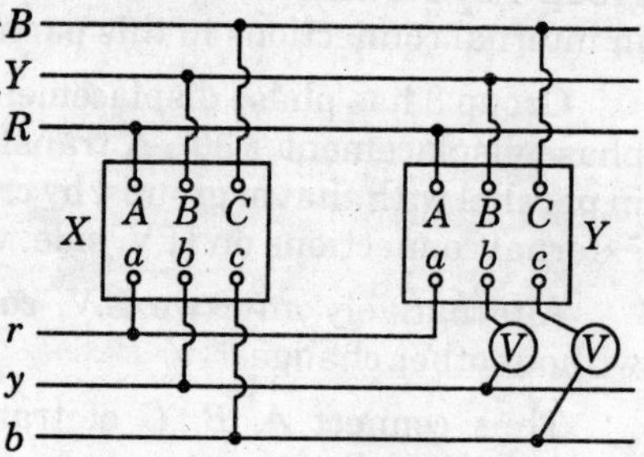


Fig. 17.2. Polarity check on 3-phase parallel transformers.

further measurement are necessary between terminals *a*, *y* and *b*, *r*. If for these measurements voltage is zero, then permanent connections are made accordingly between secondary terminals and secondary bus bar by cross-connection.

**Three Phase Transformers.** (Figs. 17.2 and 17.3). For three phase transformers, the following steps are essential during planning stage and before starting the installation.

1. Study name plates of each transformer.

2. Confirm whether the polarity, voltage ratio, vector diagram, vector group, terminal markings, kVA ratings, percentage impedances of both the transformers are acceptable for parallel operation. If not, dot not connect further.

After verifying, the above aspects, the transformers are installed and connections are completed. The other commissioning steps are taken. Before switching on the final circuit-breaker for paralleling, the following steps are taken.

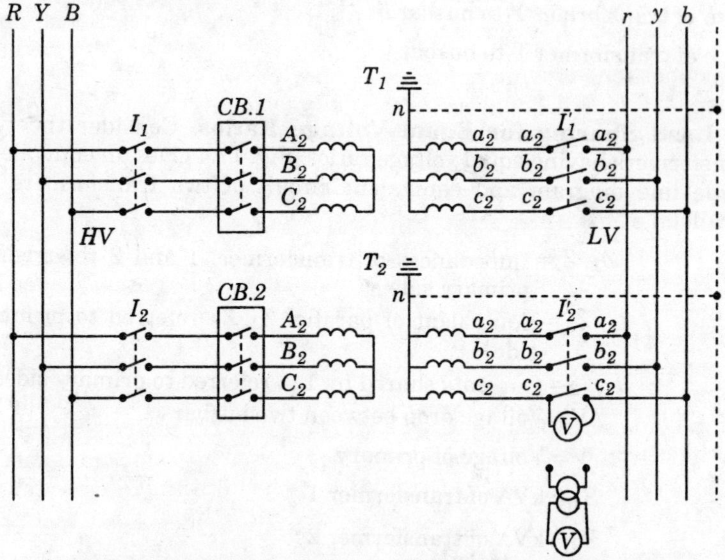


Fig. 17.3 Checking polarity before paralleling of 3 phase transformer.

3. Connect primary terminals of each transformer to corresponding bus-bar as follows:

| *Bus-bar* | *Primary of Transformer 'X'* | *Primary of Transformer 'Y'* |
|---|---|---|
| $\overline{R}$ | *A* | *A* |
| $\overline{Y}$ | *B* | *B* |
| $\overline{B}$ | *C* | *C* |

4. Connect secondary terminals of transformer $X$ and transformer $Y$ as follows:

| *Bus-bar* | *Secondary of Transformer 'X'* | *Secondary of Transformer 'Y'* |
|---|---|---|
| $\overline{r}$ | $a$ | $a$ |
| $\overline{y}$ | $b$ | $b$ |
| $\overline{b}$ | $c$ | $c$ |

5. Measure voltage between secondary terminal of transformer $Y$ and corresponding bus-bar, *i.e.*, voltage between

Terminal $b$ and busbar $\overline{y}$

Terminal c and busbar $\overline{b}$.

If these voltages are zero, make permanent connections.

If these voltages are of twice the phase value, cross-connect as follows after checking voltage zero

$b$ of transformer $Y$ to busbar $\overline{b}$

$c$ of transformer $Y$ to busbar $\overline{y}$

**Load Sharing for Equal Voltage Ratios**. Consider the two transformers having equal voltage ratios. Fig. 17.4 gives an equivalent single line diagram and equivalent circuit of two transformers in parallel. Let

$Z_1, Z_2$= Impedances of transformer, 1 and 2 referred to primary side

$Z_e$ = Equivalent of parallel $Z_1, Z_2$ referred to primary side

$I_1, I_2$ = Currents shared by 1, 2 referred to primary side.

$\Delta V$ = Voltage drop between two busbars

$V$ = Voltage of primary

$S_1$ = kVA of transformer 1

$S_2$ = kVA of transformer 2

$S$ = Total kVA = $S_1 + S_2$

$$\Delta V = I_1 Z_1 = I_2 Z_2 = I Z_e$$

$$\frac{1}{Z_e} = \frac{1}{Z_1} + \frac{1}{Z_2} = \frac{Z_1 + Z_2}{Z_1 Z_2}$$

Load shared by transformer 1 = $V I_1$

Load shared by transformer 2 = $V I_2$

Total load $= VI = VI_1 + VI_2$

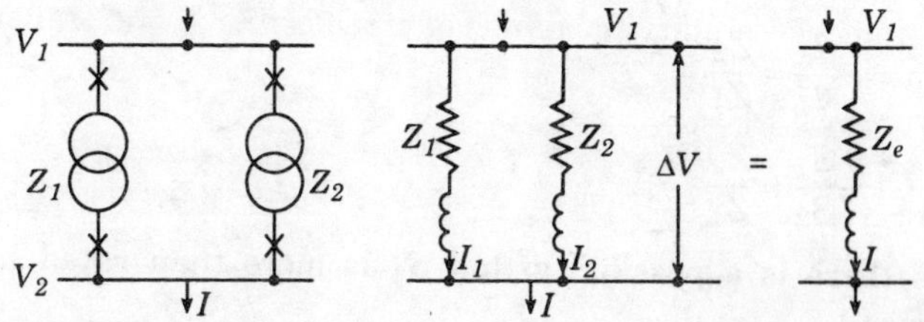


(A) Single line diagram (B) Impedance diagram referred to $V_1$
(C) Equivalent of $B$ referred to $V_1$
$\Delta V$ = Voltage drop in parallel transformers
$Z_e$ = Equivalent impedance of $Z_1$, $Z_2$ referred to primary.
Fig. 17.4. Parallel operation of two transformers.

$$I_1 = \frac{IZ_e}{Z_1} = I\,\frac{Z_2}{Z_1 + Z_2}$$

$$S_1 = VI_1 = VI\,\frac{Z_2}{Z_1 + Z_2}$$

$$I_2 = \frac{IZ_e}{Z_2} = I\,\frac{Z_1}{Z_1 + Z_2}$$

$$S_2 = VI_2 = VI\,\frac{Z_1}{Z_1 + Z_2}$$

Let $S_1$ = Nominal kVA of Transformer 1

$$= VI_1 \times 10^{-3} = VI\,\frac{Z_2}{Z_1 + Z_2} \times 10^{-3}$$

$S_2$ = Nominal kVA of Transformer 2

$$= VI_2 \times 10^{-3} = VI\,\frac{Z_1}{Z_1 + Z_2} \times 10^{-3}$$

Combined load on two transformers

$$S = S_1 + S_2$$

Also $S_1/S_2 = Z_2/Z_1$

$$I_1/I_2 = Z_2/Z_1.$$

The transformers share the load in accordance with the relative ratios of their impedances. For load sharing within rated kVA the percentage impedances of the two transformers should be almost equal. The breaker capability on both sides of the transformers should be checked as parallel operation of the transformers reduces the circuit impedance and increases the fault current.

**Load Sharing for Unequal Per cent Impedances.** If transformer 1 has too low per cent impedances than that of transformer 2, in parallel operation the following ratios would be too high.

$$\frac{I_1}{I_1} = \frac{Z_2}{Z_1}$$

$$\frac{S_1}{S_2} = \frac{Z_2}{Z_1}$$

Thus there is a possibility that $S_1$ is more than rated kVA of transformer 1.

As per usual design practice, smaller transformers have lesser per cent impedance. Hence when a smaller transformer is connected in parallel with the larger transformer, there is a possibility of overloading of the smaller transformer. Three possible solutions are:

— To limit overall load such that $S_1$ is within rated $kVA_1$

— To add series reactance externally in the circuit of transformer 1.

— Modifying transformation ratios.

# 18

# Tap-Changer and Voltage Control

## 18.1 VOLTAGE CONTROL IN NETWORK (POWER SYSTEM)

The voltage of busses in generating stations, switching sub-stations and receiving sub-stations should be held within permissible limits. The voltages of distribution lines and supply points to consumers should be held at constant rated values (with permitted deviation) under fluctuating load conditions. The task of voltage control is closely associated with fluctuating load conditions and corresponding requirements of reactive power compensation (kVAr Compensation), and tap-changing.

## 18.2 PERMISSIBLE VOLTAGE VARIATION

During heavy loads (or low power factor loads) the IX drop in transmission and distribution lines increases and the *receiving-end voltages decrease.*

**Table 18.1. Reference Values of Voltage Limits in A.C. Network**

| *Class* | *System Voltage* | *Highest Voltage* | *Permissible Lowest System Voltage* |
|---|---|---|---|
| | *Line to line R.M.S.* | *Line to line R.M.S.* | *Line to line R.M.S.* |
| LV (1 ph.) | 240V | 264 V | 216 V |
| MV | 215 V | 257 V | 374 V |
| M.V. | 3.3 V | 3.6 kV | 3 kV |
| M.V. | 6.6 kV | 7.2 kV | 6 kV |
| M.V. | 11 kV | 12 kV | 10 kV |
| M.V. | 22 kV | 24,kV | 20 kV |
| M.V. | 33 kV | 36 kV | 30 kV |
| H.V. | 66 kV | 72.5 kV | 60 kV |
| H.V. | 132 kV | 145 kV | 120 kV |
| E.H.V. | 220 kV | 245 kV | 200 kV |
| E.H.V. | 400 kV | 420 kV | 380 kV |
| U.H.V. | 760 kV | 800 kV | 750 kV |

**Note:** L.V.= Low Voltage
M.V. = Medium High Voltage
M.H.V. = Medium High Voltage
H.V. = High Voltage
E.H.V. = Extra High Voltage
U.H.V. = Ultra High Voltage

During low loads the IX drop in series reactance of lines is negligible. The shunt capacitance of transmission lines taking capacitive currents causes *increase in receiving voltages*. Thus, the sub-station bus voltages experience:

REDUCED VOLTAGE ⟷ HIGH LOAD
INCREASED VOLTAGE ⟷ LOW LOAD
NORMAL VOLTAGE ⟷ MEDIUM LOAD

Low voltages cause higher current flow through supply lines for same load causing higher line losses. Low voltages also cause increased current to deliver same power, hence increased heating of lines, motor, transformers. Below certain voltage (70 to 80% rated voltage) the motors get stalled and are tripped automatically by the overcurrent or undervoltage protection. Sustained high voltages cause failure of insulation of transformers and motors. The permissible values of upper and lower voltage limits are given in table 18.1.

Permissible variation is approximately ± 10% of Nominal Value.

## 18.3 METHOD OF VOLTAGE CONTROL

The various methods of voltage control in the network include:

— *Excitation Control* and voltage regulators in generating stations.
— Use of *Tap changing transformers* at sending-end and receiving-end of transmission lines.
— Switching-in *shunt reactors* during low-loads or Long EHV lines with non-switched shunt reactors.
— Switching-in *shunt-capacitors* during high loads or low p.f load.
— Use of *series capacitors* in long EHV transmission lines, (distribution lines in certain cases of fluctuating loads).
— Use of tap-changing transformers in factory, sub-stations, distribution sub-stations.
— Use of statics *SVAr Sources* (*SVS*) having shunt capacitor and reactor with step-less control of reactive power and voltage.
— Use of *synchronous condensers* in receiving sub-stations for reactive power compensations. (Now SVS preferred).

All the above methods are appropriately applied in respective sub-stations to achieve voltage control of various newton busses.

*Summerising* the voltage control is achieved by following methods:

*Consumer End*: Tap-changing transformer, Shunt Capacitor.

*Distribution Sub-station*: Tap-changing transformers, Switched shunt capacitors.

*Receiving Sub-station* : Tap-changing transformers, series capacitors; Switched shunt reactors,

Static VAr Sources, Synchronous condensers.

*Switching Sub-stations:* Same as above.

Switching sub-stations are added to provide compensation to very long lines at interval of 250 to 300 km.

*Generating Stations and*

*Sending-end of Transmission lines:* Off-circuit tap switches, shunt reactors, series capacitors, Excitation control.

**Compensation of Reactive Power.** Reactive Power flow ($Q$) is closely related with the voltage control.

The Apparent Power $S$ (kVA) is given by

$$S = P \pm jQ$$

where $S$ = Apparent Power, kVA

$P$ = Real power, kW

$Q$ = Reactive power, kVAr.

The various equipment in the network 'Absorb' or 'generate' reactive power.

By present AIEE convention:

*Voltamperes-reactive are obsorbed by inductive loads and Q for inductive loads is considered positive.*

*Voltampers are supplied by capacitive loads and Q for capacitive load is considered negative.*

$$S = P + jQ$$

Real power $P$ controls the active power (which converted into mechanical/heat or some other form...........(watts) and influence frequency $f$.

Reactive power $Q$ is exchanged between inductive and capacitive loads in the network and influences the voltages in the network.

The control of various bus voltages is achieved by supplying/absorbing the reactive power requirements (kVAr) of the respective busbars by means of series or shunt compensation.

**Compensation of reactive power means supplying/absorbing reactive volt-amperes.**

### 18.3.1 Effective or Reactive Power Flow on Voltages at Sending -end and Receiving-end of Transmission Line

Let $P$ = power transfer watts per phase.

$Q$ = Reactive power transfer VARs per phase.

$V_S$ = Sending end voltage Volts, phase to n.

$V_R$ = Receiving-end voltage, phase to n.

$\Delta V = V_S - V_R$....... drop in the line voltage

$R + jX$ = Series impedance of line/phase.

The relationship between $V_S$, $V_R$ and $P$, $Q$ is given by the equation:

$$\Delta V = V_S - V_R = \frac{RP + XQ}{V_R}$$

If the resistance $R$ is neglected, *i.e.*, $X > R$, then

$$\Delta V = V_S - V_R = \frac{XQ}{V_R}$$

*Hence voltage drop in line depends mainly on the flow of reactive power Q.*

The power angle $\delta$ between $V_R$ and $V_S$ is proportional to

$$\delta \propto \frac{XP - RQ}{V_R} \approx \frac{XP}{V_R}$$

If $X >> R$, *angle* $\delta$ *depends mainly on P.*

Thus.

**Voltage is mainly controlled by reactive power flow, power-angle δ is mainly controlled by real power flow. For Voltage control, the flow of reactive power through the transmission line should be controlled. The flow of reactive power is controlled by injecting required VARs into the system by means of**

— Static shunt capacitors/reactors, Static VAr Sources (SVS)
— Series Capacitors
— Shunt Reactors

Static shunt capacitors are installed near load points, load centres, receiving sub stations. They improve the power factor of current flowing through the distribution line and thereby raise the voltage at receiving end. During low loads, static shunt compensators are switched off. SVS are installed in various substations for stepless, fast control of voltage.

Series capacitors and shunt reactors are installed only when necessary for long, EHV/UHV a.c transmission lines.

Tap-changing transformers are the basic means for voltage control but they shall be supplemented by means of compensation of reactive power. Only tap-changing transformers are not adequate for voltage control of various busses in the network. Voltage control in the Network is achieved by appropriate means at each sub-station and generating station. Centralized voltage control from load despatch centre is not technically possible as the required tap-changing and compensation is necessary in each sub-station.

### 18.3.2 Tap-Changing Transformers

*The voltage control of transmission and distribution systems is obtained basically by tap-changing.*

Tap-changers are either no-load or off-load tap-changers. By changing the turns ratio of transformer, the voltage ratio and the secondary voltage is changed and voltage control is obtained. Tap-changing is the most widely used method of controlling voltages at various levels.

The voltage control of the range ± 16% can be achieved by tap-changing transformers.

**Off-Circuit tap-changing.** Occasional adjustment of voltage ratio can be made by off- circuit tap changing. These adjustments are usually for seasonal load variations of special operating requirements of local sub-stations. Typical range of the on-circuit tap-changers are: 1 ± 2½ % variation in 5–7 steps. *Daily and short-time voltage control is not possible by off-circuit tap-switch.*

Off-circuit tap-changer operation is manually executed by sub-station operator.

**On-load tap-changers.** *The daily voltage variation due to changing load, and short period voltage variations are controlled by on-load tap-changers automatically.*

*On-load tap-changing is also useful in industrial applications where variable voltage is required for the process (e.g., arc-furnace duty).*

The voltage ratio of a transformer can be varied by about ± 16% by means of on-load tap-changers.

On-load tap-changers have about 16 steps with provision of automatic voltage control. The voltage regulating equipment for automatic control of on-load tap-changer comprises a line-drop compensator, voltage sensitive regulating relay, time-delay relay etc.

A tap-changer is provided on a transformer for maintaining specified out going voltage where the incoming voltage is subjected to voltage variations. The tap-changer is mounted in/on the transformer tank. It comprises a motor driven mechanism and associated control circuit for starting and stopping the motor. The motor can be run in the direction for a *raise* tap-change or in the reverse direction for a *Lower* tap change.

*In order to initiate the tap-changing, the line / bus voltage is sensed from secondary of a V.T. by voltage sensitive relay. The voltage sensitive relay has two pairs of contacts-for 'raise' and 'Lower'. A time delay element is provided within the voltage sensitive relay or its circuit separately. The time delay relay prevents tap-changing operation during transient voltage changes and hunting of changers., Time delay can be adjusted between minimum 10 sec. to 60 sec. or more. A line-drop compensator is provided within control circuit used for regulating transmission line voltages.*

*When the line voltage varies beyond certain set value; the voltage sensitive relay connected in the Secondary circuit of V.T.A is actuated either to close 'raise' contacts or 'Lower Contacts'. The driven motor rotates in required direction to achieve tap changing.*

The motor stops automatically after changing the tap as the unit switch provided in the mechanism operates.

Line drop compensator is a replica of transmission line(Consisting of adjustable resistor and inductor elements). The current flowing through R and L of L.D.C. is equivalent to current flowing in transmission line. *The voltage drop in L.D.C. is proportional to voltage drop in transmission line.*

The voltage drop across the RL of L.D.C. is injected into main regulating voltage coil circuit. Therefore, the operation of voltage regulating relay is in accordance with the requirements of the voltage drop in the transmission line. The tap-changing is, therefore, obtained as per the transmission line requirements of changing load currents and reactive drop in the line. Thus the tap-changing by on load-tap changer provides automatic regulation of bus bar voltage. Static voltage regulating relays are avilable for automatic changing.

## 18.4 PRINCIPAL OF TAP-CHANGER

The voltage ratio of a transformer is nearly equal to the current ratio $V_1/V_2 = N_1/N_2$

By changing the turns-ratio ($N_1/N_2$), the voltage ratio can be changed in the same proportion. The secondary voltage can be varied.

One of the windings (HV or LV) is provided with several tappings. These tappings are connected to a 'tap-selector' in the tap-changer. By changing the tap-position, the appropriate number of turns are brought into circuit and desired turns ratio is obtained.

Tap-changers are of two types:

— Off-circit tap-switch — On-load tap-changer.

These names are self-explanatory.

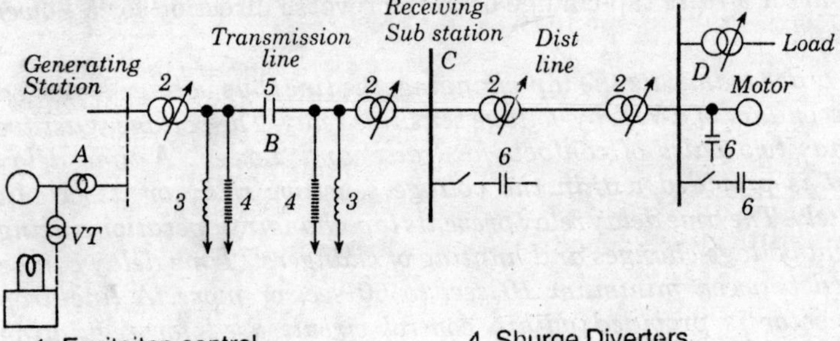


1. Excitaiton control
2. Tap Changing Transformer
3. Shunt Reactors (Switched).
4. Shurge Diverters.
5. Series Capacitors.
6. Shunt Capacitors (Switched).

Fig. 18.1. Methods of voltage control in network.

## 18.5 LOCATION OF TAP-CHANGERS (Fig. 18.1)

*Tap changer is fitted with the transformer for adjusting secondary voltage.*

Occasional adjustments in seacondary voltage can be made by *off-circuit tap-changer*. Such adjustments are seasonal load variations. The tap is changed only after opening the circuit-breaker on supply side.

Daily or short time voltage adjustment is made by means of *on load tap-changer*. The tapping of on load tap-changer can be changed without interruption in load current.

The modern practice is to install the tap-changer within the transformer tank. The tap changer is filled with dielectric oil. This oil does not get mixed with the main transformer tank oil.

There is no fixed rule regarding locating the tap-changer on primary or secondary winding.

It is generally desirable to locate the tap-changer on HV winding beacuse of smaller current. If rating of HV winding is high (400 kV) it may be difficult to insulate tap-changer components with respect to gound. Hence in such cases tap-changer may be put on LV winding or on neutral-end of HV winding.

For star connected transformer with solidy grounded neutral, the taps and the tap-changer are generally placed on the grounded neutral end of the winding. Though the winding may be of very high voltage at line end (400 kV for example), the maximum voltage to which the tap-changer at neutral end is subjected is equal to voltage age between highest tap position and neutral. By placing the taps nearer the neutral end, the voltage rating of the tap-changer can be minimised.

## 18.6 OPERATION OF A TAP-CHANGER

Refer Fig. 18.2. The winding (*W*) is provided with tappings 1, 2, 3, 4........The change over of tap-selecting switch would bring about change in the selected tap. In on-load tap-changer, the circuit of winding should not get opened, while changing the taps.

Hence while changing the tap selector, the two taps are bridged by the tap selector *via* the resistors (*R*). The resistor (*R*) limit the current in the part of winding undergoing communication *via* the tap selector. In earlier designs, reactors were used for current limiting. However, now resistors are preferred as they do not store electrical energy.

The on-load tap changer is fitted with power transformer. The winding (HV or LV) is tapped. The taps are connected to the diverter switch of the tap-changer.

The motor drive unit is initiated by a push button or voltage control relay, the tap selector changes the tap. The diverter switch diverts the current. The break in current is prevented by transition resistor bridged by the Divertor Switch.

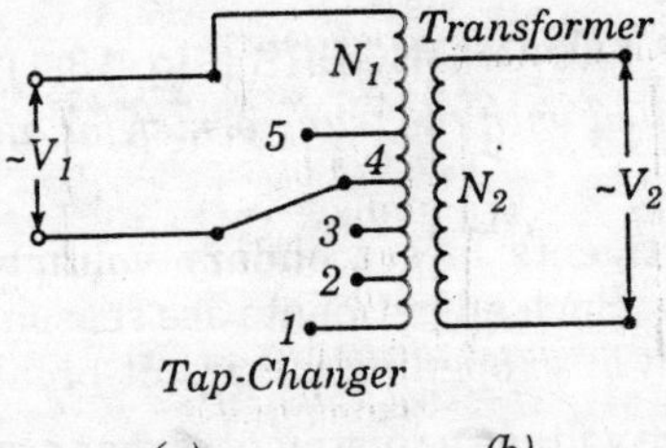


(a) (b)

By changing the tap position, the turns-ratio ($k$) = $N_1/N_2$ can be changed.

$V_1/V_2 = N_1/N_2 = k, V_2 = k \cdot V_1.$

Fig. 18.2. Principle of a tap-changer.

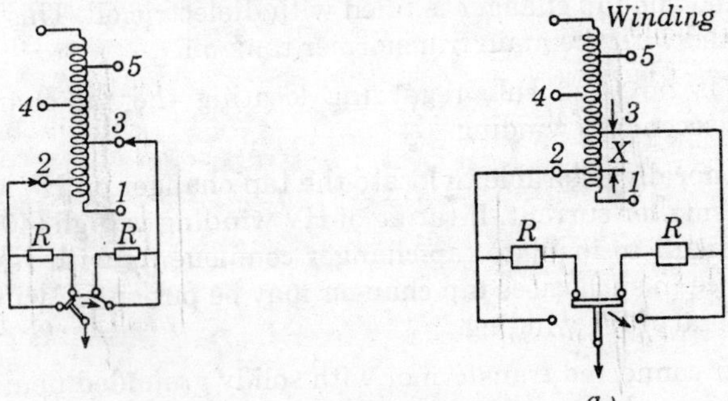


(a) (b)

(*a*) Current passing through Tap No. 2

(*b*) Current passing through Tap Nos. 2, 3 and Resistor R

Fig. 18.3. Tap-changing Process.

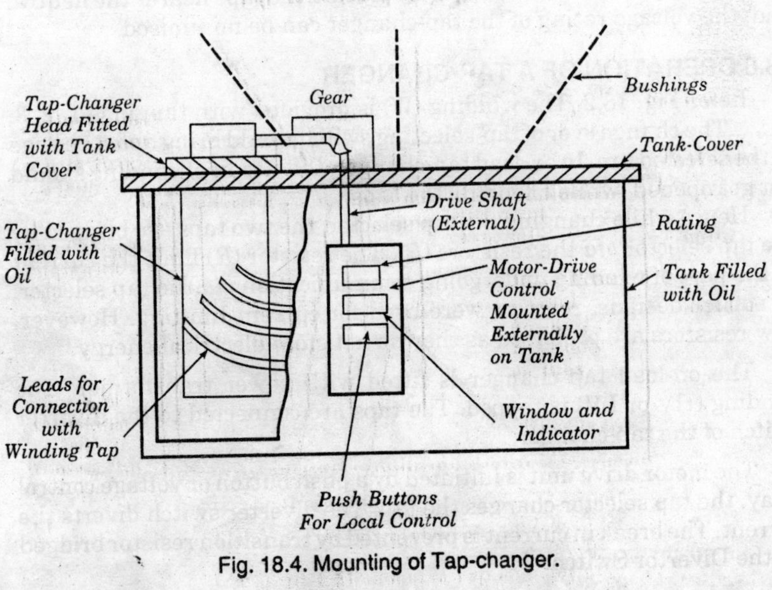


Fig. 18.4. Mounting of Tap-changer.

Refer Fig. 18.2. Initially, (*a*) current passes through Tap No. 2. Then, (*b*) Tap. Nos. 2 and 3 are bridged by the diverter switch *via* transistor Resistors *R*. The short-circuiting of winding *X* is prevented by *R*. Finally, the current passes through Tap No. 3. Tap changer operation is completed.

The sequence of operation of tap-selector and diverter switch is such that the tap is changed without interruption in the current in the main transformer winding. Hence the tap can be changed without interruption in load current, hence it is called on-load tap-changer.

## 18.7 AUTOMATIC CONTROL OF A TAP-CHANGER

The tap-changing operation is initiated by pressing the push button on the motor driver housing of the tap-changer or by a contactor operated by automatic voltage regulator. The voltage control relay operates when the line voltage increases or decreases by set amount. When the voltage control relay operates, the motor gear unit-of on-load tap-change gets a command for raise or lower. Depending upon signal, the relays and spring to complete one-tap changing operation to 'Raise' or 'Lower' the tap. To prevent tap changing operation during transient fluctuations, a time delay relay is provided in a control circuit. The time delay relay can be adjusted up to 60 seconds.

In the meanwhile the motor-gear operates and charge. The springs to keep the tap-changer ready for the next operation.

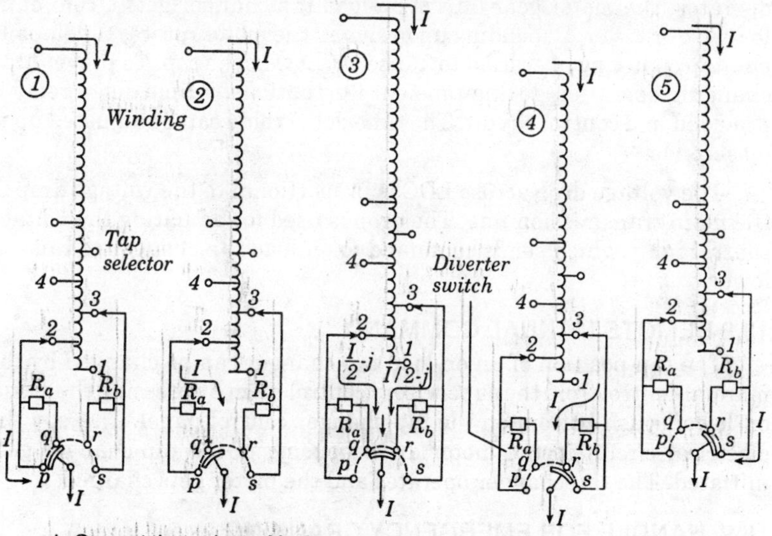


1. Current through tap No.2,
2. Current through tap No. 2. Ra,
3. Current through tap No. 2, Ra; tap 3, Rb,
4. Current through tap No. 3, Rb,
5. Current through tap No. 3.

Fig. 18.5 On-load tap-changing.

**Line-drop Compensation (LDC).** For automatic voltage control of transmission lines, the voltage control relay which gives command to on-load tap-changer is provided with line drop compensation (LDC). LDC is in a small replica consisting of R and L proportional to transmission line. The LDC connected to the secondary of CT and VT and is arranged such that variation of load current causing voltage drop in main line is simulated in the replica type LDC.

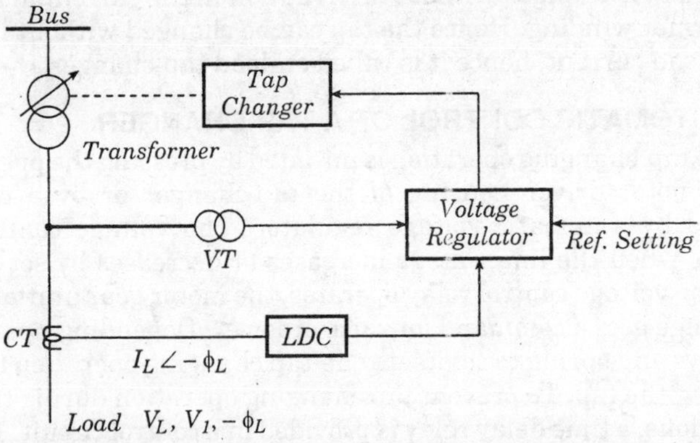


Fig. 18.6. Automatic control of on-load tap changer and LDC.

The voltage regulator relay operates when the line voltage increases or decreases by set amount. When the voltage control relay operates, the motor gear unit of on-load tap-changer gets a command for raise or lower. Depending upon signal, the motor rotates to complete one-tap changing operation to 'Raise' or 'Lower' the tap. To prevent tap changing operation during tansient fluctuations, a time delay relay is provided in a control circuit. The time delay relay can be adjusted up to 60 seconds.

The voltage drop across LDC is proportional to the voltage drop in the main transmission line. The drop is used for actuating the voltage control relay which sends command to on-load tap changer to raise or lower.

## 18.8 REMOTE MANUAL COMMAND

The tap-position of an on-load tap changer can be changed by the manual control from the supervisory control room by pressing the 'raise' or 'lower' push bottom on the tap-changer control panel. Thereby the electrical circuit in the motor drive housing of the tap-changer gets initiated. The tap-changer operates and the motor gets charged.

## 18.9. HANDLE FOR EMERGENCY CRANKING

The springs in the motor-drive housing of a tap-changer are normally charged by the motor. In case of motor or supply failure, the springs can be charged manually by the hand crank. The limit-switch provided in the assembly prevents starting of motor when the hand-crank has been placed in its position.

## 18.10. TESTS ON TAP-CHANGERS

There are separate standards for on-load tap changer and off-circuit switches. These standards give the terminologies, ratings, requirements, type tests and routine tests.

The *Type-Tests* are conducted to confirm the rating and characteristic of a tap-changer of paritcular type and design. These need special testing facilities. Type tests include:

— Mechanical operation tests and timing tests

— Dielectric tests including

1. One minute power frequency withstand voltage test
2. Lightning impulse voltage withstand.

— Temperature rise tests

— Measurement of resistances

— Short-circuit tests (short time current test)

— Breaking capacity tests and transition Resistor Tests.

The *routine tests* are necessary on each tap-changer. These include:

— Mechanical operator tests and timing tests

— Measurement of resistance

— Dielectric tests (performed with the transformer in assembled condition)

After assembly of the complete transformer, the operation of tap-changer is checked under the routine tests of power transformer.

## 18.11 PARALLEL OPERATION WITH TANSFORMERS HAVING OLTC's

If the transformers with OLTC's are to be operated in parallel, care should be taken to ensure identical transformers with identical tappings. It should be also ensured that tap-changing *command to* parallel transformers should be *simultaneous*. The voltage ratios should be changed at the same time. Both the transformers should have the same tap position.

If the tap positions are different, corrective actions should be taken either manually or automatically. For automaic control, several alternatives of different sophistication are available to prevent out-of-step operations between parallel transformers.

**Summary**

The tap-changing is used for seasonal and daily voltage variation. Off circuit tap-changers are operated after switching open the C.B. On-load tap-changers are operated during load flow. A tap-changer is a complex mechanical switching device. It is fitted in the transformer tank. It should be designed and manufactured to give a very reliable service.

# 19

# Loading of Power Transformers

The service life of a transformer is influenced by the temperature rise of windings and temperature rise of oil due to the kVA loading. The temperature rise depends upon the ambient temperature, the load cycle and the previous load status. At low ambient temperatures and about 60% rated continuous load, the transformer can have a very long service life over forty years. At higher temperatures, the life is reduced. Overloads cause excessive temperature rise and deterioration of the insulation and the oil. Overloads reduce the service life of the transformer. However, the daily load curves have periods of underload, normal load and overloads. This chapter reviews the loading criteria and the co-relation between ambient temperature, earlier load and the changed load, the maximum hot-spot temperature. The IEC guidelines for loading have been reviewed. It is assumed that the maintenance is carried out regularly and the transformer is protected against external voltage surges and through short-circuits.

The ideal loading condition for a delta/star connected transformer would have been a 3-phase balanced load which is rarely achieved with the distribution network available in suburban and metro cities in our country. So long the un-balanced load is in the range of 10% among the phases, the effect may be ignored. However, it becomes critical when the un-balanced loading goes beyond 10%. Incase, the un-balanced current for any particular transformer goes beyond 10%, the cause may be investigated for applying remedial measures on priority.

**Table 19.1. Comparison of Permissible Duration of Overloads for ON Transformers of 1950's and 1980's**

| *Base load %* | *Permissible Overloads ONAN* Transformers* | | | |
|---|---|---|---|---|
| | *1950's* | | *1980's* | |
| | *% Overload* | *Hours* | *% Overload* | *Hours* |
| 50 | 130 | 0.5 | 150 | 0.5 |
| | 115 | 2 | 140 | 2 |
| 75 | 120 | 0.5 | 150 | 0.5 |
| | 110 | 2 | 130 | 2 |
| 100 | 120 | 0.5 | — | — |
| | 110 | 2 | — | — |

*Oil Natural Air Natural Cooling.

## 19.1 PERMISSIBLE DURATIONS OF OVERLOADS

With better insulation and better internal cooling oil circulation, the permissible duration of overloads can be increased.

During 1950–1980, the design of cooling systems and insulation systems has progressed.

## 19.2 THERMAL TIME CONSTANTS OF A TRANSFORMER

The time in hours required for a transformer loaded at rated kVA and with constant temperature of cooling medium, to reach steady temperature is called the *time constant* of the transformer (Refer Table 19.2).

The windings generate heat. This is dissipated through the cooling system. When the load changes, the winding temperature changes at a faster rate than the corresponding rate of change of oil temperature. Something happens when load is thrown off. Windings cool very fast where oil cools very slowly.

**Table 19.2**
**Reference Values of Thermal Time Constants for ONAN Transformers**

| *Rated MVA* | *Nominal System Voltage on HV sided $KV_{rms}$* | | | |
|---|---|---|---|---|
| | *11* | *33* | *66* | *Above 132* |
| | *Thermal Time Constants in Hrs* | | | |
| Up to 0.05 | 3.5 | 0.5 | — | — |
| 0.05 to 0.25 | 3.0 | 4.0 | 5.0 | — |
| 0.5 to 1 | 2.75 | 3.5 | 4.0 | 5.0 |
| 1 to 10 | 2.5 | 2.75 | 3.5 | 4.0 |
| Above 10 | 2.5 | 2.75 | 3.0 | 3.5 |

## 19.3 NATURE OF THE LOAD

The kVA load fluctuates instantaneously, daily and seasonally. The average value increases over the years due to the growth in demand of electrical energy.

Thus the load on a transformer may be at times lower and sometimes higher, than the rated value.

Depending upon the location and application the kVA load varies in certain pattern called a *load curve* for 24 Hours. During some hours of the day, the load is low and during some other hours the load is high. Depending upon the applications the overloads are classified as

1. **Repeating Overloads.** (Normal load cycles). These correspond to an approximated daily load curve. The overloads occur for certain duration during the day.

2. **Emergency Overloads.** These occur due to unexpected happenings such as sudden tripping of a parallel transformer. Such emergencies are rare but overload factors are higher and loss of life is of faster time rate.

3. There are many instances when single phasing takes place. As a consequence, the current in one phase goes drastically high, causing operational problems and may lead to the failure of transformers.

## 19.4 CRITERION FOR LOADING AND PERMISSIBLE OVERLOADING

The loading of transformer is decided by permissible temperature rise of windings and oil. Permissible oil temperature is approximately 65°C and hot spot temperature of the winding is approximately 80°C at rated load with superior insulating materials and better oil, these values can be slightly higher.

*As the load on the transformer does not remain steady and varies according to the load curve, the loading of transformers becomes an important operating problem.*

The *rated output* of a power transformers is mentioned on its name plate with reference to specified temperature rise under specified test conditions. The output which can be obtained from a transformer without causing undue deterioration of the insulation may be either more or less than the name plate rating depending upon the operating conditions. *These include as ambient temperature, initial loading, cooling provisional, life expectancy etc.*

*Life expectancy reduces if the transformer is overloaded for longer durations with higher overload factor.*

Permissible duration of overload depends upon initial load, type of cooling and insulation class of transformer. Higher over loads are permissible for a shorter duration.

**Table 19.3**
**Permissible Duration of Overload ON Transformer.**
**Reference Ambient Temperature 35°C.**
**Previously on Rated Load**

| Overload % : | 125 | 150 | 175 | 200 | 300 |
|---|---|---|---|---|---|
| Duration (minutes) : | 125 | 45 | 15 | 10 | 1 |

**For sub-station transformers, overload protection is generally arranged to initiate alarm/trip the breaker on the basis of temperatures of oil as follows:**

| Switch-on Fans | : | Oil temperature 60°C |
|---|---|---|
| Sound/alarm | : | 90°C |
| Trip | : | 100°C |

If the transformer is previously on part load the permissible duration of overloads would be different as indicated in Table 19.4.

**Table 19.4**
**Permissible Duration of Overload Reference Ambient Temperature 35°C, Previously on Part Load**

| Base load % | 50 | | 75 | | 100 |
|---|---|---|---|---|---|
| Overload % | 140 | 150 | 130 | 150 | Table 19.1 |
| Duration Hrs. | 2 | 0.5 | 2 | 0.5 | |

## 19.5 EFFECT OF AMBIENT TEMPERATURE

Ambient temperature means room temperature or weather temperature. Ambient temperature varies with geographical location, season, hour of the day and location of the transformer (indoor or outdoor).

For given maximum temperature ($T_{max}$), the permissible temperature rise ($T_r$) depends on ambient temperature ($T_a$)

$$T_{max} = T_r + T_a$$

For higher ambient temperature, the load on transformer should be reduced. For lower ambient temperatures, the load on the transformer can be increased.

Assuming ambient temperature of 35°C, and average oil temperature on full load equal to 60°C, the permissible loading of power transformers based on ambient temperatures is given in the following table:

**Table 19.5**
**Loading on the Basis of Ambient Temperature**

| *Type of cooling* | *Per cent of rated kVA* | |
|---|---|---|
| | *Decrease load for each degree C higher temperature* | *Increased load for each degree C lower temperature* |
| Self-cooled.....OA | 1.5 | 1.0 |
| Water cooling.....OW | 1.5 | 1.0 |
| Forced air cooling ...OA/FA, OA/FA/FA | 1.0 | 0.75 |
| Forced oil cooling......FOA, FOW or OA/FOA/FOA | 1.0 | 0.75 |

Over loads are permissible or not depends on

— ambient temperature of air
— temperature of cooling air or cooling water
— previous load on the transformer.

Main point governing permissible over load is the average winding temperature measured by resistance method should not exceed 95°C.

The result of excessive over loads on transformer is the cellulose insulation becomes mechanically weak resulting in winding failure. The oil gets rapidly oxidised during excessive over loads.

## 19.6. AGEING OF INSULATING MATERIALS

The solid and liquid insulating materials used in a transformer are adversely affected by heat, oxygen and moisture. At higher temperatures, the solid insulating material such as cellulose, paper, press board become brittle and undergo chemical and electrical properties deteriorate. The tensile strength reduces. Their capability to withstand electrodynamic stresses during short-circuits and dieletric stresses during surge voltage waves is drastically reduced. Under normal stress condition, the insulation shows long life even with overloads. But during external short-circuits or during lightning switching surges, the insulation which had been subjected to excessive temperature, during earlier history, fails.

Oil starts oxidising and decomposing rapidly at higher temperatures. The decomposition of oil and other insulating materials at high temperature reduces the voltage withstand capability and short-circuit withstand capability of the insulation system. The change in properties with time is called *Ageing*. The life reduces in inverse proportion to the temperature of the insulation. The effect was quantified on the basis of researches during 1950–1980. Two noteworthy formulae have been recognised.

### 19.6.1. Moisture in Power Transformers

The operating temperature of a transformer normally depends on the load it feeds. The rated operating temperature occurs when a transformer feeds the rated load. The operating temperature goes beyond ratio temperature when a transformer feeds more than rated load. It reduces transformer life. The reduction in life is decided by the operating temperature and the moisture content present in the transformer. The rate of ageing in service accelerates at high temperature. It has been found that for every 6.5°C increase in operating temperature, the cellulose life reduces to half, if the moisture content in the paper is 0.3% by weight. The rate of ageing is much higher at high moisture content and remanout life reduces drastically at 5% or more moisture content in the paper.

**Oxygen.** Ageing take place due to chemical reactions between long chain glucose molecules of cellulose and oxygen. In the absence of oxygen, there will by no reaction and hence, ageing. But oxygen is always present either in the form of air dissolved in oil or paper. Though people have tried to replace air in oil by nitrogen or an electronegative gas, efforts have always failed. Alternatively, a rubber based membrane has been used with success to prevent direct contact between oil and atmosphere. The life of membrane is about 10 to 15 years. There after, it begins to allow air and water vapour to get diffused. Additionally, the chemical process of ageing forms water upto 10% of the weight of cellulose. Fitting a membrane traps water formed during this process and moisture is blocked into the system where it is a catalyst causing more rapid ageing of the insulation.

**Moisture.** Oil dissolves about 60ppm water before it saturates. Cellulose saturates at 10% moisture content in dry condition, and between 12 and 18% water content when it is oil impregnated. The presence of moisture as a *contanination* in the oil-paper insulation system compromises the dielectric strength of the paper and act as a catalyts for rapid ageing of the insulation system. Most power transformers use paper and oil as the main form of insulation.

External moisture is repeatedly drawn into a free breathing transformer as the working temperature rises and falls with the load. As paper (cellulose) ages, internal moisture is generated. The long chains of cellulose break during service and the carbon combines with any oxygen present to form carbon monoxide, carbon dioxide and water. The oil can also generate significant amount of moisture due to oxidation. The gases dissolved in oil and water remain largely in the paper where its presence contributes to further ageing.

The following are the probable ways for moisture to enter a transformer

1. Inadequate drying process
2. Leaks in tank, joints etc.
3. Internal generation

Water is bad for transformer, the specific effects of moisture are complex and not widely understood. In addition to long-term damage associated with accelerated paper ageing, the evolution of paper bubbles or free water from paper insulation can also cause short term failure.

Dissolved moisture in oil can form precipitate during rapid cool down periods and become free water, which may not redisolve. Hence, any method of moisture determination based on a single measurement without regard to these compounding factors may provide a false indication of the insulation integrity especially for transformers with cyclical load profiles.

Since hot oil is able to support more moisture than cold oil without affecting the transformer performance, percentage saturation is temperature dependent. When hot oil is cooled, the relative saturation increases and an emulsion of water and oil form. Free water may also be produced which will have a serious effect on dielectric strength of the oil and can also load to the formation of rust where it collects, typically in the bottom of main tank and conservator.

Further more, when wet paper gets very hot, for example, during a period of sustained over loading, the possibility of bubble formation arises. On heating of paper, moisture in the paper is boiled off as water vapour introducing a risk of partial discharge and electric breakdown.

Moisture in a transformer is very dynamic, moving with temperature between oil and paper. By far the greatest quantity is contained in paper, which acts like a sponge. Moisture within the transformer is shared between liquid and solid insulation (cellulose/paper) only 2% of the total moisture is dissolved in oil, and remaining 98% is trapped within paper. The moisture moves relatively rapidly from paper to oil along with the rise in temperature. With the temperature fall, the moisture moves back into the paper but more slowly. During the cooling period, water flows out of oil and goes back into paper at a rate slower than it came out.

After a period of prolonged steady temperature, the water in the paper and oil reaches equilibrium state. At that point of time, by measuring the moisture content of the oil, it is possible to estimate the quantity of water in paper from standard tables. The diffusion of water from the insulation tends to slow as the transformer tries to reach equilibrium state. The problem occurs when the oil becomes saturated, the water has no where to go. It can only flow as free water between the interface of the outer layers of the solid insulation and the saturated oil. Thus free water flows in an energised field and the consequences can be disastrous.

The present method of determining the dryness of transformer paper insulation is to measure the moisture content of an oil sample and use the well established moisture equilibrium characteristic between oil and paper insulation. However, the dynamics of moisture movement between paper and oil during temperature cycling is significant and, unless taken into consideration, can cause significant errors in moisture assessment.

Dealing with the problem of moisture in a transformer is a very important part of effective asset management. Always record the temperature when an oil sample is taken for moisture analysis. Never change oil just because it is wet. The new oil will very quickly degrade to the same condition as the old, as moisture leaves the paper to re-establish an equilibrium condition.

### 19.6.2. Montsinger's Formulae for Ageing of Insulation

This was the first formula and is called "Rule of Eight Degrees".

This was postulated by the American scientist Montsinger during 1950s. The rule states that each 8°C rise in temperature reduced the life of the insulating material by a half. This is represented by the formula

$$t = t_0 \, (2^{-\theta/8})$$

where $t$ = duration of life

$t_0$ = constant (corresponding to the length of 'normal' life)

$\theta$ = the difference in °C from the normal temperature.

This formula was derived by taking a 50 per cent reduction in the tensile strength of an insulating material as the criterion for the end of its life.

The various researchers carried out experiments by applying temperatures for certain durations of time and followed by chemical analysis and dielectric tests on the insulating material samples. The results indicated that cellulose insulating material retain their properties well beyond the arbitrary limit set by Montsinger. Impregnated Paper which has become brittle is still capable of withstanding the normal electric stresses. This capability is basically due to the impregnating oil and the barrier effect. Usually the transient oscillatory electrodynamic force during a short circuits or surges cause disintegration of the insulating material, followed by a breakdown between turns or coils.

### 19.6.3. Arhenius Formula

This formula recognises the degree of polymerisation (DP) of cellulose, short time heavy loads.

The formula is

$$t = A\, e^{-T/B}$$

where, $t$ = Time required for chemical reaction at $T$

$T$ = Absolute temperature

$A, B$ = Constants.

This formula is applicable in the temperature range 80° – 130°C.

The degree of polymerisation of a new paper is about 1250 and it reduces to about 150 for a completely crumbled paper.

CIGRE's Transformer Working Group has considered 6°C as the value for establishing the loading guide (instead of 8°C of the Motesinger's Formula).

## 19.7 HOT-SPOT TEMPERATURE

Fig. 19.1 shows the curve showing the number of hours of loading per day which would give one day loss of life (reduction in service life by one day.

By operating the transformer with hot-spot temperature of 98°C, the transformer operated for 24 hours (continuously) results in one day loss of life. Whereas increasing the hot spot temperature to 110°C, the loss of life of 1 day is reached only in 6 hours. That means 24 hours operation with hot spot temperature of 110°C would result in 4 days reduction in the service life of the transformer. If hot spot temperature is 140°C, loss of life of 1 day occurs in only 11 minutes.

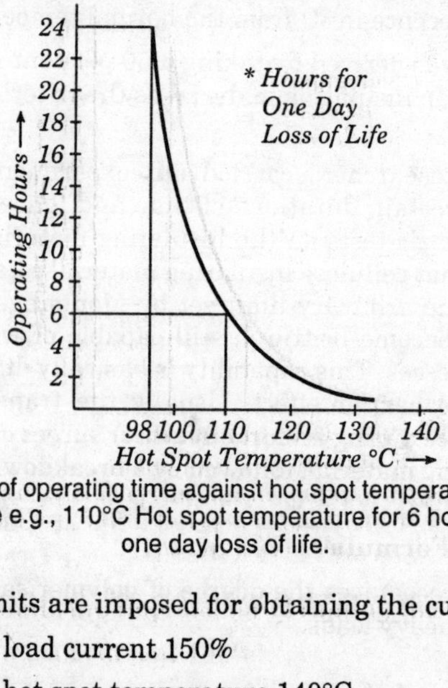


Fig. 19.1 Curve of operating time against hot spot temperature for one day loss of life e.g., 110°C Hot spot temperature for 6 hours gives one day loss of life.

Following limits are imposed for obtaining the curve.

1. Maximum load current 150%

2. Maximum hot spot temperature 140°C

3. Maximum temperature of oil in emergency loading 115°C.

Continuous operation with hot spot temperature of 98°C gives normal rate of degradation.

*The rate of degradation doubles for every 6°C increase in the hot spot temperature.*

## 19.8 IEC LOADING GUIDE

For given ambient temperature (*e.g.*, 10°C), given initial load condition *e.g.*, 50% rated load and given overload (*e.g.*, 150%), how many hours can the overload be continued safely? The answer is given in the IEC Loading Guide in the form of tables and graphs having the following variables.

1. Base Load (previous load) in terms of Load Factor $K_1$.

$$K_1 = \frac{\text{Base Load kVA}}{\text{Rated Load kVA}}$$

(Range of $K_1$ : 0 to 1.2).

2. New Load in terms of load factor $K_2$

$$K_2 = \frac{\text{New Load kVA}}{\text{Rated Load kVA}}$$

Range of $K_2$ : 0.7 to 2.

3. Ambient temperature.

*e.g.,* 0°C, 20°C, 30°C, 40°C.

4. Permissible duration of new load in hours,

*e.g.,* 0.5 Hr, 2 Hr, 8 Hr, 24 Hr.

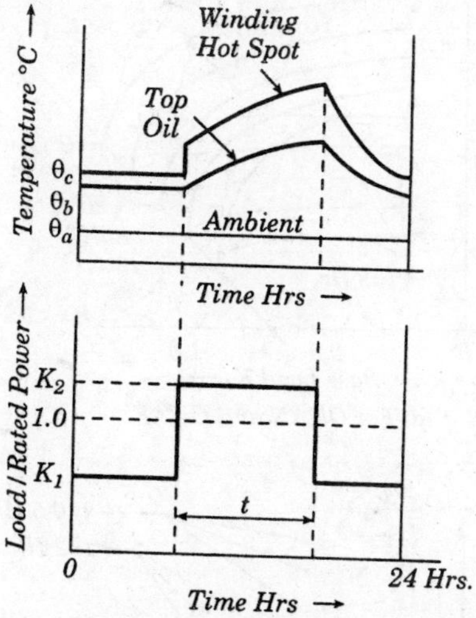


Fig. 19.2. A typical Daily Load cycle with initial load factor $k_1$ and intermediate load factor $K_2$.

From the graph for given three conditions, the fourth parameter can be determined.

## 19.9 TYPICAL DAILY LOAD CYCLE

Figure 19.2, shows a typical daily load cycle with initial load factor $K_1$, Load factor $K_2$ for $t$ hours followed for load factor $K_1$ again. Ambient temperature may be of any value between 0°C and 40°C. The corresponding oil temperature and winding hot-spot temperature curves are shown in the upper half of the figure. The duration $t$ and overload factor $K_2$ decide the maximum hot-spot temperature.

## 19.10 LOADING GUIDE CURVES

*Figure 19.3 (a) and (b)* show the graphs for loss or life for normal 24 Hr day for various values of $K_1$, $K_2$ and ambient temperature. Fig. 19.3 (*a*) is for ONAN, ONAF transformers and Fig. 19.3 (*b*) for OFAF and OFWF transformers.

For example from Fig. 19.3 (*a*) for initial load $K_1 = 0.5$ and ambient 40°C and overload factor $K_2 = 1$, the point is just near 8 Hr line. It means, the transformer can be loaded upto $K_2 = 1$ for 8 Hrs. to reach hot spot temperature of 40°C with ambient of 20°C, the transformer can be loaded upto $K = 1.1$ for 8 Hrs.

For initial load of $K_1 = 0.5$ and ambient of 40°C the transformer can be loaded upto $K_2 = 1.3$ for approximately 2 Hrs.

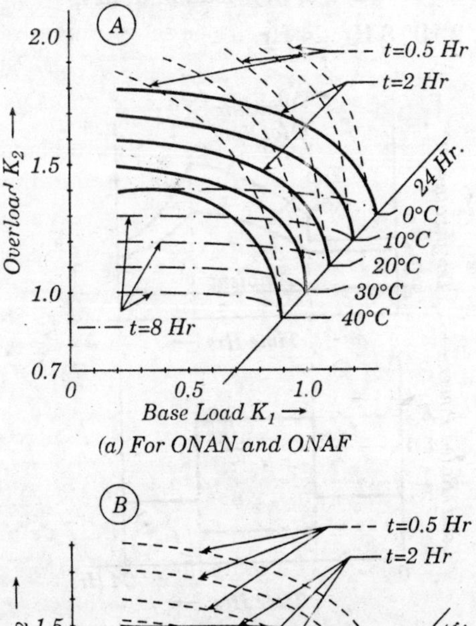


(a) For ONAN and ONAF

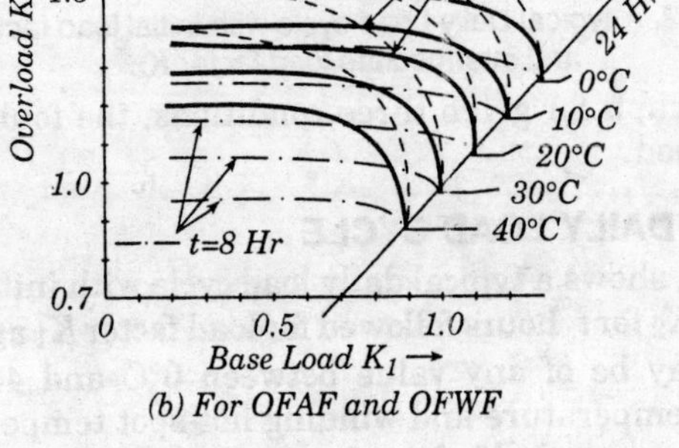


(b) For OFAF and OFWF

Fig. 19.3. IEC Guide for daily load cycles with overloads of 0.5, 2, 8 hours as a function of ambient temperature giving a normal day's loss of life.

The curves can be interpolated for other ambient temperatures or durations of overloads.

## 19.11 VARIATION IN THERMAL TIME CONSTANT OF OIL AND WINDINGS

The windings generate the heat and pass on to the Oil. Hence the winding temperature is higher than oil temperature as shown in Fig.19.2. The thermal time constants of heating of oil and heating of windings are quite different. The thermal time constant of windings are of several minutes, whereas the time constant of oil is several hours (Table 19.2). The temperature of winding rises at a much faster rate than temperature of oil.

Secondly, the variation in temperature of winding relative to that of oil is not constant. At low temperatures, the viscosity of oil is higher. Hence relative increase in winding temperature is higher (as compared with the corresponding rate of increase, temperature of oil).

## 19.12 THROUGH SHORT-CIRCUIT CONDITION

A power transformer is generally adequately protected against flow of through short-circuit currents. (short-circuit current flowing through the transformer for faults beyond the transformer).

The short-circuit current may be in one or more phases and r.m.s. value ranges between 2 to 25 times rated current. A transformer has certain inherent capability to withstand sustained short-circuit currents. If due to certain lapses, the overcurrent protection of transformer does not operate, the Buchholz relay and sudden pressure relay operate after an elapsed time in case of oil cooled transformers. The winding and oil temperature rises rapidly resulting in loss of service life which cannot be easily quantified. If short circuit current flow continues for a longer duration of time, the transformer fails due to insulation failure and winding fault.

Failure due to external short circuits for distribution transformers is quite common with the type of system available in the present distribution network. Transformers are designed to withstand shortcut forces for very short durations. In case, the external short circuit persists for more than 2 to 3 seconds, the fate of the transformer is uncertain and may get damaged due to excessive shortcut forces.

To improve upon the performance of transformer against short circuit forces, it is desirable to use proven protective equipment. Moreover suitable protection, like ACB on LV side, OCB, VCB, HRC fuses, dropout fuses etc., on HV side, as deemed fit, should be provided.

## 19.13 PROTECTIVE DEVICES AGAINST OVERLOADING

— Over-current protection
— Winding temperature indicator, alarm, and trip-out

— Oil temperature indicator, alarm and trip-out
— Buchholz relay with alarm and trip contacts
— Sudden pressure relay with alarm and trip-out contacts.
— Overfluxing protection against heating of core due to excessive magnetic flux densities.

## Summary

The loading criterion for transformer takes into account:
— Hot spot temperature
— Previous load and new load
— Ambient temperature
— Thermal time constant.

A set of curves have been recommended by IEC for certain factors $K_1$ and $K_2$ from a typical daily load cycle.

Higher hot spot temperature gives more loss of life. The overloading is done by sacrificing the life of the transformer.

Power transformer should be selected for 20% higher kVA rating than prevailing load (Ref Sec. 20.4—1).

# 20

# Ordering, Transportation, Installation and Site Testing

The alternative methods of packing at manufacture's works, transportation, handling and unloading at site have been reviewed. The methods of installation and site testing have been described.

These aspects must be considered during initial design of a larger power transformer so that transportation, handling and site erection can be done efficiently.

## 20.1 DATA COLLECTION PRIOR TO ORDERING

Transformers are installed either outdoor or indoor. Some distribution transformers are pole-mounted (out-door).

The installation aspects of the transformer should be considered at the time of ordering and project planning.

— Before ordering the transformer, the data regarding the following aspects should be obtained and used for planning the project and the substation layout.
— Requirements of electrical kVA load, application aspects.
— Location, environmental conditions, ambient temperatures, rain, dust, altitude, siesmic zone etc.
— Substation layout, voltage levels, fault-levels.
— Transport facilities, roads, etc., between the manufacturers premises and final site. Road, rail permits, availability of suitable trailors, wagons.
— Movement within substation, road, rails, curves.
— Civil engineering requirements such as the room, foundation, trenches for cabling, ventilation aspects, etc.

The data regarding transport requirements and handling facilities should be obtained. This information includes: overall dimensions, weight, lifting arrangements, transport facilities, special trailors, the transport route, roads, bridges, culverts, arches, etc., throughout the route, rail route, and requirements of special wagons, etc. The movement within substation should be precisely planned.

## 20.2 INFORMATION TO BE FURNISHED BY THE MANUFACTURER TO THE USER

The following information is generally furnished by the manufacturers to the user at the time of the enquiry:

(*a*) **Information to be furnished in all cases**

1. Name of the Manufacturer........
2. Service Continuous/short time etc.
3. Ratings Rated kVA.....Rated Voltage of HV.....kV
   Rated Voltage of LV.......kV
   Rated frequency...... Hz

Temperature rise of oil.......°C

Temperature rise of winding by resistance method......°C

4. Number of phases.......
5. **Connections** HV: LV:
   Vector Group:
6. **Tappings** HV:....per cent; LV:....... per cent
7. **No load current at rated voltage and rated frequency in all the phases.....**
8. No-load loss at rated frequency and rated voltage.......kW
9. **Load-loss** at rated current at 75°C: per cent
10. **Impedance** at rated current at 75°C...... per cent
11. **Reactance** at rated current and frequency.......per cent
12. **Efficiency** at 75°C, at Unity p.f.:
    At full load.....per cent
    At ¾th full load....... per cent
    At ½ full load...... per cent
13. Efficiency at 75°C at p.f. 0.8 lag:
    At full load......per cent
    At ¾ load.....per cent
    At ½ full load......per cent
14. **Regulation** at full load, at 75°C
    At unity p.f......per cent
    At 0.8 p.f. lag.......per cent
15. **Weights:**
    Core and windings......kg. Tank with fittings......kg.
    Oil.....kg. Total weight.......kg.
16. **Quantity of oil**........Litres.
17. Overall Dimension: Length......mm; Width......mm;
    Breadth......mm.
18. **Terminal Arrangements**: of HV and LV
19. **Reference Standard:**
20. **Remarks:**

(*b*) **Additional Information** (on request)

1. Maximum flux density at rated voltage, frequency.......
2. Load for maximum efficiency......% of full load
3. Maximum Efficiency:.......
4. Impulse withstand levels: HV.....kV peak
   LV......kV peak

5. No-load current at 110 per cent rated voltage........A
6. No load loss at 110 per cent rated voltage.....kW
7. Types of windings: HV......LV......
8. **Clearances:**
   8.1 Minimum clearances between phases:
   (*a*) in oil.....mm (*b*) out of oil.........mm
   8.2 Minimum clearance of HV to earth in oil.......mm
   8.3 Minimum clearance of LV to earth in oil........mm.
9. Minimum clearance height for lifting core and winding from tank......mm
10. Thickness of tank.......mm.

(*c*) **Shipping Details**

| *Sl. No.* | *Part to be Dispatched* | *Size* | *Weight* |
|---|---|---|---|
| | | | |

(*d*) **Details about Auxiliary Windings:**

1. Ratings.......
2. Connections......
3. Tappings......
4. Impedance.......

(*e*) **Details about Bushings:**

1. Type.......
2. Creepage distance in air......mm
3. Recommended gap setting........mm
4. Weight of assembled bushings......mm
5. Impulse withstand voltages.........kV
6. Power frequency withstand voltages.........kV.

(*f*) **Details about Tap-changer**

1. **Make**......
2. **Type**......
3. **Ratings**...
4. Quantity of oil.....
5. Rated voltage......
6. Step voltage........
7. Number of steps.....
8. **Control**.....
9. Auxiliary supply requirements......
10. Voltage control details
11. Line drop compensation details
12. Parallel operation...
13. Protective devices with tap changer
14. Weight, dimensions of tap-changer.

### (*g*) Details about Fitments on the Transformer

Details of rollers, thermometers, explosion vents, buchholz relays, CTs, inspection covers, breather, conservator, neutral grounding points, earting points, details about marshalling kiosk, etc.

### (*h*) Diagrams

The manufacturer should furnish the following diagrams:

— Terminal markings and winding connections
— Vector groups and vector diagrams
— Rating plates
— Insulation levels HV, LV, MV
— Interconnections between three single phase units forming a 3-phase bank.

### (*i*) Valve Schedule and Coolant Flow Diagram

## 20.3 RELATED ASPECTS NEEDING ATTENTION

The following important aspects need attention.

1. **Interchangeability** of transformers with a spare transformers. It is a useful practice to order and install one spare transformer so that in an event of a failure of a regular transformer, it can be quickly replaced by the spare one. However this practice is no more followed now.

2. **Spares.** Standard erection spares such as gaskets, hardware, cable boxes, fuses, etc., should be ordered along with the main equipment. The maintenance spares and spares for one overhaul should also be ordered and stocked.

3. **Substation Layout.** Transformer is the biggest, heaviest and costliest equipment in the switchyard. The bushings are long. The *clearances* should be adequate. Sufficient clearances should be available between the phase connections and nearest phase point and nearest ground point.

Large transformers are moved on their trolleys along the rails or by road trailers. Substation has well planned rail-cum-roads for taking the transformers up to the plinth and un-loading, shifting the transformer for repairs, replacing the spare transformer etc.

4. Provision of draining the oil.

5. Provision for isolating the transformers from the busbar for the maintenance. Isolators are provided on either sides.

6. **Safety Precautions.** The installation and commissioning team should take all the recommended precautions.

7. Fire protection.

8. Electrical protection against abnormal operating conditions.

9. Neutral Earthing.

10. Earthing of tank, tank cover, core etc.

11. Surge arresters for protection against lightning surges and switching surges.

## 20.4 SELECTION OF POWER TRANSFORMERS FOR A SUBSTATION

Electrical substations are of two types (1) Switching substation (2) Transformer substation. Transformer substation has two/three /four voltage levels. Transformers of corresponding voltage ratios are installed in between *e.g.*, 220 kV/132 kV/ 33 kV.

Selection of the right size of power transformers has a major impact on the substation costs since they represent the most expensive items.

Important aspects regarding specifying a power transformer include the following:

**1. Future load growth**

This determines the selection of rating in MVA. The nominal rating can be exceeded by 20% if additional cooling (or low ambient temperature) is provided. This is achieved without harming the lifetime of the transformer.

If sacrifice in lifetime can be allowed, higher intermittent loading can be considered. See, for instance, IEC Loading Guide Publ. 354 (Refer chapter 19).

**2. What voltage variations exist in the networks during different loading conditions?**

The answer determines the required regulating range. The most common solution today for substation transformers is to install an on-load tap-changer which allows adjustments while the transformer is still energized.

"Normal range" = 10 to 15 per cent.

"Normal step" = 1 to 2 per cent (*e.g.*, 1.25%, 1.67%)

**3. Does the network impose any specific requirements on the impedance of the transformer?**

The impedance of a new power transformer affects the electrical network in different ways, *i.e.*,:

1. It limits short circuit currents inversely.

2. It causes a voltage drop directly.

3. It influences system stability inversely.

4. It affects parallel operation with other transformers in the network.

In many cases it is of advantage to specify optimum impedance of the transformer giving the lowest purchase price.

**4. Preference for a cooling method**

Smaller units, say below 20 MVA, are often specified to have a self-cooled (ONAN) rating. For large units it is often more economic to choose Oil-Natural Forced Air (ONFA) or Oil Force Air-Forced (OFAF) cooling. It is then necessary to provide continuous and reliable power supply for the oil pumps and fan motors in order to be able to supply rated load.

**5. Does the environment require a low sound level? What is the limit of sound level?**

The transformers manufactured today usually fulfill the specifications of IEC/IS/NEMA standards as far as the sound level is concerned. If a lower sound level is required, special measures internal as well as external may be needed in order to reduce the noise from the core and the fans.

These include sound Absorbing Barriers/Enclosures.

**6. Does the transportation pose a limit for the weight size/type of transformer?**

Unless this question is investigated the rating/size/type cannot be finalized. This applies to large transformers.

## 20.5 TRANSPORTATION, HANDLING AND STORAGE

### 20.5.1 Transportation

Two alternatives are available for mode of transport:

1. Small and Medium Transformers: Truck.

2. Large Transformer Tanks: Road trailors; Rail Wagons.

**Despatch.** Transformer are despatched by the manufacturer by one of the following methods depending upon the size and local conditions:

1. Dried-out, filled with oil, ready for service. (Small transformer).

2. With oil covering core and coils only. (Medium transformer).

The balance space is filled with nitrogen gas.

The tank cover is always bolted into its position prior to final despatch.

The small transformer may be packed in a strong wooden packing case for despatch or may be sent without packing case depending upon conditions of transport. The terminals and fitments protruding out need careful considerations.

Protective hoods may be specially provided. For long distance transports and export jobs, special packing cases are provided for protecting the cooling tubes, tank and fitments to prevent damage during transit.

3. Without oil in the tank, filled with by nitrogen at pressure slightly above atmosphere pressure. (Large transformer).

In case of extra high voltage transformers, the HV bushings are packed separately and temporary connections are brought out for insulation resistance measurements. Some of the accessories are also packed separately.

In case of large transformers, the transport route, handling, movement, wagons, tailors, necessary permits from Railways and Road Authorities should be preplanned before finalizing tank dimensions. Wagons should be ordered or booked in advance.

**WITH OIL**

(*a*) The Transformer is filled with oil such that about 10% of the tank volume is left clear for expansion to limit the excess internal air pressure to 0.35 kg/cm$^2$. Fittings dismantled before transport are packed in packing cases in line with shipping list.

(*b*) All openings resulting from removal of fittings for shipment are sealed with suitable gasketted blanking plates during transport.

(*c*) The balance oil quantity required for the complete filling of the reactor is supplied separately.

(*d*) A transformer despatched according to this method can be stored at site or elsewhere for one year provided, that all insulating materials are covered with oil and silicagel breather is mounted and quality of oil is well maintained.

**WITH NITROGEN**

Large oil filled transformers/reactors are not normally oil filled during shipping due to weight limitations. To protect the active parts against moisture the transformer tank is filled with dry Nitrogen at a positive pressure of 0.175 kg/cm$^2$ (2.5 psi).

All openings resulting from the removal of fittings for shipment are sealed with suitable gasketted blanking plates during transport.

A transformer despatched according to this method should normally be stored upto 3 months after arrival at site or elsewhere.

For control of gas pressure and maintaining the pressure during transport and possible storage before assembling, the transformer is equipped with an automatic device. This device is called two stage $N_2$ regulator and is kept in a steel box and mounted on the frame provided on tank side for keeping two back up Nitrogen cylinders.

$N_2$ regulator reduces cylinder high pressure of 120 to 140 kg/cm$^2$ to required low pressure of 0.175 kg/cm$^2$, in two stages. One gauge provided on the first stage indicates the cylinder pressure, whereas other gauge provided on second stage indicates the tank pressure.

When tank pressure falls below 0.15 kg/cm$^2$, due to leakage/fall of ambient temperature, regulator automatically feeds the gas from cylinders, to build up required pressure in the tank.

Two back up cylinders are provided to meet the gas requirement. Normally one cylinder is kept open and the other shut. When the pressure of first cylinder falls to 10 kg/cm$^2$ immediately its valve should be closed and the valve of second cylinder should be opened.

When cylinder is required to be removed for refilling, disconnect copper tubing from cylinder valve.

Use only dry Nitrogen gas to IS:1747 with 50 ppm moisture and 1% oxygen by volume.

### 20.5.2 Nitrogen Filling for Transportation

Large transformers weighing above 50 MT are transported as follows:

— Tank filled with dry nitrogen or dry air.

— Bushings, tap-changers, conservator, Buchholz relay breather, radiators, rollers, marshalling kiosk etc., packed separately.

If the tank is of medium weight, the same is filled with oil with reduced level. The space above oil is filled with dry air or nitrogen. The space is provided for expansion of oil due to heating by solar radiation and atmospheric temperature during transport and storage. External nitrogen gas cylinders with pressure regulating valves are provided for make-up of leakage of nitrogen gas during transport and storage.

Escorts are provided for maintaining a record of gas pressure and for safe transportation and intermediate storage if any. For important transformers 'impact recoders' are fitted to the tank to record the impact during the entire journey period between manufacturers works to the final location at site.

**Instructions for Filling Dry Pure Nitrogen Gas with Back Up Cylinders (At Works)**

(*i*) Lower the oil level to the minimum necessary to dismantle the items (such as bushing and turrets) which must be removed for shipping.

(*ii*) Pull 500 mm mercury vacuum after blanking off all openings.

(*iii*) Break the vacuum by admitting dry nitrogen through a convenient valve at the top of the tank and drain the oil completely.

(*iv*) Continue to supply nitrogen until it maintains a steady pressure of 0.17 ± 0.02 kg/cm$^2$ above the atmosphere.

(*v*) Pressure of nitrogen gas shall be maintained at 0.17 ± 0.02 kg/cm$^2$ at same reference temperature. Pressure would be monitored by taking three readings within 24 hours to ensure that there is no leakage of gas.

(*vi*) Shut off the gas supply valve and fit dry nitrogen back up cylinders through nitrogen regulator valve.

### 20.5.3 Rail Transport

When possible, rail transport is preferred to road transport. Rail transport of large transformers is economical and safer. In case of transformers, where weight and dimensions exceed the limits, special well wagons are employed.

**Loading.** The manufacturers of large transformers generally have their own railway siding. The transformers are loaded on railway wagon at the works by using the cranes. In cases, separate siding facilities are not available, road trailers are used for the transport from works to loading railway station. If crane facility is not available, the transformers are *unloaded* from the trailers near the railway track on to the platform of the sufficient height built-up by wooden sleepers. Jacks and pull-lift chain-pully blocks of adequate capacity are used to slide the transformer over the pair of rails places on the sleeper-platform bridging the trailer width in full. To prevent toppling over of the trailer, the transformer tank is moved to the platform, the stage end of the trailer is supported by a sleeper pack. The transformer tank is slided on the wagon taking care to take rails for full width of the wagon. The rails may be greased for easy movement. The rollers of the transformer are removed before despatch from the works. The 'sleeper stage' should be at a slightly higher level to allow for the increases in the height of the trailer while releasing the load.

**Lifting and Jacking.** The transformer tank should be lifted by means of lugs or shackles provided for lifting. All the shackles or lugs should be used simultaneously to lift the transformer in balanced position.

The slinging angle should not exceed 60°. The wire ropes should have sufficient strength. Gunnie-cloth should be used on the slings to avoid cutting of slings due to metal-corners.

*While using the jacks the projections of the tank specially provided for the jacks should be used. The jack should never lift the valve or cooling tubes. More than two jacks must not be operated simultaneously.*

Two jacks on opposite side may be operated simultaneously and they should have firm support on the sleepers. Jacks should not be kept on load for prolonged duration.

*The transformer tank should be handled in vertical position. Every precaution must be taken to avoid over-turning.*

Loading on railway-wagon should be done symmetrically so that the weight on all the axles is distributed uniformly.

The selection of wagon and approval of loading diagram by the railway authorities must be done well in advance, wagons are booked in advance.

**Lashing.** The tank placed on the wagon is lashed on all the four sides by wire ropes or chains of adequate strength. The chain or wire-ropes are tightened using turn buckles with loading facilities. Wooden props are used. The lightness of the lashing is checked after movement over certain distance. If transhipment is carried out en-route, the lashing is checked again.

**Railway Movement Permits**

After selecting the wagon, loading diagrams are sent to railway authorities for approval. After approval, the route permits are taken from all the railway authorities over the route form the works to the site or from the port to site.

### 20.5.4 Road Transportation Large Transformer Tanks

Small and medium transformers are loaded on trucks at manufacturer's works and are transported up to the site and are unloaded. The bushings and accessories are provided with protective loads.

Large transformer tanks are transported by road trailer when rail route is not available. Alternatively, road transport is resorted to from nearest railway station (unloading point) to the site. The road trailers for transportation of large transformer tanks are multi-axle low platform trailers driven by high power tractors. Loading, lifting, lashing on road trailers is similar to that described for rail wagons. Before finalising the transportation plan, complete route survey is conducted. The following rules are applicable for finalising the road route.

1. Road width minimum 5 m
2. Bridges and culvert : Adequate strength permission from highway authorities.
3. Encumbrances along the route : Telephone, telegraph, distribution lines, trees cross beams, subways, cross roads.
4. Sharp turns : Minimum radius of turn to be verified.
5. Bearing capacity of road : To be verified especially in rainy seasons.
6. Gradients : Strength of road trailers must be ensured, for pulling up and for braking.

7. Strengthening the route : Wherever necessary the bridges, culverts are strengthened by propups of wooden pillers, steel sections etc., in consultation with the highway authorities. In some cases, bypass route is preferred instead of strengthening a culvert.

8. Many times coordination from local police may also be required for traffic control.

**Precaution during movement**

1. A pilot vehicle with tools, jacks, sleepers, chequer plates, crow-bars, wire ropes, etc. should accompany the road trailer. The crew should be of well trained staff.

2. Red flag and red light should be displayed on prominent positions in front and on the rear to warn the traffic. A pilot vehicle should ensure clear passage.

3. After certain movement, the lashing should be checked.

4. The movement speeds on good road should be less than 10 km/hr to 15 km/hr for loaded vehicle and 15 to 20 km/hr for trailer without load. For bad roads and on slopes, lesser speeds are ensured.

5. The brake system should be well maintained and carefully applied.

6. Very low speeds are used over bridges and culverts. Speeds should be gradually reduced before reaching bends, culverts, etc.

7. If the vehicle tyres get locked up in muddy soil, the trailer is anchored and the tractor is detached. The tractor is moved forward by using suitable sleepers. The tractor can then be pulled up by winches in the rear of the tractor.

**Transport by Sea or River**

For ocean transport, large vessels are used. For rivers and lakes barges are used.

The unloading on wharfs is by ships cranes.

The unloading on barges can be also by ships cranes.

While transferring from the wharf to barge/ship the cranes in the port are used.

**(B) Unloading at Site**

Small packages are unloaded with the help of a crane or a derrick with a chain-pulley block. The cranes of adequate capacity are arranged in advance. Alternatively the transformer is slided on platform formed by wooden sleepers as described earlier.

### (C) Inspection and Storage at Site

Main tank is received by road trailer. The accessories are received separately by trucks.

On arrival at site, the packing cases should be checked against the despatch particulars. Any loss of packages in the transit should be intimated to the manufacturer and insurance company.

The transformer should be unpacked and inspected for any signs of transit damage. Oil leakage should be checked along the valves, tank welds, gasketted flanges etc., Gas pressure (if gas filled) should be checked.

The transformer transit damage may be serious damage. It must be immediately reported to the manufacturer and the insurance company. The thorough inspection should be carried out jointly. Otherwise, the claims cannot be easily settled.

Externally observed damaged packages should be segregated and got inspected by surveyors of the insurance underwriters.

Following observation should be made after unpacking.

— Whether the tank sides or turbes are dented
— Any fitments are damaged
— Any oil-leakage
— Any porcelain broken
— Any scratches on tank
— Any instrument glass or observation glass broken
— Any auxiliary item damaged
— Any rust, condensation.

**Records of Delivery**

The record of delivery of packing cases and the tank should be jointly signed by the customer's and manufacturer's representative. Format No. 20.01 gives an example.

## 20.6 STORAGE

The transformers arrived at site and likely to be installed immediately do not need elaborate storage. Transformers not to be installed immediately need proper storage to avoid influx of moisture, effect of rains/dust, etc. It is preferable to store the transformers indoors, with proper covering and proper flooring. The oil should not be drained unless the provision of filling inert gas is available.

**Format 20.01**

---

**Record of Delivery to Site**

Customer's Ref.......................................

Manufacturer's Ref.....................................................................

Record of Delivery (Tank/Packing Cases)

Customer..................................Site..................................................

Transformer Serial No...........................................................................

The above Transformers has been inspected

1. The transformers proved to be delivered and assembled without known/visible transport and/or assembly damages. Possible remarks have been noted below. Alternatively, a special inspection record has been issued.

Remarks............................................................................................
............................................................................................
....................

2. The shortages are as given below:

............................................................................................
............................................................................................

These will be despatched.........................................

During the time

So that the stipulated order can be considered to be completed

Place.....................................................................................................

Date......................................................................................................

Customer's Representative Manufacturer's Representative

.............. .................... .................................. ..............

Enclosures : Test Record.........................

Inspection Record.......................

Others.............................................................

..........................................................................................................

## 20.7 HANDLING

The transformers are provided with lugs and shackles for the purpose of lifting. Before lifting the transformer, all the bolts of the cover should be tightened.

When jacks are used for lifting, the projections provided for lifting should be used.

Proper balance should be maintained while lifting the transformer.

Large tanks are moved on trolleys along the rails. Special pulling techniques are used for turning by 90° over the railcrossing.

Before lifting the transformers, the cover bolts should be tightened.

## 20.8 TOOLS AND EQUIPMENT FOR INSTALLATION WORK

The requirements vary with the size of the transformer. The requirements are as follows:

1. **Lifting Equipment.** Wire ropes, (slings), D-shackles. Derrick with chain pulley blocks (if cranes are not available), cranes of adequate capacity.

2. **Oil Filtration Plant.** The mobile plant comprises vacuum, heating, filtering equipment along with oil circulation facility. The following sizes are recommended.

| Quantity of oil in the Transformer | Litres | Up to 20,000 | Up to 50,000 | Above 50,000 |
|---|---|---|---|---|
| Capacity of the oil filteration plant | Litres/Hr | 2500 | 5000 | 10,000 |

3. **Oil Storage Tank.** Oil is received in drums. This should be filled in the storage tank. It is filtered and filtered oil is circulated through the transformer tank till enough insulation resistance and polarisation index is achieved.

4. **Vacuum Pump.** With hose, end fittings for producing vacuum of 1mm of mercury.

5. **Pressure-Vacuum Gauge.** For checking vacuum/gas pressure in the tank.

6. **Miscellaneous Tools and Instrument**

(*a*) Oil testing equipment (IS 335).

(*b*) Meggers (Mega-ohm meter) 2500 V, 1000 V.

(*c*) **Indicating instruments.** Ammeters, voltmeters, milliammeters, Wattmeters, Avometer.

(*d*) Set of spanners, hammer, plier, screw-drivers.

(*e*) Drum opener, crow bars, plier, hammer.

(*f*) Cleaning cloth, cleaning fluid, an air-compressor with hose.

— Electric lamp with cable, terminal board.
— Brushes, paint
— PVC insulated cables for connecting measuring instruments.
— Facility for minor civil works and minor repair works.

### 20.8.1 Location and Site Preparation

(*a*) Reactor shall always be placed on concrete plinth without rollers as per foundation plan drawing whereas transformer may be even placed with rollers. Therefore it is very important to refer foundation drawing before placing the transformer/reactor on final location.

(*b*) Transformer/reactor should be placed on the foundation so that easy access is available all around and diagram plates, thermometers, valves, oil gauges, etc. can be easily reached or read. Adequate electrical clearances are also to be provided from various live points of the transformer to earthed parts.

(*c*) ONAN type transformers/reactors depend entirely upon the surrounding air for carrying away the heat generated due to losses. For indoor installation, therefore, the room must be well ventilated so that the heated air can escape readily and be replaced by cool air. Air inlets and outlets should be of sufficient size and number to pass adequate air to cool the transformer. The inlets should be as near the floor as possible and outlets as high as the building will allow. Where necessary, exhaust fans can be installed for the purpose.

(*d*) The transformers should always be separated from one another and from all walls and partitions to permit free circulation of air. In this connection reference is also drawn to IS: 10028 (Part II).

(*e*) Where rollers are not fitted, level concrete plinth with bearing plates of sufficient size and strength can be adopted for outdoor transformers. To prevent the formation of rust, it is essential to avoid presence of air and water in the space between the plinth and the base of the transformer by use of cretex of similar bituminous compound.

(*f*) Where rollers are fitted, suitable rails or tracks should be used and the wheels locked to prevent accidental movement of the transformer. Where walls are provided, it should be ensured that the transformer gets a good ventilation as mentioned above for indoor transformers. Provision should be made for the emergency drainage of the oil from the transformers (e.g., in case of fire in neighbouring apparatus or bushing or the transformer tank), by surrounding the transformer plinth with sump filled with small pebbles.

### 20.8.2 Internal Inspection and Check Points for Assembling the Transformer/Reactor

**(*a*) Check-points before starting assembly:**

1. Conditions of leads.
2. Bracing, clamping of leads.
3. Connections.
4. Tapchanger checks.
5. General conditions of insulation.
6. Core check that is has not moved in transit.
7. Core-ground; this is checked with the megger after removing earth connection.
8. CTs, including the secondary leads and their passage through metal parts.
9. Check that shipping frame for bushings have been removed.

10. Check that coil position has not moved in transit.
11. Check for dirt, metal swarf, moisture.
12. Check that the bushing leads set without being too close to ground or other points of different potential.

**(*b*) Check-points during assembly**

By means of the Part list and the transformer/reactor OGA, the assembling of a fully completed transformer is carried out according to the following instructions. The following precautions are to be taken:

(*i*) Fire-fighting equipment shall be available at the oil-treatment equipment as well as at work on and adjacent to the transformer.

(*ii*) Welding work on or adjacent to the transformer shall be avoided, but if this is not possible, the work shall be supervised by fire-protection personnel.

(*iii*) Smoking on or near the transformer shall not be allowed.

(*iv*) Transformer tank, control cabinet etc., as well as assembling and oil-treatment equipment shall be connected with the permanent earthing system of the station.

(*v*) Check that there is no overpressure in the transformer when blanking plates or connection lids are to be opened.

(*vi*) All loose objects, tools, screws, nuts etc., shall be removed from the transformer cover before opening the connection and blanking lids.

(*vii*) All loose objects (tools, pencils, spectacles etc.,) shall be removed from the boiler-suit pockets etc., before starting the work through man holes.

(*viii*) Tools to be used inside the transformer/reactor -e.g., for tightening of screw-joints shall be fastened to the wrist or another fixed point by means of cotton tape or string.

(*ix*) Tools with loose sleeves and tools with catches must not be used at work inside the transformer.

(*x*) Greatest possible cleanliness shall be observed at work inside the transformer/reactor, and at handling of parts to be mounted inside the transformer.

(*xi*) Fibrous cleaning material should not be used as it can deterioate oil when mixed with it.

(*xii*) All components despatched separately should be cleaned inside and outside before being fitted.

(*xiii*) A transformer/reactor is best protected from damp hazard by circulating warm, dry, deaerated oil through it until temperature is 5° C to 10° C above ambient. This should be done before allowing external excess to the interior of the tank. The warm oil should be circulated all the time transformer is open to atmosphere.

(*xiv*) Oil pump and all joints in the oil pipe work should be airtight to avoid entrance of air through leakage joints.

(*xv*) The active part (core and winding) should be exposed to the surrounding air as short time as possible. Open therefore only one blanking plate or connection lid at a time for remounting of bushings, valves etc.

(*xvi*) Objects which-despite all precaution are dropped inside transformer/reactor, must absolutely be brought up from the equipment.

(*xvii*) Check that the oxygen content inside the transformer tank is minimum 20% if a person is to enter the tank.

### 20.8.3 Assembly of Wheels

Mounting of wheels under reactor/transformer is to be done as per roller arrangement drawing. The reactor however in service, is to be placed on plinth with anti-earthquake fastening without rollers. Transformer placement can be with or without rollers as per applicable OGA/foundation drawing.

### 20.8.4 Assembly of Bushings

In case the bushings are mounted on turrets on the transformer/reactor cover, they are either delivered mounted on their turret or–incase of large bushings dismantled from the turrets.

The turrets are often individually adapted; check therefore that they are re-mounted in correct places, which appear from the OGA drawing and part list.

Assembling of bushings is carried out according to the detailed information documents available.

### 20.8.5 Assembly of Valves

Valves which may affect the loading gauge, or will be subjected to damages, should be dismounted before delivery. Re-mount the valves the positionings appear from the OGA drawing and part list. The gasketting surfaces shall be cleaned well and new gaskets fitted. Check that all valves are closed.

### 20.8.6 Assembly of Cooling Devices

Valves which are not dismantled like shut-off valves for radiators, coolers and possible headers shall be provided with blanking plates during the transport.

Remove the blanking plates when the assembling of the coolers is to be started. Check first that the valves are closed.

Check that each radiator and possible header are assembled in the correct positions according to OGA drawing. In case of OFAF or OFWF cooler mounting shall be done as per the relevant leaflet given in Vol.I.

The shut-off valves against the transformer tank shall be closed until the oil-filling is started.

### 20.8.7 Assembly of Oil Conservator

The conservator, which may be with or without aircell is assembled either on the transformer, or on a separate frame. Before the conservator is assembled it shall be checked that belonging equipment *e.g.*, Oil-level indicator-functions satisfactorily.

The breather is connected to the oil conservator, and it is very important that joints and couplings in the pipe between breather and conservator are air tight.

### 20.8.8 Assembly of Pipe Work

Pipes with flanges for connection of conservator, radiators, as well as pipes for equalising of turrets etc., are mostly delivered completely ready for assembling according to OGA and part list.

In certain cases e.g., at a separately assembly oil conservator-certain fitting and welding of pipes and flanges on site is however required. Instruction for such assembly of external pipes is given in article 20.9.2.

### 20.8.9 Flanges, Blanking Plates

When re-mounting blanking plates, connection flanges etc., the gasketting surface shall be cleaned well and new gaskets fitted.

### 20.8.10 Accessories

Accessories like cooling fans, pumps, OLTC and components for supervision and control, oil-level indicator, flow indicators, gauges, Buchholz relay, PRV, thermometers etc. are assembled according to leaflet/description valid for the components.

### 20.8.11 Control Cabling

Re-assemble the control cables according to the drawing of wiring system and connect the cable ends to terminal blocks in instruments, terminal boxes, junction boxes and control cabinets according to valid connection diagram.

### 20.8.12 Gaskets

The sealing system normally used against oil and gas in BHEL's transformers and belonging components has rubber gaskets in grooves and nitrile rubber bonded cork gaskets at other places.

### 20.8.13 Oil Filling

The completely mounted Transformer is oil-filled and shall be treated according to specifications.

The lower and upper shut-off valves for radiators/coolers and possible headers shall be open during evacuation and oil-filling.

If coolers are placed on suspension beams, which are mounted at right angle to the tank, the suspension beams shall be supported against the ground during the evacuation. Also radiators mounted on the tank wall shall be supported in a similar way.

The hose for filling of oil is connected to the bottom valve of the transformer which must not be opened until the hose has been deaerated and completely filled with oil.

### 20.8.14 Cleaning and Painting

The transformer and its equipment are cleaned carefully from dirt, oil, lubricating grease, and damaged surfaces are touch-up painted with the primer paints and finish paints delivered.

### 20.8.15 Exchange of Bushing

When exchanging a damaged bushing or other component on the cover of a fully oil-filled transformer, we should proceed according to the following:

Close the valve in the pipe between the transformer and the oil conservator. Pump oil from the transformer tank into the oil conservator so that the oil quantity which need be drained off to lower the oil-level enough below the transformer cover is pushed to the conservator. As the oil is being transferred from tank to conservator, fill up the tank with dry nitrogen via a suitable valve on the cover or in turrets.

Exchange the faulty bushing and transfer then the oil from the conservator to the tank by opening the valve in the pipe between conservator and main tank. De-air the bushings and turrets.

## 20.9 STORING OF TRANSFORMER/REACTOR DESPATCHED FILLED WITH NITROGEN

### 20.9.1 Storing Before Complete Assembling

The storing place should be easily accessible for inspection and maintenance of the transformer. The bedding for the equipment should be larger than its bottom surface and dimensioned for the load. The transformer is placed on boardings or beams so that good ventilation is obtained underneath the transformer bottom.

Before storing, the transformer is inspected according to directions "Reception and assembling of transformer/reactors despatched partly dismantled and filled with nitrogen".

A transformer without remarks may be stored up to 3 months after arrival at the site without oil-filling. During the storing time, the inert gas (nitrogen) filling shall be maintained and pressure regulated, so that exposure of active part to atmosphere is avoided.

If the storage time is judged to exceed 3 months, the transformer should be provided with oil conservator including oil-level indicator and breather, and oil-filled. "Oil filling under vacuum". Certain valves must be re-mounted to enable the oil-filling being carried out. Furthermore, at the time at oil-filling of a completely assembled transformer, certain rules in practice must be complied with absolutely.

Wherever possible it would be most desirable to keep the transformer energized even at a low voltage so that its temperature is higher than the ambient temperature. The low voltage may be applied under open circuit or short circuit conditions. It may be ascertained whether partial cooling is required in such a case. The oil quality should also be periodically monitored. If for some reason, oil filling cannot be carried out after a storage period longer than 3 months, the nitrogen pressure shall be maintained and supervised carefully. If the storage time without oil exceeds 18 months manufacturer should be consulted about measures to be taken.

### 20.9.2 Storing of Components and Accessories Before Complete Assembling

Independent of the duration of the storing time, the directions below apply for dismounted components and accessories, as well as for material to be used in connection with the assembling work.

**(*a*) Storing indoors**

In such a room, the following articles should be stored:

(*i*) Insulation material as paper, pressboard, bakelite, wood, cotton tape etc.

(*ii*) Insulated details as paper-insulated conductors, pressboard insulated shielding bodies etc.

(*iii*) Chemicals as solvents, glues, varnishes, hardeners etc.

(*iv*) Breathers, drying agents.

(*v*) Terminal boxes, connection boxes, control cabinets.

(*vi*) Gas relays, oil-level indicators, thermometers, pressure valves etc.

It is very important that the pipe is tight. Possible leakage will cause moisture on the transformer with the service disturbances.

Mounting of the breather pipe shall be as per OGA drawing.

### 20.9.3 Oil Conservator

For position of conservator along with necessary supports, refer OGA drawing.

### 20.9.4 Oil Conservator Pipe

The pipe has dimension 80 mm usually and has welded flanges. The pipe shall be painted internally with a yellow, oil-resistant paint, and externally with a paint specified on the drawing. The pipes shall always incline upwards minimum 2/3 degrees from the transformer.

### 20.9.5 Equalising Pipes

The pipe system in connection with the transformer cover is as a rule manufactured in workshop. The pipe between transformer and conservator may be pre-assembled.

The pipe is provided with weld-flanges. No pipe part is allowed to be so long that internal inspection and cleaning is difficult to carry out. Besides straight extensions, each pipe part may contain one bend.

The pipes shall always be placed with minimum 2/3 degrees inclining upwards from the transformer. Internal surface treatment is with yellow oil resistant paint. External surface treatment is made as specified on the drawing as per specification. Cleanliness is extremely important.

### 20.9.6 Coolers

The positioning of the radiators/coolers is indicated on OGA drawing. These are positioned so that the highest point of the oil-pipe system is always positioned below the bottom level of the conservator.

The pipe system is provided with filter valves at the start and finish to enable pumping the oil through the system.

All places where air may be collected are provided with air release plugs/valves.

### 29.9.7 Cooler Pipes

The pipe having dimensions as per OGA drawing and may be provided with weld-flanges, expansion joints. No pipe part is allowed to be so long that internal inspection and cleaning will be difficult.

The pipes shall be placed so that air release plugs will be positioned at the highest point of the pipe part. The pipes shall be painted internally with a yellow, oil-resistant paint and externally according to the paint as per specification.

## 20.10 INSULATING OIL, QUALITY AND TREATMENT

### 20.10.1 Quality

The oil to be filled in transformer generally complies with the requirements of the customer's specification. The characteristics of fresh oil as per IS : 335 "Specification for New Insulating Oil".

## 20.11 CIVIL WORKS AND CONSTRUCTIONAL ASPECTS

The dimensions, out-line drawings, data about weights, foundation plans etc. are obtained from the manufacturer for finalising the civil layout of the substation including the location of the transformer, road-cum-rails etc., *The bus-work and external clearances are finalised in three dimensions by taking into account the final dimensions of the transformer, cooler, bushings etc.*

For **indoor installtion**, the following aspects should be considered:

— Ventilation

— Noise level

— Space required for movement, maintenance, etc.

— Trenches for cables.

**Minimum clearances** between the transformer and the walls should be as follows:

— Walls on all four sides: 1.25 metres

— Walls on three sides: 1 metre

— Walls on back side only: 0.5 metre.

The clearance of 0.5 metre (minimum) should be provided between the top most point of the conservator and the roof.

**Ventilation Area:** Outlet: 2 $m^2$ per 1000 kVA,

Inlet: 1 $m^2$ per 1000 kVA, minimum.

**Permissible Noise Level.** Method of installation and sound proofing enclosures depend upon the location and permissible sound levels.

For **outdoor installations**, the clearances between live parts and neighbouring structures, equipment etc., should be maintained as per electricity rules. In heavily polluted atmosphere, indoor installations should be preferred.

The civil construction includes:

— Transformer, foundations, cooler foundation, Radiator foundation, fire-proof walls, sound-proofing enclosures

— Road-cum-rails

— Oil sump

— Trenches for cables and oil piping

Following aspects are applicable in general for both outdoor and indoor transformers.

**Foundation.** Simple, firm and levelled foundation is necessary for transformers. The base should be horizontal. The foundation should be able to withstand the load.

The level of concrete plinth for outdoor transformer should be above the maximum flood level. The suitable rail-tracks should be provided where rollers are used with transformers.

After bringing in final position, the wheels should be locked to prevent movement.

The separately mounted coolers need a foundation at appropriate location.

**Facility for drainage of oil.** Indoor transformers having oil capacity of more than 2000 litres should be provided with soak pits.

Outdoor transformers having oil capacity of more than 9000 litres should be provided with drainage facility.

**Cabling.** Power cables and control cables should never be run in the same conduit or cable tray. Power cables are at higher voltage than control cables. If run in the same conduit or tray, electric stress will reduce the life of the control cables. Further, more loss in power cables will also be harmful to control cables. D.C. control cables, a.c. protection circuit cables and a.c. power cables should be segregated (separated) from each other.

Routing of a.c./d.c. protection cables and a.c. power cables should be pre-planned so that cross-over is minimum.

Cables may be carried along the walls, clamped, on vertical supports at regular intervals depending upon cable size.

Cable trays may be made of galvanized iron or aluminium sheets.

**Cable boxes.** If the transformer is fitted with cable boxes, and is to be connected by paper insulated power cable, cable ends should be sealed. The cable boxes should be filled with oil or compound.

**Main power connections.** For medium voltages, cables connection or bare conductor connection is used. For indoor installations, the cable connection is preferred.

Bare connections may be for outdoor installations. Bare connections are not preferred for indoor installations. When required, segregated phase bus-ducts may be used for transformer.

In generating stations, isolated phase bus-ducts are used for generator-transformer connections.

For bare connections, rigid or flexible type aluminium/ACSR conductors are preferred. For rigid conductors of more than 4 metre length, expansion joint is preferred to take care of expansion taking place due to temperature rise.

While using copper to aluminium connection, suitable bimetal connectors are used to prevent corrosion.

While making aluminium joint, the surface oxide layer should be cleaned with emery and anti-oxidising grease should be applied immediately. The joint should then be made. (The oxide film on aluminium surfaces is insulating and increases the resistance of joint resulting in local heating and at times open circuit).

**Bushings.** The bushings are inspected for cracks. Gaskets are inspected. Bushings are lifted carefully as recommended by the manufacturer and then installed. The nut-bolts should be tightened in a recommended sequence by torque spanners.

## 20.12 FIRE PROTECTION

General guidance is provided in IS 1646—1997. Adequate precautions should be taken during substation planning and construction stage to limit the spreading of fire in the event of accidental ignition of the transformer oil. The transformer units, oil filled switchgear, other electrical equipments, cable trenches etc., should be segregated in groups such that burning oil does not spread and the fire is localized.

Fire proof walls are provided between transformers and between a transformer and adjucent building. Cable and cable trenches should be laid such that transformer oil does not flow through them.

Where fire risk is high, following precautions are recommended:

— Structures, partition walls etc., should be capable of resisting the effects of fire of longer duration

— Independent ventilation should be provided. So that the trunking does not communicate the fire to other halls.

— Installation of fire detection system, smoke detector system. Remote indication and alarm regarding smoke and excessive temperatures.

— Automatic disconnection of supply in the event of fire.

— Fixed or automatic fire fighting system to be installed wherever necessary fire extinguishing medium may be water, spray, carbondioxide, halon, foam. The detection system triggers the automatic release of extinguishing medium around the transformer such systems should be supplemented by portable fire extinguishers. Several units should be kept suitably.

— *Spraying water on charged transformer should be avoided. Water causes electric current flow through pipe lines.*

— For large outdoor transformers, automatic protection is provided by installation of sprinkler system activated by five detecting units. Sprinklers are activated after tripping the transformer-breakers from busbars.

## 20.13 ASSEMBLY AND CONNECTIONS

The assembly includes following operations:

1. Assembly of bushings on the tank and internal connections.
2. Assembly of tap-changers on the tank and internal connections.
3. Assembly of marshalling kiosk on the tank and connection of power cables and control cables.
4. Assembly of cooling system and associated piping, valves etc.
5. Assembly of marshalling kiosk.
6. Electrical connection-main power.
7. Electrical connection-auxiliary.
8. Electrical connection-protection.
9. Connections of neutral earthing.
10. Connections of tank earthing.

## 20.14 SAFETY PRECAUTIONS

All the basic safety rules should be followed. Some are mentioned below:

1. Before starting the installation, check slings, chains, and all lifting/pulling accessories for strength. Rusted or strained items must not be used. Following checks are essential before energising a transformer.
2. To disconnect the transformer from supply and ground the windings.
3. To disconnect both the primary and secondary. The purpose of disconnecting secondary is to eliminate and possibility of a system feed back.
4. To lock the disconnecting switches in open position.
5. To remove the fuses or fuse cut outs to a special inaccessible area so they cannot be accidently reused.
6. To check the permanently installed transformer ground.
7. To remove the tank top or manhole cover of liquid immersed transformer to relieve internal tank pressure.
8. It should be mandatory procedure that when a man enters a transformer tank a second man be on duty outside the tank. Man should not enter nitrogen filled tank.
9. No tools or other equipments are dropped or left inside tank.
10. Do not take a chance. Play safe.
11. Do not assume that a transformer is dead (de-energized).
12. To make sure all is clear before energizing, after work is completed.

**Note.** Askareb has poisonous fumes and is now banned for use in transformers and reactors.

## 20.15 SITE TESTING AND TEST RECORDS

After the above preparations, several commissioning tests are conducted on the transformer and tap-changer. The test to be carried out at site before commissioning the transformer will depend upon the voltage and kVA rating of the transformer, facilities available at site and contractual obligations.

Field Quality Plans are prepared by the manufacturer and are approved by the user. In these Field Quality Plans, the site checks and tests are listed and the formats for record are enclosed.

### Preparation Prior to Testing

Following are organised in advance:

- Field Quality Plans
- Test Record Formats
- Testing instruments
- Safety precautions and fire protection
- Transformer ready for test.

### 20.15.1 Test Schedule and Test Sequence for Site Tests

This is chosen carefully in consultation the user. Sequence should be such that minimum time is wasted and feed-back about defects, if any, is obtained through earlier tests. Tests which indicate possible internal defect are conducted in the beginning. For small and medium transformers which are despatched fully assembled and with oil, the tests are simpler and take lesser time. For large transformers above 1000 kVA, tests are more elaborate. Transformers for parallel operation need additional tests before paralleling.

Field tests are *not* for confirming design capability. Field Tests are for ensuring the health of the transformer after installation and its readyness for energising.

### 20.15.2 Schedule of Site Tests

| | |
|---|---|
| (A) General observation | —Complete transformer<br>—Control and relay panels etc.<br>—Junction boxes and marshalling kiosks |
| (B) Secondary injection tests | —Of all the protection relays |
| (C) Primary injection tests | —Tests on operation and stability of earth-fault relays on side h.v.<br>—Tests on line directional elements of high-voltage line relays<br>—Tests on high speed neutral circuit breaker.<br>—Tests on overcurrent relays on l.v. side<br>—Tests on operation and stability of earthfault relays on l.v. side<br>—Tests on operation of standby earth fault relay on l.v. side<br>—Tests on overcurrent relay on h.v. side (when current transformers are not in transformer) bushings.<br>—Voltage Compensation. |
| (D) Ratio Tests | —With 415 V applied on high voltage side, measure the voltage between all phases on the low-voltage side for every tap position.<br>—To check phasing, measure volts;<br>*A* to *a*, *b* and *c*<br>*B* to *a*, *b* and *c*<br>*C* to *a*, *b* and *c* |

*Contd...*

| | |
|---|---|
| | Where *A*, *B* and *C* are the terminals of three phase on high-voltage side and *a*, *b* and *c* are the corresponding terminals on low voltage side. |
| (E) Tripping Tests | —High voltage side breaker<br>—Low voltage side breaker<br>—Intertripping tests<br>—Winding temperature trips. |
| (F) Measure earthing resistance | |
| (G) Buchholtz relays | —Tests for angle, air injection etc.<br>—Check that there is no air in protector before commissioning<br>—When energizing, close in on 'Trip' etc.<br>—Check for stability when oil pumps are started:<br>1. at ambient temperature<br>2. at a winding temperature of 80°C or above. |
| (H) Alarm Circuits | —Buchholtz relay<br>—Oil and winding temperature thermometer set at 85°C and 100°C respectively<br>—Cooling gear failure. |
| (I) Fans and pumps | —Check that the oil valves are open in cooling circuit<br>—Check the rotation of pumps, automatic starting overload devices<br>—Check stability of Buchholtz relay |
| (J) Tap changing tests on no-load | —Check mechanism, indication, buzzer, tap-changing sequence raise and lower Ration for each tap position. |
| (L) Phasing tests | —At 415 V<br>—Between transformers in a bank<br>—To prove internal and external<br>—Connections for parallel operation<br>—On auxiliary supplied and voltages transformers |
| (M) Insulation tests (reduced voltage) | —On high and low voltage winding.<br>—On current and voltage transformer circuits, etc. |
| (N) Check oil levels | |

*Contd...*

| | |
|---|---|
| (O) Voltage Compensation test (if compensation transformers are fitted) | —Primary injection<br>—Load tests<br>—If necessary, switch-in which relays connected to correctly compensated voltages from the other transformer |
| (P) Insulation Resistance | —Main Circuit<br>—Auxiliary Circuits. |
| (Q) Additional checks if possible | —Performance on low voltage<br>—Low voltage excitation current<br>—Gradual voltage build-up test. |
| (R) Check on neutral earthing switch | —Check neutral earthing switch is closed before energising. |
| (S) Relay setting | —Set relays in control room before energising. |
| (T) Load Tests | —Connect voltmeters, ammeters wattmeters on HV, LV sides.<br>—Check performance on load<br>—Check relays do not trip. |
| (U) Tap-changer tests on load | —Check full range of taps. |

### 20.15.3 Additional Checks for Parallel Operation

For satisfactory parallel operation, transformers should have identical (*a*) phase displacement, (*b*) voltage ratio, and (*c*) percentage impedance. They should be so connected that their polarity and phase sequence are identical. Provided the polarities of the winding correspond, transformers with the following connections operate satisfactory in parallel. Connections in Group A should not be parallel with those in Group B. (Refer Ch. 16 for details)

Group A — Star/star, delta/delta and delta/zig-zag

Group B — delta/star, star/delta and star/zig-zag.

**Polarity and Phasing Out.** While connecting new transformer, special care should be taken to follow the diagram of connections supplied by the manufacturer taking into account, the phase sequence of the supply. In case of three phase transformer, if connections are not made in correct phase sequence, the outgoing supply may also be of wrong phase sequence. This would require breaking down of connections and remaking the high voltage cable connections.

Whether the phase rotation is clockwise or anti-clockwise, it should be the same for all the transformers that have to work in parallel. However, it is recommended that the standard phase sequences in accordance with the Indian and international practice, namely red, yellow and blue sequences in the anti-clockwise direction should be adopted. A positive check will help in ensuring correct external connections. The simplest way is to connect two transformers in parallel on primary sides connect the secondary terminals of one transformer to its bus-bars, and if assumed, corresponds to the equivalent terminal of the second transformers to the bus-bars, which it is assumed, corresponds to the equivalent terminals of the first transformer. After ensuring that both transformers are on the same tap, voltage readings between the remaining secondary terminals of the two transformers and the bus-bars be taken. If both readings are zero, the transformers are of same polarity and phase rotation, and the connections may now be made permanent.

In the case of star connected secondaries, and alternative arrangement to the secondary connections indicated above is to connect the star points to each other. (This connection may be *via*-earth in which case, of course, none of the secondary terminals will be connected to the bus-bars before closing).

It is also possible for the voltage reading to be double of the secondary voltage which, when the voltage reading happens to be across unlike phases. It is, therefore, necessary that care is taken to see that the range of the voltmeter is equivalent to the sum of secondary voltages of the two transformers.

For transformer operated in parallel, the load shared should not exceed ± 10 per cent of its rated output. For this, percentage impedance and the ratio resistance to reactance should be equal. *Transformer of kVA output more than three times must not be connected in parallel.* (Chapter 16 gives full details)

## 20.16 NO-LOAD OPERATION

After all the above checks and tests, the voltage is applied to the transformer on no load. The no load performance of the transformer is observed for a sufficiently long period prior to loading.

In case of parallel transformers, each transformer should be operated on-load for sufficient time. Parallelling should be done after the additional checks mentioned above have been carried out. Thereafter, the load can be switched in.

Before the voltage is applied for the first time, the following conditions shall be satisfied.

1. All protections are fully operative.
2. Fire fighting system is operative.
3. The insulation resistance, drying-out has been satisfactorily completed.
4. Phasing checks are satisfactory.
5. Tap-changer operate satisfactorily.
6. There is no leakage of oil.
7. Breaker operation must be ensured.

*When first voltage is applied, observers should see, listen and observe from a suitable location.* Control room operator should watch the transformer protection panel. The voltage is applied by closing the circuit-breaker on supply side.

## 20.17 TYPICAL FORMAT FOR SITE TEST RECORD FOR A LARGE TRANSFORMER WITH ON-LOAD TAP-CHANGER

A systematic set of Formats, ready, for filling-in are kept ready by the site test engineer. These formats are reproduced from the Field Quality Plan of the particular transformer. The Site Test Record Book to be filled in during the field test.

Format 20.02 gives the typical contents of the Site Test Record and Format 20.03 gives the final test certificate of site testing.

Format No. 20.02

---

**A Typical Contents Page of Site Test Record Book**

*__Note:__ Tests that have to be done on the transformer are marked.

| WET | TEST RECORD | CODE | S.No. |
|---|---|---|---|
| Record-Field Test | Order No. | | sheet |
| | Drg. No. | | |
| | Ref. | | |

Customer:

Site:

Order No ..........................................................

Transformer type..................................Serial No.........................

Tap changer type...................................   ........................

Driving mechanism type..........................   ........................

---

**Contents of Test Record***

1. Ratio test
   (*a*)Windings
2. Checking of vector group
3. Insulation test of
   (*a*) Windings
   (*b*) Current transformers
   (*c*) Control cabling and supply cables
   (*d*) Core.
4. Checking of bushing and turrets
   (*a*) Capacitance measurement on bushings
   (*b*) Checking of potential connection between flange-tank
5. Polarity checking on current transformers
6. Checking of winding temperature circuits
7. Oil tests.

*Contd........*

8. Operational test of supervisory equipment
9. Operational test of other equipment
   (*a*) Cooling equipment
   (*b*) De-energized tap-changer with driving mechanism
   (*c*) On-load tap-changer with driving mechanism
10. Whether customer will withness testing

---

**Format No. 20.03**

**Field-Test Certification**

---

Customer's Ref. Cert. No.........................

Manufacturer's Ref. Date...............................

Site Location :

Particulars about Transformer Tested

Above transformer has been field-tested at..........site during.......... The test record is attached herewith. The tests were witnessed by the following:

1. .....................(Manufacturer)
2. .....................(User)
3. .....................(Consultant).

**Remarks:**

1. *Transformer has been successful in field-testing and has been put on trial operation with effect from:..............*

2. *Transformer has failed. The detailed report of failure is attached herewith.*

3. Any other comment:................

**Signatures:** Manufacturer User Consultant

---

## 20.18 COMMISSIONING

### 20.18.1 Testing After Assembly of the Transformer/Reactor at Site

After the transformer/reactor has been assembled at site, it shall be tested in order to check that it has not been damaged during transport and assembly to such an extent that its future operation will be at risk. Regarding the performance of the test, refer to the testing method as per standards. The results of the test shall be documented as detailed in article 20.19 "commissioning checks-Transformers" and article 20.20 commissioning checks-Reactors.

### 20.18.2 Application of Voltage

If possible, the voltage should be increased step by step up to rated voltage. This may be done by connecting the transformer/reactor to a generator whose voltage is raised slowly. The higher the rated voltage of transformer/reactor the more important it becomes that the application of the voltage is done as described. If it is not possible to use a generator, the transformer/reactor may be connected directly to a live line.

After the first application of voltage, the transformer/reactor shall be checked carefully (gas relay, temperatures, leakages).

When the transformer/reactor has been is service for some weeks with normal working temperature, all sealing joints shall be re-tightened.

### 20.18.3 Energising

The initial magnetising current at the time of switching will be very high. This depends on the particular moment in the cycle. The transformer should always be soaked for few hours under constant care *i.e.*, keep it energized. If the breaker trips on differential, Buchholz or any other device, the cause must be investigated before re-energising the transformer or reactor. After successful charging, performance of the transformer/reactor, OTI, WTI readings should be monitored for 24 hours and ensured that they are as per loading.

### 20.18.4 Analysis of Gas

The gas connected in the relay will help to identify the nature of the fault. It is suggested that the following checks are made at convenient intervals or following the indication of accumulation of gas through alarm signal.

1. Rate of gas collection—The greater the rate of gas collection, the more severe is the nature of the developing fault.

2. Colour of the gas helps in finding the affected material as follows:

| *Colour* | *Identification* |
|---|---|
| White | Gas of decomposed paper and cloth insulation. |
| Yellow | Gas of decomposed wood insulation. |
| Grey | Gas of overheated oil due to burning of iron portion |
| Black | Gas of decomposed oil due to electric arc. |

3. Combustibility of Gas—A small amount of gas drawn through the top pet cock if brightens the flame, then the gas is combustible. Incombustible gas indicates air.

4. Chemical Analysis of the Gas—The principles of working gas analysing equipment is illustrated in the Fig. 20.1

Two solutions are prepared as detailed below and best results are obtained with freshly prepared solution.

Solution 1 : 5 gms of silver nitrate ($AgNO_3$) dissolved in 100 ml distilled water.

Solution 2 : A weak solution of ammonia in water is slowly added to 100 ml of solution 1, until a white curdled precipitate which forms first disappears in the mixture.

The gas analyser loaded with these solution is then connected to the top pet cock. Small quantities of gas collected in the relay is allowed to pass through the two solutions as illustrated.

**The results are identified as follows:**

1. Both solutions are clear : Gas is air
2. Solution 1–White precipitate turning brown on exposure to sunlight : Gas of oil decomposition.
3. Solution 2–turning to Dark brown precipitate : Gas of decomposed paper, cotton or wood insulation.

**Note:** The above information on Gas Analysis are as detailed in **IS:3638-1966.** Please refer **IS:3638-1966** for alternative method of chemical analysis.

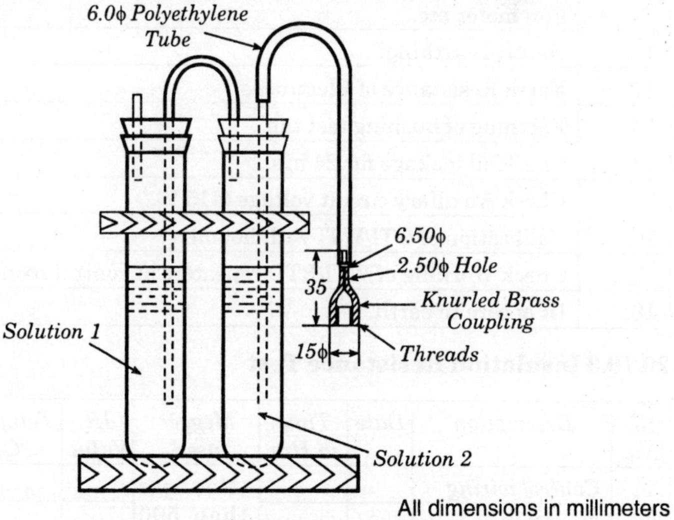


(9.5 outside diameter) of test pitcock on gas-operated relay.
Apparatus for Gas Analysis.
Fig. 20.1. Threads to suit outlet

## 20.19 COMMISSIONING CHECKS-TRANSFORMER

### 20.19.1 Scope

This schedule covers the tests to be done at site after transformer has been installed and dried out.

### 20.19.2 General

Check the following:

| *Sl.No.* | *Description* |
|---|---|
| 1. | Breather Silicagel (Blue when dry) |
| 2. | Oil in the Breather housing cup. |
| 3. | All valves for their correct opening and closing sequence. |
| 4. | Oil level in conservator tank. |
| 5. | Oil in cooling system. |
| 6. | Oil level in bushings. |
| 7. | Release air, wherever necessary. |
| 8. | Cooling accessories (Pump motors, Fan motors etc.) for direction and O/L setting. |
| 9. | Buchholz, oil level indicator, pressure gauges, thermometer, Temp. indicators etc., for operation. |
| 10. | Earthing of main tank M.Box T/C driving gear, diverter, Pump Fan motor etc. |
| 11. | Neutral earthing. |
| 12. | Earth Resistance of Electrodes. |
| 13. | Earthing of bushing test tap. |
| 14. | Check oil leakage for 24 hrs. |
| 15. | Check Auxiliary circuit voltage (415 V). |
| 16. | Calibration of OTI/WTI with hot oil. |
| 17. | Check Working of WTI/RTD repeaters at control room. |
| 18. | IR of core to earth. |

### 20.19.3 Insulation Resistance Test

| *Sl. No.* | *Description* | *Date* | *Time in Hrs* | *Megger used* | *IR Value* | *Temp. °C* | *Re-marks* |
|---|---|---|---|---|---|---|---|
| 1. | *Control wiring* | | | (Not less than 500 V megger) | | | |
| 2. | *Tap Changer*<br>(*a*) Motor<br>(*b*) Control | | | | | | |

*Contd...*

| *Sl. No.* | *Description* | *Date* | *Time in Hrs* | *Megger used* | *IR Value* | *Temp. °C* | *Re-marks* |
|---|---|---|---|---|---|---|---|
| 3. | Cooling system<br>(*a*) Motor Fan<br>(*b*) Motor Pump<br>(*c*) Control wiring | | | | | | |
| 4. | Main winding<br>(*a*) HV/E+LV<br>(*b*) IV/E+HV<br>(*c*) LV/E+HV+IV<br>(*d*) HV/IV<br>(*e*) IV/LV<br>(*f*) HV/LV | | | (Not less than 1000 V megger) | | | |

**Note:**

1. While checking these values no external line, lightning arrestors etc., should be in circuit.
2. Special care should always be taken while meggering the transformer winding to ensure that there is no leakage in the leads.

### 20.19.4 Oil Characteristics

Take necessary precaution (regarding rinsing the bottle, cleaning hand, air bubble etc.) while withdrawing the samples (Please refer IS:6855). Each sample should be free of air bubbles and should not be tested when it is hot. The sample should satisfy IS:1866.

| *Sl.* | *Oil Sample* | *Time & Condition* | | | *Mois-ture* | *Break* | *Resis-tivity at* | *Temp.* | *Rem-arks* |
|---|---|---|---|---|---|---|---|---|---|
| *No.* | *From* | *Date* | *Time* | *Wea-ther* | *in PPM* | *down Votlage in kV* | *90°C (in ohm-cm)* | *90°C* | |
| 1. | Tank<br>Top Sample<br>Bottom Sample | | | | | | | | |
| 2. | Cooling system<br>Top Sample<br>Bottom Sample | | | | | | | | |
| 3. | OLTC Diverter<br>(each phase) | | | | | | | | |

### 20.19.5 Tests on CT

1. Ratio
2. Polarity
3. Magnetising current
4. IR value.

### 20.19.6 On Load Tap Changer

| *Sl.No.* | *Description* | *Date* | *Observation* | *Remarks* |
|---|---|---|---|---|
| 1. | Visual Inspection of equipment. | | | |
| 2. | Hand operation on all taps. | | | |
| 3. | Complete wiring of the circuits | | | |
| 4. | Limit Switch | | | |
| 5. | Over running device. | | | |
| 6. | Remote Panel wiring. | | | |
| 7. | Over load Device of Driving Motor. | | | |
| 8. | Local Operation (Electrical). | | | |
| 9. | Remote Operation (Electrical). | | | |
| 10. | Tap Position Indicator. | | | |
| 11. | Step by step contractor. | | | |
| 12. | Out of Step Relay. | | | |

**Note:** While operating the mechanism on Electrical Control, check once again limit switches, step by step contractor, over running device etc., for their actual operation and ensure that they are functioning properly.

### 20.19.7 Off Circuit Tap Switch

Tap switch handle should not be left halfway and/or unlocked.

### 20.19.8 Continuity Test

Continuity between line and neutral (for neutral end TC) or line to line (for line end TC) with multimeter on all taps and phases to be confirmed.

### 20.19.9 Measurement of Winding Resistance:

| *Winding* | *Tap No.* | *Phase U* | *Phase V* | *Phase W* | *Temp.* | *Remarks* |
|---|---|---|---|---|---|---|
| HV | 1 | | | | | |
| Winding | 2 | | | | | |
| | 3 | | | | | |
| | 4 | | | | | |
| | 5 | | | | | |
| | 6 | | | | | |
| | 7 | | | | | |
| IV winding | | | | | | |
| LV winding | | | | | | |

### 20.19.10 Voltage Ratio Test

Ratio on all taps is to be checked by hand operation only. This can be done any time, once the tap changer is completely erected. Start the tap changer from lowest tap and then go on increasing tap by tap while checking the value instead of starting from normal tap.

| *Tap Nos.* | *Voltage applied* | | *Voltage Measured* | | *Ratio obtained* | *Remarks* |
|---|---|---|---|---|---|---|
| 1 | | | | | | |
| 2 | | | | | | |
| 3 | | | | | | |
| 4 | | | | | | |
| 5 | | | | | | |
| 6 | | | | | | |

### 20.19.11 Magnetisation Current

(*a*) Apply 3 phase 415 V on HV Terminals and keep LV open.

| *Voltage Applied* | | *Current measured* | | *Remarks* |
|---|---|---|---|---|
| U-V | Volts | U phase | m Amps | |
| V-W | Volts | V phase | m Amps | |
| U-W | Volts | W phase | m Amps | |

**Note:** In case of single phase transformer, apply 230V, 1 phase supply between line terminal and earth.

(*b*) Apply 3 phase 415 V on LV terminals and keep HV open.

| u-v | Volts | u phase | m Amps | |
|---|---|---|---|---|
| v-w | Volts | v phase | m Amps | |
| u-w | Volts | w phase | m Amps | |

**Note:** In case of single phase transformer apply 230 V, 1 phase between line and earth terminal.

### 20.19.12 Vector Group

Check the vector group of the transformer by connecting in a suitable manner.

| *Vector group* | *Diagram of connection* | *Diagram as connected for test* | *Remarks* |
|---|---|---|---|
| | | | |
| | | | |
| | | | |

| **Conditions to be proved** | **Voltage Measured** |
|---|---|
| 1. | 1. |
| 2. | 2. |
| 3. | 3. |

### 20.19.13 Final IR Checks

The megger readings finally after the transformer is connected to the system

Date.......................... Time........................ Temp. ............................

| *Windings* | *Megger used* | *Value obtained in Mega ohms* | *Remarks* |
|---|---|---|---|
| HV/E+LV | | | |
| IV/E+HV+LV | | | |
| LV/E+HV+IV | | | |
| HV/IV | | | |
| IV/LV | | | |
| HV/LV | | | |

### 20.19.14 Other Test

| *WTI Settting* | *Set for* | *Proved* | *OTI Setting* | *Set for* | *Proved* |
|---|---|---|---|---|---|
| Alarm | | | Alarm | | |
| Trip | | | Trip | | |
| Fan Start | | | | | |
| Fan Stop | | | | | |
| Pump Start | | | | | |
| Pum Stop if applicable | | | | | |

### 20.19.15 Protection and Alarms

Prove the tripping of associated breakers by actual operation of the various devices and relays.

**Under no Circumstances Shorting of Electrical Connections should be Done.**

| *Sl.No* | *Device* | *Set for* | | *Proved* | | *Remarks* |
|---|---|---|---|---|---|---|
| | | *Alarm* | *Trip* | *Alarm* | *Trip* | |
| 1. | Buchholz | | | | | |
| 2. | Excessive Winding temperature | | | | | |
| 3. | Excessive Oil Temp. | | | | | |
| 4. | Oil flow failure | | | | | |
| 5. | Water flow failure | | | | | |
| 6. | Differential pressure (OFWF cooling system) | | | | | |
| 7. | Fan failure | | | | | |
| 8. | Low oil level (conservator tank) | | | | | |
| 9. | Pressure relief valve | | | | | |
| 10. | Differential relay | | | | | |
| 11. | Over current relay | | | | | |
| 12. | Earth fault (REF) | | | | | |
| 13. | Instt. Earth fault | | | | | |
| 14. | Inter trip, if any | | | | | |
| 15. | Trip free check. | | | | | |

### 20.19.16 Record the following after charging

(*a*) No load current at relay terminal

U phase A
V phase A CT Ratio
W phase A

(*b*) Temperature (at the time of charging)

O.T.I °C
W.T.I °C
Ambient °C

(*c*) Maximum temperature after 24 hours. °C

## 20.20 COMMISSIONING CHECKS REACTOR

| | |
|---|---|
| Customer | W.O.No. |
| Site | Sl.No. |
| Rating | Voltage class |
| Scope | |

This schedule covers the tests to be done at site after reactor has been installed and dried out.

### 20.20.1 General

Check the following:

| *Sl.No.* | *Description* | *Remarks* |
|---|---|---|
| 1. | Breather Silicagel (Blue When Dry) | |
| 2. | Oil in the Breather Cup. | |
| 3. | All valves for their correct opening and closing sequence. | |
| 4. | Oil level in conservator tank. | |
| 5. | Oil in cooling system. | |
| 6. | Oil level in bushings. | |
| 7. | Release air, wherever necessary. | |
| 8. | Buchholz, oil level indicator, thermometer, temperature indicators etc. for operation | |
| 9. | Earthing of main tank M.Box | |
| 10. | Neutral earthing. | |
| 11. | Earth Resistance of Electrodes. | |
| 12. | Earthing of bushing test tap. | |
| 13. | Check oil leakage for 24 hrs. | |
| 14. | Check auxiliary circuit voltage (415 V). | |
| 15. | Calibration of OTI/WTI with hot oil. | |
| 16. | Check Working of WTI/RTD repeaters at control room. | |
| 17. | IR of core to earth. | |

### 20.20.2 Insulation Resistance Test

| *Sl. No.* | *Description* | *Date* | *Time in hrs.* | *Megger used* | *IR Value* | *Temp.* | *Remarks* |
|---|---|---|---|---|---|---|---|
| 1. | Control Wiring | | | 500 V | | | |
| 2. | Main Winding | | | | | | |
| (*a*) | HV/E | | | > 1000 V | | | |

**Note:**

(*i*) While checking these values no external lines, lightning arresstors etc., should be in circuit.

(*ii*) Special care should always be taken while meggering the reactor winding to ensure that there is no leakage in the leads.

### 20.20.3 Oil Characteristics

Take necessary precaution (regarding rinsing the bottle, cleaning hand, air bubble etc.), while-withdrawing the samples. Each sample should be free of air bubbles and should be tested when it is hot. The sample should satisfy IS:1866.

| *Sl.* | *Oil Sample* | *Time & Condition* | | | *Mois-ture* | *Break* | *Resistivity at* | *Temp.* | *Remarks* |
|---|---|---|---|---|---|---|---|---|---|
| *No.* | *From* | *Date* | *Time* | *Wea-ther* | *in PPM* | *down Voltage in kV* | *90°C (in ohm cm)* | *at 90°C* | |
| 1. | Tank Top Sample Bottom Sample | | | | | | | | |
| 2. | Cooling System Top Sample Bottom Sample | | | | | | | | |

### 20.20.4 Tests on CT

1. Ratio
2. Polarity
3. Magnetising current
4. IR value

### 20.20.5 Measurement of Winding Resistance

| | *Phase U* | *Phase V* | *Phase W* | *Temp.* | *Remarks* |
|---|---|---|---|---|---|
| Winding | | | | | |

### 20.20.6 Current Measurement

(*a*) Apply 3 phase 415 volts on HV Terminals.

| *Voltage Applied* | *Current measured* | *Remarks* |
|---|---|---|
| U-V Volts | U phase m A | |
| V-W Volts | V phase m A | |
| U-W Volts | W phase m A | |

**Note:** In case of single phase reactors apply 230 V, 1 phase between line terminal and earth.

### 20.20.7 Final Checks

The megger readings finally after the reactor is connected to the system.

| | *Date* | *Time* | *Temperature* |
|---|---|---|---|
| *Winding* | *Megger used* | *Value Obtained in megaohms* | *Remarks* |
| HV/E | | | |

### 20.20.8 Other Test

| *WTI Setting* | *Set for* | *Proved* | *OTI Setting* | *Set for* | *Proved* |
|---|---|---|---|---|---|
| Alarm | | | | | |
| Trip | | | | | |

### 20.20.9 Protection and Alarms

Prove the tripping of associated breakers by actual operation of the various devices and relays.

**Note:** Under no circumstances shorting of electrical connections be done.

| *Sl.No.* | *Device* | *Set for* | | *Proved* | | *Remarks* |
|---|---|---|---|---|---|---|
| | | Alarm | Trip | Alarm | Trip | |
| 1. | Buchholz | | | | | |
| 2. | Excessive Winding Temperature | | | | | |
| 3. | Excessive Oil Temp. | | | | | |
| 4. | Oil level (Low & Max.) | | | | | |
| 5. | Pressure Relief Valve. | | | | | |

### 20.20.10 Record the Following After Charging:

(*a*) No load current at relay terminal

U phase m A

V phase m A CT Ratio

W phase m A

(*b*) Temperature (at the time of charging)

O.T.I °C

W.T.I °C

Ambient °C

(*c*) Maximum temperature after 24 hours. °C

# 21

# Filtering of Oil, Filling of Oil and Drying-out

The procedure of filtering of oil, filling of oil and drying out of transformers has been described in this chapter. Typical filteration plant has been described.

## 21.1 INTRODUCTION

After completion of the assembly of the transformer; filtered oil is filled in the transformer tank by means of oil filteration plant. It should be ensured that the oil of adequate dielectric strength, purity and other properties is filled as per prescribed procedure. After filling, the oil is circulated through vacuum filteration plant several times till desired dryness, dielectric strength etc., are achieved. The details have been described in the following sections.

## 21.2 OIL SAMPLING AND TESTING

Oil is usually received in *sealed drums* or *oil tanks*. Before use, the oil should be tested. The oil samples are taken from the bottom of the drum/tank. Sample from bottom will have more moisture, sludge etc. than the sample from top. The samples should be taken allowing the oil to settle for 24 hours.

**Sampling.** The samples should be taken such that external moisture, dust, chemicals etc., do not contaminate the oil sample. The bottle should be preferably of 1 litre capacity and of clear glass with ground glass stoppers. The bottle should be clean and dry. Sample should be filled from the bottom. Oil should not be touched or exposed to air. The bottle should be sealed immediately after filling with the sample oil.

**Sampling from a drum.** Keep the drum vertical for 24 hours to allow release of air. Clean the area around the plug. Use a clean glass tube and a sampling bottle. Insert the sampling tube upto 15 mm from bottom of the drum and take the sample in the bottle. Discard the first two samples. After that the sampled oil should be released from the sampling bottle into another glass receptacle.

***Oil is* tested *as per IS 335—1972 or other relevant standard.***

Field tests on oil include:

— Moisture content (should be less than 5 ppm)

— Dielectric strength/breakdown value at certain temperature

— Other tests as per field quality plan approved by the customer.

## 21.3 PRESSURE TEST AND TIGHTNESS CHECK

After the assembly and tightning, the pressure/leakage tests are carried out to ensure that no leakage problems will be encountered during the vacuum test and after oil filling. Pressure gauge on the transformer tank cover is of range 0 to 100 kPa. The transformer tank is filled with dry nitrogen/dry air by opening the regulator valve on gas cylinders.

The slight over pressure 30 kPa is applied and regulator valve of gas cylinder is closed. Thereafter pressure readings are taken at an interval of 30 minutes. If the transformer is properly sealed there will not be significant pressure drop between consecutive pressure readings. A slight pin hole, defective sealing etc., gives pressure drop. Possible leakage points are.

— **Threading joints.** Check looseness, use PTFE tape and retighten the threaded part. Apply soap solution and see no bubbles are formed.

— **Defective gauges.** Gauges should be tested in advance. If found leaking, replace them.

— **Through flat gasket joints.** Retighten the nuts. Gasket should be squeezed uniformly.

— **Through o-ring sealing joints.** Open the joint, clean the groove. Place correctly dimensioned ring and retighten. Use recommended torque spanner.

— **Small cracks in cooling system.** Pipes, tank, cooling tubes etc., may have small cracks. Arrange Welding and reactification of leaking joint.

**Method of Leak Detection**

During pressure test, fill the transformer with air/nitrogen at 30 kPa.

Take ultrasonic leak detector and move the nozzle around the joints. The leaking joint will give distinct audio-signal. Take soap water solution and apply by brush to various sealing joints and suspected leakage points. Leaking joint will give soap bubbles.

## 21.4 VACCUM TIGHTNESS TEST

Before starting the oil filling, *Vaccum test* is conducted on the completely assembled transformer including the cooling equipment. The tank and the cooling system may be tested separately or together.

Vacuum gauge (range 0.01 to 1 kPa) should be connected to the suitable valve on the transformer cover.

Vacuum is applied by means of the Vacuum pump. The transformer is evacuated, vaccum is maintained for 12 to 36 hours. Vacuum test is carried out as follows:

1. Transformer is evacuated to 0.15 kPa.

2. Vacuum pump is closed and stop-valve to vacuum pump is also closed.

3. Readings of vacuum gauge are taken at an interval of 30 minutes.

Let $P_1$ = Pressure after 1, 2, 3, . . . Hours, kPa.

$P_2$ = Pressure after 1.5, 2.5, 3.5, . . . Hours kPa.

$\Delta P = P_2 - P_1$, kPa

= Pressure drop between consecutive readings.

$t$ = Time between two consecutive readings in minutes.

$V_m$ = Oil volume rating plate, liters.

$$\Delta P = \frac{P_2 - P_1}{t \cdot 60}, V_m \ldots \left(\frac{kP_a.l}{S}\right)$$

For proper vacuum tightness, $\Delta P \leq 3$

The vacuum is held in the transformer for 12 to 36 hours as per Table 21.1.

## 21.5 OIL FILLING UNDER VACUUM

Following alternatives are possible:

1. Fill oil from drums into separate oil-storage tank. Filter the oil in the storage tank by circulation. Then fill in the transformer under vaccum and circulate.

2. Fill the oil from the drums into tanks of the transformer and circulate. This method is used for small transformer.

### Oil Filling and Filteration Procedure

If the oil is despatched separately in drums and the drying-out of transformer is carried out without oil, the oil is filled in the tank after the following steps:

— drying out of the transformer tank; core and coils.

— filling of oil by means of oil-filtering plant into the transformer tank.

Oil samples should be taken and tested before filling the transformer tank. It should be ensured that no air pockets are left in the tank and no dust or moisture enters the oil.

Oil should be filled through the oil filtering plant and metal hoses or PVC hoses. Rubber hoses should not to be used since the sulphur in the rubber would dissolve in oil, causing dielectric strength of the oil to be lowered and also, the dissolved sulphur would attack the copper in the windings. To prevent aeration of the oil, the transformer tank should be filled through the bottom drain valve. The top-side vent should be opened so that there is no pressure build-up-and gases are expelled.

In a conservator type of transformer, the rate of oil flow should be reduced when the level is almost upto the bottom of the main cover to prevent internal pressure from rupturing the relief pipe disphragm. Enough time should be allowed (12 to 36 hours) for the oil to permeate the transformer and also the air bubbles to escape. Any air accumulated in the Buchholtz relay should be released. The sides of the transformer tank may be trapped with a hammer on all sides to release trapped-up air. An alternate method for removing the trapped air from large transformers is to keep the transformer energized at no load for about 12 to 24 hours at the end of which the air cocks on the transformer are opened to allow the released air to escape. The standing time generally recommended is as follows:

**Table 21.1, Vacuum Treatment and Oil Filteration Duration**

| *Transformer HV Rated voltage kV* | *Application of Vacuum Hours before oil filling* | *Standing time after oil-circulation and before energizing Hours* |
|---|---|---|
| <220 | 12 | 12 |
| 220 to 400 | 24 | 48 |
| 765 | 36 | 120 |

If specified vacuum tightness is not reached, the cause of leakage should be investigated. The joints should be re-checked and properly sealed.

*Vaccum filling may be used for large transformer with tanks designed to withstand vacuum. A vacuum pump may be connected to the top valve of the transformer and the oil hose to the top filter press valve. The tank shall be tightly sealed and evacuated to approximately 6 mm of mercury and the vacuum maintained for 12 to 36 hours or longer depending on the size and voltage of the transformer. The oil valve may then be opened and the oil allowed to flow slowly into the tank. The vacuum should be maintained for a specified time after the tank is full.*

*After filling and standing time, the oil is circulated under hot condition and with vacuum treatment by means of vacuum filteration plant.*

**The direction of oil circulation through the filter is shown in the Fig. 21.2.**

In vacuum filling, the oil is heated to 50° to 70°C in the filtering-plant. This temperature refers to the outlet of the filtering plant, and in let to the transformer tank. The vacuum-level in the tank should be 0.15 kPa. During oil filling, transport plastic tube may be used for vacuum/pressure gauge. Oil circulation pump should have a capacity of

2 to 5 $m^3$/Hr. The temperature of outgoing oil from filters should be approximately 70°C.

Pressure on oil pipes should be positive. Initially, maximum rate of 4.5 $m^3$/hr is applied. For final 70 mm below cover, the flow rate is reduced to 0.5 $m^3$/hr. Finally after 70 mm gap, oil filling is continued until the bushings and conservator are filled with oil. Valve on top of bushing is then closed and valve on conservator is opened oil level is adjusted.

*Cooling system* of large transformers can be filled separately.

*Vacuum proof cooling system* is evacuated for 2 to 3 hours and filled with filtered, degassified oil. The oil is circulated through the cooling system and filteration plant at least twice. After this the valves between cooling system and the transformer tank are opened.

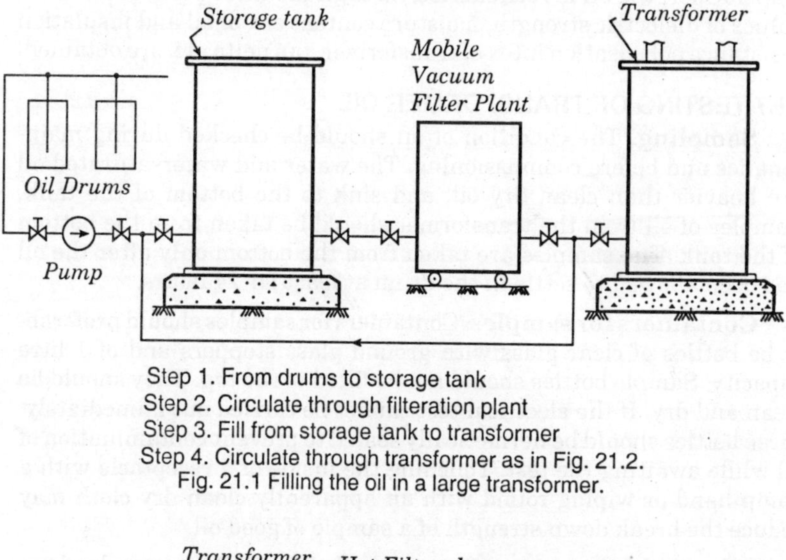


Step 1. From drums to storage tank
Step 2. Circulate through filteration plant
Step 3. Fill from storage tank to transformer
Step 4. Circulate through transformer as in Fig. 21.2.

Fig. 21.1 Filling the oil in a large transformer.

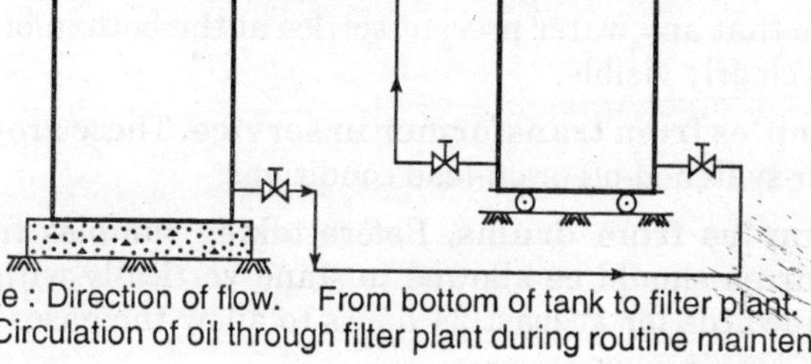


Note : Direction of flow. From bottom of tank to filter plant.

Fig. 21.2 Circulation of oil through filter plant during routine maintenance.

On-load tap-changer is filled according to the instructions for the OLTC.

## 21.6 FILLING THE OIL FROM DRUMS INTO TRANSFORMER TANK

Before filling the oil in the transformer tank, the oil is heated upto 70°C (outlet of filter and inlet to transformer) and circulated through vacuum filter. Vacuum filter removes particles above diameter up to 5 μm, air, moisture etc. *The filtered oil should have gas content less, than 0.2% and moisture less than 5 ppm (parts per million).* For this, the oil may be circulated through the filter for several hours/days. Transformer oil from drums is passed through the vacuum filter plant before filling in the tank (Fig. 21.1). After filling in the tank, the oil is circulated through the vacuum filter plant. It is filled in the transformer after the desired dryness and test values are achieved. After filling in the transformer, the oil is recirculated through the filter plant till desired values of dielectric strength, moisture content etc. of oil and insulation resistance polarisation intex of transformer, tan delta etc. are obtained.

## 21.7 TESTING OF TRANSFORMER OIL

**Sampling.** The condition of oil should be checked during maintenance and before commissioning. The water and watersaturated oil are heavier than clean dry oil, and sink to the bottom of the tank. Samples of oil from the transformer should be taken from the bottom of the tank. The samples are taken from the bottom only after the oil has been allowed to settle in the drum at least for 24 hours.

**Containers for samples.** Containers for samples should preferably be bottles of clear glass with ground glass stoppers and of 1 litre capacity. Sample bottles should not be filled to the top. They should be clean and dry. If the electrical test cannot be carried out immediately, these bottles should be hermetically sealed to prevent contamination of oil while awaiting the test. Touching the inside of a receptacle with a damp hand or wiping round with an apparently clean dry cloth may reduce the break down strength of a sample of good oil.

**Oil samples from transformer tank.** When taking samples from the tank, remove dirt from the sampling valve and plug. To ensure that the valve is clean, allow some oil to flow into a separate receptacle before collecting samples for testing. Samples should be collected in clear glass container so that any water present settles at the bottom of the receptacle and is clearly visible.

**Oil samples from transformer in service.** These are preferably taken under switched-off or on-load conditions.

**Oil samples from drums.** Before taking samples from an oil drum, the drum should be allowed to stand vertically with the bung vertically upwards for at least 24 hours to allow the gases to pass. A clean glass or brass tube long enough to reach within 15 mm of the lowermost part of the drum should be inserted, keeping the uppermost end of the tube tightly closed with the thumb. The thumb should then be removed to allow oil to enter the bottom of the tube. The top of the tube should again be tightly closed and the oil sample withdrawn. The first three samples should be thrown away. Thereafter, the samples should be obtained into a suitable container.

**Testing of Dielectric Strength of Oil.** Take standard test cell (volume 300 to 500 milli-litre, spheres 12.5 to 13 mm dia of brass/bronze/stainless steel, with 2.5 mm gap). Take the oil sample from the bottom of the transformer tank and fill it in the standard cup. Allow 20 minutes for air bubbles to vanish. Apply A.C. voltage gradually. Voltage should be steadily increased till the break down occurs between electrodes.

**Moisture, Oxygen and Impurities in Oil.** That transformer oil and winding have a tendency to readily absorb moisture from the air. The effect of water in solution in the oil will decreases the dielectric strength of the oil as well as of the insulating paper which absorbs and stores the moisture due to higher affinity of water to paper over oil.

All possible preventive steps, should therefore, be taken to guard against moisture penetration to the inside of the transformers. This will include blocking of all openings for free access of air in storage and frequent reactivation of breathers in service.

Oxygen present inside the transformer due to air remaining in oil, reacts on the insulation and the decomposition products cause sludge which blocks the free circulation of the oil. The adverse effect of oxygen, get accelerated at higher operating temperatures. The dielectric strength of oil is diminished by significantly small quantities of solid impurities. It is, therefore, a good practice to filter the oil during periodic maintenance if the break down voltage of oil is poor. Some oxidizing type varnishes readily react with transformer oil and from sludge on the windings. Synthetic varnishes having acid inhibiting properties generally preferred. This should be considered when the rewinding and replacing the coils during repairs of transformers.

**Table 21.2**

**Preferred Minimum Breakdown Values (BDV) of Transformer oil (2.5 mm Gap, 1 Min. Voltage)**

| *Oil Sample.* | *Transformer HV Side kV Rating* | | | | |
|---|---|---|---|---|---|
| Upto . | 11 | 11–33 | 66–220 | 220 | 400 |
| Fresh oil from drum | 25 | 30 | 40 | 45 | 50 |
| Oil from Transformer Tank | 20 | 25 | 35 | 40 | 45 |

## 21.8 OIL MAINTENANCE

Oil maintenance is carried out in accordance with the standard title 'Code, Practices of Maintenance of Insulating Oils'. The code refers to the contamination of oil and determination of whether the oil is suitable for further service. It also gives the procedure of treatment of oil at site.

Contamination of oil due to moisture or solids can be dealt with satisfactorily at site. Centrifugal separators are effective in removing free water and find solid impurities. Filters remove moisture, gases and soild particles. During periodic maintenance, the oil from the tank is circulated through vacuum Filter Plant several times till desired purity of oil and desired Insulation Resistance/Polarisation Index of transformer windings are achieved.

## 21.9 PURIFIERS AND FILTER PLANT FOR TRANSFORMER OIL

For filtering and purifying the transformer oil, a mobile oil purifier is used. Fig. 21.3 illustrates the main components in a typical *centrifugal type oil purifier*.

**The transformer oil is circulated through the following:**

— Heating Chamber (2) which increases the temperature of oil. There is a provision of thermostat and the heater can be set to achieve desired temperature. *Increase in temperature results in the drying-out of oil.* The outlet temperature should never exceed 80°C. The temperature range of 70°C to 75°C is preferred.

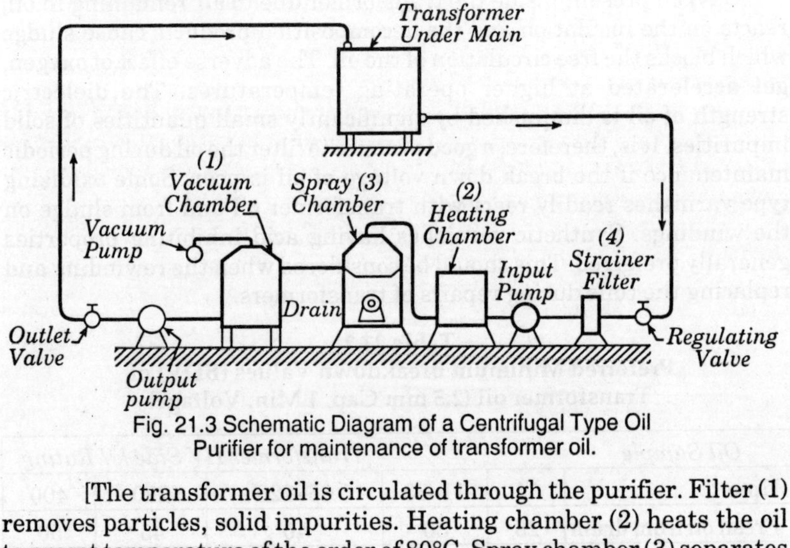


Fig. 21.3 Schematic Diagram of a Centrifugal Type Oil Purifier for maintenance of transformer oil.

[The transformer oil is circulated through the purifier. Filter (1) removes particles, solid impurities. Heating chamber (2) heats the oil to preset temperature of the order of 80°C. Spray chamber (3) separates heavy particles from the oil vacuum chamber makes the oil dry. Input pump and output pump help in circulating the oil.]

— **Spray Chamber** (3). This contains a motor driven rotating bowl. Dirty oil is admitted in the centre of the chamber into the bowl having several conical separating vanes. The bowl is rotated at a speed of 6000 rpm by means of gear motor.

**The swirling and spraying of oil causes separation of dirt particles, moisture particles from oil.** The extremely fine spray causes separation of heavier dirt particles and release of moisture and gases.

— **Vacuum Chamber** (4). The process of drying out is accelerated by application of vacuum. The oil is admitted in the vacuum chamber. The upper portion of the chamber is evacuated to about 4 mm of mercury by means of motor driven vacuum pump.

— **Strainer Filter** (1). The oil is passed through strainer/filter plates having fine mesh size. The dirt particles are separated and the oil is filtered. The filter stack comprises of several paper plates held closely together by spring loadings. The dirt particles remain on one side of the filter plates. The filter plates should be cleaned periodically.

— **Activated Alumina Filter.** (not shown). Activitated alumina balls (2 to 3 mm dia) are highly porous. They absorb moisture and chemical impurities. Oil is circulated through such filters.

The oil is circulated through the vacuum filter purifier plant for several hour still the desired dielectric strength is achieved. The Break-Down Value (BDV) of oil with 4 mm gap should be *above* 50 kV rms at 75°C.

**Stream line purifier.** In such a purifier, the oil is subjected to high pressure (6 kg/cm$^2$) by means of compressed air applied to the chamber (1). The oil is passed through a stack of several filter plates (2) made of filter paper. The dust particles remain on one side of the filter plate and filtered oil is passed on. The oil is then passed through a vacuum tank as mentioned above.

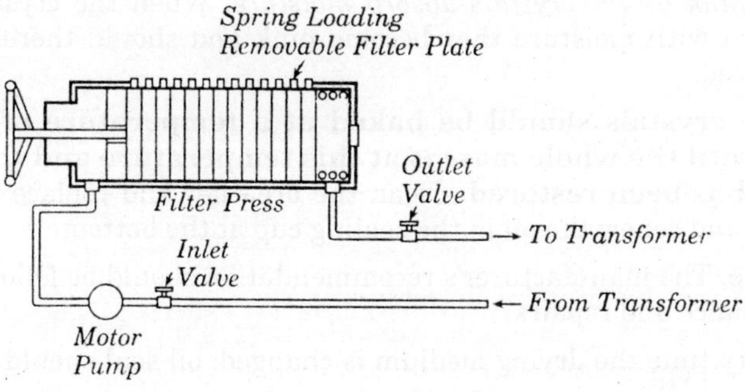


Fig. 21.4. Schematic Diagram of a filter press. (Item No.2).

Fig. 21.5. illustrates the scheme of a streamline filter.

The pressure chamber (1) is pressurised by means of compressed air. The oil is passed through the filter press (2). The filtered oil is passed through heating chamber with the vacuum chamber. Higher temperature and vacuum causes removal of moisture. The oil is circulated several times till desired purity is achieved.

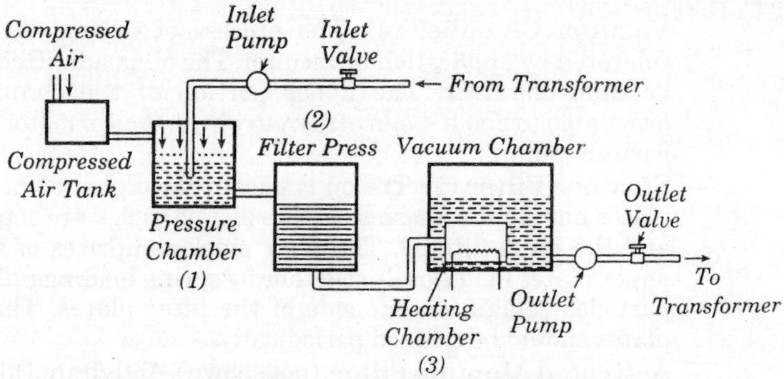


Fig. 21.5 Schematic Diagram of a Streamline filter.

## 21.10 MAINTENANCE OF SILICA GEL BREATHER

The transformer is filled with dielectric oil or dry inert-gas. In case of *oil filled transformer a conservator* is provided. It is installed at a slightly higher level than that of the tank. During higher loads, the oil in the tank expands and the level of oil in the conservator rises. *The air cushion in the conservator permits expansion and contraction of the oil in the tank without contact with moist-external air. The air cushion* in the conservator is connected to the external atmosphere via a silica-gel breather ensuring dryness of incoming air during the breathing.

**Breather.** Silica gel breathers are fitted with a sight glass through which the colour of the crystals can be seen. *The colour changes from blue to pink as the crystals absorb moisture.* When the crystals get saturated with moisture they become pink and should therefore, be reactivated.

**The crystals should be baked at a temperature of about 200°C until the whole mass is at this temperature and the blue colour has been restored.** Clean the breather and replace the dry crystals and renew the oil in the sealing cup at the bottom.

**Note.** The manufacturer's recommendation should be followed for maintenance and repairs.

Every time the drying medium is changed, oil seal should also be changed.

No work should be done on any transformer unless it is disconnected from all external circuits and the tank and all windings have been solidly earthed.

In case of anything abnormal occurring during service, maker's advice should be obtained, giving him complete particulars as to the nature and the extent of occurrence, together with the nameplate particulars in order to assist identifications.

## 21.11 DRYING-OUT OF POWER TRANSFORMERS

**Purpose.** The transformer oil and insulation is hygroscopic (absorbs moisture). If the transformer is **despatched without oil or is left idle for a long period, the oil and insulation absorbs moisture.** Drying out is necessary prior to commissioning. **If a large power transformer is idle for more than one month, drying-out may be necessary prior to re-energising.** The main purpose of the drying out is to expell the moisture from the oil, the winding insulation and the other internal parts. If the transformer is not dried-out, it cannot withstand service voltage for a long duration and its insulation may fail prematurely. Even it may not sustain a few kV voltage or rated voltage.

**Procedure of drying-out.** In the drying-out process, the transformer oil/winding is heated with application of vacuum for prolonged period (ten hours to four weeks). Periodic readings of (1) oil and winding temperature (2) Power input (3) Insulation Resistance are taken. The temperature of oil is maintained at 80°C and that of windings at 90°C.

The values of insulation resistance start falling in the beginning of the drying out process. This indicates that the moisture drops are getting distributed in the winding and the oil in form of vapour. After several hours, the insulation resistance becomes steady. This indicates that vapours are distributed in the insulation and oil. *On further continuation driving-out, the insulation resistance values start rising. This indicates that the moisture is being expelled from the windings and oil.*

The drying-out process is stopped when the insulation resistance value (hot) is more than the specified value, during the rising mode of the drying-out process and the polarisation index, dielectric strength of oil are satisfactory.

For service aged transformers up to 66 kV or so, moisture content upto 35 ppm are considered acceptable. For 66 kV upto 220 kV, the moisture content in oil upto 250 ppm is considered acceptable. For 220 kV and moisture content upto 20 ppm is considered acceptable. However the use of absolute values for water does not alway guarantee safe conditions and the % of dry weight should be determined.

**Methods of dry-out.** The power transformers may be drying out by one of the following methods:

**(1) With the tank filled with dielectric oil**

(*a*) **Induction coil method.** This method is used in USSR for smaller transformers. This is not suitable for medium and large transformers.

(*b*) By short-circuit method

(*c*) **By circulating the oil through a suitable oil filteration plant***

(*d*) By means of oil-immersed resistor-heaters.

The above methods may be supplemented by

— Application of vacuum of the order of 6 μm to 10 μm

— Circulating the oil through filter.

**(2) With the oil removed from the tank**

(*a*) by blowing hot-dry air through the tank

(*b*) by short-circuit method

(*c*) by radiating lamps placed near the winding.

Drying-out of power transformers can be carried out by means of one of the above mentioned depending upon the size/rating of transformer, site conditions, available equipment. Transformers upto about 1000 kVA and 33 kV may be dried-out without vacuum. Above this rating the drying out process is accelerated by applying vacuum of the order of 6 μm to 10 μm in the portion between the oil and the tank cover.

**Preparations for drying-out**

— Lagging the tank with fire resistance mat such as asbestos cloth, glass sheet provide external shields to prevent drought of cold air.

— Connecting thermocouples, placing thermometers, calibration, arranging measuring instruments.

— To bring-out the well insulated leads from the windings from the terminal bushings for the measurement of the insulation resistance.

— To bring-out thermocouple leads through one of the opening in the tank.

— To prepare a log-book

**Safety Precautions**

1. Earthing of tank and cover
2. Proper connections
3. Boards indicating work in progress, no tress-passing, Don't touch. No smoking, No welding etc.
4. Well ventilated room to expel moisture
5. Fire fighting equipment kept ready
6. Transformer should never be left unattended, during the drying-out process

*Most common method for filling the oil in transformer and for drying out. This is also used after prolonged idle period.

7. Use tested and healthy filteration plant having adequate capacity of vacuum pump, filter heater and circulation pump.
8. Temperature should never be exceeded beyond specified permissible limits (70°C at inlet)

### 21.11.1 Drying-out by Induction Heating Method (Fig. 21.6)

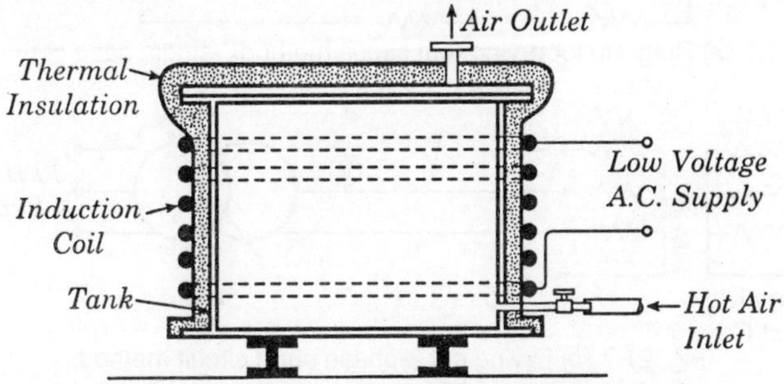


Fig. 21.6 Drying-out by induction heating method.

This simple method can be conveniently used at site. The oil is drained. The steps mentioned earlier are taken.

A magnetizing coil of sufficient cross-section, insulation and number of turns is placed around the transformer tank over the heat resistant lagging. Single-phase (A.C) current is circulated through the coil. The transformer gets heated by induced currents in the steel tank. The power required for drying out is of the order of 2.5 kW/$m^2$, where $m^2$represents surface area of the tank. Current in the coil can be calculated from the expression.

$$I = \frac{kW \times 1000}{V \cos \phi}$$

The tank temperature is raised to about 105°C during the drying-out. Simultaneously hot air may be circulated.

### 21.11.2 Short-circuit Method of Drying-Out

This method is useful for drying-out either transformer filled with oil or transformer without oil. The sides of the tank are suitably lagged. The tank cover is raised by about 320 mm to permit outlet for moisture evolved during the drying out. The l.v. winding is short-circuited. The h.v. winding is supplied with low single-phase or three phase voltage to circulate short circuit current of the order **of 85 per cent of load current.** (Refer Table 21.3). The voltage of the order of 5 per cent of rated voltage is usually adequate.

If single-phase supply is used, h.v, windings should be connected temporarily in series. Suitable ammeter, voltmeter, and fuses are connected in supply circuit as shown.

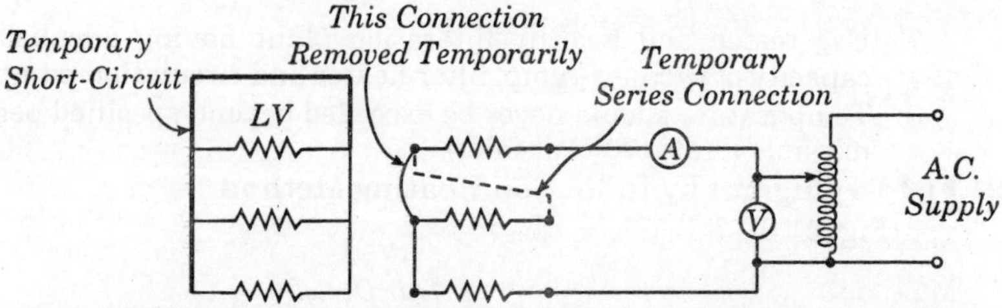


Fig. 21.7 (*a*) Diagram for drying -out circuit method—single base connection.

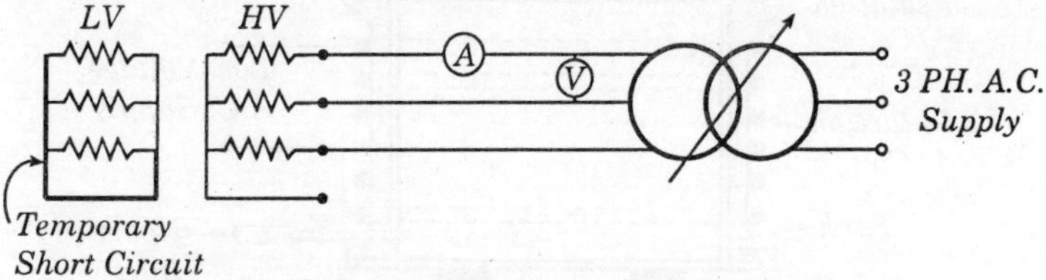


Fig. 21.7 (*b*) Drying out 3-phase short circuit method.

**Table 21.3**
**Short-Circuit Currents for Drying-out**

| *Per cent of full load current* | *Maximum top oil temp.* °C |
|---|---|
| 50 | 85 |
| 75 | 80 |
| 80 | 75 |

The short-circuit (on l.v. sides) should not be opened by mistake or by loose connection as it would give rise to dangerous overvoltages in h.v. circuit.

The oil temperatures are measured by spirit type thermometers. Mercury thermometers are *avoided* as they give error due to eddy currents in the mercury. Oil temperature should be measured at the bottom level and at the top of the oil level.

The winding temperature is measured by d.c. resistance method as follows:

D.C. resistance is measured by Voltmeter/ammeter method using a suitable d.c. voltage supply.

$$T_2 = \frac{R_2}{R_1}(T_1 + 235) - 235$$

where, $T_2$ = Temperature of winding, when hot corresponding to $R_2$ . . . . °C

$T_1$ = Temperature of winding, when cold corresponding to $R_1$ . . . . . °C

$R_2$ = D.C. Resistance, hot

$R_1$ = D.C. Resistance, cold (Ambient)

Temperature rise of winding

$$= T_2 - T_1.$$

**For this Method**

Maximum permissible winding temperature 90°C

Maximum permissible oil temperature 80°C

The oil gets rapidly deteriorated above this temperature. Insulation resistance is measured periodically during the drying-out process as mentioned.

*If short-circuit method is used for drying the transformer without oil,* the tank should be dried by hot air circulation and dry oil is filled after the drying-out of the winding and the tank.

**Short-circuit method is simple but is not satisfactory because the distribution of heat in the winding does not remove moisture from the oil easily.** Local temperatures in the hot-spot of winding may reach higher values than permissible limits.

Samples of air taken from top and bottom of tank are tested for dielectric tests and megger tests 7 times at interval of 4 hours each. After this, the ventilation is closed and temperature is maintained for 24 hours without filtering the oil. If dielectric strength is satisfactory the process is stopped.

### 21.11.3 By Circulation of Transformer-Oil through Purifier (Filtering Plant)

The modern method of drying-out of transformer consists of circulation of the transformer oil through oil filtering plant. The modern oil filtering and purifying plants are portable and have the following components:

— Vacuum tank, vacuum pump
— Heating Chamber, Heaters
— Spray Chamber
— Filter Press
— Activated Alumina Chambers
— Centrifugal Blower
— Strainer
— Pumps for Circulation of Oil.
— Temperature gauges, Pressure Gauges, temperature controllers ; Protection systems.

The oil from the transformer tank is circulated through the filtering plant for (i) removing moisture and (ii) for removing sludge, dirt and soild impurities (iii) for removing dissolved gases.

While using the oil filtering plant for the purpose of drying out; the thermostat of the filtering plant is set at out-let temperature of 90°C.

The oil is drawn from the transformer tank through a pipe dipped to the bottom of the tank. The out-let of the filtering plant is delivered back into the transformer tank at the top.

The purifier (filtering plant) is operated continuously except for one hour per day for cleaning the cones of centrifugal type of filter or filter pads of the vacuum type filter.

### 21.11.4 Oil-immersed Resistance Heater Method

The specially-made immersion heaters are dipped at several points in the tank filled with oil. The tank cover is raised by about 320 mm. The oil temperature is raised to about 85°C at top. Initially, higher currents may be used for more heat input. Subsequently, the current should be reduced to limit heat input. Low voltage supply should be used for safety purposes.

This method is easy and has several merits.

— Oil gets uniformly heated
— Top and bottom of coils get uniformly dried
— Excessive local heating of windings is avoided.
— Oil from the bottom portion of the tank gets thoroughly dried of moisture content.
— a.c or d.c source can be used.

### 21.11.5 Application of Vacuum while Drying-out

The drying-out process may be accelerated and improved by applying vacuum during the drying-out. **This method is used only when the tank is designed to withstand vacuum.**

For transformers rated 66 kV and above or 5 MVA and above, vacuum is applied while drying.

Vacuum is created directly into the transformer tank by means of a vacuum pump. The inlet of vacuum pump is connected to a suitable outlet in the upper portion of the transformer tank or cover. Vacuum of the order of 630 mm of mercury is maintained during the drying-out process. The vacuum process is used in addition to the short-circuit or resistance heating method.

Vacuum is not essential while drying-out, but the vacuum is preferable because at lower pressure, the moisture is liberated from the oil at lesser temperature, hence drying out process is accelerated.

### 21.11.6 Blowing Hot Air through Tank

The transformer without oil can be readily dried by blowing not dry, clean air (85° to 95°C) through its tank. The hot dry air is obtained by means of centrifugal air blower with filters and heating elements (15 kW for 10 $m^3$ tank). This method may be supplemented by short-circuit method. The moisture from the tank and coils are quickly removed by this method due to low humidity of hot, dry-air.

The temperature of inlet air should be between 85°C and 95°C and that of out-let air should between 60°C and 90°C.

### 21.11.7 Duration of Drying-out (general)

1 to 6 days for 11 kV transformer.
10 days to 30 days for 220 kV transformer.
15 days to 40 days for 400 kV transformer.

The drying-out process should be continued till the oil samples taken from the bottom of the tank and top of the tank have desired dielectric strength (Break-down value of 40 kV with 2.5 mm gap, (cold) and the insulation resistance is of desired value. The actual time required *will vary widely* depending upon the size of the transformer, amount of moisture and the method adopted for the drying-out, capacity of filtering plant.

| *Stage* | *Duration* | *Average Temp. of oil* |
|---|---|---|
| Initial heating up | 4–8 hour | Ambient to 80°C |
| Steady Temperaure | 6–48 hour | 80°C |
| Cool Down | 4–6 hour | 80°C to Ambient |

### 21.11.8 Precautions while Drying-out:

1. Never leave the transformer unattended during any part of the process. The transformer should be watched and observed.

2. Transformer–oil temperature should never exceed 85°C (Refer Table 21.3). The maximum temperature of anything in contact with the oil should never exceed 90°C.

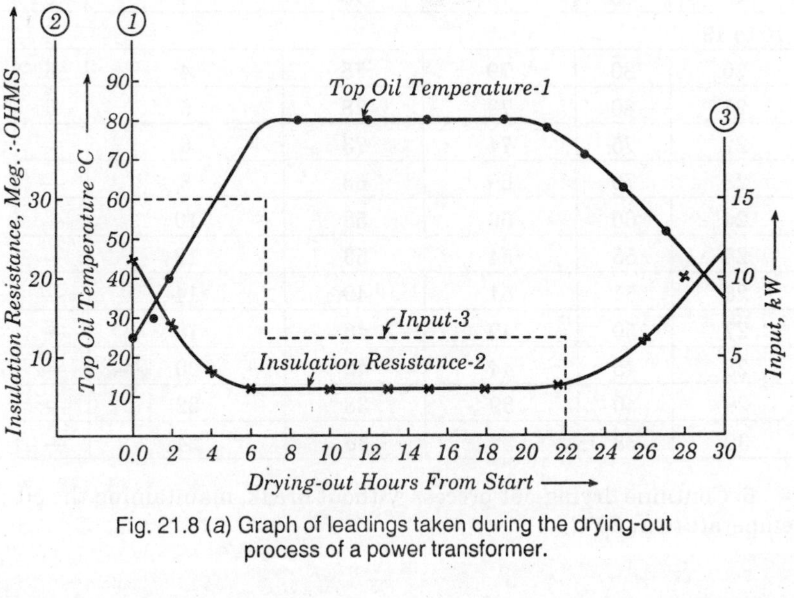


Fig. 21.8 (*a*) Graph of leadings taken during the drying-out process of a power transformer.

3. Maintain log sheet (Table 21.4).

4. Use lagging to prevent loss of heat through the tank walls and effect of cold draughts.

5. Use proper ventilation to remove the moisture given off by the transformer oil

Table 21.4

**Log Sheet of Drying out**

Details about Transformer :.............................................................

**Details about Method of Drying :.................................................**

**Date of Start:** **Date of Completion:**

| *Hours from Start* | *Top Oil* | *Temperature Bottom Oil* | *°C Average* | *Insulation Resistance Mega-ohms* | *Input kW* |
|---|---|---|---|---|---|
| 0 | 25 | 25 | 25 | 22 | 0 |
| 1 | 30 | 28 | 26 | 16 | 15 |
| 2 | 38 | 37 | 37.5 | 13 | 15 |
| 3 | 45 | 44 | 44.5 | 9 | 15 |
| 4 | 50 | 48 | 49 | 6 | 15 |
| 5 | 65 | 58 | 59 | 5 | 15 |
| 6 | 75 | 69 | 69.5 | 4 | 15 |
| 7 | 80 | 79 | 78 | 4 | 6 |
| 8 | 80 | 79 | 78 | 4 | 6 |
| 9 | 80 | 79 | 78 | 4 | 6 |
| 10 to 19 | | | | | |
| 20 | 80 | 79 | 78 | 4 | 6 |
| 21 | 80 | 79 | 78 | 5 | 6 |
| 22 | 75 | 74 | 73 | 6 | — |
| 23 | 70 | 69 | 68 | 8 | — |
| 24 | 60 | 59 | 58 | 10 | — |
| 25 | 55 | 54 | 53 | 12 | — |
| 26 | 51 | 51 | 49 | 14 | — |
| 27 | 50 | 49 | 48 | 18 | — |
| 28 | 45 | 44 | 43 | 20 | — |
| 29 | 40 | 39 | 38 | 22 | — |
| 30 | 38 | 37 | 38 | 24 | — |

6. Continue drying-out process without break, maintaining the oil temperature at 80°C.

7. Only spirit-thermometers should be used. Mercury thermometers should not be used.

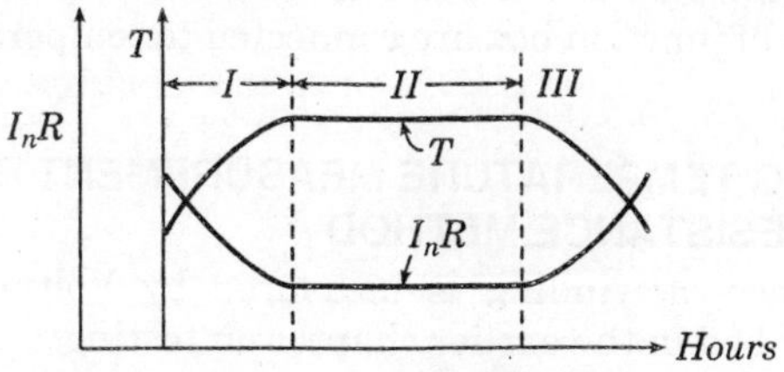

(i) Initial heating stage $I_nR$ reduces as $T$ increases
(ii) Steady stage : $I_nR$ and $T$ constant
(iii) Final stage heat input cut off $I_nR$ and $T$ reducing.
Fig. 21.8 (*b*) Indicating three stages of drying.

* (1) Refer Fig. 21.8 (*a*) for the graphs.

$I_nR$ = Insulation Resistance

(2) In the first stage of dying-out, the insulation resistance reduces. This indicates release of moisture within insulation and oil. In the second stage, the insulation resistance is steady. In the third stage, insulation resistance starts increasing indicating that moisture is being expelled.

(3) Drying out process is stopped when sufficient insulation resistance and *PI* values are reached during third stage.

(4) BDV of oil samples is measured after every four hours.

## 21.12 MEASUREMENT OF TEMPERATURE

While drying-out, the following temperatures are measured periodically:

— top oil, bottom oil — core
— coil assembly.

Temperature is measured by means of spirit thermometer, temperature indicators, thermocouples with temperature indicators is very commonly used. A thermocouple consists of a pair of wires of dissimilar metals joined at one end (hot junction). This joint is placed on the point whose temperature rise is to be measured. The other ends of wire are at lower temperature (Ambient). Thermal emf is generated in the thermocouple due to the difference in temperature between the hot junction and the cold junction. This emf is proportional to the temperature rise. The cold ends are connected to direct reading instrument which reads emf and whose scale is graduated to read °C. Several thermocouples may be used during the drying-out process.

---

* Thermocouple: Copper-constantum type: 4 mV per 100°C temperature rise; 0.5 to 1 mm diameter enameled copper, constantum. Wires are usually used.

The thermocouple wires should not come in contact with live parts. Suitable junction-box/selector box should be used. The thermocouple cold-ends are connected to the pairs of terminals in the junction box. The fixed points of junction box are connected to temperature measuring instrument.

## 21.13 WINDING TEMPERATURE MEASUREMENT BY SELF-RESISTANCE METHOD

DC resistance of winding is measured by Voltmeter/Ammeter method as described in the earlier chapter on testing.

Resistance values are measured at periodic intervals of 15 minutes. Temperatures are calculated as described with short-circuit method.

## 21.14 MEASUREMENT OF INSULATION RESISTANCE OF POWER TRANSFORMERS

Insulation resistance measurement reveals the health of insulation with respect to dryness, major defects in insulation, damage in insulation, earth faults, etc. By conducting insualtion resistance measurement tests, the subsequent high voltage tests on defective insulation can be avoided.

Insulation resistance ($I_nR$) is the resistance of insulation between two conducting parts or between a conducting part and earth. It is measured in terms of applied d.c. voltage divided by total current through the insulation, *i.e* $I_nR = V\,dc/I$. Insulation Resistance is measured by means of megger (D.C. Insulation *Tester). Megger is a d.c. megaohmmeter with a built-in motor driven d.c. generator.* The scale of megger is graduated in megaohms with lowest mark zero and highest mark infinity.

For transformer testing, the following megger voltages are recommended.

— 1000 V megger for oil-immersed transformers upto 100 kVA and all dry type transformers rated upto 1 kV.

— 2500 V megger for large transformers rated 11 kV, 33 kV, 66 kV, 110 kV, 220 kV, and 400 kV.

The line terminal of the megger (L or +) is connected to the conducting point of equipment under test. The other earth terminal (E or –) of the megger is connected to the other conducting point of the equipment under cost or to earthed tank. The motor is driven or the handle is rotated. The reading is obtained in megaohm. The insulation resistance depends upon temperature, dryness.

During the drying out process, the temperature and the insulation resistance are periodically measured.

The insulation resistance of the power transformer is measured between the following points in a sequence of tests:

1. Between 'All winding terminals connected together', and 'earthed tank'.

2. Between 'each winding' and 'tank', the remaining windings being earthed.

Two-winding transformers have HV and LV windings.

Three winding transformer have HV, MV and LV windings.

Table 21.5 gives the alternative test points for insulation resistance measurement.

**Table 21.5**
**Measurement of Insulation Resistance of Powers Transformer**

| *Short Form* | *Insulations Resistance Measurement Between* |
|---|---|
| **1. Two winding measurement** | |
| 1. HV-Tank ; LV | HV winding *AND* Tank with (LV winding and Tank earthed) |
| 2. LV-Tank ; HV | LV winding *AND* Tank with (HV winding and Tank earthed) |
| 3. HV ; LV-Tank | HV, LV winding connected together *AND* Tank with (Tank earthed). |
| **2. Three winding transformers** | |
| 1. HV-Tank ; MV ; LV | HV winding *AND* Tank with, (Tank, LV and MV windings earthed) |
| 2. MV-Tank ; HV ; LV | MV winding *AND* tank with, (Tank, HV, LV earthed) |
| 3. MV-Tank ; HV ; LV | MV winding *AND* Tank with, (Tank, HV, MV earthed) |
| 4. LV-Tank ; HV ; MV | LV winding *AND* Tank with (Tank HV, MV earthed) |
| 5. HV ; MV-Tank ; LV | HV, LV windings connected together *AND* Tank with (Tank and LV winding earthed) |
| 6. HV ; MV ; LV-Tank | HV; MV; LV windings connected together *AND* tank with tank earthed. |

## 21.15 INSULATION RESISTANCE AND POLARISATION INDEX

*Insulation resistance* of an electrical equipment refers to the resistance between conducting part and earth, expressed in megaohms. The insulation resistance can also be measured between two circuits separated by insulation.

Insulation resistance is measured by *Megger*. Megger consists of a built in megaohm meter and a d.c. generator. The generator is driven by hand or by a motor.

One terminal of megger is connected to conducting part. Other terminal is connected to earth frame (or other conducting circuit), the rotor of the generator is driven by hand or by motor.

*The reading $V_{dc}/I_{dc}$ read by the megger gives the insulating resistance value in megaohm. The scale of Megger is graduated from zero to infinity in terms of megaohms.*

When d.c. voltage is applied to the insulation, initially the insulation draws capacitive charging currents ($I_c$) in addition to leakage currents ($I_l$). Thus the Megger reads.

**Initial Megger Reading:**

$$R_0 = \frac{V_{dc}}{I_{dc}}$$

$$R_0 = \frac{V_{dc}}{I_c + I_l}$$

After continuous application of d.c. voltage, the capacitance currents reduce and only leakage current continue.

**Megger Reading after 60 seconds:**

$$R_{60} = \frac{V_{dc}}{I_l}$$

Since $I_l < I_c + I_l$

$$R_{60} < R_0$$

Hence the Megger reading after 60 sec is higher than initial Megger reading.

For good dry transformer insulation at the temperature between 15°C and 30°C, the *absorption coefficient* ($K_{ab}$) should be less than 1.3.

$$K_{ab} = \frac{R_{60}}{R_{15}}$$

should be more than 1.3, where

$R_{15}$ = 15 second Megger reading

$R_{60} \doteq$ 60 second Megger reading.

*Insulation resistance measurement reveals quality of the transformers insulation and the degree of the dryness. The subsequent high voltage tests can be avoided if insulation resistance is low.*

Before measuring the insulation resistance of an assembled transformer, its terminal bushings must be carefully wiped with a piece of dry cloth. When handling a Megger, one should observe accident prevention rules. Transformer windings possess a substantial capacitance, therefore, the current carrying parts can only be touched after electric charge has been removed from them. For this purpose, these parts should be connected to the earthed tank. When doing this, one should wear rubber gloves. It is absolutely prohibited to use a Megger to test a transformer under voltage.

The total direct current $I_{dc}$ seen by the current coil of the Megger in insulation resistance measurement has following four components:

$$I_{dc} = I_c + I_a + I_{lc} + I_{ls}$$

where $I_{dc}$ = Total current seen by the megger

$I_c$ = Charging currents of capacitance

$I_a$ = Dielectric absorption current or polarizing current

$I_{lc}$ = Conduction leakage current through the insulation

$I_{ls}$ = Surface leakage current.

$(I_c + I_a)$ flow for several seconds or minutes depending upon the size and capacitance of insulation. Their magnitude goes on reducing with time and after a few minutes $(I_c + I_a)$ become zero.

The remaining two components ($I_{lc}$ and $I_{ls}$) are constant for a given applied voltage and are the true indicators of the insulation resistance. Wet insulation increases conduction currents through the insulation. Dirty surface of insulation increases the surface leakage currents.

Since the capacitive currents and absorption currents reduce to zero after about 60 seconds, insulation resistance value after 60 seconds gives a better idea about quality of insulation.

*The ratio $R_{60}/R_{15}$ is called absorption factor.*

where $R_{60}$ = 60 seconds reading of insulation resistance

$R_{15}$ = 15 seconds reading of insulation resistance

Alternatively a 10 minute reading is taken for large transformers instead of 60 second reading.

The value obtained for 60 seconds should be higher than for 15 seconds if the material is sound. The ratio $R_{60}/R_{15}$ called the absorption factor gives a positive indication of the good condition of the insulation if it corresponds with the manufacturer's test figures. Table gives reference values for a large transformer.

Experience shows that the above methods of non-destructive testing gives reliable values of the condition of insulation, moisture, surface cleanliness and quality of insulation. It is easy to perform at site also.

**Table 21.6**
**Reference Values of Insulation Resistance**
**Power transformers, Mega-ohms**

| *Measurement* | *30°C* | | | *50°C* | | |
|---|---|---|---|---|---|---|
| Between | $R_{15}$ | $R_{60}$ | $R_{60}/R_{15}$ | $R_{15}$ | $R_{60}$ | $R_{60}/R_{15}$ |
| HV and ground | 750 | 1000 | 1.34 | 250 | 300 | 1.2 |
| LV and ground | 1000 | 2500 | 2.5 | 500 | 750 | 1.5 |
| LV and HV | 1000 | 2500 | 2.5 | 600 | 1000 | 1.67 |

**Note 1.** Insulation resistance at 50°C is lesser than insulation resistance at 30°C.

**2.** $R_{15}$ refers to 15 seconds reading of Megger. $R_{60}$ refers to 60 seconds reading of Megger.

For class A insulation, the insulation resistance in mega-ohms get halved for every 10 to 15°C rise. Therefore, the temperature should be noted and recorded every time insulation resistance is taken.

The magnitude of the insulation-resistance is not always indicative of the degree of dryness of the transformer. Therefore, use is made of an additional characteristic known as absorption factor (PI) which is the ratio of the 60 second insulation resistance to the 15 second insulation resistance, *i.e.* $PI = R_{60}'' / R_{15}''$.

For power transformers with dry insulation, the absorption factor at a temperature of 10 to 30°C must not be lower than 1.3.

The minimum permissible value of Insulation Resistance varies with the size of transformer and the voltage rating. A safe general rule is about two megaohms per kV of operating voltage, when the transformer is hot (60°). Refer Table 21.7.

**Effect of Temperature on Insulation Resistance.** *The insulation resistance depends on temperature,* therefore, when testing insulation, the temperature should also be measured. In oil-immersed transformers, the temperature, of the top oil is conventionally taken as the insulation temperature, while in dry type transformers, it is the ambient temperature that is taken as the insulation temperature.

The results of the insulation resistance measurements should be checked against the manufacturers's specifications or against the results of the previous tests. If there are no such data, the check should be made against the values specified in the standards. For new oil-immersed transformers, the 60 seconds insulation resistance as a function of the winding temperature and voltage class is given in the Table. The valves of $R_{60}$ given in the table refer to all the windings of a given transformer.

Table 21.7
Minimum Permissible Insulation Resistance $R''_{60}$
(in M ohm) for Oil-Immeresed Transformer Windings

| *Transformer* | *Winding temperature, °C* | | | | | | |
|---|---|---|---|---|---|---|---|
| *Voltage class* | 10 | 20 | 30 | 40 | 50 | 60 | 70 |
| Up to 33 kV | 450 | 350 | 250 | 150 | 100 | 70 | 50 |
| Between 33 kV and 110 kV | 950 | 650 | 450 | 270 | 180 | 120 | 70 |

## Questions

1. Explain why insulation resistance of a transformer varies with:
   — application of megger voltage
   — temperature of oil.
2. Explain the concept of 'absorption factor' with reference to drying out of a power transformer.
3. Describe the procedure of drying out of a large oil filled transformer.

# 22

# Maintenance of Power Transformers

With good preventive maintenance and proper loading, a power transformer gives a service life of over forty years. The transformers need careful preventive maintenance. The principles of maintenance, facilities required and maintenance schedules have been reviewed in this chapter.

The objective of maintenance is to ensure correct operation of transformer permanently over its designed life of 30-35 years or even longer if justified economically and technically.

## 22.1 NEED OF PERIODIC MAINTENANCE

During normal service the following effects are possible:

— Dust/Dirt collection on bushings, in control cubicle, etc.
— Rusting of various ferrous parts in transformer, cooling system.
— Loosening of terminals
— Leakage of oil through gaskets, threaded joints, sealing joints
— Gradual increase in vibration level
— Deterioration of Oil
— Loosening of internal parts, windings, laminations (rare)
— Ageing of insulation
— Choking of cooling-system valves/pipe, Defect in cooler control, etc.
— Touch-up painting by means of primer and finish paints.

As an age old saying goes: "*A stitch in time saves nine*". A regular periodic maintenance will correct the situation in-time and will eliminate the need of consequent major repair.

It is essential to have periodic preventive maintenance of power transformers by trained persons, equipped with maintenance facilities. *The earlier notation that the transformer does not need maintenance is wrong.* Transformer needs regular maintenance for satisfactory service.

*Regular preventive maintenance ensures long, fault-less and trouble-free service.* A rigid maintenance discipline ensures *long life.*

## 22.2 BREAKDOWN MAINTENANCE VERSUS PREVENTIVE MAINTENANCE

(1) *The breakdown or Corrective Maintenance* activities are undertaken after failure of an equipment. Such maintenance results in outage of circuit and supply. In general, it consists of locating the trouble, repair and recommissioning. It is very costly.

(2) *The Preventive Maintenance* is undertaken to ensure smooth and efficient working of a system equipment. Preventive maintenance is undertaken as per schedule before breakdown of a system or machine takes place.

A performance record of each critical component is maintained and biasing decisions on the service life of the component and the total number of hours of service, it has put in. Repairs or replacements are made to ensure that no breakdown occurs at any time during the service.

Preventive maintenance is carried out in planned manner. Breakdown maintenance is carried out as and when necessary.

For power transformers, preventive maintenance is recommended because failure of a transformer results in a costly and prolonged outage.

## 22.3 INSPECTION, SERVICING, OVERHAUL

Maintenance covers a wide range of activites aimed at keeping the equipment in perfect working condition for performing its function as per assigned duties. The choice of activities and schedule depends upon local requirements.

**1. Inspection.** This refers to the maintenance activity which comprises careful observation/scrutiny of the equipment without dismantling it. It usually includes visual and operational checks.

**2. Servicing.** This refers to cleaning, adjustment, lubrication and other maintenance functions without dismantling the equipment.

**3. Examination.** This refers to inspection with necessary dismantling, measurements and non-destructive tests to obtain data regarding the condition of components/sub-assemblies.

**4. Overhaul.** This refers to the work done with the objective of repairing/replacing worn-out parts and defective parts. The equipment, sub-assemblies are dismantled partly or completely. The conditions of components is inspected. Dimensions of worn-out components are measured. The components worn-out beyond acceptable limit are replaced. The assembly is followed by functional checks and measurements to ensure satisfactory operation.

## 22.4 MONITORING

The important data about large transformers in major substations is periodically scanned by automatic monitoring systems. This data (Table 22.1) is communicated to control room as well as to the load-despatch centre.

The monitoring helps in taking appropriate actions depending upon anticipated service conditions such as overloads.

In advanced SCADA (Supervisory Control and Data Acquisition systems) the follow up actions are decided with the help of expert systems programmes available with the load control centre.

**Table 22.1**
**Transformer Substation Data Monitoring**

| *Data* | *Units* | *Check interval* |
|---|---|---|
| **Load on lines** | | |
| Active power | MW | 20 sec |
| Reactive power | MVAr | 20 sec |
| Apparent power | MVA | 1 min (optional) |
| **Load on transformers** | | |
| Active power | MW | 20 sec |
| Reactive power | MVAr | 20 sec |
| Apparent power | MVA | 20 sec |
| **Limiting Values of** | | |
| Minimum bus voltage | kV | 1 min |
| Maximum Transformer load | MVA | 1 min |
| Voltage on main bus | kV | 20 sec |
| Voltage on auxiliary bus | kV | 20 sec (optional) |
| Winding temperatures | °C | 15 min |
| Ambient temperature | °C | If changed. |
| Protection status | 0/1 | If changed |

The interval can be varied also.

## 22.5 MAINTENANCE MANAGEMENT

The activites include

— Planning of maintenance activites: daily, weekly, monthly, half-yearly, five-yearly schedules.
— Maintaining the log (record) of important variables
— Record of inspection and maintenance
— Organising maintenance spares
— Organising maintenance tools, tackle, consumables

— Organising skilled manpower
— Carrying-out the maintenance work as per plan.

## 22.6 GENERAL GUIDE-LINES FOR MAINTENANCE

These are applicable for routine preventive maintenance of a transformer.

**1. Dirt and Dust.** The external surfaces of all the bushings should be inspected regularly. When required, bushing surfaces should be cleaned by use of try-chloro ethelene and clean cloth. (This is possible during shut-down) control cabinet, tank surfaces, cooler surfaces, etc. should be cleaned of dust, insects, leaves and other dirt.

**2. Oil Leakage.** After energizing the transformers, certain settling may occur in the sealing joints.

The sealing-joints should be re-tightened by using appropriate torque spanners recommended in the following table. This is essential for flat gaskets which are not placed in grooves.

Table 22.2

Tightening Torques for Hexagonal Steel Nuts*

| *Dimension of Hex. Bolts* | *Surface treatment* | *Tightening torque Tol. ± 10%* | |
|---|---|---|---|
| | | *Nm* | *kpm* |
| M8 | Zinc-coated | 24.5 | 2.5 |
| M10 | | 39.0 | 5.0 |
| M12 | | 84 | 8.6 |
| M16 | | 205 | 21 |
| M20 | Untreated | 430 | 44 |
| M24 | | 745 | 76 |
| M40 | | 1 520 | 155 |
| M36 | | 2 650 | 270 |

*Torque spanners have adjustable handle. The torque applied corresponds to the setting. The over tightening or under-tightening is avoided.

**3. Rust Removal and Touch-up Painting.** This activity should be done during regular maintenance shut-down. Rust damages are removed and surface treatment restored to original state by means of primer and finish paints.

**4. Oil Filteration and Moisture Removal.** Transformer oil absorbs moisture easily. Moisture absorption is prevented by means of following alternatives:

(*a*) *Oil conservator with rubber sack* (rubber bellow): The system consists of an oil conservator with a built-in rubber sack as a separating wall between the transformer oil and the surrounding air.

(*b*) *Oil conservator with breather.* The moisture absorption prevented by a breather connected to the conservator. The active drying agent (silica gel) should be exchanged or regenerated when 2/3 of the agent has been pink by absorbed moisture.

The breather contains also an oil-lock that prevent spontaneous air circulation. This lock should be filled with oil to level specified.

(*c*) *Oil-level indicator for oil conservator.* The transformer oil conservator is provided with an oil-level indicator graduated from 0 to 1. The correct oil-filling level is specified on an information plate that is placed on the transformer plate panel. At an oil temperature of +20° to 45°C, the conservator should be half filled. If the level exceeds the value 'full', oil must be drained off. If the value is low, oil must be filled in. Normal oil level should be at 35°C mark.

(*d*) *Gas-operated Relay (Buchholz Relay).* Faults such as flash-over, short-circuit and local overheating normally result in gas-generation. The gas-bubbles gathering in the gas-operated relay affect a float-controlled contact which gives an alarm signal.

Rules for sampling and a preliminary evaluation of the properties of the gas collected, and other information about the gas relay functions are given relevant standards.

(*e*) *Venting.* Certain transformers are provided with venting nipples on higher level components in order to remove possibly trapped air in the oil system. These nipples should be checked specially after the installation of the transformer, or after an inspection that implies opening of the oil system.

(*f*) If the oil has been exposed to moist air due to prolonged storage, moisture content and dielectric withstand tests shall be carried out. If values are low, oil should be filtered.

(*g*) *Sludge and Acid in Oil.* Oil which has not been too much oxidised may be regenerated by circulation through the filtering machine. However for smaller transformers; filterations is not economical.

The oil filtration should be preferably carried out whether transformer is warm and the viscocity of oil is low. The oil filtration or exchange should be as complete as possible. Old oil should not mixed with new oil as the new oil will get infected and will age-up quickly.

**5. Temperature Supervision.** The service life of a transformer depends on temperature of core, winding and oil. It is therefore essential to keep a watch on the winding temperature continuously. In automatic monitoring system, the winding temperatures and oil temperatures are scanned and monitored, continuously. When temperatures approaches limits, the alarm will be sounded. If temperature further increases, transformer should be tripped.

(*a*) Overloads. The transformers can be overloaded during lower ampient temperatures. Overloads should be judged by winding temperatures and oil temperatures. Temperature of windings rise more rapidly due to lower time-constant of winding. Therefore, winding temperatures should be supervised during overloading.

If the temperature in a transformer shows a tendency of rising without a corresponding increase of the load has occurred, this may be caused by a reduction of the cooling ability of the cooling equipment (dirt, dust). However, firstly the thermometer should be checked.

(*b*) *Thermometer for measuring of top-oil temperature.* The thermometer consists of a cylindrical sensing body with a flange, a capillary tube, and a thermometer housing with dial and contact-device. The measuring system is filled with a liquid, which changes its volume at temperature variations, and affects springy bellows. The movements of the bellows are transferred to the pointer and signal contacts *via* a link system. The thermometer is provided with 4 signal contacts of micro-switch type. The contacts can be set independently of each other.

(*c*) *Winding-temperature indicator.* The thermometer system consists of a sensitive body with assembling details, a capillary tube and a thermometer housing, which contains a scale with an indicating pointer and a maximum temperature pointer, heating and adjusting resistor, as well as contact-device for four micros-switches.

(*d*) *Remote control of winding temperature.* For remote control of winding temperature resistance-temperature device with a heating element built into the same housing is used. The heating element is fed by the secondary current of a current transformer.

For setting of the heating element, there is a parallel-connected adjustment resistor installed in the control cabinet.

(*e*) *Bushings.* Bushing porcelains surface should be cleaned of dust and dirt regularly. In areas where air carries salt, cement, dust, smoke chemical substances; the cleaning should be more frequent. Bushing oil-level should also be watched regularly.

(*f*) *Terminal Connections.* Inspect visually. If dirty, clean and tighten the terminal connections by using torque spanners. Check that terminal conductor does not produce tension on the equipment.

(*g*) *Off-load Tap Switch.* During overhaul, the movable parts of operating mechanism are lubricated. If transformer is disconnected from supply and is not in use for a long time, operate the off-load tap switch to all positions and then re-set.

(*h*) *On-load Tap-changer.* O.L.T.C. requires regular maintenance as given in Table 22.3.

For frequently operating O.L.T.C. the maintenance frequency shall be higher.

**6. Cooling Equipment.**

(*a*) *Radiators, Oil-Air Coolers: Air side.* The cooling surfaces shall be inspected regularly and when required cleaned from dust, insects, leaves or other airborne dirt. This is especially important in case of fan-cooling. The cleaning is suitably carried out by means of water flushing at high pressure.

(*b*) *Radiators, Coolers for Oil-Air, Oil Water Oil-side.* Normally, no measures are necessary for keeping the internal cooling surfaces clean as long as the oil is in good condition. If, however, sludge formation has set in, the sludge may deposit on horizontal surfaces in radiators and coolers. If such a case, the radiators and coolers should be flushed internally with clean oil in connection with oil exchange.

If the sludge does not loosen, flush with petrol etc., and then with oil.

(*c*) *Coolers for Oil-water, Water Side.* The coolers should be inspected regularly. All coolers can be cleaned by pulling out the tube packets and thus making them accessible for cleaning.

Depending on the condition of the cooling water, the time intervals between inspections vary very much. Suitable intervals are determined by experience.

(*d*) *Air Fans.* The fan-motors are generally provided with permanent-lubricated bearings and double sealing rings. The motor bearings are axially clamped with spring-washes. If the sound-level of the fan increases, we should firstly re-tighten all mounting supports.

(*e*) *Valves, flow-indicators, pressure meters* during periodic maintenance, these components of cooling system should be checked as per instruction manual.

(*f*) *Control Cabinet.* The components should be checked visually and then as per instructions in the manual.

**7. Bushings.** Bushing porcelains shall be cleaned from dust and dirt regularly. In areas where the air contains impurities as salt, cement dust, smoke or chemical substances, shorter intervals are required.

**8. Connections.** In order to avoid prohibited temperature rises in the electrical connections of the transformers/reactor, all screw-joints should be checked and re-tightened according to schedule enclosed.

**9. Accessories.** Separate leaflet/instructions should be followed for various fittings (as applicable) for Fans, Pumps, Flow indicators, Pressure Gauges, Oil Gauge, Pressure reducing valve, OLTC, Off circuit tap switch, OFAF/OFWF Coolers etc.

**10. Control of Oil.** The oil in a reactor provides an electrically insulating and a cooling medium. The service reliability of an oil-immersed transformer/reactor is therefore mainly, depending on the oil quality. In service, oil is subjected or normal deterioration due to the conditions of use mainly due to air, water and solid particles/sediment.

The oil should be maintained as per the guidelines of IS:1866. Periodicity of test and permissible limits for important parameters of oil-electric strength, water content, resistivity, tan-delta, neutralization value, sediment and precipitable sludge, flash point and interfacial tension should be checked. Health of reactors can be effectively monitored by Dissolved Gas Analysis (DGA) technique described. This technique helps in detection of incipient faults in reactors.

**Guidelines for the Characteristics of Oil to be Obtained Before Energizing New Transformers Using New Insulating Oils According to IS: 335-1983**

| *SL. No.* | *Characteristic* | *Equipment Voltage* | *Permissible Limit Satisfactory For Use* |
|---|---|---|---|
| (i) | Electric strength (breakdown voltage kV) | Below 72.5 kV<br>72.5 kV and less than 145 kV<br>145 kV and above | 40 kV (rms) min<br>50 kV (rms) min<br>60 kV (rms) min |
| (ii) | Specific resistance (resistivity ohm-cm at 90°C) | All voltages | $1 \times 10^{12}$ ohm-cm (min) |
| (iii) | Dielectric dissipation factor (tan δ) at 90°C Max. | All voltages | 0.05 |
| (iv) | Water content, ppm Max. | Below 72.5 kV | 25 ppm |
| | | 72.5 kV and less than 72.5 kV | 20 ppm |
| | | 145 kV and above | 15 ppm |
| (v) | Interfacial tension at 27°C (Min) N/m | All voltages | 0.030 |
| (vi | Dissolved gas content | 145 kV and above | |

## 22.7 PART-WISE MAINTENANCE SCHEDULE

During periodic maintenance, the parts of the transformer need cleaning, re-tightening, touch-up painting, lubricating, topping-up, etc. Table 22.3 gives a list.

### Table 22.3
### Part-wise Maintenance-Supervision Schedule for a Large Transformer

| *Part* | Inspection check | *Actions* | *Frequency** |
|---|---|---|---|
| Tank, cover, conservator | Dirt, dust<br>Oil leakage | Cleaning<br>Re-tightening | AI<br>EI, WI |
| | Surface treatment | Touch-up painting | AI |
| Broather | Colour silica-gel | Possible exchange | MI |
| Breather, oil lock | Water in oil | Possible exchange | MI |
| Conservator | Oil level | Reading | WI |
| Gas-operated relay | Oil level | Possible venting | MI |
| Venting nipples | Possible encl. air | Venting | UI |
| Oil | Oil samples | Possible filtering | QI |
| Thermometer, top oil | | Reading | WI |
| Winding temperature indicator | | Reading | WI |
| Remote control of winding temperature | Functional check | | AI |
| Cooling equipment, air-side | Dirt, dust | Cleaning | AI |
| Cooling equipment, oil-side | Dirt, dust | Cleaning | US |
| Cooling equipment, water side | Dirt, dust | Cleaning | US |
| Cooling equipment | Water flow | | MI US |
| Fans, pumps | Function | | QI |
| Fans | Sound-level | Possible re-tightening | EI, US |
| Flow-indicators and Pressure meter for | Function | Reading | DI |
| Oil and water | Dirt, sludge | Cleaning | DI |
| Control cabinet, relays | Function | | AI |
| Control cabinet, heat | Function | | QI |
| Bushings | Oil leakage | Re-tightening | EI+US |
| Bushings | Dirt, dust | Cleaning | AI |

*Refer foot-note on page 417.

*Contd......*

| *Part* | Inspection check | *Actions* | *Fre-quency** |
|---|---|---|---|
| Bushings, connections | Contact-joints | Re-tightening | EI+AI |
| De-energized tap-changer | Function | Lubricating | AI |
| On-load tap-changer | Function | Possible replacement* | AI |
| O.L.T.C., oil | Oil sample | Possible replacement** | AI, US |
| O.L.T.C., oil-level indicator | Level | Reading | WI |
| O.L.T.C., thermostat | Function | | AI |
| O.L.T.C., pressure relay | Function | | AI |
| O.L.T.C., driving mechanism | Dirt, dust | Cleaning | AI |
| O.L.T.C., automatic | Function | | AI |
| O.L.T.C., contacts | Contacts | Possible replacement** | US |
| O.L.T.C., counter | No. of operations | | US |

*Frequency: AI=Annual inspection
EI=About 1 month after taking into service
QI=Every three months
MI=Monthly inspection
WI=Weekly inspection
US=When required, Un-scheduled inspection

**Number of operations is a deciding factor.

## 22.8 MAINTENANCE SPARES AND MAINTENANCE FACILITIES

These are recommended by the manufacturer and decided by the user. The number of identical transformers in a substation or in the area covering the operation and maintenance wing should be known for deciding the spares to be stocked. These include

- — Nitrogen cylinders, couplings, valves, pipes, etc.
- — Oil, silica-gel
- — Set of hardware
- — Gaskets of various types
- — Insulating lapes, crape papers
- — Power cables and Control cables
- — Set of instruments and fitments
- — Set of oil valves and Set of pipe fittings, etc.

*Major Maintenance Facilities for* transformer maintenance are usually organised centrally for a group of substations. These include:

— Oil Filterations plants and accessories
— Transformer handling facilities
— Maintenance workshop
— Tools and tackle
— Testing facilities, etc.

## 22.9 INSPECTION, REPAIRS, OVERHAUL

Maintenance is considered in three categories:

— Routine Inspection and Minor Repairs
— Medium Repairs
— Major Repairs and Overhauls.

The object of preventive maintenance of transformers is to obtained long, trouble-free life and ensure high reliability.

**Routine Preventive Maintenance and Minor Repairs.**

This includes preventive maintenance work which does not call for opening of the transformer cover. It includes visual inspection: checking of fitments, checking of level of oil, cooling system, fastenings, control circuit, oil levels, leaks, etc. The insulation resistance values are measured. The BDV* of oil samples is measured. The gas sample obtained from Buchholtz relay is analysed.

The nut-bolts are tightened, the porcelain surfaces are cleaned. Silica gel in the breather is replaced. The external fitments are repaired wherever necessary. The oil level is brought to desired value. The oil is filterised. Minor repair work is carried out by the operating personnel in power stations and sub-stations.

**Medium Repair Work.** This includes dismantling the transformer for inspection/repairs of the core-coil assembly. The sub-assemblies are inspected and repaired as necessary (e.g., repair conservator tank, tap-changer, cooling system, sealing gaskets, etc.) The gaskets are replaced, if necessary. The defects revealed in routine maintenance are removed during the minor repair work. The other minor repairs and maintenance mentioned earlier is also carried out.

**Major Repair Work and Overhauls.** Major repair work is carried out after a serious internal fault or after a prolonged service (8 to 10 years).

Overhaul is carried out if the transformer has been in service for several years and has been subjected to severe overloads. Severe prolonged overloads will result in weakening of coil insulation and deterioration of oil. Overhaul may also be carried out if the transformer has seen through a short-circuit of longer period.

---

*BDV=Break Down Voltage.

This involves opening-up of the transformers, replacement of windings and insulation, tightening of the core laminations, replacement of winding connections, replacement of bushings, etc. Such repair works require complete dismantling of the transformer. Major repair work is carried out by trained personnel, in a planned manner preferably in a well equipped repair-workshop.

Tap-changer has complex mechanism with springs, movable parts, arcing parts and oil. The overhaul of a tap-changer should be done by the manufacturer/with the help of manufacturers trained staff.

## 22.10 MAINTENANCE FREQUENCY: DAILY, MONTHLY, YEARLY

Small unattended distribution transformers and industrial transformers are practically maintenance free. Large important high voltage, high capacity transformers need regular preventive maintenance. The notations used in the schedules of transformer maintenance includes the following:

— Routine daily inspection ...DI
— Routine weekly inspection ...WI
— Routine monthly inspection ...MI
— Quarterly inspection ...QI
— Annual inspection ...AI
— Un-scheduled maintenance (whenever required) ...US
— One month after commissioning ...EI

**1. Daily Inspection (DI)**

1.1. Check tank and radiators for unusual noise, oil and water leaks.

1.2. Check oil level in main tank bushings.

1.3. Check relieve vents whether normal or open.

1.4. Check whether cooling water is flowing, whether oil circulation pump is operating when necessary, whether fans start when necessary.

1.5. Check relay panel temperature indicators and confirm normal condition.

1.6. Check position of tap-changer.

1.7. See that all control/alarm/power/supply circuit switches are closed and fuses in the circuit are well placed.

**2. Monthly Inspection (MI)**

2.1. Check oil level in main tank, oil filled bushing etc. If oil level has fallen down below specified level for given temperature, the cause of leakage should be determined.

Oil level varies with change in oil temperature.

2.2. Check and record oil temperature.

2.3. Check bushing surface for signs of chipping dirt, oil film etc.

2.4. Check presence of nets, vines, shrubs etc., in the neighbourhood of transformers.

2.5. Check terminal connections, earthing connections for tightness.

2.6. Other checks mentioned in daily check.

**3. Annual Inspection**

3.1. Check foundation for cracking and settling. A slight shift of the transformers may break bushings or connecting oil or water lines. See that rail stops are firm in place to hold transformer in position on the rail. Check transfer car and matching of its rails with transformer deck rails at each position. Point metal work as needed.

3.2. Clean dirt and oil from radiating surfaces. Repaint as necessary. Stop excessive vibration of radiator tubes, tighten loose or vibrating parts. Check for unusual internal noises. Inspect oil and water piping, valves and plugs. Manipulate radiator cut off valves to see that they are in operating condition and secure in the open position. See that all oil drain valves which can be operated without wrenches are plugged or locked to prevent unauthorized opening.

3.3. See that relief diaphragm is in operating condition and closes tightly. The non-shattering-type diaphragm should be actuated to see that it is not stuck shut from rust or paint. Make sure that material used in shattering-type diaphragm is not too thick or tough to be broken by reasonable internal pressure. See that screens and baffles in the vents or breathers are not obstructed or broken. If breathers are of dehydrating type, check chemicals and replace if depleted.

3.4. Clean dirty gauge glasses and connection. Check oil level indicators and relays for proper operation. Replenish oil if below normal. Drain out and replace bushing oil if dirty or discoloured.

3.5. Check external supply and drain piping for leaks. Flush out cooling coils of heat exchanger water passages with air and water. Test coils for leaks by applying air pressure to coils and absorbing for bubbles rising in oil and drop in air pressure with supply valve closed, or use a hydrostatic pressure test. A pressure of about 75 pounds per square inch is recommended. If water scale is present, circulate a solution of 25 per cent hydrochloric acid and water through the coils until clean. Then flushout thoroughly. Clean external surfaces of coils.

3.6. Check flow indicators and relays for proper operation.

3.7. Clean and test water tubes similar to cooling coil, check for oil and water leaks.

3.8. Check motors and control for fans and pumps.

3.9. Check calibration of temperature indicators and relays, check and clean relay contacts and operating mechanism.

3.10. Check setting and operation of regulator and relay, see that gauges are indicating properly.

3.11. Check for gas leaks by applying liquid soap on all joints valves, connections, etc., with gas pressure raised to the maximum recommended by the transformer manufacturer.

3.12. Clear porcelain with water, chlorothene, or other suitable cleaner. Repair chipped spots by painting with lacquer approved by manufacturer. Inspect gaskets for leaks tighten bolts, check power factor, check oil sample from bottom of bushing for dielectric strength and presence of water which may be entering at top. Replace or replenish oil if necessary.

3.13. Check top settings and adjustments at terminal board to see that they agree with diagrams. Check insulation resistance of wiring with devices connected. Check ratio and phase-angle adjustments of potential devices if changes have been made in secondary connections and bushing.

3.14. Tighten all bus and ground connections. Refinish joint contact surfaces if they have been overheating. Inspect ground cable to see that it is not loose or broken.

3.15. Lower the oil level to atleast the top of the core. Inspect for sludge on core and windings. Inspect under side of cover for moisture and rust and clean up. Check connections at terminal board, tighten all bolted connections, cord bolts, etc., within reach.

3.16. Inspect contacts and clean if reachable on internal inspection. If not reachable for visual inspection, check each position with Wheatstone bridge across winding to defect poor contact.

3.17. Inspect tap-charger as per instruction-book. Drain oil from contact compartment, clean and refinish contact surfaces. Check contact spring pressure. Check contact operating mechanism Tighten connections and other bolts.

3.18. Check motor check and adjust brake, check gears, shafts, and lubrication.

3.19. Check condition of contacts and refinish if burned or corroded. Check contact springs, operating rods, and levers check closing and opening position with respect to position of main contacts.

3.20. See that positions indicated correspond to position of main contacts. Check remote electrical indicators for correct operation, obstruction to movement of pointer, etc.

3.21. Check operation counter for correct registration.

3.22. Run tap changer or regulator through several complete cycles both control relay and manual control, and observe contacts and mechanism for proper operation.

3.23. Inspect fuses or circuit breakers on all power, control and alarm supplies to anxiliary equipment and devices. Check and tighten wiring connections at all terminal points. Inspect wiring for open circuits, short circuits, and damaged insulation. Check insulation resistance of wiring with devices connected.

3.24. Check the insulation resistance between each winding and ground. Disconnect all external leads at the bushing leads terminals except where the connecting leads can be suitably isolated at adjacent disconnecting switches, for this test. Inspect wiring for open circuits, short circuits and damaged insulation. A similar test using a capacitance bridge is recommended where such an instrument is available.

3.25. Check the dielectric strength of the insulating oil in the main and auxiliary tanks and oil filled bushings.

The acidity of the insulating oil in the main tank should be checked at intervals of less than 5 years. Transformers operating at high temperatures or showing signs of sludging or dark colour of the oil should be checked more frequently. Oil may be checked in the field with a dielectric test kit or samples sent to Laboratory.

## 22.11 UN-SCHEDULED MAINTENANCE

If the transformer has been properly maintained and not overheated and barring internal failure, it should not require untanking within the normal life. If sludge has been allowed to form due to overheating and oxidation of the oil, the transformer should be untanked and the core, coils, oils passages, tank and water cooling tubes washed down with clean oil under pressure to remove sludge and other accumulations which prevent proper circulation of the oil. Inflammeable liquids should not be used in cleaning the core, coils, or inside of tank. While untanked, check for loose laminations, core bolts, insulating blocks etc., and other pertinent features on the check list.

The necessity for filtering and/or reclaiming the insulating oil will depend on the results obtained from the oil dielectric and oil acidity tests. It may be more economical to replace the oil in small transformers rather than filter and reclaim it.

## 22.12 MAINTENANCE OF UNATTENDED TRANSFORMERS

Major sub stations having transformers rated 1 MVA and above are usually attended at all time. Such installation can have hourly, weekly, monthly inspection.

Medium size transformers between 0.5 MA and 1 MVA are used in smaller sub-stations. They can also have daily, weekly and monthly maintenance.

Small transformers below 500 kVA are often installed in unattended sub-stations. Such transformers can have 6 monthly maintenance.

**Table 22.4. Check List of Maintenance of Power Transformer**

| *Activity* | *Large Transformer (About 1 MVA)* | | *Small Transformer (Upto 1 MVA)* | | |
|---|---|---|---|---|---|
| | *Attended* | *Unattended* | *Attended* | *Unattended* | |
| Dielectric Strength of oil | AI | AI | AI | | AI |
| Bushings | MI AI | AI | MI | AI | AI |
| Tap Changer or Regulator | DI AI | AI | MI | AI | AI |
| Motor and Drive Housing | AI | AI | | | |
| Auxiliary and Limit Switches | AI | AI | | | |
| Position Indication | AI | AI | | | |
| Operation Counter | WI AI | WI AI | | | |
| Operation | AI | AI | | | |
| Tanks and Radiators | DI AI | WI AI | MI | AI | AI |
| Main Terminal and Ground Connections | DI AI | WI AI | MI | AI | AI |
| Terminal Board and Connections | AI | AI | | AI | AI |
| Foundation | AI | AI | | AI | AI |
| Piping of Oil and Water | DI AI | WI AI | WI | AI | AI |
| Plug and Valves | DI AI | WI AI | WI | MI | MI |
| Oil Levels | DI AI | MI AI | WI | AI | AI |
| Vents and Breathers | DI AI | MI AI | WI | AI | AI |
| Relief Vents | DI AI | MI AI | WI | AI | AI |
| Water Cooling Piping | AI | MI AI | | AI | AI |

*Contd...*

| *Activity* | *Large Transformer (About 1 MVA)* | | *Small Transformer (Upto 1 MVA)* | | |
|---|---|---|---|---|---|
| | *Attended* | *Unattended* | *Attended* | *Unattended* | |
| Flow Indicators and Relays | DI AI | MI AI | DI AI | AS | |
| Heat Exchangers | AI | | | | |
| Oil Pumps | DI AI | MI AI | | | |
| Cooling Fans | DI AI | MI AI | DI AI | | |
| Temperature Indicators | US | MI US | WI AI | AI | |
| Core and Coils | AI | MI AI | US | US | |
| Internal Inspection | | | AI | AI | |
| Power Supplies and Wiring | DI AI | MI AI | | | |
| Insulation Resistance | AI | AI | AI | AI | |
| Oil Filteration | US | US | US | US | |

*DI=Daily Inspection* *WI=Weekly Inspeciton* *MI=Monthly Inspection* *AI=Annual Inspection* *US=Unscheduled*

**Table 22.5. Typical Maintenance Schedule for Transformers upto 1000 kVA**

| *Frequency of Inspection* | *Inspection* | *Inspection Details* | *Action required if conditions are unsatisfactory* |
|---|---|---|---|
| 1. Hourly | Load (amperes Temperatures) voltage | Check against rated figures | Start fan if necessary |
| 2. Daily | Dehydrating breather | Check that air passages are clear. Check colour of silica-gel | If silica gel is pink change, may be reactivated for use again |
| 3. Monthly | Oil level in transformer | Check transformer oil level | If low, top up with dry oil, Examine transformer for leaks. |
| 4. Quarterly | Bushings | Examine for cracks and dirt deposits | Clean or replace |

*(Contd...)*

| | | | |
|---|---|---|---|
| 5. Yearly | Oil in transformer | Check for dielectric strength and water content. Check for acidity and sludge. | Take suitable action to restore quality of oil. |
| Yearly | Earth Resistance | | Take suitable actions if earth resistance is high. |
| Yearly | Relays, alarms, their circuits, etc. | Examine relay and alarm contacts, their operation, fuses, etc. Check relay accuracy etc. | Clean the components and replace contacts and fuses if necessary. Change the setting, if necessary. |
| 6. Yearly of after internal fault | — | Overhaul, inspection, lifting of core and coils. | Wash by hosing down with clean dry oil. |

**Table 22.6. Typical Maintenance Schedule for Transformers above 1000 kVA**

| *Frequency of Inspection* (1) | *Inspection* (2) | *Inspection Details* (3) | *Action required if conditions are unsatisfactory* (4) |
|---|---|---|---|
| 1. Hourly | Ambient temperature | — | — |
| Hourly | Winding temperature | Check that temperature is reasonable | If abnormal heating, shut down the transformer and investigate if heating is persistently higher than normal. |
| Hourly | Oil Temperature | | |
| Hourly | Load (amperes Voltage) | Check against rated figures | — |
| 2. Daily | Oil level in transformer | Check against transformer oil level | If low, top up with dry oil, examine transformer for leaks |
| Daily | Oil level in bushing | — | — |
| Daily | Leakage of water into cooler | — | — |
| Daily | Relief diaphragm | — | Replace if cracked or broken |

*(Contd...)*

| *Frequency of Inspection* | Inspection | *Inspection Details* | *Action required if conditions are unsatisfactory* |
|---|---|---|---|
| Daily | Silicagel breather | Check that air passages are free. Check colour of active agent. | If silicagel is pink change by spare charge. The old charge may be reactivated for use again. |
| 3. Quaterly | Bushing | Examine for cracks and direct deposits | Clean or replace |
| Quaterly | Oil in transformer | Check for dielectric strength and water content. | Take suitable action to restore quality of oil. |
| Quaterly | Cooler fan bearings, motors and operating mechanisms | Lubricate bearings. Check gear box. Examine contacts Check manual control and interlocks. | Replace burnt or worn contacts or other parts. |
| 4. Yearly | Oil in transformer | Check for acidity and sludge. | Filter or replace |
| Yearly | Insulation resistance | Measurement | Filteration of oil |
| Yearly | Oil filled bushings | Test Oil | Filter or replace |
| Yearly | Gasket joints | | Tighten the bolts evenly to avoid uneven pressure |
| Yearly | Cable boxes | Check for sealing arrangements for filling holes. Examine compound for leaks. | Replace gaskets, if leaking |
| Yearly | Sugar diverter and gaps | Examine for crack and dirt deposits | Clean or replace |
| Yearly | Relays, alarms, their circuits, etc. | Examine relay and alarm contacts, their operation, fuses, etc. Check relay accuracy etc. | Clean the components and replace contacts and fuses, if necessary. Change the setting if necessary. |
| Yearly | Earth Resistance | — | Take suitable acting; if earth resistance is high. |
| 5. Yearly | Above 1 MVA | Overall inspection including lifting of core and coils. | Manufacturers work or maintenance workshop |

## 22.13 TROUBLES WITH POWER TRANSFORMERS AND POSSIBLE CAUSES OF FAILURE

The transformer may fail due to any of the following reasons:

— **System disturbances** beyond the stipulated limits, e.g., sustained overvoltage, underfrequency, through short-circuit not cleared by breaker, repeated short circuits, failure of protective devices, switching or lightning surges, sustained over loads, over fluxing, etc.,
— Lack of Maintenance
— Improper operation, overloading
— Manufacturing defect or weakness
— Testing can prevent this
— Poor quality of oil, moisture in oil
— Inadequate drying, poor oil due to overheating.
— Hostile environments such as extremely low temperatures causing high viscosity or extremely high ambient temperature causing overheating; conductive dust on insulator surfaces causing flashovers.

*Transformes failure,* can be categorised as

1. Failure due to temperature rise. This may be due to
— Overloads
— High ambient temperatures
— Failure of cooling system
— Through short-circuit currents.

2. Failure of insulation due to switching surges or lightning surges, partial discharges.

3. Failure due to moisture or dirt in oil.

4. Failure of components e.g., tap-changer.

5. Other causes, e.g., d.c. component, harmonics etc.,

Troubles in magnetic circuit are usually dormant. They are not detected by usual tests on windings *i.e.*, ratio test, winding resistance test, winding meggering etc., However, no-load measurements reveal higher losses. Core to earth insulation resistance measurement also reveals core bolt insulation condition. Major problem with core requires a major repair at manufacturers works.

**Table 22.7 Transformer troubles (Except on-load tap changer)**

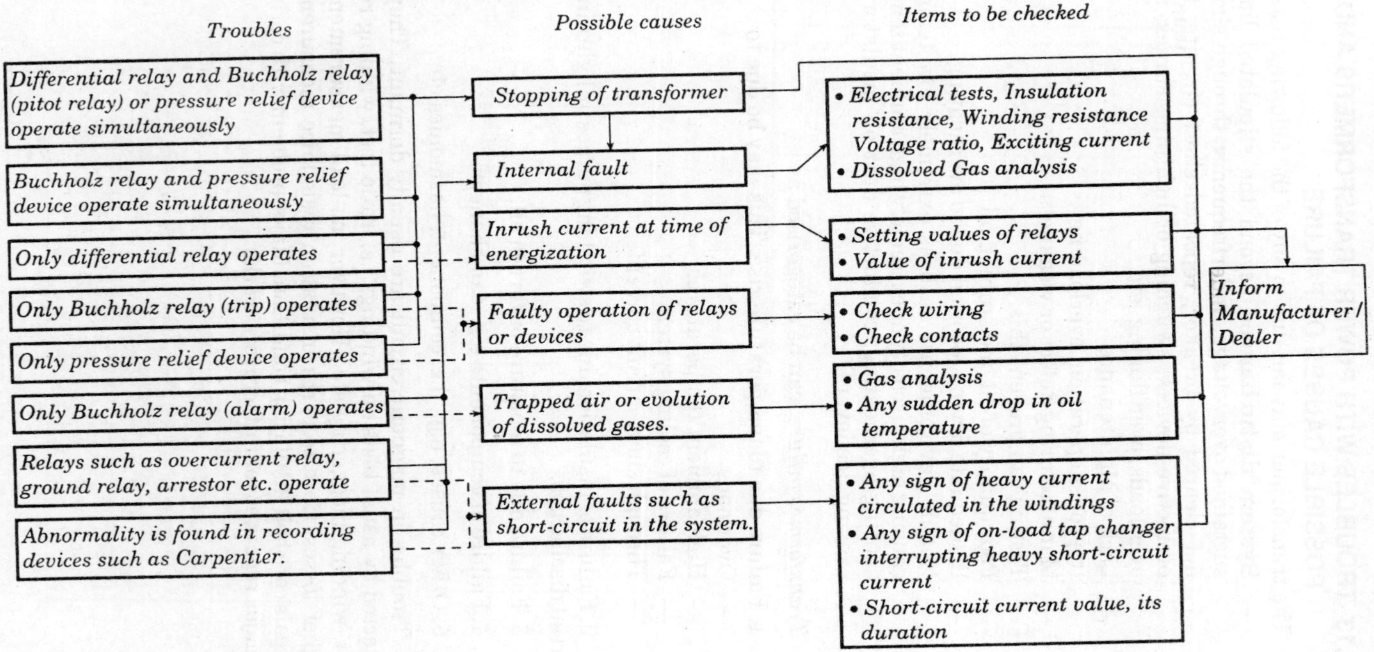

**Table 22.8 Transformer troubles (In case of on-load tap changer)**

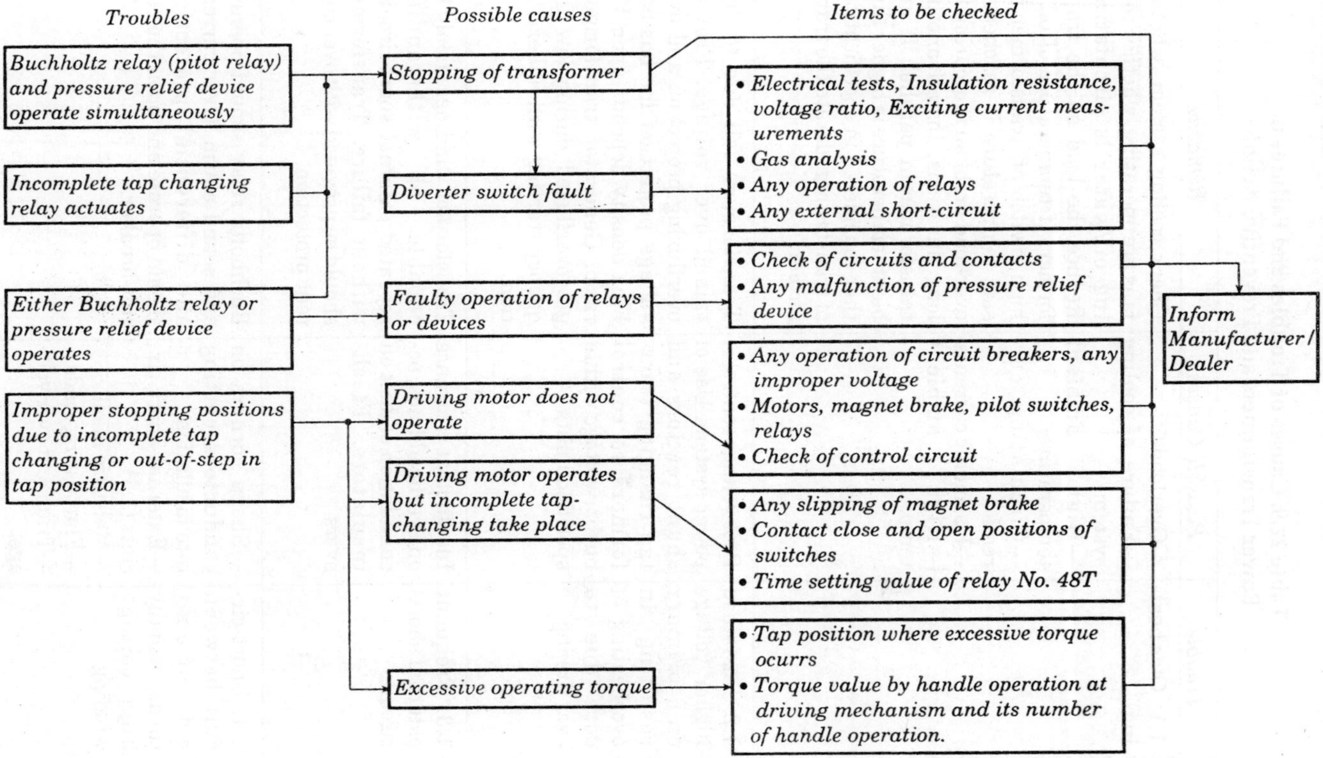

**Table 22.9. Causes of Troubles and Failures in Power Transformers and Preventive Actions**

| *Trouble* | *Possible Causes* | *Remarks* |
|---|---|---|
| 1.1. Overheating | —Overloads<br>—Failure of cooling system<br>—High ambient temperature<br>—Circulating currents<br>—Harmonic currents<br>—High ambient temp. | Check cooling system, whether fans are operating, whether cooling oil/water is circulating. Reduce the load on the transformer. If temperature of oil is high, switch off transformer till safe temperature is reached. If over-load problem is occuring for long durations, install another transformer in parallel. If ambient temperature is higher than that considered in specifications of transformer, derate the transformer. |
| 1.2. Sustained higher voltage on primary resulting in overheating of core due to over fluxing. | Poor voltage control of power system. Use of shunt reactors and tap changing transformers to control busbar voltage within specified limits. | Transformers fail due to sustained over voltage. Provide overfluxing protection and over voltage protection for bus-bar. Flux density depends upon $V/f$ ratio. Generator transformers get overfluxed during low frequency starting with full excitation. |
| 1.3. Frequent external short-circuits | Insufficient clearance on overhead lines, accumulation of dust on insulators. Flash-overs | Transformer windings should be capable of withstanding repeated external short-circuits without failure. Transformer should be provided with over current protection. |
| 1.4. Short-circuit between adjacent turns, usually high voltage winding. | —Sharp corners on conductors cutting into insulation.<br>—External short circuits (1.3)<br>—Moisture in oil.<br>—Fluctuating loads<br>—Transient over voltage. | Buchholtz relay should operate and sound alarm. Over current and differential protection should operate and open the circuit-breaker. |

| *Trouble* | *Possible Causes* | *Remarks* |
|---|---|---|
| 1.5 Internal short circuit. | —Substained overload and insulation failure.<br>—Fault in tap changer.<br>—Failure of end turns of coil due to over voltage surges.<br>—Bad solder joint causing local overheating and open circuit.<br>—Ageing of insulation, abration of insulation resulting in internal short circuits. | —Overcurrent protection.<br>—Earth-fault protection.<br>—Differential protection<br>—Back-up by Buchholtz relay, sudden pressure relay, winding temperature relay, oil temperature relay etc. |
| 1.6. Moisture in oil | —Moisture in the oil while filling.<br>— Breather saturated.<br>—Defective seals. | Oil should be filtered. Silica-gel should be replaced, gaskets should be replaced. Transformer should be dried out. |
| 1.7. Rapid deterioration of oil | —Excessive overloading<br>—Presence of moisture<br>—Poor quality of oil | Cause should be determined and corrective action to be taken. Analysis of gas pin-points the type of insulation decay. |
| 1.8. Carbon and other conducing particle in oil | —Sparking in oil, excessive temperature of coil. | Conducting particles line up on insulation surface causing reduction in insulation resistance and failure by tracking. Transformer needs over-hauling. |

**Table 22.10. Troubles with Core and Magnetic Circuit**

| *S.No* | Class of Trouble | *Description* |
|---|---|---|
| 1. | Failure of insulation of bolts used for clamping core and yoke. | Failure of insulation of bolts used for clamping the core and yoke causes heavy circulating currents resulting in core heating. |
| 2. | Vibrations in core and tank. | The loose core clamping bolts and bolts between core and structure results in vibration of core. This results in excessive and unacceptable noise. |

| *S.No* | Class of Trouble | *Description* |
|---|---|---|
| 3. | Excessive core heating, high magnetising currents. High in-rush current. | Excessive heating of core result in temperature rise of winding. |
| 4. | Failure of core bolt insulation | Over-fluxing and temperature rise of core, core-bolts. Moisture absorption and dielectric failure. |
| 5. | Over-fluxing of power transformer, Melting of core bolts, burning of core bolt insulation, burning of insulation between laminations. Excessive leakage flux and vibrations in tank. | Flux density depends on $V/f$ ratio. **The generator transformers and auxiliary transformers fail by overfluxing if excitation is maintained during starting or stopping the unit**. Over-fluxing relay should be provided for protection of generator transformer. This relay is connected in excitation circuit. It prevents overfluxing condition. |

## 22.14 TROUBLE SHOOTING & INVESTIGATION OF TROUBLES

An alert maintenance engineer and the expert team for investigation have the following means for identifying the possible trouble or failure.

1. Log-book record. Record of event recorder, fault recorder.
2. Control-panel and relay panel.
3. Analysis report of gas samples from Buchholz relay.
4. Analysis of sludge from oil.
5. Insulation resistance measurement report regarding quality of oil and insulation. Loss angle/tan δ measurement report.
6. Partial discharge test report.
7. Checking of phase to earth and phase to phase insulation by megger. The failure analysis is like an expert detective work.

*Insulation resistance measurements* indicate the health of the transformer insulation and oil. It also indicates phase to ground fault/phase to phase fault/core-insulation failure.

Loss angle measurement and comparison with earlier record indicate the health of insulation.

*Partial discharge measurements* give possible location of partial discharges within the transformer.

*Analysis of gas sample from Buchholz* gives indication of type of insulation deterioration.

*Operation of alarm and trip contacts of gas-pressure relays* indicates excessive oil temperature of oil possible due to through faults not detected by differential protection.

*Operation of transformer protection* gives indication regarding the type of abnormal condition (such as overload) or type of fault such as an earth fault or phase fault within the transformer.

In the event of a transformer failure, a team comprising of (1) Relay testing engineer (2) Operation and maintenance engineer (3) System analyst (4) Design engineer etc., carry out a *joint inspection*. The possible causes are listed. The possibilities are eliminated by logical analysis and clues. Thereafter the most probable cause is ascertained.

Often complete site-tests are repeated and the results are compared with earlier records. The remedial actions are:

— Repair of transformer at site or at manufacturer's works. This needs detailed planning.
— Prevention of similar failures in future by appropriate actions such as:

1. Improved operation/maintenance schedule.
2. Improved protection.
3. Improved system design.

Feedback should be given to other substations operation and maintenance staff.

### 22.14.1. Condition Monitoring

Condition monitoring is very important tool which can be a great help in improving the effectiveness and efficiency of maintenance.

The main objective of condition monitoring is to measure the amount and rate of deterioration of degradation of transformer as time passes.

The purpose of condition monitoring to attend to the failures, which can be prevented with a consequence of safety and cost. It also enables maintenance to be performed according to the measured condition of a transformer. With condition monitoring, we can also estimate the remaining life of transformer from its present condition and rate of degradation, allowing the transformer to be used closer to the end of their life and it helps in formulating the replacement strategy.

The degadation time scale is an important factor in decision making process and has a major influence on the way in which we perform monitoring.

Many external factors are responsible for changes in a transformer over a period of time. The most important are the action of air, oxygen and moisture on the insulation material. Oxidation of oil increases with temperature and presence of catalyst. It results in formation of acid and polar products causing an increase in dissipation factor (tan $\delta$). The presence of moisture in oil reduces its dielectric strength, particularly when the water is in suspension or absorbed by solid materials.

The prolonged action of heat on cellulose insulating materials cause a chemical change, a rupture of molecular chain aggravated by the presence of humidity which greatly reduces mechanical strength of organic materials such as paper and oil and are very liable to degradation under stress provided by PDS.

*Furanic Compounds* formed in transformers are solely turned by the degradation of the cellulose insulation. In some cases, they tend to accumulate providing a sense of the historic ageing of a cellulosic insulation. However these compounds can be significantly degraded by high temperature associated with incipirent faults in the presence of high oxygen.

### 22.14.2 Degree of Polymerization (DP)

The degree of polymerization closely relates to the mechanical properties of the paper. The paper in transformer varies in uniformity of ageing not only over the time but spatially and ageing depends on temperature, water and oxygen content gradients, polar contaminants and by-products.

DP for new paper is approximately between 1000 and 1400 and 200 may be considered as the end of life of paper. At 200 DP, transformer may withstand electrical stresses but not mechanical stresses due to short circuit etc., Unfortunately, the insulation paper's insulation cannot be sampled from a working transformer. With some care, the continued use of laboratory analysis for dissolved gas in oil, furanic compounds in oil, degree of polymerization and oil quality can greatly aid in the assessment of the condition of the insulation in transformers. Dissolved gas analysis is routinely used as these detect a wide range of problems, while tests for furanic compounds and DP are used to assess the condition of the solid insulation. With the help of these tests, we can predict the life of transformer.

Furanic compound data are useful to confirm or complement dissolved gas in oil tests. DP data while providing a good sense of the degree of ageing of the insulation, is complimented by tests for furanic compounds and dissolved gas analysis of oil which may detect an over heating condition not found with paper samples selected.

When paper is relatively wet and aged, furan analysis must be applied with care. Manytimes, furan analysis method and frequency response analysis method are used to confirm the defect.

## 22.15. ONLINE INSULATION INTEGRITY MONITORING

Recently, on line monitoring has been introduced for transformers. On line insulation monitoring for transformers is desirable because of the following reasons:

1. It maximises up time and unnecessary maintenance outages are eliminated.

2. Interval testing is fine if done regularly. Yet, many times, the interval between tests is too long to detect an impeding failure. Relying on interval testing it can be harmful, as it is not known by user when problem starts and how rapidly it progresses. On line monitoring tests continuously notify about the impending problems in time.

3. On line monitoring avoids sudden failures that forces shutdown, leading to production loss, or wide area power outage. Depending on the extent of damage, the disruption could last for weeks. Changes in bushing capacitance and power factor are indicative of insulation deterioration.

### 22.15.1 Online Monitoring of Transformers

Transformers are a vital part of any transmission and distribution system. Monitoring transformers for problems before they occur can prevent faults that are costly to repair and result in a loss of service. Considerable costs are associated with transformer failure, especially if such failure happens without warning, and no action for a planned outage can be taken. Without redundancy, there can be huge losses in terms of produced energy, process downtime, penalties, and more. Therefore, preventing in-service transformer failures has a profound economical impact, as well as the ability to deliver a reliable power.

Current monitoring systems can provide information about the state of a transformer, but are either off line or very expensive to implement. On-line transformer diagnostics is the key to greatly reduce the cost and increase the reliability of providing the needed electrical energy to a growing society. Remote transformer monitoring and diagnostics are growing in popularity among electric utilities. The need to simplify transformer monitoring and prevent thermal damage is driving electric utilities to adopt online monitoring and diagnostics.

The condition of oil-paper insulation system is the main diagnostic indicator that influences failure-free operation of transformers. Monitoring of such characteristics, which concern in the failure of transformer is necessary when safe and reliable operation is required.

Transformer oil undergoes varying degrees of aging or deterioration under normal operating conditions. The rate of ageing will be contingent upon the magnitude of the electrical, thermal, and mechanical stresses. Insulation breakdown in the windings, from coil-to-coil or coil-to-ground, will result in arcing. Under arcing stress, the oil will generate solid carbon, which will form sediment, decreasing the heat dissipation capability. Furthermore, arcing stress will cause a decrease in the dielectric strength of the oil. Therefore, a sensor that can provide an assessment about the condition of oil inside transformers or breakers would be an excellent means for relative diagnostics of the equipment.

Hydrocarbon molecules constituting the transformer oil experience strong electric field in presence of occluded species like oxygen and moisture. Progressive damage to the oil is on account of build-up of polar/polarizable oxygenated hydrocarbon molecules generated by electric field assisted oxidative chemical reactions. Dielectric permeability of the oil, thus, increases at a very slow rate.

Slow build up of oxidation products as a result of chemical reactions with oxygen and moisture from environment under the prevailing service conditions and physical ingress of polar molecules such as water cause the dielectric permeability of the service oil in any transformer to increase with time.

### 22.15.2. Parameter Monitoring

Installing monitoring equipment on transformers is usually done for two reasons, namely, (1) monitoring important transformer functions that can help in detecting the developing faults before they lead to a catastrophic failure and (2) monitoring transformer functions can allow for a change from periodic to condition-based maintenance.

Transformer monitoring mainly involves data acquisition, sensor development, data analysis, and the development of causal links between measured values and failures of transformers. The main transformer parts that need monitoring are insulation quality, winding temperatures, oil quality, and mechanical moving parts such as on-load tap changers (OLTC). Monitoring the windings and insulation systems for gas-in-oil and partial discharge are crucial; temperature and load monitoring on the other hand, is regarded as base information and should be included in any type of transformer monitoring.

On-line gas sensors are typically the first choice in designing full time monitoring systems for dissolved gas analysis (DGA); simply because the technique of analysis is well established and accepted, and the sensor is truly capable of detecting a wide range of failure types.

The load capability of a transformer is limited by the hot spot of the windings. The hot spot is typically calculated indirectly from measurements of oil temperatures and load current. An alternative method involves fibre-optic temperature sensors that are installed in the winding during the manufacturing process. These sensors come in two varieties-fibers which measure the temperature at a single point, and distributed fibers that measure the temperature along their length. All of these systems involve high costs; in particular, the distributed fibre sensor is the most expensive to install and can only be applied to new transformers.

The condition of the insulation can also be judged from other parameters as well, such as moisture levels and particulate content. Data interpretation with these parameters is not straightforward, but new techniques are being developed using software to analyze the large body of historical data available and identify patterns of progression towards failure. If similar deterioration is detected for a transformer in service, remedial action can be taken.

Other types of online sensors have also been investigated. Examples of such systems are online measurements of the moisture content of the oil, static charge in oil, optical sensors and pump monitoring. Also on-line measurements of the moisture in the cellulose by optical fiber techniques are being studied. In general, these systems do not have a strong coupling to important and frequent failure modes.

As mentioned above, the dielectric constant of oil goes up with its degradation. In one of the methods, this oil is used as medium between the capacitor plates. This capacitor is used in one oscillator. As the quality of the oil changes, the frequency generated by the oscillator also changes. With all other factors remaining unchanged, the digital pulse frequency at the output of oscillator is governed by the dielectric permeability of the oil that acts as the dielectric medium in the capacitor assembly. The pulse frequency changes sensitively with the change in dielectric permeability and, hence, the reduction in measured pulse frequency with respect to the fresh oil is a measure of dielectric degradation of the used oil during service.

Hence, the change in frequency indicates the condition of oil. Frequency can be measured by any of the commercially available hand-held frequency meter. However, for a detailed study, the frequency data as a function of time can also be recorded through a PC using a laboratory developed interface hardware and software. The capacitance, with such oil as the dielectric medium, is a function of the extent of contamination. Hence, the frequency at the output of an oscillator, configured with this capacitor in the timing circuit, decreases as the oil quality deteriorates. Precise frequency data permits monitoring of very minute shifts in dielectric permeability, hence enabling early detection of onset and progress of degradation in the quality of service oil.

The sensing element is a capacitor assembly which is constructed out of circular polished stainless steel discs profiled by wire cut EDM. The discs are closely spaced with uniform gaps and are electrically separated from the adjacent ones by flat Teflon rings over the supporting rod. The miniature pulse generation electronics is enclosed within a small cylindrical enclosure placed close to the sensing element and fixed on the same side of the mounting flange. A dielectric type pulsating temperature sensor is also provided close to the sensor. Thus the sensors and the associated signal generation electronics remain immersed within oil for the on-line device.

In another method, the principle of light absorption by oil is used for determining the oil condition. It is being claimed that this will be the cost effective method. This monitoring system, based on absorbance of light, has the potential to be an online diagnostic tool that can provide early detection of potential abnormalities without going through the expense of DGA. Furthermore, given that light absorption at different wavelengths may correspond to different failure modes, this new monitor has the potential for detection of multiple failure modes simultaneously. Finally, given its operational principles and the required hardware and software, this monitoring system can provide an inexpensive approach to transformer diagnostics. Through this online monitoring system, light is passed through the oil of the transformer and tested for absorbance. Experimental results have demonstrated that by using different wavelength, one could determine the difference between an acceptable or unacceptable sample of oil. Based on a priori determined absorbance levels of sampled oil, associated with different transformer failure modes, a database can be created that would be used with this monitoring system. Samples of failed transformer oils show a trend of increasing absorbance levels. Additional wavelengths can be identified, which provide more information about the state of the transformer and make the system more versatile in simultaneously determining the cause of different faults.

### 22.15.3. Utilization of Online Monitoring

Many electric utilities are reluctant to use on-line transformer monitoring devices because of the high cost involved in the installation of such systems. However, these systems are important for ensuring the smooth operation of electric power transmission networks. Many utilities such as electricity boards, PGCIL (Power Grid Corporation of India Limited) have started using online monitoring of transformers in our country.

Online monitoring of transferors is the emerging technology and it will take some time to mature. The use of online monitoring of transformers is likely to increase in recent future as its use helps in detecting the faults at an early stage. This avoids sudden failure and helps in planning maintenance. Transformer life also increases. As mentioned above, many approaches are being invested by researchers all over the world and the best and the cheapest one will be able to survive.

**Summary**

The maintenance is planned. Maintenance Management includes organising, staff, facilities, spares planning, follow-up and monitoring. The objective is to have preventive maintenance for long trouble-free service life with minimum overall cost. Maintenance includes

— Daily inspection, weekly inspection, monthly inspection, quarterly inspection, yearly inspection, unscheduled inspection.

— Major repairs, overhaul.

Maintenance includes filtering the transformer oil. For this the transformer oil is circulated through vacuum filteration plant till desired Insulation Resistance and dielectric strength value is achieved.

During *periodic maintenance*, the various parts of the transformer are inspected, checked and repaired. During *overhaul,* the assemblies are dismantled and worn-out parts are replaced. Over-hauls need well equipped maintenance workshops, skilled personnel, relevant drawings, spares etc.

# 23

# Protection and Fitments

The various possible internal and external *abnormal conditions* and their harmful effects on transformers have been reviewed.

The principles of *protective relaying* and switchgear for transformer protection are illustrated.

Protective and monitoring *fitments* on the transformer, tap-changer and man-machine interface for operation and control of a transformer have been described.

## 23.1 OBJECTIVES OF TRANSFORMER PROTECTION AND MONITORING

During the service of a transformer, there can be occassional internal and external abnormal conditions and faults. Some abnormal conditions such as overloads require timely actions by the operators to prevent a major failure. Many overload protection also takes care of this.

Some other abnormal conditions such as faults within the transformer or beyond the transformers need immediate automatic appropriate tripping of circuit-breakers so as to prevent extensive damage to the transformer and the associated installation. These protective functions for the transformers and associated equipments are carried out by switchgear and protective devices and associated fitments on the transformer.

Three principle aims are:

**1. Protection against external disturbances.** When external short-circuits, external overvoltages, external surges, external overloads occur in the system, the transformer should not be subjected to excessive stresses. It should be adequately protected. *Transformer is the most vulnerable equipment in the substation and the network.* The system design should be such that the short-circuit levels and insulation levels are properly graded and coordinated with the transformer withstand levels.

**2. Protection of the transformer and associated system against internal faults.** If the fault is within the transformer, heavy fault currents will tend to flow from busbars to the fault.

The fault currents should be automatically stopped by opening the circuit breakers from either sides quickly and reliably. Thereby the damage to the transformer and other system components such as CTs, Busbars, Generators etc., is minimised..

**3. Monitoring of transformer continuously.** This is done automatically or manually by periodic checks on voltages, currents, temperatures etc., and warn against possible abnormal condition in advance, thereby the operator can take corrective action. Automatic

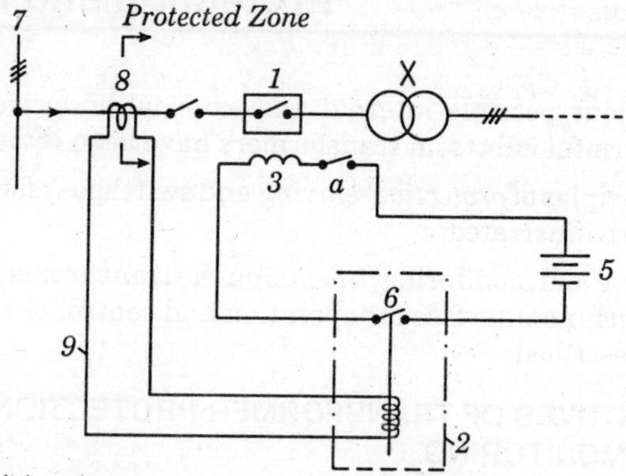


1. Circuit-breaker
2. Relay
3. Trip coil of c.b. (Shunt Release)
4. Trip circuit
5. Battery
6. Relay Contacts
7. Busbars
8. Current transformer
9. Pilot-wires

*a* Auxiliary switch contacts

*x* Protected power transformer.

Fig. 23.1 Protection principle.
Circuit-breaker control for single-in feed. For fault in or *X* for overcurrents beyond (8), the circuit-breaker (1) is tripped. Protected zone is beyond (8) and is not bounded beyond the transformer. Protection is non-unit type.

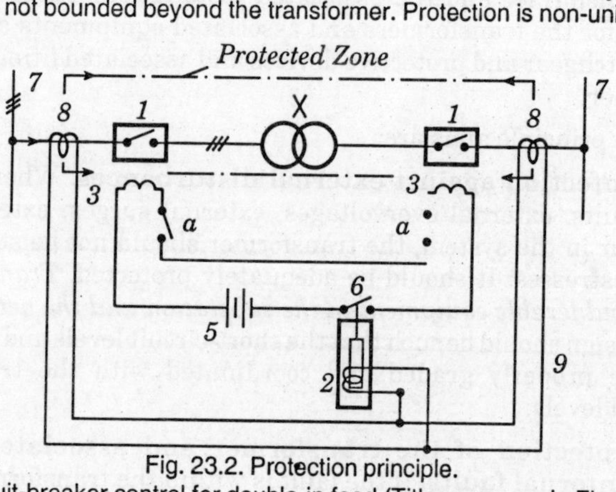


Fig. 23.2. Protection principle.
— Circuit-breaker control for double-in feed (Titles same as in Fig. 23.1.)
For fault in X, circuit-breakers (1) both the sides are tripped simultaneously Protected Zone is bounded by CTs on either sides. Protection is unit type and exact.

monitoring system called SCADA (Supervisory Control and Data Acquisition system) is provided for large AC Networks. (Ref. Sec. 22.4)

## 23.2 PRINCIPLE OF PROTECTIVE RELAYING

The protective relaying senses the abnormal conditions and gives an alarm or isolates that part from the healthy system. Thus when a fault occurs in a transformer, it is automatically isolated from the network by means of switchgear and protection.

There are two distinct circuits:

1. *Main power circuit* through which power flows through the transformer. This is at voltages corresponding to voltages of HV and LV circuits.

2. *Control/protection circuits.* These are at low voltages. They include:

(*a*) *DC auxiliary circuit* in which circuit-breaker auxiliary switch contacts, battery and relay contacts etc., are connected, and

(*b*) *Pilot wires* between CTs and relay measuring circuit.

Figs. 23.1 and 23.2 illustrates the scheme of protective circuit.

The essential components are:

— Protective Relays (6)
— Circuit-breakers (1) connected in main power circuit
— CTs (8), Primaries are connected in main power circuit with the secondaries connected to pilot wires (9)
— Battery supply (5) and DC trip circuit for energising trip coil (3) of circuit-breakers (1)
— Pilot wires between CT secondaries and protective relay circuits (9).

The relays are compact, self-contained devices which respond to abnormal condition. The relay distinguish between normal and abnormal condition. Whenever an abnormal condition develops, the relays close its contacts. Thereby the trip circuit of the circuit-breaker is closed. Current from the battery supply flows in the trip-coil of the circuit-breaker and the circuit-breaker opens and the faulty part is disconnected from the supply. The entire process, occurrence of fault-operation of relay-operating of circuit-breaker-removal of faulty part from the system', — is automatic and fast.

Circuit-breakers are automatic switching devices which can interrupt normal currents and fault currents.

The functions of protective relaying include the following:

— To sound an alarm or to close the trip circuit of circuit breaker so as to disconnect a transformer during an abnormal conditions which include over-load, under-voltage, temperature rise, unbalanced load, reverse power, under-frequency, short circuits, etc.

— To disconnect the abnormally operating transformer so as to prevent the subsequent faults, *e.g.* over-load protection protects the transformer and prevents insulation failure.
— To disconnect the faulty transformer quickly so as to minimize the damage *e.g.* if a transformer is disconnected immediately after a winding fault, only a few coils may need replacement. If the fault is sustained, entire winding may get damaged and the transformer may be beyond repairs.
— To localise the effect of external fault by disconnecting the fault part, from the healthy part, causing least damage to the healthy transformer.
— To isolate the transformers for through fault condition.

## 23.3 CIRCUIT-BREAKER CONTROL

Figures 23.1 and 23.2 illustrate the scheme of circuit-breaker control for transformer protection and switching. When a fault occurs in the transformer '*X*', fault power starts flowing from the busbar (7) towards the faulted transformer. The CTs (8) are connected on supply side. Increase in secondary currents produces corresponding increase in the primary currents. The overcurrents is sensed by the relay (2).

If the relay current is above threshold value, the relay is actuated and it closes its contacts (6). Current flows from the battery (5) in the trip circuit (4). As the trip coil of the circuit breaker (3) is energized, the circuit-breaker operating mechanism is actuated and it operates for the opening operation. Auxiliary switch *a* is important item in the circuit. As the circuit-breaker contacts open, the auxiliary switch contacts also open and the trip-circuit is opened by the auxiliary switch contacts.

In case of a single in-feed, (Fig. 23.1) a single circuit-breaker on supply side is opened.

In case of double in-feed, (Fig.23.2) the circuit-breakers on both the sides are tripped simultaneously.

After opening of the circuit-breaker, isolators are opened and the transformer is completely isolated from the live busbars. The cause of tripping is investigated.

## 23.4 PROTECTIVE ZONES AND LOCATIONS OF CTs

A part of the system protected by a certain protective scheme is called protective zone or zone of protection. The entire power-system is covered by several protective zones and no part of the system is left unprotected.

The boundary of a protective zone is determined by the location of current transformers. Hence, current transformers are located such that the circuit-breakers are covered in the protective zones.

The zones can be precisely identified in unit systems, such as circulating current differential protection of transformers. Unit system is one in which the protection responds to faults in the protected zone alone, and it does not respond to through faults (faults beyond the protected zone). For example, in Fig. 23.2, the protective zone bounded by CTs is definite and protection operates only for internal faults.

Non-unit systems, such as over-current protection, do not have exact zone boundary. For example, see Fig. 23.1.

Each zone has certain protective scheme and each protective scheme has several protective systems. *e.g.*, overload, short-circuit, undervoltage, overfluxing, earth fault protections, etc.

## 23.5 CHOICE OF PROTECTIONS

Protective relaying is necessary for every power transformer plant. The choice of protection depends upon several aspects such as type and rating of the transformer, its importance, location, probable abnormal conditions, cost, etc. Between generators and the final load points, there are several transformers of various ratings. Each needs certain adequate protection. The protective scheme depends on the size of the transformer. For small transformers, simple protective devices such as fuses are employed. For medium size transformers, O.C. relays are used. Large transformers differented protecting as primary protective.

**For small distribution transformers, only drop-out fuse link may be adequate.** The cost of protection itself may be more-than the cost of the transformer. Hence, no special protection is provided. When we want transformer not to fail under any condition, other protection are provided in such cases.

For large generator transformers, over-current, differential, over fluxing, earth-fault, Over-temperature, Buchnolz, Sudden pressure relays and Surge Arresters are essential. In addition, monitoring system, data collection and data logging etc., are also provided, in large substations and the data regarding transformer is scanned periodically and communicated to the data loggers and control room computer.

## 23.6. PRIMARY AND BACK UP PROTECTION

Primary protection (Main protection) is the essential protection provided for protecting an equipment machine. As a precautionary measure, an addition protection is generally provided and is called 'Back-up Protection'. The primary protection is the first to act and the Back-up protection is the next in the line of defence-meaning, if primary Protection fails, the back-up protection comes into action and removes the faulty part from the healthy system. Back-up protection is provided for the following reasons:

If due to some reason, the Main protection fails, the *back-up protection* serves the purpose of protection. Main protection can fail due to failure of one of the components in the protective system such as

primary protection fails, there must be an additional protection, otherwise the fault may remain uncleared, resulting in disaster.

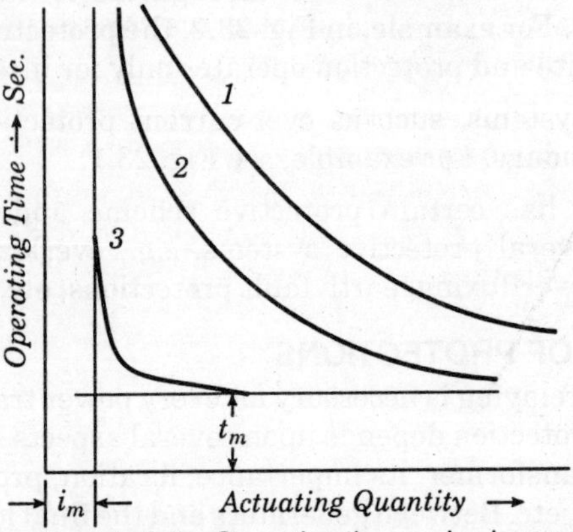


1, 2. Inverse time characteristic. Operating time varies inversely with the operating quantity.

3. Definite-minimum time characteristic operating time has definite minimum time $t_m$ and definite threshold value of operating quantity $i_m$.

Fig. 23.3. Operating time characteristics of protective relays.

Primary protection for the transformer covers the transformer itself. The back-up protection may cover the transformer plus the busbars, transmission line etc.

## 23.7 TIME CHARACTERISTICS OF PROTECTION AND PROTECTION COORDINATION

Three types of time characteristics are shown in Fig. 23.3.

For overloads and back-up protection, characteristic 1, 2 are preferred.

For internal faults such as phase to ground fault and phase to earth fault characteristic 3 is preferred.

Main and back-up protection should be coordinated.

## 23.8 RELAY TIME AND FAULT CLEARING TIME

Fault clearing time is the time between the instant of fault and instant of final are interruption (in circuit breaker).

Fault clearing time is the sum of relay-time and breaker time.

Fault Clearing Time = [Relay Time] + [Breaker Time]

| Relay Time ↓ | | Breaker Time ↓ |
|---|---|---|
| Fault Instant To Closing of relay contacts | + | Closing of relay contacts To Final Arc extinction in C.B. |

The relay-time is the time between the instant of occurrence of fault and the instant of closure of relay contacts. Or, it is the time between the instant when the operating quantity reaches the pick-up value and the instant of closure of relay contacts.

Though fast fault clearing is desirable, time lag is purposely provided in majority of protection systems for the following purposes :

— To permit discrimination between main and back-up protection.

— To prevent the operation of relay during transients, starting currents,permissible load fluctuations, etc.

The relay-time of fast relays is of the order of a few cycles and that of inverse time relays can be adjusted between about 40 seconds to 60 seconds. The circuit-breaker time for slow circuit-breakers is of the order of 5 cycles and that of fast circuit-breakers is of the order of 2 cycles to 3 cycles.

Static Relays of $\frac{1}{2}$ cycle or one cycle are now available.

*Primary protection* is by fast instantaneous relays having no international time lag. Protection time is less than 10 cycles.

*Backup protection* may be by inverse time overcurrent and earth fault relays. Protection time may be a few seconds to several minutes depending upon the time delay selected. The greatest the time for back-up protection to operate, the greater will be the damage in the system. Operation of backup protection isolates larger part of network. Hence it is preferable to have *local back-up rather* than *remote back-up*.

## 23.9 ABNORMAL CONDITIONS AND STRESSES

Power transformers are used in high voltage systems for transferring large loads. They are subjected to voltage stresses, current stresses, thermal stresses and electromechanical stresses during their operation.

*Voltage stresses* are caused by normal voltage, power frequency overvoltage, impulse overvoltages. They affect the internal and external insulation.

*Current stresses* are caused by normal currents, overload currents and short-circuit currents flowing through the transformer windings. The current stresses result in

— Temperature rise

— Electromagnetic forces.

*Environmental effects* are caused by alternate variation in the ambient temperature, atmospheric dust and pollution etc.

*Mechanical Stresses.* During external short-circuits, windings bushings are subjected to dynamic forces.

**Magnetic Stresses.** During high flux densities, during magnetising current inrush, magnetostriction, etc., cause magnetic stresses in core.

## 23.10 ABNORMAL CONDITIONS EXTERNAL TO A TRANSFORMER

These are classified depending upon the waveform and duration of overvoltages and over currents. The cause is in the system and not in the transformer. These include:

**Overcurrents.** The two categories are

— Overloads above 1 p.u. and last for several minutes to several hours

— Short-circuit currents of several times load currents and last for a few cycles only till the protective systems interrupt them.

Overcurrents have the following causes and range:

1. **Switching-in of Transformer.** Peak value of first current loop when switching-in, duration several cycles.

$$I_0 = 3\sqrt{2} \text{ to } 8\sqrt{2}\ I_n$$

$$I_n = \text{Rated current.}$$

2. **Motor Staring Currents.** R.M.S. value or starting current:

$$I_d = 3 \text{ lo } 7\ I_n$$

Duration is several seconds.

3. **Short Circuit at the Secondary.** R.M.S. value of short-circuit current:

$$I_{sc} = 6 \text{ to } 25 I_n$$

duration several cycles.

The effects of overcurrent include the following:

1. Drop in secondary voltage, due to $IX$ drop in the transformer.

2. High temperature rise of the windings and oil.

3. Electrodynamic forces involving high stresses in the transformer windings.

**Overvoltages.** These vary widely in waveform and amplitude.

Accordingly they are classified as

— **Temporary Overvoltages.** These are of power frequency. The amplitude varies between 1.0 p.u. to 1.2 p.u. and duration is of few cycles to several minutes. The cause is reactive power flow resulting in voltage drop/voltage rise in transmission lines. The methods of voltage control include tap-changing of transformers and shunt compensation. (Refer Chapter on voltage control.)

— **Lightning and Switching Surges.** The transformer is protected by use of surge arresters. Details covered in Chapter 24.

Lightning surges last for a few tens of microseconds.

Switching surges last for several hundred microseconds. Surge Arresters are installed near transformer and on incoming overhead lines and exposed busbars etc.

**Other Network Phenomena**

— Flow of Third Harmonic Currents, higher harmonic currents
— Flow of d.c. component currents
— Ferro-resonance condition, etc.

## 23.11 PROTECTION PRACTICES AND SIGNIFICANT ASPECTS

**(1) Overcurrents.** They affect insulation life by temperature-rise and mechanical stresses. Protective devices are:

1. Winding temperature indication and alarm, allows full use of transformer overload capacity.

2. Oil temperature indication and alarm, winding temperature may be excessive.

3. Time delay overcurrent relays, may isolate too rapidly on large and too slowly on small overcurrent.

Differential relays do not respond to overcurrents other than internal short-circuit currents.

**(2) External Faults in Connected Systems.**

1. System protection to isolate faulty network, transformer impedance to limit through-put. Transformer overcurrent protection protects the transformer.

**(3) Internal Faults.**

1. Instantaneous O.C. and E.F. relays.

2. Buchholtz relay to give alarm and initiate isolation. However, this is too slow and not very sensitive.

3. Relays or fuses, high setting necessary for discrimination; restricted earth fault relays give full discrimination but respond only to earth fault.

4. Differential protection fully discriminative. It can be very fast and sensitive.

**(4) Overvoltages.** These affect insulation stress.

External,due to atmospheric causes:

1. Insulation coordination and grading of surge arresters.

2. Protective gaps to lower surge crest voltage, disturb service continuity.

3. Cable connections to overhead lines, lower steepness of surge wave-front.

Internal due to harmonics and/or resonance with system capacitance, switching overvoltages. Following aspects are important.

1. Delta-connected tertiary stabilising winding.

2. System insulation coordination.

(5) **Short-Circuits within Transformer.** Causes extensive damage due to high fault current. The transformer is disconnected by action of instantaneous overcurrent protection and differential protection.

(6) **Incipient faults below oil level.** These generate gases. Buchholz relay in installed between the tank and the conservator. It is a gas actuated relay which gives an alarm on incipient fault. For serious faults, the relay causes tripping of breakers.

The choice of protection for any given power transformer depends upon the number of factors, such as its size, importance, and whether it has on-load or off-load tap changer, whether it is operated single or in parallel, etc.

## 23.12 CHOICE OF PROTECTION SYSTEMS

The choice varies widely depending upon the size of transformer, rated voltage, cost of transformer and importance of location. The general guide-lines are given in Table 23.1 choice is decided on the basis of local conditions.

In very important substation, where a transformer shutdown is not desirable, complex, costly protection by advanced digital static relays and close monitoring is recommended.

For small distribution transformers, a shutdown can be taken for repairs. Therefore a costly, complex protection system is not preferred. A simple and cheaper protection system by HRC Fuses or over current and earth-fault relays is considered.

**Table 23.1**
**Power Transformer Protection**

| *Abnormal condition* | *Protection* | *Remarks* |
|---|---|---|
| 1. Incipient fault below oil level. | Buchholz relay (Gas actuated relay). | Buchholz relay for transformers of rating 500 kVA and above. |
| 2. Large internal faults phase-to-phase, phase-to-ground. | 1. Buchholz relay trips the circuit-breaker. | Buchholz relay slow and less sensitive. |

*(Contd...)*

| *Abnormal condition* | *Protection* | *Remarks* |
|---|---|---|
| | 2. Percentage differential protection. | Percentage differential protection for transformers above 5 MVA. |
| | 3. High speed high set over current relay. | |
| 3. Saturation of Magnetic circuit.* | 1. Overfluxing protection with voltage regulator. | For generator transformer and unit auxiliary transformer. |
| | 2. Over-voltage protection of busbars. | With busbar protection. |
| 4. Earth faults | 1. Differential Protection. | For transformers of and above 5 MVA |
| | Earth fault relay in residually connected circuit | (*a*) Instantaneous restricted E.F. relay. (*b*) Time lag E.F. relay. |
| 5. Through faults (External faults feeding through the transformer | 1. Graded time lag overcurrent relay. 2. HRC fuses, Drop-out fuses. | Protection of transformers. Small distribution transformers up to 500 kVA. |
| 6. Overloads | 1. Thermal over-load relays. 2. Temperature relays. 3. Overcurrent relays with inverse characteristic. | Fans started at certain temperature. Alarm and tripping actions later. |
| 7. —High voltage surges due lightning switching | 1. Horn gaps. | Not favoured for important transformer. |
| —Ferroresonance | 2. Surge aresters. | Recently ZnO Arresters introduced, preferred |

*V/F factor for generating transformer increases during manual starting. Therefore, overfluxing relay is connected with voltage regulator of generator unit.

**Table 23.2. Protection for Transformers of Various Ratings**

| | |
|---|---|
| Small, Distribution Transformers | Only HRC fuses for earth faults protection and phase fault protection. Over load protection generally not provided. |
| | For more important transformers of above 500 kVA. Over current relays are used. |
| | Instantaneous earth fault relays for transformers above 500 kVA. |

*(Contd...)*

| | |
|---|---|
| Transformer in important locations, rating 500 kVA above. | Restricted earth fault protection, over current protection, earth fault protection. Temperature Gauges, Buchholtz. |
| Transformer of about 5 MVA and above. | Differential protection, Restricted earth fault protection, Over current protection, Over fluxing protection, Buchholtz relays, sudden pressure relays, Temperature Gauges and temperature relays, Monitoring systems. Directional over current protections of parallel transformers. |

**Table 23.3**
**Protections of Associated Circuit Elements which may give Back-up Protection to Transformers.**

| | |
|---|---|
| Busbar protection | —Short-circuit protection and earth fault protection |
| | —Undervoltage protection |
| | —Overvoltage protection |
| | —Surge arresters |
| | —Over current protection |
| Line protection | —Short current-protection |
| | —Earth-fault protection |
| | —Surge arrester protection |
| | —Reverse power protection |
| Generator-Transformer Unit | —Unit differential protection<br>—Other protections |
| | —Overfluxing protection. |

## 23.13 BUCHHOLTZ RELAY (GAS ACTUATED RELAY)

**Principle.** The incipient faults in transformer tank below oil level actuate Buchholtz relay so as to give an alarm. The arc due to fault or sparks causes decomposition of transformer oil. The product of decomposition contain more than 70% of hydrogen gas, which being light, rises upwards and tries to go into the conservator. The Buchholtz relay is fitted in the pipe leading to the conservator. The gas gets collected in the upper portion of the Buchholtz relay, thereby the oil level in the Buchholtz relay drops down. The float, floating in the oil in the Buchholtz relay tilts down with the lowering oil level. While doing so the mercury switch attached to the float is closed and the mercury switch-closes the alarm circuit. Thereby the operators know that there is some incipient fault in the transformer. The transformer is disconnected as early as possible and the gas sample is tested. The testing of gas gives clue regarding the type of insulation failure. Buchholtz relay gives an alarm so that the transformer can be disconnected before the incipient fault grows into a serious one.

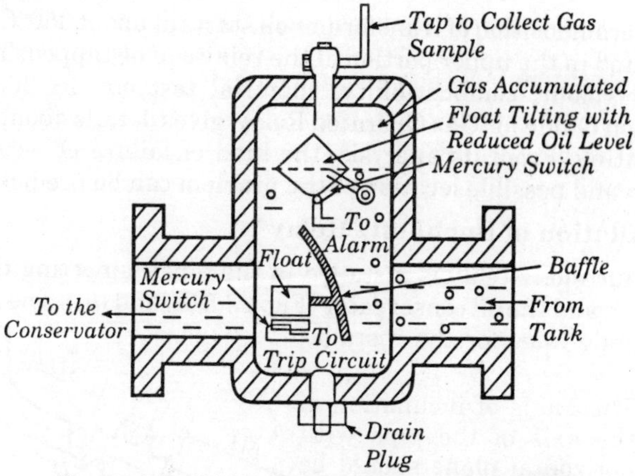


Fig. 23.4. Buchholtz Relay (Gas Operated Relay).

When serious short circuits occur in the transformer, the pressure in the tank increases. The oil rushes towards the conservator. While doing so it passes through the Buchholtz Relay. The baffles (plates) in the Buchholtz relay get pressed by the rushing oil. Thereby they close another switch which in turn closes the trip circuit of circuit-breaker. Thereby the transformer is removed from service.

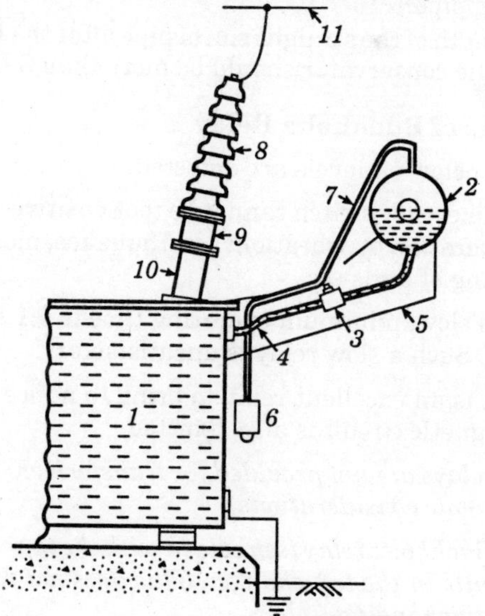


1. Tank
2. Conservator
3. Buchholtz
4. Pipe (1) to (2) and with (3)
5. Bracket for (2)
6. Breather filled with Silica-gel
7. Pipe between (2) and (6)
8. Bushing
9. CT mounted on (10)
10. Turret
11. Overhead flexible bus in substation.

Fig. 23.5 (*a*) Installation of Buchholtz Relay, Conservator, Breather, etc.

The decomposition of transformer oil starts at about 350°C. The gas accumulated in the upper portion of the relay can be tapped. The gas is tested for colour, combustibility, chemical test etc. IS 3668—1966 'Application Guide for Gas Operated Relay' gives details about analysis and mounting. From its analysis, the kind of failure or weakness in insulation and possible location of the problem can be predicted.

**Installation of Buchholtz Relay***

The Buchholtz relay is installed in the pipe connecting the transformer tank and the oil conservator [Fig. 23.5 (*a*) and (*b*)]. The following are the guide lines for the installation:

— The angle of inclination of the axis of the pipe with horizontal plane should be between 10° to 11°.

— The length of the straight run of the section of pipe between the relay and the transformer tank should be more than 5*D* (*D* is the internal diameter of the connecting pipe.)

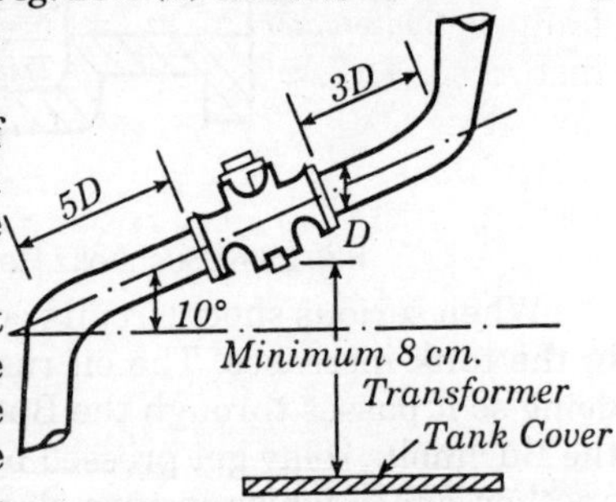


Fig. 23.5. (*b*) Insulation of Buchholtz Relay-pipe.

— The length of the straight run of pipe after the Buchholtz relay up to the conservator should be more than 3 *D*.

**Limitations of Buchholtz Relay**

Only faults below oil levels are detected.

Setting the mercury switch cannot be too sensitive otherwise there can be a false operation by vibrations, earthquakes, mechanical shocks to the pipe, sitting of birds etc.

The relay is slow, minimum operating time is 0.1 second, average time 0.2 second. Such a slow relay is unsatisfactory.

However, it is an excellent relay to bring to notice incipient fault. Sparking in magnetic circuit is also detected.

*Buchholtz relays are not provided for transformers below 500 kVA. (This is for economic considerations).*

*A separate Buchholtz relay is provided with the tap changer to detect the incipient faults in the tap-changer. This does not respond to small arcing during tap-changing.*

*The normal pipe bore diameter is recommended by Standards as 25 mm for transformers upto 100 kVA, 50 mm for between 1000 to 10,000 kVA and 80 mm for above 10,000 kVA.

## 23.14 BIASED DIFFERENTIAL PROTECTION. CIRCULATING CURRENT DIFFERENTIAL PROTECTION.

The *differential protection* responds to the vector difference between two similar quantities. In protection of transformer, CTs are connected at each end of the transformer. Refer Fig. 23.6. The CT secondaries are connected in star or delta and pilot wires are connected between the CTs of each end. The CT connections and CT ratios are such that currents fed into the pilot wires from both the ends are equal during normal conditions and for through faults. During the internal faults such as phase to phase or phase to ground, the balance is disturbed. The out-of-balance current ($\mathbf{I_1 — I_2}$) flows through the relay operating coils. To avoid unwanted operation on through faults, restraining bias coils are provided in series with pilot wires. The ampere-turns provided by bias coil or restraining coil are proportional to $\left(\frac{\mathbf{I_1 + I_2}}{2}\right)$.

The restraining torque increases through with current and relay does not operate due to the difference in CT ratios for high values of short circuit currents. High speed relay element is provided in the Differential System.

Fig. 23.6 (*a*) illustrates the principle and Fig. 23.6 (*b*) gives the operating characteristic. During normal operation the currents circulate in pilot wires without any differential current.

An additional restraining coil is provided in the relay. The restraining coil gets a current proportional to $(I_1 + I_2)/2$ whereas the operating coil gets the differential current $(I_1 - I_2)$.

The restraining current increases with through current. As a result, the relay is restrained against wrong operation which would have occurred due to CT inaccuracies, CT saturation, difference in pilot wire lengths, initial current inrush, short circuits beyond the transformer protection zone, etc.

The relay unit is instantaneous and is not provided with any time-lag.

The relay responds instantaneously to earth faults and phase-to-phase faults within the protected zone. The protected zone is between the CTs on the two sides.

Differential relay does not responds to:

— Turn-to-turn faults in the same winding.
— Overloads
— Faults beyond CTs
— Overvoltages
— Temperature rise.

### CT Connections and Pilot Wires

The CT connections should be such that the resultant currents fed into the pilot wires from either sides are displaced in phase by an angle equal to the phase shift between the primary and secondary currents. To get this arrangement, the following rules are followed:

— Secondaries of CT's on star connected side of power transformer are connected in delta [Fig. 23.9 (*a*)].

— Secondaries of CT's connected on delta side of power transformer are connected in star [Fig. 23.9 (*b*)]. With such arrangement, the phase displacement between currents gets cancelled with the phase displacement due to star/delta connections of CT secondaries, and the current fed to pilot wires from both sides are in phase during normal conditions.

— In both cases, three currents transformers are required at each side of the protected transformer. The connections of CT secondaries are such that during normal conditions and for external faults, no current should flow through the relay operating coils. Secondary current circulates through pilot wires and restraining coils.

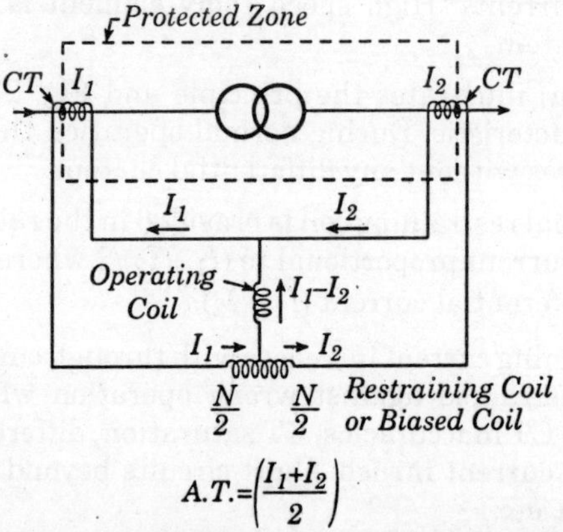


Fig. 23.6. Per cent differential relay. (Biased differential relay).

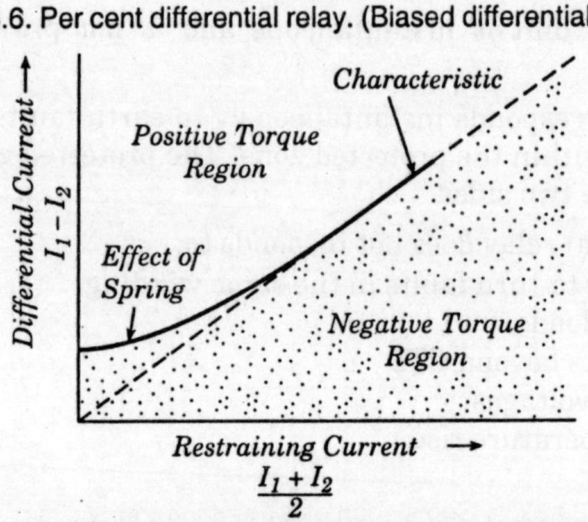


Fig. 23.7. Operating characteristic of differential relay.

Fig. 23.8 shows the complete circuit of circulating current differential protection.

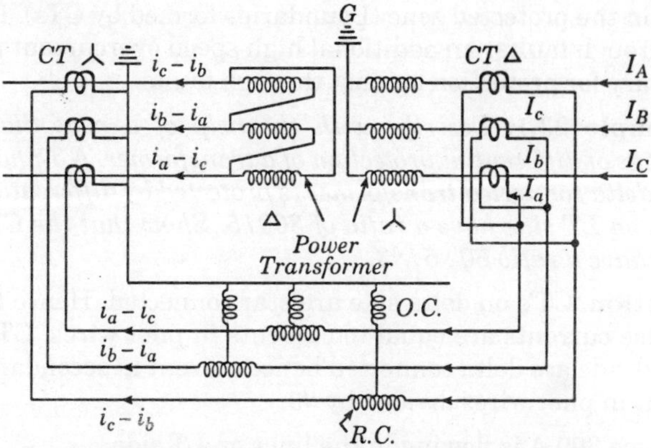

Fig. 23.8. Differential protection of delta star transformer.

**Protections provided.** The differential protection provides instantaneous protection (less than 0.1 seconds and no intentional time-delay) against.

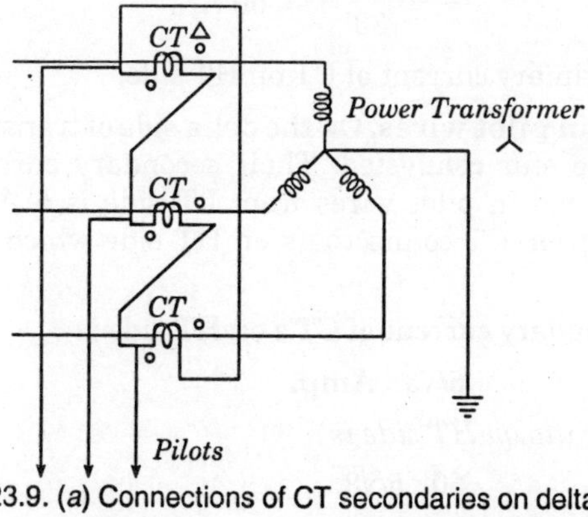

Fig. 23.9. (*a*) Connections of CT secondaries on delta side.

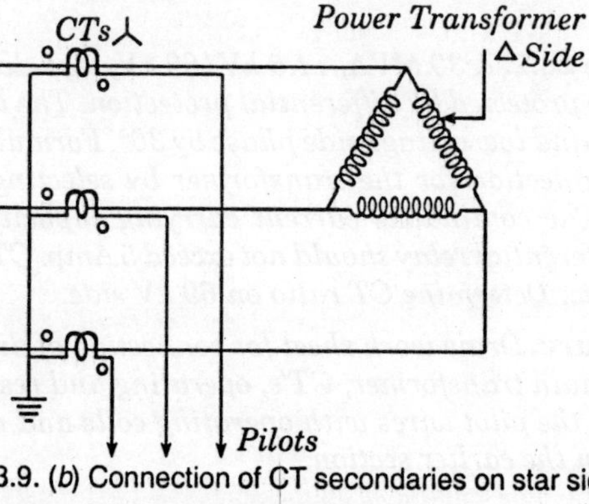

Fig. 23.9. (*b*) Connection of CT secondaries on star side.

— Phase to phase faults
— Phase to ground faults

within the protected zone (Boundaries formed by CTs). It *does not* detect through faults. An additional high speed overcurrent protection is necessary for protection against through faults.

**Example 23.1.** *Describe with the help of a neat diagram the connections of differential protection of a transformer. A 3-phase 33 / 6.6 kV star / delta connected transformer is protected by differential system. The CT's on LT side have a ratio of 300 / 5. Show that the CT's on HT side will have a ratio 60 : 5 / √3.*

**Solution.** CT's on delta side are star connected. Hence the secondary phase currents are equal to currents in pilot wires. CT's on star connected side are delta connected hence current in secondary is equal to current in pilot wires divided by $\sqrt{3}$.

Assume 300 A is flowing in the lines on LT side

$$\sqrt{3} \times 6.6 \times 300 = \sqrt{3} \times 33 \times I$$

$$I = \text{current in HT lines}$$

$$= \frac{6.6 \times 300}{33} = 60 \text{ A.}$$

which is primary current of CT on HT side.

**Currents in pilot wires.** On the delta side of transformers the CT secondaries are star connected. Their secondary current is 5 Amp. Hence current fed in pilot wires from LT side is 5 Amperes. Same current is fed from CT connections on HT side which are delta connected.

Hence secondary current of CT's on HT side is

$$5/\sqrt{3} \textbf{ Amp.}$$

*Hence CT ratio on HT side is*

$$60 : 5/\sqrt{3}.$$

**Example 23.2.** *A 30 MVA, 11.5 kV / 69 kV, star-delta power-transformer is to be protected by differential protection. The high voltage side phase lags behind low voltage side phase by 30°. Formulate the complete differential protection for the transformer by selecting CT ratios, CT connections. The continuous current carrying capacity of restraining coils of the differential relay should not exceed 5 Amp. CT ratio is 3000 / 5 on 11.5 kV side. Determine CT ratio on 69 kV side.*

***Procedure.** *Draw work sheet for connection of differential relays showing the main transformer, CT's, operating and restraining coils of CT's. Connect the pilot wires with operating coils and restraining coils as described in the earlier section.*

*Calculate the full load current of transformer on HV side and LV side. Select CT ratio.*

**Solution.** Calculate full load current for a 30 MVA, 11.5 kV star/69 kV delta power transformer.

**On 11.5 kV Side**

$$I_p = \frac{30000}{\sqrt{3} \times 11.5} = 1506 \text{ A.}$$

$$\text{CT ratio } \frac{3000}{5} = 600 \qquad \text{(Given)}$$

$$I_s = \frac{1506}{600} = 2.51 \text{ A.}$$

Since 11.5 kV side is star connected, CT secondaries will be delta connected. *Hence current fed into pilot wires* from 11.5 kV side CT secondaries is

$$\sqrt{3} \times 2.51 = 4.35 \text{ A.}$$

**On 69 kV Side**

$$I_p = \frac{30000}{\sqrt{3} \times 69} = 251 \text{ A.}$$

CT ratio to be selected

Current in secondary of CTs=Current in pilot wires in 69 kV side current in star connected CTs = 4.35 A

| | |
|---|---|
| Hence CT ratio on 69 kV side | = 251/4.35 = 57.7 |
| Select CT ratio | = 60 |
| Secondary current | = 5 A |
| Primary current | = 60 × 5 = 300 A |
| CT ratio on 69 kV side | = 300/5 (Final) **Ans.** |

**Phase Displacement**

There is an inherent phase displacement between vectors representing the voltage induced in high voltage winding and low voltage winding having same marking letter and corresponding neutral points, in case of star-delta transformers. Hence the load currents on H.V. side are displaced in phase with respect to load currents of corresponding phase on L.V. side. The power transformers are grouped according to the phase displacement, *e.g.*,

Group 1 : Star-star, Phase displacement = 0°

Group 2 : Star-star, Phase displacement = 180°

Group 3 : Delta-star, Phase displacement = Minus 30°

Group 4 : Delta-star, Phase displacement = Plus 30°

**(Refer. IS : 2026-1962)**

In the circulating current differential protection, the phase displacement in line currents on two sides, introduces phase difference in secondary currents of CT's on two sides.

By choosing appropriate CT ratios and by connecting CT secondaries on star connected side in delta (Fig. 23.9 *a*) and CT secondaries on delta connected side in star (Fig. 23.9 *b*). The currents fed into the pilot wires are equalised in phase and in magnitude.

The polarity of CT connections should be such that current fed into pilot wires from the two ends circulates in a closed current and do not oppose each other.

In case of D.D connected transformers also CTs are connected in λ on both sides to take care of zero sequence currents.

**Magnetizing current inrush.** When the transformer is energized, initially there is no induced e.m.f., the condition is similar to switching of an inductive circuit. The resistance being low, a large inrush of magnetizing currents take place. The magnitude of this current inrush can be several times that of load current. The magnitude of inrush currents depends on circuit conditions and voltage at the instant of switching. Maximum peak values equal to 6 to 8 times the rated current can occur.

The factors which influence the magnitude and duration of magnetizing current inrush include.

— size of transformer
— size of power system
— type of magnetic material in the core
— residual flux in the transformer before switching in
— how the transformer is energized.

The inrush currents decays rapidly for the first few cycles and then very slowly. Sometimes they take 4 to 6 seconds to subside. In high resistance path, the inrush currents decay more rapidly.

Inrush currents are seen only by the primary side CTs. They do not reflect on secondary side.

The inrush of magnetizing current will, therefore, cause the operation of differential protection system unless some special modification is done.

Formerly, the relay was provided with time lag of 0.2 second. By this time the inrush will vanish and relay does not trip unnecessary. But what about the protection of the transformer during this period?

While commissioning, one does not know whether there is a fault or not. Providing a time lag is therefore risky. There are several reported incidents that the relay was tripped due to internal fault during switching on for the first time. The engineers thought that the relay has

---

Ref. Switchgear and Protection, book by Khanna Publishers.

tripped due to magnetizing current inrush. They made the relay inoperative and switched on the transformer. Since there was a fault and relay was inoperative the transformer was damaged.

Next development was desensitizing the relay for a short period of 0.1 second during switching. After this time, the shunt across the relay coil is removed. This method also leads to the same danger mentioned above. The latest method adopted in transformer protection is *Harmonic current restraint.*

**Harmonic Restraint and Harmonic Blocking in Differential Protection**

The initial inrush of magnetizing currents have a high component of even and odd harmonics. Table 23.4 gives a typical analysis.

Harmonic component of short circuit currents is negligible. This principle is used for restraining the relay from operation during initial current inrush. The harmonic restrain differential relay remains sensitive to fault currents but does not operate due to magnetizing currents.

Table 23.4

| *Harmonic components in magnetizing current* | *Amplitude as a % of Fundamental* |
|---|---|
| 2nd | 63.0 |
| 3rd | 26.8 |
| 4th | 5.1 |
| 5th | 4.1 |
| 6th | 3.7 |
| 7th | 2.4 |

The operating coil of the relay receives fundamental component of current only. The restraining coil receives rectified sum of fundamental and harmonic component.

Thereby, inrush currents having more harmonic content give more restraining torque and the relay does not operate.

**Harmonic blocking.** The harmonic component of inrush current is used for blocking a separate blocking relay whose contacts are in series with the contacts of the differential relay. The blocking relay contains a 100 Hz blocking filter in operating coil and 50 Hz blocking filter in restraining coil. During inrush currents, the 2nd harmonic component is predominant and the blocking relay is blocked. The blocking relay contacts remain open.

During short circuits, 50 Hz component is predominant. Hence blocking relay operates and relay contact circuit is closed.

## Differential Protection of Three-Winding Transformer

The principle of differential protection can be adopted for three winding transformer. Fig. 23.9(*c*).

To achieve current balance in pilot wires, ratio adjusting (current balancing) transformers are used in some schemes. The relay unit used in such protection have two restraining coils and one operating coil.

The connections should be such that, during normal current and through faults, the restraining coils get restraining current.

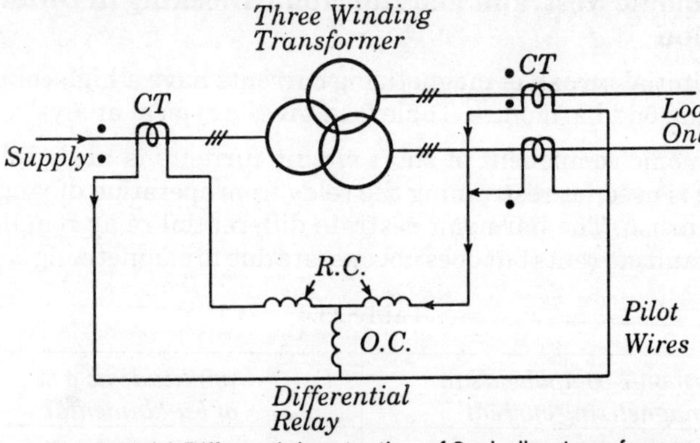


Fig. 23.9 (*c*) Differential protection of 3 winding transformer
R.C.=Restraining coil
O.C.=Operating coil.

**Differential Protection of Auto-transformers.** The principle of differential protection can be applied to three phase auto-transformers.

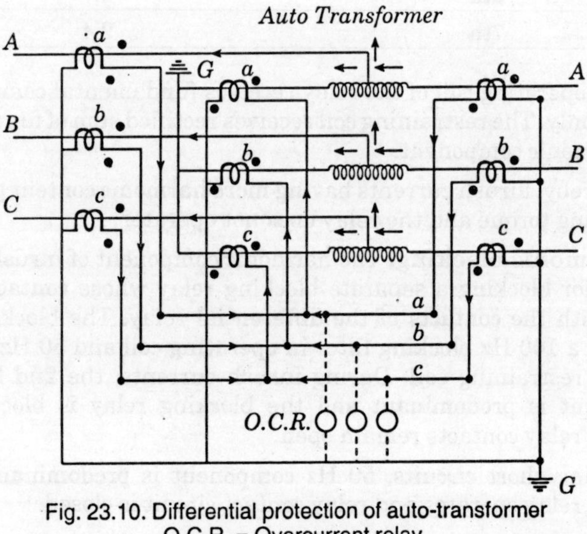


Fig. 23.10. Differential protection of auto-transformer
O.C.R. = Overcurrent relay.

The connections of CT secondaries differs for earth-fault protection alone and combined phase faults and earth fault protection.

Fig. 23.10 illustrate the scheme.

The Kirchhoff's current law states that the vector sum of component currents entering (or leaving) a point in electric circuit is zero. Thus the CT secondaries can be so connected that during normal condition and external faults, the vector sum of currents in relay operating coil is zero. During internal faults, this balance is disturbed and relay operates.

## 23.15 PROTECTION OF GENERATOR-TRANSFORMER UNIT AND MAIN TRANSFORMER

In thermal power stations, Generator is directly connected to the Main Transformer to form a unit. Presently, use of generator circuit breakers is also inversing.

The three large electrical equipments in the 'Unit' include:

— Generator
— Main Transformer
— Auxiliary Transformer.

The scheme of Generator transformer Unit Protection comprises the following:

— Primary Protection and back-up protection of generator
— Primary and back-up protection of main transformer
— Primary and back-up protection of unit auxiliary transformer (service transformer)
— Combined protection for generator and main transformer *i.e.*,

1. Generator differential protection.
2. Main transformer differential protection.
3. Unit auxiliary transformer differential protection.
4. Overall differential protection.
5. Generator protection.
6. Unit auxiliary transformer protection.
7. Main transformer protection.

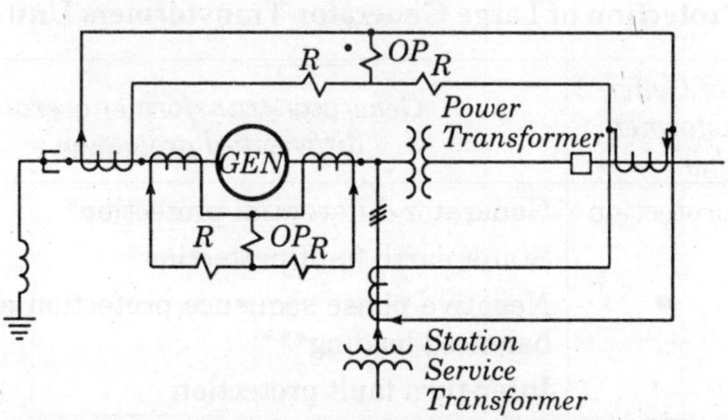


Fig. 23.11. Differential Protection of unit type Generator-Transformer systems. (Single line diagram) R-Restraining Coil OP-Operation Coil.

The scheme of Generator transformer Unit Protection comprises the following (Ref. Table 23.5).

- — Primary Protection and back-up protection of generator
- — Primary and back-up protection of main transformer
- — Primary and back-up protection of unit auxiliary transformer (service transformer)
- — Combined protection for generator and main transformer. The basic layout of generator connections has been illustrated in Fig. 23.2.

**Combined Differential Protection for Generator Main Transformer**

In the protection scheme, the differential protection generally covers the generator and main step-up transformer. Separate differential protections are provided for generator and for unit auxiliary transformers (Ref. Table 23.5).

The zone of combined differential protection may include generator stator winding, main step-up transformer and the bus-bar connections. A separate set of CT's is provided for this protection. The CT's at neutral side are star connected and CT's on HT side of main step-up transformer are delta connected. A third set of CT's is provided on the Teed-off to unit-auxiliary transformer. The CT's on Teed-off connection are necessary to compensate for the load current in Teed-off connection. These CT's are connected in parallel with the CT's of combined differential protection (Fig. 23.11).

Generally it is not practicable to cover the unit auxiliary transformer in the generator main transformer differential protection due to following reasons:

- — Zone of protection should not too large.
- — Burden on CT's increases.
- — Rating of unit auxiliary transformer is generally 1/10th main generator and it is difficult to select relay setting.

**Table 23.5**
**Protection of Large Generator-Transformers Unit**

| *Protection of Generator-Transformer together* | *Generator-transformer overall differential protection* |
|---|---|
| Generator protection | Generator differential protection*<br>Stator earth fault protection*<br>Negative phase sequence protection against-unbalanced loading***<br>Inter-turn fault protection<br>Reverse power protection |

*Contd...*

| *Protection of Generator-Transformer together* | *Generator-transformer overall differential protection* |
|---|---|
| | Field failure protection**<br>Rotor earth fault protection<br>Temperature sensors in slots***<br>Overcurrent relays in stator and rotor circuits<br>Surge arresters for generator overvoltage protection |
| Protection of unit-auxiliary transformer | Differential protection*<br>Restricted earth fault protection*<br>Buchholtz relay<br>Overcurrent protection<br>Winding and oil temperature sensors<br>Overfluxing Protection |
| Protection of main transformer | HV Overcurrent Protection*<br>HV Restricted earth fault Protection*<br>Buchholz relay<br>Winding and oil temperature sensors<br>Surge arresters on HV side<br>Overfluxing Protection |
| Preventive measures —Sound alarm on control panel | Continuous monitoring of outlet temperature of gaseous of liquid coolants<br>Flow monitors<br>Low boiler pressure alarm/trip<br>Lubrication oil failure<br>Emergency trip<br>Low vacuum |

## 23.16 EARTH-FAULT PROTECTION OF DISTRIBUTION TRANSFORMER FED THROUGH A 3-CORE CABLE BY ZERO SEQUENCE RELAY

Figure 23.12 shows the circuit diagram and Fig. 23.13 shows the details of connections. Fig. 23.14 illustrates the principle. In absence of an earth fault in the transformer or the supply cable, the current in the secondary of zero sequence CT is negligible. Under balanced load and without earth fault,

$$I_r \propto I_a + I_b + I_c \cong 0$$

*Trip generator c.b., close throttle valves, open field c.b., open auxiliary c.b.

**Close emergency throttle valves, main c.b. opend only after of interlock reverse power relay.

***Trip main circuit breaker only.

However during an earth fault on load side of zero sequence CT,

$$I_r = I_a + I_b + I_c = 3I_{a0}$$

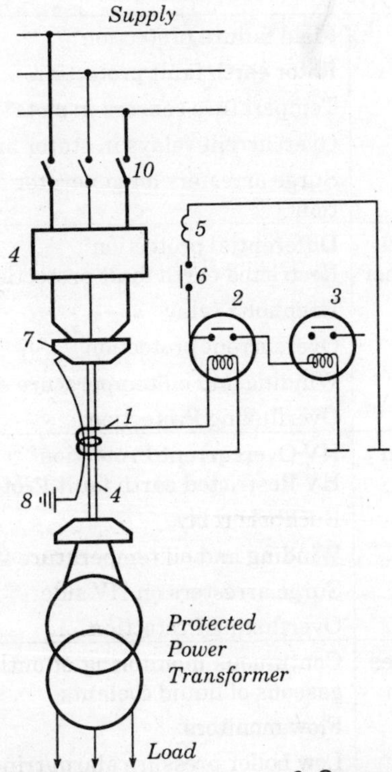


1. Core balance CT
2. Overcurrent relay
3. Time delay relay
4. Circuit-breaker
5. Trip coil of 4
6. Auxiliary switch
7. Cable terminal box
8. Earthing connection
9. Vacant
10. Isolator.

Fig.23.12. Circuit diagram of transformer protection by zero sequence relay core balance protection.

where $I_{a0}$ = zero sequence component. The relay connected on secondary side of Zero-sequence CT (core balance CT) operates. The earthing connection from cable pot to earth (4) should be passed through the eye of the CT core to eliminate error due to sheath currents $I_{sh}$.

[*Note.* During an earth fault $I_a + I_b = I_c \neq 0$, Flux $\phi$ in core $\neq 0$; Zero sequence current flows.]

## 23.17. OVERCURRENT PROTECTION AND EARTH FAULT PROTECTION OF POWER TRANSFORMERS

Overcurrent protection and earth fault protection is provided as a main protection for medium transformers where differential protection is *not* provided.

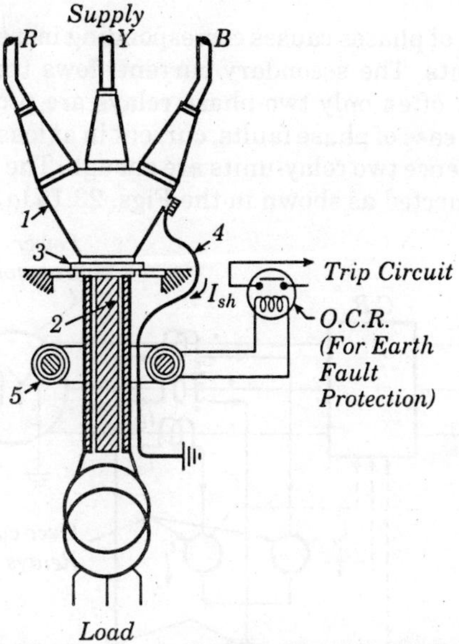


1. Cable terminal box
2. Sheath of 3 core cable connection to (1)
3. Insulator support for 1
4. Earthing connection passing through 5
5. Core balance CT.

Fig. 23.13. Details of connections of core balance protection. (connection 4 should pass through eye of 5 to avoid error due to sheath currents of 2).

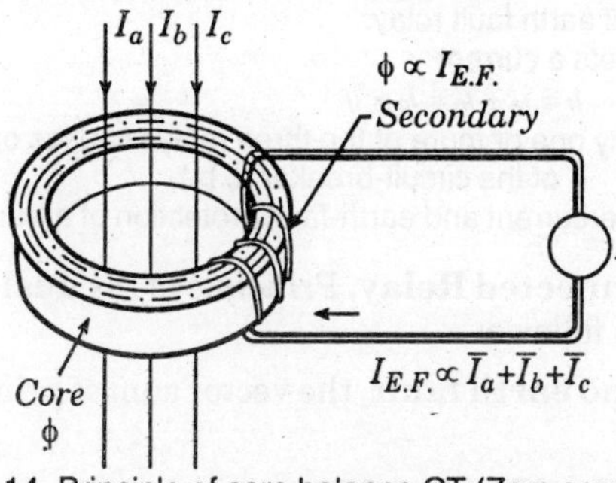


Fig. 23.14. Principle of core balance CT (Zero sequence CT) for earth fault protection.

Differential protection is generally uneconomical for power transformers below 1 MVA. In such cases, overcurrent protection is employed as main protection against phase faults. For transformers above 1 MVA, if differential protection is used as a main protection, overcurrent protection is used in addition, as a back-up for sustained through faults. Earth fault protection is provided in addition to phase fault protection.

**Combined Earth-fault and Phase-fault Protection.** It is convenient to incorporate phase-fault relays and earth-fault relay in a combined phase-fault and earth-fault protection Fig. 23.15. The increase in current of phases causes corresponding increase in respective secondary currents. The secondary current flows through respective relay-units. Very often only two-phase relays are provided instead of three, because in case of phase faults, current in at least any two phases must increase. Hence two relay-units are enough. The earth-fault relay is residually connected as shown in the Figs. 23.15 (*a*) and (*b*).

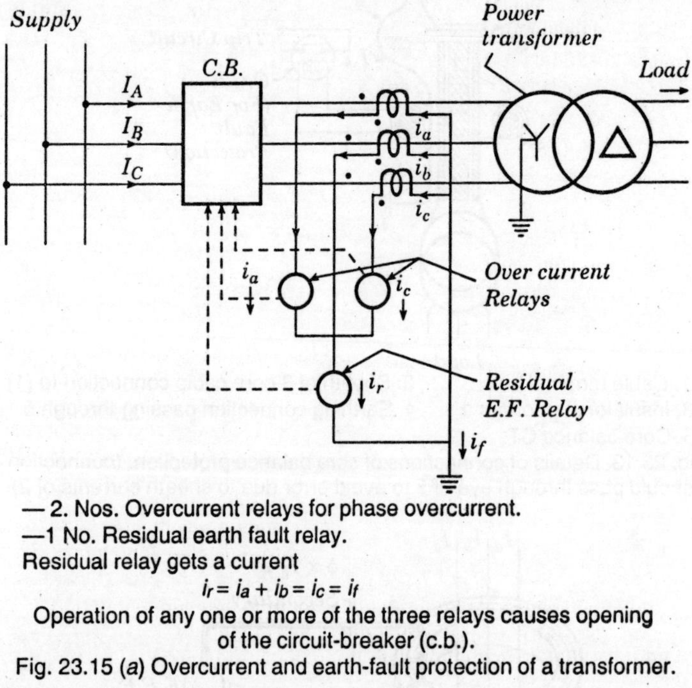


— 2. Nos. Overcurrent relays for phase overcurrent.
—1 No. Residual earth fault relay.
Residual relay gets a current

$$i_r = i_a + i_b = i_c = i_f$$

Operation of any one or more of the three relays causes opening of the circuit-breaker (c.b.).

Fig. 23.15 (*a*) Overcurrent and earth-fault protection of a transformer.

**Residually Connected Relay.** Principle of residual connection of CT secondaries is as follows:

**When there is no earth fault,** the vector sum of primary currents of CTs is zero. *i.e.,*

$$I_A + I_B + I_C = 0$$

Therefore vector sum of secondary currents of CTs is zero

$$i_a + i_b + i_c = 0$$

**If there is an earth fault** is any one or more primary side phases *A, B, C,* this balance is disturbed. The out-of balance secondary current $i_r$ flows through the residual circuit. This is called residual current $i_r$ given by

$$i_r = i_a + i_b + i_c$$

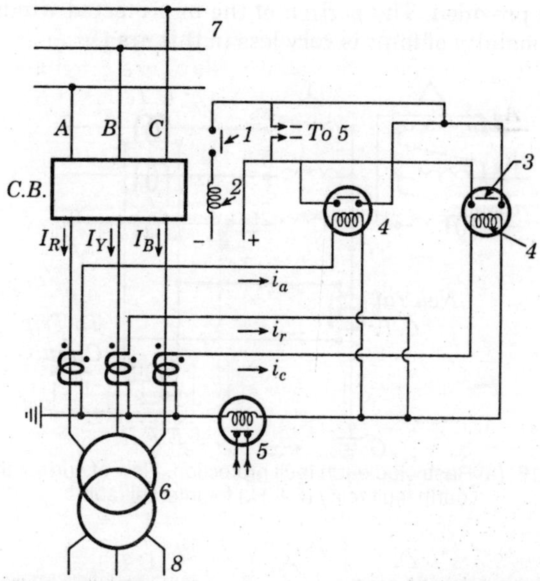


1. Auxiliary switch contacts
2. Trip coil of C.B.
3. O.C. relay contacts
4. O.C. relay coil
5. E.F. relay contacts (which should also close trip circuit-connections not shown)
6. Power transformer to be protected
7. Supply side busbars
8. Load side.

Fig. 23.15 (*b*) Connection details for OC and EF protection.

The earth fault relay is connected in the residual circuit. If $i_r$ is above threshold value, the relay operates. Hence it gives earth fault protection.

Residual relay can operate for earth faults beyond transformer protection zone. Hence for some transformers restricted earth fault relay is preferred.

## 23.18 RESTRICTED EARTH FAULT PROTECTION COMBINED WITH OVERCURRENT PROTECTION

Transformer earth fault protection should not operate for faults beyond the transformer protection zone. This is ensured by the restricted earth fault protection. Fig. 23.16 ($a$) shows the connections of CTs and flow of actuating current through the relay coil during internal earth faults.

During external faults, no current flows through the earth fault relay [Fig. 23.16 ($b$)]. When differential protection is provided, what is the used of providing REF protection? Differential protection does not cover the full winding. Some portion of the winding remain unprotecting because of basing. REF protection covers more portion of the winding.

Hence, it is provided. The portion of the unprotected winding is very less and probabilty of fault is very less in this area.

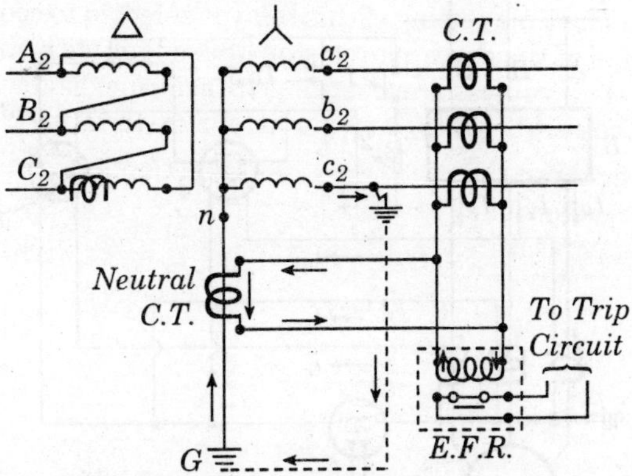


Fig. 23.16. (*a*) Restricted earth fault protection. Flow of current through earth fault relay (E.F.R.) for internal fault.

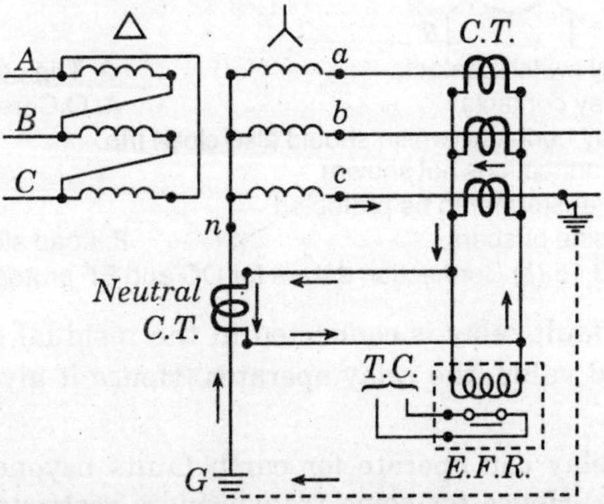


Fig. 23.16. (*b*) Relay does not operate for external earth fault.

## 23.19 PROTECTION OF RECTIFIER TRANSFORMER

Rectifier transformer windings have AC side terminals and rectifier side terminals. The characteristics of load on the transformer depends upon the type of connections and the load on the rectifier itself. Static protection system having overload characteristics closely above rectifier normal load characteristic is preferred.

— Buchholtz relay

— Overload protection. Very inverse or extremely inverse over-current relays for protection of rectifier transformer.

— Faults in rectifier:

(*a*) HRC fuses for protection of rectifier

(*b*) Overload relays on primary side of transformer as a back-up.

## 23.20 PROTECTION OF GROUNDING TRANSFORMER

(Fig. 23.17)

The CT secondaries are delta connected. An overcurrent relay with time lag (1) is inserted in the delta. The zero sequence currents circulate in this delta. The time setting of this relay is selected to coordinate with thermal rating of the earthing resistor (if used) or with time setting of other earth fault relays. The earthing transformer is disconnected by opening the circuit-breaker, on a persistent earth fault.

The other three relays (2) provide protection against faults in the grounding transformer. These are instantaneous relays, set between 25 to 50 per cent of continuous current-rating of grounding transformer.

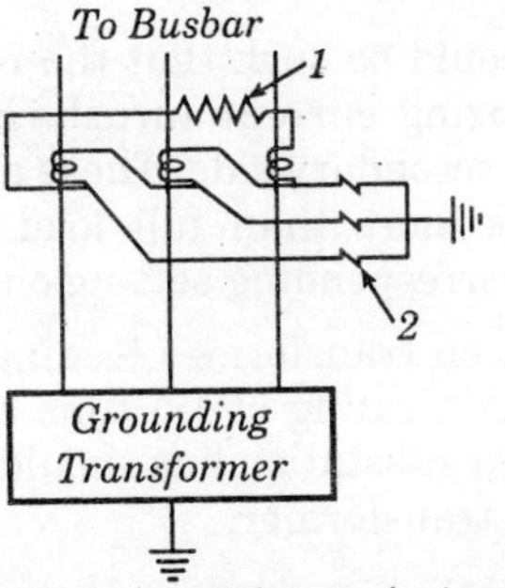


1. Relay providing delayed protection against external faults.
2. Relays providing protection against internal faults.

Fig. 23.17. Protection of a grounding transformer

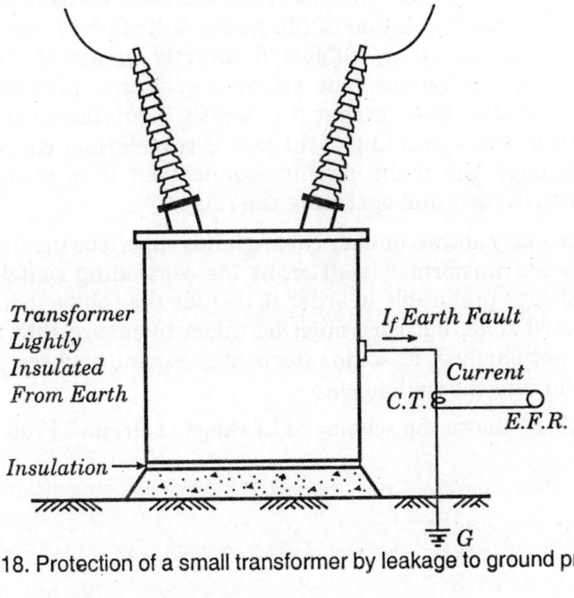


Fig. 23.18. Protection of a small transformer by leakage to ground principle.

Buchholtz relay is also used. Earth fault protection is provided by residually connected relay (not shown in the figure).

## 23.21 PROTECTION OF ARC FURNACE TRANSFORMERS

Furnace transformers are subjected to repeated short circuits during the melting process. Inverse time overcurrent relays are provided for both phase faults and earth faults.

Induction type inverse overcurrent-relays arc used for short circuit and overcurrent protection of Furnance Transformer. The setting is such that for current of the order 300 to 400 per cent of full load current, faster tripping is obtained. For overcurrent of the order of 150 per cent, enough time delay provide so that the relay does not trip during normal current surges.

The time delay should be such that the relay should not operate during initial magnetizing current inrush. High speed overcurrent relays are provided on secondary side. These are set to pick up instantaneously for currents more than full load secondary current but slightly less than the corresponding setting on relays on HT side.

**Note.** The substation transformer feeding the arc furnace transformer should have MVA rating of 1.5 time arc furnace transformer rating. The fault level at substation bus should be at least 80 times the MVA rating of furnace transformer.

## 23.22 LEAKAGE-TO GROUND PROTECTION FOR SMALL TRANSFORMERS

Leakage-to-frame protection is a very simple system suitable for small power transformers. It consists of a current transformer slipped over the earthing-connection of the power transformer casing, with a single-overcurrent, relay connected directly across the secondary through a setting-resistor. The power-transformer is mounted on a concrete or similar base so that it is lightly insulated from earth. An earth-fault in either winding of the power-transformer causes current to flow through the main earthing-connection, thus energising the current transformer and operating the relay.

The primary and secondary cable-glands should be insulated either at the power-transformer itself or, at the controlling switchgear; the latter is always preferable in order to include the cables themselves in the protected zone, but care must be taken to ensure that the cable-sheath is not earthed, at some intermediate point between the power transformer and the switchgear.

Fig. 23.18 shows the scheme of Leakage of Ground Protection.

## 23.23 OVERLOAD PROTECTION

The permissible overload and their duration depends upon the type of cooling and insulation class of transformer. Higher over-loads are permissible for a shorter duration.

**Permissible Duration of Overload**

| Overload% : | 125 | 150 | 175 | 200 | 300 |
|---|---|---|---|---|---|
| Duration (Minutes) : | 125 | 45 | 15 | 10 | 1 |

Hence for sub-station transformers, overload protection is generally arranged to initiate alarm. In unattended stations, over-load protection is arranged to trip the breaker after a requisite time delay.

The transformers with utility equipment are prone to sudden overloads. (Furnace transformers, transformers for motors). The overload protection for such transformers is also given requisite time delay.

While selecting the overcurrent protection of transformer, the following aspects need consideration:

— Magnetizing current inrush: Inverse relays are not affected by the current inrush as they have enough time lag. Instantaneous overcurrent relays should be high set to avoid maloperation.

— The fault currents on primary side and secondary side of power transformers are different for phase-phase faults. Lower value should be selected for setting of overcurrent relays.

— Primary full load current should be considered while setting the overcurrent relay.

— The setting of inverse overcurrent relay is generally 125 per cent of transformer rating to take care of normal overloads. Enough time delay should be provided as per the application.

— The setting of instantaneous overcurrent relay on primary side should be more than asymmetrical value of fault current for 3-phase fault on secondary side of transformer. This setting is generally adequate to take care of magnetizing current inrush.

— Same set of current transformers should not be used for differential protection and overcurrent protection.

— For small distribution transformers below 500 kVA, over-current protection may be provided simply by the fuses on H.V. side, as such transformers are installed in unattended sub-stations, circuit breakers and relays are not provided.

## 23.24 PROTECTION OF TRANSFORMERS IN PARALLEL

The following protections are necessary in case of transformers operating in parallel:

— Overcurrent protection

— Earth-fault protection

— Directional overcurrent and directional earth fault relays on secondary side to prevent the healthy section feeding into faulty section.

Fig. 23.19 illustrates the scheme. The feedback is prevented by operation of directional overcurrent relay of faster setting. By operation of this directional overcurrent relay, the corresponding CBs are quickly tripped and the feedback from healthy section is prevented. The current coils of d.o.c. relay and o.c. relay on secondary side may be connected in series.

## 23.25 EXTERNAL SHORT-CURRENT (THROUGH FAULTS)

As per the various standards on distribution transformers, power transformers and regulating transformers, the transformer should be capable of withstanding the mechanical and thermal stresses caused by external short-circuits with following conditions:

— the magnitude of r.m.s. value of symmetrical current in any winding does not exceed 25 times the base current in that winding.

— the duration of external short-circuit is limited to time period indicated in the Table 23.6. (intermediate values obtained by interpolation)

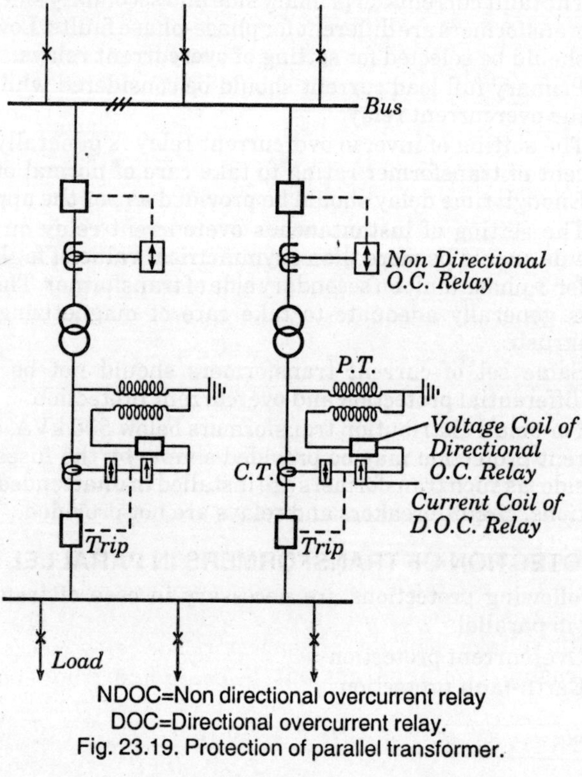


NDOC=Non directional overcurrent relay
DOC=Directional overcurrent relay.
Fig. 23.19. Protection of parallel transformer.

Table 23.6*
Permissible Duration of Through Fault Currents

| *R.M.S. Value of Symmetrical current in a winding (Times base current)* | *Time period in seconds* | *Transformer % Impedance* |
|---|---|---|
| 25 | 2 | 4 |
| 20 | 3 | 5 |
| 16.6 | 4 | 6 |
| 14.4 | 5 | 7 |

Through faults are not detected by differential protection of transformer. If the through faults persist of longer duration, the transformer gets damaged by thermal stresses. The through faults are detected by overcurrent relays, overcurrent relays with undervoltage blocking, zero sequence protection, negative sequence protection.

The setting of overcurrent protection for through faults covers transformer, station busbar and portion of a transmission line. The overcurrent protection for through faults provides back-up protection to differential protection for internal faults.

The overcurrent due to faults are accompanied by voltage drop, negative phase sequence currents. Earth faults are accompanied by zero phase sequence currents.

## 23.26 OVER-FLUXING PROTECTION

(Fig. 23.20)

The flux density '$B$' in transformer core is proportional to $V/f$.($B \propto V/f$). Power transformers are designed to withstand ($V_n/f_n \times 1.1$) continuously, where $V_n$ is normal highest r.m.s. voltage and $f_n$ is standard frequency. Core design is such that higher $V/f$ causes higher core loss and core heating. The capability for higher $V/f$ values is limited to a few minutes.

| $\dfrac{v/f}{v_n/f_n}$ | 1.1 | 1.2 | 1.25 | 1.3 | 1.4 |
|---|---|---|---|---|---|
| Duration of Withstand limit (minutes) | Continuous | 2 | 1 | 0.5 | 0 |

High $V/f$ can occur in Generator Transformers and Unit-auxiliary transformers if full excitation is applied to generator before full synchronous speed is reached. $V/f$ relay (Volts/Hertz) relay is provided in the automatic voltage regulator of generator. The relay blocks and prevents increasing excitation current before rated frequency is

*Ref. ANSI C 57 12.00–1968.

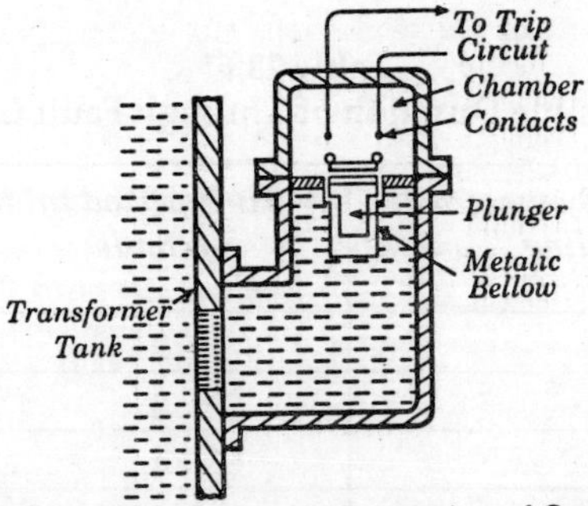


Fig. 23.20. Characteristic of Over Fluxing Protection of Generator Transformer and Unit Auxiliary Transformer (Dark Line) Dashed line shows the design value. $V/f$ = Actual Volts per Hz ratio $V_n/f_n$ = Normal Volts per Hz ratio. For the ratio $(V/f)/(V_n/f_n)$ above the dark line, the overfluxing relay operates.

reached. Hence overfluxing protection is provided with generator transformers. It may not be needed for network transformer.*

In *V/f* relay, resistance and capacitance are connected to secondary of *VT*. The voltage drop across the resistance is a function of *V/f*, where *V* is the line to earth voltage and *f* is frequency. This voltage is fed to the 'Volts per Hertz' relay.

The magnetic flux in the transformer core is a function of *V/f*. Hence the relay senses magnetic flux condition. Overfluxing relay is provided with enough time lag. Overfluxing relay is not necessary for substation transformers. In substations, frequency relays are provided for load shedding at distribution levels.

## 23.27 SAFETY DEVICES AND FITMENTS WITH POWER TRANSFORMERS

The electrical protection systems can sense the abnormal conditions by measuring current/voltage. Besides electrical relays, a power transformer can be provided with the following safety and monitoring devices.

- — Fluid level gauge
- — vacuum gauge
- — pressure/vacuum switch
- — sudden pressure relay
- — pressure relief value
- — fluid temperature indicator
- — hot spot temperature indicator
- — gas temperature indicator
- — combustible limit relays etc.
- — conservator and
- — Breather

*Overvoltage relays should be provided in bus-bar protection to avoid transformer failure due to over-fluxing.

The application of these devices depends upon the type of transformer.

**Table 23.7**
**Protective and Safety Devices for Power Transformers**

| Device | *Type of Transformer* | | |
|---|---|---|---|
| | *Oil filled* | *Dry Ventilated* | *Dry Sealed* |
| 1. Fluid level gauge | * | | |
| 2. Vacuum gauge | * | | * |
| 3. Pressure relief valve | * | | |
| 4. Sudden pressure relay (rate of rise pressure relay) | * | | |
| 5. Pressure/vacuum switch | * | | * |
| 6. Fluid temperature indicator | * | | |
| 7. Hot spot temperature | * | * | * |
| 8. Gas temperature indicator | | | * |

**Rate-of-Rise Pressure Relay.** (Fig. 23.20). Rate of rise pressure relay does not respond to static pressure. It responds only to rate of rise pressure resulting from internal arcing. The main pressure sensing element is a pressure actuated micro-switch mounted inside a metallic below. Static pressures do not squeeze the bellow. Dynamic pressure squeeze the bellow and operate the micro-switch.

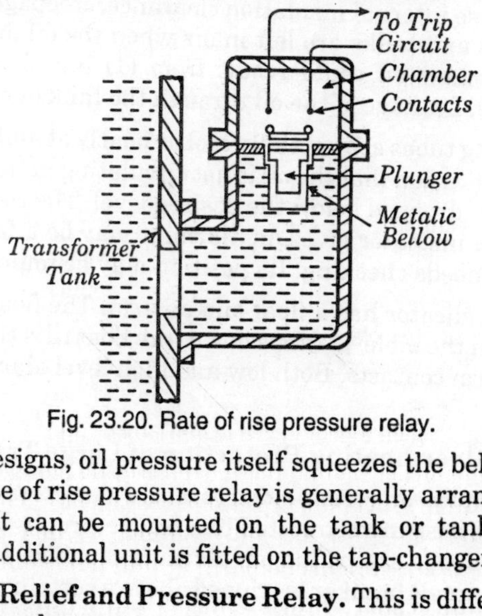


Fig. 23.20. Rate of rise pressure relay.

In some designs, oil pressure itself squeezes the bellow filled with special oil. Rate of rise pressure relay is generally arranged to trip the transformer. It can be mounted on the tank or tank cover of the transformer. Additional unit is fitted on the tap-changer cover.

**Pressure Relief and Pressure Relay.** This is different from rate of rise pressure relay.

Pressure relay and pressure relief device is mounted on transformer tank. It releases gas pressure to the atmosphere during.

— high overload peaks
— Prolonged overloads
— arcing faults within oil.

The pressure relief valve is spring loaded and has a seal-seat. (Fig. 23.21*a*). When the pressure inside the tank increases above a certain valve, the force on movable sub-assembly exceeds the spring force and the valve operates (Fig. 23.21*b*). The alarm contacts are closed. After release of pressure the valve may be manually reset (not shown in figure).

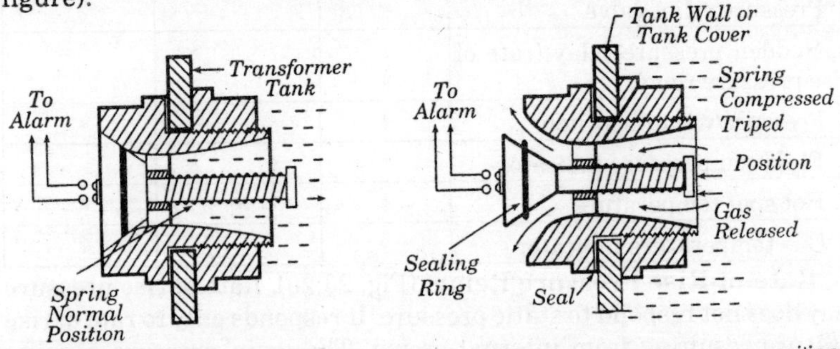


(*a*) Pressure relay-sealed position. (*b*) Pressure relay-open position.

Fig. 23.21

**Low Oil Level Fluid Level Gauge.** Low oil level is a harmful condition because internal insulation clearance, creepage etc., between leads, bushings and tanks are left in air when the oil drops below the specified level. Low oil could result from (1) initial mistake to fill sufficient oil (2). Leakage of the oil through the tank or cooling system.

If the cooling tubes are partially cool or nearly at ambient temperature, it is an indication that the oil is not circulating in the cooling tubes and oil level has dropped below the desired level. The cooling tubes are warm and level indicator gives an alarm, it may be a false alarm and level indicator needs checking. Its position may be improper.

The level indicator has a float and an arm. The float is suspended in the oil. When the oil level drops down, the float tilts the arm thereby closing the alarm contacts. Both low and high level alarm contacts are provided.

### Thermal Over-heating Protection of Large Transformers

Thermocouples or resistor temperature detectors are kept near each winding. These are connected to a bridge circuit. When temperature increases above safe value, an alarm is sounded. If measures are not taken, the circuit breaker is tripped above a certain set value. Some typical settings for oil temperatures are as follows:

Switch on fans : 60°C
Alarm : 90°C
Trip : 110°C

**Oil Temperature Indicator Thermometer.** An oil thermometer, which is similar for all oil-filled transformers, can be considered as a partially effective protective device when equipped with alarm contacts connected to give remote warning of abnormally high oil temperature. Its location is such that it naturally monitors the hottest fluid that exists in the transformers. The same thermometer is often used to start fan motors on transformers equipped with automatic air blast to increase the name plate kVA rating.

The thermometer cannot be relied upon as a fault-detecting device. Transformer oil has a much longer time constant than the windings themselves, hence in many times more sluggish in response to changes in loading losses which directly affect winding temperature, Thus the thermometer's temperature warning will vary between too conservative or too pessimistic, depending on the rate and direction of change in loading.

Alarm contacts used in conjunction with a oil thermometer are adjustable but are typically set in a sequence that brings on fans at a liquid temperature of 60°C and actuate a switch contact should the temperature reach 90°C. For a typical design at 30°C ambient, the fans are brought into operation at about 90 per cent rated load whereas the alarm is given at about 130 per cent rated load. These percentages will vary with each manufacture for each design and are dependent upon the actual ambient temperature. The percentage loadings will be somewhat lower at ambients above 30°C and higher at ambient under 30°C.

Switches are usually capable of readjustment through a range of + 10°C, thus allowing compensation for some of the factors mentioned above.

**Hot Spot Thermometer.** (Winding Temperature Device) The thermometer bulb is located in a pocket near the winding. The bulb is surrounded by non-circulating oil. The bulb is also heated by a small heater connected across CT secondary. Thereby the heat given to the bulb is a function of load current as well as the temperature of oil near winding. The device is matched with heating curve of the transformer winding.

The reading of hot spot thermometer is rated to actual thermal condition of transformer than that of oil temperature indicator. However due to the necessity of closely matching its artificial bimetal gradient to the theoretically hottest spot winding gradient, a short time heavy overload will often register higher on the dial than a long-time light overload.

## Summary

*The abnormal conditions* include: Overloads, excessive temperatures, overvoltages, overfluxing, under-voltage, failure in cooling system, failure in auxiliary voltage supply, etc.

*Faults* include: internal faults and through faults.

*Faults* are phase to phase or phase to ground faults or open circuit faults.

Transformers are provided with protective relaying and protective fitments.

The choice depends on size of transformer and probable abnormal conditions. Most common conditions are (1) Overload (2) Earth fault (3) Phase faults (4) Through faults.

# 24

# Power Transformers in Substations and Generating Stations

Basic aspects regarding the transformer substation layouts, neutral earthing, surge protection etc., have been described.

The layout of main transformer, auxiliary transformer and station service transformer in thermal power station switchgards have been illustrated.

**Part A. The Power Transformers in Switchyards**

## 24.1. TRANSFORMER SUBSTATION

In power transmission network, there are generally two types of substation, *the switching station* and the *transformer station.* Spare capacity for lines is not extensive due to the fact that it is very costly. Spare transformer capacity, however, is more common.

Transformer substation has two/three/four voltage levels *e.g.,* 400 kV/220 kV/132 kV/33 kV, with power transformers of appropriate kV and kVA ratings between consecutive voltage levels.

The main purpose of an outdoor transformer station switch-yard is to control the power flow, that is to connect it from incoming lines, often *via* busbars, to either outgoing lines in the same voltage system or *via* power transformers to plants having other service voltages, etc.

## 24.2. SINGLE LINE DIAGRAMS OF SWITCHYARDS

The single-line diagram can be regarded as one of the important documents. It gives a clear picture of the switching possibility, the functional location of apparatus, etc. The most costly and important equipment in the switchyard is the power transformer. A single line diagram indicates the equipment by their symbols. The main circuit, busbars, c.b., isolators, CTs, VTs, SAs, Neutral Earths etc., are indicated.

## 24.3. BUSBAR LAYOUTS FOR A TRANSFORMER SUBSTATION

The layout drawing gives the physical (geometrical) picture of the switchyard. It shows the type solution, for example, the busbar arrangement (if any), whether a high or a low built design has been chosen, etc.

Almost every transformer station will sooner or later be subject to modification and extension. Clarity and flexibility, therefore, have high priority in transformer station design.

Some usual bus arrangements used for transformer substations include the following:

— Without busbar
— Single busbar
— Main-and transfer busbars
— Duplicate busbars
— Duplicate and transfer busbar
— Double circuit-breaker
— Breaker and a half

Two arrangements are described here*.

**Duplicate Busbar Scheme** (Fig. 24.1). The system has two identical (symmetrical) busbars, *i.e.*, one busbar can be used as a complete stand-by for the other. This will guarantee uninterrupted operation in the event of a busbar fault.

The duplicate busbar system is one of the more common types. It is considered suitable for interconnected systems with high demands on switching flexibility.

**Main Busbar with Transfer Busbar** (Fig. 24.2). The transfer busbar (*T*) is chiefly used for facilitating maintenance of a line circuit breaker with uninterrupted service. The line will then be connected to the transfer busbar through the bus coupler. The bus coupler circuit breaker served as line breaker during the maintenance period.

As there is usually spare transformer capacity in a switchyard having more than one busbar, power transformer bays are seldom equipped for connection to the transfer bus.

The line circuit breaker, especially for voltage systems of 132 kV and above, is often provided for high-speed auto-reclosing. Line faults are to about 80% arc faults. Therefore, if the line can be de-energized for about 0.3 second, the arc will be extinguished and the line re-closed with hardly any noticeable service interruption.

For the power transformer, with its more direct and shorter connection to the busbar, auto-reclosing is usually not considered necessary. The purpose of the transformer circuit breaker is to disconnect the transformer upon internal faults as well as upon bus-bar faults.

## 24.4. ROADS AND ROUTE FOR TRANSPORTATION

The internal roads and approach roads should be wide enough and should have large radius of curves at bends to facilitate movement of road trailers and unloading of transformer tanks.

---

*Refer : Electrical Substation Practice, Book Khanna Tech, Publications.

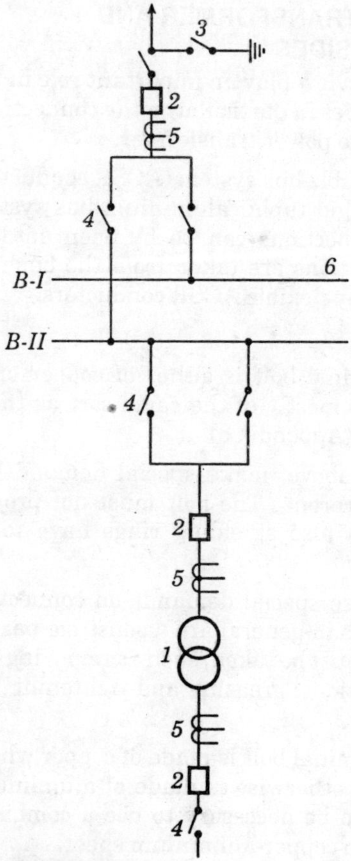


1. Transformers
2. Circuit-breakers
3. Earthing switches
4. Isolators
5. CTs
6. Busbars.
B-I. Main bus
B-II. Duplicate bus.

Fig. 24.1. Transformer connections in duplicated busbar scheme.

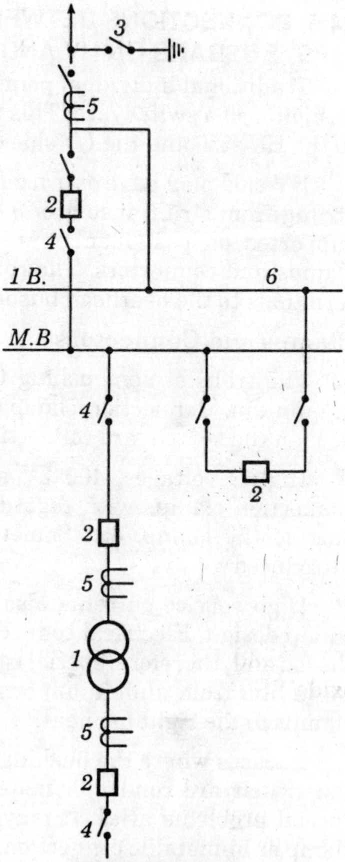


B.M. = Main bus
T.B. = Transfer bus.

Fig. 24.2. Transformer connections in main and transfer bus scheme.

The routes of the transportation roads in relation to power transformer locations is an essential factor in the switchyard layout. For example, a transportation road in front of the transformers gives a different appearance to the switchyard than what would be the case with the road behind the transformers.

The layout will be different if the HV and LV connections are made from opposite sides or if both are made from the same side.

## 24.5 CONNECTIONS BETWEEN TRANSFORMER AND BUSBARS ON HV AND LV SIDES

Traditional/individual points of view play an important role in the designing of a switchyard. This applies in particular to the connections to the HV side and the LV side of the power transformer.

HV side may have *overhead* flexible bus system (ACSR conductors strung from strain insulators) or rigid tublar aluminium bus system supported on post insulators. Connections can be by open outdoor clamps and connectors. The connections are taken from the bushing terminals to the overhead busbars by flexible ACSR conductors.

### Clamps and Connectors

The transformer bushing terminal bolt is either of copper or of aluminium. Connection clamps are mostly of the same sort as those used in the switchyard connections (Appendix 8).

Higher voltages, 400 kV and above, make special demands on connection clamps with regard to corona. The bolt must not project outside the clamp. etc. Sometimes also shielding rings have to be introduced.

High service currents also make special demands on connection clamp design. Electrical connections in general are a sensitive part of the job and, therefore, special care must be taken, such as removing the oxide film from aluminium connections, greasing and tightening the clamps to the right moment.

In cases where the bushing terminal bolt is made of copper whilst the switchyard conductor material otherwise is made of aluminium, special problems arise. It may then be necessary to use a combined clamp or bi-metallic connection with copper-aluminium sheet.

**Cables.** As the conductor on the LV side, both oil-impregnated cables and PEX cables are being used. Naturally these connections have different appearances. The PEX cable can be connected more or less directly to the bushing terminal. Usually copper or aluminium bars are connected to the bushings and then the cable is connected to the bars.

## 24.6 EARTHING GRID

To limit step and touch voltages to safe values and to control the influence of short-circuit currents on the telecommunication installations, a strong earthing network is required. This applies especially, to effectively earthed systems with high earth-fault currents.

The earthing grid itself, in this case, is generally made of 40 mm dia mild-steel rods buried to a depth of 0.5 meter. The effectively earthed power transformer neutral points are connected to the earth grid by means of *duplicate 120 mm*$^2$ *copper wires*. The earth wire from the transformer housing is connected directly to the earth grid.

To further decrease the earthing resistance, the earth grid is often connected to a number of so called earthing pits.

**Equipment Earthing.** Tank is connected to the earthing grid by two earthing conductors.

**Neutral Earthing.** Following alternatives are available:

— *Effective (solid) Earthing.*

Effectively earthed neutrals shall be connected to the earth grid with duplicate earth wires, each being dimensioned for the earth-fault current in the station.

However if earth fault currents are unacceptably high, solid earthing is not preferred. In such cases impedance earthing is preferred.

— *Impedance Earthing.*

One of the most common ways of impedance earthing in networks under the 145 kV level is the arc-suppression coil earthing system. Usually in this application also a neutral resistor is connected in parallel to the coil (neutral reactor) to protect the neutral points against overvoltages.

In the event of an earth-fault in the system, the neutral resistor is disconnected instantaneously and gives the neutral reactor of the system the opportunity to extinguish the arc. After 1.5 to 2 seconds, the resistor is reclosed.

## 24.7 SURGE ARRESTER PROTECTION

Surge arrester are connected near the transformer terminals between phase and ground. The surge arresters provide protection against voltage surges due to lightning and switching. Details are covered in Chapter 25.

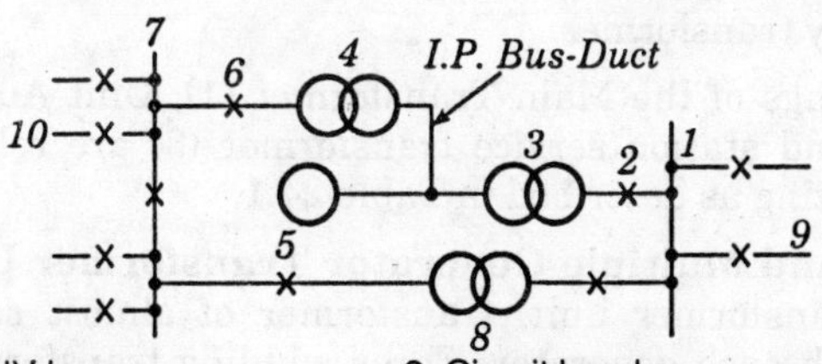


1. EHV bus
2. Circuit breaker
3. Main transformer
4. Auxiliary transformer of unit
5. Generator
6. Auxiliary C.B.
7. Auxiliary bus
8. Station service transformer
9. EHV yard
10. Auxiliary system.

Fig. 24.3. Single line diagram-Unit system of generator-transformer connections in thermal power stations (Refer Fig. 24.3 for scheme without 8).

## 24.8 POWER TRANSFORMER CONNECTIONS IN THE UNIT SYSTEM OF GENERATOR CONNECTIONS

In thermal power stations, generators of following ratings are commonly used.

| | |
|---|---|
| 60 MW | 11.8 kV |
| 120 MW | 13.8 kV |
| 500 MW | 22 kV |

Generator unit upto 500 MW have been installed in India.

Unit concept is universally adopted.

In units systems, the generator is connected to its transformer to form a unit. The unit is connected to HV bus through a HV circuit-breaker (Fig. 24.4). The use of generator circuit breaker is also being common as of today.

The station service auxiliaries and power required for starting is supplied at a lower voltage can be taken from H.V. Bus. But in that case another transformer having high ratio is necessary to step down the voltage to station service supply voltage.

The principle of unit connection which is now used extensively in thermal power stations, require a station service transformer which is separate from the unit and which obtains its supply from the high voltage system (Fig. 24.4) or from a separate network. Once the generator has reached synchronous speed, it is switched into network by means of high voltage circuit-breaker in unit lay out. The station services supply is immediately switched over from the station service transformer to the unit auxiliary transformer which branches off between the main transformer and generator. Many times, station load is divided on 50%-50% basis between station service transformer and unit auxiliary transformer.

The ratings of the Main Transformer (1), Unit Auxiliary Transformer (2) and station service transformer (3) are related with the generator rating as described in Table 24.1.

**Single and Multiple Generator Transformer Unit.** In single generator-transformer unit, transformer of almost same rating is provided with each generator. Three winding transformers are used where two values of high voltages are required.

In multiple generator-Transformer unit, two or three generators are connected to a generator bus. Transformer is connected between the generator bus and high voltage bus (Fig. 24.5). Such scheme can be adopted in small hydro-electric power stations.

However, this scheme is not very common in modern thermal stations due to high capacity of modern turbo-generator (500 MW and above).

When two secondary voltage levels are to be fed, three winding transformer is used (Fig. 24.4).

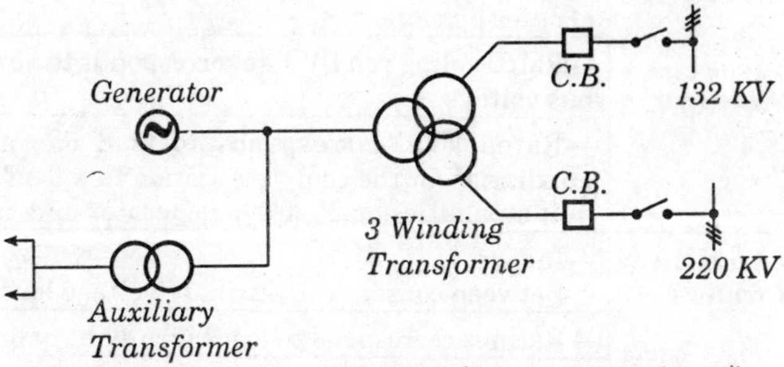


Fig. 24.4. Connections of 3-W transformer to generator unit.

**Table 24.1**
**Summary of Power Transformers in a Generating Station**

| *Title* | *Particulars* |
|---|---|
| **1. Main transformer of Generator Unit** | —One for each generator unit<br>—Rated voltage on LV side corresponds to rated generator voltage |
| | —Rated voltage on HV side corresponds to rated voltage of HV Bus. |
| | —Rated 3 phase rating corresponds to the rating of generator unit.<br>—Usually outdoor type. |
| | —LV terminals connected to generator terminals via isolated phase bus system. |
| | —HV terminals connected to outdoor busbars by flexible ACSR coductors via overhead flexible bus. |
| | **Alternatively.** To $SF_6$ Gas insulated. Substation (GIS) via $SF_6$ gas insulated bus system. |
| | —Purpose to feed power to the grid. |
| **2. Unit Auxiliary Transformer** | —HV side at rated voltage corresponding to generator rated voltage. |
| | —LV side corresponds to rated voltage corresponding to auxiliary bus voltage *e.g.*, 6.6 kV. |
| | —Rated kVA app. 15% of generator rating. |
| | —Usually outdoor. |
| | —Purpose to feed power to generator auxiliaries of that unit. |
| | —One for each unit. |

*(Contd...)*

| | |
|---|---|
| **3. Station Service Transformer** | —One for each group of generators<br>—Rated voltage HV: corresponding to rated voltage of outer busbars. |
| | —Rated voltage on LV side corresponds to auxiliary bus voltage |
| | —Rated kVA corresponds to load of common auxiliaries for the complete station flux load of one unit auxiliaries, app. 20% of generator unit rating. |
| **4. Auxiliary Transformers** | —Indoor<br>—Between consecutive auxiliary voltage levels |
| | —Ratings correspond to loads on auxiliary bus. |
| | —Usually dry type preferred. |

**Switching sequence for starting.** Before starting the generator unit, the boiler auxiliaries, turbine auxiliaries and other auxiliaries are started by taking power from main bus *via* station service transformer.

The generator is brought to rated speed, frequency without giving excitation current and building-up terminal voltage. After reaching synchronous speed, the excitation is gradually increased to till terminal voltage reaches rated value.

After establishing synchronous conditions of voltage, frequency on phase angle, phase sequence between generator and main bus, the generator transformer unit is synchronised with bus-bar by closing main circuit breaker.

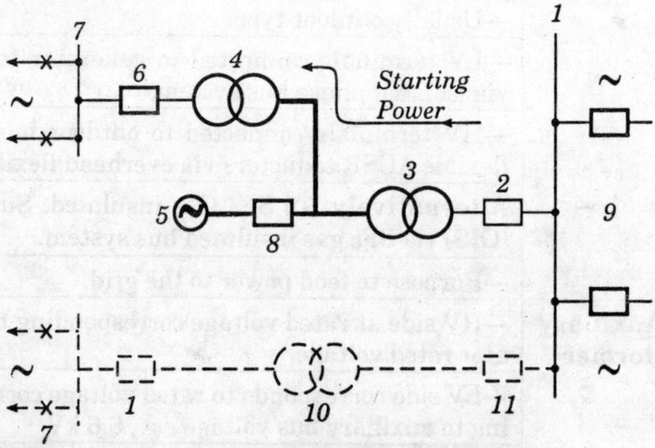


1. EHV bus
2. Circuit breaker (EHV)
3. Main transformer.
4. Auxiliary transformer.
5. Generator.
6. Auxiliary C.B.
7. Auxiliary bus.
8. Generator circuit-breaker.
9. EHV-outdoor switchyard.

**Note.** Station Service Transformer (10) is eliminated shown by dashed.

Fig. 24.5. Scheme of unit generator transformer connection with use of *Generator Circuit-Breaker* (8)

The input to turbine is gradually increased. Later, the unit auxiliary circuit breaker is closed. The generator starts feeding its unit auxiliaries. The load on the generator gradually increased by increasing input to turbine.

## 24.9 SCHEME EMPLOYING GENERATOR CIRCUIT-BREAKERS

In the conventional unit scheme of thermal power stations, the starting power is taken from the grid *via* the station service transformer. Therefore station service transformer is essential for starting the first generator unit. For high unit capacity power station, another layout shown in Fig. 24.5 is preferred in which the station Service Transformer is eliminated. Starting power is taken from the main bus via the main transformer, with the generator circuit-breaker open. After bringing-up the speed and then excitation, the generator unit is synchronised with the main bus by closing the generator circuit-breaker.

After synchronising, the generator unit supplies power to the main bus and auxiliaries. Thus the use of generator circuit breaker eliminates the need of a separate high capacity station service transformer.

## 24.10 AUXILIARY POWER TRANSFORMERS

The auxiliaries in the thermal power station include (1) generator auxiliaries (2) boiler auxiliaries (3) station service auxiliaries. The auxiliaries include motors of various ratings, pumps, conveyer belt systems, auxiliary lighting supply, etc. The power required by auxiliaries ranges from 6 to 8 per cent of station MW rating. In 200 MW unit class power station, the auxiliaries are at 6.6 kV and 415 V. In 500 MW unit class power station the auxiliaries are at 11 kV, 6.6 kV, 3.3 kV and 415 V. The auxiliary system has two/three or four voltage levels.

Auxiliary transformers are necessary between each consecutive voltage level. Fig. 24.6 shows a scheme of Auxiliary supply system in a thermal power station. Usually the auxiliaries for a unit are categories as unit auxiliaries. Auxiliaries common to the station are called station auxiliaries.

Auxiliary loads of various voltage ratings are supplied from auxiliary transformers at respective voltage level bus. *Indoor Dry type power transformers are preferred.*

The auxiliaries connected with the unit are called "Unit Auxiliaries", and are supplied by generator *via* the unit auxiliary transformer.

The auxiliary of the station common to all the units are called Station Auxiliaries. These are fed through the station service transformer.

## 24.11. ISOLATED PHASE BUS-DUCTS FOR CONNECTION BETWEEN GENERATOR AND MAIN TRANSFORMER AND UNIT AUXILIARY TRANSFORMER

The conductors between generator, unit transformer, unit-auxiliary, transformer are enclosed in hollow, tubular aluminium enclosures. These enclosures are continuous and are connected in star and earthed at each end. The conductors are supported on epoxy

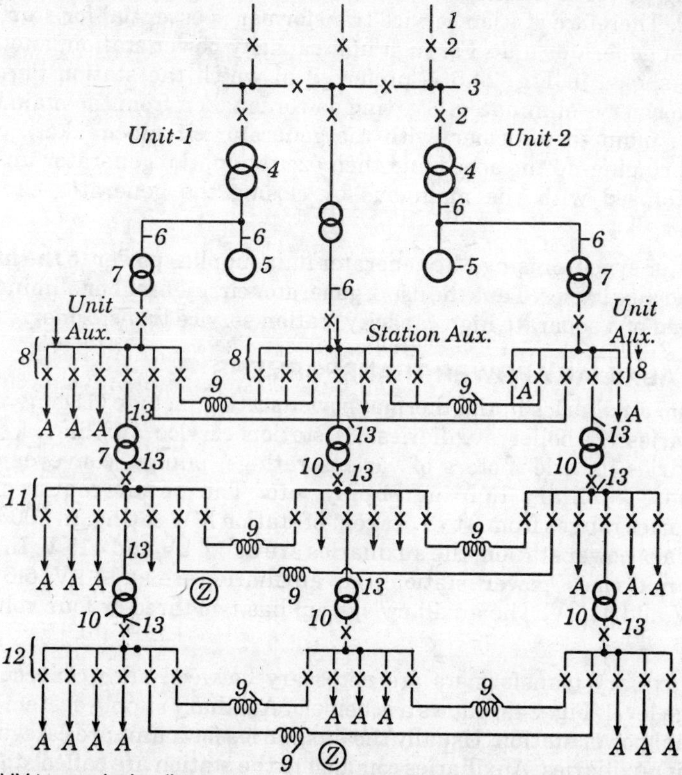


1. EHV transmission line.
2. EHV switchgear generally outdoor.
3. EHV bus, generally outdoor, sectionalised.
4. Main transformer of generator transformer unit (outdoor) Rating almost equal to that of 5.
5. Turbogenerator (indoor).
6. Isolated phase buses, continuous type.
7. Unit auxiliary transformer (rating about 6 to 8%, that of 5).
8. Auxiliary switchgear (say 12 kV).
9. Current limiting reactors, switched during emergency or starting.
10. Auxiliary transformers.
11. Auxiliary switchgear (say 7.2 kV).
12. Auxiliary switchgear (415 V).
13. Metal enclosed conductor.

*A* = To auxiliary equipment *X* = Switchgear

*Z* = These interconnections are generally omitted.

Fig. 24.6. Transformers in thermal power stations. Connections with generator unit and busbars.

insulators within the enclosures. Such a system is called Isolated Phases Bus System and is used in all thermal power stations having generator rating of 60 MW and above. The eddy currents induced in the enclosures flow longitudinally in the enclosures. Thereby they produce associated magnetic field outside and within the enclosures. This field interacts with the field of the main conductors. As a result, in case of isolated phase bus system, the magnetic field is substantially reduced, outside the enclosures. Thereby electrodynamic forces between main conductors during external short circuits are substantially reduced. (To about 5% of their value without enclosures). Therefore, the insulator design is simplified. Heat is produced in the encloures as well as in the conductors. Upto normal current ratings of 18 kA, air natural cooling may suffice. Between 18 kA and about 25 kA normal current rating forced air cooling is preferred. Above 25 kA conductors are water cooled.

## Summary

The transformers are the costly and large equipment in Main Substations and Generating stations. The associated Circuit-Breakers and layout aspects must be well known to the transformer designers. Alternatives are available to simplify and economise the layouts and satisfying future requirements of load growth.

# 25

# Surge Arrester Protection

In 1950's the failure rate of power transformers was high as surge arrester technology was not yet developed. Today, superior surge arresters and understanding of transient phenomena permit satisfactory surge protection of power transformers. Methods of connections have been described along with principles of application.

## 25.1 INTRODUCTION

Transformers are subjected to overvoltages. The insulation level of a transformer should be coordinated with the protective levels of the surge arresters and spark gaps. Neutral earthing at each voltage level is necessary from the considerations of overvoltages and earth fault protection.

The insulation requirements of power transformer are determined by the transient overvoltages. Overvoltages surges or transients are voltage waves of magnitude higher than normal value and these persist for a short duration. Overvoltages transients occur due to several causes, Important causes are:

— Lightning surges
— Switching surges
— Faults, Arcing grounds
— Travelling Waves etc.

Overvoltage transient last for a few tens/hundreds microseconds. They are characterised by high rate of rise, high peak value and are dangerous for insulation.

## 25.2. LIGHTNING SURGES

These originate with a lightning stroke on overhead line or outdoor equipment. The wave travels along conductors and reaches the substations. The lightning waves are represented by standard lightning impulse wave (1/50 microseconds wave). The *external clearances* of the electrical installations are designed to withstand lightning surges of specified magnitudes. Each electrical equipment is designed and tested to withstand certain specified lightning impulse voltage wave.

To protect the electrical transmission lines and equipment from the hazards of lightning strokes, the following measures are taken:

— Use of overhead shielding wires (earth wires) for overhead transmission lines, substations and all outdoor installations.
— Use of lightning masts

— Use of spark-gaps (now not preferred)
— Use of Surge Arresters (These were formerly called lightning arresters).
— Use of neutral earthing, equipment earthing.

For each transformer winding, the following characteristics are specified:

— Rated voltage
— Basic Lightning impulse withstand voltage level (BIL)
— Switching Impulse Withstand Level (SIWL)
— Minimum external clearances and creepage distances
— Power frequency 1 minute withstand level.

The basic lightning impulse withstand levels for each power frequency voltage level are recommended by the IEC and IS. These values are generally based on the recommendations of the CIGRE working groups, statistical data, analystic studies and experiments. *The basic impulse voltage levels of various equipment at each voltage level are coordinated with reference to the protective characteristic of surge arresters.*

**For Voltage upto 275 kV** rms phase to phase, the design of line insulation and apparatus insulation with respect to clearances, voltage stress on surface of conductors, insulation design, impulse withstand level etc., are generally based on the required basic lightning impulse withstand level.

## 25.3 SWITCHING SURGES

These occur with the opening or closing of circuit breakers under various switching operations due to the transient exchange of energy between the inductance and capacitance.

**In medium voltage range** (1 kV to 36 kV) switching surges occurring during following duties of circuit breakers are significant:

— Low inductive current switching current chopping
— Capacitor switching-restrikes
— Motor switching, current chopping
— Switching of inrush currents of transformers
— Switching of reactor currents.

The following measures are taken to reduce the switching surges:

— Use of suitable circuit-breaters such as VCB, $SF_6$ CB having pre-insersion resistors while closing and opening resistors while opening.
— Use of RC surge suppressors
— Use of Surge Arresters.

**In EHV range** (245 kV and above), the type of circuit breaker and transient overvoltage occur during various switching duties like opening of unloaded transmission line, clearing short line fault, closing of unloaded line, autoreclosing, switching of inrush currents of transformers, reactor switching etc. The standard specify the maximum limit of peak transient switching voltage.

**In EHV range,** the transformer-insulation design is influenced by the requirement of switching impulse withstand levels.

The standard switching impulse test (250 μs/2500 μs) is specified for power transformer windings rated 220 kV and above. *A transformer is tested for switching impulse test, full lightning impulse wave and chopped lightning impulse wave as per the relevant standards.*

The transformer insulation is stressed severely due to switching surges and lightning surges. *End-turn insulation* is stressed severely during the initial rise of impulse wave. After a few micro-seconds, the transient oscillations occur within the winding and peak voltage is higher in the middle. This phenomenon is described in Chapter 12.

## 25.4 SURGE ARRESTERS

By installing suitable surge arresters near transformer terminals, the transformer windings are protected from lightning and switching voltage surges.

Surge Arresters are generally connected between phase and earth in substations, distribution system, near transformer terminals and near terminals of large rotating machines. In isolated neutral systems, a surge arrester is connected between transformer star neutral and ground to give a path for surge to discharge to the ground.

The surge arresters discharge the excessive *surge voltages to ground and protect the transformer insulation system.* The transformer insulation level can be selected economically.

The *gapped, silicon carbide surge arresters* are being used since 1950's. During 1960's *gap-less Zinc Oxide Arresters* (ZnO Arresters) of superior characteristics have been developed. ZnO arresters have higher energy absorption capability and superior *V/I* characteristic. They are being increasingly preferred.

## 25.5 INSULATION COORDINATION

The protective level of the surge arresters is selected such that these are below the impulse withstand level of the protected transformer. This is called insulation coordination. At each voltage level, there are several electrical apparatus and a few surge arresters. **The insulation levels of various apparatus at each voltage level are selected with reference to the protective characteristics of surge arrester at that voltage level.** Also the various consecutive voltage levels are linked with each other through transformers. Hence the insulation levels of various voltage levels need coordination. Thus the insulation coordination deal with:

— Selection of voltage levels.
— Selection of impulse withstand levels.

— Selection of protective levels for each voltage levels.
— Coordination of protective levels between consecutive voltage levels.
— Choice of protective level characteristics of surge arrester with respect to basic impulse withstand level of the apparatus at each voltage level.

Power—frequency overvoltages last for a long period of the order of seconds or minutes. Transient overvoltages discussed in this Chapter last for a few tens/hundreds of microseconds.

## 25.6. PER-UNIT OVERVOLTAGE, SWITCHING OVERVOLTAGE FACTOR

Let $U_n$ = Rated normal line-to-line rms system voltage

$U_m$ = Rated highest system voltage, rms line-to-line

$\frac{\sqrt{2}U_n}{\sqrt{3}}$ = Peak of rms voltage, phase to ground for nominal system voltage

$\frac{\sqrt{2}U_m}{\sqrt{3}}$ = Peak of rms voltage, phase to ground for highest system voltage

Then any voltage higher than the voltage $(\sqrt{2}/\sqrt{3})\,U_m$ is called *overvoltage*.

$(\sqrt{2}/\sqrt{3})\,U_m$ is considered as 1 per unit. Overvoltage is specified in terms of per unit by overvoltage factor $K$

$$K = \frac{U}{(\sqrt{2}/\sqrt{3})\,U_m}$$

where $U$ = Actual peak overvoltage.

$K$ = Per-unit overvoltage or overvoltage factor.

Any voltage higher than the voltage $(\sqrt{2}/\sqrt{3})\,U_m$ is called *overvoltage*.

The insulation of transformers should withstand the over voltages occurring due to internal and external causes.

The over-voltages are of two categories:

— Power frequency voltages
— Impulse voltage surges due to lightning and switching.

The sustained power-frequency over-voltages occur due to regulation, Ferranti effect, etc.

The type of earthing (solid/resistance) influences the magnitude of over-voltages. For system above 145 kV the magnitude of internal over-voltages is significant. These are caused by switching transients and travelling waves.

Impulse voltage surges occur due to lightning and switching. The wave lasts for some hundreds of microseconds.

The performance of insulation is verified by power-frequency tests and impulse tests.

The surge arresters (lightning arresters) divert the transient over-voltages to earth and protect the transformer insulation.

## 25.7 TERMS AND DEFINITIONS

1. **Normal system voltage** of system is the r.m.s. line to line voltage by which the system is design *e.g.*, 11 kV, 220 kV etc. ($U_n$).

2. **The highest system voltage** of the system is the highest r.m.s. voltage (line to line) which can be sustained under normal operating condition at any point on the system ($U_m$).

*e.g.*, 12 kV, 245 kV corresponding to above values.

3. **Overvoltage.** The time dependent voltage between phase and earth of value exceeding $(\sqrt{2}/\sqrt{3})U_m$.

4. **Switching Overvoltage Factor K**

$$K = \frac{\text{Peak switching overvoltage}}{\text{Peak voltage of highest system voltage}}$$

$$= U/\sqrt{2/3}\,U_m$$

5. **Coefficient of Earthing** at a given location of the system

$$= \frac{\text{Highest rms voltage of healthy line to earth}}{\text{Line to line rms voltage}}$$

6. **Effectively Earthed System.** It is a power system whose coefficient of earthing is below 80 per cent.

7. **Non-effectively Earthed System.** Whose coefficient of earthing is above 80 per cent.

8. **Lightning Arrester or Surge Arrester.** A device connected between phase and earth or between phases to protect electrical equipment from transient overvoltages and to limit the duration and amplitude of the follow current.

## 25.8 PROTECTIVE RATIO, PROTECTIVE MARGIN

The protection of equipment against impulse voltages waves by means of Surge arresters is expressed in term of Protective Margin.

$$\text{Protective Ratio} = \frac{\text{Impulse Withstand Level of Equipment}}{\text{Protective level of Surge Arrester}}$$

Separate protective ratio is specified for

(1) Lightning Impulse wave.

(2) Switching Impulse wave.

Protective Ratios are usually above 1.2.

Protective Margin = Equipment Withstand Level–Protective level of Surge Arrester

Protective Margin may be expressed in terms of per cent of Equipment Withstand level.

Protective levels are different for Lightning Impulse and Switching Level.

$$\frac{\text{Lightning Impulse withstand level}}{\text{Switching Impulse withstand level}} = 1.2$$

## 25.9 INSULATION COORDINATION

To determine the appropriate insulation levels ot transformers, to select the settings of coordinating gaps, to select the correct lightning arresters at various locations etc., the electrical engineer needs knowledge of insulation coordination.

The IEC-71-1 definition of Insulation Coordination is as follows:

*Insulation co-ordination is correlation of insulation of equipment and circuit with the characteristic of protective devices such that the insulation is protected from overvoltages.*

While designing a transformer, the overvoltages should be given due consideration. Insulation coordination consists of steps taken to prevent damage to electrical equipment due to overvoltages and to localize the flashovers to points to discharge over-voltages at such points, where they will cause minimum damage. This is achieved by correlating the insulation strengths of line, switchgear, transformer, machines etc. and the characteristics of the overvoltage protective devices such as rod gaps, surge arresters: **The impulse withstand level of system components and the impulse protective level to protective devices are correlated.**

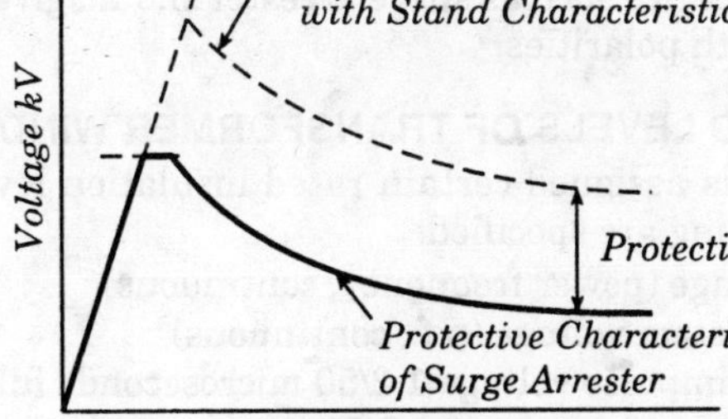


Fig. 25.1. Principle of surge arrester application for transformer protection. (Protective characteristic of the surge arrester is below the withstand characteristic of the transformer with certain margin).

The protective level of surge arrester should be lower than the withstand level of the transformer. (Ref. Fig. 25.1).

## 25.10 INSULATION LEVEL OF A TRANSFORMER WINDING

'Basic Insulation Level' is a term which includes the following characteristics of a transformer winding

— Power frequency voltage withstand level.
— Lightning impulse voltage withstand level for full wave and for chopped wave.
— Switching impulse voltage withstand level (applicable to transformer windings rated 220 kV and above. Each winding (HV, LV, MV) will have its own insulation level. It covers bushings tap-changer, windings etc., at the respective level.

These withstand levels together characterise the insulation level of a transformer winding.

The withstand level of a transformer is given in terms of impulse voltage wave of specified amplitude, duration and waveshape drawn on voltage/time characteristic.

Time is in microseconds and voltage in kV. The word 'impulse' is used for test wave and surge for actual wave in the electrical network.

The following points should be kept in mind while coordinating the insulation in the sub-station:

1. Surge arrester should have the lower protective level. The residual voltage should be less than transformer insulation strength.

2. The voltage time withstand curves of individual equipment should be taken into account. To withstand voltage characteristic of all the equipment, there should lie above the protective characteristic of surge arrester, with enough margin.

3. The insulation coordination should be based on worst possible atmospheric condition as regards rain, humidity, pollution and snow. Standards (such as IEC) should be followed.

The protective device such as surge arrester should give protection against waves of both polarities.

## 25.11. WITHSTAND LEVELS OF TRANSFORMER WINDINGS

A transformer is assigned certain rated insulation level for each winding. The following are specified:

— Rated voltage (power frequency, continuous)
— Highest system voltage (p.f., continuous)
— Lightning impulse voltage 1.2/50 microseconds full wave
— Lightning impulse voltage 1.2/50 microseconds chopped wave, chopping on wave front or wave tail as specified
— Switching impulse voltage (250/2500 microseconds)
— Power frequency 1 minute withstand level.

For each rated voltage of winding, corresponding withstand levels are specified. Table 25.1 gives standard insulation levels and test voltages for power transformer windings.

**Table 25.1**
**Standard Insulation Levels and Test Voltages for Power Transformer Windings**

| *Highest system voltage kV r.m.s.* | *Power-freq. test kV r.m.s.* | *Impulse test voltage kV, p* | | | *Power frequency test voltage, kV, r.m.s.* | | |
|---|---|---|---|---|---|---|---|
| | | *Standard 1* | | *Standard 2* | *Standard 1* | | *Standard 2* |
| Less than 1.1* | 2.5 | | | | | | |
| 1.1* | 3.0 | | | | | | |
| 3.6 | 8.0 | | 45 | | | 16 | |
| 7.2 | 15.0 | | 60 | | | 22 | |
| 12.0 | 25.0 | | 75 | | | 28 | |
| 17.5 | 36.0 | | 95 | | | 38 | |
| 24.0 | | | 125 | | | 50 | |
| 36.0 | | | 170 | | | 70 | |
| 52.0 | | | 250 | | | 95 | |
| 72.5 | | | 325 | | | 140 | |
| 100.0 | | 450 | | 380 | 185 | | 150 |
| 123.0 | | 550 | | 450 | 230 | | 185 |
| 145.0 | | 650 | | 550 | 275 | | 230 |
| 170.0 | | 750 | | 650 | 325 | | 275 |
| 245.0 | | 1050 | | 900 | 460 | | 395 |
| 300.0 | | | | 1050 | | | 460 |
| 362.0 | | | | 1175 | | | 510 |
| 420.0 | | | | 1425 | | | 630 |

*No impulse tests

## 25.12. TRANSIENT PHENOMENA IN TRANSFORMER WINDINGS

For lightning and switching surges, the transformer winding appears as a combination of inductance and capacitance. As the surge approaches the winding, the end-turn insulation gets higher voltage stress than the insulation in the middle of the winding. However, after a few microseconds, the oscillations within winding result in higher voltage stress in the middle of the winding. Thus during the first few microseconds, the highest voltage stress points change from end turns to the middle of the winding and the maximum value may be 3 to 5 p.u.

The waveform and maximum values of transient voltage go on varying with time and along the winding and the variation is influenced by the waveshape of the surge and the winding parameters.

## 25.13. PROTECTIVE DEVICES AGAINST TRANSIENT OVERVOLTAGES

The transient overvoltages travel from transmission lines; circuit-breakers, busbars towards the transformer. The protective device bypasses the overvoltages and protects the transformer insulation. Various protective devices are provided in the substation to protect the transformer insulation.

**Table 25.2. Protective Devices Against Lightning Overvoltages**

| *Device* | *Where applied* | *Remarks* |
|---|---|---|
| 1. Rod gaps | Across insulator string, bushing insulators. | —Difficult to coordinate<br>—Create dead short circuit<br>—Cheap |
| 2. Overhead Ground wires (earthed) | —Above overhead lines<br>—Above the sub-station area | Provide effective protection against direct strokes on line conductors, towers, sub-station equipment |
| 3. Surge Arresters | —On incoming lines in each sub-station<br>—Near terminals of Transformers and Generators<br>—Near motor and generators terminals. | —Diverts overvoltages to earth without causing short-circuit<br>—Used at every voltage level in every sub-station and for each line<br>—Gapped type or<br>—ZnO Gap-less type |

## 25.14 ROD GAPS OR COORDINATING GAPS

These are, used for insulators, equipment and bushings. The conducting rods are provided between line terminal and earthed terminal of the insulator with an adjustable gap. The medium of gap is air. The rods are approximately 12 mm dia or square. The gap is adjusted to breakdown at about 20% below flash-over voltage of insulator. The distance between are path and insulator should be more than 1/3 of the gap length.

Precise protection is not possible by rod gaps. The break-down voltage varies with polarity, steepness and wave-shape of the wave. The power frequency currents continue to flow even after the high voltage surge has vanished. This creates an earth fault only to be interrupted by circuit-breaker. Operation of rod gap, therefore, leads to discontinuity of supply. The advantage of gap is low cost and easy adjustment on site. For more precise operation, surge arresters are used.

**Table 25.3. Typical Insulation Levels, Clearances and Coordinating Gap Setting in Sub-Stations**

| *System voltage kV r.m.s.* | *Impulse withstand voltage kV p.* | *1 min, 50 Hz voltage withstand kV r.m.s.* | *Minimum clearance to earth cm* | *Minimum clearance between phases cm* | *Coordinating gap settings* cm* |
|---|---|---|---|---|---|
| 6.6 | 60 | 22 | 20.4 | 25.4 | 5 × 1 |
| 11 | 75 | 29 | 20.4 | 25.4 | 5 × 1½ |
| 22 | 125 | 55 | 25.4 | 30.5 | 2½ × 2½ |
| 33 | 170 | 75 | 36.6 | 43 | 5 × 3⅔ |
| 66 | 325 | 140 | 70.8 | 29 | 37 |
| 132 | 650 | 275 | 114 | 127 | 65 |
| 275 | 1050 | 400 | 214 | 250 | 115—120 |
| 400 | 1560 | 680 | 305 | 356 | 150—175 |

1. Nominal voltage : Phase to phase voltage kV r.m.s.
2. Higher rated voltage : Highest r.m.s. phase to phase voltage.
3. Clearances : Gap between the conducting parts along a stretched string.

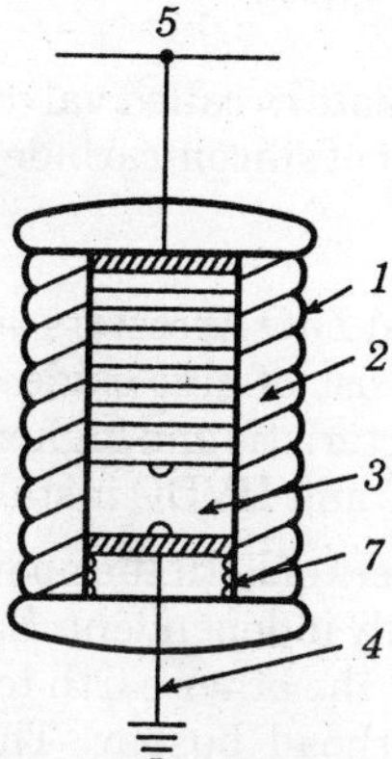


1. Porcelain Housing.
2. Silicon-carbide discs (in conventional arrester).
3. Gapunit (in conventional arrester).
4. Earth connection.
5. Line connection.
6. Zinc-Oxide discs (in MOA).
7. Springs.

Fig. 25.2 (*a*) Conventional Gapped Arrester.

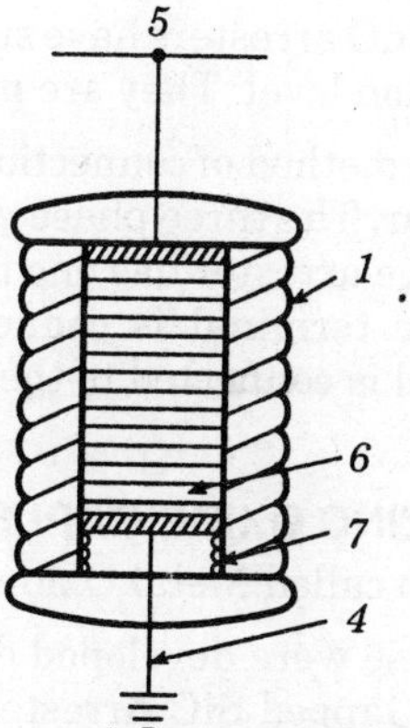


Fig. 25.2 (*b*) Metal-oxide Arrester without Gap.

*With the development of Surge Arresters, the practice of providing co-ordinating gaps in sub-stations is no more preferred.

## 25.15 SURGE ARRESTERS (LIGHTNING ARRESTERS)

*Surge Arresters* are usually connected between phase and ground (Fig. 25.2) to protect the apparatus insulation from lightning surges and switching surges (impulse voltage waves).

The resistor blocks in the surge arrester offer low resistance to high voltage surge and divert the high voltage surge to ground. Thereby the insulation of protected installation is not subjected to the full impulse wave. The surge arrester does not create short-circuit like rod gaps and retains the residual voltage across its terminals. Surge Arrester discharges current impulse surge to earth and dissipates energy in the form of heat.

A counter is connected between the lower terminal and station earth. Operation of surge arresters is registered on the counter.

After discharging the impulse wave to the earth, the resistor blocks in the surge arrester offers a very high resistance to the normal power frequency voltage and acts as open circuit. Surge arresters are not against temporary power frequency overvoltages. They provide protection against impulse voltage waves.

The following types of surge arresters are used:

1. **Gapped Silicon-carbide Surge Arresters** called valve type or conventional Gapped Arresters. These consist of silicon-carbide discs in series with gap units.

2. **Zinc-Oxide Gapless Arresters** called ZnO Arresters or Metal-oxide Arresters. These are gapless and consist of zinc-oxide discs in series. ZnO arresters have superior *V/I* characteristic and higher energy absorption level. They are preferred for EHV and HVDC installations.

The method of connection of surge arresters of both the above types is similar. The three phase units are physically independent. Each pole of a surge arrester has one line terminal and the other earth terminal. The line terminal is connected to the overhead busbar. The earth terminal is connected to the station earth.

## 25.16. ZINC OXIDE GAPLESS SURGE-ARRESTER

Also called Metal Oxide Arrester (MOA)

These were developed during 1970's and are now preferred to the earlier Gapped SiC Arresters in many applications. The conventional Silicon-carbide Arresters have a characteristic of $I = \text{k}V^x$. where $x$ is approximately 5. The arresters need a gap. The gap is associated with variation in spark over and are quenching problem. The SiC Arresters have lower energy absorption capability.

In case of *ZnO arrester,* the material for resistor is Zinc-oxide, Bismuth oxide and Cobalt oxide, in sintered disc form.

The value of $x$ is more than 20. The energy absorbing capability is very high. The arrester does not need gaps.

The resistor discs are made-up of grains of ZnO ($n$-type material) grains sintered with the flux of insulation oxide such as $BiO_2$ along with other materials like CaO, $MnO_2$, $Cr_2O_3$.

The composition and manufacturing process is a trade secret of manufactures. The characteristics vary with the composition. The characteristic is approximately

$$I = kV^x = kV^{40}$$

High value of index $x$ gives near ideal characteristic to the surge arrester. Fig. 25.3 show the voltage-current characteristic of conventional SiC elements and of ZnO elements (Metal Oxide Arrester-MOA).

### V/I Characteristics of Metal Oxide Arresters

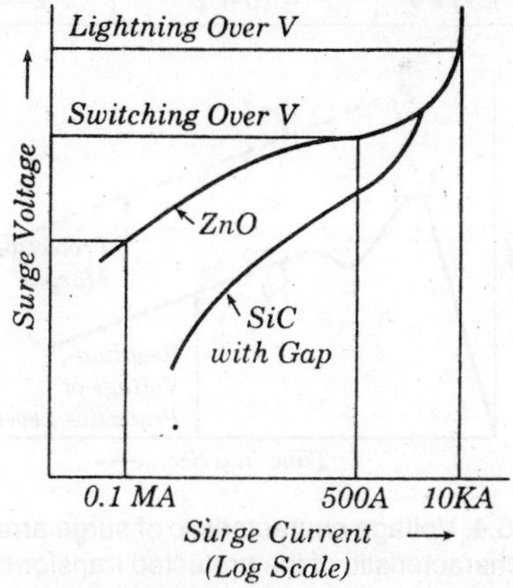


Fig. 25.3. V/I characteristic of ZnO arrester and SiC arrester.

The metal oxide arresters have a superior characteristics as shown in Fig. 25.3. The $V/I$ characteristic of ZnO Arrester is almost flat. Below certain voltage, the MOA does not conduct at all. Above this voltage, it starts conducting and the characteristic is almost flat. Therefore, the protection can be precisely selected. Thus with MOA, it is possible to have a very small margin between the discharge voltage of the MOA and the insulation level of the protected equipment.

For service voltage, current through ZnO arrester is only a few milliamperes. The $V/I$ characteristic becomes flat and then rises again.

The flat portion is useful in deciding the level, difference between the protected apparatus characteristic and the arrester characteristic. A small margin can be kept with ZnO arresters.

**Normal Leakage Current in ZnO Arresters**

Due to higher flat *V/I* characteristic above certain voltage, the normal leakage current in ZnO arresters is only a few milliamperes. Hence, there is no much temperature rise. Characteristics of arresters are not affected. Secondly, there is no need of spark gap to stop leakage current or follow-up current.

**Energy Absorption Capability of ZnO Arresters**

The surge arrester has to dissipate the energy equal to

$$W = \int vi\, dt \text{ joules.}$$

Typical values of energies to be dissipated in HV station type surge arresters are as mentioned in the Table 25.4.

**Table 25.4**

| *Rated voltage kV r.m.s.* | Upto 36 kV | 72.5—420 | above 420 |
|---|---|---|---|
| *Energy Capability kJ/kV* | 4 to 4.2 | 7.2—7.8 | 13 |

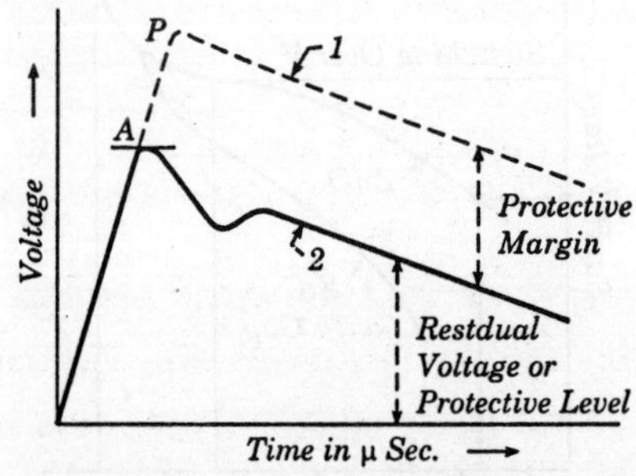


Fig. 25.4. Voltage characteristic of surge arrester.
1. Withstand characteristic of the protected transformer insulation.
2. Protective characteristic of surge arrester.

## 25.17. GAPPED SIC ARRESTERS (VALVE TYPE ARRESTERS)

These type of arresters are getting replace by recent ZnO arresters.

Surge arrester is connected between line and earth. Conventional Gapped Arrester consists of resistor elements in series with gap elements. The resistor elements (Silicon-carbide) offer non-linear resistance such that for normal frequency power system voltages, the resistance is high. For discharge currents, the resistance is low. The gap units consist of air gaps of appropriate length. During normal voltages, the surge arrester does not conduct. When a surge-wave travelling along the overhead line comes to the arrester, the gap breaks down. The resistance offered being low the surge is diverted to the earth. After a few microseconds, the surge vanishes and normal power frequency voltage is set up across the arrester. The resistance offered by resistors to this voltage is very high. Therefore, gap current reduces and voltage across the gap is no more sufficient to maintain the arc. Therefore, the current flowing to the earth is automatically interrupted and normal condition is restored. This high voltage surge is discharged to earth. Hence the insulation of equipment connected to the line is protected.

Figure 25.4 illustrates the operation of a surge arrester. When a lightning surge travelling along the transmission line reaches the terminal of the surge arrester, at a particular voltage (instantaneous value) *A*, depending upon steepness of wave front, the SA sparks over. The voltage is called impulse sparkover voltage. Hence the surge is diverted to earth through the SA and insultatison on subtation side is not subjected to peak voltage *P*. After breakdown, the voltage across SA does not drop to zero like in rod gaps because of the series resistors. The voltage across the gap remains at residual value for a short time. *Hence line to earth voltage remains at residual value during discharge.* A portion of wave proceeds further but the peak and steepness of wave front are reduced.

After short time of the order of some microseconds, the wave is discharged and normal frequency voltages appear across the SA. The normal voltage is not enough to maintain the arc in the gap units and the arc extinguishers. The SA restores the original condition.

## 25.18. INSTALLATION OF SURGE ARRESTERS

Surge arresters are installed in following locations:

1. As first apparatus for each incoming line in the substation; between each phase and earth.

2. Near terminals on HV side of each transformer, between phase and earth.

3. Near LV side of each transformer between phase and earth.

4. Between transformer neutral and earth (optional).

5. Between tertiary terminal and earth for each phase of tertiary winding of a transformer.

6. For phase-to-phase across delta connected transformer winding.

The surge arrester is installed on galvanised steel structure, one for each phase.

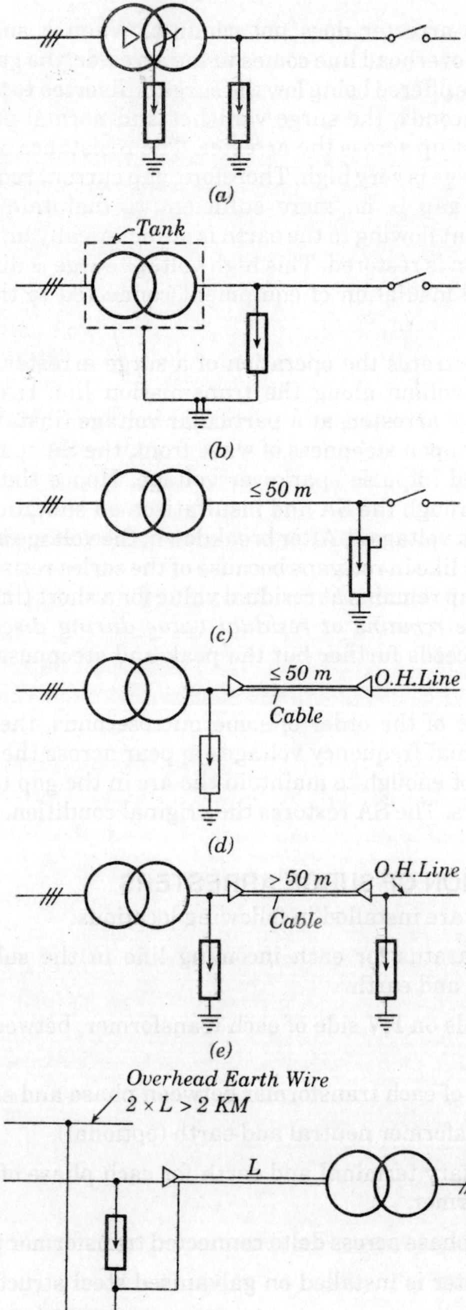


Fig. 25.5. Standard methods of connecting surge arresters for protection of power transformers. Single line diagram.

The surge arresters must be installed on supporting structures in a vertical position and arranged so as the exclude any accidental contact with them. Buses connected to the arrester must not exert pressures on the latter in excess of 25 kgf.

Prior to mounting surge arresters, it is necessary to check clearances between their current carrying parts and other elements of the electrical insallation (earthed and current carrying parts of other devices, walls, guards, etc.), for compliance with specified values.

Following rules are applicable for surge arrester protection of power transformers.

1. **Transformers in non-effectively earthed systems and neutral available** (Fig. 25.5 A). For non-effectively earthed systems and where the transformer neutral is available, a surge arrester must always be installed in the neutral point. One more arrester is installed near the terminals of the transformer. Fig. 25.5. A. shows a single line diagram.

2. **Earthing of surge arrester and transformer tank** (Fig. 25.5 B). The arrester must be connected to the earthing grid with shortest possible conductor. The transformer tank shall be connected to same earthing point.

3. **When the transformer is connected to overhead bus.** (Fig. 25.5 C). The distance between transformer and arrester shall normally not exceed 50 meter.

For lines on wooden poles with unearthed cross-beams and/or earth wire available, the arrester shall be placed near the transformer.

4. **When the transformer is connected to an overhead line via cable.** (Fig. 25.5 D, E, F).

4.1. *For a cable up to a length of 50 meter.* The arrester shall be placed at the transformer side of the cable. (Fig. 25.5 D).

4.2. For a cable with a length of more than 50 meter an arrester shall also be placed in the other end of the cable. (Fig. 25.5 E).

5. **Transformer connected with enclosed cable.** Connect the surge arrester at the termination of O.H. line (Fig. 25.5 F). Overhead earth wire and shield of cable are also earthed.

## 25.19. EFFECT OF NEUTRAL EARTHING

If the neutral point of the system or the transformer itself is earthed, surge voltages are discharged to earth and voltage distribution along windings is less severe. Hence neutral earthing helps in discharging the surges to ground and reducing the voltage stresses on winding insulation. (Ref. Ch. 26).

## 25.20. CLASSIFICATION OF SURGE ARRESTERS BASED ON DISCHARGE CURRENT RATING

The surge arresters are classified according to their rated discharge currents and rated voltages.

Table 25.5
Classification of Surge Arrester

| | *Station type* | *Line type* | *Distribution type* |
|---|---|---|---|
| Standard normal discharge current (amperes) peak | 10,000 | 5000 | 2500 : 1500 |
| Voltage rating kV r.m.s. | 3.3—245 | 3.3—123 | Upto 3.3 |
| Application | Large power-Station and Large Sub-station | Intermediate, Large Sub-station, Medium Power Station | Distribution system ; Rural Distribution |

**Calculation of Discharge Current of Arrester.** The choice of discharge current to be used in insulation coordination depends on whether or not the intallation is shielded against direct strokes. In shielded stations, the incoming lines must also be shielded for atleast half a km from station. With such shielding, the voltage magnitude of the surge at the start of the protected zone is usually assumed to be a 1.2 times the negative critical flash over (CFO) of the line. Making the conservative assumption of zero attenuation during wave travel from the start of the shielding to the station, the maximum discharge current can be calculated as

Discharge current,

$$I_A = \frac{2.4 \times (\text{Line CFO}) - \text{Arrester discharge voltage}}{\text{Line–surge impedance}}$$

conservative estimates of discharge currents in shielded stations are:

Table 25.6

| *Normal system voltage, kV* | *Highest system voltage, kV* | *Surge current, A* |
|---|---|---|
| 66 | 725 | 5,000 |
| 132 | 145 | 5,000 |
| 220 | 245 | 10,000 |
| 400 | 420 | 15,000 |
| 750 | 765 | 20,000 |

## Summary

Surge arresters have lower protective level (kV) for discharging lightning surges and switching surges to earth and reduce the stresses on the transformer windings below their withstand levels.

ZnO arresters are being preferred to earlier SiC gapped arresters.

Surge arresters are connected near transformer terminals, phase to ground (in addition to those near line terminals).

Surge Arresters protect the transformers from surge voltages provided, they are correctly installed and their protective level is below the withstand level of the transformer winding.

# 26

# Neutral Grounding, Arc-Suppression Coil, Third Harmonic Current Flow and Tertiary

Neutral Grounding is an important system problem which influences :

— Insulation levels
— Earth fault protection
— Flow of third harmonic currents
— Safety.

Basic aspects have been discussed with reference to the power transformer neutrals.

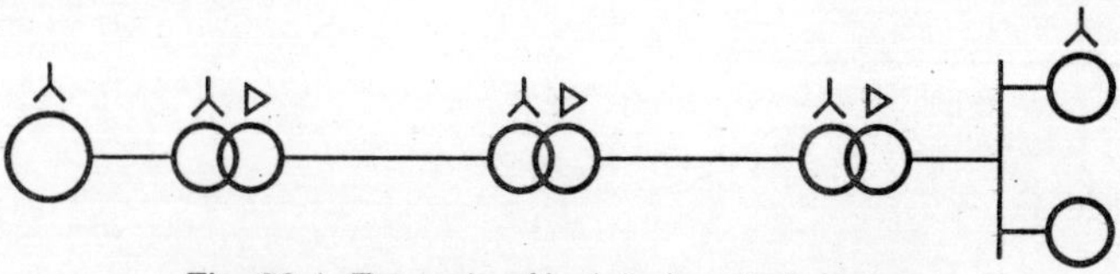

Fig. 26.1. Example of isolated neutral system.
(Not preferred in modern installations exception ; Continuous process plant)

Part I of this chapter deals with System Neutral Grounding with reference to transformer Neutrals.

Part II deals with Third Harmonic Magnetizing Currents and associated phenomena and delta tertiary winding.

## 26.1 INTRODUCTION TO SYSTEM NEUTRAL GROUNDING

Figure 26.1 shows an *isolated neutral system.* The neutral point of the transformer or the generator are without earthing; such systems are not used in modern supply systems due to disadvantages mentioned in Table 26.1 column 2.

Modern three-phase AC supply systems are with neutral grounding. The advantages are mentioned in Table 6.2. Methods of neutral grounding are:

(1) Solid Grounding.
(2) Reactor Grounding
(3) Resonant Grounding
(4) Resistor Grounding.

Ref. Fig. 26.7. All the systems having any of the above type of grounding are *called Grounded Neutral Systems.* The advantages of Grounded Neutral Systems are mentioned in Table 26.1, Column 3.

*Considering the several advantages, it has become a universal practice to ground the neutral of star connected winding of power transformer at least at one point at each voltage level as shown in Fig. 26.2.*

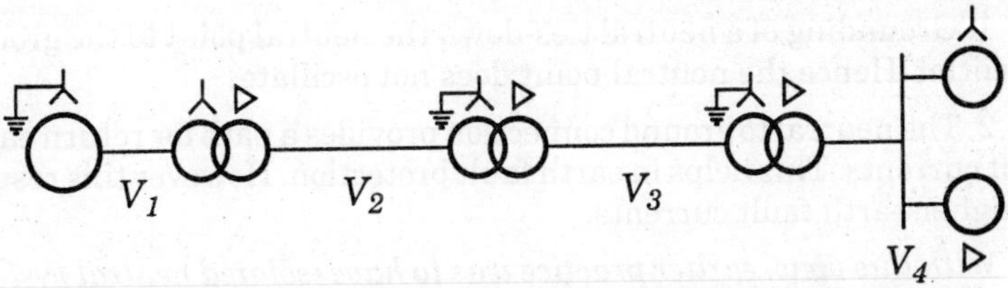


Fig. 26.2. Example of a Grounded Neutral System. (Each voltage level is provided with at least one grounded neutral. Neutral Grounding is provided preferably at the supply end).

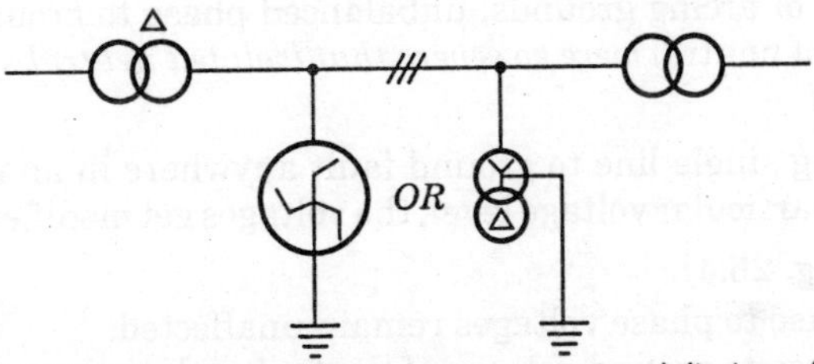


Fig. 26.3. Use of a Zig-zag Transformer or a star-delta transformer specially for System Neutral Grounding.

If due to delta connections, a star point is not available at any of the voltage levels, a *Special Neutral Grounding Transformer* is installed. Alternatively a star-delta transformer is installed. The neutral point of the star connected winding is earthed.

From Figs. 26.2 and 26.3, the close intimacy between transformers and the system neutral grounding can be visualised. The neutral grounding influences (1) Insulation levels (2) Flow of earth fault currents (3) Flow of harmonic currents in the no-load magnetizing currents. Hence, they play a very vital role in transformer design and network application.

Apart from the insulation coordination, earth fault protection and discharge of lightning overvoltages to earth etc., the neutral grounding provides a ready path to the flow of third harmonic zero sequence currents in a star connected winding and thereby influences the emfs in the three phases and currents in three phases. For star-star winding a special tertiary delta winding is provided for circulation of third harmonic current.

## Part I—System Neutral Grounding

### 26.2 COMPARISON OF ISOLATED NEUTRAL SYSTEM AND GROUNDED NEUTRAL SYSTEM

In Isolated Neutral System, there is no electrical connection between any of the phases and the earth.

In Grounded Neutral System, the neutral of star point is grounded.

1. Grounding of a neutral ties-down the neutral point to the ground potential. Hence the neutral point does not oscillate.

2. The neutral to ground connection provides a path for return earth fault currents. This helps in earth fault protection. However this results in higher earth fault currents.

*With this view, earlier practice was to have isolated neutral system.* In such a system, in absence of neutral to ground connection, earth fault currents used to be too low. Even an earth fault could be tolerated due to its low value. But during earth faults on the isolated neutral system, the problem of arcing grounds, unbalanced phase to ground voltages, oscillations of neutral *were so severe that isolated neutral systems were discontinued.*

3. During single line to ground fault anywhere in an ungrounded system at a particular voltage level, the voltages get modified as follows: **(Ref. Fig. 26.4).**

- Phase to phase voltages remain unaffected.
- Phase to ground voltage of the faulty phase goes down.
- Phase to ground voltage of the healthy phases increases to almost $\sqrt{3}\,V_{ph.}$, resulting in overstressing of insulation of the two healthy phases everywhere at that voltage level.

The insulation of all the motors, cables, transformers etc. gets continuously overstressed and unless the equipment are designed to withstand such stresses, these equipment will fail though the earth fault was remote and fault current is negligible.

- In an isolated neutral system, the lightning surges and switching surges are not dissipated to earth. The insulation gets overstressed and may fail. Hence it is essential to earth the neutral point of an isolated neutral system through a surge arrester. Table 26.1 gives the comparison.
- In some continuous process plants such as steel plants, aluminium plants etc., single phase to earth fault is deliberately tolerated without tripping the process. In such schemes, isolated neutral system is preferred. However insulation levels of transformers, motors, cables breakers etc. are $\sqrt{3}$ times the usual levels.

**Table 26.1. Comparison between Isolated Neutral System and Grounded Neutral System**

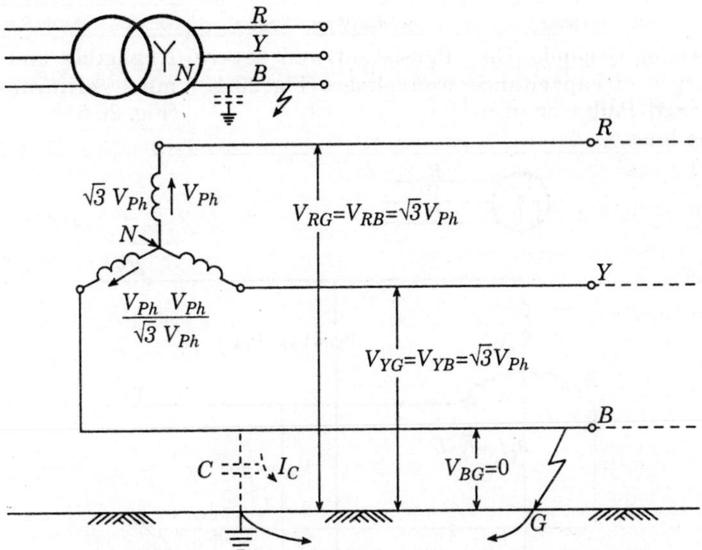


1. Effect of earth fault on phase *B* on voltages to earth of healthy phases *R* and *Y*.
2. Capacitive Current $I_C$ feeds arcing grounds *BG*.

Fig. 26.4. Isolated neutral system.

**Table 26.1. Comparison between Isolated Neutral System and Grounded Neutral System**

| *Phenomena* | *Isolated Neutral System* | *Grounded Neutral System* |
|---|---|---|
| 1. Earth fault currents. | Negligible | High |
| 2. Earth fault protection. | Difficult | Simple (Fig. 26.6) |
| 3. Safety associated with discharge of overvoltages and disconnection of faulty parts. | Unsafe | Safer |
| 4. Neutral point | Unstable oscillates | Stable |
| 5. Voltages during single line to ground faults. | Phase to ground voltages of healthy phases increase to phase to phase value (Fig. 26.4) | Phase to ground voltages of healthy phases remain at their usual value (Fig. 26.5) |
| 6. Insulation levels | Higher | Lower |
| 7. Third Harmonic currents. | No path | Path available |
| 8. Surge voltages due to lightning. | No path. Special Surge Arrester necessary between neutral and ground | Discharged to earth. Path available. |

*(Contd...)*

| *Phenomena* | *Isolated Neutral System* | *Grounded Neutral System* |
|---|---|---|
| 9. Arcing Grounds (Discharges of capacitance through faults on-overhead lines. | Persistent and severe overvoltages (Fig. 26.4) | Negligible and almost eliminated (Fig. 26.5) |

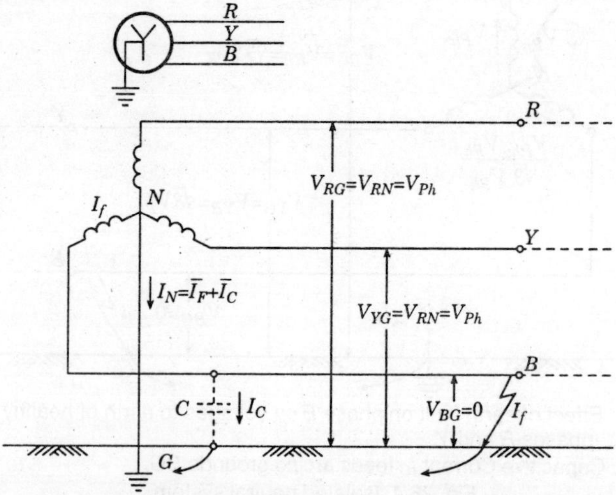


Fig. 26.5. With neutral grounding, during an earth fault on phase *B*, voltages of *R* and *Y* remain unchanged.

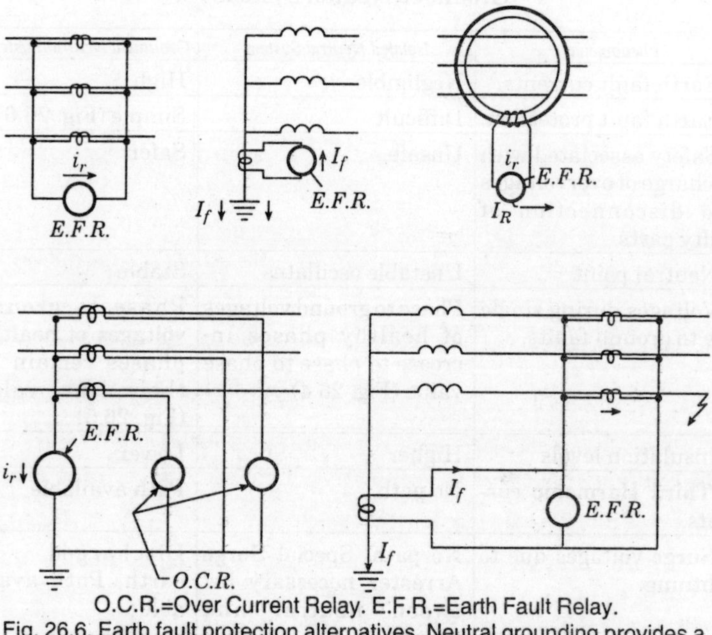


O.C.R.=Over Current Relay. E.F.R.=Earth Fault Relay.

Fig. 26.6. Earth fault protection alternatives. Neutral grounding provides a path for earth fault current $I_f$. The earth fault protection alternatives are quite simple.

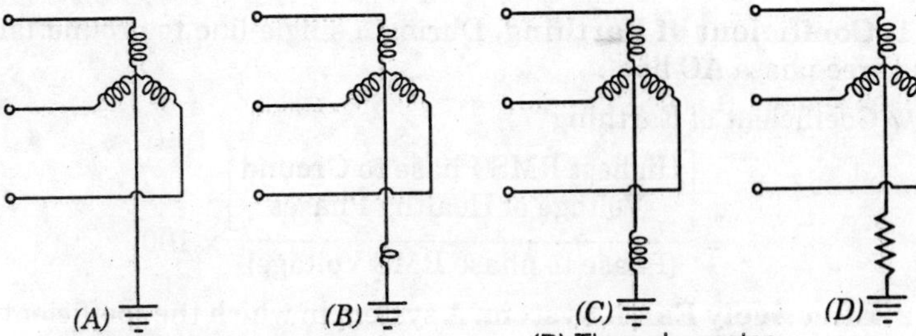


(A) Solid (B) Through reactor
(C) Through Arc-suppression coil (D) Through resistor

Fig. 26.7. Alternative methods of neutral grounding.

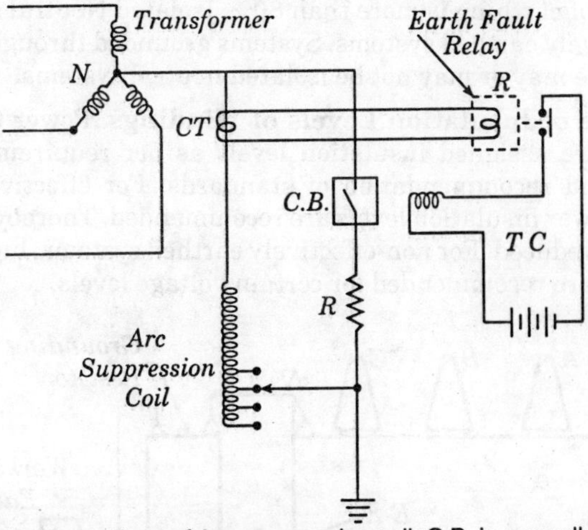


Fig. 26.8. Connections of Arc suppression coil. C.B. is normally open. Flow of earth fault current initiates the closing of C.B. and arc suppression coil is shunted through R.

## 26.3 METHODS OF NEUTRAL GROUNDING

The alternatives are shown in Fig. 26.7 and include the following.

- — Solid grounding
- — Resistance grounding
- — Reactor grounding
- — Resonant grounding (Arc-suppression coil, Peterson Coil, Ground fault neutraliser)

The choice depends upon the required limit of earth fault current, the coefficient of earthing, capacitive currents to be neutralized, etc.

## 26.4 COEFFICIENT OF EARTHING

The insulation level of a transformer winding is 'full' or 'reduced' depending upon whether the system is 'effectively earthed' or 'non-effectively earthed'.

The definitions are as follows :

**1. Coefficient of Earthing.** During a single-line to ground fault on a three phase AC line,

% Coefficient of Earthing

$$= \frac{\begin{bmatrix}\text{Highest RMS Phase to Ground} \\ \text{Voltage of Healthy Phases}\end{bmatrix}}{[\text{Phase to phase RMS Voltage}]} \times 100$$

**2. Effectively Earth System.** A system in which the coefficient of earthing is below 80% of solidly earthed system is an effectively earthed system.

**3. Non-effectively Earthed System.** A system in which the coefficient of earthing is more than 80%. Isolated Neutral systems are non-effectively earthed systems. Systems grounded through resistance or reactance may or may not be isolated neutral systems.

**Choice of Insulation Levels of Windings.** Power transformer windings are assigned insulation levels as per requirements of the network and recommendation of standards. For effectively earthed systems, lower insulation levels are recommended. Thereby the insulation cost is reduced. For non-effectively earthed systems, higher insulation levels are recommended for certain voltage levels.

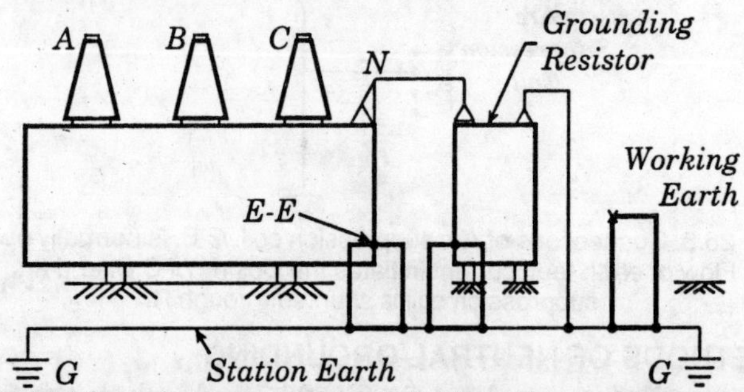


Fig. 26.9 (*a*) Transformer neutral grounded through a *resistor* or a *reactor*. Tank is also grounded as shown by *EE* (Equipment earthing)

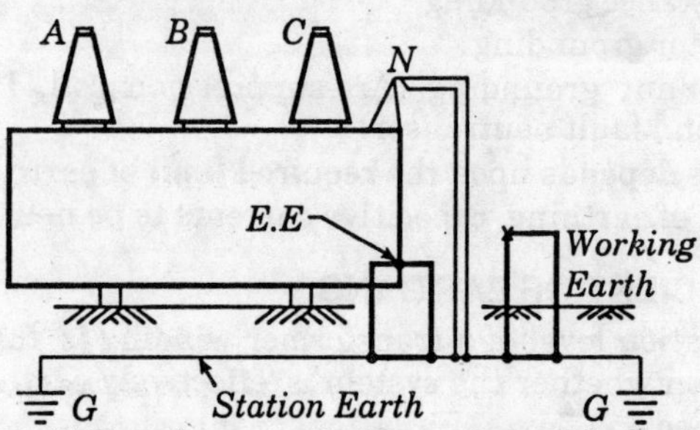


Fig. 26.9. (*b*) Transformer neutral grounded solidly. Tank is also grounded as shown by *EE* (Equipment earthing).

## 26.5 HOW TO GROUND A TRANSFORMER NEUTRAL

The neutral point of a three phase star connected winding is brought at the neutral bushing. This point is connected to station earth either directly or *via* a neutral grounding resistor or reactor as shown in Fig. 26.9.

If Arc-Suppression coil is used, the connections are as shown in Fig. 26.8. *The taps of the arc suppression coil are selected automatically on the basis of inductance required to compensate capacitive earth fault currents.* The arc suppression coil is short-time rated (*e.g.* 10 sec.). Hence after a time delay of about 8 seconds, if the earth fault current is continuing, the circuit breaker (*CB*) is closed and arc suppression coil is bypassed. The earth fault current flows through resistance *R*.

## 26.6 NEUTRAL EARTHING REACTOR AND ARC SUPPRESSION COILS (SINGLE PHASE DEVICE)

### 26.6.1 Neutral Grounding Reactor

The Neutral Grounding Reactors are connected between neutral point of 400 kV/800 kV reactors and earth, where the neutral of shunt Reactor is suitable for 145 kV class insulation.

The reactors are oil immersed type ONAN cooled (oil immersed with natural air cooling) with continuous rating of 10/15 Amps and a 10 sec. rating as indicated in the Rating Data sheet. As continuous losses of the reactors are negligible, reactor tank surface is adequate for dissipation of these losses. Hence radiators are not provided.

Considering linear impedance characteristic requirement upto rated short time current a core less design with magnetic shielding of CRGO sheet has been made. The magnetic circuit, therefore consists of rectangular frame of CRGO steel lamination packets of adequate area. Area of magnetic circuit is selected such that saturation does not take place under short time current. A rigid clamping structure is provided for clamping of magnetic frame and a very low flux density is used to minimize the vibration and achieve linear impedance characteristic.

The graded disc type concentric winding suitable for a rated voltage of 145 kV and basic insulation level of 550 kV has been provided without core inside. Winding is held in position by way of special insulation structure inside winding and finally kept under pressure between top and bottom yokes of magnetic frame. Return path of flux is provided by way of two return limbs.

The line terminal is taken out through the tank cover via 145 kV, 800 Amps OIP condenser bushing provided with suitable terminal connector. The neutral lead is taken out through the tank cover via a 36kV, 630 Amps porcelain bushing.

The tank is of welded mild steel plate construction shot blasted on the inside and outside to remove scales before painting. The tank is painted on the inside with yellow paint and its outside surface is painted with two coats of primer paint and finishing coat, of light grey paint to shade 631 of IS:5. This is a standard painting scheme followed for all equipment.

The fittings include a conservator with a magnetic oil gauge, pressure relief device, drain and filter valves, sampling valves, thermometer pockets, Buchholz relay, temperature indicator for oil and silicagel breather.

These reactors are designed for mounting directly on plinth.

Single-phase reactors are often used, alone or in conjunction with resistors, to connect the neutral point of a transformer to earth.

Reactors of relatively low impedance are used to limit earth fault current. High impedance reactors are used as arc-suppression coils to compensate for the capacitive current appearing in the case of line-to-earth fault in the network.

*An arc-suppression coil may be provided with a secondary winding for connection of a resistor or with an auxiliary winding for measuring purposes.*

## 26.7 SPECIFICATIONS AND RATINGS

IEC 287, Reactors covers neutral grounding reactors and arc suppression coils. (Ref. Ch. 31).

**Terms and Definitions**

1. *Rated voltage* ($V_{1N}$). The highest r.m.s. voltage at rated frequency for which a reactor is designed. Neutral earthing devices are single phase devices.

For high impedance reactors, *e.g.* arc-suppression coils, the rated voltage is usually taken as the line-to-neutral voltage of the network unless operating conditions justify the selection of a different value.

For low impedance neutral earthing reactors, the rated voltage is specified by the purchaser taking into account the highest voltage which can exist across its terminals under fault conditions in the network.

Thus if $Is$ is short-circuit current flowing through neutral under worst condition of line to ground fault. $Z_L$ is impedance of neutral grounding reactor, $V_{NG}$ is the maximum neutral to ground voltage.

$$V_{NG} = Is\, Z_L$$

2. *Insulation levels.* The insulation level of a single-phase neutral-earthing reactor or an arc-suppression coil corresponds to the maximum voltage which may appear at the neutral of the associated system or transformer. It depends on $V_{NG}$ described above.

For the earth end of the coil, selection of a reduced insulation level may be appropriate (graded insulation).

The values of insulation levels are selected from standard specifications.

3. *Rated current of an arc-suppression coil.* The value of current which the apparatus is designed to carry at rated voltage at rated frequency with the reactor arranged for maximum current principal tapping or maximum air gap as appropriate).

4. *Rated short-time current of a single-phase neutral-earthing reactor.* The fault current which the apparatus is designed to carry for a specified duration. Depending on their duration, several rated short-time currents may be specified.

5. *Rated loading time.* The duration for which the apparatus is designed to carry the rated current or the rated short-time current.

The rated loading time of a neutral-earthing reactor of low impedance shall be specified by the purchaser. If not specified, it is assumed to be 3 s.

If the rated loading time of an arc-suppression coil is up to 25, the coil is a short-time duty type. If it is longer, the coil shall be designed for continuous duty.

The rated loading time of short-time duly coils is specified by the manufacturer.

6. *Rated impedance.* The impedance of the reactor is equal to the ratio of rated voltage to rated current or rated short-time current.

7. *Rated power of an arc-suppression coil.* The rated power is the apparent power obtained when rated voltage is multiplied by rated current.

$S = V_{LN} \times Is$

$Is$ = Rated current

$V_{LN}$ = Rated voltage

**Rating Plate Data for Neutral Grounding Reactor and Arc Suppression Coil**

The following data is generally given :

1. *Arc-suppression coil*-Type... or
   *Single-phase neutral-earthing reactor*-Type...
2. Number and year of the specification.
3. Manufacturer's name.
4. Manufacturer's serial number.
5. Year of manufacture.
6. Rated power (for arc-suppression coils only).
7. Rated frequency.
8. Rated voltage.
9. Rated current (for arc-suppression coils only).

10. Measured impedance for maximum and minimum setting, if applicable.
11. Rated short-time current (for single-phase neutral-earthing reactors only).
12. Rated loading time.
13. Type of cooling.
14. Class of temperature of dry type apparatus, and temperature rise if non-standard.
15. Insulation level, separately for the earth end of winding where appropriate.
16. Total mass *.
17. Mass of insulating oil*.
18. Untanking mass*.

## 26.8 TESTING OF NEUTRAL GROUNDING REACTOR

These are similar to the tests on transformers, series reactors and shunt reactors have a reference to IEC-76 and IES-287... Type tests, routing tests and special tests are as follows :

**1. Measurement of winding resistance (routine test).** As per IEC Publication 76, on power transformers and IEC 287 for reactors.

**2. Measurement of current (routine test) and impedance.** As per IEC 76.

Measurements of arc-suppression coil are made over the whole range of adjustment, preferably at rated voltage and frequency. Should this be impracticable, the measurement method is subject to agreement on the understanding that the test voltage be chosen as high as possible and that test at different voltages be made for the purpose of extrapolation.

**3. Test of temperature rise (type test).** As per IEC Publication 76.

This test is performed at rated voltage and frequency.

For single-phase neutral-earthing reactors of low impedance, for which a rated loading time less than 10 s has been specified, a temperature-rise test is not required. Instead the final temperature is calculated in the same way as that for transformers under short-circuit conditions, as per IEC Publication 76. An initial temperature of +40°C is assumed for calculations.

**4. Inter-turn overvoltage withstand test (routine test).** Arc-suppression coils with graded insulation shall be tested with a voltage across the winding equal to twice rated voltage.

*Arc-suppression coils with graded insulation* shall be tested with the reduced insulation terminal earthed and the other terminal raised to the appropriate test voltage.

---

*If above 5 MT.

Arc-suppression coils with tappings or variable air gap shall be set for minimum current.

Low *impedance single-phase neutral-earthing reactors* shall be tested as series reactors.

The method of test is as per IEC Publication 76.

When the test between turns is impracticable, the test shall be replaced by an impulse voltage test with an increased duration of the front of the impulse wave.

*Separate-source voltage-withstand test (routine test).* As per IEC 76. The test voltage are be Tables 26.1 and 26.2, for the specified insulation levels of the apparatus. Series 1 values shall be chosen for oil-immersed apparatus and Series 2 values for dry-type apparatus.

*Impulse-voltage withstand test* (*type test*). As per IEC 76. The test voltages are taken from table I and II, Clause 4, for the specified insulation levels of the apparatus. Unless otherwise specified, the front duration of the impulse wave shall be 10 $\mu s$.

**Tolerances**

— Current ± 5% or rated value
— Impedance ± 20% of rated impedance.

## 26.9 EQUIPMENT EARTHING (BODY EARTHING)

'Earthing' is connecting to ground. The non-current carrying parts are earthed for safety of personnel and to make earth fault detection simpler. Earthing of non-current carrying parts such as tank, cabinets, structures etc. is called Equipment Earthing. This is for entirely different purpose than neutral earthing.

Fig. 26.9 (*a*) and (*b*) item *EE* show equipment earthing. Two earthing strips are provided between the earthing pad on the transformer tank and the station earthing system.

There should not be two earthing pads as there would be local circulating currents through the tank and return earth.

The resistance of connection between the earth pad and the station earthing system should be low. Hence, cross-section of earthing strips and the joints should be well cleaned before final tightening and antioxidizing jelly should be applied.

In some transformer, the tank is in two halves. These should be joined by a short-circuiting links to provide effective joint between the top and bottom tanks.

The bottom housing of CTs and VTs should be earthed.

The lower terminal of surge arrester should be connected to station earthing system by earthing rods of large cross section.

## Part 2—Third Harmonic Magnetizing Currents

**Fourier series.** Any non-sinusoidal periodic function such as (1), Fig. 26.10 can be obtained by algebraic sum of component periodic sinusoidal functions of various frequencies called (Fundamental 1 + other harmonics).

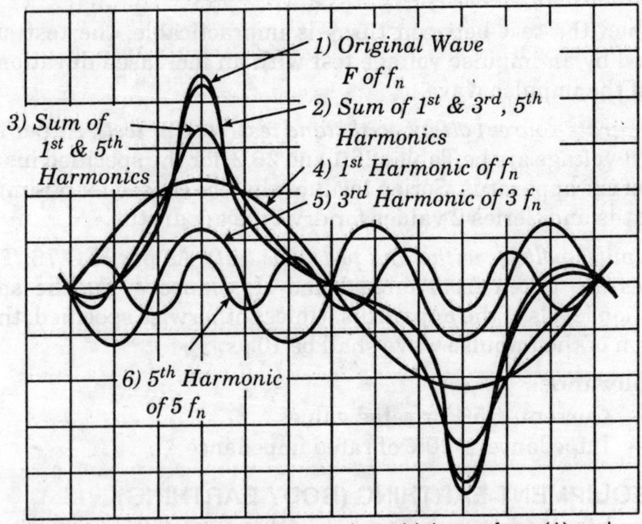


Fig. 26.10. Original periodic non-sinusoidal waveform (1) and Harmonics (4), (5) and (6).

## 26.10 HARMONIC IN MAGNETIZING CURRENT OF TRANSFORMER

Refer Fig. 26.10 illustrating the concept of 'Fourier Series'. A non-sinusoidal periodic function can be resolved into a mathematical series containing several sinusoidal functions called a fundamental and harmonics. If the magnetizing flux density $B$ is sinusoidal, the magnetizing current is non-sinusoidal. The analysis of the non-sinusoidal periodic waveform of magnetizing current shows that it contains substantial amount of third harmonic component and fifth harmonic component. (Fig. 26.15) typically 44% of third harmonic, 16% of fifth harmonic and 3% of seventh harmonic current.

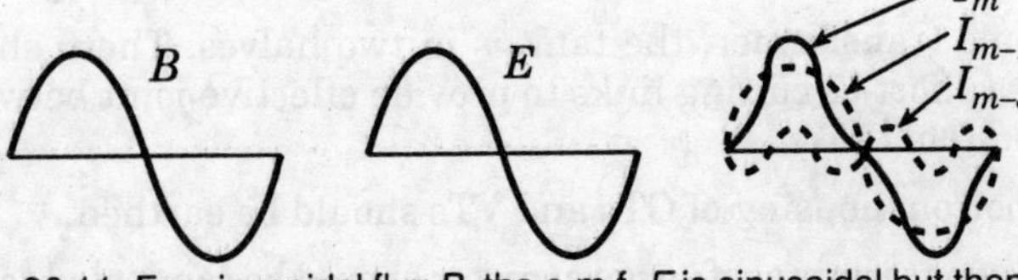


Fig. 26.11. For sinusoidal flux $B$, the e.m.f. $E$ is sinusoidal but then the magnetizing current $I_m$ is non-sinusoidal and contains fundamental ($I_{m-1}$) and predominant third harmonic ($I_{m-3}$).

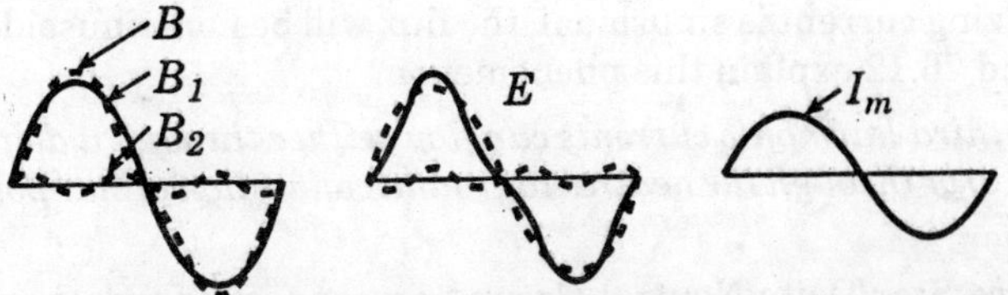


Fig. 26.12. By sinusoidal magnetizing current $I_m$ the flux $B$ is non-sinusoidal (flat topped) and emf is also non-sinusoidal (peak topped)

*The third harmonic component is the largest* and unless care is taken the problems are faced in the form of distorted voltage waveform.

Figure 26.13 ($A$) and ($B$) shows a hysteresis loop of flux density ($B$) *versus* magnetizing current ($I_m$). The corresponding waveforms are shown in Fig. 26.13 ($B$).

Flux and magnetizing current are non-linear with each other. Hence, if the magnetic flux ϕ (hence induced EMF) is sinusoidal, the magnetizing current $I_m$ will be non-sinusoidal. Alternatively, if the

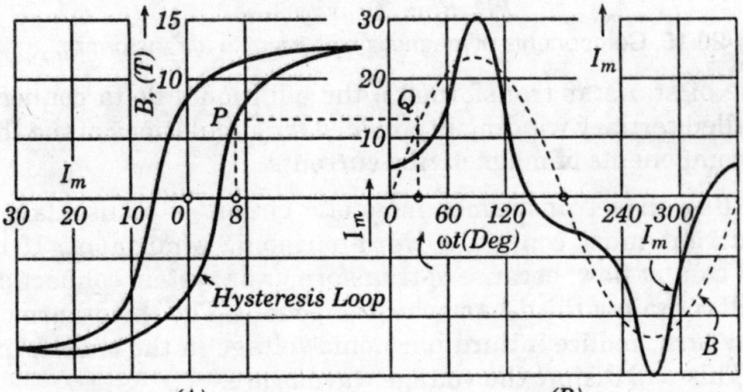


Fig. 26.13. ($A$) Hysteresis loop ($B$) Sinsusoidal $B$ ($E$ not shown) Nonsinusoidal Magnetizing current.

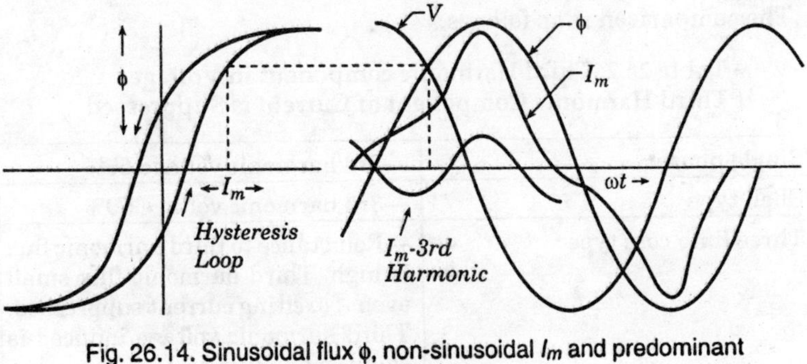


Fig. 26.14. Sinusoidal flux ϕ, non-sinusoidal $I_m$ and predominant Third Harmonic $I_{m-3}$.

magnetizing current is sinusoidal, the flux will be non-sinusoidal. Figs. 26.11 and 26.12 explain this phenomenon.

*The third harmonic currents can flow, either through a delta winding (26.16) or through the neutral to ground connection of star point (Fig. 26.17).*

Hence Star/Delta/Neutral Grounding connections, determine the path for the third harmonic currents and the core constructions, 3 limb/5 limb. Core type of shell type determines the path of flux of 3rd harmonic.

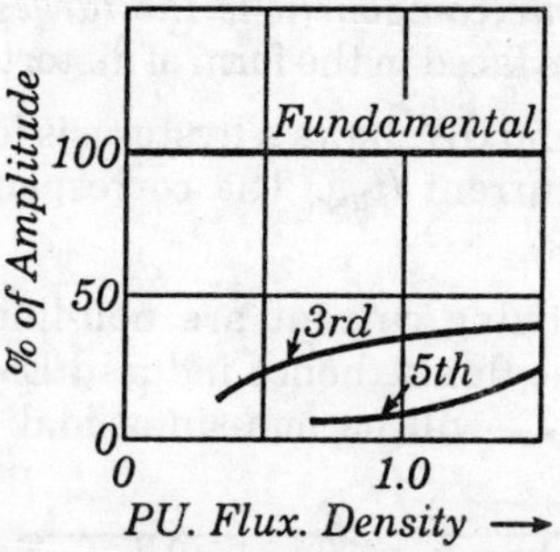


Fig. 26.15. Components of magnetizing current in a transformer.

In case of star/star transformers, the additional delta connected winding called tertiary winding is provided for circulations of the third harmonic components of magnetizing currents.

If the flux in a transformer magnetic circuit is sinusoidal, the exciting current must contain a third-harmonic component. If this component cannot flow, because of transformer or system connections, the flux will contain a third-harmonic component. The third-harmonic flux will, in turn, induce a third-harmonic voltage in the transformer windings. This will distort the voltage waveform.

*When the third harmonic current is suppressed, the magnitude of the third-harmonic voltage induced in a transformer winding, will vary between 5 and 50 per cent depending upon the type of transformers core (3 limb / 5 limb / shell).*

The comparison is as follows.

**Table 26.2. Third Harmonic component in Voltages if Third Harmonic Component of Current is Suppressed**

| | |
|---|---|
| 1. Single phase | —3rd harmonic voltage 50% |
| 2. Shell type | —3rd harmonic voltage 50% |
| 3. Three limb core type | —Reluctance to third harmonic flux is high. Third harmonic flux small even if exciting current suppressed. Third harmonic voltage induced is small (maximum 5%) |

From the above discussions, we conclude the following :

1. With sinusoidal flux and therefore sinusoidal EMF, the no-load current (magnetizing current) contains a substantial third harmonic.

2. With sinusoidal waveform of no-load current (exciting current) the flux and therefore induced EMF will contain predominant third harmonic, therefore the waveform is flat topped.

| Flux | | EMF | | Magnet Current |
|---|---|---|---|---|
| Non-sinusoidal | ⇌ | Non-sinusoidal | ⇌ | Sinusoidal |
| Flux | | EMF | | Magnet Current |
| Sinusoidal | ⇌ | Sinusoidal | ⇌ | Non-Sinusoidal |

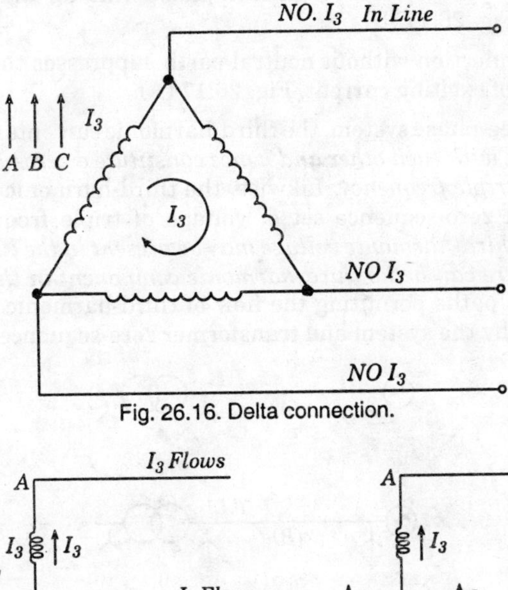


Fig. 26.16. Delta connection.

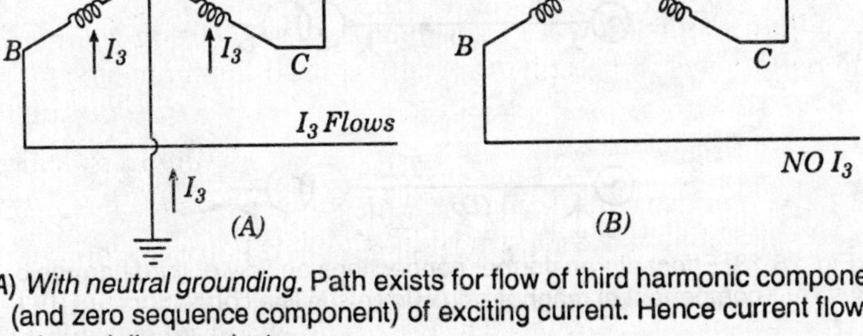


(*A*) *With neutral grounding.* Path exists for flow of third harmonic component (and zero sequence component) of exciting current. Hence current flows through line conductors.

(*B*) *With isolated neutral.* No path. Hence third harmonic currents are absent from line conductors.

Fig. 26.17. Star connection.

## 26.11 STAR AND DELTA CONNECTIONS

It is seen that third harmonics must occur in either the magnetizing current or the voltage of a transformer. The exciting current will take the shape imposed by the particular connections used. It is always preferable to have at least one delta-connected winding in a three-phase transformer bank. *The delta connection will provide a path for the flow of third-harmonic currents and will minimize the third-harmonic current in the external circuits.* This is very desirable because third-harmonic currents in the external circuits may, under some conditions, cause telephone interference.

Star connection with neutral grounded will provide path for third harmonic currents to flow. Hence with star connected neutral, third harmonic current flows through each phase winding and through line conductor. Fig. 26.17 (B).

Star connection without neutral earth suppresses third harmonic component of exciting current. Fig. 26.17 (A).

In a three-phase system, the third-harmonic currents of each phase are in phase *with each other and hence constitute a zero-sequence set of currents of triple frequency.* Likwise, the third-harmonic voltages will constitute a zero-sequence set of voltage of triple frequency. *Thus, although a third-harmonic voltage may be present in the line-to-neutral voltages, there can be no third-harmonic component in the line-to-line voltage.* The paths permiting the flow of third-harmonic currents are determined by the system and transformer zero-sequence circuits.

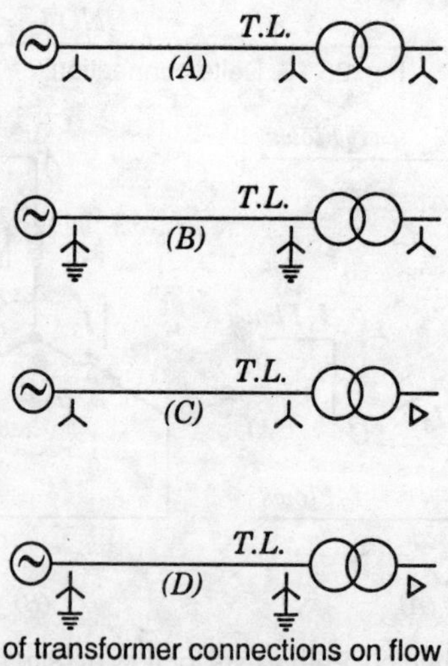


Fig. 26.18. Effect of transformer connections on flow of third harmonic component of magnetizing currents in line conductors.

**Effect of Transformer Connections** (Fig. 26.18.). The path for flow of the third harmonic currents through line conductors depends on transformer connections (star/delta) at sending-end and receiving end. Table 26.3 shows various combinations.

In Fig. 26.18 (A), both ends are with star/star. There is no path for the third harmonic currents to flow. *The third harmonic component in magnetizing current is suppressed. Hence, there will be third harmonic component in line to line voltages at that voltage level.* Voltage waveform will be flat-topped. Fig.26.17. (B) shows both end stars with neutral grounded. Third harmonic currents find a path through return earth. Third harmonic component of the magnetizing current is not suppressed. Flow of third harmonic current will make the magnetizing current waveform non-sinusoidal. As a result the flux in the core and therefore line to line EMFs will be sinusoidal. This is desirable and essential as the EMF must be sinusoidal. However flow of third harmonic current through line conductors will cause telephone interference if telephone lines are in parallel and running close to the overhead lines.

With delta connection in the winding at receiving end transformer [Fig. 26.18 (C) and (D)], third harmonic currents flow through closed delta and third harmonic voltages will be eliminated.

In Fig. 26.18 (C) there is no path for third harmonic currents. Hence third harmonic currents are eliminated frcm line.

In Fig. 26.18 (D), neutrals at both ends are earthed. Third harmonic currents have a path to flow. However because of close delta on receiving-end secondary, the third harmonic component has a ready path to circulate and they need not flow through the line conductors. Small content would be present if the impedance of line to third harmonic currents is low.

This general analysis applies to 3 phase two winding transformer and 3 phase transformers.

Same principle applies to three phase three winding transformers if used on receiving-end side.

## Part 3—Tertiary Delta

In a star/star three phase transformer unit, an additional delta connected tertiary winding is provided for flow of zero-sequence components (due to single phase loading, unbalanced loading) and flow of third harmonic component of no-load (magnetizing) current. if the third harmonic content in the flux (therefore in EMF) is to be avoided *i.e.* EMF waveform is to be made more sinusoidal rather than flat topped, a tertiary must be used in any form of star-star transformer (shell type/core type).

**Table 26.3. Effect to Connections on Third Harmonic Current Flow**

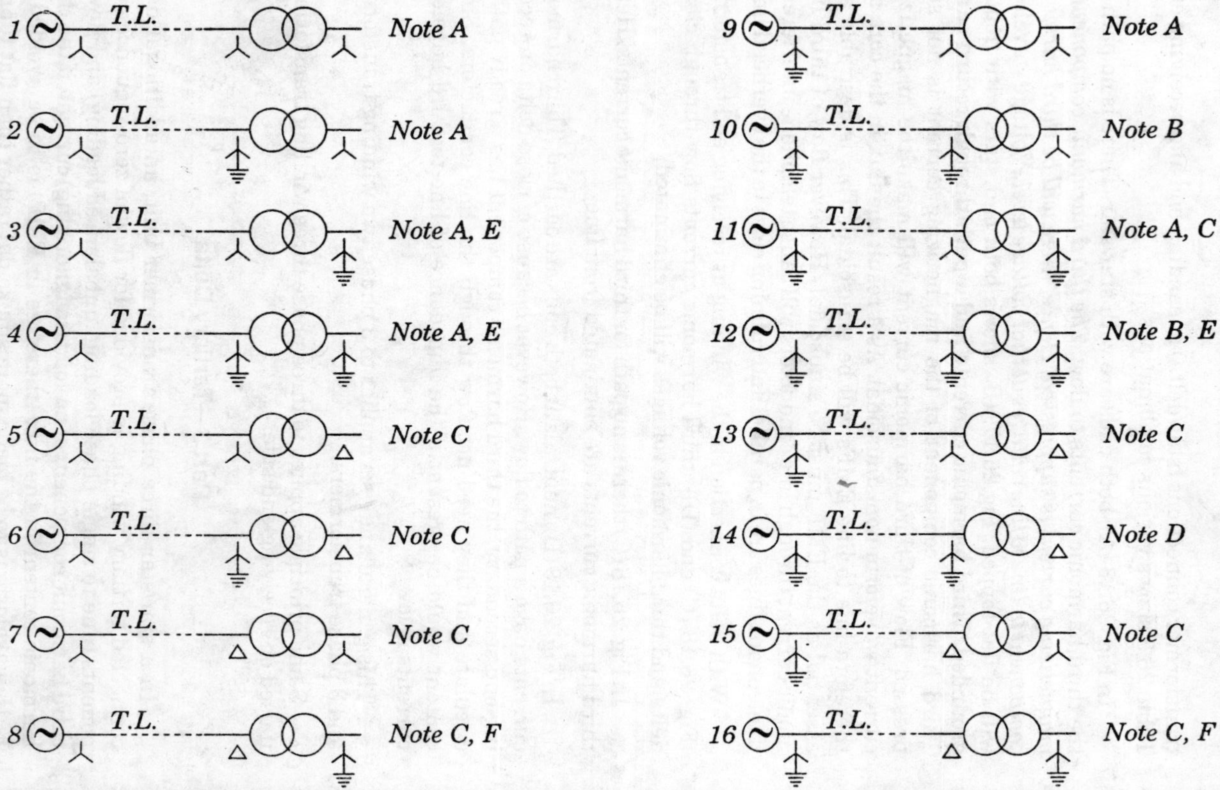

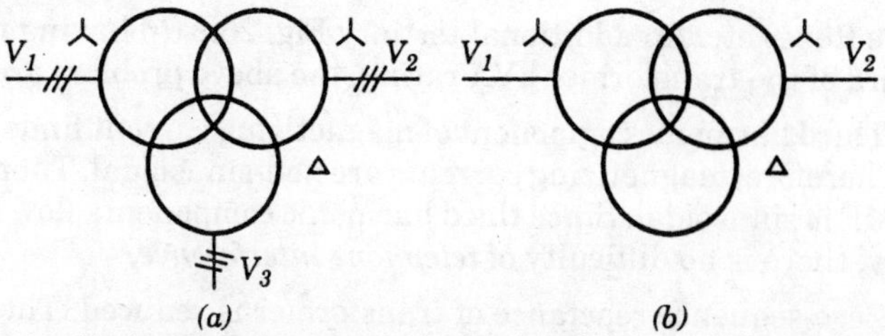


Fig. 26.19. Tertiary delta is essential for a otherwise two winding transformer. Delta tertiary makes it a three winding transformer either
(*a*) with third voltage level ($V_3$)
(*b*) without third winding terminals

Note. In case delta is to be loaded (as in *a*) the delta winding is designed for sharing load current plus third harmonic currents under external earth faults on any of the windings.

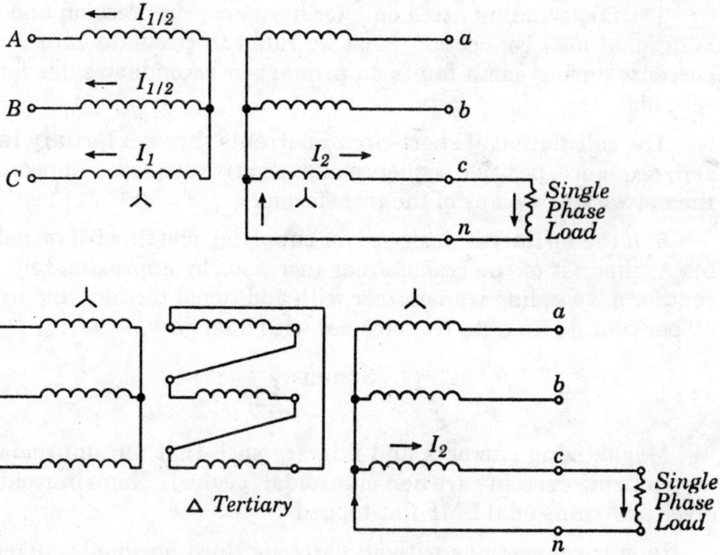


Fig. 26.20. Use of delta tertiary for flow of current during single phase loading.

It has been a very well established practice to provide a delta tertiary to star/star transformer with following purposes :

1. **Stabilization of Neutral Point Voltages.** In case of unbalanced load (*e.g.* single phase load on one phase and neutral of star secondary) the neutral point would get displaced. The distribution of currents in three primary phases without tertiary is shown in Fig. 26.20 and is $I_1$, $I_1/2$, $I_1/2$. The current flowing in unloaded phase primaries is purely magnetizing current and causes saturation of core, deformation of phase voltages and shifting of neutral point, heating of core due to

leakage fluxes etc. An additional tertiary Fig. 26.8 (*b*) having rating of one third of the transformer kVA rating, the above problem are solved.

2. Third harmonic component of magnetizing current finds a closed path. Therefore, magnetizing currents are non-sinusoidal. Thereby flux and EMF is sinusoidal. Since third harmonic components flow through tertiary, there is no difficulty of *telephone interference.*

3. Zero-sequence reactance of transformer is reduced. The ratio of $Z_0/Z_1$ reduces to less than three.

4. Reactance of transformer is increased. The reactive power absorbed from the system increases but fault current reduces.

5. Tertiary can be used for connecting additional auxiliary loads at lower voltages. SVS systems, auxiliary loads etc. can be connected to tertiary terminals.

Tertiary winding fitted only for harmonic suppression and not for additional load connection must be rated to circulate zero sequence currents during earth faults on primary or secondary sides for a few seconds.

The calculation of short-circuit currents through tertiary involves zero-sequence, positive sequence and negative sequence impedances of the network as well as of the transformer.

6. If the tertiary is designed for supplying one third of transformer MVA, the cost of the transformer increases by approximately 15 per cent for a 2 winding transformer with additional tertiary and by about 40 per cent for an auto-transformer with a tertiary.

## Summary

Magnetizing currents and flux are such that for sinusoidal flux, magnetizing currents are non-sinusoidal (peaked). Non-sinusoidal flux gives non-sinusoidal EMF flat-topped.

In star connections without earthing third harmonic current has no path.

In star connection with neutral earthing, third harmonic currents do flow.

In delta connection third harmonic currents do flow.

For star-star transformer delta tertiary is a must.

Ungrounded Neutral system is no more preferred as it has several drawbacks.

## Questions

1. State the principle of flow of magnetizing current in following windings and corresponding line terminals.

— Star without neutral ground
— Star
— Delta.

2. Explain the purpose of delta tertiary.

3. What are the benefits of grounded neutral system.

4. For a single line to earth fault on phase *A* of three phase ungrounded system (*A, B, C*) what would be the voltages

(1) $V_{AB}$, $V_{BC}$, $V_{CA}$.

(2) $V_{AN}$, $V_{BN}$, $V_{CN}$.

Notes Reg. Table 26.3, P. 526.

**Flow of Third Harmonic Current Through Transmission Lines**

| *Note* | *In Tr. Line On Generator Side* $I_3$ | *In Tr. Line On Load Side* $I_3$ |
|---|---|---|
| *A* | No | No |
| *B* | Yes | No |
| *C* | No | No |
| *D* | Yes | No |
| *E* | No | No |
| *F* | No | No |

# 27

# Auto-Transformers

Auto-transformers are well known for their reduced size and economic use of material. Unfortunately, the low impedance and the direct connection between HV and LV go against their wide spread use in networks. The basic aspects and applications have been elaborated.

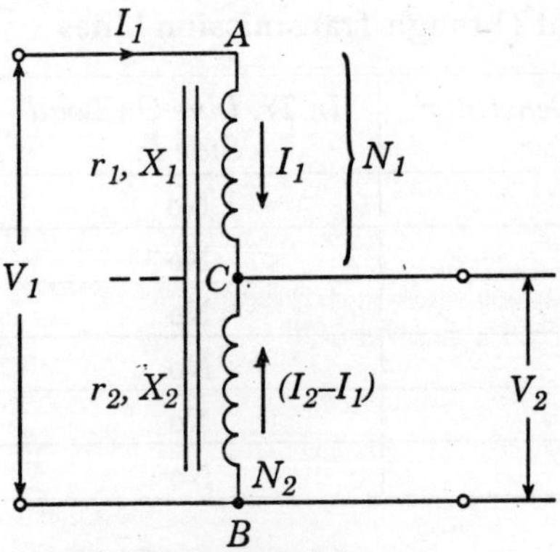


C = Common point
AC = Series winding
CB = Common winding
$V_1$ = HV side voltage
$V_2$ = LV side voltage.
Fig. 27.1. Single phase auto-transformer.

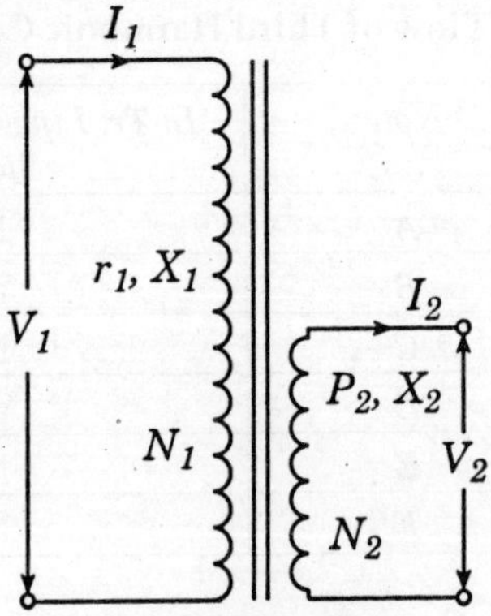


$V_1$ = HV side voltage
$V_2$ = LV side voltage.
Fig. 27.2. Single phase two-winding transformer.

## 27.1 INTRODUCTION

In an auto-transformer, the primary winding and secondary winding have a common part. The secondary is connected electrically to the primary at a common point (*C*) (Fig. 27.1). The following terms are applicable :

— *Common Winding.* The part of the winding common to the HV and LV windings.

— *Common Terminal.* The terminal which is common to HV and LV winding.

— *Series Winding.* Winding other than common winding.

Figure 27.2 shows a single phase auto-transformer. Fig. 27.3 shows a three-phase star connected auto-transformer. Most three phase auto-

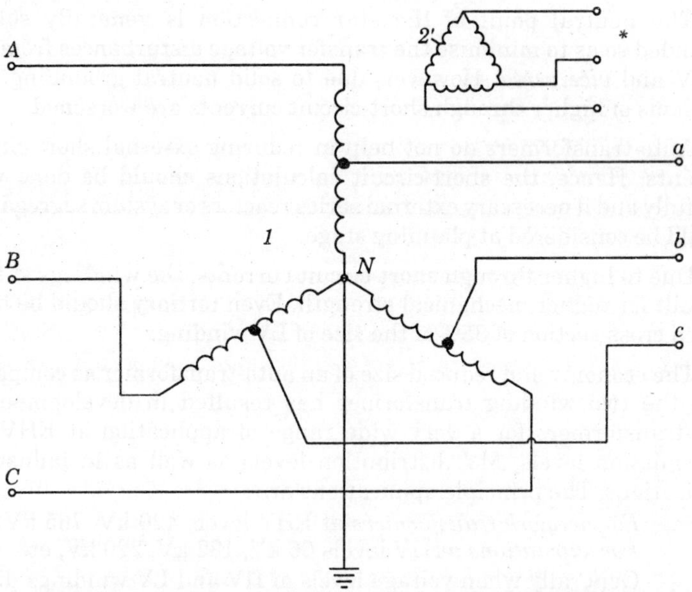


Fig. 27.3. Three phase auto-transformer star winding with neutral solidly grounded. Delta tertiary wound on the same core for providing path for third hormonic magnetizing currents.
1. Auto-transformer, star/star. 2. Delta tertiary.
*Leads and terminals (optional).

transformers are star connected and it is a usual practice to add an additional delta winding called *'Tertiary'*. The purpose of delta tertiary is to provide an internal path to the third harmonic currents required for excitation and thus eliminating them from the AC network. The delta tertiary also helps to stabilize the neutral with reference to line voltage.

Compared with a two winding transformer, the auto-transformer has lesser weight, lesser size and lesser cost. Hence it is preferred in certain situations after considering other system problems, when $V_1$ and $V_2$ do not differ widely.

In ordinary two winding transformer, the HV and LV windings are insulated from each other. The energy is transferred by inductive coupling. The high voltage surges pass from HV to LV sides (or *vice versa*) by inductive/capacitive couplings. In an auto-transformer, the HV winding is connected to LV winding. Hence high voltage surges pass from HV to LV (or *vice versa*) directly. This is the greatest drawback of auto-transformers.

In auto-transformers, the impedance of windings is lesser and the through short-circuit currents would be higher. Therefore, means are necessary to limit the through short-circuit currents to safe values.

The neutral point of the star connection is generally solidly grounded so as to minimise the transfer voltage disturbances from HV to LV and *vice versa*. However, due to solid neutral grounding, the problems of higher through short-circuit currents are worsened.

Auto-transformers do not help in reducing external short-circuit currents. Hence, the short-circuit calculations should be done very carefully and if necessary external series reactors or system segregation should be considered at planning stage.

Due to higher through short-circuit currents, the windings should be built for higher mechanical strength. Even tertiary should be built with a cross-section of 35% of the size of LV winding.

The economy and reduced size of an auto-transformer as compared with the two winding transformer has resulted in development of auto-transformers for a very wide range of application at EHV-AC transmission levels, MV distribution levels as well as in industrial applications. The principle applications are :

- *For network transformers* at EHV levels 420 kV, 765 kV etc. *For substations* at HV levels 66 kV, 132 kV, 220 kV, etc.
- Generally when voltage levels of HV and LV windings differ only by one step, *e.g.* 220 kV/132 kV.
- *For system inter-connections*
- *For starting* of synchronous motors, induction motors etc. *For variable LV or HV supply. Variacs*
- *As regulating transformers* for obtaining very wide range of low secondary voltages for industrial applications such as traction, furnaces, electrolysis plants etc.

A very wide choice is available for the tappings on the auto-transformers. Thus, suitable choice of tappings must be made for obtaining the following alternatives :

- Fixed voltage ratios between HV and LV
- HV voltage fixed, LV variable
- LV voltage fixed, HV variable
- HV voltage, LV voltage widely varying with need for coarse and fire voltage control
- For starting purpose with LV voltage increasing from lower value to higher value within certain specified time.

Auto-transformers offer unique advantages for industrial applications as well as network applications. Therefore they are being used from 765 kV down to 220 V. They have advantages and disadvantages which restrict their applications compared with two winding transformers.

## 27.2 BASIC PRINCIPLE

Figure 27.2. shows a *two-winding single phase transformer*. Current $I_1$ flows through the primary and current $I_2$ through secondary.

The two windings are insulated from each other. Energy flow is by magnetic induction. The volt-amperes of primary and secondary are almost equal *i.e.*

$$V_1 I_1 = V_2 I_2$$

For comparison, Fig. 27.1 shows an auto-transformer. It has a common point $C$ between primary and secondary windings.

Primary is not insulated from secondary. If $I_2$ is the current on secondary load side, the current flowing through the common winding is $(I_2 - I_1)$.

In case of two winding transformer current $I_2$ flows through secondary winding but in case of auto-transformer $(I_2 - I_1)$ flows through common winding.

Consider single phase auto-transformer shown in Fig. 27.1. Neglect magnetizing current. Total number of turns is $N_1$. Common winding turns are $N_2$. Neglect losses.

Let $I_2$ = Output current (Load current)

$V_2$ = Output voltage (voltage across common winding)

Then $I_1$ = Input current

$= I_2(N_2/N_1)$

$V_1$ = Input voltage

$= V_2(N_1/N_2)$

Current is common winding $= I_2 - I_1$.

Hence cross-section of common winding can be smaller assuming same current density (A/mm$^2$) for the conductor.

The ratio of conductor material of auto-transformer ($G_a$) and two winding transformer ($G_t$) be $G_a/G_t$.

$$\frac{G_a}{G_t} = \frac{I_1 (N_1 - N_3) + (I_2 - I_1) N_2}{I_1 N_1 + I_2 N_2}$$

$$= 1 - \frac{V_2}{V_1}$$

With same current density for entire conductor in the windings, the ratio of conductor materials is as follows.

$$\frac{\text{Conductor material for auto–transformer}}{\text{Conductor material for 2–W transformer}} = 1 - \frac{V_2}{V_1}$$

where $V_2$ is output voltage and $V_1$ is supply voltage.

The core is as large as two-winding transformer core.

With $V_2/V_1 = \frac{1}{2}$ the ratio of copper becomes

$$\frac{\text{Conductor material for auto–transformer}}{\text{Conductor material for 2–W transformer}} = 1 - \frac{V_2}{V_1}$$

$$= 1 - 0.5 = 0.5$$

*i.e.*, only 50% material would be enough. Overall cost of transformer would however be only about 65% of equivalent two-winding transformer.

The reduction in copper depends on $V_2/V_1$. As $V_2$ approaches $V_1$, the reduction in copper increases. For example if $V_2$ is 15 kV and $V_1$ is 20 kV, the ratio of coppers is 1–15/20=0.25. Copper requirement is reduced to 25%.

## 27.3 RELATIVE SIZE

The relative size of an auto-transformer with a fixed transformation ratio $V_2/V_1$ (where $V_2 < V_1$) to equivalent two-winding transformer is given by

$$K = 1 - \frac{V_2}{V_1}$$

*The reduction in size of auto-transformer relative to two-winding transformer increases as $V_2$ approaches $V_1$.*

In other words with same amount of material, an auto-transformer will have higher MVA rating than equivalent two-winding transformer.

For throughout of 5 MVA, the relative sizes of two-winding transformer and auto-transformer are as follows:

| | *Transformer without regulation* | *Transformer with 15% regulation* |
|---|---|---|
| Two-winding transformer | 5 MVA | 5.9 MVA |
| Auto-transformer $V_2/V_1$ = 20/30 kV | 1.67 MVA | 2.5 MVA |
| Auto-transformer $V_2/V_1$ = 20/10 kV | 2.5 MVA | 3.38 MVA |

The auto-transformers are preferred for substations when $V_1/V_2$ is near unity, *e.g.* 132 kV/220 kV, 420/765 kV.

The reduced cross-section of common winding makes auto-transformers physically smaller, less costly, more efficient than the two-winding transformer of the same circuit kVA rating.

## 27.4 THREE-WINDING AUTO-TRANSFORMER

Figure 27.3 shows a circuit of a 3 ph. 3-W auto-transformer. It is usually star connected with grounded neutral. A third delta connected tertiary-winding is wound on the same core to carry the third harmonic component of exciting current. Delta tertiary winding could be of smaller rating when it is designed to carry only third harmonic currents.

However during ground-faults on the network higher currents flow through tertiary.

As per well accepted practice, delta-tertiary-winding is designed for 35% of auto-transformer equivalent two-winding kVA rating (Not circuit kVA rating).

## 27.5 EQUIVALENT SIZE OF AUTO-TRANSFORMER

This term is used for comparison of size of an auto-transformer with that of two winding transformer of the same output.

For winding or a part of a winding, the VA rating is a product of maximum current and maximum voltage in service.

For a complete transformer, the two winding equivalent is the half the sum of the power ratings of all the winding. For a two winding transformer VA rating of primary and secondary winding is the same equal to

$$V_1 I_1 = V_2 I_2 = \frac{V_1 I_1 + V_2 I_2}{2}$$

A three winding transformer, has two-winding equivalent $VA_e$ is given by

$$VA_e = \frac{V_1 I_1 + V_2 I_2 + V_3 I_3}{2}$$

An auto-transformer with voltage ratio $V_2/V_1 (V_2 < V_1)$ has relative to a two-winding transformer of same output is

$$K = 1 - \frac{V_2}{V_1}$$

When $V_2/V_1$ approaches unity, the reduction in size of auto-transformer increases for the same output.

## 27.6 ADVANTAGES OF AUTO-TRANSFORMERS

1. When voltage ratio $(V_2/V_1)$ is near unity, auto-transformer of the same output as two-winding transformer has smaller size, lesser cost, higher efficiency, lesser losses etc.

2. If $S$ is the VA rating, linear dimensions vary as $S^{0.25}$, weight and volume as $S^{0.75}$.

3. Short-circuit impedance reduces in proportion to the equivalent rating. This is beneficial for voltage regulation during changing loads.

4. For large EHV transformers for interconnection between two systems, the rating is of several hundred MVA.

The usual two winding transformers in three-phase units are larger, heavier and may not be transportable. Three single phase two windings would be necessary. However, with auto-transformer a single three phase unit has smaller size and lesser weight and it may be transportable on given route from manufacturer's works to the site.

## 27.7 CHOICE OF AUTO-TRANSFORMERS

Compared with two-winding transformer of same output, an auto-transformer has

1. Lower size, lesser material, lesser cost.

2. Lower losses, higher efficiency.

3. Lesser transport size*, transport weight.

Hence a single three phase auto-transformer unit may be transportable whereas three phase two-winding transformer unit of same output may be beyond permissible transport limits. Hence for large EHV interconnecting transformers rated above 500 MVA, auto-transformer units may be considered favourably.

4. Lower percentage reactance (leakage reactance). Hence better voltage regulation, lesser voltage drop.

5. Several alternatives for tap-changing (Refer Sec. 27.8).

6. Can be used for obtaining variable voltage supply during starting, speed control, power control etc.

7. Are preferred for system interconnections at different voltage levels *e.g.* 220 kV/400 kV. The saving in transformer cost is significant.

## 27.8 DEMERITS OF AUTO-TRANSFORMERS

Auto-transformers have following inherent disadvantages which restrict their application as a usual power transformer. Care should be taken in specifying an auto-transformer with respect to

— Insulation levels and surge arrester protection
— Neutral earthing
— Short-circuit currents and withstand capabilities
— Triple harmonic current path and delta-tertiary
— Reduced reactance and transient disturbances on HV and LV sides.

These aspects have been summarised below :

1. *Insulation levels and surge arrester protection* (Fig. 27.3).

Common point and electrical connection between HV and LV winding results in transmission of high voltage lightning surges and switching surges form HV to LV and vice-versa. Both HV and LV are subjected to highest stresses. Hence surge arresters are necessary on HV side, on LV side and on neutral to ground.

---

* Size reduce as follows :

$S$ = Power transfer

—Dimensions = $S^{0.25}$

—Volume = $S^{0.5}$.

2. Auto-transformer neutral should be earthed. It should not be kept floating.

3. Auto-transformer windings need higher insulation than that of a two-winding transformer.

4. Short-circuit reactance of an auto-transformer is $1/K$ times that of equivalent two winding transformer where $K = (1 - V_2/V_1)$.

For example if $V_2/V_1 = 0.5$ and % $X$ of a two-winding transformer is 6%, the %$X$ of equivalent auto-transformer would be $6\% \times (1 - 0.5) = 3\%$ only. The short-circuit current during external short-circuits would be doubled.

5. As a result of higher short circuit currents, the auto-transformer windings need higher mechanical strength than that of two-winding transformer.

6. Tertiary winding is necessary. Tertiary gets higher currents during external short-circuits. Hence special means should be adopted to increase zero sequence impedance of delta tertiary or neutral grounding neutral impedance for auto-transformer.

7. Delta connected Auto-transformers have floating (imaginary) neutral. This gives disturbances and unbalances in phase voltages. Hence delta connected auto-transformers are not preferred.

8. Type of grounding of auto-transformer neutral should be same as that for system neutral (solid/resistance/reactance).

## 27.9 AUTO-TRANSFORMER TAPPINGS AND METHODS OF CONNECTIONS

Applications demand the tappings of auto-transformer for regulating either $V_1$ or $V_2$ or both $V_1$ and $V_2$.

It is not desirable to place the taps adjucent to the line terminals particularly for voltage above 15 kV because of the extra insulation required for the end-turns. If taps are provided here, they would require extra padding throughout the tapped section. Also tapping near end turns would form the weakest portion of the winding. This can be avoided by providing the taps in the middle of the winding as shown in Fig. 27.8.

Several alternatives are available. The choice depends on the range of variation, whether $V_1/V_2$ or both $V_1$ and $V_2$ are variable.

Figure 27.4 shows an auto-transformer connection without tapping. The voltage ratio $V_1/V_2$ is fixed. This type of connection is used for fixed $V_1$ and fixed $V_2$. This is a simplest Auto-Transformer.

Figure 27.5 shows a special auto-transformer which gives a very-wide variation in voltage $V_2$ for given fixed HV voltage $V_1$. For large

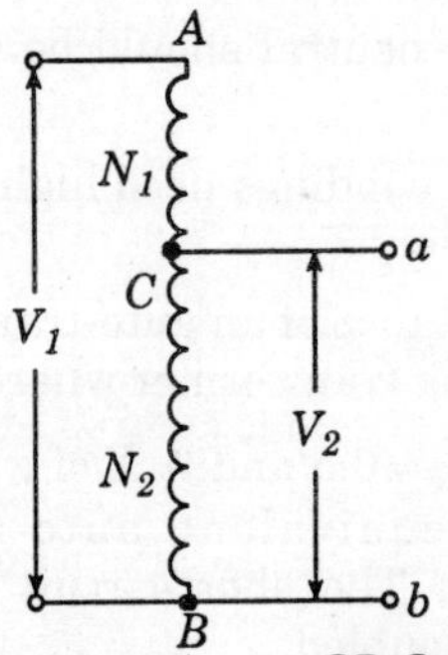


*AC*=Series winding
*AB*=Terminals of HV winding
$N_2$=Turns of common winding
$V_1$=Primary voltage
*CB*=Common winding
$N_1$=Turns of series winding
C=Common point.
$V_2$=Secondary voltage

Fig. 27.4. Single phase Auto-Transformer without tapping.

adjustments, course taps are changed. Fine adjustment of $V_2$ is obtained when tap near neutral is used.

The $V_2$ can be varied over a wide range.

Such an arrangement is used for Auto-Transformers which have to supply variable low voltage ($V_2$) from high value (tap 0) to low voltage (tap 3). The applications include furnaces, traction duty, rectifier plants etc.

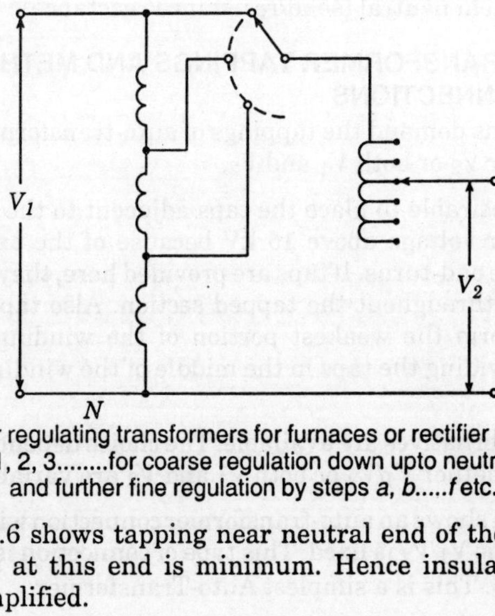


Fig. 27.5. For regulating transformers for furnaces or rectifier plants, several steps 1, 2, 3........for coarse regulation down upto neutral point and further fine regulation by steps *a*, *b*.....*f* etc.

Figure 27.6 shows tapping near neutral end of the winding. The voltage stress at this end is minimum. Hence insulation in tapped winding is simplified.

Figure 27.7 shows a booster transformer combined with an auto-transformer (Further details in Chapter 28).

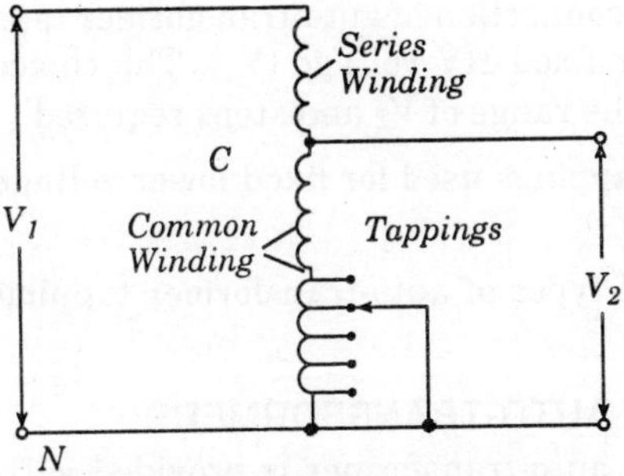


Fig. 27.6. Tapping at neutral-end. Tappings provided near neutral-end which is less exposed to high voltage surges coming from line terminal.

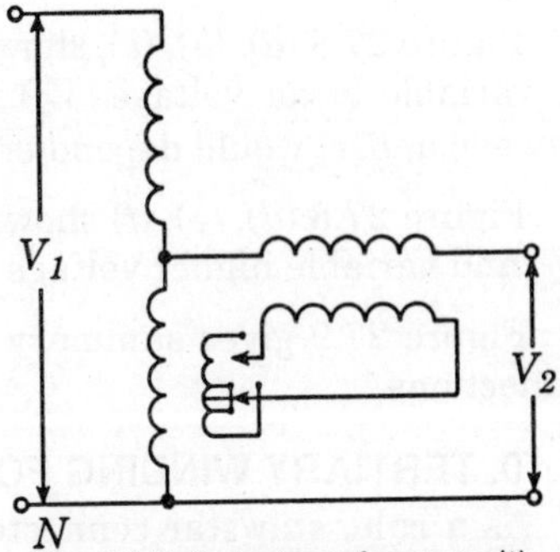


Fig. 27.7. Auto-transformer with booster transformer. The booster transformer is excited by the auto-transformer.

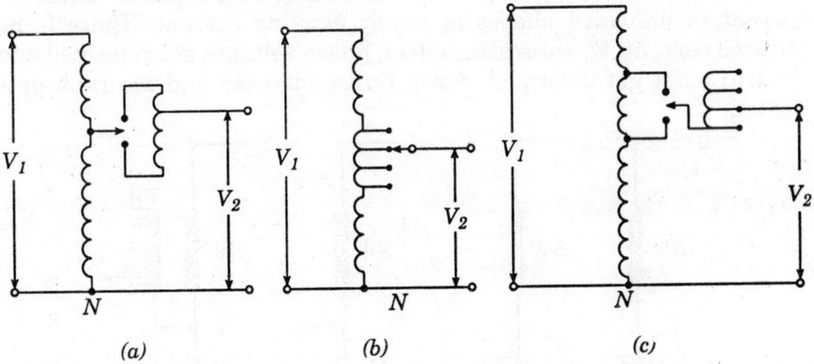


Fig. 27.8. (*a,b,c*) Connections and Tapping for fixed $V_1$ and variable $V_2$. $V_1$ higher level and $V_2$ lower level. Choice between *A, B, C* depends on tapping range.

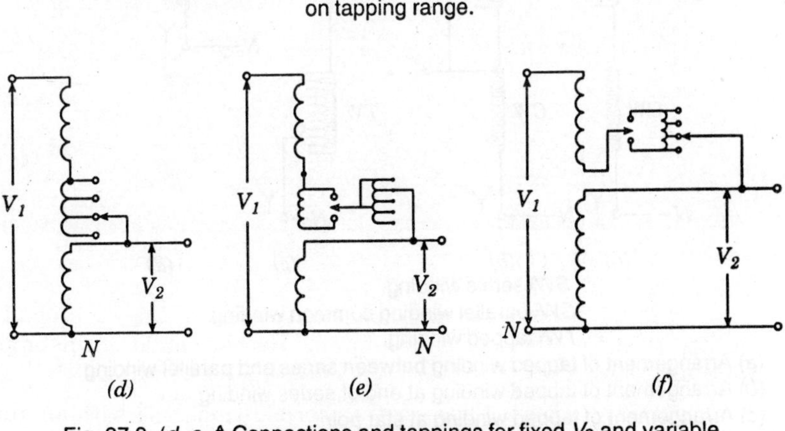


Fig. 27.9. (*d, e, f*) Connections and tappings for fixed $V_2$ and variable $V_1$, $V_1$ is higher level and $V_2$ is lower level.

Figure 27.8 (*a*), (*b*), (*c*), shows connection of auto-transformer taps for variable lower voltage ($V_2$) for fixed HV voltage ($V_1$). The choice between *a, b, c,* would depend on the range of $V_2$ and steps required.

Figure 27.8 (*d*), (*e*), (*f*) show tappings used for fixed lower voltage ($V_2$) and variable higher voltage ($V_1$).

Figure 27.9 gives summary of types of auto-transformer tapping connections.

## 27.10. TERTIARY WINDING FOR AUTO-TRANSFORMERS

As a rule, star/star connected auto-transformer is provided with delta-tertiary for following purposes :

1. *Stabilising the phase-to-phase voltages during unbalanced loads on secondary side (e.g. single phase loads).*

Without a tertiary (Fig. 27.11 *a*) during single phase loads the current in unloaded phases is purely exciting current. There is no induced current. By saturation effect, phase voltages get deformed and neutral point get deformed. Stray fluxes increase and the tank gets heated.

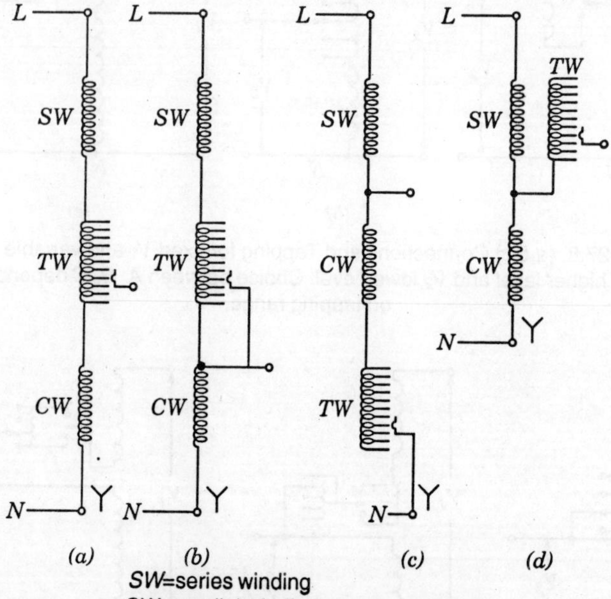


*SW*=series winding
*CW*=parallel winding common winding
*TW*=tapped winding.

(*a*) Arrangement of tapped winding between series and parallel winding.
(*b*) Arrangement of tapped winding at end of series winding.
(*c*) Arrangement of tapped winding at star point.
(*d*) Arrangement of tapped winding in fork-connection at low-voltage terminal.

Fig. 27.10. Types of auto-transformer connections with tappings.

By incorporating a delta tertiary (Fig. 27.3 and Fig. 27.11 *b*), the balanced ampere-turns are obtained in all the three phases of tertiary. These windings are on the same core. Hence the magnetising currents are balanced in all the three phases. The problem of shifting of neutral and unbalanced voltages is eliminated.

For normal conditions, the rating of tertiary winding is one third of the transformer throughput rating. However during phase to ground short-circuits in the network, the currents in delta-tertiary increase and the delta-tertiary is designed for 35% of throughput rating of the transformer.

2. *Suppression of third harmonic currents due to no-load current in neutral to ground circuit when neutral is earthed.* (Fig. 27.3) Such currents produce electro-magnetic disturbances in low voltage unshielded telephone cables, in the neighbourhood. Shielded telephone cables are not affected.

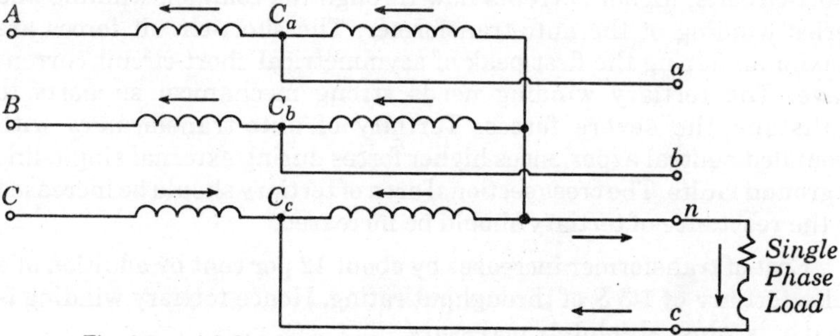


Fig. 27.11 (*a*) Single-phase load on a star-star auto transformer results in circulation of third harmonic currents in star windings

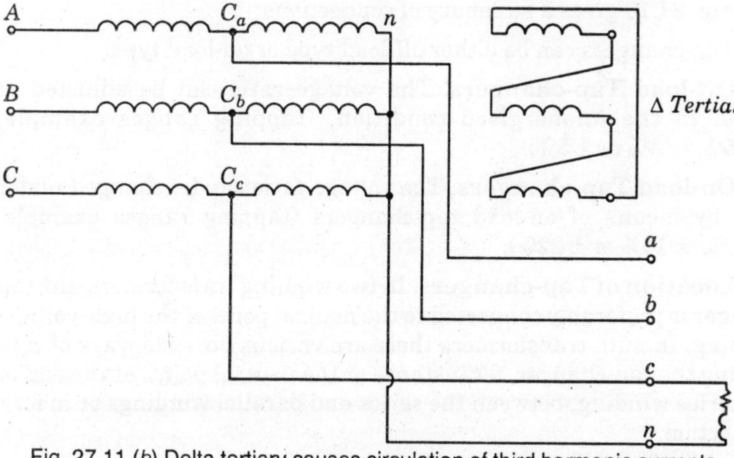


Fig. 27.11 (*b*) Delta tertiary causes circulation of third harmonic currents in delta tertiary.

Delta-tertiary eliminates the flow of third harmonic no-load current in neutral to ground connection. Also CRGO sheet steel and modern core constructions has low magnetizing current and this problem is not as serious as it used to be in 1950's.

3. *Reduction in zero sequence reactance.* With the use of delta tertiary, the ratio of $X_0/X_1$ becomes less than three. In delta circuit, zero-sequence reactance $X_0$ is reduced by 5 to 15%.

4. Increase of *kVAr*. Delta-tertiary gives additional reactive power absorbed by the transformer and also additional stored reactive energy to the system.

5. Tertiary can be used for supplying auxiliary loads at reduced voltage.

*Short-circuit forces in tertiary.* The design of tertiary is governed by short-circuit forces during external short-circuits. During external short-circuits, higher currents flow through the common winding and series winding of the auto-transformer. The short-circuit forces are maximum during the first peak of asymmetrical short-circuit current wave. The tertiary winding needs strong mechanical supports to withstand the severe forces. Tertiary of auto-transformers with grounded neutral experiences higher forces during external single-line to ground faults. The cross sectional area of tertiary should be increased or the reactance of tertiary should be increased.

Cost of transformer increases by about 12 per cent by addition of a delta tertiary of 1/3 *S* of throughput rating. Hence tertiary winding is used only when absolutely necessary.

## 27.11 TAPPING AND REGULATION OF VOLTAGE RATIO

Fig. 27.10 gives a summary of connections.

Tap-changers can be either off-load type or on-load type.

**Off-load Tap-changers.** The voltage ratio can be adjusted in steps, in the unenergised condition, (tapping ranges example, ± 2.5%, ± 4% or ± 5%).

**On-load Tap-changers.** The voltage ratio can be changed under load by means of on-load tap-changers (tapping ranges example, ± 11%, ± 16% or ± 22%).

**Location of Tap-changers.** In two winding transformers, the tap changer is preferably connected to the neutral point of the high-voltage winding. In auto-transformers there are various possible ways of connecting the tap-changer, for instance at the neutral point, at the end of the series winding, between the series and parallel windings or in fork connection.

**Regulating Transformers-Booster Transformers.** In special cases two-winding, auto-or booster transformers are combined for the purpose of regulation of the voltage ratio under load for instance, in booster transformer sets (Ref. Chapter 28).

**Induction Regulators, Moving-Coil Regulators.** In the case of induction regulators, moving-coil regulators, etc. continuous regulation of the voltage ratio is possible (Ref. Chapter 28).

## Summary

Auto-transformers have reduced size, reduced cost but need more design provision for insulation coordination, neutral grounding, delta-tertiary, short-circuit-strength etc.

Auto-transformers are chosen only after detailed study of following:

— Short-circuit-current and strength
— Method of neutral grounding
— Insulation levels
— Transformation ratio (0.5 to 2)
— Balanced loads
— Third harmonic currents.

## Questions

**1.** State whether correct or wrong :

— Auto-transformers is preferred only for low voltage single phase loads.
— Auto-transformer is preferred when voltage ratio is less than 3 : 1.
— Auto-transformer has low impedance compared with usual two winding transformer.
— Tap-changers are not used with auto-transformers.
— Auto-transformers are of smaller size than equivalent 2-winding transformers.
— Tertiary delta is necessary for star connected auto-transformers.
— Auto-transformers are used for arc furnaces.

**2.** State the demerits of auto-transformers. Even then in which specific applications are they preferred and why ?

# 28

# Regulating Transformers for Phase Angle Control

The normal application involve power transformers with tap-chargers for in-phase voltage control. In case of parallel circuits and system interconnections, special *phase regulating transformers* are sometimes necessary. The application of regulating transformers involves detailed study of requirements of *in-phase, quadrature* and *phase-angle voltage control* requirements and the choice of auto-transformer two winding transformer and supplementary transformers. The details have been described with the help of schematic diagrams and vector diagrams.

## 28.1 INTRODUCTION

In some applications in power transmission, it becomes necessary to introduce certain *phase angle regulation* with or without variation in the magnitude of voltage. The change in voltage magnitude is easily achieved by usual tap-changing transformers. The phase angle regulation requires a specially connected regulating transformers called phase-angle transformers or phase angle regulating transformers.

Booster transformer is a type of phase angle transformer in which one of the transformer windings is connected in series with the main circuit and the excitation is taken from other windings. The voltage is injected in the line for phase angle control.

Three applications of phase angle transformers or regulating transformers are

1. Tie-line (Interconnection) power control. This requires phase-angle regulation.

2. In parallel circuit (loop system) to match the phase angle of one circuit with that of other circuit for proper load sharing. This requires magnitude and phase regulation.

The regulating transformers are used in conjunction with tap-changing transformers/auto-transformers/booster transformers and automatic control systems. The possible requirements include

1. Voltage magnitude control only. This is achieved by tap-changing transformer or auto-transformer.

2. In-phase voltage control only. This is same as (1) above.

3. Quadrature phase voltage control only.

4. Combination of In-phase and Quadrature voltage control.

The requirements are met by selecting appropriate connections of windings of the regulating transformers. Several types of connections are possible for obtaining the required phase angle regulation.

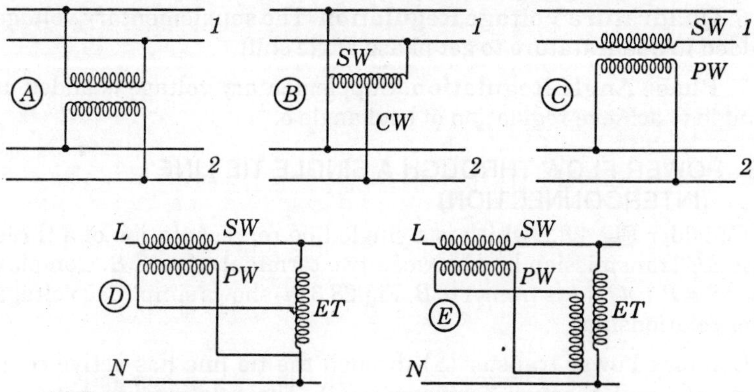


(*a*) Two winding transformer (*b*) Auto-transformer
(*c*) Booster transformer
(*d*) Booster-transformer with Exciting Auto-transformer (ET)
(*e*) Booster transformer with Exciting two winding-transformer (ET)
1. Circuit-1 2. Circuit-2
Fig. 28.1. Types of transformer connections PW = Parallel winding. CW = Common winding, SW = Series winding.

## 28.2 TERMS AND DEFINITIONS.

(Fig. 28.1 *a* to *e*)

1. **Auto-Transformer.** The primary and secondary windings are connected at a point conductively. Primary and secondary windings have a common part.

2. **Two Winding Transformer.** Primary and secondary windings are insulated from each other.

3. **Booster Transformer.** One of the windings is connected in series with the circuit in order to later its voltage magnitude/phase. The other winding is an energizing winding which is electrically separate from the series winding.

Figure 28.1 illustrates the connections referred above. Booster transformer set consists of an exciting transformer (an auto-transformer or a two-winding transformer) and a booster transformer. The parallel winding of the booster transformer is supplied by the secondary of the exciting transformer.

4. **Phase Regulating Transformer.** A single transformer unit or a combination of a main transformer and a supplementary transformer for shifting the phase angle of output voltages.

The phase shifting may be achieved by tap-charging.

5. **In-phase Voltage Regulation.** Only magnitude of output voltage is regulated without change in phase angle.

6. **Quadrature Voltage Regulation.** The supplementary voltage is added in quadratature to get phase angle shift.

7. **Phase Angle Regulation.** Supplementary voltage is added at an angle to achieve regulation of load angle $\delta$.

## 28.3 POWER FLOW THROUGH A SINGLE TIE LINE (INTERCONNECTION)

Consider Fig. 28.2 which is a single line representation of a three phase AC transmission line between two terminals $A$ and $B$. Complex power $S = P \pm jQ$ flows from $A$ to $B$. Fig.28.3 ($a$) shows simplified voltage vector relationship.

Complex Power transfer ($S$) through the tie line has active component ($P$) and reactive component ($Q$). The relationship between $V_A$, $V_B$ and $P$, $Q$ is given by the following well known equations:

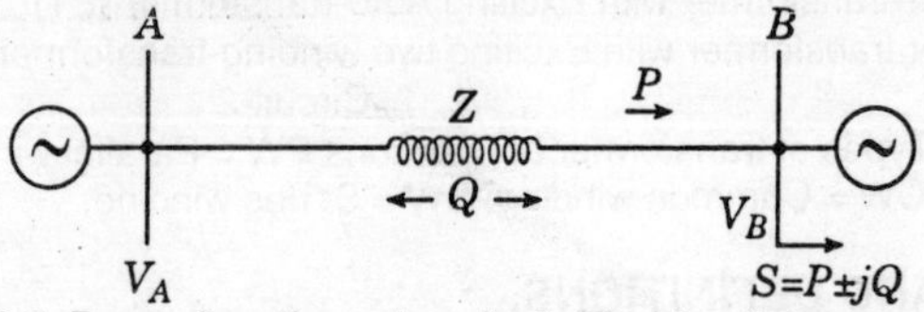


Fig. 28.2. Power flow through a single Tie-Line (interconnector).

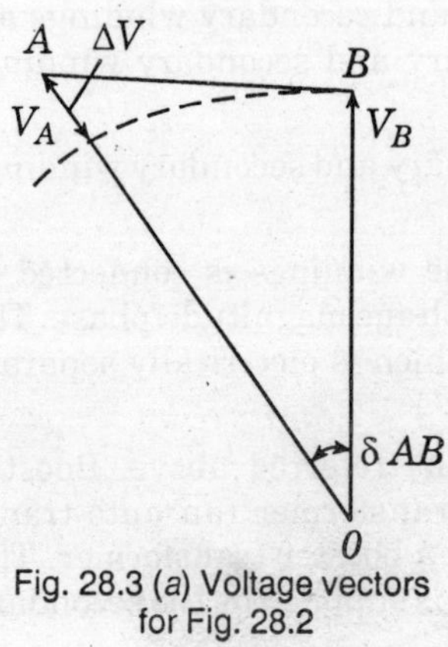


Fig. 28.3 ($a$) Voltage vectors for Fig. 28.2

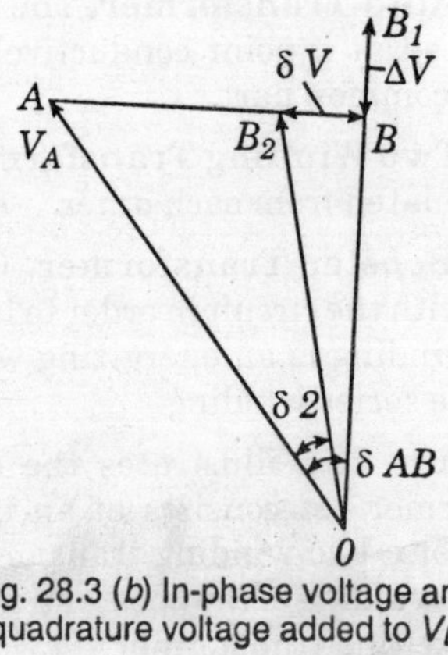


Fig. 28.3 ($b$) In-phase voltage and quadrature voltage added to $V_E$.

## 28.4 POWER FLOW DIRECTION - SINGLE INFEED LINE

Take a simple system shown in Fig. 28.5. We shall identify the parameters which determine the direction of power flow. Let $Z$ be the impedance of the tie line, $Z = R + jX$. Let the load $S = P \pm jQ$ be connected to terminal $B$, at voltage $V_B$. Generator is connected to terminal $A$. In this situation the active power $P$ can flow only from the generator to the load *i.e.* from $A$ to $B$. Reactive power $Q$ can however flow from $A$ to $B$ or $B$ to $A$ as the load can either generate or absorb the reactive power.

From this simple situation, the following conclusions can be drawn assuming line resistance $R$ is negligibly small. The vector diagram Fig. 28.6 gives the relationship between the in-phase and quadrature components and power angle δ.

1. For transmitting active power $P$, a phase shift δ is necessary between voltage vectors $V_A$ and $V_B$.

2. Power flow $P$ is approximately proportional to sin δ *i.e.* $P$ is proportional to quadrature component of voltage drop ($\delta V$).

3. Reactive power $Q$ depends on magnitudes of voltages $V_A$ and $V_B$. The transmitted reactive power $Q$ is approximately proportional to the in phase component of voltage drop ($\Delta V$).

$\Delta V$ is the measure of voltage drop ($V_A - V_B$).

Fig. 28.6 shows the vector diagram indicating inphase and quadrature voltaged drops.

In system such as in Fig. 28.4, it is generally sufficient to install a transformer $T_1$ at the sending-end for regulating the voltage loss $\Delta V$ *i.e.* in-phase regulation. A tap changing two-winding transformer or a tap-changing auto-transformer would be sufficient for single in-feed lines.

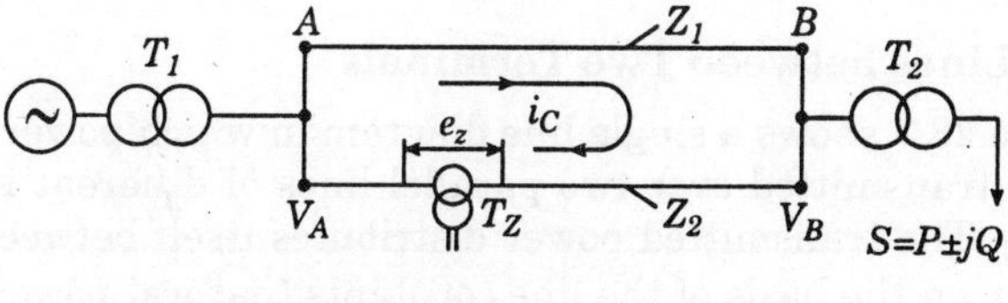


$T_1$, $T_2$ = Step-up and step-down transformers
$AB$ = Parallel lines
$Z_1, Z_2$ = Line impedances
$T_Z$ = Supplementary transformer
$e_Z$ = Supplementary voltage
$i_C$ = Circulating current
$S = P + jQ$ = Apparent power transmitted

Fig. 28.7. Power transmission along two parallel lines with different line impedances.

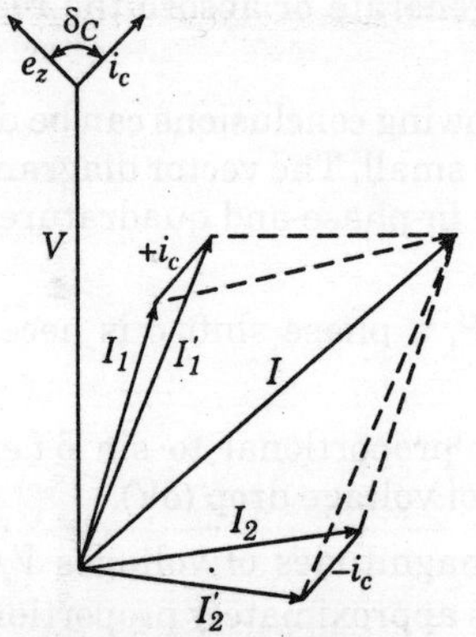


$I$ = Total current burden
$I_1$, $I_2$ = currents in the two lines in accordance with natural distribution.
$i_c$ = Circulating current
$I'_1$, $I'_2$ = Imposed current distribution
$V$ = Voltage at the point on the line where the supplementary transformer is connected (reference voltage)
$e_z$ = Supplementary voltage
$\delta_C$ = Phase angle system (loop).

Fig. 28.8. Vector diagram of current in transmission system of Fig. 28.6.

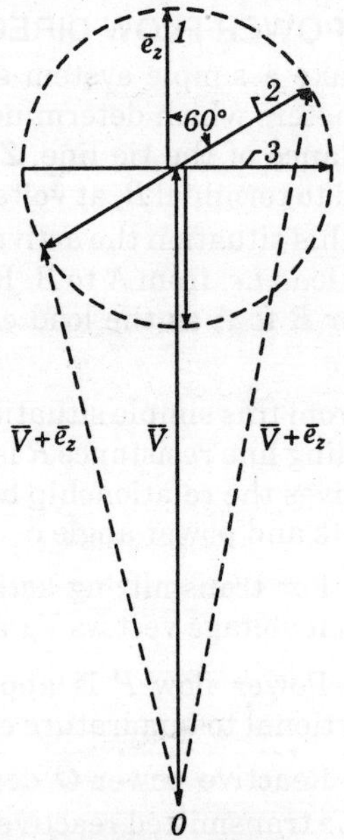


$V$ = Reference voltage
$e_z$ = Supplementary voltage
1 = In–phase shifting
2 = Phase-angle shifting
3 = Quadrature phase shifting

Fig. 28.9. Phase position of supplementary voltage.

## Parallel Lines between Two Terminals

Figure 28.7 shows a single line diagram in which power from $A$ to $B$ is to be transmitted over two parallel lines of different impedance $Z_1$ and $Z_2$. The transmitted power distributes itself between the two lines solely on the basis of the line constants (natural power distribution). If the lines are suitably dimensioned for this natural distribution, the system can be operated without difficulty. If this is not the case, the desired power distribution can be achieved by introducing supplementary voltage $e_z$ at any point in the network.

This *supplementary voltage* $e_z$ produces a circulating current $i_c = \dfrac{e_z}{Z_1 + Z_2}$ in the network which is superimposed on the natural distribution (Fig. 28.8). Altering the phase position of the supplementary voltage also changes the phase position of the predominanlty inductive circulating current. In this way one can influence the distribution of active or reactive power between the two lines, as required.

An extra transformer $T_z$ is needed to produce the supplementary voltage. This is termed an in-phase, phase-angle or quadrature phase shifting transformer, depending on the phase position of the supplementary voltage (Fig. 28.9). Its type rating, is determined by the throughput capacity and the supplementary voltage needed. The necessary type rating, however, is often also influenced by other factors, such as short-circuit strength.

The best known form of voltage regulation is in-phase shifting. This is found with every regulating power transformer. Phase-angle and quadrature shifting are justified only in special cases. They have been used increasingly in Europe for controlling the power distribution in parallel lines and voltage systems, as well as in loop systems.

**Possible Connections of Phase Regulating Transformers.** Several possible connections are available for the generation of the supplementary voltage and injecting it in the line. The choice depends upon the particular system requirements. The most important parameters are

— range of control
— power flow direction
— throughput capacity
— voltage level.

Some possible connections are described below.

*In-phase, Phase-angle or Quadrature Phase Shifting Individually.* If only one of three forms of shifting is required, this can be solved with just a single transformer.

Basic kinds of connection are illustrated in Figs. 28.10, 28.11 and 28.12.

*In-phase voltage shifting.* Fig. 28.10 shows connections of a single three-phase auto-transformer with tappings on series winding for in-phase voltage shifting.

For tap 1, shows supplementary voltage $e_z$ is maximum. Voltages $A'$, $B'$, $C'$ is higher than voltages $A$, $B$, $C$ by in-phase component $e_z$ added by the supplementary voltage.

As described in Fig. 28.1, in-phase shifting is necessary for compensating $IX$ drop in a long line.

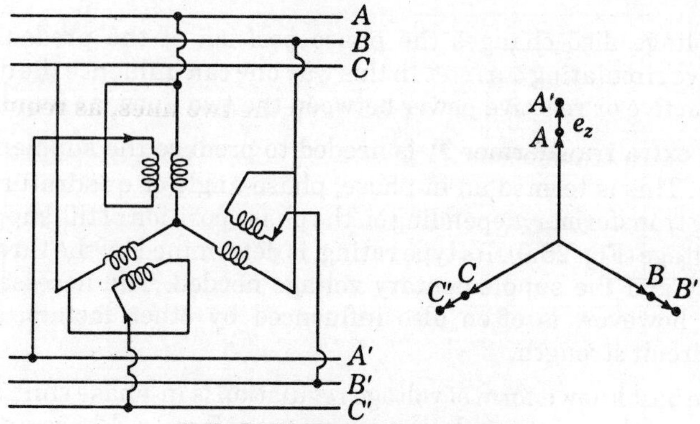


A, B, C = Voltage reference system
$e_z$ = Supplementary voltage
A′,B′,C′ = Voltage increased by $e_z$

Fig. 28.10. Connection for direct in-phase regulation.

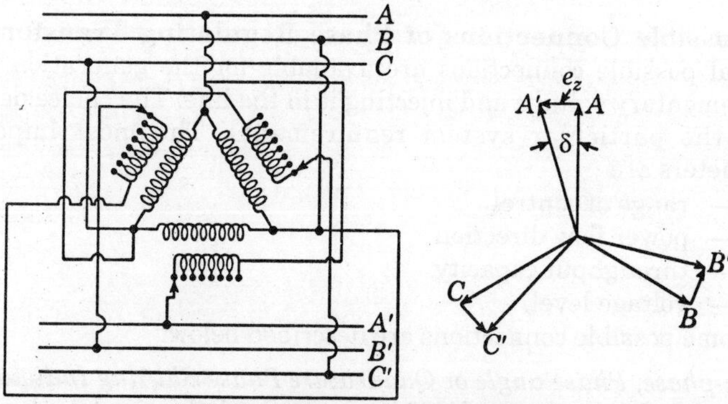


A, B, C = Voltage reference system
$e_z$ = Supplementary voltage
A′,B′,C′ = Phase-shifted voltage system
δ = Phase angle.

Fig. 28.11. Connection for direct quadrature phase regulation.

**Phase-Angle Regulation.** Fig. 28.12 shows connections for direct phase angle regulation. The method of deriving the supplementary voltage is different than that in Fig. 28.11. The supplementary voltage $e_z$ is added at a phase angle θ to the reference voltage. Thereby the angle δ changes with change in $e_z$. The supplementary voltage $e_z$ is changed by means of the taps on the series winding of the auto-transformer. Fig. 28.12 also shows the vector relations. The voltages $V_A'$, $V_B'$, $V_c'$ are lesser than $V_A$, $V_B$, $V_C$.

**Direct Quadrature Phase Regulation.** Fig. 28.13 shows connections of a single regulating transformer for direct quadrature voltage

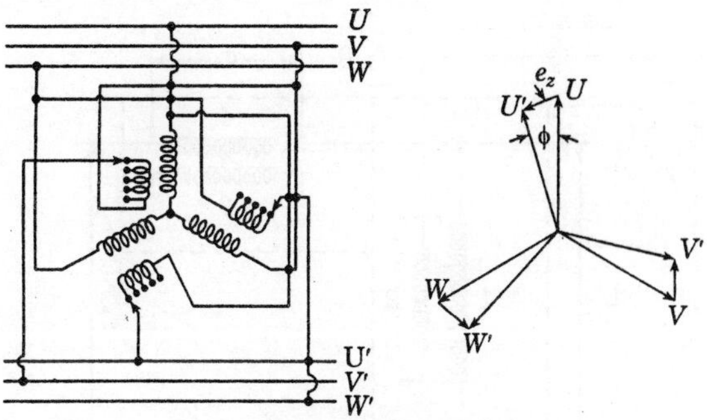


$U$, $V$, $W$ = Voltage reference system
$e_z$ = Supplementary voltage
$U'$, $V'$, $W'$ = Phase-shifted voltage system
$\varphi$ = Phase angle

Fig. 28.12. Connection for direct quadrature phase regulation.

regulation. Supplementary voltage $e_z$ is in quadrature with reference $V_A$. Increase or decrease in $e_z$ by tap-changing results in change in the magnitude of $V_A'$, $V_B'$, $V_C'$ as well as phase angle δ.

The transformers shown in Figs. 28.10, 11, 12 do not differ materially mechanically or electrically from the power transformers with tap-changers. In general, phase control is obtained by deriving supplementary voltage from one phase and inserting it in the same phase or other phase.

*Use of two transformers for phase angle control.*

Refer Fig. 28.13 (*a*).

Two transformers are often necessary for reasons of dielectric or short-circuit strength.

The first (exciter) transformer (*A*) serves to supply the second (supplementary or series) transformer (*B*). It is quite possible to use an existing power transformer to provide excitation for the supplementary transformer. With a supplementary transformer, it is possible to employ both direct regulation (in the series winding of the supplementary transformer) and indirect regulation (in the secondary winding of the exciter transformers).

The desired phase-position of the supplementary voltage is obtained by suitably combining the connection arrangements in the exciter and supplementary transformers (see Table 28.1 for examples). By applying control in both directions (bucking and boosting) one can change the sign of the supplementary voltage or of the phase angle. Fig. 28.13 (*B*) gives the vector relationships.

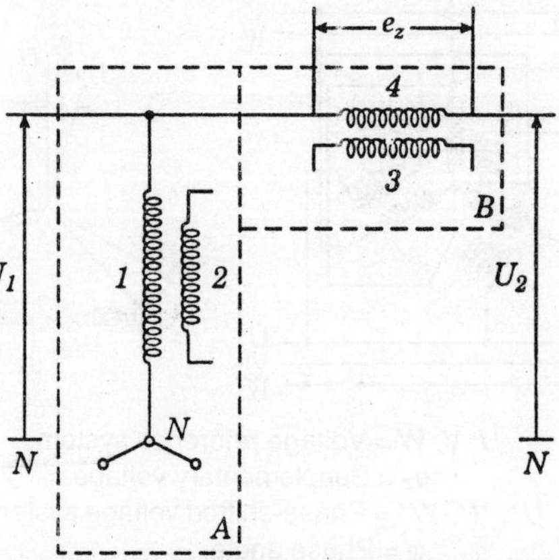


Method with two transformers, single-phase diagram, for in-phase, phase-angle or quadrature phase regulation.

*A*=Exciter transformer
*B*=Supplementary transformer
1=Primary winding of *A*
2=Secondary winding of *A*
3=Excitation winding of *B*
4=Series winding of *B*
(*a*) in-phase regulation
(*b*) phase-angle regulation
(*c*) quadrature phase regulation
*U*=Reference voltage
$U_1$=Regulated voltage
$e_z$=Supplementary voltage
δ=Phase angle.

Fig. 28.13 (*b*) Vector diagrams for voltage regulation.

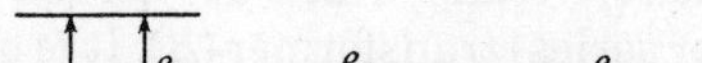


Fig. 28.13 (*a*) In-phase (*b*) quadrature (*c*) phase-angle.

Regulation of Transmission Line.

**Table 28.1. Combinations of Connections for Obtaining Required Phase Position of Supplementary Voltage in Fig. 28.13 (*b*)**

| | *Winding No.* | *Phase supplementary In-phase a* | *Position of voltage Phase angle b* | *Quadrature C* |
|---|---|---|---|---|
| Exciter | 1 | Star | Star | Star |
| Transformer | 2 | Delta | Delta | Delta |
| Supplementary | 3 | Delta | Star | Delta |
| Transformer | 4 | Star | Star | Star |

*Auto-transformer and supplementary series transformer combination forming a regulating transformer.*

Figure 28.14 shows a simplified circuit-diagram of a regulating transformer for voltage control. The exciting transformer is a three phase star connected auto-transformer with automatic tap-changer. The supplementary series transformer injects supplementary voltage $e_z$ in the line voltage

$$\overline{U}_{A}' = \overline{U}_{A} + \overline{e}_z$$

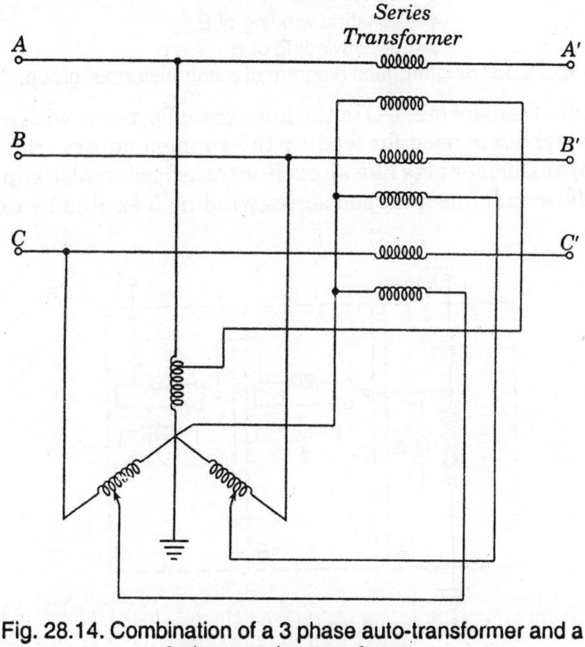


Fig. 28.14. Combination of a 3 phase auto-transformer and a 3 phase series transformer.

Ref. Fig. 28.13 (*b*) for vector diagram principle.

*Auto-transformers with in-phase or phase angle shifting.*

Figure 28.15 shows a combination of one main auto-transformer *A* and one supplementary transformer *B* for both phase angle and in-phase shifting. This is a single phase detail of Fig. 28.14 with additional tertiary winding.

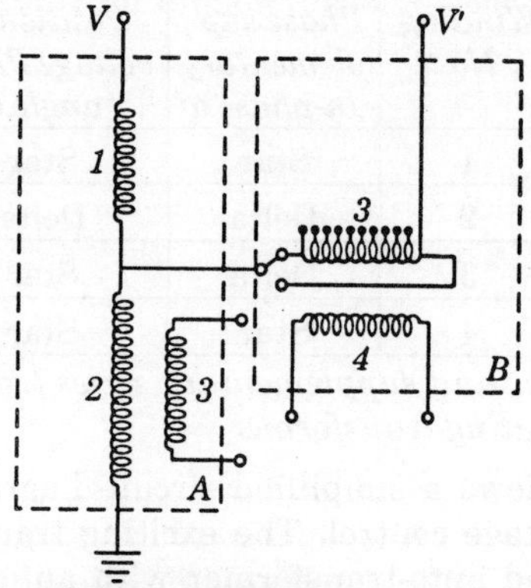


*A*=Main transformer
*B*=Supplementary transformer
1=Series winding of *A*
2=Parallel winding of *A*
3=Tertiary winding of *A*
4=Excitation winding of *B*
5=Series winding of *B*

Fig. 28.15. Single-phase diagram of autotransformer group.

The main transformer (*A*) in the auto-transformer is with a tertiary winding (3) which is used for feeding the supplementary transformer. The main transformer acts like an exciter transformer; also supplementary transformer *B* has a tapped series winding 5 excited by excitation winding 4.

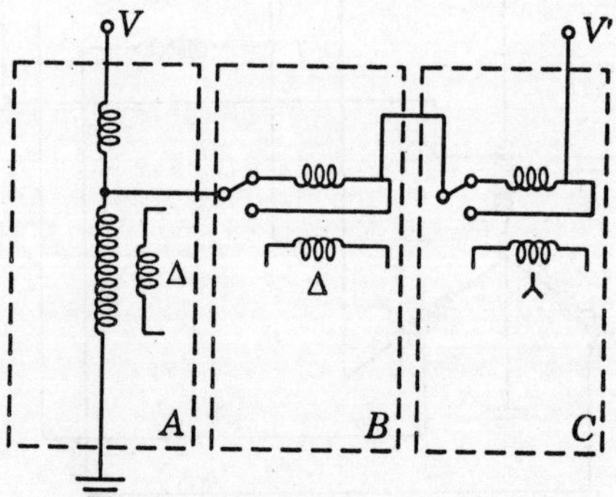


*A*=Main transformer
*B*=In-phase supplementary transformer
*C*=Quadrature supplementary transformer.

Fig. 28.16. Single-phase diagram of autotransformer group with independent in-phase and quadrature phase regulation.

Several combinations of schemes are possible. Fig. 28.16 shows another scheme for independent voltage control and phase angle control. The main transformer (*A*) has three windings (Delta, Star, Star). The supplementary series transformer receiver supplementary controlled voltage $e_z$. The phase angle and magnitude can be controlled either simultaneously or independantly. For the latter control, the tap-changers of main transformer should be independent and should be controlled separately.

**Choice of Tertiary Voltage.** An important detail when planning an autotransformer group with supplementary transformer is selecting the tertiary voltage.

The choice is governed by the answers to the following questions :

— Must a load or power source of prescribed voltage be connected to the tertiary winding ?

— Is a busbar system necessary ?

**Prescribed Tertiary Voltage.** If a local network, shunt reactor, synchronous capacitor or a generator is connected to the tertiary winding, the voltage is already specified. A busbar system and circuit-breaker is then required. The entire installation must be sized for the short-circuit power occurring on the tertiary side.

Actual (natural) tertiary short-circuit powers are of the order of 2000 to 3000 MVA. The available rated breaking capacities of circuit-breakers in the relevant voltage range are approximately.

| | |
|---|---|
| 1000 MVA for rated voltage | 12 kV |
| 1500 MVA for rated voltage | 24 kV |
| 2500 MVA for rated voltage | 36 kV |
| 3600 MVA for rated voltage | 52 kV |
| 5000 MVA for rated voltage | 72.5 kV |

It follows from this that at the lower voltage a series reactor must be provided to limit the short-circuit current.

**Free Choice of Tertiary Voltage.** A busbar system is needed if the supplementary transformer is required to provide facilities for both in-phase and phase-angle shifting, and possibly also quadrature regulation. The busbar system must then have a number of isolators. In this case, the most economical solution is to be found at higher voltages because the price of the installation is affected more by the short-circuit current than by the voltage. Care must always be taken during switching operations that the circuit does not close even for a short time, with the exciter winding of the supplementary transformer open-circuited.

**Applications Reviewed**

1. **Parallel lines, loop Circuit.** Fig. 28.17 shows parallel transmission lines. The impedances $Z_1$ and $Z_2$ are different resulting in circulating current $I_c$ in the loop which will give additional $I_c^2\, R$ losses. The load sharing $I_1$ and $I_2$ will also be different. By introducing a

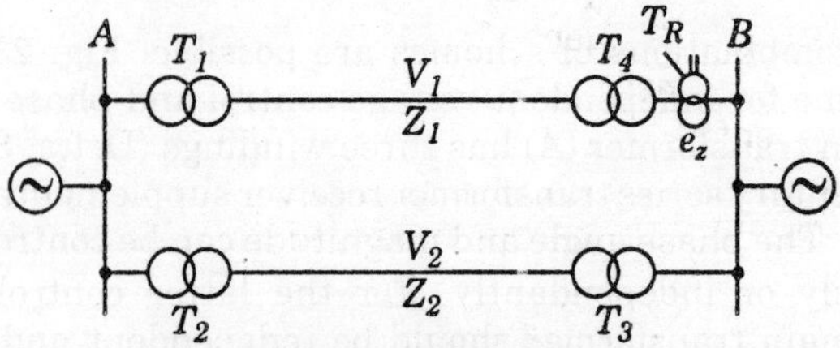


$Z_1$ = Impedance of circuit I'

$Z_2$ = Impedance of circuit II

$T_1, T_2, T_3, T_4$ = Tap-changing transformer

$T_R$ = Phase regulating transformer

$e_z$ = Supplementary voltage

Fig. 28.17. Parallel circuits at different transmission voltage

Regulating Transformer $T_R$ (with in-phase and/or quadrature control) the situation can be corrected.

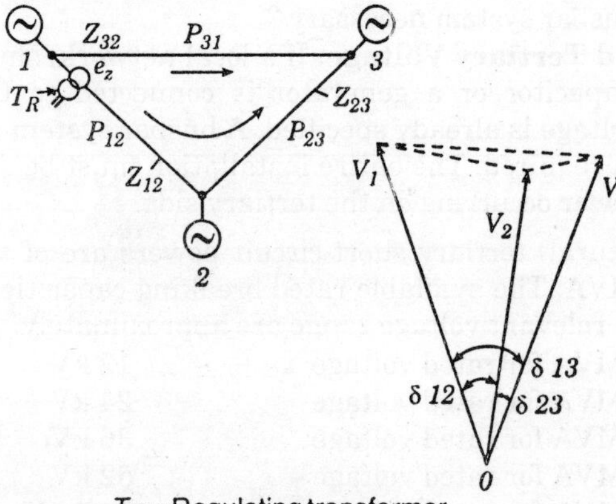


$T_R$ = Regulating transformer

$P_{1-2}, P_{2-3}, P_{3-2}$ = Power Exchange

$Z_{1-2}, Z_{2-3}, Z_{3-2}$ = Impedances

$V_1, V_2, V_3$ = Busbar voltages

$\delta_{12}, \delta_{23}, \delta_{32}$ = Power angles

$e_z$ = Supplementary voltage

$$P_{1-2} = \frac{V_1 \cdot V_2}{X_{12}} \sin \delta_{12}$$

$$P_{2-3} = \frac{V_2 \cdot V_3}{X_{23}} \sin \delta_{23}$$

$$P_{3-2} = \frac{V_3 \cdot V_2}{X_{32}} \sin \delta_{32}$$

Fig. 28.18. Three independently controlled AC systems interconnected by Tie-lines 1-2, 2-3, 3-2 vector relationship for Power-Angles.

**2. Three or More System Interconnections.** Ref. Fig. 28.18 in which three independently controlled AC Networks are interconnected by tie lines 1-2, 2-3 and 3-1 ; having different impedances. The purpose of tie-line control is to supply power from surplus area say (1) to deficit area (say 2).

Normally increase in generation of area 1 will feed power to area 2 by natural adjustment of power angle $\delta_{12}$. However, power flow from 1 to 3 would also get adjusted and increase in generation of 1 will result in :

Total Generation = Total Load

$$\Sigma G = \Sigma L$$

$$G_1 + G_2 + G_3 = L_1 + L_2 + L_3$$

(neglecting losses)

Power will flow from 1 to 3 *via* the loop depending upon the impedances of parallel path.

If a regulating transformer is installed in the tie line, the phase angle between say 1 and 2 can be adjusted to obtain required power flow between 1 and 2 as seen from Eqn.

$$P_{12} = \frac{V_1 \cdot V_2}{X_{12}} \sin \delta$$

$V_1$ and $V_2$ cannot be changed beyond close permissible limits. $X_{12}$ can be changed by changing series capacitors. Alternatively, a regulating transformer in the line 1, 2 can be used for adjusting phase angle $\delta_{12}$ to get desired power flow between 1, 2. Similar method can be used for controlling power between tie-lines 2, 3 and 3, 1.

As large EHV AC systems with several interconnections have been introduced, the need for control of power transfer through individual interconnectors becomes more complex. The solution is found by installing phase regulating transformers with automatic in-phase and or quadrature voltage phase control in the tie-line circuits.

### Summary

Regulating transformers are used for obtaining in-phase/quadrature/combined phase regulation. There are various types of connections. Application are in parallel lines, interconnected lines, industrial plants.

### Questions

1. Explain the principle of in-phase voltage control and quadrature voltage control.
2. State applications of voltage regulating transformers.

# 29

# Neutral Grounding Transformers

Neutral grounding transformers (earthing transformers) are either zig-zag type or star-delta type. They are applied for grounding power system neutral when no other neutral point is available at a particular voltage level. The salient aspects about grounding transformers have been illustrated.

## 29.1 INTRODUCTION

In the three-phase AC system, the system neutral must be grounded at least at one point on every voltage level (Ref. Ch. 26). The neutral-point is taken from star connected generator neutral or star connected transformer. However if such a point is not available at a particular voltage level due to delta connected transformers, the *neutral grounding transformer* is installed at that voltage. Alternatively, a *star-delta transformer* is installed without loading the delta.

A grounding transformer (earthing transformer) is a transformer intended only for obtaining neutral to ground connection in a three phase AC system. *The grounding transformer does not serve the usual transformer functions of stepping-up or stepping down the voltages.*

A grounding transformer is short-time rated. (10 sec. to 1 min) Therefore, their size is small and they do not need cooling tubes or radiators.

## 29.2 STAR-DELTA TRANSFORMER USED AS A GROUNDING TRANSFORMER

Ref. Fig. 29.1. Conventional star-delta transformer without, any load on delta secondary can be used as a neutral grounding transformer for the voltage level of star-side winding. This simple method is used for emergency if a suitable star-delta transformer is available. The ratings of the star-winding to carry short-time currents should be confirmed.

## 29.3 CONNECTIONS OF A GROUNDING TRANSFORMER

Figure 29.2 shows the circuit for connecting a zig-zag Grounding Transformer to obtain the system neutral at voltage level of the three phase line ABC. The circuit breaker is used in association with the protective relays for the neutral grounding transformer.

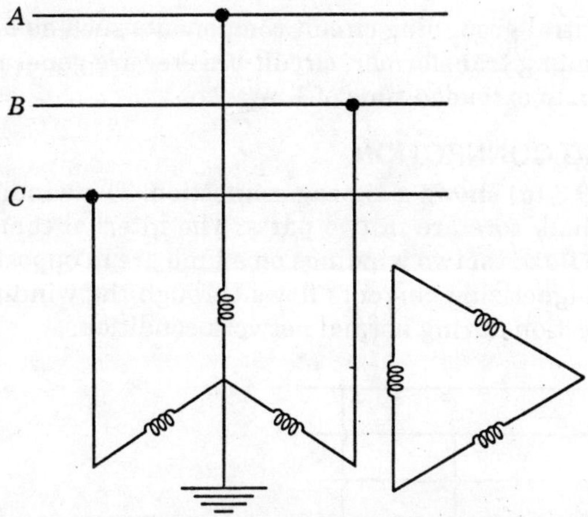


Fig. 29.1 Star-delta transformer used for neutral-grounding Delta side is not loaded. (Neutral point is then available at voltage level corresponding to the star side).

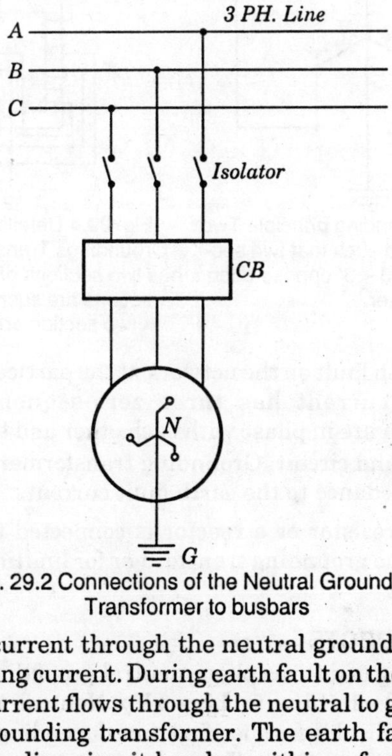


Fig. 29.2 Connections of the Neutral Grounding Transformer to busbars

The normal current through the neutral grounding circuit is only a small magnetizing current. During earth fault on the three phase line, the earth-fault current flows through the neutral to ground connection of the neutral grounding transformer. The earth fault in the line is interrupted by the line circuit-breaker within a few seconds (for distribution systems) and within a few cycles in EHV system. Hence the ratings of neutral grounding circuit components such as busbars CTs, neutral grounding transformer, circuit breaker are generally of short-time of 10 sec. to extended time of 1 minute.

## 29.4 ZIG-ZAG CONNECTION

Figure 29.3 (*a*) shows a zig-zag connection. The windings on each of the three limb core are in two parts. The internal connections are such that the fluxes of two windings on a limb are in opposition. Hence very small magnetizing currents flows through the windings and the neutral connection during normal network condition.

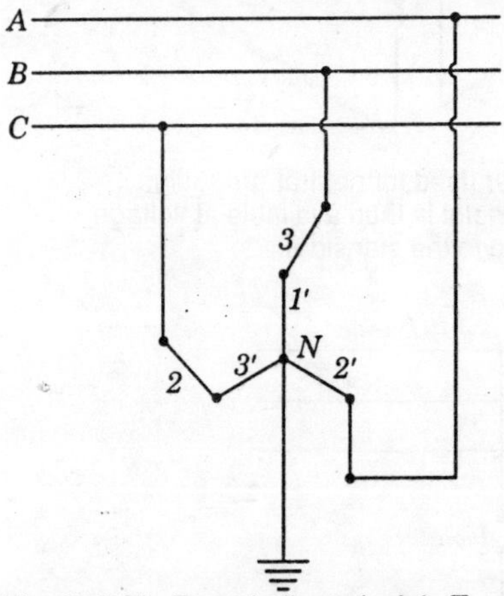


Fig. 29.3 Zig-Zag winding principle Two stars are connected such that two sections 1 – 1′, 2 – 2′, 3 – 3′ oppose each other.

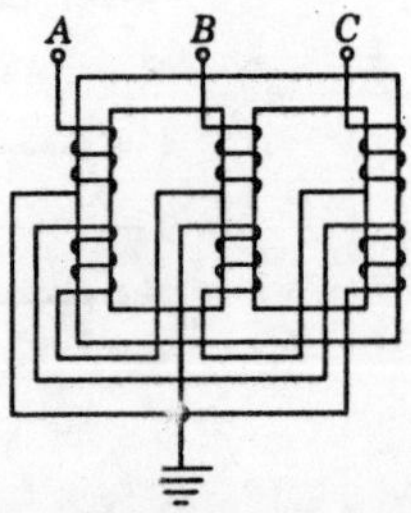


Fig. 29.4 Details of windings of a Groundings Transformer. Each limb has two sections of windings. The connections are such that the fluxes of two section are in opposition.

During an earth fault on the network at the particular voltage level, the earth fault current has three zero-sequence components $I_{AO}, I_{BO}; I_{CO}$ which are in phase with each other and they flow through the neutral to ground circuit. Grounding transformer offers very little zero sequence impedance to the earth fault currents.

Sometimes a resistor or a reactor is connected in the neutral to ground circuit of the grounding transformer for limiting the earth fault current.

## 29.5 DESIGN ASPECTS

The kVA rating of a three phase neutral grounding transformer is given by the product (Line to Line kV × Neutral to Ground Fault Current) and is applicable for specified time depending upon the protection of line against earth fault. Typical short time ratings for Neutral Grounding Transformers are

For Distribution systems = 1 minute
For Transmission system = 10 seconds.

Rated voltage of the neutral grounding transformer is the line to line highest system voltage for which the neutral grounding transformer is intended.

As the neutral grounding transformers are short-time kVA rated, their size and cost is lesser than those of continuously rated transformers of same capacity.

**Equivalent Two-Winding Transformer Rating.** The size of neutral grounding transformer is expressed in terms of equivalent 2-winding transformer rating as follows :

$$S_G = V_{L-L} \times I_n \text{ kVA}$$

where $S_G$ = Nominal kVA rating of neutral grounding transformer

$V_{LL}$ = Line to line rated kV

$I_n$ = Rated Short-time currents, neutral to ground

$S_\alpha$ = Equivalent two winding transformer kVA

$S_\alpha = S_G \times K_3$

for a three phase grounding transformer unit. $K_3$ depends upon the short-time duration. Table 29.1 gives the values of $K_3$ for Grounding Transformers.

**Table 29.1**
**$K_3$ Factors for Equivalent Two Winding Transformers**

| *Short-Time Duration* | *Star / Delta* | *Rated Voltage of Grounding Transformers** | | | |
|---|---|---|---|---|---|
| | | *2 Upto 12 kV* | *22—33 kV* | *66 kV* | *132 kV* |
| 10 sec | — | 0.06 | 0.07 | 0.08 | 0.09 |
| 1 min | 0.17 | 0.1 | 0.1 | 0.1 | 0.1 |
| 2 min | 0.24 | 0.13 | 0.153 | 0.16 | 0.17 |

**Earthing Transformers and Three-phase Neutral Electomagnetic Couplers.** Three-phase neutral electromagnetic couplers are generally of the oil-immersed type. They are usually connected either in zig-zag or in star-delta ; the delta connected winding may be of the open type to permit the insertion of a resistor or reactor to adjust the zero-sequence impedance.

Earthing transformers may have a (secondary) low-voltage winding to provide an auxiliary supply to a substation. Such a secondary has a

*1. Rated voltage. The voltage for which the apparatus is designed.

rated power and is covered by IEC Publication 76 for power Transformers.

Three-phase couplers and earthing transformers provide an artificial neutral and are used for the following purposes :

1. to earth an otherwise unearthed system ;
2. to connect single-phase loads between lines and neutral :
3. to connect an arc-suppression coil ;
4. to limit the current during a line-to-earth fault due to the impedance of the coils and the possible additional resistors, permitting selective protection.

### Ratings and Specifications

Unless operating conditions justify the selection of higher value, the rated voltage of an earthing transformer is deemed to be the line-to-line voltage of the associated system.

**2. Continuous rated current.** The current in the neutral which the apparatus is designed to carry continuously, when it is energized at rated voltage and frequency. This quantity is only specified when the apparatus is designed for the connection of single-phase loads between the neutral and the line terminals.

A continuous rated current in the three phases may be specified when a load is connected to a secondary winding.

**3. Rated short-time current in the neutral.** The current in the neutral which the apparatus is designed to carry for a specified duration.

The rated short-time current is associated with a line-to-earth fault, the apparatus being energized at rated voltage.

Depending on their duration, several rated short-time currents may be specified.

**4. Zero-sequence impedance.** The impedance in ohms per phase at rated frequency corresponding at the appropriate reference temperature to the flow of rated short-time current between the line terminals connected together and the neutral.

**5. Ability to withstand rated short-time current and temperature rise.** Earthing transformers and couplers should be capable of withstanding the rated short-time current for the specified duration. (*e.g.* 1 sec.).

The permissible temperature rises depend on the duty. In the case of single-phase loading, the temperature-rise limits are the same as for transformers and, when used with an arc-suppression coil, the temperature-rise limits are the same as for the arc-suppression coil. If the earthing transformer or coupler limits the earth-fault current, the same temperature rise shall be valid as for a transformer during short-circuit.

**6. Insulation Level.** The insulation level of a neutral to ground reactor is selected on the basis of its rated voltage and corresponding withstand levels of power frequency voltage and impulse voltage.

The neutral terminal may have reduced value.

The line terminal may have higher value.

Thus the Neutral Grounding Transformer winding may have graded insulation.

**Rating Plate Data for Neutral Earthing Transformer or Neutral Electromagnetic Coupler**

The title should be clearly marked.

The rating plate shall show the following information.

1. Earthing transformer or coupler-type.......
2. Number and year of the specification.
3. Manufacturer's name.
4. Manufacturer's serial number.
5. Year of manufacture.
6. Rated frequency.
7. Rated voltage.
8. Continuous rated current.
9. Connection.
10. Measured zero-sequence impedance (ohms per phase).
11. Rated short-time current and specified duration.
12. Rated voltage and power of the secondary winding, if any.
13. Type of cooling.
14. Class of temperature of dry type apparatus, and temperature rise if non-standard.
15. Insulation level, separately for the earth end of the winding when appropriate.
16. Total mass.
17. Mass of insulating oil.
18. Untanking mass.

**Testing of Grounding Transformers.** Type tests, routine tests, special tests are similar to those for Power Transformers and series reactors. They include the following :

| *Title* | *Type Test* | *Routine Test* |
|---|---|---|
| 1. Measurement of winding resistance. | | * |
| 2. Measurement of zero sequence impedance. | | * |
| 3. Measurement of load losses and no-load losses. | | * |
| 4. Tests on temperature rise | * | |
| 5. Inter-turn overvoltage withstand test. | | * |
| 6. Separate source voltage test. | | * |
| 7. Impulse voltage withstand test. | * | * |
| 8. Short-circuit withstand test—special test. | * | |

**Short-circuit Withstand Test on Grounding Transformers or Neutral Electromagnetic Coupler.** The short-circuit test is intended to control the mechanical behaviour of the apparatus under short-circuit conditions.

The earthing transformer or coupler shall be connected to a symmetrical three-phase supply, and a short-circuit shall be thrown between one phase terminal and the transformer neutral so synchronized that maximum asymmetry of the short-circuit current is obtained. The supply voltage shall be so adjusted that the first peak value of short-circuit current reaches $1.8 \times \sqrt{2}$ times the highest rated short-time current r.m.s. value, unless otherwise specified.

Ten successive applications of short-circuit current shall be made, each having a duration of ten cycles.

The ability of the apparatus to withstand the test shall be determined by visual inspection, by repetition of the dielectric tests at 75% of the original value, and by a check measurement of the zero-sequence impedance.

**Note**-By agreement between purchaser and manufacturer, a three-phase test may be replaced by a single-phase test of equal severity.

## Summary

Grounding transformers/earthing transformers have zig-zag winding on three leg core with opposing winding sections on each leg.

They are short time rated.

The specifications are covered by IEC 289.

## Questions

1. State the need of neutral grounding transformers.

2. Explain zig-zag connection on a three leg core of an earthing transformer.

3. How many bushings will be required for a grounding transformer for a three phase system ?

4. Why is the earthing transformer short-time rated ?

5. State whether correct or wrong :

— Earthing transformer is required at each voltage level.
— Earthing transformer requires a tertiary winding.
— The secondary of a earthing transformer is with a tap-changer.
— Earthing transformer is connected between the neutral and earth.
— Earthing transformer is generally air-insulated.

6. How to obtain a system neutral for earthing if a zig-zag earthing transformer is not available but several other transformers are available in neighbouring store ?

# 30

# Arc-Furnace Transformers and Induction Furnace Transformers

The furnace transformers of special design features are used in the following installations:

— Single phase indirect arc furnaces
— Three phase direct arc furnaces
— Mains frequency induction furnaces, etc.

The secondary voltage is low. Secondary currents are high. The secondary voltage is varied over a wide range during the furnace operation. The electrical schemes have been described with particular reference to the furnace transformer.

## 30.1 ARC FURNACE TRANSFORMERS FOR SINGLE PHASE INDIRECT ARC FURNACES

**Indirect Arc Furnaces** are small single phase units of melting capacities of a few tens of kg per hour. The rating of furnace transformer is approximately 1.2 kVA per (kg/hr) melting rate.

Furnace load is single phase fluctuating type. Supply is three phase or single phase depending upon furnace size. Series inductor with tappings is provided on supply side of furnace transformer. In addition the following provisions are also necessary.

1. Switchable capacitor banks for phase load balancing.
2. Switchable capacitors for shunt compensation.

In an *indirect arc furnace*, the arc is between two electrodes above the metal bath. The load is of single phase. If the electrodes are supplied by a single-phase two-winding transformer, there will be fluctuations in supply side voltage with unbalance in three phase voltages and unstable neutral point. Hence, the single phase load should be connected to a special three-phase to single phase transformer having unequal turns ratios for one of the phase to be loaded. In addition, there should be static balancing of three phases by means of inductor, capacitor sets as shown in Figs. 30.4 and 30.5.

## 30.2 A THREE PHASE DIRECT ARC FURNACE TRANSFORMERS

All large arc furnaces above 1 MT/hr melting rate are *three phase direct arc furnaces*.

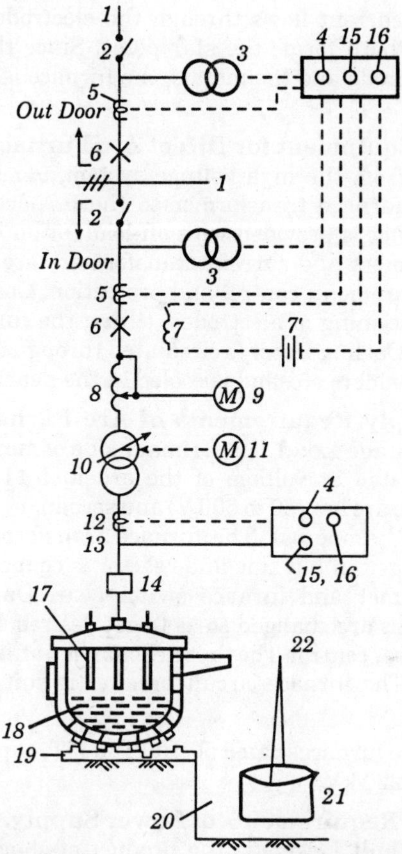


| | |
|---|---|
| 1. High Voltage Supply | 2. Isolator (Disconnector) |
| 3. Potential Transformers | 4. Measuring Instrument |
| 5. Current Transformers | 6. Furnace Circuit Breaker |
| 7. Trip Circuit for 6 | 8. Tapped Reactor |
| 9. Motor for Tap Changing | 10. Furnace Transformer |
| 11. Off Load Tap Changer | 12. Current Transformers |
| 13. Voltage Connections | 14. Flexible Cables |
| 15. Ammeters, etc. | 16. Voltmeters, etc. |
| 17. Electrodes | 18. Furnace |
| 19. Rocker | 20. Pouring Pit |
| 21. Laddle | 22. Slings with Overhead Crane |

Fig. 30.1 Electrical scheme for a direct arc furnace (Single line diagram)

A typical 3 phase arc furnace has three electrodes. They are connected to the secondary of the furnace transformers by means of flexible high current cables. (Fig. 30.3). During the furnace operation, the electrodes are continuously positioned automatically for obtaining current balance.

The electric current flows through the electrodes into the metal bath. The metal bath forms the star point. Since the arc is directly between the electrode and the metals, the furnace is called *Direct Arc Furnace.*

**Electrical Equipment for Direct Arc Furnace.** (Fig. 30.1) The supply is taken from the high voltage system, *via* Isolator, Furnace circuit breaker, furnace transformer to the furnace electrodes. The *furnace transformer* is provided with off-load, or on load tap changer. Voltage transformers and current transformers are provided for the purpose of measurement, control and protection. Control systems are provided for positioning of electrodes, tilting the furnace, lifting and swinging of roof. Cooling water is circulated through furnace shell, roof rings, electrode holders etc. and is cooled in the nearby cooling pond.

**Power Supply Requirements of Arc Furnace Plants—Nature of Arc Furnace Load.** The primary side of medium size furnace transformer is rated at voltage of the order of 11 kV, 33 kV. The secondary voltage are low (80 to 500 V) and secondary currents are high (several thousand amperes). The furnace transformer is fitted with off-load tap changer on h.t. side and reactor is connected between the furnace transformer and furnace switch-gear. During the furnace operation, the taps are changed so as to get desired secondary voltage for purpose of power control. The taps are changed after opening furnace circuit breaker. The furnace circuit breaker is suitable for repeated operation.

For very large furnaces rated 50/100/150 MT, supply may be taken at 66 kV/132 kV/220 kV.

**Fault Level Requirements of Power Supply.** Fault level (short circuit level or Fault Power) is the product of short circuit current, actual system voltage and factor $\sqrt{3}$ for the case of three phase circuits. It is the apparent power that would flow in case of a three phase short circuit as a given point of the power system.

While selecting the power supply for an arc furnace plant, the fault level at the point of connection of the furnace should be adequate. Hence, the power line should be taken from the sub-station bus having adequate fault level. If the fault as a bus is inadquate the power should be taken from the bus of yet higher voltage level having desired fault level. The expression given below can be taken as a guide rule.

$$Sa = K \cdot 80, T \text{ mva}$$

where Sa = Fault level at the point of connection of Furnace transformer. (MVA)

$T$mva = Nominal rating of furnace transformer (MVA)

$K$ = Multiplying factor to take into account, the number of arc furnaces in the plant

$K = 1$ for one furnace

$A = 1.2$ for two furnaces

For example, if furnace transformer rating is say, 5 MVA, then the fault level of supply at point of connection of the furnace plant should be above $5 \times 80 = 400$ MVA. Therefore, power for arc furnace plant should be supplied directly from a major receiving station or power station bus *via* independent transmission line.

**Choice of Voltage.** The choice of voltage for feeding the arc furnace plant is determined by the voltage-levels of the buses in the sub-station and their fault levels. The fault level requirements of the supply are calculated as described above.

**KVA Rating of Intermediate Step-down Transformer which feeds the arc furnace plant.** The furnace transformers are given a nominal kVA rating such that they can be safely overloaded by about 20% during the melt down periods. In other words:

$$(T \text{ mva}) \max = 1.2\ (T \text{ mva}) \qquad \ldots(2)$$

where,

$(T \text{ mva})$ = Nominal MVA rating of the furnace transformer.

$(T \text{ mva}) \max$ = The rated apparent power the furnace transformer can supply.

While selecting an intermediate transformer (if any) Eq. (2) should be considered. Hence the rating of the intermediate step-down transformer (if any) should be more than 1.2 times the furnace transformer rating. If the intermediate transformer feeds two furnace transformers, its rating should be more than 1.2 times the sum of the nominal ratings of the two furnace transformers.

**Furnace Transformer.** Furnace transformer is the 'heart' of the furnace installation. It is a power transformer with 11 or 33 kV voltage primary and low voltage secondary. The secondary currents are very much high (between 1000 A and 10,000 A). The secondary is frequently short-circuited. Frequent current surges occur during the melting periods. Due to the above aspects, the design of furnace transformers is quite different from that of usual power transformers. The furnace transformer is ruggedly built. *The secondary is permanently delta connected.* The secondary voltage are low in the range between 70 to 550 volt. The secondary voltages are changed by means of tap changer on HV side. The primary is provided with six point tap changer. *There is also a provision of delta star switching. Thus, six secondary voltages are available corresponding to the six tap position of primary with delta connection and six more with star connection.* The several secondary voltages are useful in controlling the rate of heat input to the furnace. During the initial melting period, higher secondary voltage is tapped to obtain higher rate of heat input. The taps are subsequently changed to get lower secondary voltages, as the melting continues.

Typical Ratings of 3-Phase Direct-Arc Furnace Transformer

| *Capacity Metric Tons** | *Furnace transformer Rating* | *Reactor coil Rating* | *Secondary voltage between electrodes* | *Circuit breaker breaking capacity* |
|---|---|---|---|---|
| | *kVA* | *kVA* | *V* | *MVA* |
| 1 | 800 | 200 | 120.....70 | 250 |
| 10 | 4000 | 1000 | 220.....90 | 500 |
| 25 | 8000 | 1600 | 280....100 | — |
| 50 | 20000 | 2000 | 400....110 | — |

*Refer to melting rate tons/hr.

The furnace transformer rating is given in MVA, there is no definite rule regarding the rating of the furnace transformer to be used with a particular furnace. However, the melting rate obtainable from the arc furnace depends upon the capacity of the transformer. As a thumb rule, for smaller, the kVA of the furnace transformer can be approximately taken as 800 kVA per 1000 kg/hr melting rate. For bigger furnaces, the kVA figure is reduced.

The inherent reactance of furnace transformer is between 4 to 6 per cent. In case of small furnace transformers upto 7500 kVA, this reactance is not enough to limit the current surges within desirable limits. Hence the transformers are provided with series reactors.

**Series Reactors**

The reactors connected in the primary circuit provide the necessary reactance to stabilise the arc. In small furnace transformers of the size upto 1000 kVA, the reactor is built inside the transformer tank. For larger transformers, the reactor is separately installed as indicated in Fig. 30.1.

**Tap Changer**

Off load tap changer is relatively cheaper. *However the circuit breaker should be opened every time before changing the tap.*

On load tap changers are popular in Europe. Six point tap changer are used for furnace transformers. The secondary voltages of a furnace transformer can be conveniently changed so as to control the heat input. A typical set of secondary voltages for a 40 ton furnace is *e.g.*

282, 242, 220, 199, 165, 115 V.

**Furnace circuit-breaker.** Before changing the off-load tap-changer, the circuit-breaker should be opened. After the changing the tap the circuit-breakers closed again. Hence the circuit-breaker should be suitable for repeated operating duty.

## 30.3 WINDING ARRANGEMENT ALTERNATIVES FOR DIRECT ARC-FURNACE TRANSFORMER

**Tap Changer on HV Side.** Fig. 30.2 shows the details of the furnace temperature connections preferred upto 10 MVA rating. The HV supply is rated 11 kV/22 kV/33/66 kV depending upon the short-circuit level required for the furnace installation. By varying the taps on HV side, the secondary voltage is varied.

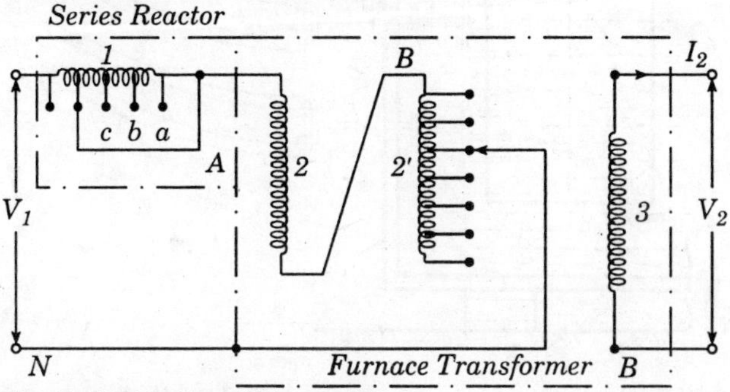


A—Series reactor with tap-switch
B—Auto-Transformer N—Neutral of 3 Phases.
$V_1$ HT supply e.g. 11 kV, 33 kV, 66 kV, 132 kV
$V_2$ LT Supply to furnace e.g. 60 V to 500 V,
2, 2' Primary 3 Secondary.

Fig. 30.2 Furnace Transformer (schematic single phase representation of 3 phase System.)

**2. Auto-Transformer on HV Side.** This arrangement shown in Fig. 30.2 is preferred when supply voltage is of 60 kV/110 kV/132 kV/220 kV direct upto the furnace plant and the furnaces are of high capacity e.g. 20/25/50/80/100/150 MT Auto transformer with variable secondary voltage given an economical solution.

## 30.4 DESIGN ASPECTS OF ARC FURNACE TRANSFORMERS

**Core :** Usually three limb core with CRGO laminations and 45° mitred joints. The laminations are held by glass-fibre bands and external tie rods. Punched holes in laminations are not permitted.

**HV Windings.** These are tapped windings like usual power transformer HV tapped winding.

**LV Winding.** LV winding is of low voltage (70 to 550 V) and high current (several thousand Amperes) and high fluctuating currents. Number of turns is small. Hence *parallel, layer winding* is preferred. The conductors are of large cross sectional area made up with continuously transposed multi-stranded conductor. LV winding is placed on outer side (unlike in usual power transformer).

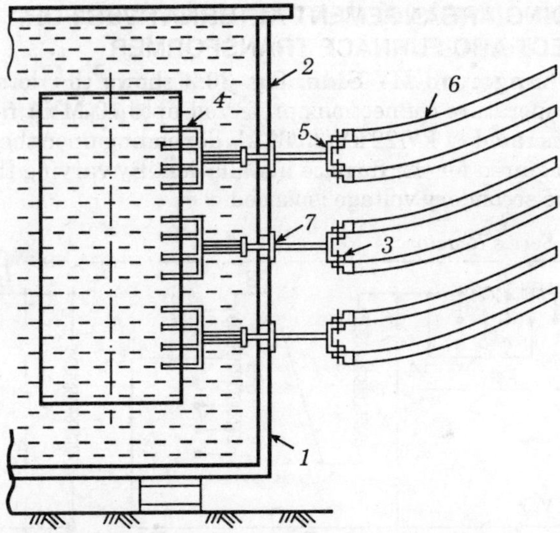


1. Tank cover
2. Tank Wall
3. High current terminal
4. Leads form LV winding
5. Connector (Internally oil cooled)
6. Flexible cables between 5 and the electrode holder on the furnace.

Fig. 30.3 LV high current connections of arc furnace transformer.

**Terminal Connections.** Secondary side of furnace transformer is rated for low voltage and high fluctuating currents. It is necessary to have large number of flexible stranded insulated cables between the LV terminal and the furnace electrodes holder terminal. During the operation,the electrode holder gets continuously positioned in vertical direction. The secondary cables oscillate at random due to electromechanical forces and the oscillatory motion of the electrode holders.

HV Connections of furnace transformer are taken through busducts to the outdoor switchyard.

**Internal Leads of LV.** (Fig. 30.3) These are special design considering the high current and low voltage. The several parallel paths are taken to LV terminals. LV terminals are oil cooled and have several holes on terminal plate to enable connections of flexible cables between the LV terminals and the furnace electrode holder. The terminals are fixed on strong epoxy insulating plates.

**Cooling.** OFWF is preferred for large furnaces. Oil is forced through all the parts of the windings. The heat from oil is exchanged with the cooling water in the oil to water heat exchanger.

## 30.5. TRANSFORMERS FOR MAINS FREQUENCY, CORELESS INDUCTION FURNACE

**Main frequency (line frequency) coreless induction furnace** operates on 50 Hz supply and does not need the costly frequency conversion equipment. These furnaces have become very much popular with cast iron and aluminium foundaries. They can be used, depending upon the design, for melting various grades of cast iron, steel, alloys, aluminium, magnesium etc. The electrical equipment for mains frequency furnace comprise mains side circuit breaker, furnace transformer, starting contactor, direct contactor, compensation system balancing system, measurement and control panel etc. The scheme for electrical connections is shown in Fig. 30.4.

The power supply requirements of mains frequency induction furnaces are simpler than those of arc furnaces. Phase load balancing equipment are installed as shown in Fig. 30.5. The power factor is maintained above 0.8 lag by means of capacitors. For furnaces upto of about 500 kW, the transformer is designed voltage rating to suit customers requirement. It may be mentioned here that HT supply is generally available at a cheaper rate and it may be economical to take the HT supply, though initial cost is higher.

**Table 30.1**
**Mains Frequency Induction Furnace Transformer Data**

| Capacity kg | 350 | 500 | 850 | 1250 | 2000 | 3000 | 4500 |
|---|---|---|---|---|---|---|---|
| Transformer Rating nominal, kV | 225 | 360 | 450 | 675 | 975 | 1350 | 1875 |
| HV side Supply | HT/LT | HT/LT | HT/LT | HT | HT | HT | HT |
| LV Voltage Rating (Single Phase) Volts. | 415 | 415 | 550 | 540 | 1000 | 1000 | 1100 |

Referring to Fig. 30.4, the LT or HT supply (1) is taken as per the choice, to the primary of the furnace transformer (3), *via* the main circuit breaker (2). The over current protection and under voltage protection (18) is provided on supply side. The primary side of the furnace transformer is provided with a few taps (3) to permit selection of primary turns to suit the service voltage. These connections are permanently made. The secondary is provided with about six taps (4) and a motor driven off-load tap changer (5). The power to load section can be taken *via* the starting contactor (7) which supplies power *via* the starting resistors (6). The direct contactor (8) is based on the size of furnace, on the process adopted, pouring temperature etc. The energy consumption is more for the first heat and reduces for the subsequent heats.

The furnace coil (9) is connected to two phases. The compensation section comprises fixed capacitors (13) and switchable capacitors (14).

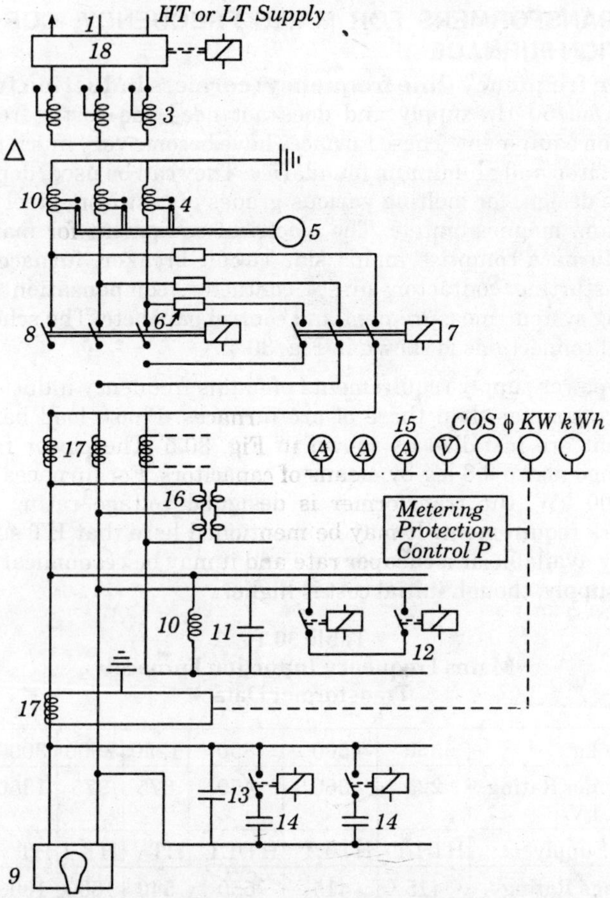


1. Supply, HT or LT as per customer's requirement
2. Circuit breaker trip coil
3. Primary side taps (fixed)
4. Secondary side taps
5. Geared motor for 4
6. Starting resistors
7. Starting contactor
8. Direct contactor
9. Furnace (single phase)
10. Choke for balancing
11. Fixed capacitor for balancing
12. Switchable capacitors for balancing
13. Fixed capacitor for compensation
14. Switchable capacitors for compensation
15. Measuring instrument
16. Potential transformers
17. Current transformers
18. Over current under voltage protection

Fig. 30.4 Mains frequency coreless melting furnace scheme.

The switchable capacitors are put on and off according to a programme such that the power factor is maintained between 0.8 to 1. The balancing section comprises the chock (10), capacitor (11), switchable capacitors

(12). The current transformers (17), potential transformers (16) are provided on the secondary side and measuring instruments are provided for measurement of current in three phases, coil voltages power factor, power energy consumed.

The protection on the supply side comprises HRC fuses, thermal over current relay, under voltage release. On low voltage side, generally no electrical protection is provided. The transformer is fitted with Buchholz realy temperature indicators. Audible and visual signals, alarms are provided in the cooling water scheme.

The switching, changing taps, supervision of temperature etc. can be performed from the measurement and control panel installed near the furnace, on the platform. The furnace power, hence the heat input is controlled by changing the voltage applied to the furnace coil by means of the tap changer. The load section is disconnected while changing the off circuit tap-switch.

**Furnace Transformer for Coreless Mains Frequency Induction Furnace.** The furnace transformer is usually three phase star-star with tap-changer of LV side and off-circuit tap-switch on HV side. The LV side neutral is grounded. Delta-tertiary may be provided on the core to provide path to third harmonic magnetizing currents.

The starting resistors are used while switching-in to reduce inrush currents.

The load is single-phase inductive load. For obtaining a balanced load on three phase supply network, a balancing scheme is connected

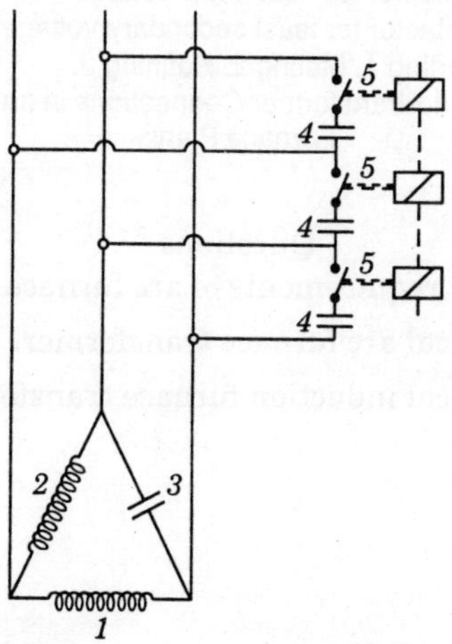


1. Furnace Coil 2. Inductor
3. Capacitor 4. Switchable capacitor
5. Contactors for 4.

Fig. 30.5. Balancing set for connection in induction furnace plant (Items 10, 13, 14 in Fig. 30.4)

to the three phases on LV side. (Fig. 30.5). The currents drawn from three phases get uniformly balanced. As the load on the furnace coil changes, switchable capacitors are switched-in to maintain the balance.

**Auto-Transformer Connection with Contactors for Stepped Switching.** For small induction furnaces, single phase auto-transformers with tappings switched in by contactors can be used. Fig.30.6 shows the scheme.

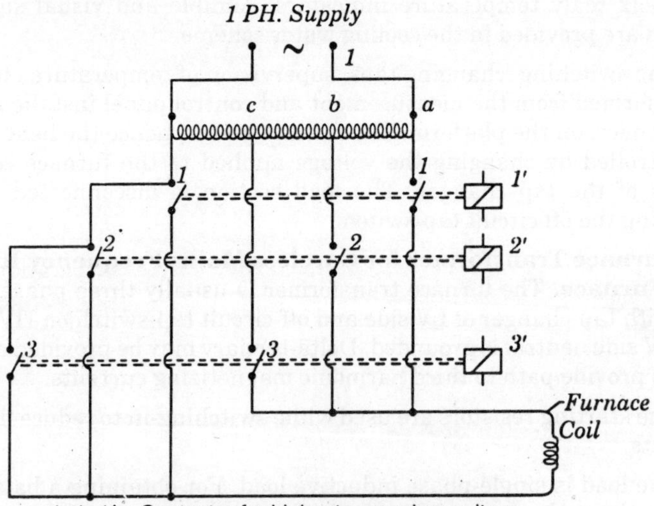


1, 1, 1′ = Contactor for highest secondary voltage
2, 2, 2′ = Contactor for next lower voltage
3, 3, 3′ = Contactor for least secondary voltage.
Sequence : Starting 1, Meting 2. Refining 3.

Fig. 30.6. Auto-transformer Connections in an Induction Furnace Plant.

## Questions

1. Explain supply requirements of arc furnace plant.
2. Describe a typical arc furnace transformer.
3. Describe a typical induction furnace transformer.

# 31

# Shunt Reactors and Series Reactors

Shunt Reactors are used for providing shunt compensation to long EHV-AC lines. The application, design aspects, specifications, ratings, testing requirements etc. have been described.

*Current Limiting Reactors* (*Series reactors*) are used for limiting short-circuit currents, current surges etc.

As they are connected in series with the power circuit, they offer impedance to the flow of normal current and short-circuit current. They are used in strategic locations to limit the short-circuit level. They are also used with fluctuating loads and with rectifiers for smoothing the current waveforms.

Neutral Grounding Reactors are installed along with star-connected transformer or generator for providing reactance in series with neutral to ground path, thereby to limit the earth fault current.

Arc suppression coil is a tapped neutral grounding reactor used for varying the reactance in the neutral to ground circuit.

A reactor has predominantly inductive coil along with insulation system, magnetic gapped core or air core, bushing or terminals, steel enclosure or with open to sky construction, oil insulation or air insulation. The types include

— Oil Immersed Reactors
  - With Gapped Iron Core
  - Without Iron Core (Core less)

— Air Insulated Reactors
  - Without Iron Core.

*Oil Immersed Reactors* have many features similar to those of an Oil Immersed Power Transformer.

*Air Insulated Reactors* are simpler outdoor/indoor large coils installed on insulators and insulating/non-magnetic support structure.

Various types of reactors are covered by the same standards (e.g. IEC 289 : Reactors) and they have similar configurations.

## 31.1 INTRODUCTION

*Reactors are equipment of transformer family. A reactor has a predominantly inductive coil.*

Reactors are used in the power system (network) for current limiting and for compensation of reactive power and for system neutral grounding. There are three types of reactors (1) Series reactors, connected in series for current limiting and (2) Shunt reactors, connected in shunt, for compensation of reactive power. (3) Neutral grounding reactors.

**Oil Immersed Reactors** are similar to transformers in external appearance and have some design features similar to those of power transformers. *e.g.* bushings, tanks, cooling system, fitments, etc.

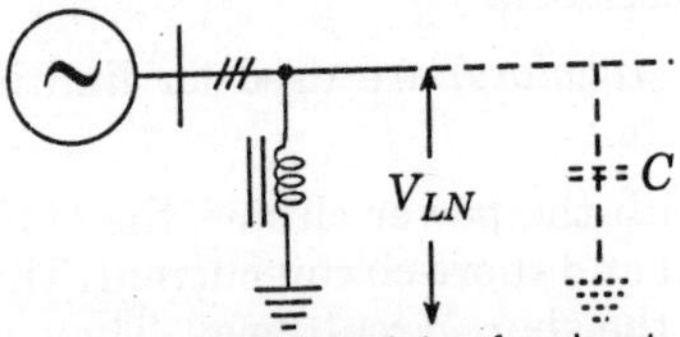


Fig. 31.1. (A) Principle of a shunt reactor (single phase representation).

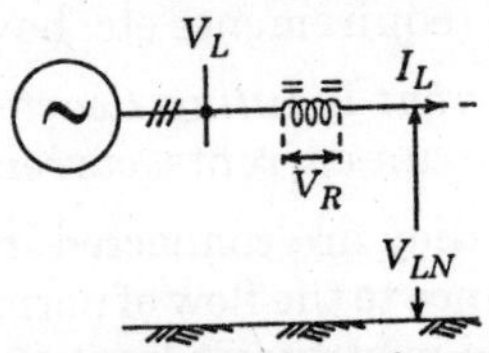


Fig. 31.1. (B) Principle of a series reactor (single phase representation).

Air-core dry type reactor looks like a large coil.

Figure 31.1 *(A)* shows a single line representation of shunt reactor. Voltage $V_{IN}$ comes across each phase of a shunt reactor connected across phase and neutral. For three phase system, a three phase reactor is necessary. It will have three line terminals and one neutral terminal (Ground terminal).

Figure 31.1 *(B)* shows a single line representation of a series reactor. The reactor coil (one per phase) is connected in series with the power circuit. The complete coil is at normal voltage $V_{IN} = V/\sqrt{3}$ with respect to earth.

Voltage across the reactor is $V_R = I_L X_L$ where $I_L$ is the line current and $X_L$ is reactance of the reactor. During through short-circuits $V_R$ increases.

Considering the similarity of construction, design features, specifications etc. of various types of reactors, the standards such as IEC 289 apply to the following:

**Types of Reactors**

— series reactors, such as current-limiting reactors and load-sharing reactors;
— shunt reactors :
— single-phase neutral-earthing reactors, arc-suppression coils ;
— three-phase neutral electromagnetic couplers and earthing transformers.

*Considering similarity between Oil Immersed Transformers and the Oil Immersed Reactors, the standards such as IEC 298 apply to Reactors unless it is mentioned otherwise. The ratings, tests, etc. are similar in many respects.*

## 31.2 DEFINITIONS AND TYPES

1. **Reactor.** A predominantly inductive coil.

2. **Series reactor.** A reactor intended for series connection in a system, either for limiting the current under system fault conditions or for load-sharing in parallel circuits.

3. **Shunt reactor.** A reactor intended for shunt connection in a system to compensate for capacitive current.

4. **Single-phase neutral earthing reactor.** A single-phase reactor intended for connection between the neutral of a transformer and earth for limiting the line-to-earth current under system fault conditions.

5. **Arc-suppression coil.** A single-phase neutral earthing reactor intended for compensating the capacitive line-to-earth current due to a single-phase earth-fault.

6. **Three-phase neutral electromagnetic coupler and earthing transformer.** A three-phase reactor or transformer intended for connection in a system without neutral so as to provide for an artificial neutral.

Earthing transformers may in addition supply a local network such as the auxiliaries of a substation.

7. **Oil-immersed reactor** is one in which the coils and magnetic circuit are immersed in an insulating oil.

8. **Dry-type reactor** is one in which the coils and magnetic circuit are neither impregnated with a insulating fuild nor immersed in an insulating oil.

9. **Current-limiting reactor.** A current-limiting reactor is a reactor intended for limiting the current that can flow in a circuit under short-circuit conditions, or under other operating conditions, such as motor starting, synchronizing, arc stabilization, capacitor switching, etc.

10. **Series reactor.** It is connected in series with the power circuit. It is called current limiting reactor in certain application.

11. **Bus reactor.** A bus reactor is a current-limiting reactor for connection between two different buses or two section of the same bus for the purpose of limiting and localizing the disturbance due to a fault in either bus.

12. **Feeder reactor.** A feeder reactor is a current-limiting reactor for connection in series with an alternating-current feeder circuit, for

the purpose of limiting and localizing disturbance due to a fault in either bus.

13. **Starting reactor.** A starting reactor is a current-limiting reactor for limiting the starting current of a machine or device

14. **Synchronising reactor.** A synchronising reactor is a current limiting reactor for connecting momentarily across the open contact of a circuit-interrupting device for synchronising purpose.

15. **Paralleling current-limiting reactor.** A paralleling reactor is a current-limiting reactor for correcting the division of current-between parallel connected transformers or circuit which have unequal impedance voltages under short-circuit conditions.

16. **Neutral grounding reactor.** A reactor connected between neutral point of a star connected winding and the earth to limit earth fault currents.

17. **Smoothing reactor (AC).** A reactor connected in series with the supply to smoothen out surges in current due to fluctuating loads (such as an arc furnace or a welding transformer).

18. **Smoothing reactor (DC).** A reactor connected in series with the AC/DC convertor on DC side for smoothening DC current waveform.

19. **Series filter reactor.** A series reactor in series with a capacitor for blocking certain harmonic frequencies and passing some harmonic frequencies.

20. **Bypass reactor.** A reactor used in the bypass circuit of series capacitor. The reactor limits inrush currents when capacitor is bypassed.

21. **Shunt reactors for shunt compensation.** Reactors connected between phase and ground at terminal substations and in intermediate substations of long EHV-AC lines for compensation of line to ground capacitive currents.

22. **Shunt reactors for AC harmonic filters.** Reactors connected along with capacitor in phase to ground circuit to eliminate certain harmonics from the main circuit.

23. **Shunt reactor in SVS scheme.** Shunt reactor in static VAr. source. The current in the shunt reactor is controlled by the thyristor control.

Static VAr Source (SVS) is used for Dynamic Voltage control. The reactor current is increased during low loads on long AC lines.

## Part I—SHUNT REACTORS

### 31.2.1 SHUNT REACTORS

Shunt Reactors are used in high voltage systems to compensate capacitive generation from long lightly loaded overhead lines or extended cable systems and also for control of dynamic overvoltages.

Gapped core construction is preferred for high system voltages over coreless construction due to the high energy density that can be achieved in gapped core construction. The core sections between consecutive air gaps are moulded in epoxy resin to prevent movement between individual laminations. The spacers forming the air gaps are blocks of ceramics with a high modules of elasticity and the whole stacking of core modules is cemented together during the assembly to form a solid column without possibility of rocking, or rubbing between individual parts.

The core segments are of radial laminated configuration. The radial laminations prevent fringing flux from entering flat surfaces of core steel which would result in eddy current overheating and hot spots.

Five limbed core construction is adopted to achieve high zero sequence impedance. In addition to the three gapped core limbs with windings, there are two continuous outer return limbs. The two unwound side limbs help in achieving zero sequence impedance approximately equal to the positive sequence impedance. Other construction type can be a three limbed construction. For single phase reactors e.g. 800 kV class middle leg wound with two return legs type of construction is adopted.

Interleaved disc winding are used for rated voltages 220 kV and above. This type of winding configuration provides better impulse voltage distribution. For lower voltage classes a continuous disc winding or a multi layer helical winding are used. The tank is rectangular in construction with flat cover welded to the tank rim at top. The associated cooling control equipment is housed in a tank mounted weather proof marshalling box.

### 31.3 APPLICATIONS OF SHUNT REACTORS

The purpose of reactor (also termed a compensating or shunt reactor) is to compensate the capacitive charging power of three phase high-voltage lines. There are a number of reasons for doing this:

- improve stability of transmission
- reduce power-frequency and transient overvoltages in the system and
- prevent self-excitation of generators when connecting open circuited lines.

Fig. 31.2 shows four principle applications of shunt reactors.

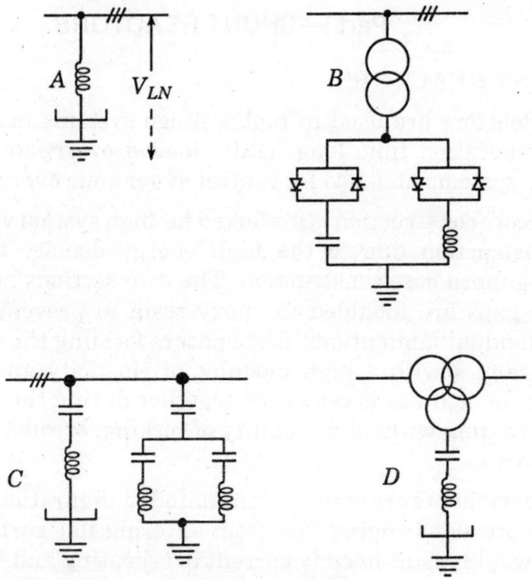


(A) Shunt reactor for direct connection.
(B) Shunt reactor in static VAr source.
(C) Shunt reactor for harmonic filters.
(D) Shunt reactor connected to tertiary winding for shunt compensation. (capacitor is used only in case of filters).

Fig. 31.2 Applications of shunt reactors.

**Table 31.1**
**Applications of Shunt Reactors**

| *Application* | *Connection* | *Remarks* |
|---|---|---|
| 1. Shunt compensation | 1. Direct<br>2. Through C.B.<br>3. Via Tertiary | — For long EHV line<br>— At sending-end<br>— At receiving-end<br>— At intermediate sub-stations. |
| 2. AC hormonic filters | 1. Shunt RLC circuits<br>2. Separate filter branches tuned to certain characteristic harmonic, e.g. 5th, 7th, High pass | 1. On AC side of thyrister controlled devices.<br>2. On AC side of rectifiers. |

With the growth of 400 kV lines and 765 kV AC lines the need for shunt compensation reactors increases. Table 31.2 gives the MVAr ratings of shunt reactors for EHV-AC lines.

**Table 31.2. MVAr Ratings of Shunt Reactors for 100 km Length of 50 Hz AC Lines***

| $E_{max}$ (kV) | 245 | 345 | 420** | 525 | 765 | 1100 |
|---|---|---|---|---|---|---|
| MVAr | 20 | 40 | 60 | 100 | 250 | 550 |

*For 60 Hz, MVAr increases by 20%.

**In India, standard values are 50, 63, 80 MVAr units at 420 kV.

## 31.4 THREE METHODS OF CONNECTIONS

Fig. 31.3 explains the following :

(*a*) Shunt reactor directly connected to transmission line. This method in preferred for EHV-lines for two reasons.

1. Reactor switching is a severe duty on circuit breakers for high voltages. Suitable circuit breakers are not available at 400 kV, 765 kV.

2. While switching in or out the line, the reactor must be in the circuit to ensure compensation.

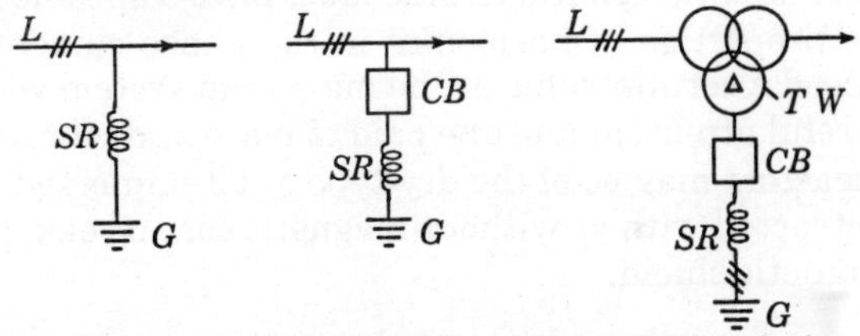


(A) Directly to busbars/line without any switching device.
(B) Through a Circuit-Breaker.
(C) To the Tertiary winding of a transformer.
Fig. 31.3. Three methods of connecting shunt reactors.

(*b*) **Shunt Reactor Connected with a Switching Device.** The switching device capable of reactor switching must be available. Reactor switching is a difficult duty for circuit-breakers due to :

— high stored energy in reactor corresponding to the chopping of current ($i_e$)

$$W_e = \frac{1}{2} i_c^2 L \text{ joules}$$

— high switching overvoltage factor above 3 p.u. which is not permissible.

For voltage levels below 245 kV, $SF_6$ circuit-breakers have been developed to meet above requirements. If a circuit-breaker is available, switchable reactor scheme (Fig. 31.3 *B*) is preferred as an independent protective zone for shunt reactor would be possible. C.B. for reactor switching are with opening resistors.

In absense of the circuit-breaker, for the shunt-reactor faults, the line breaker would be tripped.

(*c*) **Shunt Reactor Connected to Tertiary Terminals** (Fig. 31.3. C).

The advantages are

1. A circuit-breaker can be incorporated at lower voltage level.

2. Cost of shunt reactor is reduced. However the choice between the three schemes is finalised after detailed technical and economic feasibility studies.

For EHV-AC lines scheme *A* is preferred. For HV-transmission and distribution circuits scheme (*C*) is preferred.

## 31.5 SPECIAL FEATURES OF SHUNT REACTORS

The rating data are taken as power, voltage and frequency. From the thermal standpoint, the reactor must be designed for the maximum continuous system voltage. Compared with a transformer, a reactor has the following distinctive features.

— in the over-excited condition (overvoltages in the system) the magnetization characteristic must have a specific form
— the proportion of harmonics in the phase current must not exceed a certain value at the maximum system voltage
— Careful attention must be paid to noise and vibrations.

Shunt reactors may be of the dry-type or oil-immersed type. They may be constructed with or without magnetic core or electromagnetic shield or magnetic shield.

## 31.6 MAGNETIZATION CHARACTERISTIC

There are two basically different kinds of high-voltage shunt reactor, namely with or without a magnetic core in the centre of the winding. The magnetization characteristic of both types is, strictly speaking, not exactly linear.

In the case of an air-core reactor, however, saturation occurs at a higher voltage and is less pronounced than in a reactor which has a magnetic core. It has therefore become customary to speak of linear characteristics (air core reactor) and nonlinear characteristics (reactors with magnetic cores).

For a low-voltage reactor intended for connection to the tertiary winding of a transformer, the magnetization characteristic is of no practical significance. *The studies of h.v. transmission systems indicate that it is better to use reactors with a nonlinear characteristic. Their main advantage is that reactance drops as voltage increases, and so the reactive power absorbed, i.e. the degree of compensation, is higher.*

For compensation of EHV-AC lines, oil-immersed shunt reactors with gapped magnetic core in the centre are generally preferred (Fig. 31.4)

For shunt filter reactors, the voltage across filter branch gets divided across capacitor (on line side and reactor) (on earth side) Air-core reactors are preferred.

Since, the magnetization characteristic has substantial influence on the price of a reactor, it is essential that the characteristic should be exactly defined between customer and supplier. A typical magnetization characteristic is shown in Fig. 31.5. The curve is defined by the following.

— Duty point $\phi_n$
— knee point $\phi_k$
— slope of unsaturated region, $\alpha_1$
— slope of saturated region, $\alpha_2$

Defining the characteristic includes specifying the knee point $\phi_k$, *i.e.* the point of intersection of the two straight lines defined by tan $\alpha_1$ and tan $\alpha_2$. The slope of the lines is governed by the rated data

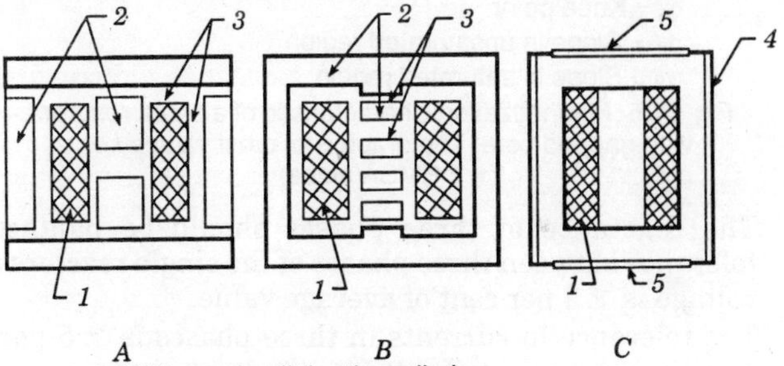


A. With gap in all the three limbs.
B. With gap in only central limb.
C. Without magnetic core.
(1) Coils (2) Magnetic core
(3) Air gaps (4) Conducting shield
(5) Conducting shield.

Fig. 31.4. Configuration of cores for shunt reactors.

of the reactor in the unsaturated region (tan $\alpha_1$), and by the air inductance of the winding in the saturated region (tan $\alpha_2$).

Considering $\phi_n$ as 1 p.u., the reactors are designed to get knee point $\phi_k$ between 1.2 and 1.3 p.u. although some designs are with $\phi_k$ between 1.15 and .15. It should be remembered that the position of the knee has a decisive effect on the price of the reactor.

The magnetization curve is plotted for crest values of exciting current $\hat{I}$ and crest valve of flux $\hat{\phi}$. (or exciting voltage $\hat{E}$).

— If $\hat{E}_m$ is the high system voltage crest value (e.g. $\sqrt{2} \times 245/\sqrt{3}$ for 220 kV class) the reactance of the reactor should remain linear at least upto 1.3 $\hat{E}_m$, sometimes 1.5 $\hat{E}_m$ is specified.

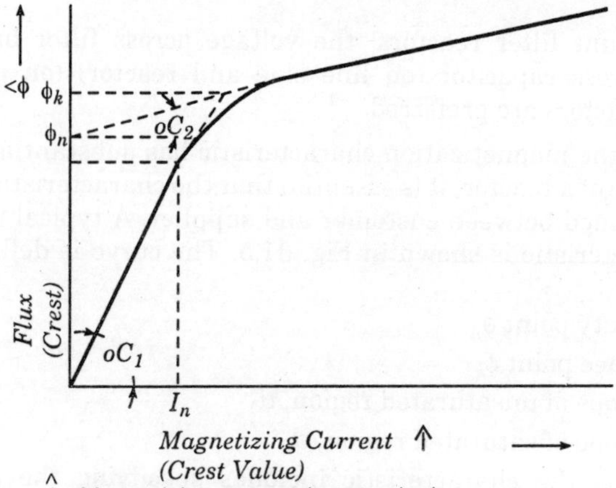


$\hat{I}$ = Magnetizing current (crest value)

$\phi$ = Inductive flux (crest value)

$\phi_n$ = Duty point

$\phi_k$ = Knee point

$\alpha_1$ = Slope in unsaturated region

$\alpha_2$ = Slope in saturated region

Fig. 31.5. Magnetization Characteristic of a shunt reactor with gapped core. The graph is of crest values *i.e.* ($\sqrt{2}$ RMS Values)

— The reactance of three phases should be balanced. The tolerance between three phases of the single reactors at rated voltage is ± 2 per cent of average value.

— The tolerance in currents in three phases is ± 5 per cent of rated current at rated voltage.

## 31.7 NEUTRAL CURRENT AND ZERO-SEQUENCE IMPEDANCE

If required zero-sequnce impedance is only 55 to 65 per cent of positive sequence impedance, a three-limb constructions is suitable. If required zero sequence impedance is 90 to 100% of positive sequence impedance, a five-limb construction is used.

In three phase reactors, the third harmonic currents flow continuously through the neutral to ground circuit during normal service. The three phases should have least deviation in magnetization curves. The design of magnetic core and the magnetization characteristic is such that third harmonic currents through neutral are only about 1% of rated current during normal voltage.

## 31.8 SINGLE PHASE UNITS AND THREE PHASE UNITS

Figure 31.6 shows a single phase shunt reactor. It has one coil and two terminal bushings. Fig. 31.7 shows a three phase shunt reactor. It

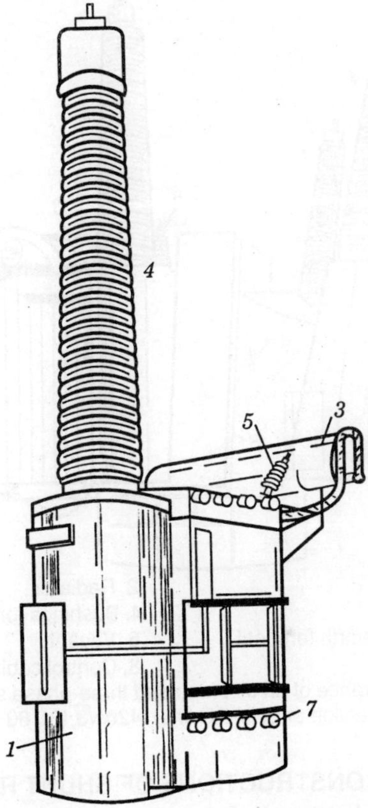


1. Tank
2. Radiator (not shown)
3. Conservator
4. Bushing for line terminal
5. Bushing for earth terminal
6. Vacant
7. Connections for cooler.

Fig. 31.6 Appearance of an oil immersed single phase shunt reactor for shunt compensation of EHV-AC lines 135 MVAr, 525/√3 kV, 60 Hz.

has three terminal bushings for line terminals and one terminal bushing for neutral terminal.

Single units have following merits:

— Zero sequence impedance can be made equal to positive sequence impedance by suitable design parameters of core.

— one reactor units can be kept as a spare without high investment.

For voltage of 400 kV and belows single three phase units can be built easily to required specifications. For 765 kV and above three single phase units are preferred due to above technical requirements.

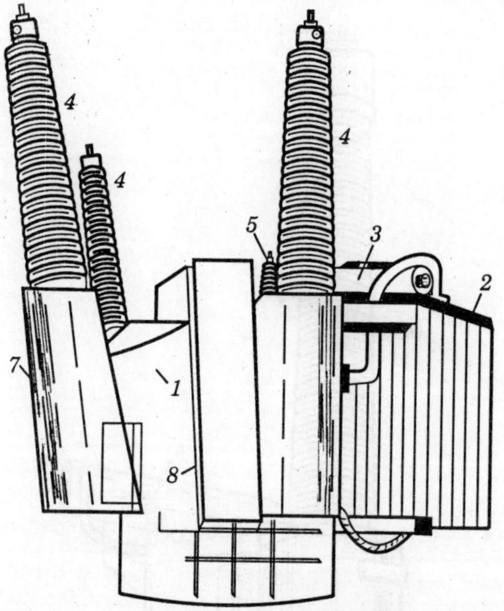


1. Tank
2. Radiator
3. Conservator
4. Bushings for line terminals
5. Bushing for earth terminal
6. Vacant
7. Turret
8. Control cabinet.

Fig. 31.7. Appearance of an oil-immersed three-phase shunt reactor for shunt compensation of EHV-AC line. (420/$\sqrt{3}$ kV, 60 MVAr, 50 Hz)

## 31.9 TYPES OF CONSTRUCTIONS OF SHUNT REACTORS

— The following types of constructions are common. The choice depends upon the rated voltage, rated kVAr and the cost.

1. **Oil-Immersed with Gapped Core**
   — Single phase unit
   — Three phase unit

This is further classified as

— ONAN, ONAF, OFAF etc. depending upon type of cooling.

2. **Oil-Immersed coreless.**
   — Single phase unit
   — Three phase unit

This is further classified as ONAN, ONAF, OFAF etc.

3. **Dry Type Shunt Reactors.**

Try Dry-Type or Oil-Immersed Type shunt reactors are designed for following alternatives:

1. Outdoor Type
2. Indoor Type
3. Semi-outdoor Type.

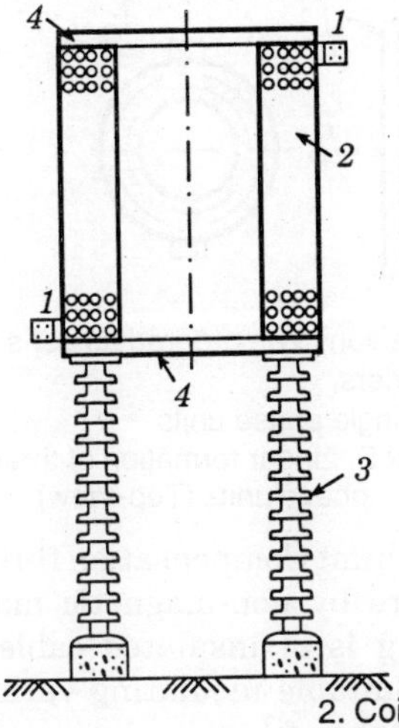


1. Terminals
2. Coil
3. Post Insulators
4. Insulating brackets.

Fig. 31.8. Configuration of one pole of an outdoor Air-Core, Core-less shunt Reactor. Such reactors are used for AC filters

## 31.10 DRY TYPE SHUNT REACTORS

Figure 31.8 illustrates the configuration of a a dry type outdoor or indoor shunt reactor in single phase unit.

Figure 31.9 shows plan views of a three-phase bank with triangular formation.

In coreless reactor, there is no iron core or iron parts. The flux density is much lower than in gapped-core reactor. The get the same flux, the diameter of core-less reactor coils should be much larger. The flux density is maximum near inner turns and minimum near outer turns. The open, dry type coreless reactors are used for lower voltages

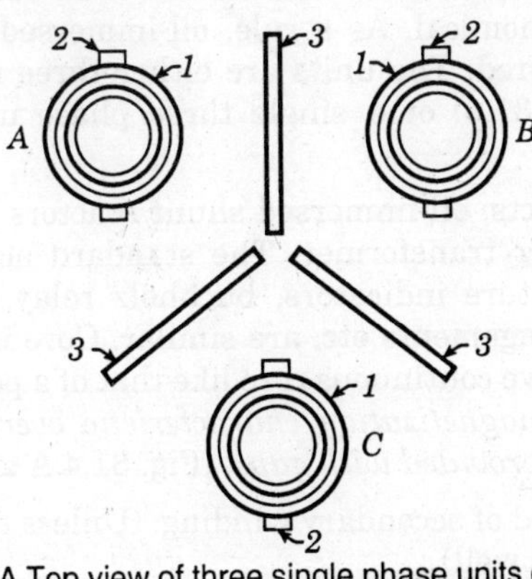


Fig. 31.9 A Top view of three single phase units of Air-Core shunt reactors in a triangular formation

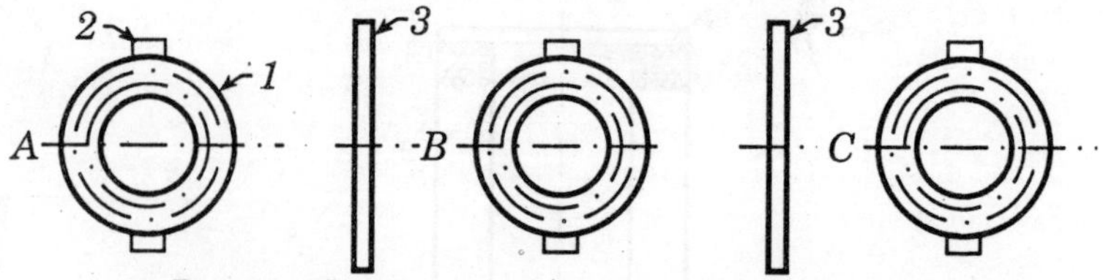


1. Reactor coil
2. Terminal (Position to be ordered as per substation layout)
3. Fire-proof barriers.
A, B, C, Three single phase units

Fig. 31.9 B. Linear formation of three single phase units (Top-View).

(AC Filter Reactors or Shunt Compensation through tertiary). The rigid supports to the coil are by non-magnetic materials and insulating materials. The winding is of insulated cables having continuously stranded conductors. Suitable insulating varnish is provided around the external surfaces of the coil.

The entire reactor coil is supported on post insulator columns which are designed to withstand impulse voltages and power frequency voltages corresponding to the voltage class of the shunt reactor.

Upper terminal of the shunt reactor is connected to the busbars or filter capacitor. The other terminal (star point) is connected to station earth along with the corresponding terminals of other phases.

Cross-section of conductor is designed on the basis of rated current and rated short-time current. The windings are designed as per required insulation strength and ampereturns.

## 31.11 CONSTRUCTION OF GAPPED-IRON CORE OIL IMMERSED SHUNT REACTORS

For higher voltages (400 kV, 765 kV etc. ) and higher MVAr ratings (20 MVAr and above, see Table 3.2) the size of air-core reactor becomes too big and uneconomical. As a rule, oil-immersed gapped iron core reactors are preferred. The units are either three numbers of single phase units (Fig. 31.6) or a single three phase unit (Fig. 31.7) as discussed earlier.

In many respects, oil-immersed shunt reactors are similar to the oil-immersed power transformer. The standard accessories such as bushings, temperature indicators, buchholz relay, sudden pressure relay, sealing arrangements etc. are similar. Core is different. Shunt reactor does not have continuous core like that of a power transformer. *To ensure linear magnetization characteristic over a wide range of voltage, the core is provided with gaps.* (Fig. 31.4 A and B)

There is no need of secondary winding. (Unless the reactor is used as a transformer as well).

The shunt reactor has one winding per phase, which is connected between line terminal and earth.

The gapped core is built by radial core sections moulded in epoxy resin.

The moulded type sections of gapped core ensure that laminations do not get dislocated.

Between consecutive core sections, ceramic spacers having high dimensional accuracy under pressure are placed.

The moulded core sections and the ceramic spacers are accurately positioned and cemented together under pressure to get single sturdy column (limb) suitable insulating tie rods and clamping beams are provided to get rigid core and to maintain pressure on the core sections in the gapped limb.

In a single-phase shunt reactor, unit two concentric cylindrical coils are provided on the central gapped limb, one near the upper yoke and the other near lower yoke. The magnetic fluxes of the two coils oppose each other.

In three phase shunt reactor unit, three plus three coil sections connected as described above are placed concentrically on the central

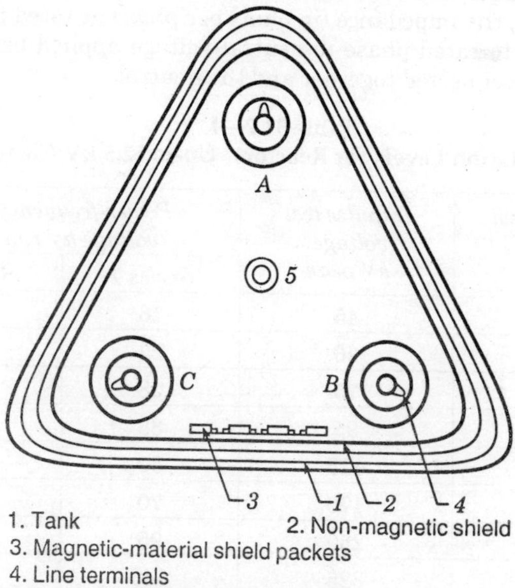


1. Tank 2. Non-magnetic shield
3. Magnetic-material shield packets
4. Line terminals
5. Neutral terminals (at the centre)
A, B, C, Reactor Coils

Fig. 31.10. Top-view of a core-less oil-immersed three-phase shunt reactor.

limb. Individual phase coils are connected as in the case of single-phase shunt reactor.

Another popular configuration used for oil-immersed core-less. Three phase shunt reactor is shown in Fig. 31.10. The three windings are placed vertically in triangular formation without a core. The tank provides the enclosure.

## 31.12 PARTICULAR REQUIREMENTS OF SHUNT REACTORS

1. **Rated voltage.** The highest voltage at rated frequency which the apparatus is capable of withstanding continuously and for which it is designed.

**Note.** The rated voltage of a shunt reactor has to be specified by the purchaser. It may be less than the maximum system voltage depending on the operating conditions. e.g. 245 kV shunt reactor. It is convenient to express the voltage rating as 245 : $\sqrt{3}$.

2. **Rated power.** The apparent power specified for service at rated voltage. It is expressed in kVA or MVA.

3. **Rated current.** The current for which the apparatus is designed as derived from the rated voltage, the rated power and a factor depending on the number of phases.

4. **Zero-sequence impedance.** For star-connected polyphase shunt reactors, the impedance (in ohms per phase at rated frequency) corresponding to rated phase-to-neutral voltage applied between the line terminals connected together and the neutral.

**Table 31.2—I**

**Insulation Levels for Reactors* Up-to 72.5 kV Class**

| *System highest voltage kV r.m.s.* | *Impulse test voltage kV peak* | *Power-frequency test voltage kV r.m.s,.* | |
|---|---|---|---|
| | | *Series 1* | *Series 2* |
| 3.6 | 45 | 16 | 21 |
| 7.2 | 60 | 22 | 27 |
| 12 | 75 | 28 | 35 |
| 17.5 | 95 | 38 | 45 |
| 24 | 125 | 50 | 55 |
| 36 | 170 | 70 | 75 |
| 52 | 250 | 95 | — |
| 72.5 | 325 | 140 | — |

5. **Insulation levels.** For the line terminals, insulation levels correspond to those specified for transformers. The neutral terminal of a star connected reactor may have reduced insulation level.

*Test value for application to the line terminals.

Thus shunt reactor may have two different insulation levels : Higher insulation for line terminals and reduced insulation level for neutral terminal.

Standard insulation levels are recommended by IEC 289 Reactors. Insulation levels in general correspond to those specified for transformers (IEC Publication 76). Unless otherwise specified, test voltages are in accordance with Tables I and II.

**Table 31.2—II**
**Insulation levels for Reactors Above 100 kV Class**

| *System highest voltage kV r.m.s.* | *Impulse test voltage kV peak* | | *Power frequency test voltage kV r.m.s.* | |
|---|---|---|---|---|
| | | | *Series 1* | *Series 2* |
| | *Full insulation* | *Reduced insulation* | *Full insulation* | *Reduced insulation* |
| 100 | 450 | 380 | 185 | 150 |
| 123 | 550 | 450 | 230 | 185 |
| 145 | 650 | 550 | 275 | 230 |
| 170 | 750 | 650 | 325 | 275 |
| 245 | 1050 | 900 | 460 | 395 |
| 300 | – | 1050 | – | 460 |
| 420 | – | 1425 | – | 630 |

## 31.11 VIBRATIONS AND NOISE

The alternating magnetic field passes through air-gaps and steel. This causes tremendous forces of attraction between adjucent core sections. These high magnitude forces also alternate along with the alternating magnetic flux.

In a reactor, unlike a conventional transformer, the main magnetic flux passes through two media–steel and air.

Noise and vibration are, therefore, caused not only by magnetostrictive, forces, but also by Maxwellian forces of attraction, and these are generally very considerable. The latter act especially as axial compressive forces on the magnet columns. To prevent the columns from resonating, a hard material has to be used for the air-gap spacers. In addition, continuous high compression of the columns must be maintained during operation.

The spacers between adjucent core-sections should be of high compression strength, high dimensional stability. The construction of core limbs and yoke should be such that the core does not become loose.

The vibrations originating in the core are transferred to the tank walls and supporting components ; through coil and the core-base. Anti-vibration pads are used at the core-base between the core and the tank-base. The tank walls are provided with stiffners whose location, thickness etc. is determined after advanced vibration analysis. The earlier generation of shunt reactors had severe physical vibration and noise. After research and development, the vibration and sound levels have been reduced.

## 31.13 RATING PLATE DATA FOR SHUNT REACTORS

The following data should be given on the rating plate.

The name of the equipment 'SHUNT REACTOR' shall be clearly marked on the name plate.

1. Shunt reactor-Type...
2. Number and year of the specification.
3. Manufacturer's name
4. Manufacturer's serial number.
5. Year of manufacture.
6. Number of phases.
7. Rated power.
8. Rated frequency.
9. Rated voltage.
10. Regulating range, if any.
11. Connection.
12. Measured impedance per phase at rated voltage.
13. Zero-sequence impedance, if required.
14. Type of cooling.
15. Class of temperature for dry-type reactors, and temperature rise if non-standard.
16. Insulation level, separately for the earth end of the winding where appropriate.
17. Total mass.
18. Mass of insulating oil.
19. Untaking mass.

## 31.14 TESTS ON SHUNT REACTORS

The general requirements of Type Tests, Routine Tests and Special Tests are similar to those of IEC 76 for power Transformers.

**Table 31.3 Testing of Shunt Reactor**

| *Test and Remarks* | *Type Test* | *Routine Test* |
|---|---|---|
| 1. **General Requirements for type, routine and special tests.** Remarks : As per IEC-76 for Power Transformers. | | |
| 2. **Measurement of winding resistance.** As for Power Transformer. | | * |
| 3. **Measurement of loss and current** | * | |

(Contd...)

| *Test and Remarks* | *Type Test* | *Routine Test* |
|---|---|---|
| 4. **The loss and the current should preferably be measured at rated voltage and frequency.** As the power-factor of a shunt reactor is normally very low, loss measurements using wattmeter methods may be subject to considerable errors ; hence a bridge method or a calorimetric method with proper precautions may be used to advantage. | * | |
| The loss in the various parts of the reactor cannot be separated by measurement ; it is thus preferable, in order to avoid corrections to reference temperature, to perform the measurement when the average temperature of the windings is practically equal to the reference temperature. If this is impracticable, the additional loss shall be deemed independent of temperature. | | |
| 5. **Test of temperature rise.** This test is performed at rated voltage and frequency. Ref. IEC-76 | * | |
| 6. **Inter-turn overvoltage withstand test.** Ref. IEC-76. When such test is not possible on large reactors, the test is replaced by impulse voltage test. | * | |
| 7. **Separate-source voltage -withstand test.** Table 31.2—I and II give the test voltages for the specified insulation level of the reactors. Series I values shall be chosen of *oil-immersed reactors and Series II values for dry-type reactors.*<br>For the test between winding and earth, both ends of the phase winding under test are connected together. The ends of the other phase windings are earthed. The test voltage is applied between the ends of the winding under test and earth.<br>For the test between turns, the test voltage is applied to each end of the phase winding in turn, whereas the other end is earthed through a resistor, the value of which is chosen to suit the service conditions but must not exceed 500 Ω. The ends of the other phase windings are earthed during the test.<br>*If surge diverters are connected in parallel with a series reactor*, the impulse test voltage between turns may be reduced subject to agreement. Its level must be at least 1.3 times the protective level of the surge diverters. The surge diverters are removed during the test. | * | |

| *Test and Remarks* | *Type Test* | *Routine Test* |
|---|---|---|
| 8. *Short-circuit current withstand test (special test).* The short-circuit withstand test is designed to prove mechanical capability at rated short-time current, and in the case of reactors with magnetic core or shield to measure the impedance corresponding to the rated short-time current. It consists of two applications of rated short-time current each of a duration of ten cycles, the first peak having a crest value of $1.8 \times \sqrt{2}$ times the r.m.s value. (Certain service conditions may result in asymmetry factors less than $1.8 \times \sqrt{2}$). Three-phase reactors should be subjected to two three-phase tests : one with maximum asymmetry of the short-circuit current in the central phase, the other with maximum asymmetry in an outside phase. | — | |
| The ability of reactor to withstand the test shall be determined by remeasuring the impedance, by visual inspection and by repetition of the routine dielectric tests at 75% of the initial value. The thermal behaviour under rated short-time current is ascertained according to the formula in IEC Publication 76. If difficulty is encountered in measuring the impedance at rated short-time current, a test with symmetrical current may be agreed upon. To obtain an accurate result, it is necessary to keep the voltage and current constant for several cycles, and to do this it may be necessary to test at a reduced current. The current for this test should exceed the current required to saturate the core or shield. | | |
| 9. **Impulse-voltage withstand test.** the impulse-voltage test is a type test for reactors designed for exposed situation. It is a routine test when the inter-turn overvoltage test is not practicable. Table 31.2 I and II is generally applicable for testing of shunt reactors. Test voltage will be for respective insulation level of the reactor. | * | * |

## 31.16 TOLERANCES

Following tolerances are generally acceptable for shunt reactors.

1. **Tolerance on current at rated voltage and rated frequency.** ± 5% of rated current.

2. **Loss.** Shall not exceed by more than 15%.

3. **Allowable harmonic Content in reactor current.** For shunt reactors intended to be directly earthed, the maximum allowable crest value of the third harmonic component of the reactor current shall be

3% of the crest value of the fundamental when the reactor is energized at rated voltage with a sinusodial waveform.

## Part 2—SERIES REACTORS

## 31.14 GENERAL REMARKS

Series reactors may be dry type or oil-immersed type. They may be constructed with or without magnetic core or electromagnetic shield or magnetic shield.

Series reactors are being used in electrical networks for over fifty years for limiting short-circuit currents. The basic principle has been described in sec. 31.1 and 31.1 (*b*).

## 31.15. APPLICATIONS OF SERIES REACTORS

Figure 31.11—1 to 13 gives a summary of series reactor applications, described below.

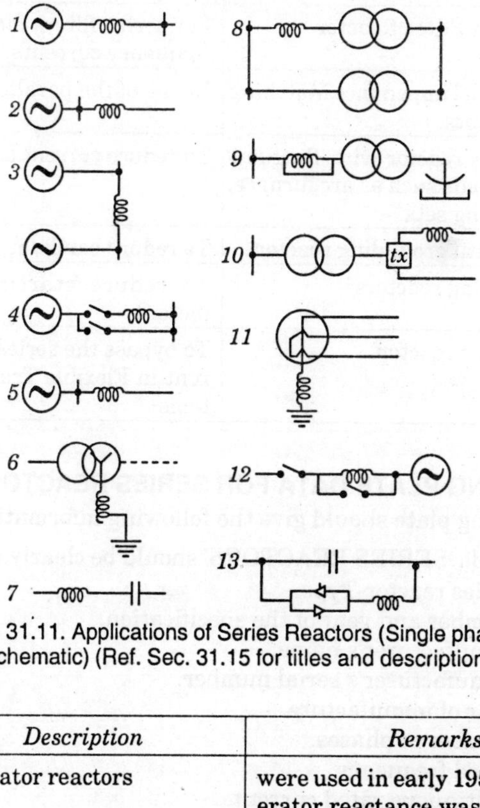


Fig. 31.11. Applications of Series Reactors (Single phase Schematic) (Ref. Sec. 31.15 for titles and description).

| *Sl.No.* | *Description* | *Remarks* |
|---|---|---|
| 1. | Generator reactors | were used in early 1950s when generator reactance was not adequate to limit short-circuit currents. |

*(Contd...)*

| *Sl.No.* | *Description* | *Remarks* |
|---|---|---|
| 2. | Line reactors | were used in early 1950s when circuit-breakers were not of enough breaking capacity to interrupt short-circuit currents. |
| 3. | Busbar Reactors | Connected between bus-sections to limit short-circuit currents. No more needed as breakers of high capacity are available today. |
| 4. | Synchronising Reactors | Generators (or two sources) are synchronised through a reactor. |
| 5. | Damping reactor | To reduce steepness of surge currents (No more favoured). |
| 6. | Arc suppression coil, (Ground Fault Neutralizer): | For resonant earthing. Neutral to ground reactor. |
| 7. | Series Filter Reactor | For series filters for blocking high frequency currents. |
| 8. | Parallel impedance Matching Reactors. | In one of the parallel circuits. |
| 9. | Series reactor with fluctuating loads such as arc furnace, welding sets. | To reduce current surges. |
| 10. | Neutral grounding reactor. | To reduce earth fault currents. |
| 11. | Starting reactors | To reduce starting current of motors. |
| 12. | Bypass reactor | To bypass the series capacitor current in Flexible Transmission systems. |

## 31.16 RATING PLATE DATA FOR SERIES REACTOR

The rating plate should give the following information :

The words 'SERIES REACTORS' should be clearly marked.

1. Series reactor-Type.
2. Number and year of the specification.
3. Manufacturer's name.
4. Manufacturer's serial number.
5. Year of manufacture.
6. Number of phases.
7. Rated frequency.
8. Continuous rated current.
9. Measured impedance at continuous rated current.
10. Rated short-time current and specified duration.
11. Type of cooling.

12. Class of temperature for dry-type reactors and temperature rise if it is not a normal value.
13. Insulation level.
14. Total mass.
15. Mass of insulating oil
16. Untanking mass.

## 31.17. TERMS AND DEFINITIONS FOR SERIES REACTOR

(Refer sec. 31.2 also).

1. **Series Reactor.** It is an inductance coil connected in series with the system for one of the following purposes :

— Limiting current during fault condition.
— Limiting current during synchronising, load sharing, fluctuating loads, etc.

2. **Continuous Rated Current.** The r.m.s. value of current which the reactor can carry continuously, with temperature rise of current carrying parts and other parts, within specified limits, [e.g. 800 A].

3. **Rated Short-time Current.** The symmetrical r.m.s. value of fault current which the reactor can carry for specified short time [e.g. 40 kA for 1 sec.]

4. **Rated Impedance.** Impedance expressed in ohms per phase at rated frequency or in per unit specified for the reactor.

5. **Rated Over Current Factor.** The ratio of rated short time current to continuous current, e.g. 25.

6. **Rated Through-put kVA.** $\sqrt{3}$ × Rated voltage × Rated current (for 3-phase reactors).

7. **Rated Voltage.** The line to line service voltage for which the reactor is designed. It is expressed in kV, rms.

8. **Short Circuit Rating.** The reactor should be capable of withstanding the mechanical and thermal stresses during short circuit at its terminals for a specified period of time e.g. 1 sec.

The temperature rise during short circuit should be such that it does not alter the chemical proportion of the core etc.

9. **Rated Insulation Level.** The withstand values of Impulse Voltage Test and Power Frequency Voltage Withstand Test for which the reactor is designed.

Each rated voltage has corresponding insulation level.

## 31.18 TYPES AND CONSTRUCTIONAL DETAILS

Following types are common :

— Dry Type or Immersed Type
— With gapped iron core or without iron core

— With electromagnetic shield or without electromagnetic shield
— with magnetic shield or without magnetic shield

The constructional details described in sec. 31.9 for shunt reactors apply to series reactors with following changes.

— Cross sectional area of conductors for series reactors is larger.
— The phase to ground insulation for the complete series reactor (line terminals) corresponds to required insulation level.
— The construction of coil, support structure is mechanically strong to withstand through short-circuit current. (*e.g.*, 25) times normal current and ($\sqrt{2} \times 1.8 \times I_{sc}$) as peak value.

## 31.19 SELECTION OF SERIES REACTORS

While selecting a series reactor, following aspects should be considered

1. **Type.** Dry or oil-Immersed.
   Type of cooling,
   Type of shielding, etc.
2. Number of phases 1 or 3
3. Whether Indoor or Outdoor or Semi-outdoor.
4. Reactance in ohms at rated frequency at (1) rated current (2) rated short-circuit current.
5. Rated voltage, Rated insulation levels.
6. Normal current rating, short-time current rating, duration.
7. Ability to withstand peak short-circuit current.

Unless otherwise specified, is applicable on the under-standing that the rated short-time current in the reactor shall not exceed 25 times the continuous rated current for a period not exceeding 3s.

8. Rated throughput kVA.

## 31.20 TESTING OF SERIES REACTORS

The classification of type tests, Routine Tests, Special Tests, for series reactors is same as that for power transformers (IEC 76) following table gives details:

**Table 31.4. Testing of Series Reactors**

| | *Type test* | *Routine test* |
|---|---|---|
| **1. Measurement of winding resistance**<br>—As for power transformers, IEC 76 | | * |
| **2. Measurement of impedance** | | * |

*(Contd...)*

| | *Type test* | *Routine test* |
|---|---|---|
| (*a*) The impedance of a single-phase series reactor shall be measured at rated frequency by applying a voltage which results in the circulation of the continuous rated current.<br>(*b*) The impedance of a three-phase series reactor shall be measured at rated frequency by applying to the star-connected phase-windings a system of symmetrical voltages which results in the circulation of currents, the average of which corresponds to the continuous rated current. The impedance shall then be taken as:<br>$\dfrac{\text{Phase–to–phase applied voltage}}{\text{Continuous rated current} \times \sqrt{3}}$<br>(*c*) The impedance of series reactors which have neither magnetic core nor shield of magnetic material may be measured at a lower value of current. | | |
| **3. Measurement of loss.** The measurement of loss requires special care due to the low loss angle. An appropriate method (wattmeter bridge or other)shall be adopted by the manufacturer. | | |
| For reactors without core or shield (magnetic or electromagnetic) the test method is as in IEC Publication 76, for Power Transformers. In the case of other reactors the losses in their different parts cannot be separated by measurement. It is thus preferable to measure the loss with the average temperature of the windings practically equal to the reference temperature. If this is impracticable, the additional loss of reactors with magnetic core or shield shall be deemed independent of temperature. If these reactors have more than 30% additional loss, measurement should be performed, if possible, at continuous rated current. | | |
| **4. Impulse voltage withstand test.** The impulse-voltage tests are type tests for reactors designed for exposed situation,<br>This test is devised to check the ability of the reactor to withstand steep-wave impulse-voltages between turns of the winding and between the winding and earth.<br>The test voltages are from Table 31.2, Table I and II, for the specified insulation level of the reactor. | * | * |

*(Contd...)*

| | Type test | Routine test |
|---|---|---|
| **5. Separate source voltage withstand test.** | | * |
| (1 Min. power frequency test). The test shall be applied for 1 min. between the following parts: (1) the winding and earth; (2) the windings of different phases. The test voltages shall be taken from Table 31.3, Table I and II, for the specified insulation level of the reactors. Series 1 values shall be chosen for oil-immersed current limiting reactors and Series 2 values for dry-type reactors. | | |
| **6. Temperature rise test.** This is performed at rated current and rated frequency as per IEC 76 for power transformers. | | * |
| **7. Inter-turn overvoltage withstand test.** When a test between turns is practicable, it shall be performed at an increased frequency. The duration in seconds shall be 120 times rated frequency divided by test frequency. The test shall be made at a voltage corresponding to twice the steady state voltage appearing across the reactor at rated short time current. | | * |

If this not feasible test (4) is performed.

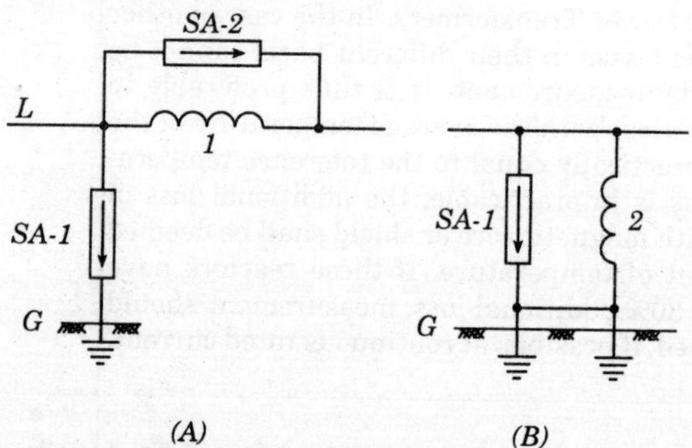


(*A*) *Series Reactor.* SA-2 Against voltage surge across the series reactor. SA-1 Against line to ground voltage.
(*B*) *Shunt Reactor.* SA-1—line to ground.

Fig. 31.12. Surge arrester protection.

## 31.24. TOLERANCES

**Current limiting reactors:**

— Impedances ± 20% of rated impedance
— Load sharing reactors ± 7.5% of rated impedance
— Impedances of three phase shall not deviate by more than 3%.
— Tolerances on loss ± 15% of declared value.

## 31.21. SURGE ARRESTER PROTECTION

Surge arresters (ZnO type) are connected across each phase of reactor winding (Fig. 31.12). The withstand level of reactor is coordinate with the protective level of the surge arrester.

For *shunt reactor* (2) full phase to ground voltage (across the reactor coil) comes continuously across the surge arrester (SA-1). Hence, protective level of SA-1 should correspond to withstand level of the shunt reactor (2). For series reactor (1), SA-1 provides phase to ground surge protection. SA-2 provides surge protection against high voltages during through short-circuit currents. ($V = IX$).

### Summary

The reactors have several types such as series, shunt, neutral grounding, filter, bypass etc. and applications for compensation, current limiting, filtering, limiting ground currents etc.

There is a similarity in the oil immersed reactors and oil-immersed transformers.

Standard specifications for reactors (such as IEC 289) cover series reactors and shunt reactors.

### Questions

1. State clearly the difference between:
   — Series reactors and Shunt reactors with regard to normal current and rated voltages.
2. Fill in the gaps.
   (*a*) Series reactors are used for the following applications.
   (1).........(5)........
   (*b*) Shunt reactors are used for the following applications
   (1).........(5)........
3. Explain the construction of gapped core oil immersed reactor.
4. State whether correct or wrong.
   (*a*) Series reactor is connected between phase and ground.
   (*b*) Shunt reactor is connected between transformer tertiary and ground.
   (*c*) Capacitors are connected in series with series reactors and in parallel with shunt reactors.
   (*d*) Series reactor neutral must not be grounded.
   (*e*) Shunt reactor neutral must not be grounded.
   (*f*) Surge arresters are provided across the reactors for protection against lightning surges.
5. State Rating plate data of a shunt reactor.
6. Can a series reactor be used as a shunt reactor? Why?

# 32

# Distribution Transformers

Conventional distribution transformers are of standard designs and are manufactured in lots. In India transformers up to 11 kV, 500 kVA in single phase and three phase versions are identified as the distribution transformers. (In USA upto 67 kV and 500 kVA). This chapter covers the types, specifications, fitments, test requirements and applications.

## 32.1 DEMAND FOR DISTRIBUTION TRANSFORMERS

Table 32.1 gives the data for India. The annual MVA production of distribution transformer constitutes about 40% of total transformer production. The growth rate per year is approximately 20%. Therefore, distribution transformers are very important in power sector.

**Table 32.1. Production of Transformers in India**

| *Year* | *Distribution transformers, Million MVA* | *Power transformers Million MVA* | *Total transformers, Million MVA* |
|---|---|---|---|
| 1988–89 | 15.44 | 24.15 | 39.59 |
| 1989–90 | 19.3 | 28.20 | 47.5 |
| Annual Growth | 25% | 17% | 20% |

## 32.2 RATINGS

Ratings of distribution transformers are standardized in various countries. The main ratings include kV rating and kVA ratings. Table gives the standard ratings in India and Table 32.2 gives the standard ratings in USA. With the growth of the distribution system, the voltage levels, kVA levels and fault levels in distribution systems go up.

**Table 32.2. Standard Ratings of Distribution Transformers in USA**

| *Single Phase Transformers* | |
|---|---|
| kVA rating | 5, 10, 15, 25, 37, 50, 75, 100, 167, 250, 333, 500 |
| HV winding | 2400 V to 67000 V |
| LV winding | 120 V to 7980 V |

*(Contd...)*

| *Three Phase Transformers* | |
|---|---|
| kVA rating | 30, 45, 75, 112, 150, 225, 300, 500 |
| HV winding | 2400 V to 67000 V star |
| LV winding | 208 V to 13200 V star |

## 32.3 STANDARDIZATION

Distribution transformers have been standarized in various countries with respect to

— kV ratings
— kVA ratings
— Winding connections (Star/Delta etc.) and connection diagrams
— Type of bushings
— Terminals, sizes, makings
— Rating plates
— Mounting details
— Fitments, accessories
— Mechanical features etc.

In India, **IS 1180** "Distribution transformers up to and including 11 kV, 500 kVA". is being followed.

## 32.4 TYPES OF DISTRIBUTION TRANSFORMERS

Types may be identified on the basis of service e.g.,

1. For overhead distribution system. These are designed for pole mounting or ground mounting outdoor.
2. For underground distribution system these are mounted in indoor underground substations.
3. Indoor distribution transformers.

Type may be identified based on design features.

1. Conventional oil immersed.

2. Dry type.

3. Completely Self Protected Type (CSP) Distribution Transformer.

Convention distribution transformers are without fuse, surge arresters switching devices. CSP distribution transformers have built-in protective devices against lightning surges, over loads, earth faults, etc.

## 32.5 TAP-CHANGING PROVISION

No taps are normally required to be provided on these transformers. Taps, however, may be provided if specifically desired by the purchaser.

The standard tapping ranges, when taps are provided, are as follows:

| | *Up to and Including 25 kVa Rating* | *Above 25 kVA Rating* |
|---|---|---|
| Winding tapped | Secondary | Primary |
| Number of tappings | 2 | 5 |
| Tappings at | + 5 per cent | $\pm 2\frac{1}{2}$ and ± 5 per cent |

Tap-changing shall be carried out with the transformer off-circuit as follows:

1. By means of links for transformers up to 25 kVA.

2. By means of an externally-operated switch with mechanical locking device and a position indicator. Arrangement for padlocking shall also be provided for transformers above 25 kVA.

## 32.6 MOUNTING ARRANGEMENTS

Standard dimensions are provided on transformer base. (*e.g.*, foundation holes at 415 mm × 415 mm square corners. The transformer base is of two 75 mm × 40 mm × 460 mm long channels.

Mounting is either on plinth slightly above ground level (with complete fencing on all the four sides) or on pole-structure on raised platform.

## 32.7 PERMISSIBLE TEMPERATURE RISE

| | |
|---|---|
| Top oil 50°C | (by thermometer method of measurement) |
| Windings 55°C | (by resistance method of measurement) |

## 32.8 WINDING CONNECTIONS

As per *Indian practice.* The primary winding shall be connected delta and the secondary winding star [vector symbol Dyn 11 (see IS : 2026 (Part IV)-1977*)], so as to produce a positive phase displacement of 30° from the primary to the secondary vectors of the same phase. The neutral of the secondary winding shall be brought out to a separate insulated terminal.

## 32.9 DESIGN FEATURES

*The Tank.* Tanks are rectangular box shape of adequate strength to withstand possible pressure build up in the tank.

The exterior of the transformer tank and other ferrous fittings shall be thoroughly cleaned, scraped and given a priming coat and two finishing coats of durable oil and weather-resisting paint or enamel. All steel screws, nuts and fasteners exposed to atmosphere shall be either galvanised or cadmium-plated.

In USA, cylindrical or oval cross-section tanks are used traditionally.

Plain tanks are used upto 50 kVA. For higher kVA ratings, fins, cooling tubes, detachable radiators are used.

*Core.* Three legged cores with CRGO steel strips are preferred. Mitred inter-leaved joints are used for reducing exciting current, core loss, weight of core.

Windings are concentric cylindrical windings with LV near the core and HV on outer side.

As distribution transformers are subject to frequent overloads, external short-circuits, lightning surges etc., the windings are more ruggedly built. The windings are designed to carry higher peak loads for shorter duration and continuous lower overloads for long duration. In other words, the windings are designed to carry higher than rated continuous current, insulation system is thermally up-rated with better cooling, prior ageing etc.

Vacuum oil treatment is provided for the complete unit to achieve higher impulse voltage withstand in recent transformers aluminium winding is being used instead of copper winding particularly for LV circuits.

## 32.10 STANDARD FITTINGS

Fig. 32.1 shows three views of a typical distribution transformer with standard fittings in following serial order. These are applicable for oil-immerse distribution transformers rated 40 kVA and above.

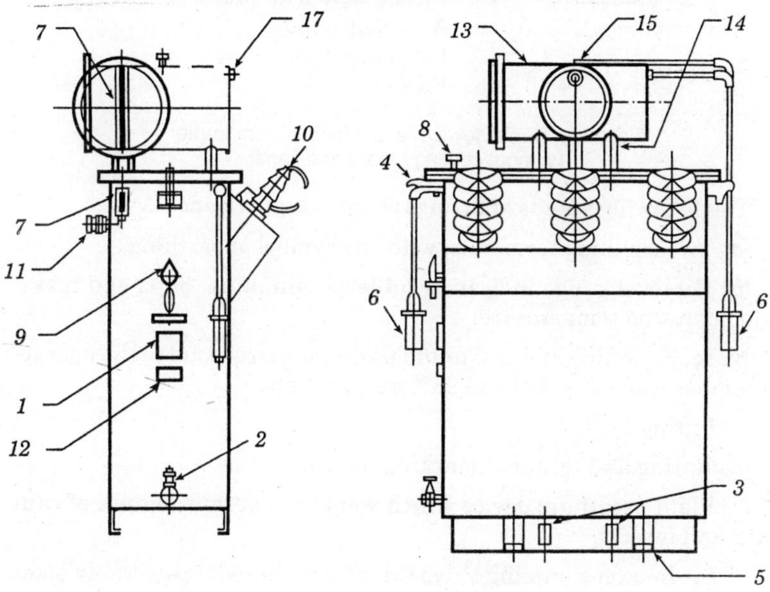

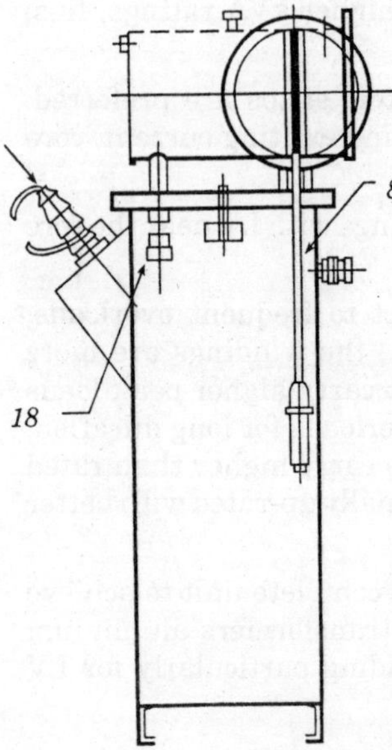


1. Rating plate.
2. Drain plug or drain valve.
3. Two earthing terminals.
4. Lifting lugs.
5. Platform mounting arrangement.
6. Silica-gel-Breather.
7. Oil gauge.
8. Thermometer pocket.
9. Off-circuit tapping switch.
10. HV bushings with arcing horns.
11. LT bushings.
12. Diagram plate.
13. Conservator.
14. Conservator drain plug.
15. Filling hole with plug.
16. Air release plug.
17. Plain breather.
18. Filter valve.

Fig. 32.1. Three views of a distribution transformer (without cooling tubers and finns)

The following standard fittings should be provided:

(*a*) Two earthing terminals, with the symbol of earthing

(*b*) Oil level gauge indicating oil level minimum, 30°C and maximum operating temperature,

**Note.** Minimum and maximum positions correspond to the operating temperature of – 5°C and 98°C respectively.

(*c*) Lifting lugs,

(*d*) Rating and terminal marking plates,

(*e*) Plain breathing device which would not permit ingress of rain water and insects,

(*f*) Drain-cum-sampling valve (M 20 size thread*) perferably steel with plug, (*g*) Thermometer pocket (for transformers of rating above 25 kVA), and

(*h*) Oil-filling hole (M 30 size thread*) with cover (for transformers without conservator).

**Note.** The bottom drain valve and filling hole may be used for filtration purposes also.

**Extra Fittings.** The following shall be available as extra fittings at the option of the purchaser if specified when inviting tenders:

(*a*) Dehydrating breather in lieu of plain breathing device,

(*b*) Filter valve (M 30 size thread*), and

(*c*) Thermometer pocket (for transformers of rating 25 kVA and below).

A conservator of appropriate dimensions is fitted with distribution transformers rated 50 kVA and above. The pipe between main tank and the conservator should be of 20 to 50 mm internal diameter.

**Bushings.** The transformers are fitted with three high voltage and four low voltage outdoor type bushings of appropriate voltage and current ratings. The electrical characteristics of high voltage bushings shall conform to respective standards.

If required (by the purchaser) a suitable cable-end box may be provided on the secondary side.

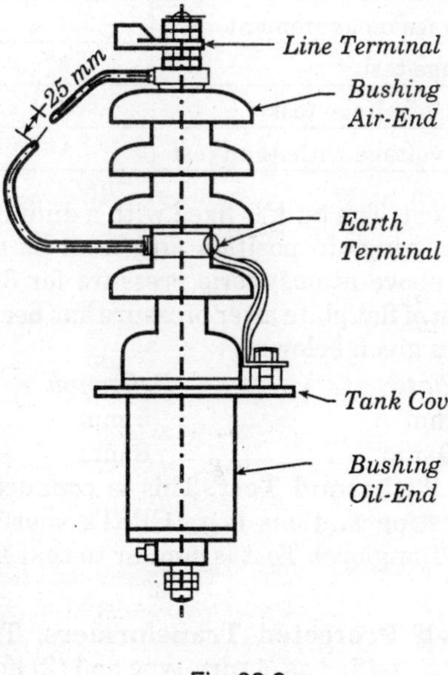


Fig. 32.2.

In some applications, the secondary side is connected to underground power cable. In such cases, a suitable cable-end box is provided on LV side instead of LV bushings. Fig. 32.2 shows a typical bushing for distribution transformers. For bushings exposed to overhead distribution lines, suitable surge arresters are provided across the line terminal and earth terminal. Alternativelly arcing gaps are provided as shown in Fig. 32.2.

**Impedance.** The percentage impedance of distribution transformers is 4% approximately.

**Testing.** Type tests, routine tests and special tests are performed on distribution transformers as per recommendations of standards (*e.g.* IS 1180). The summary is as follows:

**Table 32.2. Summary of Tests on Distribution Transformers**

| *Title* | *Type Test* | *Routine Test* |
|---|---|---|
| 1. Winding resistance measurement | * | * |
| 2. Temperature rise test | * | * |
| 3. Measurement of impedance | * | * |
| 4. Short circuit withstand test | * | * |
| 5. Air pressure test | * | * |
| 6. Voltage ratio and vector relationships | * | * |
| 7. No-load loss and no-load current | * | * |
| 8. Insulation resistance measurement | * | * |
| 9. Induced overvoltage test | * | * |
| 10. Lightning impulse voltage test | * | * |
| 11. Separate source voltage withstand test | * | * |

**Air Pressure Test.** The tank is fixed with a dummy cover with all fittings including bushings in position and shall be subjected to air pressure of 35 kPa above atmospheric pressure for 30 minutes. The permanent deflection of flat plate after pressure has been released shall not exceed the values given below:

| *Length of Plate* | *Deflection* |
|---|---|
| Up to 750 mm | 5 mm |
| 751 to 1250 mm | 6 mm |

**Short Circuit Withstand Test.** This is conducted in specially built high power testing stations (*e.g.*, CPRI's short circuit testing station, Bhopal and Banglore). Test is similar to that for power transformers.

**Completely Self Protected Transformers.** The distribution transformers can be classified as (1) dry-type and (2) liquid-filled-type. The dry-type distribution transformers are air-cooled and air insulated.

The liquid-filled-type distribution transformers can be further classified as (1) oil-filled and (2) synthetic liquid filled.

The distribution transformers employed in overhead distribution systems can be classified as:

1. Conventional transformers.
2. Completely self-protecting (CSP) transformers.
3. Completely self-protecting for secondary banking (CSPB) transformers.

The Conventional transformers have no integral protection against lightning, fault, or overload protective devices provided as a part of the transformer. The completely self-protecting (CSP) transformers are, self-protecting against lightning surges, overloads, and short circuits. Lightning arresters mounted directly on the transformer tank, provide the protection against the lightning and line surges. The overload protection is provided by circuit breakers inside the transformer tank. The transformer is protected against an internal fault by internal protective links located between the primary winding and the primary bushings. CSPB distribution transformers are designed for banked secondary service. They are built similar to the CSP transformers, but they are provided with two sets of circuit breakers. The second set is used to sectionalize the secondary when required.

**MV Transformers.** Transformers rated upto 33 kV are used in consumer substations distribution stations, in auxiliary supply systems have MV supply on primary and LV load on secondary side. The methods of connections include the following:

**Medium Voltage**

- — Dry cables,
- — Single-phase oil filled cables,
- — Three-phase oil filled cables
- — Overhead conductors.

**Low Voltage**

- — Bars when the board of LV substation is near to the transformer
- — Cables when the LV substation is distant.

According to a survey carried out for failed distribution transformer of ratings 16, 25, 63 and 100 kVA, the following defects have been observed.

| | |
|---|---|
| Manufacturing defect | — 75% |
| Storage/transportation issues | — 5% |
| Operational problems | — 10% |
| Maintenance practice | — 7% |
| Unknown Causes | — 3% |

From the above, we see that manufacturing defects are the major cause of transformer failures. We can improve this by going for stage wise inspection at the manufacturing stage itself by short circuit and heat run tests. In case of doubtful results type tests should be conducted on random samples.

**Selection of transformer.** While selecting a transformer, one should consider the total operating and not the purchase price. If one purchases a cheap transformer, it will have high losses resulting in more total operating cost for whole life of the transformer. The total operating cost consists of the purchase price and the operating cost for the whole life of the transformer. The interest should be considered for the service period of the transformer and various options should be considered for selecting the transformer.

## Summary

In India Distribution Transformers rated up to 11 kV, 100 kVA are standardized. The standardization includes shape, bushing dimensions, rated kVA, rated kVs, connections, fitments etc. In USA distribution transformers up to 67 kV and 500 kVA are standardized in similar manner.

The load conditions on distribution transformers are more severe. They can be mounted indoor/outdoor on plinth or on pole.

## Questions

1. What is the main difference in the production technique of distribution transformers and of power transformers.
2. What is completely self protected distribution transformers?
3. Which are the various of mountings of distribution transformers?

# 33

# Current Transformers (CTs)

Current transformers are either indoor epoxy cast or outdoor porcelain clad type. Upto 11 kV, indoor epoxy cast CTs are installed in MV metalclad switchgear. For 33 kV and above, porcelain clad oil immersed CTs are preferred. CTs are very important in electrical installations. Accuracy classes include

— protective CTs
— measuring CTs.

## 33.1 INTRODUCTION TO CURRENT TRANSFORMERS AND VOLTAGE TRANSFORMERS

Instrument transformers include current transformers (CT) and voltage transformers (VT). VTs are also called potential transformers.

**Current transformers** are used for reducing/stepping down a.c. current from higher value to lower value for measurement/protection/control.

**Voltage transformers** step down AC voltage from higher value to lower value for measurement/protection/control.

Both CTs and VTs have low VA rating and are, therefore, not used for power transfer. The difference between instrument transformers and power transformers is mainly in their VA rating. Power transformers have high kVA rating (500 kVA, 1000 kVA..... upto 1000 MVA). Instrument transformers have rating of only a few tens of VA (*e.g.*, 10 VA, 30 VA, 100 VA, 150 VA).

The *Current Transformers (CT)* step down AC current to a low value (1 A, 5 A). The accuracy of the current ratio required for measurement and for protection is different. Accordingly CTs are called

— Measuring CTs and
— Protective CTs.

Likewise. VTs are also classified as:

— Measuring VTs and
— Protective CTs.

The VTs are of two distinct designs:

(1) Electromagnetic (2) Capacitor type.

## 33.2 TYPES OF CTs

There are two classes of instrument transformers :

1. *Measuring current transformers* used for measurement purposes.

2. *Protective transformers* used for protective and control systems.

*Protective currents transformers* are used with overcurrent protection, earth fault protection, differential protection, impedance protection etc.

*Measuring current transformers* are used with ammeters, wattmeters, kVA meters and kWh meters for reducing current to 1 ampere or 5 amperes.

## 33.3 RATED CHARACTERISTICS CTs

1. *Rated primary current.*
2. *Rated short time current (primary).*
3. *Rated secondary current.*
4. *Rated exciting current.*
5. *Rated burden.*
6. *Current error or ratio error.*
7. *Phase angle error.*
8. *Composite error.*
9. *Accuracy class.*
10. *Overcurrent factor.*
11. *Insulation level (primary).*

The definitions regarding current transformers are as follows:

1. **Rated primary current.** The value of primary current on which the performance of the current transformer is specified by the manufacturer. It is in Amp. rms.

Rated primary current is assigned after conducting heat run tests.

2. **Rated short-time current (primary).** It is defined as r.m.s. value of a.c. component which the CT can carry for rated time without damage due to thermal or electrodynamic stresses.

3. **Rated secondary current.** The value of secondary current marked on the rating plate. It is in Amp. r.m.s.

4. **Rated exciting current.** The r.m.s. value of current taken by the secondary-winding of a C.T. when sinusoidal voltage of rated frequency is applied to secondary with primary winding open circuited.

5. **Rated Burden.** The burden assigned by manufacturer at which the C.T. performs with specified accuracy.

6. **Current error or Ratio error.** The percentage error in the magnitude of the secondary current is defined in terms of current error.

7. **Phase angle error.** The phase angle between primary current vector and the reversed secondary current vector.

8. **Composite error.** The r.m.s. value of the difference $(k_n i_s - i_p)$ integrated over one cycle under steady condition, given by

$$\text{Composite error} = \frac{100}{I_p}\sqrt{\frac{1}{T}\int_O^T (k_n i_s - i_p)^2\, dt}$$

where
$k_n$ = Rated transformation ratio
$I_p$ = Primary current, r.m.s.
$i_p$ = Primary current, instantaneous
$i_s$ = Secondary current, instantaneous
$T$ = Time of one cycle, in sec.

9. **Accuracy class.** The class assigned to the current transformer with the specified limits of ratio error and phase angle error.

10. **Overcurrent factor.** The ratio of rated short-time current to rated primary current.

11. **Insulation level (primary).** Insulation level of the C.T. refers to the withstand values of

— Power frequency withstand voltage kV r.m.s.
— Impulse withstand voltage $kV_p$.

## 33.4 ACCURACY CLASS

It is the class assigned to the current transformer with the specified limits ratio error and phase angle error.

The accuracy classes are as follows:

**Limits of Error and Accuracy Class**

| *Accuracy class* | *Current error rated primary current* | *Phase displacement at rated current* | *Composite error rated accuracy limit primary current* |
|---|---|---|---|
| | Per cent | Minutes | Per cent |
| 5 P | ± 1 | ± 60 | 5 |
| 10 P | ± 3 | — | 10 |
| 15 P | ± 5 | — | 15 |

The current transformers are marked as follows:

[*e.g.*, 30/5 P 10]

First number: Output in VA (*e.g.*, 30).

Second number: Accuracy class (*e.g.*, 5 P).

Last number: composite error (*e.g.*, 10).

## 33.5 BURDEN OR IMPEDANCE ON CT

*Impedance* of secondary circuit expressed in ohms, power factor is called *burden.* But it is usually expressed in terms of apparent power in kVA and rated secondary current at specified power factor. This power factor is not the power factor of secondary current of CT.

The circuit connected to the secondary winding is termed as 'burden' of the current transformer. If the term 'load' is used, it refers to the primary current magnitude. Burden is expressed preferably in terms of impedance of the circuit connected to the secondary and its resistance and reactance. The British method is to specify the burden on the CT in volt-amperes at rated secondary current at specified power factor.

Thus we may express the burden in the following two forms. *e.g.*, 0.5 ohm impedance or 12.5 volt-amperes at 5 amperes. Let rated burden $B$ volt-amperes at rated secondary $I_s$ amperes. Then, the ohmic impedance of the burden $Z_b$ can be calculated as follows

$$Z_b = \frac{B}{I_s^2} \text{ ohms.}$$

**'Burden' of CTs and VTs refer to the maximum load in voltamperes (VA) which may be applied across the secondary terminals, without the ratio and phase angle errors exceeding the permissible limits.** The burden depends upon the number of instruments or relays connected and their individuals burdens typical values are:

**Burdens of Individual Instruments/Relays**

| | *Potential (110 V)* | *Current (5 A)* |
|---|---|---|
| Indicating voltmeter/ammeter | 2 to 10 VA | 0.5 to 5 VA |
| Watt-hour meters and recording instruments | 3 to 5 VA | 5 to 7.5 VA |
| Thermal overcurrent relays | — | 2 to 12 VA |

*e.g.*, if a CT has to feed an indicating ammeter (10 VA) a record-wattmeter (5 VA) and an overcurrent relay (6 VA) the total burden would be 12 VA. If the resistance of the connecting leads (go and return) is 0.2 ohms, it's burden would be

$$= I^2R, \textit{ i.e.}, 5^2 \times 0.2 = 5 \text{ VA}$$

Therefore, the total burden on the CT would be 17 VA.

The rated burden could also be expressed in terms of impedance in ohms instead of voltamperes. Thus a 15 VA burden would be equivalent to a 0.6 ohm impedance burden with respect to 5 amp secondary or 15 ohm impedance in return to a one ampere secondary.

If burden power factor is cos $\phi$, $L$ = VA burden

$$R_b = Z_b \cos \phi \text{ ohms}$$

$$X_b = \sqrt{Z_b^2 - R_b^2} \text{ ohms.}$$

**The Standards VA Burdens Ratings for CTs and VTs**

| | *V.T.* | *C.T.* |
|---|---|---|
| Instrument transformers | 10, 15, 50, 100, 200 | 2.5, 5, 7.5, 15, 30 |
| Protective transformers | 50, 100, 200 | 2.5, 5, 7.5, 10, 15, 30<br>P.F. 0.7 lag |

Refer Fig. 33.1, giving characteristic of $I_m$ *vs.* $V_2$. It is also called excitation curve of CT. The excitation curve may be sub-divided into four main regions (*i*) from origin to ankle point (*ii*) from ankle point to knee (*iii*) knee region (*iv*) saturation region. Knee point is defined as where a 10% increases in flux density cause 50% increase to exciting ampereturns. Protective current transformer generally operate over working range of flux density extending from the ankle-point to the knee region or above, while the measuring current transformer has the flux density in the region of ankle point only.

Prior to saturation, the flux density in core is proportional to ampere-turns. On reaching saturation, magnetising inductance becomes low and, the total primary current is utilized in exciting the core alone and a, therefore, the secondary output CT disappears. The saturation continues till the primary transient current is reduced below saturation level. On energy in saturation zone, the CT behaves an open circuited.

It is difficult to avoid saturation during short circuit condition. The effect of saturation, is the reduced output, hence reduced speed of over current relays. In differential relays, the saturation disturbs the balance and stability of protection is affected.

Current transformer saturation curve is generally plotted in secondary volts *vs* exciting current measured in secondary. For the required magnitude of secondary voltage, the degree of saturation can be seen from the curve and is also indicated by magnitude of exciting current to produce this voltage.

## 33.6 OPEN-CIRCUITED SECONDARY OF CT

An important aspect in CT operation is, the voltage appearing across open circuited secondary. Normal voltage across secondary of a 15 VA CT with current of 5 A, 15/5=3 V.

However, if by mistake, secondary is open circuited, the voltage across the secondary rises to a high value. The peak value may reach some kilovolts. Open circuiting of secondaries results in zero secondary current, hence reduced back e.m.f., the working flux $\phi$ increases and core gets saturated. The secondary e.m.f. increases due to increased flux.

The primary gets overheated and the core also gets over heated. Voltages are induced in the secondary by electro-magnetic induction. The peak value of the secondary on open circuit may be several times the r.m.s. value since the core is saturated and waveform of voltage is distorted. This may cause danger to personnel working on secondary side. Therefore, when primary current is flowing, secondary should never be disconnected. In bus zone protection, a non-linear resistor may connected across secondary to limit the peak voltage to safe value.

The precautions to be taken while using current transformers are as follows:

The current transformer differs from other transformers that the primary winding is designed for connection in series with the line current at all times.

The secondary circuit of a current transformer should never be open circuited when there is current flowing in the primary winding. Under open-circuit condition, the primary current becomes exciting current which will cause a high voltage to be induced in the secondary winding as it has more turns. This voltage may be sufficient to puncture the

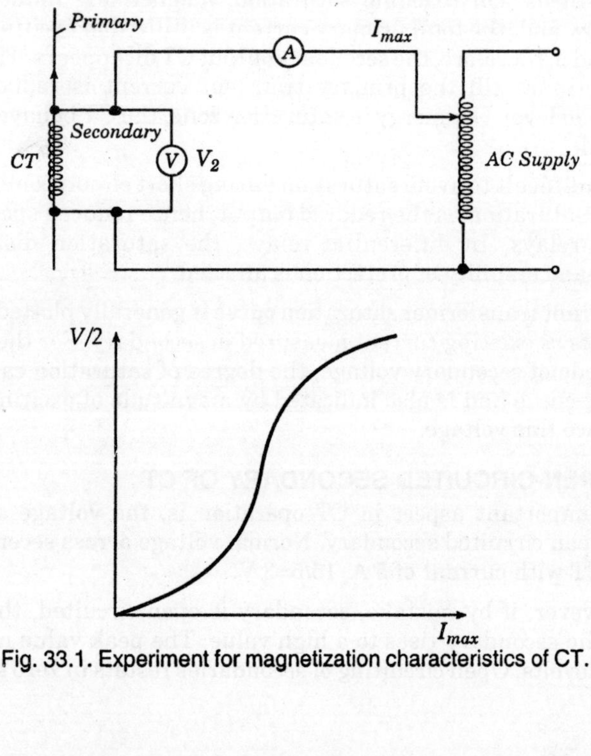

Fig. 33.1. Experiment for magnetization characteristics of CT.

insulation, and it presents the hazard of a dangerous high-voltage shock to anyone who may come in contact with the open circuit secondary.

Therefore, those working with current transformers must always make certain the secondary winding circuit of a current transformer is closed.

All current transformers should have there secondary winding grounded in service because an electrostatic field will build up in the secondary winding.

It should be clear that for the rated burden and the rated secondary current, a definite secondary e.m.f. will be required which will correspond to definite flux level in the core. Though a CT may have a rated output (say 20 MVA), is corresponds to the rated secondary current (say 5 A) and, hence, a rated secondary e.m.f., in this case, approximately 4V. 20 MVA could otherwise mean 20 A at 1V or 20 V at 1A. The first will mean overcurrent and may probably burn the CT and the second may mean saturation of the CT that has a saturation factor of the order of 5. This disapproves the misconception that the CT operation is safe and correct so long as rated VA burden does not exceed.

If the secondary winding gets open circuited while the primary winding is carrying current, a very high flux density is established which leaves behind residual magnetism of considerable magnitude. Similarly, a heavy transient short circuit current of a symmetrical nature has a large DC component and if the current is interrupted before this component has decayed (as is possible with modern high speed circuit breakers), it will leave behind residual magnetism of high order.

The high value of remant magnetism can thereby affect the performance of protective CT's operation during fault conditions to an extent that may cause mal-operation of the connected relays.

**Demagnetisation.** If a CT core is known to have got magnetised, its demagnetisation can be brought about simply in any one of the following ways:

(*i*) By passing alternating current through the primary winding and slowly reducing it to zero; the secondary winding being left open.

(*ii*) By passing an alternating current through the primary winding with a suitable resistance connected across the secondary terminals and reducing the resistance gradually.

(*iii*) By passing an alternative current through the secondary winding and gradually reducing it to zero, the primary winding being left open. It is usual to raise the flux density initially to near saturation and then to reduce it to zero over a period of about 1 minute in case of 50 $\mu s$ supply.

## 33.7 TESTING OF CTs

Tests on CTs can be classified as type tests and routine tests. Type tests can conducted on one or first few CTs of each type, to confirm the design and rating. Routine are conducted on each CT before despatch.

**Type Tests**

— Verification of terminal markings and polarities.
— Short time currents tests
— Temperature rise tests
— Impulse voltage test (for outdoor CTs) on primary
— Power frequency voltage withstand test on primary
— Overvoltage inter-turns test, etc.
— Error measurement.

**Routine Tests**

— Verification of terminal markings and polarities.
— High voltage power frequency voltage withstand test on secondary.
— Overvoltage inter turns tests.
— Determination of errors and accuracy class.

Furthermore tests are performed on protective systems by injecting current in primary. Thereby the correctness of polarity connections and stability of protection is ascertained. Some test on CTs are briefly described below:

1. **Error Measurements.** The error measurements are carried out in two different methods namely,

(*a*) Direct method

(*b*) Comparison method.

In direct method, two ammeters are used. One is connected to measure the primary current. The other to measure secondary current.

In comparison method a sub-standard CT is taken, whose errors are known. The CT under test is compared with the sub-standard CT. There are several methods based on comparison principle. These are not given here.

Specially designed tests equipment is available for testing CTs.

2. **Turns Ratio Tests.** The usual method is to measure magnitudes of primary and secondary currents near rated secondary current with a low value of secondary burden.

3. **Exciting Currents.** Exciting current is measured for several secondary e.m.fs. This is accomplished by applying voltage to the secondary winding, the primary and other windings being open circuited.

4. **Current transformers for balanced differential protective scheme.** The CTs are connected in test circuit. The spill current is measured, for through faults.

5. **Polarity Tests.** If at any instant, current is entering the primary from $P_1$, the current should leave secondary from terminal marked $S_1$. A set-up shown in the figure can show whether the polarity marking are correct or not. When the key is pressed, current enters the primary through terminal $P_1$, the voltmeter connected as shown, should read positive.

6. **Insulation Tests.** These are conducted according to BS/IS/IEC, specified power frequency voltages are applied to primary for one minute. Impulse tests are conducted on high voltage current transformers. For secondary circuit tests, voltage of 2 kV, 50 Hz is applied for one minute between secondary terminals and ground.

7. **Overvoltage Interturn Test.** In this test secondary winding is open circuited. Rated frequency, rated primary current is flow through primary for about one minute. The secondary winding is then checked to see if the insulation has passed the test.

## 33.8. STANDARD RANGE OF CTs

The rated primary current should be selected from standard values. The value should be so chosen that it is suitable for all normal currents and permissible over load currents in the primary circuit.

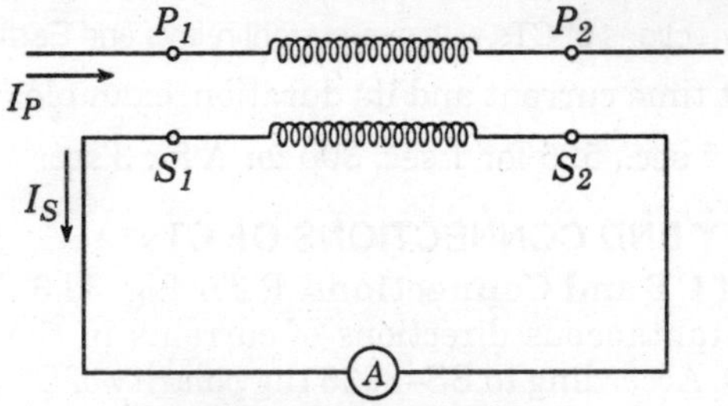


$P_1$ and $P_2$ : Primary terminals
$S_1$ and $S_2$ : Secondary terminals.
Fig. 33.2. Polarity of a CT.

Current transformer operating a high-set instantaneous over-current relay may be selected for higher rated primary current, thereby the required accuracy limit may be reduced.

Referring values of rated primary currents: 0.5–1–2.5–5–10–12.5–15–20–25–30–40–50–60–75–150–125–150–200–250–300–400–500–600–750–800–1000–1250–3000–4000–5000–6000–7500–10000 Amperes.

Reference values of rated secondary currents: 1–2–5– Amperes

Reference values of rated output:
2.5–5–7.5–10–15–30 VA and up.

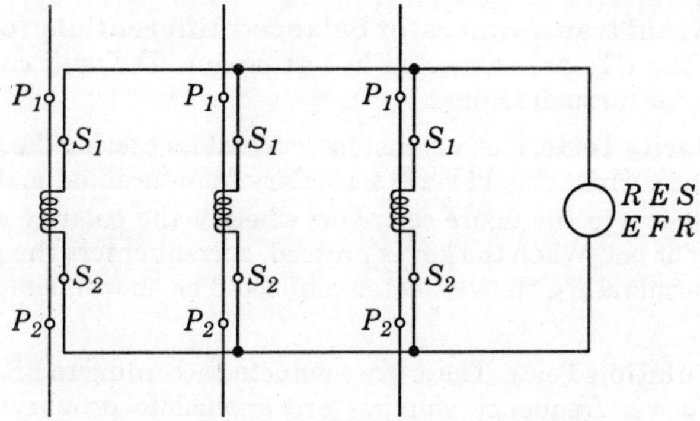


Fig. 33.3. Connection of CTs for Residual earth for relay.

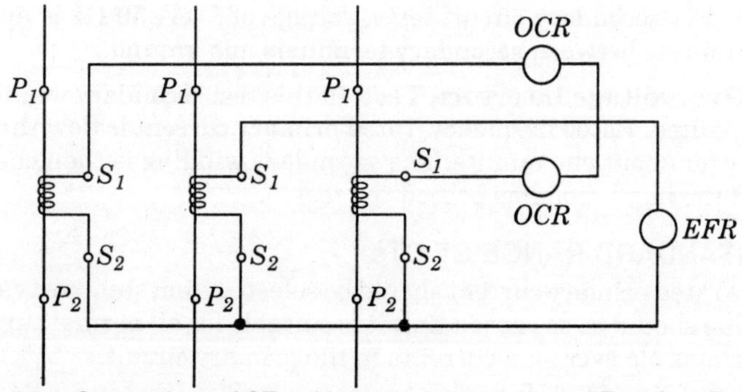


Fig. 33.4. Connections of CTs with overcurrent relays and Earthfault Relay.

Rated short time current and its duration, example:

750 A for 0.5 sec., 525 for 1 sec, 300 for A for 3 sec.

## 33.9 POLARITY END CONNECTIONS OF CTs

**Polarity of CT and Connections.** Refer Fig. 33.3. Polarity gives the relative instantaneous directions of currents in the primary and secondary leads. According to BS–3938 the polarity of CT is marked as:

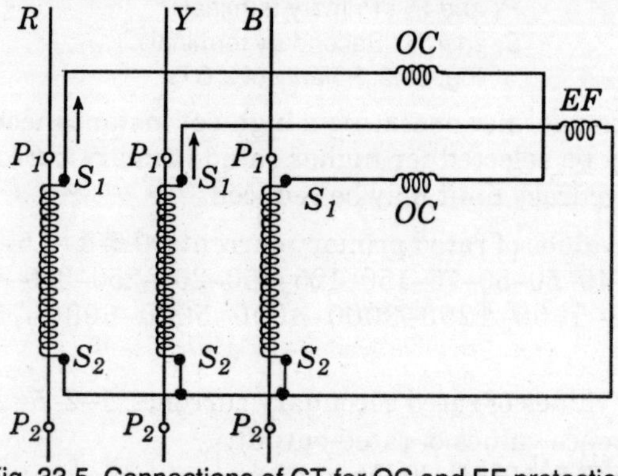


Fig. 33.5. Connections of CT for OC and EF protection.

If instantaneous current flows from $P_1$ to $P_2$ as marked by the arrow, the instantaneous currents will flow from $S_1$ to $S_2$ through the Earth Fault Relay (EFR).

## 33.10 CONNECTIONS OF CTs FOR OVERCURRENT AND EARTH FAULT PROTECTION

A normal practice is to have two overcurrent relays and one earth fault relay for protection of feeders. The CT for earth fault protection is connected in residual circuit. During no earth fault condition, the

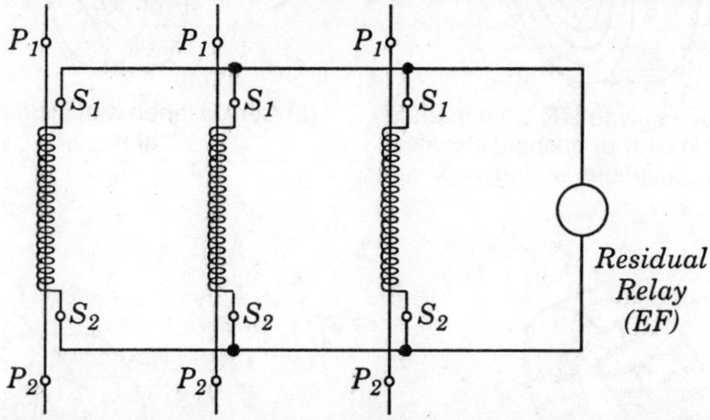


Fig. 33.6. Connection of CT for EF protection by residual relay.

current in residual circuit is zero. Hence earth fault relay does not operate. During earth fault the residual current flow initiating operation of earth fault relay.

## 33.11 CONSTRUCTIONS AND DESIGN ASPECTS OF CTs

Like any transformer, a CT has the following:

— Primary circuit and its insulation
— Secondary circuit and its insulation
— Magnetic core

But there is a vast difference in the construction of a power transformer and current transformer because current ratio and turns ratio is very high *e.g.*

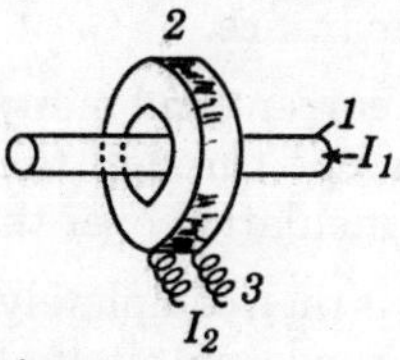


1. Bar primary
2. Secondary wound on toroidal core
3. Secondary leads

Fig. 33.7. CT with bar primary.

$$I_1/I_2 = 1000/5.$$

where $$I_1/I_2 = N_2/N_1 = 1/k$$

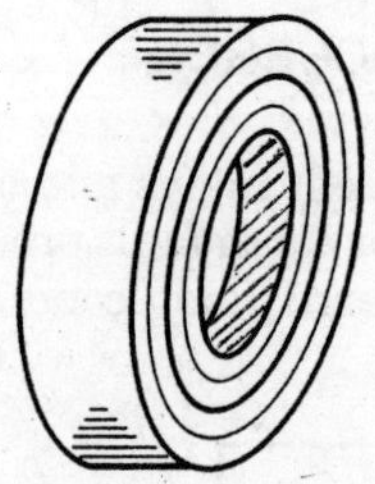

(*a*) Core of ring type CT, Core made of Nickel-iron alloy or oriented electrical steel continuous wound strip.

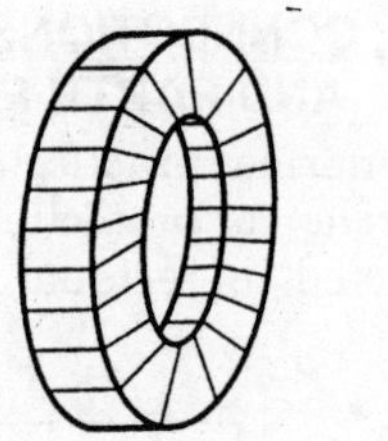

(b) Core is taped with insulating tape.

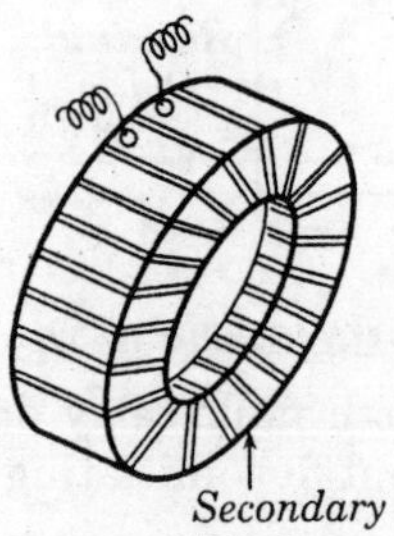


(*c*) Secondary winding conductor wound on the taped-core by means of hand-winding or toroidal winding machine.

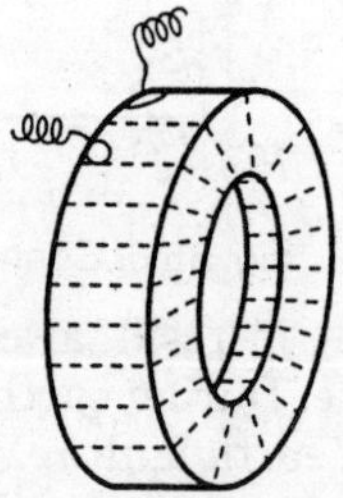

(*d*) Exterior tape is then provided with circumferential insulating wraps.

Fig. 33.8. Development of a ring type CT in sequence *a-b-c-d*.

The primary has only one turn or a bar. (Fig. 33.7). The bar primary passes through the eye of the core. The bar is at full phase to ground voltage of the power circuit and carries full current of the power circuit. Hence the primary bar conductor should have sufficient cross-section and sufficient phase to ground insulation, phase to ground creepage and phase to ground external clearance.

The secondary has low current and many turns. It is wound on the core. Since the primary passes through the eye of the core and the secondary is wound on the insulation over the core.

The secondary winding is then completely wrapped by external tape with or without exterior ring ends and circumferential insulating wraps [Fig. 33.6 (*a*) to (*d*) gives the development.]

## Current Transformer for High Voltage Installations

Separately mounted post-type CT's are suitable for outdoor service. They are usually installed in the outdoor switch yard. The primary

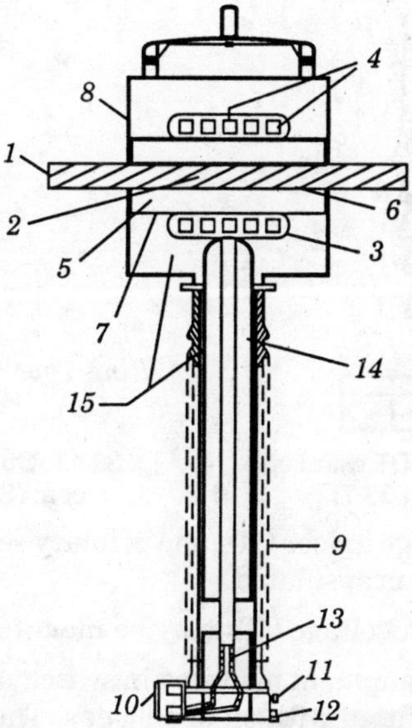


| | |
|---|---|
| 1. Primary terminal | 2. Primary bar |
| 3. Secondary windings | 4. Secondary cores |
| 5. Condenser on 2 | 6. Conductive coating on 1 |
| 7. Conductive layer on 5 | 8. Expansion chamber for oil |
| 9. Porcelain | 10. Secondary terminal box |
| 11. Drain plug for oil | 12. Earthing pad |
| 13. Secondary leads | 14. Insulation on 13 |
| 15. Oil filling of $SF_6$ gas filling | 16. Vacant. |

Fig. 33.9. Outdoor EHV or HV CT with Top-Core

conductor is at high voltage with respect to earth. Hence it is insulated by means of an insulator column filled with dielectric oil. The secondary of CT is just like the ring type CT described earlier.

Two types of current transformers are used. The hair-pin type have the secondary winding located at the bottom of the Porcelain insulator. For the top core type the secondary winding, is located on the top of the Porcelain insulator.

The voltage stress between primary (high voltage) and secondary (low voltage) is very high. This calls for graded insulation over the primary.

The primary conductor is provided with condenser type graded insulation.

For high voltage CTs the entire enclosure may be filled with $SF_6$ gas or dielectric oil. For medium and low voltages, porcelain enclosures are used for outdoor applications.

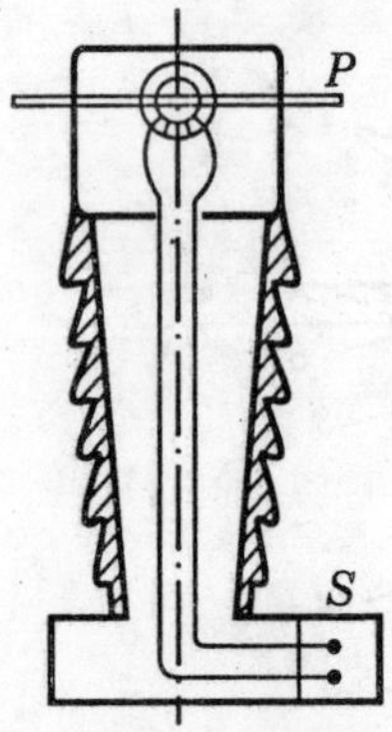


Fig. 33.10. Outdoor DT with Top Core (See Fig. 33.7)

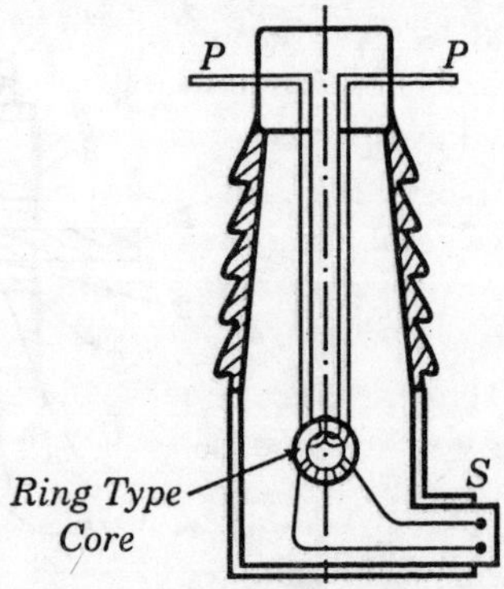


Fig. 33.11. Outdoor CT with bottom core (See Fig. 33.10)

In medium voltage indoor CTs, the primary secondary and the core may be epoxy-resin encapsulated.

**Mounting.** High voltage CTs may be mounted as follows:

1. As separate equipment mounted in switchyard. The CT will have porcelain enclosure fitted with oil or $SF_6$ gas. These CTs are installed on galvanised steel structures of app. 2.5 m height.

2. **Mounted on turret of bushings of power transformer.** The bushing has central conductor provided with condenser enclosure and supporting flange etc. The ring type cores of CTs are slipped over the central conductor. The secondary winding is provided over the ring core. A bushing may have one or more CT cores depending upon measurement and protection requirement.

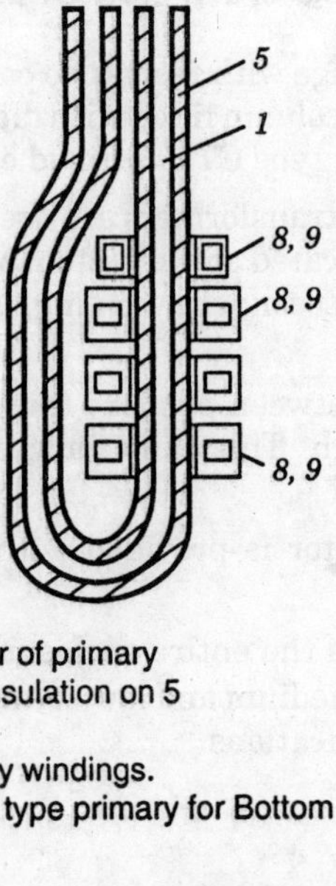


1. Conductor of primary
5. Graded insulation on 5
8. Cores
9. Secondary windings.

Fig. 33.13. Hair-pin type primary for Bottom core CT (Fig. 33.9)

3. CTs mounted inside Medium Voltage Switchgear. These are generally epoxy resin encapsulated CTs. These CTs are housed in the switchgear panel.

**Core.** The ring type core is made of high grade CRGO Nickel-iron sheet steel strips of high saturation flux density. The strips are continuously wound on winding machines. Alternatively the core may be formed interleaved laminations place in rectangular manner.

The core is sprayed with epoxy resin insulation or is passed through epoxy resin fluid bed to have resin encapsulation. Over such a core required additional insulation of craft paper may be provided. The secondary conductor with its insulation is wound on the insulated core. The secondary winding is then completely wrapped by external paper tape and circumferential insulating wraps. In synthetic resin encapsulated version, the complete unit is encapsulated in epoxy resin (with due care for providing flexible epoxy resin for withstanding short-circuit stresses on conductors.)

**Major Insulation.** The primary conductor is at rated voltage ($V_L/\sqrt{3}$) with respect to the secondary winding. Since the gap is very small, the primary conductor is provided with condenser insulation having alternate layers of tin foil and craft paper like those for a bushing conductor. The insulation should be designed to withstand:

— Power frequency voltage stresses
— Lightning impulse voltage
— Switching impulse voltage
— Short-circuit thermal and mechanical stresses.

The ring-core may be supported on porcelain hollow insulators having adequate clearance, adequate external creepage and with internal filling of dry insulating oil or $SF_6$ gas.

The secondary leads are brought down to terminal box at ground level.

**Secondary leads.** The secondary winding and leads are designed for low voltage and low current. Therefore, the secondary is of lower crosssection conductors. The leads are brought to ground level and connected to the terminal board. From here connections are taken to protection panel and measurement panel.

### Summary

CTs are either (1) indoor type or (2) outdoor type.

Indoor CTs are generally mounted in Metal Clad Switchgear

Outdoor CTs are mounted on galvanised structures.

The secondaries of the protective CTs are connected to pilot wires in the circuits of over current protection, earth fault protection, impedance protection etc.

The secondaries of measuring CTs are connected to ammeters wattmeters, kVA meters etc.

CTs are mounted on turrets of large transformers.

## Questions

1. State the difference between medium voltage indoor CT and outdoor CT.
2. Describe construction of an outdoor CT.
3. Describe construction of a ring-core CT.
4. State essential ratings of a CT.

# 34

# Voltage Transformers

Voltage transformers are either electromagnetic type or capacitor voltage divider type. The VTs are very important for measurement, control and protection. The essential aspects about VTs and CCVTs have been described.

For voltages of 72-800 kV, capacitor voltage transformers (CVTs) are used. The CVTs consist of a capacitor voltage divider and an intermediate voltage transformer. A CCVT has a dual function as a measuring transformer and a coupling capacitor for carrier frequencies.

## 34.1 APPLICATIONS AND TYPES OF VTs

Voltages such as 3.3 kV, 6.6 kV.....etc. need to be stepped down for measurement, protection and control. For this purpose voltage transformers (Potential Transformers) are necessary.

Voltage transformers (potential transformers) are used for measurement and protection. Accordingly, they are either measuring type or protective type voltage transformers. They may be either single phase or three phase. Voltage transformers are necessary for voltage, directional, distance protection. The primary of voltage transformer is connected directly to power circuit between phase and ground depending upon rated voltage and application. The volt-ampere rating of voltage transformers is lesser as compared with that of power transformers.

There are two types of constructions:

— Electromagnetic potential transformer in which primary and secondary are wound on magnetic core like in usual transformer.

— Capacitor potential transformer, in which the primary voltage is applied to a series capacitor group. The voltage across one of the capacitor is taken to auxiliary voltage transformer. The secondary of auxiliary voltage transformer is taken for measurement of protection.

**Specifications for Voltage Transformers.** The following aspects should be determined while selecting the current transformer.

1. Rated primary voltage.
2. Rated secondary voltage.
3. Rated burden.
4. Supply frequency

5. Number of phases.
6. Class of accuracy.
7. *Insulation* level. Power frequency and impulse voltage withstand.
8. Limits of dimensions, types of construction etc.

**(A) Rated Characteristics**

(*a*) *Rated voltage*
(*b*) *Rated transformation ratio*
(*c*) *Rated secondary voltage*
(*d*) *Residual voltage*
(*e*) *Phase error*
(*f*) *Ratio error*
(*g*) *Voltage factor.*

**Terms and Definitions of VTs**

(*a*) **Rated Voltage.** The voltage marked on the rating plate of the voltage transformer. The method of connection of primary winding to system and system voltage should be considered while selecting the VT of correct primary voltage rating.

There are several values of standard primary voltages. These have a reference to standard system voltages.

(*b*) **Rated transformation Ratio.** The ratio of rated primary voltage to rated secondary voltage.

(*B*) **Rated Secondary Voltage** *e.g.*, $110/\sqrt{3}$ V.

(*c*) **Rated Secondary Voltage.** *e.g.*, $190/\sqrt{3} = 63.5$ V or $110/\sqrt{3} = 190$ V. It is the value of secondary voltage marked on the rating plate.

(*d*) **Residual Voltage.** Vector sum of three lines to earth voltages, *i.e.*,

$$V_{RES} = V_{RN} + V_{YN} + V_{ZN}$$

(*e*) **Residual VT.** A three phase VT or a group of 3 single phase residually connected VTs in which residual voltage appears across secondary terminals when three-phase voltage are applied to primary windings.

(*f*) **Ratio Error.** Percentage ratio error sometimes called percentage voltage error is given by

$$\% \text{ R.E.} = \frac{100\,(K_n V_s - V_s)}{V_p}$$

where $K_n$ = Normal ratio
$V_s$ = Secondary voltage
$V_p$ = Primary voltage.

(*g*) An alternate method describe the ratio is to specify the ratio factor (V.R.F.)

$$\text{V.R.F.} = \frac{K_p}{K_n}$$

$$K_n = \text{Normal ratio } \frac{V_p}{V_s}$$

$$K_p = \text{Voltage ratio } \frac{V_p}{V_s} \text{ actual.}$$

$$\text{V.R.F.} \simeq 1 - \frac{\%\ \text{R.E.}}{100}$$

**Accuracy Glass and Limits and Phase Errors for Voltage Transformers**

| *Accuracy Classes* | *0.9 to 1.1. times rated primary voltage 0.25 to 1.0 times rated output at 0.8 lag p.f.* | | *Application* |
|---|---|---|---|
| | *Voltage error % (per cent) (+ or –)* | *Phase error minutes (minutes) (+ or –)* | |
| 1.2 | 0.1 | 3 | Measurement |
| 0.2 | 0.2 | 15 | |
| 0.5 | 0.5 | 20 | |
| 1.00 | 1.0 | 40 | |
| 3.0 | 3.00 | 120 | Protection |
| 5.0 | 5.00 | 300 | |
| 10.0 | 10.00 | — | Residual VT only |

**Application of VTs Depending upon Accuracy Class**

| *Accuracy Classes* | *Applications* |
|---|---|
| 0.1 | Precision testing in standard laboratories |
| 0.2 | Sub-standard instruments in laboratories |
| 0.5–1.0 | Industrial metering |
| 3.00 | Voltmeters |
| 5.00 | Under voltage relays, overvoltage relays other relay where phase angle is not important. |
| 10.00 | Directional relays where phase angle is important. |

**Note.** (1) Class 3.0 and 5.0 VTs are recommended for protection.

(2) Class 5.00 and 10.00 is recommended only in Residual VTs.

### (D) Burdens on Voltage Transformer

Burdens are specified in voltamperes at a rated secondary voltage at a particular power factor. Let rated secondary voltage be $V_s$. The ohmic impedance of burden be $Z_b$. Volt-ampere burden = $P$

$$Z_b = \frac{V_s^2}{P} \text{ ohms.}$$

Let burden power factor be cos $\phi$

$$R_b = Z_b \cos \phi$$
$$X_b = Z_b \sin \phi$$
$$Z_b = \sqrt{R_b^2 + X_b^2}$$

The total burden on a VT should be less than the rated burden of VT.

Table on the next page gives rated burdens of bushing type potential transformer device. The capacitor voltage transformer output is upto about 200 VA. While that of wounded type is upto about 500 VA. The standard values being: 10, 25, 50, 75, 100, 150, 200, 500 VA.

**Example.** *A voltage transformer with rated secondary voltage of 110 V has normal output of 1 A, lead loop resistance is 0.1 ohm. Calculate the voltampere output of the voltage transformer when the relay takes 0.1 ampere at 110 volts.*

**Solution.** Total voltamperes

= Voltamperes for relay + Voltamperes or leads

$$= 110 \times 0.1 + (0.1)^2 \times 0.1$$
$$= 11 \text{ VA.} \quad \textbf{Ans.}$$

### (F) Reference Values of Burdens on VT's

| *Rated Voltage kV* | | Rated Burden Volt-ampere |
|---|---|---|
| *Phase to phase* | *Phase to ground* | |
| 115 | 66.4 | 25 |
| 138 | 9.74 | 35 |
| 161 | 93 | 45 |
| 239 | 133 | 80 |
| 287 | 166 | 100 |

### (G) Typical Values of Burdens Imposed by Different Measuring Instruments and Relays on Voltage Transformers

| | |
|---|---|
| Voltmeter | 5 VA |
| Voltage coil of Watt-meter | 5 VA |
| Voltage coil of kWH meter | 7.5 VA |
| Voltage coil of Synchroscope | 15 |

| | |
|---|---|
| Under voltage/over voltage Relay | 5 VA |
| Voltage coils of electromagnetic relays | 3–10 A |
| Static relays. | 0.02–0.2 VA |

The total burden on a VT is vector sum ($r$ and $jX$) of component burdens on secondary *e.g.*, burden on a VT for under voltage protection would be the sum of burden of relay coil, pilot wires. The VA rating should be such that the total burden is less that rated burden, for pick-up condition. If the VT is overloaded beyond its rated burden, the errors will increase. The burden of a relay varies for various settings. The VA rating of VT should not be far greater than the burden. Because the accuracy of VT at very low burdens (25% rated burden) is not guaranteed.

**(H) Connection of VT**

There are three types of connections, V-V, Star-Star and Star Open Delta. (Residually Connected) VT.

(1) **V–V Connection.** This connection is used only for measurement and generally not for production. Two VTs are used. Primaries are connected in V, secondaries also in V. There is no path for zero sequence voltages arising from earth faults.

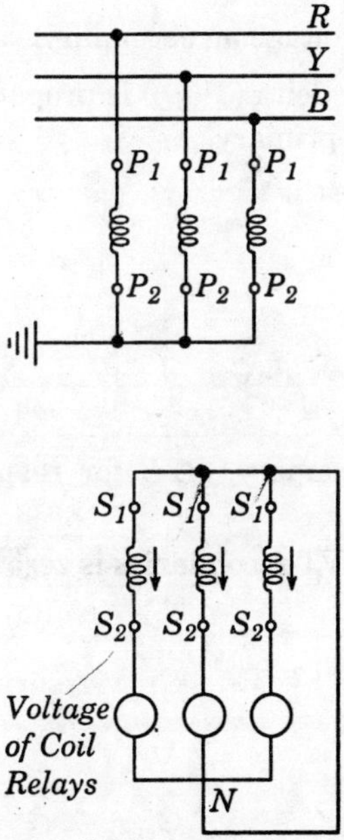


Fig. 34.1. VT Connection star-star

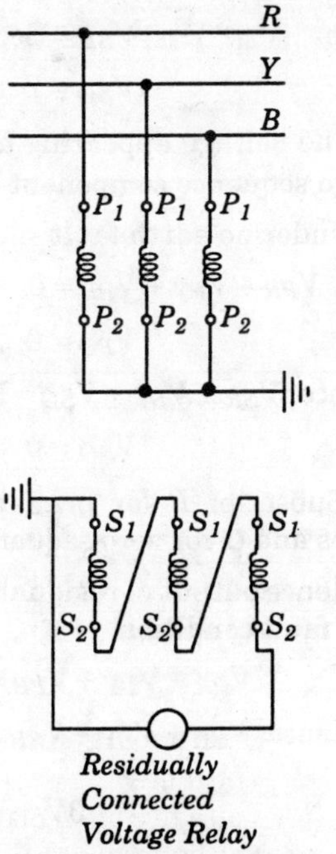


Fig. 34.2. Residual connections of VT secondaries.

(2) **Star-Star Connection.** Either there separate transformers or a single three limb transformer are used. Primaries are connected in star, secondaries, also connected in star.

Each primary phase winding is connected to phase to earth voltage of supply circuit which is transformed in secondary.

The neutral point of load is connected to neutral point of secondaries. The neutral point of primary is solidly earthed with such connections.

*If primary neutral is not earthed*, the zero sequence component of voltages (due to earth fault) cannot flow through primary windings. Hence phase to earth voltages of system which contain zero sequence component do not get truly transformed.

Hence the earth fault on the system cannot be sensed or the secondary side of VT in voltage restrained overcurrent fault protection in impedance protection for earth faults.

**I. Residually connected VT (Zero Sequence Voltage Filter)**

Primary windings are connected in star and star point is earthed. The secondaries are connected in series with the load.

$$V_{SR} + V_{SY} + V_{SB} = 3V_{SO}$$

where, $V_{SR}, V_{SY}, V_{SB}$ = Secondary voltages

$V_{SO}$ = Zero sequence voltage on secondary.

The voltage appearing across broken delta ($3V_{SO}$) is proportional to zero sequence component of voltage on primary.

Under no-earth fault

$$V_{PR} + V_{PY} + V_{PB} = 0$$

$$V_{PO} = 0$$

Hence $V_{SR} + V_{SY} + V_{SO} = 0$

$$V_{SO} = 0$$

(Subscript $P$ for primary, $S$ for secondary, $RYB$ for respective phases and $O$ for zero sequence).

Hence output of residually connected VT secondaries is zero under earth fault condition.

$$V_{PR} + V_{PY} + V_{PB} = 3\ V_{PO}$$

Hence, $V_{SR} + V_{SY} + V_{SB} = 3\ V_{SO}$

$$3V_{SO} = \frac{3\ V_{PO}}{K_n} = V_r$$

$V_r$ = Residual voltage flowing through the load connected across residually connected VT secondary.

$K_n$ = Voltage Ratio.

The residually connected VT, the star point of primary must necessarily be earthed.

Residually connected VT is used for supplying.

1. Voltage coil of voltage restrained overcurrent earth fault protection.
2. Restricted earth fault protection.
3. Directional earth fault protection.
4. Distance earth fault protection.
5. Earth-fault alarm relays.

One point on secondary is necessarily earthed for safety, in case the primary comes in contact with secondary.

The residually connected VT may have three single phase units or one three phase five limbed unit.

Accuracy class of residually connected VT is 5.00 or 100.

**Types of Construction of VTs**

(1) Electromagnetic Voltage Transformer, oil filled or epoxy resin encapsulated.

(2) Capacitor Voltage Transformer (CVT)

## 34.2 ELECTROMAGNETIC VOLTAGE TRANSFORMER

Potential transformer is similar to a conventional transformer with additional care taken to minimise errors of transformation, and the power transformed is low. The construction of a PT largely depends on the rated primary voltage. For voltages upto 3.3 kV, dry type transformers with varnish impregnated taped windings are quite satisfactory. For higher voltages, it is a practice to immerse the core and winding in oil. Recently windings are impregnated and encapsulated in synthetic resin. With this development, dry type PTs are available for voltage higher than 3.3 kV. Cast resin insulated PTs are available for voltages upto 66 kV.

The core of a smaller voltage transformer is usually made up of normal *T, U, E, I, L,* shaped laminations when hot rolled steel is employed.

For larger single phase units cut *C* core is used of oriented sheet steels.

The electromagnetic VT are either indoor or outdoor, porcelains are necessary for outdoor VTs.

The electromagnetic VT for residual connections should have five limbs.

For voltages above 76 kV, electromagnetic VTs are generally in cascade-connection. They employ a number of series connected primary coils on separate cores, with coupling coils link primary coils so as to

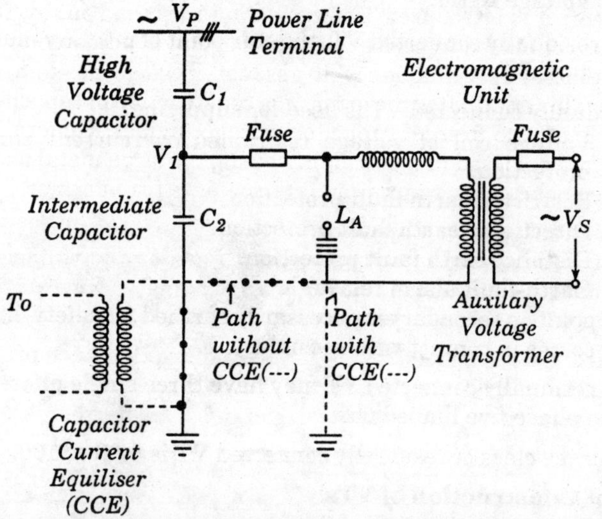


Fig. 34.3. Connections of Coupling Capacitor Voltage Transformer (CCVT).

keep the effective leakage inductance at a low value. Such an arrangement is coveniently housed in a porcelain enclosure.

However, capacitor Type VT is more economical. For high speed distance protection, electromagnetic voltage transformer is preferred.

The secondary leads should have low impedance, to reduce voltage drop.

## 34.3 CAPACITOR VOLTAGE TRANSFORMERS (CVT)

Capacitor voltage transformers are used for line voltmeters, synchroscopes, protective relays, tariff-meter, etc. They are less accurate but are cheaper.

The performance of capacitor voltage transformer is inferior to that of electromagnetic voltage transformer. Its performance is affected by the supply frequency, switching transients magnitude of connected burden, etc. The capacitor voltage transformer is more economical than an electromagnetic voltage transformer when the nominal system voltage increases above 66 kV.

The carrier current equipment can be connected *via* the capacitor of the capacitor voltage transformers. Thereby there is no need of separate coupling capacitors.

Capacitor type VT is used for voltages 66 kV and above. At such voltages, cost of electromagnetic type VTs tends to be too high. The capacitors connected in series act like potential dividers **provided the current taken by the burden is negligible compared with the current passing through the series connected capacitors.** However the burden current becomes relatively larger and ratio error and also phase error is introduced. Compensation is carried out by 'tuning'. The reactor connected in series with the burden is adjusted to such a value that at supply frequency it resonates with the sum of two capacitors. This eliminates the error. The construction of capacitor type VT depends on the form of capacitor voltage divider. Generally, h.v. capacitors are enclosed in a porcelain housing. A large metal sheet box at the base encloses the tuning coil intermediate transformer.

In CCVT (Coupling Capacitor Voltage Transformer). The same equipment serves the purpose of coupling capacitor and voltage transformer simultaneously. Fig. 34.3 shows a schematic diagram for one pole of a CCVT.

A typical CCVT for 400 kV class has total capacitance of 1500 to 2000 pF and approximately 34000 pF between the tapping point and earth. The voltage ($V_1$) across the primary of the intermediate transformer would be approximately

$$V_1 = \frac{2000}{34000} \times \frac{400}{\sqrt{3}} \text{ kV}$$

The secondary voltage of intermediate transformer is 63.5 V phase to neutral.

**Ferro-resonance in CVT.** If the natural frequency of the circuit of CVT primary and the supply network is less than about 50/3, it is possible that oscillations are set up between the inductance of intermediate transformer and capacitance of the line. The harmonic oscillations build up progressively resulting in increase in secondary voltage by 1.2 to 1.5 times the rated secondary voltage.

Hence ferro-resonance due to CVT should be prevented. While designing CVTs, the following aspects should be considered.

1. Enough cross-section of core of intermediate VT.
2. Linear portion of magnetization curve of intermediate CVT to be used.
3. Air gap in intermediate VT core.
4. Damping resistance across the secondary circuit.

## 34.4 TESTING OF CVTs

These include the following:

1. Measurement of error.
2. Core loss measurement.
3. Insulation tests:
   - Power frequency applied voltage tests for 1 minute.
   - Induced voltage tests.
   - Impulse voltage withstand test.
   - Switching surge withstand test.

— Insulation resistance measurements.

4. Polarity test.
5. Ferroresonance tests (special tests).
6. Transient response test (special test).
7. Tests on secondary circuits and on intermediate transformer.
8. Tests on coupling capacitor (special tests).

**$SF_6$ Gas Insulated CTs and VTs.** In GIS (Gas Insulated Subtations). The CT and VT are in separate metal enclosed modules. The enclosures of the module are of aluminium or stainless steel. The internal parts are supported on epoxy resin cast insulators.

The core, primary and secondary are with insulation which is compatible with $SF_6$ gas. The enclosures are filled with $SF_6$ gas at a pressure of 3 kg/cm$^2$. The module is sealed from other adjucent modules by use of neoprene rubber or viton O-seals placed in the grooves in the flanges. When assembled, the O-rings are sqeezed by about 20% diameter and give gas-tight sealing. The gas pressure in the module is monitored by the gas monitoring system.

Outdoor $SF_6$ filled CTs and CVTs are porcelain housed and filled with $SF_6$ gas. They are installed in outdoor yards on galvanised steel structures like usual oil filled CTs and CVTs.

## Summary

VTs are either *indoor* VTs housed in medium voltage switch-gear or *outdoor* type installed in HV switchyards. Indoor VTs upto 11 kV are generally epoxy encapsulated. Outdoor VTs may be of capacitor type (CVT) or electromagnetic (EMVT). The accuracy class include.

— Measuring VTs.

— Protective VTs.

The CCVTs combine function of coupling capacitor and voltage transformers.

## Questions

1. **Fill in the gaps:**

1.1. The construction of CVT includes main coupling capacitor and............

1.2. Electromagnetic VTs are used when accuracy desired is ............ than that obtainable from CVT.

1.3. For 66 kV and above..........type VT is preferred.

1.4. VTs are installed as follows

(*a*) upto 11 kV, indoor VTs in................

(*b*) 11 kV outdoor VTs on............

(*c*) 400 kV outdoor VTs on............

(*d*) $SF_6$ insulated metal enclosed VTs in...........

2. Explain connection of VTs in residual form.

3. Explain connections of VTs for measurement of voltages.

4. Explain construction of a CCVT and the occasion of ferroresonance.

5. Explain construction of an electromagnetic VTs.

6. State essential difference in construction of a CT and a VT for same voltage class.

# 35

# Other Special Transformers

Following special transformers have been described in this chapter:

— Small Transformers.
— Welding Transformers.
— High Voltage Testing Transformers.
— HVDC Convertor Transformers.
— Rectifier Transfomers.

## 35.1 SMALL TRANSFORMERS (BELOW 5 kVA)

Small transformers are produced in large numbers for

— electronic circuits
— auxiliary low voltage systems
— toys etc.

Earlier, open type of construction was used. This has been superseded by hermetically sealed construction of the transformer with oil filling or dry air filling in the metal enclosures.

The connections are taken out through metal/ceramic seals soldered to the containers. For indoor applications, epoxy encapsulation is preferred.

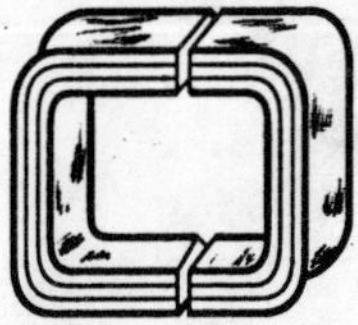

*Cut C Core*

Fig. 35.1. Cut C core for small transformers. (For toroidal core refer Ch. 33)

The core is either of shell type, core type, ring type or cut-C type. Laminations are placed in required manner or the strip is continuously wound, to form the closed magnetic circuit. The core pins are with insulating coating.

Several sizes, shapes, configurations are possible.

*Tape-wound cores*, are used for low output cores such as those for CTs, saturation core transformers, output transformers, switching-device transformers etc. High performance cores are of higher cost. Very thin cold rolled silicon steel or thin nickel-iron may be used.

High temperature dielectric coating and dielectric insulation by glass fiber, silicon-varnish etc. are used over the core.

**Ferrite (moulded Ceramic) Cores.** These are used in several intricate shapes such as E, I, cut-C, toroid etc., by sintering process. Ferrite toroid gives most optimum performance. The material used for ferrites include metal powders, ceramic having high saturation flux densities, low hysteresis loss, (low carbon steels, silicon steels, cobalt iron alloys, cobalt vanadium iron). High frequency ferrites have high saturation flux densities even at high frequencies where conventional silicon sheet steel material are not suitable. (For low and intermediate frequencies, conventional Cold Rolled Silicon sheet steels are used in strip form or lamination form).

**Choice of Cores.** In power transformers and distribution transformers, cores are of CRGO sheet steel. For small transformers, the choice is very wide in terms of core shape, material, process. The choice depends upon.

— frequency
— VA rating
— Continuous or intermittent operations *e.g.*, for a bell, the operation is intermittent.

For low output small transformers used for low frequency applications (*e.g., l.f.* amplifiers) high inductance is achieved by using high saturation flux density material having high permeability. Thereby the number of turns is reduced. Choice is (1) Toroids (2) Cut-C cores of CRGO steels.

Cut-C cores are preferred when d.c. component is present in the flux.

Cores illustrated in Fig. 33.8 for CTs are used for other low VA transformers of power frequency and low frequency.

For high flux varieties, nickel iron cores of various forms are used. Various commercial alloys like superaloy, unmetal having high permeabilities and high saturation flux densities are applied for low input voltage transformers.

**Windings.** Bobbin type continuously wound cylindrical winding described in Fig. 11.2 is wound over the limb of the core. The insulated wires are wound layer after layer in the form of a bobbin with it without interlayer insulation. The wire itself has insulation layer of its own. Additional insulation is provided for mechanical and electrical strength and to maintain the shape of the winding. Interlayer insulation may be of 'Craft Paper'.

Some insulation is required between two windings. Insulation should not be overdimensioned from thermal considerations.

**Mounting.** The factors to be considered include

— Heat dissipation from all the parts of the winding. Heat goes upwards.
— Ventilation
— Electrical field coupling
— Magnetic coupling.

When two transformers are installed in close proximity, the axis of cores should be placed at right angles. Shielding should be provided when required.

**Table 35.1.**
**Example of a Small Transformer Data**

| Type : Two winding | | |
|---|---|---|
| Input volts 110 | | |
| Frequency 50 Hz | | |
| Efficiency 85 % | | |
| Core Laminated Silicon Steel CRGO. | | |
| *Weight:* | *Window dimensions:* | |
| *Ratings* | *Primary winding* | *Secondary winding* |
| Voltage, V | 120 | 6.5 |
| Amperes | 1.6 | 29.5 |
| Turns | 280 | 15.16 |
| VA | 192 | 192 |

## 34.2 WELDING TRANSFORMERS

The arc welding needs electric power source. *AC arc welding needs* simple welding transformer with regulator. The current characteristic should satisfy the welding arc characteristic. The *V/I* characteristic of the source welding transformer and regulator is a drooping characteristic (*V* reduces with increase in current). This should match with arc characteristic. Arc voltage reduces with decrease in arc length and increase in arc diameter (increase in current). The *V/I* value at a point of coincidence of source characteristic and arc characteristic gives the operating point (Ref. Fig. 35.2).

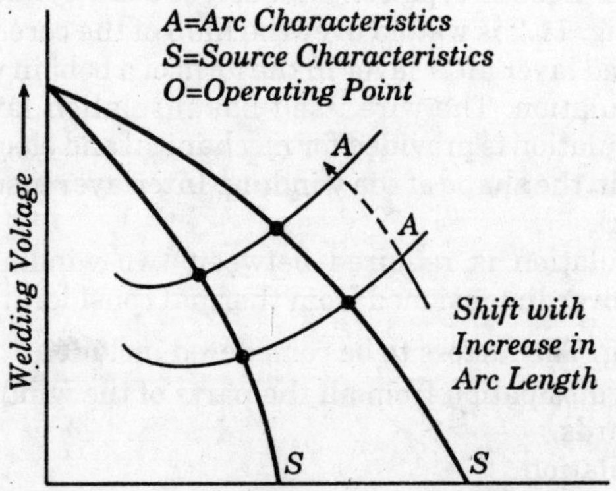


Fig. 35.2. Arc characteristic for welding.

The operating point *O* is obtained at the intersection of the arc characteristics (*A*) and the sources characteristics (*S*).

The arc characteristics (*A*) depends upon the electrode material and is shifted upwards by increasing arc length. The source characteristic is 'drooping' and can be shifted by means of regulator of welding transformer or excitation current of DC welding generator.

**Welding Transformer and Regulator.** AC arc welding voltage is in the range of 20 to 40 V and currents upto 1500 A. The stable arc requires drooping *V/I* characteristic of source (*V* on *Y*-axis *I* on *X*-axis). The source is formed by a welding transformer in series with a choke-regulator. The choke is often with air-gap so as to operate it below saturation level. Welding transformers are generally designed as single phase units.

**Arc-Welding Transformers.** There are many types arc ratings of arc-welding transformers, which supply 50-hertz single phase current to the arc used in the manual or machine (automatic) welding and surfacing of metals.

A welding transformer set converts a 220 or 440 volt supply into power at 40 to 100 volts, which is required for the arc-welding process and incorporates means of adjustment whereby the welding current can be varied continuously within suitable limits. Welding transformer sets are usually made oil filled and consist of the transformer proper (core, windings) and a variable reactor (choke) to control the secondary current of the transformer. Auxiliary equipment includes an ammeter, terminal boards to connect the primary winding to the supply mains and the secondary, to the welding circuit and a capacitive filter to bar the radio interference produced by the transformer during welding.

Welding transformer sets are put out both in the form of integrated units with the transformer and reactor placed in a common shell (monocarcase or one-body welding sets) and as sets made up of transformers and reactors encased individually (two-body welding sets). In the former case, the transformer and reactor windings are placed on a common core. Fig. 35.3 illustrates schematically the circuit arrange-

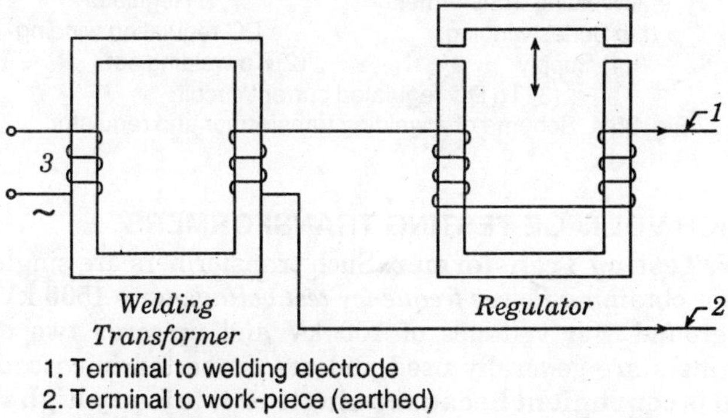


1. Terminal to welding electrode
2. Terminal to work-piece (earthed)
3. Single phase low voltage supply.

Fig. 35.3. Welding transformer with current regulator.

ment and operation of a two-body welding set. In this figure, welding transformer and regulator are shown. The welding current is varied by changing the air gap in the regulator core. As the gap is reduced, the reactance in the welding circuit is increased, this bringing down the current and *vice versa*.

Welding transformers are generally designed as single phase units with secondary voltage in the range of 70 and 100 V AC (rms). Adjustable reactor connected in series is used for current control. Some reactance is incorporated in the welding transformer itself, usually shunt capacitors are provided on the primary side for p.f. correction.

Figure 35.3 shows a regulator (adjustable series reactor). The core gap is adjusted by the handle at the disposal of the operator. Reduction in the gap increases the reactance and decreases the welding current.

Figure 35.4 shows another type of regulator. The welding transformer (*A*) supplies current to welding set (2) *via* saturable reactor (*B*). The DC current is central regulating winding (*c*) is regulated by external means. Increase in current in (3) gives increased DC component in the core and it leads to saturation of the core. The reactance reduces. The welding current increases. By varying DC current in the regulating winding, the welding current supplied to (2) can be easily controlled.

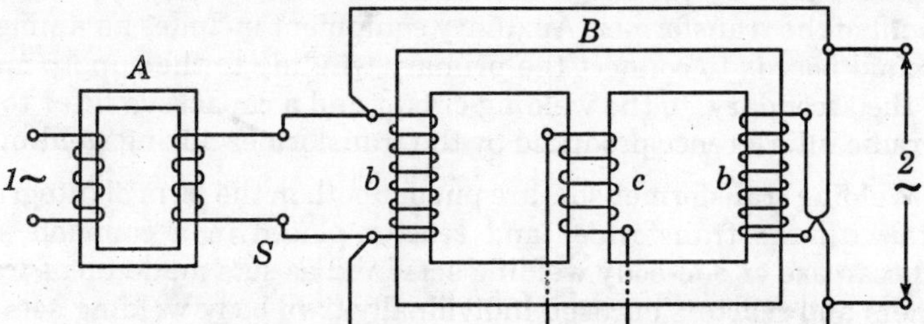


*A* Welding transformer *B* Regulator
*b*, *b* Series winding *c* DC regulating winding
(1) Supply (2) To welding set.
(3) To DC regulated current circuit.

Fig. 35.4. Scheme of a welding transformer and regulator.

## 35.3 HIGH VOLTAGE TESTING TRANSFORMERS

**H.V. Testing Transformer.** Such transformers are single phase units. For obtaining *Power frequency test voltage* upto 1500 kV, r.m.s. ph. to ground. For voltages of 100 kV and upwards two or more transformers are generally used and are connected in *cascade*. **The method is convenient because a single unit for very high voltage is very large and costly.** Cascade condition gives flexible test conditions. Cascade connection is illustrated in Fig. 35.5. These are single phase units.

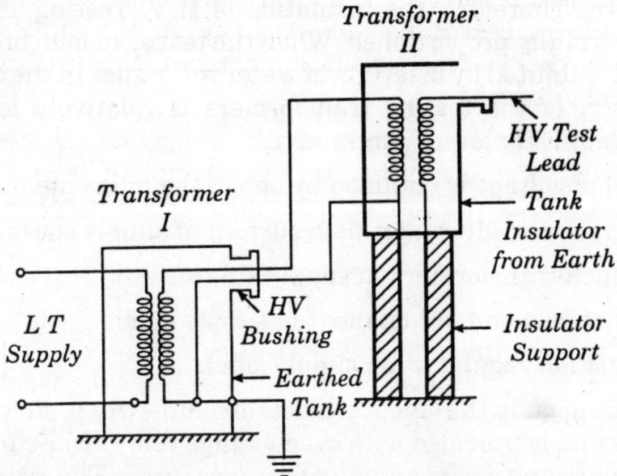


Fig. 35.5. High-voltage testing transformer (cascade connected, single phase transformer for obtaining high voltage at power frequency).

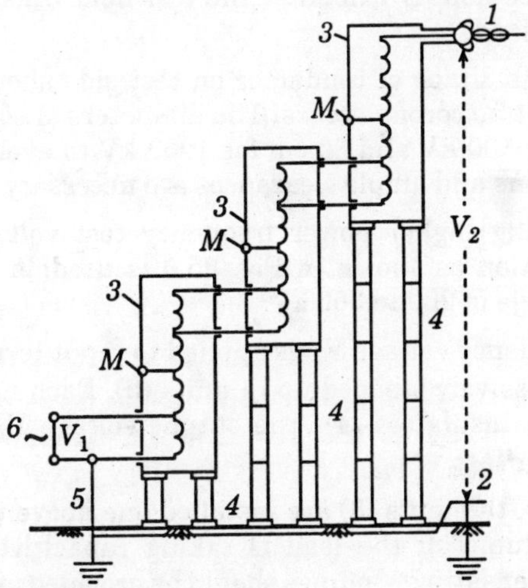


1. HV lead connected to apparatus under test.
2. Earth lead connected to earth point of apparatus under test and ground
3. Single unit of HV transformer
4. Insulator column.
5. Earthing of supply neutral
6. Single phase LV supply at 50 Hz.

Multi-unit cascace connected high voltage transformer (for single phase p.f. voltage withstand tests on HV equipment).

Fig. 35.6. Cascade connection of HV testing, transformer. *M* = Connection to metal tank.

The testing transformers are specially designed. They are subjected to transient overvoltage during their operation when the test piece breaks down. Therefore, the insulation of H.V. Testing Transformer should be carefully proportioned. When the test specimen breaks down, the current is limited by insertion of water resistance in the circuit. The kVA capacity of the testing transformers is relatively low because current is relatively low (1 Amp.).

Control of voltage is obtained by one of the following methods:

(1) Variation of alternator field current of supply source.

(2) Tapped transformer (on supply side).

(3) Resistance and inductance (on supply side).

(4) Induction regulator (on supply side).

The swithgear in the layout consists of main-switch, circuit breaker, gate switch and is provided with over-voltage relay, over current relay, interlocks earthing facility and safety measures. The gate switch is placed on the gate of screen enclosing the test field. It disconnects the supply to the transformer and earths the primary as soon as the gate is opened. Hence nobody can enter the test field when the HV transformer is energized.

The size and shape of conductor on test side should be carefully designed so that no corona occurs. The diameters of conductors are at least 2.5 cm for 100 kV and 30 cm for 1000 kV to avoid corona under normal conditions and ample clearances are necessary.

For obtaining higher power frequency test voltages multi-unit cascade connection as shown in Fig. 35.6 is used. A unit may have secondary voltage of 200 to 300 kV.

Power frequency voltage $V_1$, is applied to input terminals (6). This voltage is successively stepped up in units (3). Each unit is insulated from ground by insulators (4). The output voltage $V_2$ is supplied to apparatus under test.

Now-a-days, the units (3) are installed one above the other to get one vertical column. If the load is taking capacitive currents, the additional compensating windings should be provided in the HV testing transformers.

## 35.4 HVDC CONVERTER TRANSFORMERS

In HVDC terminals, 12-phase convertors are used universally. For each six pulse convertor one three phase two winding transformer with three secondary terminals is used. The primary is called 'AC side and secondary is called valve side. One twelve pulse convertor bridge is formed by connection of two six pulse convertors in series on DC side. The necessary phase shift between the two six-pulse convertors is obtained by connecting two convertor transformers as follows:

— One in star-star
— Other in star-delta. Ref. Fig. 35.7

The twelve pulse convertor gives twelve pulses per an AC cycle.

**Special Features of a Convertor Transformer**

— High speed, reliable, on-load tap-changer with 24 (or more) steps and regulation of + 17.5 and – 12.5% (or more). The tap changers operate frequently and should need only modest maintenance.
— Specially built low loss, low noise core. The magnetic circuit is suitable for higher *V/f* ratios and higher harmonic content.
— Exceptionally long bushings to achieve desired creepage distances.
— Very special design of insulation system and windings.
— Higher percentage impedance to limit short-circuit currents during convertor operation.
— High reliability essential.

**General Description**

Convertor-transformers are essentially designed as special high voltage power transformers. However during the operation, the windings connected to valves have a d.c. potential to ground in addition to the induced a.c. voltage. This d.c. potential (due to connection to high voltage d.c. valves) requires different insulation design and winding design. The current harmonics give eddy current losses. Hence, the winding is with more parallel paths than the normal power-transformer winding.

The losses of convertor transformers should be kept low without increasing the size and weight beyond the transportation limitations. The low loss is achieved by use of superior quality cold-rolled grain oriented silicon iron laminations for the core. The core construction is also with special design to avoid losses.

The convertor transformers are specially designed power transformer of high MVA rating (*e.g.*, 300 MVA). The special requirements and features are described above.

For one 12-pulse convertor bridge, the following alternative combinations are possible

(1) 2 Nos, 3 ph, 2 winding Transformers (Fig. 35.6)

(2) 3 Nos, 1 ph, 3 winding Transformers

(3) 6 Nos, 1 ph, two winding Transformer.

The choice depends upon transport limitations and other economic and technical factors.

A twelve pulse unit requires two three phase convertor transformers; one connected star-star and the other connected star-delta with such a combination, phase shift of 30° elec. between two six-pulse units connected in series can be obtained to get a 12 pulse convertor.

The core of single phase convertor transformer is usually of 4 limb construction. This permits lower height.

The on-load tap changers is of special design. Tap changer tank is mounted on the convertor transformer tank. The OLTC is most vital and critical switching device in an HVDC substation.

Windings are specially designed so as to give capability to withstand high dielectric stresses. Valve side windings are subjected to DC stress and AC stress.

The harmonic content in current causes additional leakage flux. It produces eddy current loss and hot spots in winding and surrounding tank. Spacing between winding and core, winding and tank is carefully selected.

Noise is controlled by special design features of core design and tank design. Noise should be within specified limits.

Main tank is ruggedly built. It is usually of rectangular box shape with beam stiffners on the sides. Tank is subjected to high mechanical stresses during transportation.

Bushings on DC side and AC side are longer than usual bushings. Creepage distances are more to avoid flash overs due to tracking.

Convertor transformers has two sets of three phase windings (Fig. 35.7).

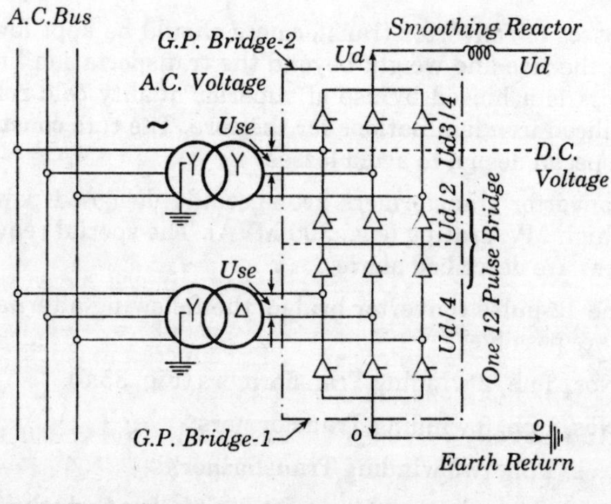


Fig. 35.7. Connections of two, three phase convertor transformers to a 12 pulse convertor bridge.

— *Line winding.* This is connected to AC busbar and supplied with 3 ph. 50 Hz, AC voltage. This is also called AC line side winding.

— *Valve winding.* This is connected to convertor bridge.

Convertor transformers are oil filled and the cooling is generally OF, AF (Oil Forced, Air Forced), Coolers are mounted beside convertor transformer. Oil is circulated through the tank and coolers by means of oil-pumps.

Convertor transformers are located on AC yard side of valve hall with valve side bushings of convertor transformer taken through the wall (Figs. 10.4 and 10.5). This permits shorter bushings with lesser creepage corresponding to indoor insulator creepage.

Convertor transformers are protected by surge arresters against lightning and switching surges, and power frequency over voltages during operation.

The preliminary design of convertor transformers tank is finalised after survey of transport route from manufacturers works to the final destination to sites. The assembled transformer tanks are heavy (200 *T* to 450 *T*) and require special railway wagons, road trailers. Tank is transported with nitrogen filling.

Convertor transformers are costly units and usually one spare transformer is provided at each terminal station.

Principles of power transformers design apply to convertor transformers also. However, additional factors are many.

**MVA Rating**

The required MVA rating of a convertor transformer is given by

$$S = \frac{P}{(n \cos \phi)} \times K$$

where $P$ = MW rating of one pole.

$S$ = MVA rating of one convertor transformer

$n$ = No–of convertor transformers per pole

$\cos \phi$ = p.f. on AC side

$K$ = Overload is factor, say 1.2

Sending-end convertor transformers have a higher MVA rating than at receiving end (line losses are deducted in calculation of $P$ at receiving end).

**Insulation Levels**

The DC side winding is subjected to DC voltage and AC voltage. The most stress occurs during polarity reversal on DC side.*

**Typical Ratings.** MVA continuous 300 MVA frequency AC side 50 Hz. Reactance 18.5%. Type of cooling OF AF.

---

*Refer "EHV-AC and HVDC Transmission Engineering and Practice". Khanna Publishers

**Table 35.2**
**Summary of Special Design Features of Convertor Transformers**

| *Requirement* | *Feature* | *Remarks* |
|---|---|---|
| 1. Higher voltage between winding and earthed core | Larger gap between winding and yoke. More insulation | Increase in radial leakage flux at ends of winding. |
| 2. Higher radial leakage flux at end. | Special design of end turns | More eddy current losses in end turns. |
| 3. Precise commutating Reactance for satisfactory convertor operation | Closely matched commutating reactance $X_{CR}$ of transformer winding in commutating path | —Reduction in commutating current to and rate of rise to safe valve—Reduced non-characteristic harmonics. |
| 4. Lower noise level | —The harmonics in magnetic flux produced high frequency magneto striction. | Noise level is maintained below 87 dB (A). |
| | Core is made of superior grain-oriented silicon steel sheets, core construction is superior | Noise due to core vibrations is reduced. |
| | Low speed fans for coolers | Noise of fans is reduced. |
| 5. DC component in valve side winding voltage | DC side winding connected to various points on valve bridge get DC voltage | Extra strong winding and insulation system for valve side winding. |
| 6. Varying DC side voltage with fixed AC side voltage | DC side voltage varies with load but AC side voltage is almost constant | Tap position changed to get various DC side voltages. |
| | Multi step fast, automatic tap changer having wide range. | Tap changer operates frequently. |
| 7. Bushings | Valve side bushings need high creepage | Usually the valve side bushing is taken through valve hall wall. |

## 35.5 RECTIFIER TRANSFORMERS (RECTOFORMERS)

1. **Applications.** Rectifiers convert AC to DC and comprise (1) suitable combination of rectifier transformers (2) suitable combination of diode rectifiers or thyristor (controlled) rectifiers. Wherever the DC power is used, rectifiers are necessary *e.g.*,

— Rectifier plants for Aluminium smelters and chemical plants
— Rectifier plants for DC traction supply
— Rectifiers for DC auxiliary supplies in power stations, substations
— Rectifiers for motor control

The following combinations prevail.

— Low secondary voltage (a few volts) and high secondary currents (several throusand amperes)
— Low voltage low current
— High voltage low current
— High voltage high current.

The required rectification is obtained by suitable combination of rectifier transformers and the rectifiers. The rectifier transformers with have AC voltage in the supply and AC flux in the core. But the DC side is connected to DC voltage which gives an additional DC component in the core. The following requirements determine the rectifier transformers design.

— Pulse number and method of connections. (Fig. 35.7 shows a 12 pulse waveform)
— DC side voltage, current
— AC side voltage and current
— kVA or MVA per transformer unit
— Neutral earthing on AC and DC sides
— Worst voltage stress
— Worst current stress
— Type of control for DC power.

In some cases, additional regulating transformers are used on supply side to get a wide range of voltage supplied to the primary.

Following types of rectifiers and convertors are used in industry.

**Table 35.3 Types of Convertors and Rectifiers**

| *Type of circuit* | *Applications* |
|---|---|
| 1. **Semi-conductor rectifiers** | — Full range of output power |
| — Selenium rectifiers<br>— Silicon rectifiers | — High power electrolysis<br>— Railway power supply<br>— Traction motors in AC traction system. |
| 2. **Line-commuted single quadrant converters with thyristors** | — Control of small motor drives<br>—Battery chargers |

| *Type of circuit* | *Applications* |
|---|---|
| 3. Semiconductor rectifiers with transductors | —Narrow setting range rectifier applications. |
| 4. Line commuted single and Double convertors<br>—with mercury arc converters (now obsolete)<br>—Thyristor convertors | —DC Motor drives of high power |
| 5. Self-commuted Inverters | —For supply to AC equipment from DC supply *e.g.*, in DC traction in which DC power supply is available from mains or from battery. |
| 6. Static AC convertors<br>—Thyristor convertors | —Variable frequency AC motor control<br>—Speed control of small motors |
| 7. Controlled DC supplies | —DC drives<br>—DC speed control<br>—DC traction. |
| 8. HVDC Transmission | See Sec. 35.3 |

2. **Comparison between AC Power Transformers and AC/DC Rectifier or Convertor Transformers**

(*a*) DC side of rectifier transformer has a ripple. Ripple depends on pulse number of rectifier.

The DC values depend on pulse number of the rectifier.

A *pulse number* is a characteristic of rectifier or converter connections. It refers to total number of successive commutations per cycle of an AC wave (360°elec.)

**Table 35.4. Effect of Pulse Number for DC Values**

| *Voltage Ratios* | | *Pulse Number* | | | |
|---|---|---|---|---|---|
| *—Relation of DC Values*<br>Form Factor : | *P = 1* | *P = 2* | *P = 3* | *P = 6* | *P = 12* |
| **Effective Value** | | | | | |
| Mean Value<br>Rectifier Peak Factor : | 1.57 | 1.11 | 1.07 | 1.0009 | 1.00005 |
| **Peak Value** | | | | | |
| Mean Value | 3.14 | 1.57 | 1.21 | 1.05 | 1.05 |

As seen from the table, increase in pulse number improves DC form. The presence of pulse on DC *side* produces *harmonics* on DC side and these get reflected on AC side by induction. Hence the rectifier transformers have harmonic content in DC current, flux and AC current/voltage.

The harmonics cause additional heating of windings and core. Hence suitable derating factor should be provided for this heating.

(*b*) As secondary current is fed to the rectifier and is usually high and *constant*, the rectifier transformer acts as a constant current transformer. For fixed kVA, the voltage of secondary is varied for fixed secondary current.

(*c*) Low secondary voltage and high secondary current requires the secondary having several parallel LV windings, (*e.g.*, 4 nos.). This is not required in normal power transformers.

(*d*) For heavy secondary currents, the secondary terminals have large cross-section and the secondary side has heavy bus system at low voltage.

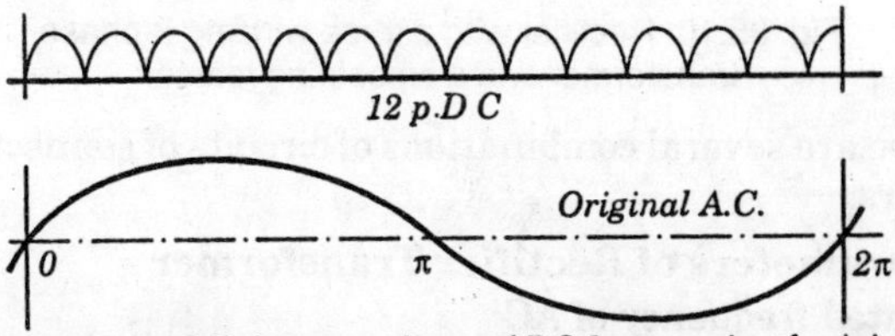


Fig. 35.7. A 12 Pulse waveform of DC [one cycle of original AC wave gives 12 pulses on DC side]

(*e*) In some designs the following associated equipment are enclosed in the same tank:

— Regulating transformer for regulating AC supply voltage to primary.
— Transductor for smooth voltage control on DC side.
— Interphase transformer for connection between two rectifier output terminals.

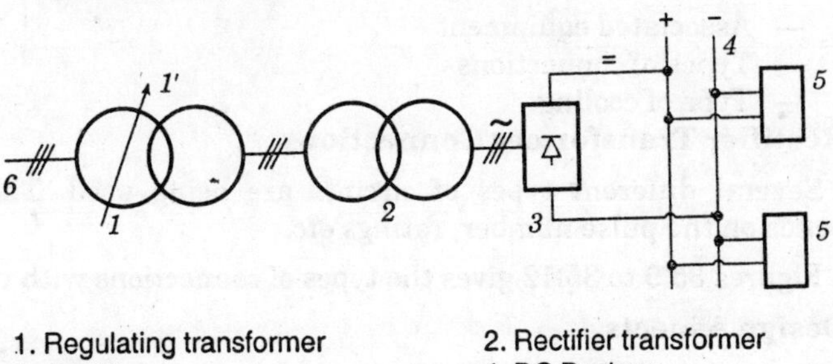


1. Regulating transformer
2. Rectifier transformer
3. Rectifier
4. DC Busbars
5. DC load.

Fig. 35.8. Scheme of a rectifier plant.

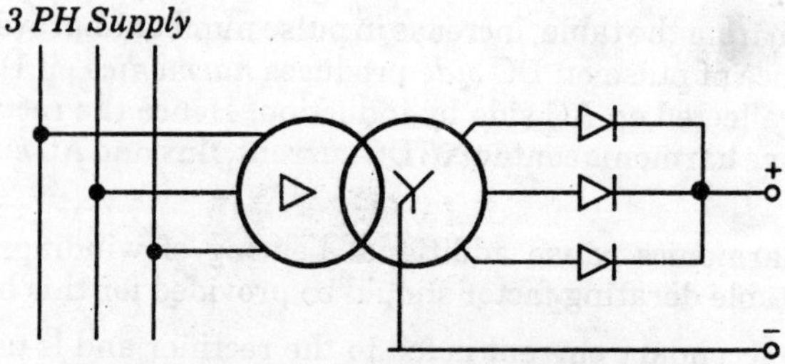

Fig. 35.9. Rectifier with three phase transformer.

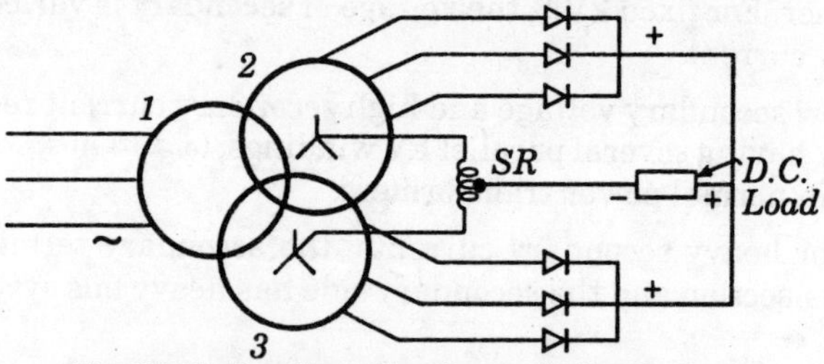

Fig. 35.10. Rectifier with a three winding 3-phase transformer and a smoothing reactor.

(*f*) There are several combinations of circuits of connecting rectifier transformers.

**3. Main Parameters of Rectifier Transformer**

— Rated frequency of AC
— Rated kVA
— Rated current of primary
— Rated current of secondary
— Rated voltage of primary
— Rated voltage of secondary
— Number of primary phases (*e.g.,* 3)
— Number of secondary phases. (*e.g.,* 3)
— Number of commutating groups connected in series on DC side.
— Associated equipment
— Types of connections
— Type of cooling.

**4. Rectifier Transformer Connections**

Several different types of circuits are being used. The choice depends on the pulse number, ratings etc.

Figures 35.9 to 35.12 gives the types of connections with remarks.

**5. Design Aspects.**

The complete rectifier installation has the following:

— Rectifier transformer (Main Transformer)
— Regulating transformer

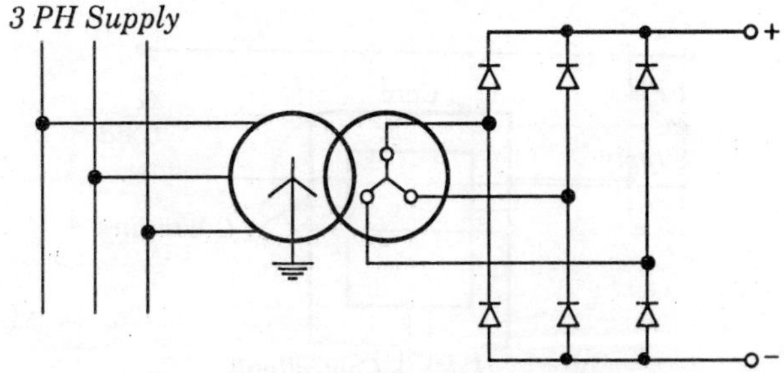


Fig. 35.11. A 6-Pulse bridge connection

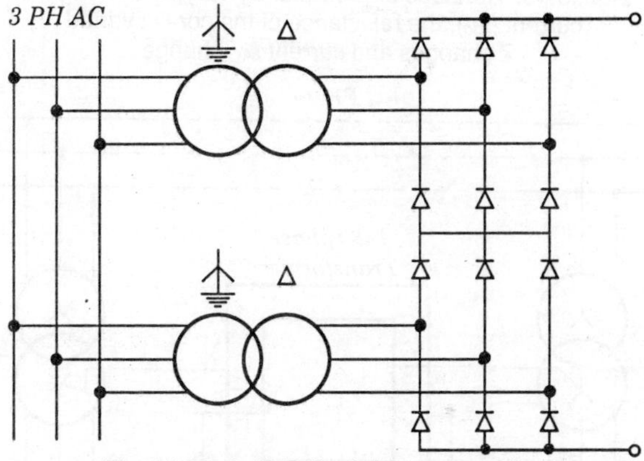


Fig. 35.12. A 12-Pulse bridge connection

— Interphase transformer
— Transductor.

The main supply is taken to the primary of the regulating transformer.

The regulating transformer receives power from mains at mains supply voltage and supplies to rectifier transformer primary. The regulating transformer is either a two winding transformer with on load tap-changer or an auto-transformer with a on-load tap changer. *Tap-changing is automatically controlled to achieve the variation in the output voltage of rectifier voltage for obtaining power control.* Thus for higher power output of rectifier, higher voltage tap of regulating transformer is selected.

Very wide range of tappings may be called for. (For smaller units tap-changer may be provided on the rectifier transformer HV side itself). However this is not economical for large installations.

Rectifier transformer receives power from regulating transformer and feeds power to the rectifier unit.

Rectifier units are connected in series to get desired DC power at load end.

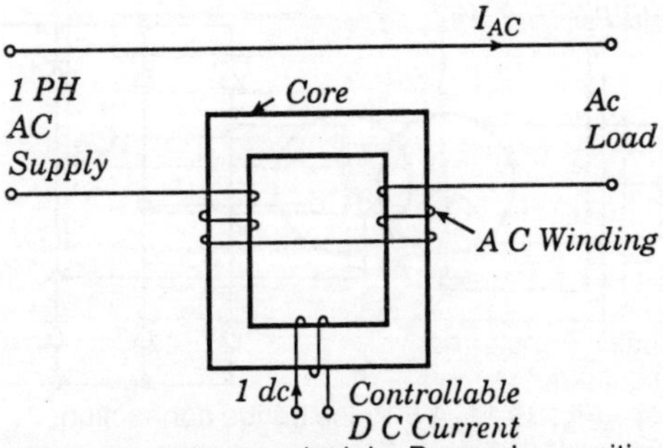


Fig. 35.13. Transductor principle. By varying exciting DC current ($I_{dc}$), the reluctance of the core is varied Z changes and current $I_{AC}$ changes

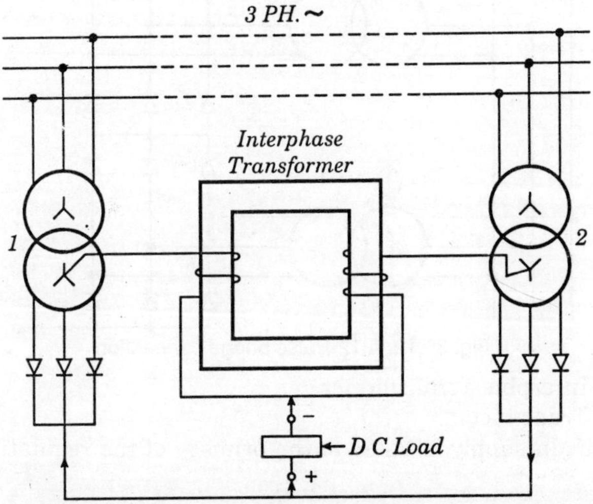


Fig. 35.14. Use of interphase transformer. The difference in DC currents of 1 and 2 is absorbed by the interphase transformer. Circulating currents between 1 and 2 are reduced.

**Interphase transformers are necessary between two parallel recfifier transformers on rectifier side to absorb the differences in DC voltages and reduce circulating currents through windings.** They have a core with windings. The reactance in the path absorbs the differences in voltages of two rectifier transformers and limits the circulating currents.

**Transductors.** It has a core with controlled DC winding. By varying the current in DC winding the flux in the core is varied by using the non-linear portion of magnetization curve.

The typical layout of a rectifier, regulating transformer, transductor is shown in Fig. 35.15.

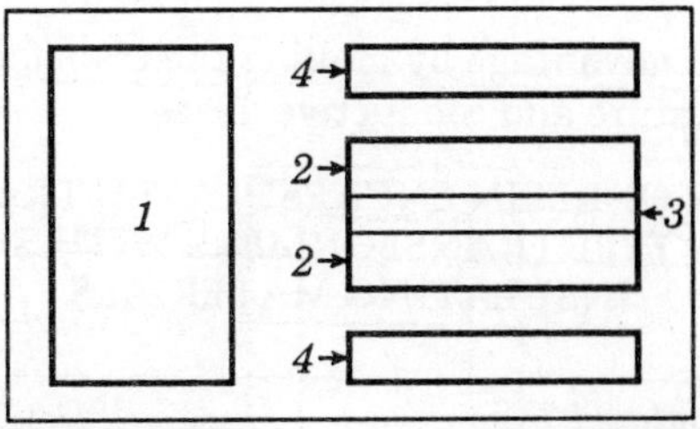


1. Regulating transformer 2. Rectifier transformer
3. Interphase transformer 4. Transductor

Fig. 35.15. Typical layout of a rectifier plant.

## DRY TYPE TRANSFORMER

Oil and Transformer have been synonymous since the origin of the manufacturing techniques of Transformers.

Oil, particularly from MINERAL base was the result of continuous research by electrical engineers, who were posed with the problem of handling high voltages as well as heat transfer in large sizes of Power Transformers.

Until the 20th century, transformers were made with their active parts merely immersed in a bath of oil required to obtain both cooling as well as insulation.

As the conciousness to conserve oil became emphatic, various oil saving techniques were developed, right from "Externally welded Round Cooling tubes on a sleeker tanks to the latest most modern Pressed Steel Radiators".

The advent of plants in early 20th century for manufacturing synthetics, chemicals, rubber etc., (fire hazard) together with development of mining of underground coal in gassy mines classified the conventional oil cooled transformers as unhealthy for use in installations which have HIGH FIRE RISKS.

The inflamable property of mineral based oil paved the path towards the development of non-inflammable synthetic liquids such as Pyrochlor, Clophen, Sovtool and other Polychlorinated biphenyls for use in the place of mineral oil, for such special applications. However, recent research on these hi-brid liquids revealed their inherent built-in nature repulsive natures namely the Non-Bio-Degradability and CORROSIVE/which necessitated the development of the polymer family product viz; Epoxy resins.

With the advent of polymer technology and its increasing application in the electrical engineering field, resin found its way into a liquidless concept of manufacturing transformers for less fire-hazardous requirements. Epoxy resins did have such better strength both electrically as well as thermally and the special technique of encapsulation offered added advantage by making the transformer (active part) impervious to moisture and conductive dusts.

## COMPARISON OF RESIN ENCAPSULATED TRANSFORMERS TO DRY TYPE TRANSFORMERS WITH SPECIAL INSULATING MATERIALS

| *Resin Encapulated Type* | *Dry Type* |
|---|---|
| I. *Sturdiness and Life Span* | |
| Possibility of developing very fine cracks during transport and even during the life time of the transformer is very high. These cracks lead to a major insulation failure. | Not present since the coils are insulated with flexible insulating materials. |
| II. *Maintenance and Repairs* | |
| Extremely expensive due to following reasons:<br>1. The coils are cast in resin and in the event of even a minor defect, the whole coil has to be scrapped.<br>2. The cost of a coil is nearly 30% more than that of an equivalent dry type with special insulation. | The coils can be attended with ease and reinforced at places of damage if necessary. In case of a damaged coil, the recovery is very high due to the absence of resin casting. |
| III. *Creepage In Dust and Coal Filled Atmosphere* | |
| The only creepage available is the plain surfaces of the coil. These plain vertical surfaces do not have any protected area to break the creepage path in the event of conductive dusts accumulating on a semi dry surface, similar to the conditions commonly expected in India | The creepage available on the surface of the coil is nearly three times when compared to that of cast coil. Further they are broken up with a number of protected area so that even in the worst condition, they do no give a continuous creepage path for conductive dust collected on the surface of coils during operation. This is achieved by the special design of coils which are always of continuous disctype. This very special advantage of dry type design of ours has made it possible to use these transformers safety in open conditions, even in coal dust, handling and off shore drilling platforms, cranes etc., in Sweden and other European countries. |

| *Cast Coil* | *Dry Type* |
|---|---|
| IV. *Thermal Distribution In Windings* | |
| Due to the restricted ventilation facilities available in a cast coil and its type of sealed construction, it is impossible to physically determine the location of the hot spot. Many assumptions about the location of the hot spot in this construction has been proved erroneous. This leads to erroneous determinations and monitoring of, safe operating temperature of the unit, leading to costly burn outs. | Ample ventilation is available. Determination of hot spots and controlling of safe operating temperature is extremely easy and eliminates burn outs. |
| V. EFFICIENCY | |
| Cast coils design suffer from the inherent defect of a comparatively larger frame size which means higher cost, higher losses and higher space and requirements for the same use without any additional qualities while at the same time they are highly prone to the above mentioned drawbacks. | Smaller frame size, lesser cost and space for the same purpose with much better utility, serviceability, reliability and economy. |
| VI. | |
| Resin is not totally non inflammable. It is only fire retardant. | The insulating materials used are totally non inflammable. |

With the improved quality of insulations used, this construction of Dry Type transformers perhaps can be more trust worthy for operations in heavily dust laden/carbon polluted atmosphere.

4. Perhaps the only advantage of Resin Encapsulated (Cast Coil) Transformer is a Notion that important active parts of winding *i.e.*, the coils are safely embedded in a robust encapsulation of resin, with substantial thickness. In fact, this is not so, since the advanced technology with superior silicone based insulating materials have better properties compared to resin and these materials do not involve a non reversible chemical change in its structure as in the case of a resin encapsulated transformer. This makes the dry type transformer extremely versatile and accessible to accurate evaluations on their performance predications, and technically as well as economically ideally suited for the most demanding duty conditions.

5. The Blanketing effect of Resin encapsulated coil requires, special design condisderations, affecting their cost economics and performance (loss figures) between comparable sizes.

Presently a number of Europe based manufacturers have perfected the technique of DRY TYPE (Plain, non-encapsulated) Transformers using improved insulating materials, which have superior thermal and electrical properties than resin.

Some of the important handicaps of CAST COIL designs are enumerated below and a detailed comparitive study of the two designs discussed are separately appended.

1. Encapsulation essentially is a process of mixing and curing of resin, this involves shrinkages by which any hairline cracks may originate at some portion of encapsulations. If cracks escape detection during routine test, they can eventually develop into a major failure.

Also such designs are highly prone to transit damages, causing expensive replacements and delays, since rework is not possible with an encapsulated coil.

2. The thickness of resin involved in insulating the surface of coils acts against its cooling facilities. This creates un-balanced thermal distribution in coils.

Since the conductor (windings) is not accessible by any means for physical inspection or measurement of temperature, the assumptions made on the hottest region of the transformer coil will have to be heavily depended upon in ascertaining the HOTSPOT TEMPERATURE during temperature rise tests.

In recent studies, it has been found that the hottest portion as such a coil need not be at one third the length of coil from Top, but could be any where. This can cause serious problem to the life of such a Transformer.

3. The straight resin encapsulated surface of a coil offers less creepage unlike the Dry Types since the latter is made with disc type coils with radiel ducts for cooling offering extra, protected creepage surfaces.

Even though the dry type construction of higher kVA Transformers had been developed during the early forties by prominent research oriented transformer manufacturers in Europe and USA, the quality of solid insulating materials available in those days prevented the use of dry type concept beyond certain optimum rating as well as voltage class.

All over the globe the synthetic liquids replaced mineral oil in prefered environments. Later, the Epoxy Resin filled (nationally presumed as resin Cast Coil type) Transformers had gained grounds despite the abnormal differential in cost.

Even though an equipment encapsulated in resin is not physically for further study and investigation, without causing severe damage to the same, this was the only alternative then available. With the recent development of Silicone based insulating materials with admirable thermal and electrical qualities, improvements in the design of dry type transformers were triggered off with this new family of insulting materials which proved beyond doubt its adaptability in place of resin.

Specialists in the DRY TYPE (CAST COIL) Transformer are well advanced with techniques for making resin encapsulated coils. In fact, most of these techniques involve winding the glass yarn along with mixed resin, on a transformer coil and then curing, instead of CASTING THEM. Therefore, strictly speaking, these are not CAST, but encapsulated.

Like oil, which experienced limitations beyond 100°C, the resin is now forced with limitations beyond 150°C.

The RESIN ENCAPSULATED versionshad firmly gripped, the transformer market, until the development of the latest classes of H and C insulations.

The users of high temperature grade transformers are becoming more aware of the latest development of the more economic, non-resin encapsulated Transformers, which are even superior in comparison.

The need which replaced synthetic liquid transformers with resin encapsulation is now replacing resin encapsulation with Dry Type transformers incorporating the hi-brid insulating materials.

Even though the dry type construction of higher kVA Transformers had been developed during the early forties by prominent research oriented transformer manufacturers in Europe and USA, the quality of solid insulating materials available in those days prevented the use of dry type concept beyond certain optimum rating as well as voltage class.

All over the globe the synthetic liquids replaced mineral oil in prefered environments. Later, the Epoxy Resin filled (nationally presumed as resin Cast Coil type) Transformers had gained grounds despite the abnormal differential in cost.

Even though an equipment encapsulated in resin is not physically for further study and investigation, without causing severe damage to the same, this was the only alternative then available. With the recent development of Silicone based insulating materials with admirable thermal and electrical qualities, improvements in the design of dry type transformers were triggered off with this new family of insulating materials which proved beyond doubt its adaptability in place of resin.

Specialists in the DRY TYPE (CAST COIL) Transformer are well advanced with techniques for making resin encapsulated coils. In fact, most of these techniques involve winding the glass yarn along with mixed resin, on a transformer coil and then curing, instead of CASTING THEM. Therefore, strictly speaking, these are not CAST, but encapsulated.

Like oil, which experienced limitations beyond 100°C, the resin is now forced with limitations beyond 150°C.

The RESIN ENCAPSULATED versionshad firmly gripped, the transformer market, until the development of the latest classes of H and C insulations.

The users of high temperature grade transformers are becoming more aware of the latest development of the more economic, non-resin encapsulated Transformers, which are even superior in comparison.

The need which replaced synthetic liquid transformers with resin encapsulation is now replacing resin encapuslation with Dry Type transformers incorporating the hi-brid insulating materials.

VOLTAMP DRY-TYPE TRANSFORMERS

In Technical Collaboration with

**MORA TRANSFORMATOREN GMBH, GERMANY**

FOR SAFETY AND ENVIRONMENTAL CONSIDERATIONS

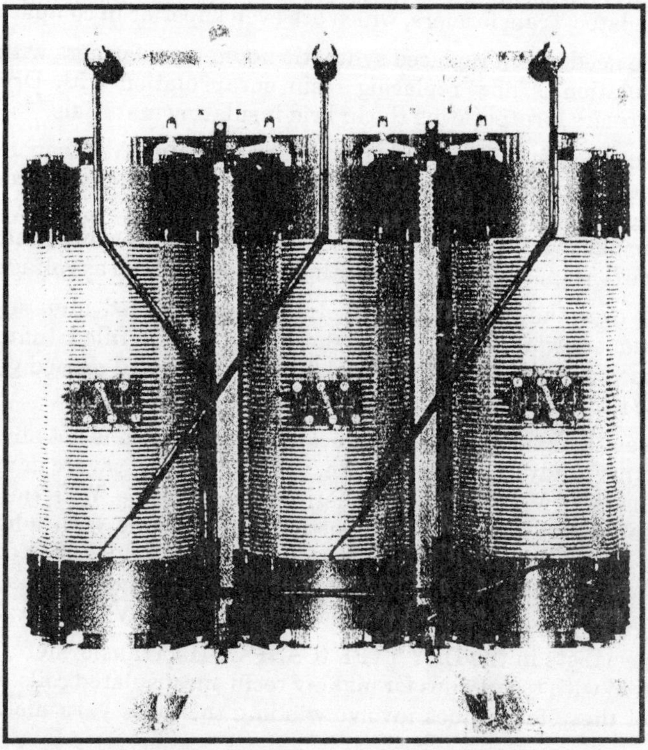

## BACKGROUND

- 35 years presence
- ISO 9001 accredited
- More than 20,000 installations
- Range upto 50 MVA 132 KV
- Extensively Type Tested range
- Branches in 13 cities

## NEW PRODUCT

- Launching Dry Type
  Transformers in Technical Collaboration with M/S MORA Germany

- More than 15,000 MORA
  Dry Type Transformer installations giving satisfactory service all over the world
- Mora's clientele includes
  ABB (Germany, Sweden, Austria), Siemens (Germany, Mexico), Wartsila (Finland), AEG (Germany, China) Mercedes, and others in Germany and Europe

**OUR STRENGTH IN OIL FILLED TRANSFORMERS**

- Supplies to World Renowned
  Industries Groups–Reliance, Haldia Petrochemicals, Indian Petrochemical Corporation, Gas Authority of India
- Supplies to various Industries
  Fertilizers and Chemicals–GSFC, IFFCO, GACL Refineries and Petrochemicals–DHDS Projects of Refineries MRPL Steel and Aluminium, Cement Power Plants, Textile, Pharmaceutical Industries, Pulp and Paper mills.
- Approved by leading Multinational and
  National Consultants.
  *Multinationals*
  Bechtel, Chemtex, Humphreys and Glasgow, Lloyds, Toyo, ABB, Siemens
  *National*
  EIL, NTPC, TCE, DCL.
- Multinational Companies who have sourced transformers form us
  Daelim, Hyundai, FAG, ICI, General Motors ABB, Siemens
- **Exports**
  28 Nos. 2,2.5 and 10 MVA Transformers to Jakarta (Indonesia)

## Voltamp Dry Type Transformers
## For Fire Safety and use in polluted atmosphere

**Do not:**

- Catch Fire • Sustain fire
- Add large quantity of combustible materials
- Generate Heavy Smoke • Propagate Fire

**Applications:**

- Refineries • Off-shore systems • Power plants
- Theatres • Hotels • High Rise Buildings
- Concert Halls • Hospitals

**Advantages over other non cast dry type transformers:**

- Vacuum impregnated windings
- No partial Discharge
- Can be used outdoors (when suitably enclosed)
- No accumulation of dust
- Less combustible material contents

## COMPARISON OF DIFFERENT TYPES OF TRANSFORMERS

| *Characteristics* | *Voltamp Resin Impregnated Dry Type* | *Oil filled Transformer* | *Resin Cast Dry Type Transformer* |
|---|---|---|---|
| 1. Operational Safety | No Fire Hazard | FIRE HAZARD | No Fire Hazard |
| 2. Location | Near Load Centre | Away from workshop for fire safety | Near Load Centre |
| 3. Cabling Cost | Low. As part of LT Cabling is replaced by HT Cabling | High. All Cabling by High Cost LT Cabling | Low. As part of LT Cabling is replaced by HT Cabling |
| 4. Relative Combustible material contents | 1 | 70 – 120 | 5 – 10 |
| 5. Typical Combustible Material Contents 11 kV/1000 KVA | 130 kWh | 9, 100 to 15,,600 kWh | 650 to 1300 kWh |
| 6. Smoke Generation | Very Little | Very heavy | Some times considerable |
| 7. Possibility of repair | Yes | Yes | Failed coils have to be discarded |
| 8. Susceptibility to Partial Discharges | Negligible as impregnated under Vacuum | Generally negligible when well designed | Significant even when coils are cast under Vacuum. Affects insulation life |
| 9. Suitability for Indoor use | Suitable as no fire risk | Suitable when fire risk is duly guarded | Suitable as no fire risk |
| 10. Suitability for Outdoor use | Suitable when enclosed in IP 45 enclosure | Suitable | Suitable when enclosed in IP 45 enclosure |
| 11. Class of Insulation and permissible Winding Temp. Rises | F – 90°C<br>H – 115°C | A – 55°C | F – 90°C<br>Class H generally not available |

| *Characteristics* | *Voltamp Resin Impregnated Dry Type* | *Oil filled Transformer* | *Resin Cast Dry Type Transformer* |
|---|---|---|---|
| 12. Suitability for occasional overloads | Class F suitable with provision of fan cooling. However fan adds to the noise and energy loss and a rotating component requiring maintenance OR Class H but being normally used as Class F Difference between Class H & Class F temp. rises being used for overloading. | Suitable with provision of fan cooling however fans add to the noise and a rotating component requiring maintenance | Class F suitable with provision of fan cooling. However fan adds to the noise and energy loss and a rotating component requiring maintenance |
| 13. Suitability for low ambient temperatures | Suitable for ambient temp up to minus 30°C | Special oil required having pour point of minus 40°C | Suitable for ambient temp up to minus 30°C |

## Amorphous Metal Core Transformers–Design Features And Advantages

*Use of amorphous metal cores reduces the core losses to approximately 25% of the core losses taking place in a CRGO steel core transformer of the same rating.*

Transformer designers have always aimed at reducing the losses taking place in a transformer. There are mainly two types of losses, that is, core losses and copper losses occurring in a transformer. Core losses are load independent and copper losses are load dependent. It means that full core losses keep on occurring even when there is partial or no load on the transformer. In view of this, it was very much desirable to reduce the core losses.

The first breakthrough in core loss reduction occurred in 1930 when cold rolled grain oriented (CRGO) silicon steel core was developed. It reduced the core losses by about for times. The second breakthrough, in core loss reduction, occurred about 25 years ago when amorphous metals were used for transformer cores. Use of amorphous metal cores reduces the core losses to approximately 25% of the core losses taking place in a CRGO steel core transformer of the same rating.

In conventional metals, the atoms forming the substance arrange in a regular, repeating pattern called a crystal. This crystalline structure isn't perfect, as it contains numerous small defects. These imperfections usually serve to strengthen the metal. Of course, if the imperfections grow too large, the metal begins to weaken and eventually breaks.

## AMORPHOUS METALS

Amorphous means without shape and these metals don't have crystalline structure like other magnetic materials. All the atoms in amorphous metal random arrange, thus giving it higher resistivity (about 3 times more) value than that for crystalline counter parts. Higher resistivity gives lower loss at all frequencies. The losses are the lowest among the known magnetic materials.

As the atoms in amorphous metal are arranged in a random chaotic order, this lack of structure means that the strength of small defects is present throughout the entire substance, creating an exceptionally strong material. With great strength comes exceptional hardness, a property that is highly desirable for structural applications. Because of absence of crystalline structure, amorphous alloys are magnetically soft, that is, they possess lower coercivity, lower core loss, and higher permeability. This random order gives rise to other amazing properties as well. As there is no crystalline structure to keep intact, we can't machine amorphous metals so easily to create a desired shape or part. It is possible to heat the material and inject into a special mould, much like some plastics. It is also easily turned into foam. That is, it can be readily mixed with air to create a permanent, lightweight, but strong material suitable for insulation, soundproofing, fireproofing, or a host of other applications.

There are no grains, grain boundaries or grain orientations in these metals. These have essentially one phase with chemical homogeneity. Amorphous metal used for transformers has slightly lower density than the crystalline material of the same composition. These metals are magnetically soft resulting in a large magnetization for the same excitation. The hystereses losses are also lower due to easy domain

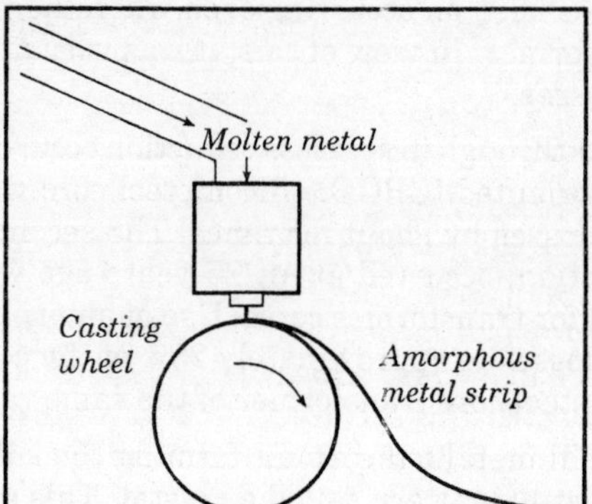

movement as it has no grain boundaries. Saturation flux density is only 1.6 Tesla for these metals, whereas for CRGO steel, it is about 2 Tesla.

## MANUFACTURING

Amorphous metals are prepared by cooling the molten metal at about million degrees per second. The fast cooling doesn't give the atoms enough time to rearrange into stable structure. Hence, for manufacturing amorphous metal, we should be able to cool molten liquid metal rapidly to prevent crystallization of the material during solidification from the molten state. The cooling rate should at least be $10^6$ Kelvin per second to prevent crystallization of the cast strip. Amorphous metal strip fabrication requires continuous quenching and solidification of the molten metal on a moving metal substrate such as rotating wheel. To achieve so high cooling rate, we require high heat transfer coefficient at the interface of the molten metal and the chill substrate, and a thin metal cross-section.

The low viscosity of the molten metal is desirable. Actually, the success of quenching process depends on metal composition, strip geometry, wheel speed and viscosity of the molten metal. Fabrication of amorphous metal is less costly than manufacturing of CRGO steel strips as the number of steps involved are less.

## AMORPHOUS METAL CORE

A magnetic core in a transformer provides an easy path for flux in order to facilitate flux linkage, or coupling between two or more magnetic elements. Energy storage in a transformer core is an undesirable phenomenon. With high permeability core material, energy storage is minimal. Eddy current losses in a core are given by the following:

Losses in W/kg $= \dfrac{g^2 B_m^2 t^2 f^2}{6\,\rho d}$ where $B_m$ is maximum flux density in Wb/m$^2$, $t$ is lamination thickness in meters; $f$ is frequency in cycles/sec, $\rho$ is resistivity in ohm-meters and $d$ is the density in kg/m$^3$. Eddy current losses are inversely proportional to the resistivity of the core material. Thus, the higher the resistivity of the core material, the lower will be the eddy current losses. As the resistivity of amorphous metals is about 3 times more than CRGO steel, eddy current losses are about three times less. Lamination thickness (about 15 thousandth of an inch) is also less in case of amorphous metal cores; this further reduces the eddy current losses.

Destruction factor is a measure of the losses in transformer core after it has been used in a transformer in comparison with the losses of the base material. Destruction factors of 0–50% are quite common when working with CRGO cores. Destruction factor is lower in case of amorphous metal cores.

Packing factor is per cent volume (or fraction) occupied by the magnetic material in the core. Amorphous metal core higher pack factor in the range of 82–88%. The packing factor is also proportional to the width of the ribbon. Wider strips exhibit lower pack factor relative to narrow strips. C and E cores are manufactured from narrow strips; hence, the core pack factor may be > 84%.

While manufacturing a distribution transformer, it is normal practice to fabricate core and coils independently. It requires that the core must be formed with a joint so that the core can be opened to accommodate pre-wound coils. To produce a jointed core, magnetic core material in sheet form is cut and layered around a mandrel. Although the overall core shape is a closed loop, each layer of the core contains a gap. After annealing the core to relieve the residual stresses from the assembly process, each layer of the gapped core is opened to a U shape. The layers of the gapped core are then threaded into the pre-wound primary and secondary coils and reassembled into the original closed shape.

Although this technique has been fully adapted to grain oriented silicon steel, it was not immediately applicable to this, hard amorphous metal. The sheer number of layers of thin amorphous metal ribbon in the finished core coupled with excessive wear to the blades used to cut the hard amorphous metal forced alternate approaches to transformer designs. The earliest amorphous metal core transformers contained simple, continuous spiral wound cores. With no gaps or the joints in the core, it was necessary to assemble the primary and secondary coils by winding insulated wire through the center and around the legs of the closed core. The amorphous metal core delivered core loss energy savings of 60–80%. The approaches of winding the coil about a finished core or cutting and stacking thousands of amorphous laminations were not economically convincing.

Several methods were tried to overcome this problem and finally cut-wound cores were found suitable for these transformers. To simulate the thickness of a silicon steel sheet, a process referred to as "pre-spooling" produced multiple layered packages of amorphous metal layer ribbon. Multiple coils of single layer thickness amorphous metal ribbon were simultaneously unwound and combined to form a strip of multiple layer thickness. The maximum capacity of these transformers is 2500 kVA in foreign countries and 1000kVA in our country. Many transformer manufacturers are collaborating with foreign manufacturers to take know-how from them and start manufacturing these transformers in India.

The cost of amorphous metal core transformers is higher than CRGO steel transformers by 25% approximately. It, therefore, needs to be demonstrated that the life cycle cost or total operating of these transformers will be less than or equal to that cost of standard transformers to justify their use Amorphous metal core transformers save energy by reducing no load losses by 60 to 70%. Since percentage impedance of amorphous metal core transformers is lower than equivalent rating CRGO core transformers, the short circuit current will increases proportionally. Therefore, electrical distribution equipment associated with amorphous metal core transformers must be increased in size to withstand the increased short circuit current. The resulting energy conservation may be offset by the increased cost of the associate equipment. Therefore, one should carry out techno-economical study before deciding to go for amorphous metal core transformers.

# References


'Transformer Reference Book', (B), Allis Chalmers, USA, 1951.

'Transformer Engineering', (B), 2nd Ed., by Blume, Camilli et all, John Wiley, 1951.

'Transformers for Electric Power Industry, (B), Westinghouse, 1960.

'J and P and Transformer Book', (B), 9th Ed. Johnson & Phillips Ltd., 1961.

'Alternating Current Machines', (B), M.G. Say, Halsted, New York, 1976.

'Transformer Response to System Switching Voltages', (P), Degeneff et all, IEEE Tran., PAS-101, p 1457, June 1982.

'Dielectric Tests for EHV Transformers', (P), Kaufman et all IEEE Tran. PAS-87, p. 135 Jan. 1968.

'Loading Transformers by Temperature', AIEE Trans. 49 April 1930.

'Dynamic Response of Power Transformers under Axial, Short Circuit Forces', (P), IEEE Trans. PAS-92, p. 1558, and p. 1567, Sept. 1973.

'EHV-AC and HVDC Transmission Engineering and Practice', (B), S, Rao, Khanna Publishers, Delhi 1990.

'Testing, Commissioning, Operation and Maintenance of Electrical Equipment', (B), S. Rao, Khanna Publishers, 2005.

'Introduction to Instrument Transformers', (B), Jenkins, McGraw Hill, 1968.

'Electrical Substation Practice–EHV-AC, HVDC, $SF_6$GIS',(B), S Rao, Khanna Publishers, Delhi.

'Switchgear and Protection', (B), Sunil S. Rao, Khanna Publishers, Delhi.

'Transformers', Literature, Courtesy, ASEA Sweden, 1984.

'Electrical Engineer's Reference Book', (B), 14th Ed., Laughton and Say, Butterworth, 1985.

'Large Transformers with Five Limb Cores' (P), Brown Boveri Review, Nov., 1972.

'Shunt Reactors for EHV Systems' (P), *ibid.*

'Regulating Transformers' (P), *ibid.*

'Reference Book of Transmission and Distribution', (B), Westinghouse, 1950.

'Transformers', Literature, Courtesy, Mitsubishi, Japan, 1988.

'Transformers', Literature, Courtesy, Brown Boveri, Switzerland, 1986.

# Index

## D

## J



## K



## L



## M

## Q



## R



## S

## T